Library of
Davidson College

Peacemaking
in Early Modern Europe

Peacemaking in Early Modern Europe

Cardinal Mazarin
and the Congress of Westphalia,
1643–1648

Derek Croxton

Selinsgrove: Susquehanna University Press
London: Associated University Presses

© 1999 by Associated University Presses, Inc.

All rights reserved. Authorization to photocopy items for internal or personal use, or the internal or personal use of specific clients, is granted by the copyright owner, provided that a base fee of $10.00, plus eight cents per page, per copy is paid directly to the Copyright Clearance Center, 222 Rosewood Drive, Danvers, Massachusetts 01923. [1-57591-017-9/99 $10.00+8¢ pp, pc.]

Associated University Presses
440 Forsgate Drive
Cranbury, NJ 08512

Associated University Presses
16 Barter Street
London WC1A 2AH, England

Associated University Presses
P.O. Box 338, Port Credit
Mississauga, Ontario
Canada L5G 4L8

The paper used in this publication meets the requirements
of the American National Standard for Permanence of Paper
for Printed Library Materials Z39.48-1984.

Library of Congress Cataloging-in-Publication Data

Croxton, Derek, 1969–
    Peacemaking in early modern Europe : Cardinal Mazarin and the Congress of Westphalia, 1643–1648 / Derek Croxton.
      p.   cm.
    Includes bibliographical references and index.
    ISBN 1-57591-017-9 (alk. paper)
    1. Peace of Westphalia (1648) 2. Mazarin, Jules, 1602–1661.
3. Alsace (France)—History. 4. France—Foreign relations—Germany.
5. Germany—Foreign relations—France. I. Title.
D271.F8C76   1999
940.2′41—dc21   98-35304
                                                                                               CIP

PRINTED IN THE UNITED STATES OF AMERICA

Contents

Preface	7
Acknowledgments	13
List of Abbreviations	15

Part I: Peacemaking and Warmaking in Mazarin's France

1. Introduction: Negotiating While Fighting	21
2. The Decision Makers	28
3. The Military Tool, Part I	56
4. The Military Tool, Part II	72

Part II: The Road to Peace

5. Introduction: From *Guerre couverte* to the Conference Table, 1630–1644	97
6. 1644: France Alone	108
7. 1645: Mazarin Gains Confidence	138
8. 1646: Triumph and Continued War	196

Part III: Conclusion

9. Mazarin as Negotiator and Strategist	259
Notes	282
Bibliography	370
Index	387

Preface

Wherever I go now, I am told that diplomatic and military history are on the upswing. It is true that there is some evidence of this. Sociologists in particular seem more interested than ever in *Bringing the State Back In*[1], and in particular in studying the influence of war on state formation. This is not just a matter of a new generation, but of changing attitudes; as the author of another recent work admits, "once upon a time, the study of war annoyed me to tears."[2] Even France, home of the *Annales* rebellion against *"l'histoire événementielle"* so many years ago, has witnessed something of a revival of interest, led by Lucien Bély.[3]

Despite these indications, however, diplomatic history is still generally regarded as peripheral. Probably more typical of current attitudes than the aforementioned works is the reaction of a fellow graduate student to whom I explained that my dissertation topic was French policy at the Congress of Westphalia. "But how do you sell that?" he asked skeptically.

The answer is that the topic addresses two matters of vital moment: peacemaking and state-building. As an example of peacemaking, French policy at Westphalia elucidates an important case in the history of war termination and offers new insights into how states assess their needs, modulate their demands, and resolve their differences in negotiations. As a study of state-building, it explains the process by which one territory and group of people were transferred from one government to another, and why precisely that territory got transferred and no other. My original interest in this subject focused on the latter aspect: how France acquired rights in Alsace. One of the directions of recent research on early modern state formation has been the existence of "composite monarchies" and the attempts to incorporate newly conquered territory into a state.[4] But while scholars have been interested in the fate of territories once they have been united, there has been no general study on how these territories came to be joined together in the first place. The few relevant, scattered comments suggest that more territory changed hands as the early modern period progressed, and that the composition and shape of the state system was far from determined in the mid-seventeenth century.[5] The existence of a "Military Revolution" affecting strategy adds an additional reason for a volatile state system, arguably favoring states that adapted successfully to the new conditions over those that did not, and thus potentially leading to the transfer of territories toward the states with more advanced military systems.

The fate of Alsace in the Peace of Westphalia could hardly form a more appropriate case study for territorial change in early modern Europe. First, the border between France and the German territories to the east has been one of the most disputed in history, not only in diplomacy and war, but in historical and legal scholarship as well. Second, France and the Empire were at opposite ends of the path toward state formation, with France as one of the more centralized states in Europe, and the Empire so decentralized that it only marginally qualified as a "state." Third, while the question of French control of Alsace has been studied extensively, these works only serve to simplify and concentrate the present work, and not to overlap with it. The great books by Wolfgang Hans Stein on Richelieu's protection policy and by Georges Livet on the French intendancy focus on the periods immediately preceding and succeeding the actual negotiations leading up to the Peace of Westphalia, when the title to Alsace was officially transferred to France.[6] Other studies by Karl Jacob, Alfred Overmann, and Konrad Repgen on the treaty terms transferring Alsace to France help clarify an extremely complicated legal situation, without delving into the broader context of the negotiations.

The way is thus clear for a more extensive study of the negotiations over Alsace between France and the Empire from 1643 to 1648. When I began, I thought for a time that I might find that the Alsatians played a significant role; after all, their laws, religion, and language were profoundly affected by their *Anschluß* with France, so one might expect them to have taken an interest in determining their fate.[7] While it is true, however, that their appeals to the other Imperial states helped introduce ambiguous wording into the treaty that limited French control for another forty years, in fact the bulk of the treaty provisions had little to do with their desires and a great deal to do with the decisions of statesmen in Paris, Munich, and Vienna.[8] As Rodolphe Reuss has expressed it, "The representatives of the Alsatian towns were not long in perceiving that the fate of their province would be decided, not in a public discussion, not in diplomatic plenary assemblies, but behind the scenes, so to speak, of the Congress."[9]

The fate of Alsace, then, was a matter chiefly of power politics. This study therefore focuses on the role of the ultimate arbiter of power, military force, in shaping French territorial demands. There has been surprisingly little discussion, either in historical or in theoretical works, of the role of the military in negotiations. It is almost axiomatic that the military situation molds the diplomatic settlement—that, in other words, the spoils go to the victor. On the other hand, states almost inevitably hand back territory in the final treaty, which makes the exact relationship between military and diplomatic success both problematic and interesting. Why, for example, did France insist on Alsace but not on Lorraine, which she had occupied for even longer? It may appear that part of a small province—which is what France gained at the Peace of Westphalia—was scant compensation for a "victor" of the Thirty Years' War, an impression that is becoming ubiquitous in modern historiography. The conclusion of the present study, however, contradicts this impression and suggests a standard for victory more in accord with the historical context.

I was once warned that this project would be *Kleinarbeit*—that is, delving into minutiae. To my pleasant surprise, however, it has been anything but that. While there is inevitably a certain amount of detail work involved in any study of this sort, I did not spend the bulk of my time studying French propositions at tremendous length to discover minor alterations here and there. There are two main reasons for this. First, the French were never so precise as to warrant an extremely close study of what they said. What was mentioned one time might be said in quite different terms another time without the writer having changed his mind at all; he simply did not bother to express himself accurately. Moreover, the specific details that were included in propositions were often changed at the last minute by the writer, so it is not necessarily possible to discern changes in Mazarin's policy by studying the exact wording of propositions deposited with the mediators in Münster. Second, the "over-the-table" negotiations covered such a relatively brief span of time—from January to September of 1646—that "detail work" formed only a relatively small proportion of the whole. The fact that the French negotiating position remained only broadly defined prior to this time meant that this study had to be equally broad to understand it.

The ideal essay, it has been said, should contain two different themes, like a Bach fugue. This book actually contains three, a decision that I hope is justified by its length. The first is the military campaigns themselves, the hard facts around which diplomacy had to operate. To make sense of the military situation, the historian has to come to terms with the "Military Revolution" without becoming drowned in the ocean of ink that has been spilled on it in the past ten years. Geoffrey Parker's seminal 1988 book has spawned a great deal of fruitful research in a short period of time, but also some sharply differing opinions on the nature of military organization and change in the early modern period. Using extensive research into the French and Bavarian campaigns, I offer my own interpretation of the strategic options available to Mazarin and his opponents, an interpretation that has led me to differ with a disturbingly large body of historiography. I am sure that this, too, will attract a certain amount of disagreement.

The second theme of this book is Mazarin the diplomat. Like the Military Revolution, Mazarin has attracted increasing attention in the past decade or so. The major difference is that, while the Military Revolution has led to new and exciting ways of examining armies, navies, and state power, Mazarin is often treated in a cursory fashion by those interested in him only tangentially. He almost seems to be riding the wave of Richelieu research which seeks to divorce his predecessor from raison d'état and identify him less as a forward-thinking centralizer and more as a man of his times. Based on the interesting work done on Richelieu, I expected to confirm the new interpretation of Mazarin; to my surprise, however, I found him to be as rational a figure as I could imagine, one as firmly devoted to raison d'état as Richelieu was ever claimed to be.

The third theme, and the main reason for the research, links the other two: the effect of the military campaigns on Mazarin's negotiating position, in particular his territorial demands. Since I found this influence to be so much less than I had expected, my book became as much an attempt to explain the *lack* of influence as to explain what influence existed. This entails a thorough understanding of how Mazarin perceived the war, but also an appreciation of the international system in the 1640s. There was a specifically diplomatic dynamic operating in the negotiations leading up to the Peace of Westphalia which, though influenced by military considerations, operated largely by its own rules. This book therefore provides a glimpse of one aspect of the evolving state system at the intersection of peacemaking and state-building.

* * *

Notes on Terminology

Personal names are rendered in the original language where this is not too awkward.

Place names are given in their standard English form; thus, Munich instead of München, and Hesse-Cassel instead of Hessen-Kassel.

Dates are always given according to the Gregorian calendar.

Coming up with names to designate the two opposing sides is problematic. In keeping with the usage of the times, I have chosen to call French, Swedish, and Hessian forces "allied" or "coalition," and France and Sweden together as "the two crowns." Their opponents are described as "Habsburg" or "Imperial," sometimes with the addition of "Bavarian" when this is not evident from the context. The terms *Imperials* and *Imperialists* are both acceptable according to Webster's Unabridged Dictionary, but I have chosen the former primarily because "Imperialists" has modern connotations that I wish to avoid.

Since contemporaries made little effort to distinguish "the Empire" from "Germany," at least in everyday usage, I have also used them interchangeably for increased variety.

The word "estates" will always refer to the estates of the Empire unless specifically noted.

Describing the territory of the German Southwest in general creates a large problem because it was not unified. I have tried to refer to Imperial Circles where this is accurate (usually the Swabian Circle), but at times I have had to resort to "modern Baden-Württemberg" as the only accurate term.

Because Hesse-Cassel plays a major role in the story while Hesse-Darmstadt appears only briefly, I have used the shortened forms "Hesse" and "Hessian" to refer to Hesse-Cassel except when this would be ambiguous.

Similarly, "Oxenstierna" used by itself will always refer to Johann, the Swedish ambassador in Osnabrück, and not to his father Axel, the chancellor.

I was planning to elaborate at length on the distinction between various words for "truce" and "armistice" (trêve vs. suspension; Waffenstillstand vs. Waffenruhe), but I found that contemporaries did not really make much of a distinction, if any, in using them; I have therefore used them interchangeably. (Cp. Heyner, 77.)

The French word "demande" is usually translated as "request," "petition," or "application." However, it would make little sense to speak of the French "territorial requests" at the Congress, so I have used "territorial demands" as the more natural translation. Readers should be aware, however, that the term "demands" has a harsher connotation in English than in French.

Acknowledgments

Since this book started as my dissertation, it seems appropriate to begin with my examiners: John Lynn, Paul Bushkovitch, Paul Schroeder, the late Donald Queller, and above all my advisor, Geoffrey Parker. Each has provided me with useful advice that I have incorporated into the book in one form or another. Orest Ranum, who read the manuscript for Susquehanna University Press, offered some penetrating comments that helped shape the final version. I also benefitted from conversations or correspondence with Paul Sonnino, David Parrott, Dennis Showalter, Geoffrey Treasure, John Rule, Andrew Lossky, Kathrin Bierther, and Konrad Repgen. Professor Repgen was kind enough to permit me to use the facilities of the Vereinigung zur Erforschung der Neueren Geschichte, without which this book would have taken much longer and been much more expensive. I would also like to thank Dr. Karlies Abmeier, head of the VENG during my stay there, and particularly Anuschka Tischer, who helped me on numerous details of French policy, and whose friendly conversation kept me going during long work days in Bonn. All the archivists were helpful, but those at the Hauptstaatsarchiv in Munich were especially understanding. I could not have completed my research without funding from the Deutscher Akademischer Austauschdienst, the U.S. Army, and Yale University, particularly Paul Kennedy and International Security Studies. Uppsala University International Summer Session kindly provided me a scholarship and an opportunity to learn Swedish. My parents deserve special commendation for their support, financial as well as moral. Last but not least, all of my friends gave helpful advice and encouragement, especially my wife Tanya, who also served as an editor and (when necessary) cattle prod.

List of abbreviations

AG	Archives de Guerre
All.	Allemagne
APW	Acta Pacis Westphalicae
BM	Bibliothèque Mazarine
BN	Bibliothèque Nationale
CP	Corréspondance politique
KAA	Kurbayern, Äußeres Archiv
KGR	Kurbayern, Geheimer Rat
KS	Kasten Schwarz
Mf	Manuscrits français
NBG	Nouvelle Biographie Générale

Peacemaking
in Early Modern Europe

Part I
Peacemaking and Warmaking in Mazarin's France

1
Introduction: Negotiating While Fighting

"PEACE SETTLEMENTS TEND TO REFLECT FACTS ESTABLISHED ON THE ground," one could hear George Will say during the height of the crisis in Bosnia. It seems logical that military campaigns would have a decisive effect on negotiations, yet it is the rare war that ends in an *uti possidetis* treaty (that is, one in which each side keeps the territory that it occupies militarily). By what process, then, does the military situation—the "facts established on the ground"—get translated into a peace settlement?

To begin with, peace is rarely imposed by one contestant or by an outside power, for the most common ending to armed conflict is negotiated settlement.[1] This point is sometimes forgotten in the aftermath of the unconditional surrender imposed in World War II, yet the limited wars of the past half-century have usually been resolved by negotiations, for example in Korea.[2] Moreover, the practice of concluding a cease-fire during the talks, which flourished between the Peace of Utrecht in 1711–12 and the Peace of Versailles in 1918–19, is increasingly rare.[3] Negotiating while fighting is thus a fact of life. The military situation, therefore, does not translate directly into a treaty, but must be mediated via negotiating positions taken up by both sides. Despite this indirect connection, however, scholars have paid surprisingly little attention to the dynamics of making peace while a war is still in progress.

To study the effects of military campaigns on negotiations, this book investigates the policy of Cardinal Mazarin at the Congress of Westphalia. Historians have a long tradition of neglecting the last half of the Thirty Years' War: in general works on the war, the years from 1618 to 1635—which cover just over half the war—often get three-quarters or more of the coverage.[4] In part this is understandable: those years were marked by a very complicated diplomatic situation that is hard to convey in a small amount of space.[5] Yet the heavy coverage devoted to the first half of the war tends to give the impression that the last part, which is relatively "neat" in that the powers were pretty well lined up on each side in a military struggle, is well understood.

Nothing could be further from the truth. Militarily, there is no modern account of the campaigns of the last years of the war. It is possible to read, in otherwise respectable works, such blatantly false statements as that France recaptured Freiburg in 1644.[6] Though tactics and strategy had evolved from the methods of Gustavus and Wallenstein, there is no general study of them, and correspondingly little understanding. Even the methods of raising and financing armies evolved from the famous system developed by Wallenstein, though historians have paid but little attention to them thus far.[7]

The diplomatic side has been almost equally understudied. Admittedly, since the publication of Fritz Dickmann's monumental work, *Der Westfälische Frieden*, nearly forty years ago, this important treaty—the most important between Verdun in 843 and the Congress of Vienna in 1814–15—has received increasing scholarly attention. Nevertheless, large gaps in our understanding still remain: the role of the peace in the origins of state sovereignty and international law is widely debated, and the effect of balance of power ideas has barely begun to be investigated.[8]

One important limitation in recent studies is that they have tended to concentrate on German states, an understandable bias considering that most scholars working on them are themselves German. To understand the Congress fully, however, a better understanding of the policies of all powers—particularly the French, Spanish, Dutch, and Swedes—is needed. France, the only state with armies in both the Low Countries and the German heartland, was a particularly important fulcrum of power, yet there is not a single study of French policy at Westphalia—the only major power so neglected.

Cardinal Mazarin, the French first minister, is the perfect symbol for this oversight: caught between two giants of French history, Richelieu and Louis XIV, he is usually a mere epilogue to the one or prologue to the other; his most-frequently cited accomplishments are completing Richelieu's objective of subduing the Habsburgs and laying the groundwork for Louis XIV's extraordinary reign.[9] Corresponding to this historical neglect, there is no adequate biography of Mazarin, especially for his early years in power. Most biographies, such as those by Karl Federn, Paul Guth, and Geoffrey Treasure, concentrate heavily on the Fronde, while Mazarin appears as only a secondary character in Pierre

Goubert's recent, *annalistes*-style work.[10] Predictably, the romantic aspects of Mazarin's career—his tremendous wealth, his library, and above all his still-unsolved relationship with the Queen Regent—have dominated historiography to the detriment of serious study of his policies.[11]

Recent revisionist historiography on the Military Revolution, on Cardinal Richelieu, and on Mazarin himself highlight the need for a study of Mazarin's policy at the Congress of Westphalia. A whole line of recent historians, including William Church and Joseph Bergin, have questioned whether Richelieu was as single-mindedly interested in reason of state as he has been supposed to be; at the same time, David Parrott and Jeremy Black have led a new attack on the Military Revolution in general, and on French military efficiency in particular.[12] Where does this leave Mazarin, generally acknowledged not only to have succeeded Richelieu but to have carried on his policies as well? And where does this leave the French achievement at Westphalia?

Mazarin, the Peacemaker?

Mazarin has been the beneficiary of one of the most successful historical rehabilitations ever. In his own day considered a deceitful and ambitious, if effective, schemer, he has now been hailed in the title of one recent biography as "a man of peace in the Baroque age."[13] It was probably inevitable that the negative picture of Mazarin that arose from the Fronde would be corrected over time and perhaps even over-corrected, but the change has been so dramatic and so fast that it is nevertheless remarkable. Adolphe Chéruel, Mazarin's most important modern defender, published his seminal *Histoire de France pendant la minorité de Louis XIV* in 1879, but it was only after World War II that pro-Mazarin works became the rule rather than the exception. Beginning with Saint-Aulaire's 1946 biography, Mazarin has been portrayed as something approaching, and even at times surpassing, a pacifist. Saint-Aulaire himself even credited Mazarin with the success of the American Revolution: after all, if France had not been allied with Spain, she could not have defeated Britain at sea; and if Mazarin had not arranged for the marriage alliance between Louis XIV and Maria Theresa, France would not have been allied with Spain in the 1770s.[14]

It was Maurice Schumann who, in 1959, first attributed Mazarin's peacefulness to his internationalism. While for Saint-

Aulaire, Mazarin was a French nationalist, for Schumann he was "Mazarin Européen," a moderate who refused to impose French domination on Europe.[15] This interpretation has become the new orthodoxy in the last fifteen years with the publication of Georges Dethan's *Mazarin: Un homme de paix à l'âge baroque, 1602–1661,* Madeleine Laurain-Portemer's "Questions Européennes et Diplomatie Mazarine," and Andrew Lossky's *Louis XIV and the French Monarchy,* and it is explicitly endorsed in Geoffrey Treasure's recent biography.[16]

It is easy to see how Mazarin might be remembered primarily for making peace—after all, his greatest diplomatic accomplishments were the Peace of Westphalia in 1648 and the Peace of the Pyrenees in 1659. Yet Mazarin has not been praised simply for concluding the wars that he inherited, but for being a moderate internationalist to the core. Thus, Andrew Lossky has written that "Mazarin was moved by the medieval ideal of the *Res publica Christiana* and . . . he regarded himself as a public servant of this Christian Commonwealth"; he praises Mazarin for his fundamental moderation; and claims that Mazarin's international outlook has been responsible, in part, for the "bad press" he has received from "votaries of the nation state." Georges Dethan, the grandnephew of Chéruel and an even more vehement defender, writes that Mazarin's diplomatic oeuvre "was essentially pacific," and adds that "the thing that really strikes the historian when he rereads the texts of the treaties inspired by Mazarin's diplomacy . . . is the moderation that characterizes them."[17] At their most absurd, historians such as Saint-Aulaire and Paul Guth have deified Mazarin, calling him the "prince of peace" and making even more blatant comparisons to Jesus Christ.[18]

Concomitant to this reassessment of Mazarin as a moderate peacemaker rather than an aggressive state builder is a reevaluation of French success at the Peace of Westphalia. David Parrott's widely read dissertation on military administration under Richelieu challenged the notion that France was militarily ascendant from the moment it entered the Thirty Years' War, and in other works he and Jeremy Black have extended the criticism of the French war effort into the 1640s and 1650s.[19] Historians have increasingly seen French success as a product of inefficient brute force that did not lead to decisive results; as Orest Ranum explains it, the Habsburgs had, in a sense, "been defeated militarily; but the powers that had defeated them were so exhausted by their efforts that they risked losing in negotiations what they had gained in battle."[20] Since the French had failed militarily, then, the results of the Peace of Westphalia have increasingly been viewed as an unhappy compromise that accomplished little; in Lossky's succinct phrase, "French military efforts in the Thirty Years War brought meager tangible results."[21] Though less entrenched than the image of Mazarin as peacemaker, this, too, has become the new orthodoxy.

> "The conferences advanced or retreated according to the vicissitudes of the combats, and our most persuasive ambassador . . . was the news of a new victory."
> —Victor Cousin[22]

A peace treaty is the product of two different sets of forces, one diplomatic, and the other military; and the dual revision of Mazarin's peace policy and the French war effort has challenged both aspects of France's role at the Congress of Westphalia as it has been traditionally understood. By investigating the effects of military success and defeat on the French negotiating position at the Congress of Westphalia, both Mazarin's peace policy and the level of French success at the conference come into sharper focus. Nowhere has the influence of military campaigns on diplomatic negotiations been more forcefully affirmed than at Westphalia.[23] The extraordinary length of the negotiations, and the fact that no truce was concluding while they were taking place, created the possibility that military operations would affect the outcome of the peace more than in other wars. But rather than analyze the relationship between fighting and peacemaking, scholars have typically merely indicated its sinister effects—for example, Peter Englund's melodramatic claim that "soldiers had been prisoners of the system for many years, and now it seemed that even the diplomats had been captured in its irrefutable logic. No one controlled the war anymore. It was the war that controlled them."[24]

Historians who agree with the general sentiment that military affairs began to dominate the negotiations—and they are legion—almost always insist that along with fluctuating military success came instability in negotiating, and hence delay. In other words, the decision to negotiate and fight at the same time delayed peace. According to Pierre Goubert, for example, the talks dragged on "above all because everyone watched the changing fortune of arms on the various fronts, and its very evolution strongly influenced the negotiations and the successive, difficult, and complex decisions."[25] Or, in R. R. Palmer's more bluntly expressed model, "The negotiations dragged on, because the armies were still fighting, and after each battle one side or the other raised its terms."[26]

In spite of their differences, Goubert and Palmer seem to agree that there was a crisis in leadership, since statesmen could not or would not look beyond their own short-term interest to the long-term benefits of peace. No doubt the weight of such a responsibility weighed heavily on those in charge, for, on the highest level, both military and diplomatic strategy merge into a single whole managed by one person. As Clausewitz expressed it,

> To bring a war, or one of its campaigns, to a successful close requires a thorough grasp of national policy. On that level strategy and policy coalesce: the commander-in-chief is simultaneously a statesman . . . On the one hand, he is aware of the entire political situation; on the other, he knows exactly how much he can achieve with the means at his disposal . . .

He continued by quoting Napoleon that "many of the decisions faced by the commander-in-chief resemble mathematical problems worthy of the gifts of a *Newton* or an *Euler*."[27]

Ironically, Mazarin, the French statesman who fulfilled this dual role, has been hailed as an innovator in his integration of military and diplomatic factors. The Baroque is noted for combining different kinds of art, and it seems appropriate that Mazarin, the man who introduced opera to France, should be remembered for his ability to combine military and diplomatic aspects of statesmanship. "For the first time," wrote Gaston Zeller of the acquisition of Breisach and Philippsburg, "the idea of a strategic frontier inspired . . . our diplomacy,"[28] while Georges Livet has called Mazarin "the man for the hour, for this period when diplomacy and war went hand in hand."[29] Not only did he let military concerns influence his goals for the peace, but he also recognized the centrality of military force in obtaining those goals; as he once wrote to the duc de Longueville, the German army was "the door through which we should enter the peace."[30]

Mazarin has traditionally been portrayed as cynically exploiting French military success to obtain more and more territory for France; as Treasure's biography states bluntly, "with each report of victory he urged [the plenipotentiaries] Servien and d'Avaux to ask for more."[31] Only the Fronde, so the story goes, forced him to make peace in 1648 rather than pressing French advantages still further. But what was Mazarin? Was he a Machiavellian statesman out to expand French borders at any price, or an internationalist interesting in securing peace for the *Res publica Christiana*? Was he a poor statesman who failed to look beyond the immediate gains of a military campaign, or a skillful and original thinker who integrated war and diplomacy? To answer these questions, this book looks at the French negotiating position in light of the military campaigns. It seems at first like a straightforward enough task, perhaps even a dull one; after all, most historians take it for granted that any state will increase its demands as its military situation improves and decrease them when it suffers defeats. The truth, however, is much more enigmatic in this case: battlefield results hardly registered at all on the French negotiating position. Instead of tracking the day-to-day changes in French policy as news from the front filtered in, therefore, the book confronts several deeper questions: Why did Mazarin not increase his demands? What factors did affect his negotiating position? What was his military strategy, and why did it not have a greater influence on his negotiating position than one would expect?

Thus, this study is fundamentally centered on the effects of the military campaigns on the French negotiating position; but in order to do so, it delves deeply into Mazarin's overall strategy and its determinants. Part 1 explains the context of the war and the negotiations, particularly emphasizing the limitations of both and the options that were available to Mazarin and his opponents. Part 2 then follows the negotiations chronologically up to the preliminary treaty in September 1646. Finally, the conclusion assesses Mazarin's strategy and its success; evaluates the role of military campaigns in his negotiating position and suggests other influences; and offers a new explanation for the length of the conference.

2
The Decision Makers

THE MOST POWERFUL MAN IN FRANCE AFTER THE DEATH OF RICHElieu in 1642 was Cardinal Jules Mazarin. His name sounds French enough, but in fact he was born in 1602 with the name of Giulio Mazzarini, a subject of the king of Spain. Mazarin's foreignness has colored interpretations of him ever since: to his contemporaries, it meant that he was a devious Italian in the mold of Machiavelli; to recent historians, it means that he was a holdover who still believed in the unity of Christendom and who restored peace to a war-torn Europe. One of the purposes of this study is to rescue Mazarin from his liminal status as a foreigner and to explain his actions in terms that he would have understood. Parts of both views of him—as a calculating power-politician and as a moderate internationalist—will appear, but neither will dominate his personality as they have in previous historiography.

Mazarin studied at the University of Alcalá in Spain, and, upon his return, raised troops to serve under the pope. In 1628 he entered papal diplomatic service, and earned an international reputation just two years later by his dramatic intervention announcing the conclusion of the Peace of Cherasco between French and Spanish forces preparing for battle. He met Richelieu in the same year and maintained contact with him in the ensuing decade.

Mazarin's grip on power in 1643, when this study begins, appeared particularly tenuous. He had only been made a cardinal in 1641, and, for that matter, had only been a French citizen since 1639. Richelieu had not made any particular arrangements for a successor,[1] and although Louis XIII accepted Mazarin as his first minister, his death in May 1643 left the monarchy in the hands of the four-year-old Louis XIV and his mother, Anne of Austria. The elder Louis did not trust his wife, who was the sister of Philip IV of Spain, so his will stipulated that the government should be run by a council during his son's minority. Nevertheless, Anne was able to convince all concerned parties—Parlement and the *grands* (important nobles)—that it would be in their best interests if she were to have full power. In a special inaugural *lit de justice* (in which the Parlement registered an edict in the presence of the king) held on 18 May, Parlement officially negated her husband's will (which was probably illegal anyway) and gave Anne unrestricted control of the regency.[2]

Mazarin's authority therefore rested almost exclusively on the confidence of the queen, a lifelong foe of Richelieu. Instead of ridding herself of Mazarin and seizing sole power, however, Anne continued to rely on him. There are two main reasons for this apparently surprising situation. First, Anne herself was unfit to govern by both training and temperament; and Mazarin was the only person she could trust to manage things properly during the delicate first months of the regency. Second, Mazarin was not Richelieu. Whereas Anne had quarrelled with the reserved, apparently sinister Richelieu, she became closely attached to the more open Mazarin. The cardinal and the queen, who were approximately the same age (Anne was Mazarin's senior by less than a year), grew into an intimate friendship that some thought crossed the line into an outright sexual relationship. While this would not be entirely unthinkable—their passionate, encoded correspondence makes one suspicious—it seems unlikely. The two needed each other, complemented each other well, and evidently engaged in a great deal of gallantry; but there is no evidence of a physical relationship.[3]

Nevertheless, it is beyond question that Anne was devoted to Mazarin and trusted him implicitly. The Venetian ambassador, Nani, reported in 1648 that Anne "depends on the will of her favorite with such absolute resignation that she does not hold other opinions, does not speak in other voices, does not profess other counsel unless they come completely established from Mazarin." But even Ruth Kleinman, who states as one of the goals of her biography of Anne to get away from the hitherto romanticized picture and show her as an active player in politics, has to conclude that "the established pattern of their collaboration" was simple: "he proposed and she followed."[4]

If the base of Mazarin's power was secured by his close personal relationship with Anne, he still had to contend with other political forces. As usual in a change of government, powerful factions opposed to the previous régime demanded a reckoning and sought to take advantage of the weakness of the new government to establish their own control. One of Mazarin's first actions was to recall those exiled by Richelieu; but they liked Mazarin—Richelieu's protégé—little more than his predecessor. A group calling itself the *Cabale des Importants* sought to assassinate Mazarin in his first year in office; besides this threat, Mazarin also had to contend with a major peasant rebellion in the Rouergue.

These were serious threats to a new government, especially one resting on the unstable foundation of a regency, but Mazarin weathered them with relative ease. Enghien's victory over the Spaniards at Rocroi on 19 May, just five days after the accession of Louis XIV, was not only an important symbolic triumph for the regency, but helped permit Anne and Mazarin to overturn Louis XIII's will and to pre-empt any who might have been thinking of taking advantage of a foreign invasion to foment rebellion. Over the first years of his ministry, Mazarin's authority only seemed to increase, such that by the middle of 1646, he could write that "France is more calm than it has ever been, calm down to the least point that one could desire of her to conclude a glorious peace."[5]

Mazarin exercised active control through his preponderant influence in the *Conseil d'en Haut*.[6] This body, which took on added importance in the minority of the king, was composed nominally of ten members, but only six attended with any regularity. The most powerful members of the council were the two princes of the blood: Gaston d'Orléans, brother of Louis XIII and uncle to the young Louis XIV, and Henri, prince de Condé. Gaston, known simply as "Monsieur," was second in line for the throne after the king's younger brother, Philippe. Although he did not have the same authority that he had enjoyed under Louis XIII, when he was for a long time the heir apparent, he still commanded considerable influence, not least in his role as *lieutenant général* of the kingdom. However, he relied heavily on his advisor, the Abbé de la Rivière; and since de la Rivière was in Mazarin's pay, Gaston could be kept more or less under control. Moreover, Monsieur spent even beyond his own prodigious resources, and hence needed to dip into state funds on occasion to remain solvent. Condé, or "Monsieur le Prince," was succeeded by his more famous son Louis, duc d'Enghien (later known as the "Grand Condé"), in December 1646. Both father and son were more obstreperous, at least in the 1640s, than Gaston; but since the Condé family struggled with the Orléans for preeminence, Mazarin was able to play one off against the other in order to maintain his own control. For instance, in 1644, the year after Enghien's great victory at Rocroi, Mazarin gave command of the main army in Flanders to Gaston; and he did the same in 1645. By thus promoting the rivalry between Condé and Orléans, Mazarin kept the two families more worried about each other than about his own government. Moreover, the younger Condé was so anxious to acquire military glory that he was usually at the front fighting, and thus could not participate in council meetings during campaigning season.[7] The other members of the council, such as the *Surintendant des Finances*, Bailleul (an office later held by Michel Particelli d'Hémery and then by the maréchal de La Meilleraye) and the *garde des sceaux*, Pierre Séguier, were more easily cowed. The plenipotentiaries, Longueville and d'Avaux, were of course in Münster and not able to sit (Servien only became a minister in 1648).[8]

Unfortunately, no records of council meetings survive, so we cannot be sure exactly how much authority Mazarin exercised in particular matters.[9] It is clear that some councillors, particularly Gaston and Condé, dared oppose him, at least outside of official council meetings. Mazarin once complained, for instance, that someone in the council—most likely Condé—was claiming that France desperately needed peace. Since such public proclamations ran directly counter to the official policy of affecting a lack of interest in peace in order to convince the Habsburgs of the need for concessions, Mazarin was naturally irritated by them. "After all," he wrote to the plenipotentiaries, "with one man building and the other destroying, I leave it to you to decide whether it is very easy to complete a building."[10] Yet Mazarin was surprisingly tolerant of dissension, writing, on another occasion, that "it is impossible to prevent some people from making contrary statements, not that they lack zeal for the good of the state, but because they believe that the expedients we adopt are not the best to achieve it."[11]

Nevertheless, there was a marked difference between what powerful members of council stated publicly and the actual decisions taken by the council. Mazarin was content to let the nobles vent their frustrations on the side so long as they did not interfere with his control of policy making. He still had Anne's favor, and, as he noted to the plenipotentiaries, "All of this [dissension] does not, thank God, have any effect on the Queen's spirit."[12] And when he deemed opposing statements too threatening, Mazarin quickly put the dissenters in their place: both Gaston and Condé wrote humble letters to the plenipotentiaries early in 1646 in which they stated that they no longer doubted that peace would be made soon by Mazarin's policies. Both announced that they accepted the decisions made by the council "all of one voice," and Condé added that "all my sentiments, . . . conform entirely to the resolutions approved . . . in the council."[13] All evidence suggests that Mazarin never lost an argument in the council.[14]

Mazarin therefore exercised effective control of the decision-making processes of the government. Not only that, but he also kept a tight rein over those subordinates who were close to him physically. As time went on, he encroached further and further on duties previously delegated to Michel Le Tellier and Henri de Loménie, comte de Brienne, the secretaries of state for war and foreign affairs, until eventually they became little more than staff officers.[15] And, while Mazarin recognized the limitations of time and distance and did not try to micromanage the negotiations, it was still true that any minister that resisted his policies—such as d'Avaux—was dismissed. The Venetian ambassador, Nani, described Mazarin's control most succinctly: "Frankly, it may be said that the king has the name, the queen the shadow, the council the prospect, but Cardinal Mazarin the substance and the effect of absolute command"; and on another occasion, he wrote that "the absolute direction of the kingdom, of the forces, of the arms, of the treasury all depend on the will of the Cardinal."[16]

Admittedly, Mazarin's decisions were circumscribed by many factors. He sought to appease the grandees with important military appointments, and in all cases his commands were of course subject to local interpretation and implementation (see below on Mazarin's managerial style and on time and distance problems). Mazarin also felt compelled to act in certain ways because he was heading the government during a regency and because he was a foreigner by birth. No signs of weakness could be countenanced that would call into question his own loyalty or make it seem that the regency was achieving less for France than a king himself might have done. As Mazarin admitted to d'Avaux,

> it is true that my status as a foreigner obliges me to do more than if I had been born French, and that the Queen also is obliged similarly, being the sister of the king of Spain, because without this quality she would be advised to give in more than she does.[17]

Mazarin was thus subject to the pressures of "public opinion," at least as far as the upper nobility was concerned.[18] His ministers were surprisingly unanimous in believing that a revolt in France during Louis XIV's minority was inevitable; in 1646, Longueville even predicted the year correctly.[19] Already during the *lit de justice* annulling Louis XIII's will, a Parlementary leader supplicated "the king and the queen to make peace, which alone could end the misery of the people."[20] Yet Mazarin was not worried about a popular rebellion; indeed, he brushed aside enemy threats to break off the conference and thereby incite unrest among the peace-starved French population.[21] On the other hand, his decision not to trade away French rights to Navarre (which were essentially a dead letter anyway) was largely based on the public outcry he feared would ensue at the relinquishing of an old French possession.[22] Similarly, after the battle of Freiburg, Mazarin only reluctantly gave up the idea of recapturing the town, which he felt the public would expect after a victorious battle (chapter 6). At least his foreignness could not be exploited effectively by the enemy. In fact, Mazarin felt that Spanish attacks on him made him more loved among the French than anything else, and he was happy to see them republished in France.[23]

Yet if Mazarin was concerned about public opinion and was willing to yield on lesser matters, he nevertheless pushed through a negotiating policy of great sternness in the teeth of the opposition of many Frenchmen, including some of the most powerful nobles.[24] Moreover, Mazarin's negotiating stance, particularly toward Spain, became more unyielding over time. In 1643 and 1644, Mazarin's position was still relatively insecure, and he was consequently more cautious, following in the path laid out by Richelieu; by 1646, Mazarin had become confident of his position both inside and outside of France, and became correspondingly more strident.[25]

France's negotiating position was, to a great extent, Mazarin's negotiating position. It may therefore be understood by examining the factors influencing Mazarin, and, to a lesser extent, his ministers. In other words, we are certainly dealing with a "rational actor" who made decisions based on analysis of factors. Undoubtedly Mazarin was subject to input from his inferiors; however, there is no question of competing subgroups fashioning policy haphazardly according to their own interests. Of tantamount importance is the fact that Mazarin made all the final decisions.[26] Moreover, Mazarin considered political factors almost exclusively—or, at the least, gave political factors absolute priority over other factors (see below, conclusion).

Richelieu had originally intended for Mazarin himself to be a plenipotentiary to the conference, along with the comte d'Avaux. When Richelieu died and Mazarin became the first minister, he thought of choosing Chavigny, the recently disgraced council member, as his replacement. However, Chavigny wavered, at first desiring to be permanent ambassador to Rome (which was considered more prestigious), but eventually choosing simply to remain in Paris. In his place, Mazarin selected Abel Servien, who had been in disgrace since 1636 and who was only recalled in May on the death of Louis XIII.[27] D'Avaux and Servien were typical of Mazarin's diplomatic appointments in that both were from the upper strata of the *noblesse de robe*.[28] For purposes of prestige, however, the duc de Longueville, a sword noble of royal blood, was to serve as head of the delegation.

The lowest ranking French plenipotentiary—Abel Servien, marquis de Sablé et Bois-dauphin, comte de la Roche-Servien—paradoxically exercised the greatest influence on the negotiations. He had a keen, impatient mind that was capable of breaking any issue into its component parts, as his numerous memoranda demonstrate. He was also efficient at separating important matters from unimportant ones; he claimed, for instance, that just as it was better to stand firm on the crucial issues surrounding the acquisition of Alsace, it was better to be accommodating on the question of an indemnity.[29] At the same time, he was intensely jealous and not at all ingratiating—certainly great weaknesses in a diplomat.[30] Servien was an experienced minister, having served at the peace talks at Cherasco in 1630–31 and as *secrétaire d'état de la guerre* until 1636, when he was disgraced. He was devoted to Mazarin, who had given him a second chance after his long exile from court.[31]

Servien's partner was Claude de Mesmes, comte d'Avaux. Also an experienced diplomat, he had served as representative to Venice and Denmark, and had negotiated the preliminary treaty in Hamburg that had paved the way for the congress in Münster and Osnabrück. Even his enemies, such as Henri de La Court, had to admit that he was a skillful negotiator.[32] He spoke fluent German as well as several other languages, and was already popular in Germany from his other visits there. By virtue of his earlier appointment and his title of *ministre*, D'Avaux had a higher rank than Servien in the delegation (and hence was always mentioned first in royal letters, received the first visit from foreign representatives, and the like). Moreover, he would have been powerful even were it not for his ambassadorship, since he was one of the two *surintendants des finances* (a function that, however, he could not effectively perform while in Münster), while his brother Henri de Mesmes was a president of the Parlement of Paris. D'Avaux supported a magnificent train that was the envy not only of foreign ambassadors, but of Servien as well.[33]

D'Avaux and Servien are often seen as polar opposites: d'Avaux the *dévot*, interested in promoting Catholic interests in the Empire and in favor of compromise; Servien the rationalist, interested in promoting the good of the French state at all costs and in favor of a hard line. There is some truth to this picture, for d'Avaux was certainly more worried about the fate of Catholicism in the Empire, and he was particularly well-disposed toward Bavaria. Servien, by contrast, was coldly rational when it came to negotiations. He quite honestly told Mazarin that "I have no other interest before my eyes than that of the State, of the service of the Queen, and that of His Eminence": religion played no obvious role in his diplomacy.[34] But while he aggressively pursued France's aggrandizement, it is probably an exaggeration to claim, as does Dickmann, that his policy was "reckless."[35] Servien was ruthless, to be sure, but he had the sense to be careful about whom France was offending. At the same time, d'Avaux (and Longueville) fully supported the acquisition of Alsace. If the acquisition of Alsace was a step of unprecedented ambition (which is debatable), at least the French ministers were united behind it; it was not something foisted by Servien on his colleagues and his superiors. D'Avaux's immense personal piety did not prevent him from supporting the war for raison d'état, and he was considered a friend of Protestant Sweden ever more than the *politique* Servien.[36]

Whether they held opposite political views or not, it is true that the two French ministers had begun quarrelling even before they got to Münster.[37] The immediate cause of their disagreement is unclear, but the deeper cause was that Servien was jealous of d'Avaux's superior status and extravagant display (which Servien could not afford). It is impossible to say precisely who was to blame, but it is clear that d'Avaux was more compromising in the beginning. As the senior representative, he had originally been in charge of drafting their common letters to court, but surrendered the responsibility to Servien at great expense to his own authority. Later, he would claim that Servien often presented him with already completed letters, giving him only minimal opportunity to make changes before sending them to Paris.[38] The feud between the two ministers grew increasingly bitter in the middle of 1644; after stern orders from court, it went through a period of quiescence, but flared up again at the beginning of 1645. D'Avaux refused to participate in drafting the letters to court, and Servien complained bitterly that

> when a negotiation is long, having multiple negotiators hurts more than it helps, because one likes to contradict or to destroy that which

the other has proposed or advanced. I have seen people who prefer to act than to let others act, but I have never seen anyone besides Monsieur d'Avaux who prevents others from working on things with which he refuses the charge himself. If it does not please the Queen to use her authority occasionally to order flatly those things that she judges necessary for her service, she will never be well served.[39]

D'Avaux, hoping that Mazarin would request that he stay, and perhaps even force Servien to retire, eventually tendered his resignation.

It was a serious miscalculation. Instead of begging him to stay, Mazarin merely wrote that he was sorry to see d'Avaux leave. Chastened, d'Avaux was forced to respond that he had determined to remain a little longer for the good of the king's service, and eventually the resignation was quietly forgotten—but d'Avaux's position in the embassy had been permanently lowered.

The outcome of this episode had been virtually inevitable. D'Avaux supported opinions contrary to Mazarin, while Servien depended entirely on the Cardinal.[40] Servien was not above writing that he wished Mazarin had not given his own opinion on an item at the same time that he requested Servien's, since "I have such a profound veneration for his opinions and I have always seen them succeed so happily that I abandon mine blindly when I find them contrary."[41] Mazarin returned Servien's faithfulness by giving him special consideration. He solicited Servien's opinion separate from the others, and sent him additional money without the knowledge of d'Avaux.[42] As he noted in one letter, "If I were to send some special message to one of you without telling the others, it would be sooner to you, for all sorts of reasons, than to the others . . ."[43] Against statements such as this, Mazarin's bland comment that d'Avaux was "one of my best friends" seems decidedly insincere.[44]

In addition to his special favor, Servien had a further, decisive advantage over d'Avaux: his nephew Hugues de Lionne, who served as Mazarin's personal secretary, and later as the *secrétaire des commandemens de la reine.*[45] Lionne not only intervened personally for Servien with Mazarin, but also supported him in a variety of more devious ways. When Maximilian of Bavaria wrote in praise of d'Avaux, for example, Lionne informed Servien that "he wasted his time, because I am the only one who has seen it, and I am not in a hurry to mention it."[46] Lionne also did not hesitate to pass along the contents of d'Avaux's letters to Servien where he felt it could be of assistance.[47] And when Servien submitted his own letter of resignation shortly after d'Avaux's, Lionne wisely withheld it, figuring that it would only irritate Mazarin (see below, chapter 7).[48]

D'Avaux was aware of his disadvantage, but could pose little against it.[49] At court, his friendly ties to Brienne were not as useful as Servien's relationship with Lionne, not only because Brienne and d'Avaux were not as intimate, but also because Brienne exercised relatively little influence compared to Lionne.[50] True, he was secretary of state for foreign affairs; but it was Mazarin who made the decisions, and Lionne had Mazarin's ear much more than Brienne did. Brienne did serve d'Avaux well on occasion, once even withholding a letter of resignation, but he could not stop Servien from having the preponderant influence.

D'Avaux was the more popular among foreign delegations, both allied and enemy. His support among the Bavarians was predictable given his sympathy for German Catholics. But even the Swedes favored d'Avaux, writing in March 1645, that he was essential because of his knowledge of the people, his ability to speak German, and the fact that he was generally well-liked. Servien, who had been expecting Swedish support against d'Avaux, was bitterly disappointed by this sudden endorsement.[51] Yet Swedish and Bavarian support, though nice, could not help d'Avaux much in internal power struggles. What he really needed was another ally within the government.

Such an ally seemed to fall providentially into his hands just as his recall request had put him at his deepest disfavor: the leader of the French delegation, Henri II d'Orléans, duc de Longueville, who arrived in Münster on 30 June 1645. Longueville had been sent in large part to end the bickering between Servien and d'Avaux, which had become so severe that it was interfering with the negotiations. Servien at first complained that Longueville favored d'Avaux, and feared being overruled by his two colleagues.[52] However, he soon realized that Longueville was not as partial as he had thought, and even d'Avaux had to admit to Brienne that he had no special relationship with Longueville.[53]

Longueville, who had married Enghien's sister in 1642, had been the governor of Normandy since 1619, and had commanded the *Armée d'Allemagne* in 1640 and later led the army in Piedmont.[54] Undoubtedly an ambitious man, he was judged by Nani to have spent too much effort chasing after titles.[55] One particularly troublesome incident occurred on the death of the duc de Brézé, the *amiral de France*. Longueville wanted the office, and complained bitterly to Mazarin when Anne kept it for herself.

Mazarin reacted defensively, and tensions between the two ran very high for a time.[56] Longueville eventually left Münster in February 1648, of his own accord, annoyed with Mazarin's policies and the sluggish progress of the negotiations. Later, he (and his more famous wife) participated in the Fronde.

Longueville has traditionally been regarded as a mere figurehead who played no significant part in the talks.[57] While it is very difficult to determine the input that each delegate had in the negotiations, it seems likely that Longueville's role has been downplayed excessively. He was not only the head of the delegation in title, but also maintained the balance between Servien and d'Avaux, who were usually at odds: whichever side Longueville supported was likely to be approved. Moreover, Mazarin sent Longueville long letters containing important orders supplementing the official royal memoranda. Longueville evidently shared the information with his colleagues, but did not allow them to read the letters, thereby making him a vital intermediary between the court and his subordinates.[58] It is true that some of his ideas, such as the acquisition of Strasbourg, were far-fetched; on the whole, however, he was a capable diplomat whose ideas were by no means despised by Mazarin.

A number of other officials assisted the French delegation. To begin with, each representative had his own secretaries. More significantly, Théodore de Godefroy, the royal historiographer, was attached to the delegation as a whole, and advised them in the complicated historical and legal questions surrounding the Imperial constitution and the French demands in Alsace and Lorraine.[59] The marquis de St. Romain served as resident in Münster and acted as a factotum for the embassy, carrying a message to court and even travelling to Sweden.[60] The most important assistants were the series of residents in Osnabrück, who kept the embassy up to date on the Swedish negotiations and the discussions by the German estates there. The first man in this post was the baron de Rorté; he was replaced in 1645 by Jean de La Barde, who was in turned succeeded in 1646 by Henri Groulart, the sieur de La Court.[61] Of these, St. Romain and de La Barde were openly under d'Avaux's protection, a situation that he exploited as much as possible. De La Court, on the other hand, was nominated by Servien, and depended on him.[62]

The trains of the French ambassadors were enormous: d'Avaux maintained over 200 in his house, Servien over 119.[63] These included at least five secretaries each, numerous pages, a priest, a surgeon, barbers, cleaning women, and assistants to look after the horses, among others; they do not include the eighteen nobles and six noble women that d'Avaux brought along to attend himself and his wife (Servien brought only four). D'Avaux's following was said to be as large as that of the five Habsburg diplomats put together.[64] This extraordinary display was partly to increase the prestige of the French crown; but it was also partly practical. Servien explained to de La Court the bare necessities:

> Two pages, four lackeys, a six-horse carriage, a majordomo, a good secretary and someone in addition who can write in Latin, a cook and an assistant, an office boy, and your usual valets. Voilà what is necessary. If you wish to add some gentlemen to be near you, you may do so.[65]

To support such a huge train, the plenipotentiaries received one hundred thousand livres per year from the government. Even this prodigious sum, however, was not sufficient to cover all their expenses. The plenipotentiaries not only maintained their own households, but also had to spread around money as bribes (which they did liberally) and to cover advances to officers raising regiments for the king. As time went on, the plenipotentiaries became more involved in recruiting and needed more money for bribes, so that for a time in 1646 they were complaining about the lack of money in almost every letter.[66]

Command and Control

It was impossible for Mazarin to exercise absolute control of his delegates operating hundreds of miles away in Münster, particularly when two of the delegates, d'Avaux and Longueville, did not share Mazarin's view of the political situation. Mazarin did have a number of important factors working in his favor. To begin with, there was Servien, who was absolutely faithful and who agreed almost entirely with Mazarin's outlook. In addition, Servien and d'Avaux's quarrel prevented them from subverting Mazarin's orders deliberately. And Mazarin could always dismiss someone who began disagreeing too strongly, as when he released d'Avaux in 1648. As a last resort, Mazarin could disavow the actions of his plenipotentiaries, as Richelieu had refused to ratify the Treaty of Regensburg in 1630; but this was a desperate measure to be avoided if at all possible.[67]

Mazarin, however, rarely needed to go to such extremes, because he was well aware of the problems of distance and communication in his running of affairs, and so left his plenipotentiaries a large amount of room to make their own decisions. In spite of their differences, Mazarin had confidence in his plenipotentiaries, writing to them that

> when I gave you the liberty before the start of the campaign to do [what you wanted] more or less in many things, I considered very carefully into whose hands I committed this power, and that each of you had the zeal and the prudence necessary to know [whether] to hold firm or to diminish our demands, or even to increase them, according to whether the military campaign, which should set the negotiations in motion and regulate them, went well or poorly.[68]

It is true that Mazarin was sometimes impatient with the plenipotentiaries for not obeying orders. On one occasion, he wrote "that it was useless to issue and to reiterate orders if they were not executed," and on a different occasion he complained that the plenipotentiaries seemed to read his letters and then forget about them.[69] It is also true that Mazarin could set sharp boundaries on the plenipotentiaries' actions. For example, he disapproved strongly of their first proposition, handed over to the mediators in December 1644. He insisted on sending a second version that had been drafted at court; while the plenipotentiaries worked on the next proposition, they spent much longer on it because they were constantly soliciting advice from court, and this delayed negotiations to an extent that almost proved embarrassing for France.[70]

But this was an exception. On most occasions, Mazarin gave the plenipotentiaries significant leeway, writing, for example, "I have told you many things . . . not with the thought that you do them all, but so that in their diversity you can choose what you believe the most useful."[71] This flexibility extended to accepting less (or more) than the plenipotentiaries' official orders called for. As Mazarin closed one letter, "I have already frequently noted that I will not hesitate at all to approve and to advise Her Majesty of all the things that you believe that we must concede in order to have peace"; even more bluntly, he told Longueville that "you can act without any imaginable scruples."[72]

The plenipotentiaries did not hesitate to take advantage of this maneuvering room, even when it entailed making decisions that contradicted Mazarin's own plans and altered the course of the negotiations significantly. This is most evident in the decision to demand Philippsburg in May 1646, after Mazarin had repeatedly emphasized his desire to make peace as soon as possible. As they confidently wrote after concluding the preliminary treaty in September 1646, "If we have violated our orders, Your Majesty will have enough goodness to pardon us for it."[73] Mazarin's emphatic decision not to negotiate in writing underscored the confidence he had in his subordinates, and made effective central control all the more difficult.

Not only did Mazarin permit his plenipotentiaries considerable room for interpreting and even altering orders; he also frequently requested their advice and shaped his policy according to it. Indeed, when they did not tell him their opinion, he complained to them.[74] It is not uncommon to see ideas emanating from Münster being repeated in official memoranda a few weeks later. For example, Longueville once commented to Venetian mediator Alvise Contarini, in defending France's claim to Breisach, that France would not accept a province "that one could take from her in four days"; Mazarin found this so pithy that he took it up word for word in his own letter a week later.[75] Servien's ideas, expressed in long, methodical memoranda, were regularly borrowed by Mazarin. As Lionne wryly commented to Servien on one occasion, "We have received your memorandum from the 14th of this month. You will recognize this easily by several items included in the royal memo."[76] Often the plenipotentiaries were divided; but when they shared the same opinion, they almost always prevailed. They unanimously rejected Mazarin's idea of a truce on the Italian front, and also combined to warn Mazarin that Bavaria was not so well-intentioned toward France as he might to think. The one occasion on which Mazarin blatantly ignored the persistent warnings of his plenipotentiaries was on the proposed exchange of Catalonia for the Spanish Low Countries—with disastrous consequences (chapter 8 below).

Communication and Deception

The orders sent from Paris came from three sources: Brienne, Mazarin, and the monarch. The most official orders were those signed by, or in the name of, the king or queen.[77] Such letters were not actually written by the infant king or his mother, but rather had been approved by the French council acting in their name. Nevertheless, the "official" letters emanating from the council did not differ much, if at all, from Mazarin's private opinions, expressed in his own letters to the plenipotentiaries. It is true that he was careful to distinguish the two types of orders;

in one letter, for example, he elaborated an argument for keeping Alsace and the Three Bishoprics as fiefs, but concluded by adding that "all this is only my personal opinion, not yet having spoken of it either with Her Majesty or in the council."[78] However, it seems clear that in observing strict formality on these matters, Mazarin was either protecting himself from potential recriminations, distinguishing carefully between fixed orders and mere proposals, or simply using the technical existence of a higher authority as a means of excusing his own decisions; for he dropped several hints, some subtle and some unequivocal, indicating his control over matters. In discussing d'Anctoville's mission to the Elector of Trier (see chapter 8), Mazarin cautioned Longueville that "Her Majesty having left here two days ago, I cannot tell you that she has approved it, because I have not been able to tell her about it yet"; however, he continued, "I would dare assure you in advance that [she will approve it] without question, and that the money will be paid with great pleasure."[79] And on another occasion, he wrote in one of his personal letters that "I have elaborated myself in the king's memorandum on the subject of Bavaria to such an extent that there is nothing left for me to add."[80] Moreover, though Mazarin complained on occasion about the actions of individual council members, he never objected to the decisions of the council, even on trivial matters—a sure sign that its decisions and his were identical. Mazarin's personal letters to the plenipotentiaries therefore complement royal letters, explaining them and sometimes adding informal orders; the two types of instructions must both be seen as elaborations of Mazarin's own thought, the one more official, the other less so.

In addition to these two sources, Brienne sent weekly orders to the plenipotentiaries derived from the conclusions of the council. Though never substantially at odds with Mazarin's views, Brienne's confusing, often contradictory letters led to occasional misunderstandings. Servien complained that Brienne was well-intentioned,

> but he has a way of expressing himself that most often makes nonsense of his thoughts, and he sends us orders so obscure and that contradict themselves so much on the most important points that we do not know what to do. If subaltern ministers located at a distance do not receive clear orders, it is difficult for them to be able to perform their duties well.[81]

Mazarin had a low opinion of Brienne's abilities, and attempted to have a body set up to handle outgoing correspondence with the plenipotentiaries, but withdrew this attempt in the face of Brienne's objections. Servien's own request that Mazarin read Brienne's outgoing letters was rejected by Mazarin on the grounds of its impracticability; Mazarin did, however, read all official incoming mail to Brienne.[82] Although Brienne continued to write his official letters, from late 1644 Mazarin increasingly took it upon himself to write directly to the plenipotentiaries. Therefore, Brienne's letters lost importance and became largely repetitions of the information sent in Mazarin's correspondence and in official royal memoranda. Even more significantly, Mazarin informed Longueville in 1646 that Brienne's letters did not always conform to official policy, since "he sometimes makes reflections and judgments in his dispatches that come only from him."[83]

Unlike the letters of some statesmen, which were only expressed in general terms and then drafted by secretaries, Mazarin's letters were uniquely his.[84] He did permit his secretaries to correct "the faults committed against the purity of the French language by a very busy foreigner," but otherwise he assured d'Avaux "that I write no letter on official matters to anyone that I do not dictate down to the last word."[85] Mazarin's dispatches were later praised by François de Callières, author of the celebrated 1716 work *La manière de négocier avec les souverains*, as "chef d'oeuvres of this genre. He examines in them the interests of each power in Europe and gives openings and expedients for accommodating them with surprising ability and clarity."[86]

Letters usually took between eight and ten days to travel between Paris and Münster. The time seems to have improved slightly over the course of the conference, with letters in 1644 and 1645 taking ten days, but by 1646 usually only eight. Because it was customary to write every week whether there was anything to say or not, the letters between the court and the ambassadors crossed in the mail, so orders were frequently repeated several weeks in a row until the plenipotentiaries had responded.[87] The lag time was troublesome, of course, and contributed to the length of the negotiations, but it was not nearly so bad for the French as it was for the Spaniards or the Swedes (whose letters from Stockholm to Osnabrück usually took at least three weeks).

The postal system also contributed to the surprisingly leaky intelligence apparati of states in the 1640s.[88] Though governments lacked the sophisticated intelligence-gathering techniques of modern states—microdots, hidden microphones, and spy satellites—secrets were still less safe than they are today. Hardly would a plan be made than it would be talked about in courts across Europe. The "secret" French talks with Maximilian's confessor, Vervaux, in March and April of 1645, for example, were being discussed in Münster as far back as November.[89] Similarly, the negotiations with Bavaria after Alerheim quickly became common knowledge.[90] France also had long advance warning of Bavaria's defection in 1647 (see below, conclusion).[91]

Relying on the established postal network, the plenipotentiaries sent their letters consistently every Saturday.[92] Since the couriers had to pass through enemy lines, it was all too easy for the Spanish or Imperial forces to intercept and steal the letters. This became a point of great contention in 1644, and the French threatened to cut off diplomatically protected Spanish travel through France.[93] Nor were the French innocent of intercepting enemy letters, especially in 1646 and 1648, when their armies sat firmly astride the route from Bavaria to Münster.[94] For particularly important messages, the court would send a special courier; on several occasions, Cyrano de Bergerac was employed for this purpose.[95] A person could increase the chance of his letter reaching the intended recipient by sending multiple couriers along different routes, but this only increased the chance that one of them would be intercepted. In any case, sending couriers was too expensive to be used on a regular basis.[96] Therefore, both sides relied on encoding to safeguard their messages. Rather than encoding entire letters, they would restrict themselves to key passages, often switching in and out of code several times in the same sentence. This saved time; encoding and decoding in an age without computers was a tedious process, even with a key handy.[97] Not only that, but errors in decoding were not uncommon, and some of them were surprisingly substantial. The codes were none too sophisticated, almost always simple substitution codes with one number or pair of numbers standing for one letter. The French seem to have used a greater variety of codes, with different ones for different pairs of correspondents. They also used a wide variety of symbols to represent common words and names, not just individual letters.[98]

But it was not primarily the fault of the codes or the intercepted letters that secrets were so difficult to keep. Though simple, and though possible to decipher, codes were still an extremely effective method of hiding information from the enemy. They could only be broken with time, and the fact is that most letters reached their destination without being intercepted, while those that were opened were generally read and returned on the spot, with no opportunity for breaking the code.[99] The real weak points in any government's intelligence network were spies: individuals at court, in the household of an important minister, or otherwise privy to secret information, who passed it on to a foreign state.[100] Mazarin had spies in Trauttmansdorff's household and in Madrid, as well as other rumor-gatherers in various cities in the Empire; Servien himself had installed a domestic servant in the household of the Spanish plenipotentiary Brun who passed along useful information.[101] Maximilian does not seem to have had a "plant" in Paris. However, neutrals residing at the French court gathered information as a matter of routine, so there was little that remained a complete secret. Even French allies, such as the Dutch, would occasionally leak secrets if they felt it was to their advantage.[102] Mazarin noted that when Maximilian wrote to him once via the nuncio Bagno, the Swedish resident Cérisantes and the Hessian Polhelm, "who are rather alert to such practices," figured out what was going on.[103] According to Brienne, the Venetian ambassador Nani was a particular problem, since he was anxious to report anything, and therefore often exceeded what he actually knew. Brienne conceded that the French needed "to be very discreet around the foreign ambassadors in this court."[104] Nevertheless, friendly ambassadors were essential to maintain communication with allies, and neutrals served to permit communications with enemy states.[105] Bagno, the papal nuncio in Paris, played a particularly important role. Serving as an informal mediator between Maximilian and Mazarin, he passed information and offers to Maximilian. Sometimes, however, it was hard to distinguish between his own opinions and those of Mazarin, which led to difficulties.[106] Finally, there was an active press in both France and the Empire that quickly disseminated any rumors of which it happened to learn.[107] Although the French newspaper, the *Gazette,* was subject to state censure, it generally operated on its own, and Mazarin was not always happy with what it published.[108]

In the first months of 1646, when the negotiations over French satisfaction reached their crucial stage, the French were struck by an intelligence crisis: the plenipotentiaries complained that the enemy was somehow finding out about their orders, particularly the ones permitting them to give in on Philippsburg. Servien wrote to Lionne that "we have almost never received new orders from the court without the mediators or other foreign ministers having known about them at the same time, from which we receive such a prejudice that I cannot express it"; he suspected the Venetian ambassador, Nani.[109] Servien was most vociferous in his accusations, but d'Avaux, as well, pleaded with Mazarin, "in the name of God, Monseigneur, do not let the ambassadors at court penetrate your good and holy intentions."[110]

The French court reacted first with increased security measures and then, increasingly, with disbelief. As far back as February, Brienne had noted the necessity "to restrain the knowledge of the Münster negotiations to fewer people than we have done hitherto"; he also agreed with the plenipotentiaries that Nani was a likely cause of some of the leaks. Mazarin likewise urged the plenipotentiaries to send particularly secret messages directly to him rather than including them in the official memorandum, "which is read in the council whatever care I take to prevent it."[111]

Yet after more and increasingly urgent warnings from the plenipotentiaries, the attitude of the court turned to skepticism. The decision to give in on Philippsburg was known to only four people in Paris—Mazarin, Brienne, Gaston, and Condé—and Mazarin had talked at length with Brienne about possible security leaks.[112] Lionne suggested that the traitor lay in Münster rather than in Paris; but Mazarin felt that the Habsburgs were simply making their "intelligence" up:

> As for what you write to me about the discovery of many things that should be secret, I can assure you that, after having closely examined this point from all sides, I have determined that it is impossible that [the problem] comes from here. Instead, these are ideas that are made from the conjectures formed in the place where you are by the ministers of other rulers. They sometimes turn out to be true, which is not impossible, and thus to authorize their conjectures afterward, they publish that they were informed by a good source here.[113]

This diagnosis on Mazarin's part may well have been correct. As Lionne argued in a letter to Servien, the Habsburgs had never discovered the plenipotentiaries' orders permitting them to give in on Catalonia and Portugal, "which are the two most important points of your negotiation, and it seems that, if they were in contact with someone who knew all the secrets, they would have discovered this one as well as the others."[114] What made Mazarin's explanation even more credible was that Münster and Osnabrück were full of wild rumors, most of them completely groundless. The Spaniards were particularly fond of letting it be known that they had won a battle that they had in fact lost; they would be proven wrong, but in the meantime they could make some diplomatic capital out of their advantage.[115] On the other hand, the possibility that the Habsburgs did have some inside information cannot be entirely discounted. Longueville, for example, reported that the enemy claimed to know that the French had the authority to pay up to six million livres for Alsace; and this was precisely the amount they had been authorized to pay.[116] Where the Habsburgs said that France would select one option of two, the possibility of their guessing right makes it credible that they could have been merely speculating; but to choose the exact size of the indemnity that France was willing to pay implies a source of information more certain than sheer conjecture.

If the French experienced intelligence leaks, it appears that they benefitted at least as much from their own spies as they lost from the enemy's. Longueville once wrote to Mazarin that "if you were in the secret council of the king of Spain, Monsieur, you would not be better informed of their intentions, and everything that we see here accords entirely with what it pleases you to tell me."[117] The plenipotentiaries themselves had their own sources of information, the most dramatic example of which is the early date at which d'Avaux discovered willingness of the estates to surrender Philippsburg. As early 16 July, he wrote to Mazarin that he had heard from "a person from whom I have sometimes received good information" that France was assured of Philippsburg, and at the end of August he boasted that "I know for certain that the affair has been resolved to our contentment by all the Electors' deputies, although they gave an oath not to reveal anything."[118]

The most striking example of French spying, however, is Mazarin's advance knowledge that the emperor would concede Breisach. He first informed his plenipotentiaries of this in a letter of 21 April 1646, and less than a week later followed it with a more detailed account of the proposals Trauttmansdorff would make before making the final concession. When he later also found out that Trauttmansdorff was hoping for Spain to conclude peace with the Dutch before giving in on Breisach, Mazarin took the extraordinary step of demanding that his plenipotentiaries tell Trauttmansdorff of their inside information as a means of pressuring him to give in sooner.[119] In this case, Mazarin's knowledge gave him the freedom to delay concessions longer than he might otherwise have done, and ultimately helped to secure France greater satisfaction than if the government had been operating on less certain information (see below, chapter 8).

Military information was as easy to obtain as diplomatic information, at least at a strategic level (see below, chapter 4). Yet in spite of this, and in spite of the repeated statements from Paris of how important prompt military news was for regulating the negotiations, the French plenipotentiaries were surprisingly ill-informed of the progress of campaigns. At the end of June 1646, Longueville addressed a letter to Mazarin complaining of the lack of information on the siege of Courtrai: "I beg you very humbly, Monsieur," he wrote, "to order someone from the army to write to us what is happening, so that we can know the truth. This is very important now that we are at the peak of the negotiations."[120] Then, in mid-August, the plenipotentiaries asked for a report on the siege of Lerida:

> It is not curiosity that obliges us to make this request, but rather it is extremely important that we be well-informed of the true state of the armies and of the enterprises that they are going to execute, so that we know whether to press the conclusion of the treaty more or less ...[121]

Mazarin could only respond apologetically to these complaints; "I know what it is to receive reliable news when one is in the middle of a negotiation, and particularly when the enemy has published contrary information," he wrote.[122] However, the court itself had enough trouble getting accurate intelligence with the armies so distant. The siege of Courtrai presented particularly difficulties since, he noted, "most of the couriers have been killed or taken prisoner up till now."[123] The news therefore had to be routed through Paris, and that meant delays in getting it to Münster. The situation should theoretically have been better regarding the *Armée d'Allemagne*; after all, the army was much close to Münster than to Paris, and Turenne was instructed on several occasions to keep the plenipotentiaries informed. However, he was not so diligent about writing as they would have liked, and their communication faced the same uncertainties as did that of military correspondence with Paris. The plenipotentiaries therefore generally relied on reports from Paris to find out the true state of affairs. At least Tracy, Turenne's subordinate, wrote whenever he could.[124]

Negotiating Tactics

The problem of secure communications was central because of its influence on French negotiating tactics. Naturally, if one's enemy knows what one is willing to concede, he will not settle for less. The French plenipotentiaries therefore often pretended to be discussing a point without having the authority to concede it, saying that they would write back to court and see if it were possible. Though they used this tactic many times (e.g., chapter 8, on the Alsace negotiations), they stated it most explicitly when explaining their orders to the sieur d'Anctoville concerning his mission to negotiate with the Elector of Trier over the right to garrison Philippsburg:

> We have given the sieur d'Anctoville power to promise [the Elector of Trier] up to 50,000 Reichstalers for this purpose . . . with order to accord this sum only if necessary, and to concede it by degrees in offering less and then increasing the offer as though on his own authority and without permission, but giving hope that he will receive permission later.[125]

Yet this sort of stratagem was only effective so long as the plenipotentiaries' true orders were not known. By claiming that the French representatives were operating against orders by conceding too little, the Habsburgs turned opinion in Münster against the French and applied pressure to them to give in to the full extent that they were permitted. The plenipotentiaries complained to Mazarin, but there was little he could do to counter this sort of calumny besides reiterating his strong support for the plenipotentiaries and that they were fully within their orders. So long as the Habsburg claims were credible—and they were certainly that—some people were bound to believe them.[126]

The French also preferred never to propose any deal, but instead to let the Habsburgs make offers. This was in part a matter of pride, of course, but it also served concrete negotiating goals. First, the side that made the first offer tipped his hand, allowing his opponent the first glimpse of what he was willing to concede. The side that held out longer could then demand additional conditions, pushing its opponent to concede more than he had planned. Second, the French did not even want to admit that they would discuss certain items unless they were sure they would get their quid pro quo. It was not only a matter of driving a hard bargain (although that was a part of it), but that the raising of some issues—particularly Catalonia and Portugal—put France in a diplomatic quandary. If it became known that France was willing to abandon its allies (and there is no doubt that Spain would have revealed this information at the first opportunity, as she did with the Catalonia-for-Spanish-Netherlands trade proposal), they would no longer feel safe in their French alliance, but would instead seek to make the best agreement they could with the Spanish. In this way, Catalonia in particular was almost as much of a yoke around the French neck as a helpful ally.[127] The fact that both France and her opponents (particularly the Spanish Habsburgs) tried to delay making a proposal as long as possible contributed greatly to the length of the talks.

It is commonly accepted that the negotiations were generally suspended during the campaigns while everyone waited to see what their outcome would be; as Adam Adami put it, "In winter we negotiate, in summer we fight."[128] Such a model, however, is very misleading, because some of the most important issues were resolved in the summer, at the height of the campaign: the Franco-Imperial preliminary treaty in September 1646, and the indemnity for Swedish troops in June 1648 (well after the battle of Zusmarshausen). No doubt at times statesmen did stall negotiations in the hope that their military situation would improve, as Maximilian did very successfully in the fall of 1645. At other times, a state preferred to conclude negotiations before having to risk another campaign; the emperor, the French, and the Bavarians all felt this way at the beginning of 1646, which is why negotiations proceeded at such a furious pace up until May, although in the end Sweden's unwillingness torpedoed a possible agreement. But there were also times when negotiations seemed to proceed in blissful ignorance of the advancing military campaigns, such as in 1644, or when they were conducted parallel with them, each new development reverberating through the conference, as in 1645. It would be a fatal error to concentrate only on the winter talks if one hopes to understand the progress of the negotiations.

Allies and Opponents

By far France's most important ally was Sweden, which had been bearing the brunt of the war in the Empire since 1630 and would continue to do so until peace was made. Nani, the Venetian ambassador in Paris, claimed that Sweden, "which previously France knew only by name," was now just as powerful.[129] This was an exaggeration, but Sweden's seemingly unending series of successes in the Empire must have made it appear to be true. Nani also touched on a sensitive subject when he noted that Sweden could form a powerful bloc if it allied with the Dutch and the English. There was little chance of this, but the possibility of

Sweden uniting with the Protestants in the Empire and continuing the war to ruin Catholicism there continued to haunt France right up until peace was signed.[130]

Axel Oxenstierna, the Swedish councillor and effective leader of the state during Queen Christina's minority, had tried to resist a close alliance to the French for as long as possible. He did not want to be tied to fighting for French demands, but eventually concluded that the French subsidy was too important to forego, and hence agreed to the Treaty of Hamburg on 30 June 1641. This committed Sweden and France to remain in the war until both partners had achieved their war aims.[131] Although there was some subsequent dispute over exactly what constituted reasonable war aims, the alliance held firm in spite of the great temptation provided to both sides by the Imperials, who made enticing offers first to one, then to the other in an attempt to break up the alliance. In fact, the unbreakable Franco-Swedish alliance proved to be perhaps the most decisive factor in shaping the Congress of Westphalia.

Swedish war aims consisted primarily of three things: limiting the emperor's authority; annexing Pomerania; and securing an indemnity with which to pay off their mercenary soldiers.[132] There was little here to create conflict with the French, although some problems did arise. The French did not object to the indemnity for Swedish troops, but feared making such a demand themselves because it would seem too aggressive. Swedish territorial demands created some friction when they extended beyond Pomerania, sometimes encompassing Osnabrück, Silesia, Bremen, and Verden, the last two of which Sweden actually obtained in the treaty. To counter this, France supported the rights of the Elector of Brandenburg, who was the legal heir of the last Duke of Pomerania. Their successful mediation of a division of the province between Sweden and Brandenburg in 1647 without antagonizing either was a major accomplishment. Sweden's goal of weakening the emperor's political control was shared entirely by France, and only caused difficulty when French ministers suspected a Swedish plot to create a Protestant bloc in the Empire that they could dominate, and hence become even more of a threat than the emperor himself had been. This, however, rarely led to any serious problems, mainly appearing in religious affairs.

The chief area of dispute between Sweden and France was the status of the Palatinate. Whereas Sweden wanted Karl Ludwig to be restored to all his lands and dignities, France supported Bavaria's acquisition of the Upper Palatinate and the Electoral dignity. Fortunately for the alliance, Sweden did not prove to be firmly committed to Karl Ludwig, and eventually accepted his restoration to the Lower Palatinate only and the creation of an eighth Electorate for him.[133]

The Swedish plenipotentiaries were, if possible, even more hostile to each other than Servien and d'Avaux. Johan Adler Salvius and his partner Johann Oxenstierna, the Chancellor's son, began quarrelling even before they got to the conference, just as the French had. Salvius was twenty years older, a longtime servant of the crown who had helped negotiate the Treaty of Hamburg with France and who administered the French subsidy; nevertheless, Oxenstierna enjoyed precedence because he was a member of the riksråd, a fact that galled Salvius greatly. Moreover, as the talks progressed, Salvius and Oxenstierna were drawn increasingly into two separate parties: while Oxenstierna labored to support the hard-line policies of his father, Salvius tried to convince the government to concede East Pomerania. He was able to exert considerable influence in this direction by acting through the powerful nobleman Per Brahe, or by persuading the queen herself, with whom he maintained a private correspondence. The power struggle within Sweden between Christina and Axel Oxenstierna was thus replayed in Osnabrück between Salvius and Johann Oxenstierna.[134] Moreover, there is some indication that Salvius and d'Avaux became friends, while Oxenstierna and Servien formed a bond based on their similar policies.[135] But these relationships should not be carried too far, because the French looked down on both of the Swedish plenipotentiaries, writing, for example, that Oxenstierna was "as difficult and as brutal as his colleague is importunous."[136] As time went on, all the French ministers seemed to prefer Salvius, not only because of his political views, but because of his more refined disposition.[137] Even Servien had to confess that "the friendship that I have desired to establish with [Oxenstierna] cannot stop me from saying that he has an extremely disagreeable temperament."[138] In addition to the two main representatives, Schering Rosenhane served as Swedish resident in Münster, while Christina was represented in Paris by Hugo Grotius (the great theorist of international law) and later by Marc Duncan Cérisantes.[139]

In spite of the new treaty negotiated by Servien and d'Avaux at the beginning of 1644 (chapter 6), France had less success in its alliance with the Dutch. Dutch representatives did not even arrive at the conference until 1646, and a large part of French relations with them was simply concerned with getting them to come either sooner or later (the exact policy changed several times over the course of the negotiations; chapters 4–6). When they finally did show up, it proved a disaster for the French, since the Spanish managed to engage them almost immediately in talks about a separate peace. Each province in the Dutch Republic sent its own representative to the conference, but the two most important were Adrian Pauw, the representative for Holland, and Johan de Knuyt, representing Zeeland and a personal representative of the Stadholder, Frederik Hendrik.[140]

France's closest German ally was Hesse-Cassel. The Hessian Landgrave, Amalie Elisabeth, was the only major German ruler to remain at war with the emperor after the houses of Brunswick made peace at Goslar in 1640. She maintained a balance between Sweden, Hesse's earlier ally, and France, who had been paying a subsidy since 1639[141]; her army campaigned sometimes with one ally, sometimes with another (chapter 4). Hesse's largest influence on France came through its radical interpretation of the Imperial constitution: it insisted that the Empire was an oligarchy of independent estates, which had to approve major decisions taken by the emperor. Hessian prodding convinced the French to take up this demand at the conference, with the result that all major German estates were represented there. Hesse's territorial demands became an issue after the war with Hesse-Darmstadt erupted in 1644 (chapter 7), but were not settled until 1647, after French and Swedish demands. Hesse was represented in Münster by Adolf Wilhelm Krosigk and Johann Vulteius; they maintained Winand von Polhelm as a resident in Paris, while France kept the Sieur de Beauregard as a resident in Cassel.[142] Amalie Elisabeth preserved as independent a policy as was possible given her total dependence on France and Sweden. The nadir of Franco-Hessian relations came in 1644 with the East Frisian affair, in which Hessian quarters were threatened by a local leader (chapters 6 and 7); afterward, Amalie had more reasons to complain than Mazarin, but the two states cooperated well. The French plenipotentiaries frequently reported that Hesse was a faithful ally.[143]

Almost all the other German states had either made their peace with the emperor, or had been overrun by Imperial arms. The Elector of Trier, whose imprisonment was one of the major causes of French entry into the war, was still held captive in Vienna and his lands occupied. Georg of Hesse-Darmstadt was friendly with the emperor, but remained neutral in the war until the attack by Hesse-Cassel in late 1645. The Margraves of Baden-Baden and Baden-Durlach, the first Catholic and the second Lutheran, were also neutral. Duke Roderich of Württemberg was fighting in the French army, but his lands were completely occupied save the lone fortress of Hohentwiel near the Swiss border. Mazarin did entertain a secret mission from Friedrich Wilhelm, the Elector of Brandenburg, in 1643, and later supported him in his effort to retain half of Pomerania; however, the French continued to shy away from an open alliance with the Calvinist Elector. Even in the absence of open alliances, however, the French still had to cultivate good relations with German estates, for they participated actively in the conference and voted on all decisions taken by the emperor. It is for this reason that Mazarin was anxious to undertake actions that would create a "pleasant smell"; Dickmann was not wrong to speak of the need to win "public opinion" in the Empire.[144]

France's major diplomatic initiative in the Empire in the 1640s was toward Maximilian of Bavaria, the emperor's brother-in-law and close ally. France's interest in Bavaria went back at least to 1621, even before Richelieu came to power. The states had two things in common: they were both Catholic, and they both feared an increase in the emperor's power. It was thus natural for them to ally in an attempt to create a third power bloc, Catholic and non-Habsburg, to counterbalance both the Habsburg bloc and the Protestant bloc. Two problems repeatedly hindered their cooperation, however: Bavaria was not strong enough to be France's primary military ally, and Maximilian was too faithful to the emperor to abandon him completely. It was on these rocks that the Franco-Bavarian alliance of 1630 foundered when Sweden (which was strong enough to be France's main ally) invaded Bavaria in 1632; a later attempt at reconciliation, conducted in 1640 at Einsiedeln, also collapsed. But these failures did not prevent the two states from carrying on further talks in subsequent years.[145]

Like Mazarin, Duke Maximilian I of Bavaria made all the final decisions in his state; unlike Mazarin, Maximilian had no important internal opponents, and maintained a centralized and efficient bureaucracy to carry out his commands. The French regarded Maximilian warily, unsure whether to see him as a Catholic ruler with similar goals, or a scheming prince who was only concerned with his own self-interest.[146] Mazarin inclined toward the optimistic view, but his plenipotentiaries saw Maximilian in a more sinister light. The plenipotentiaries also criticized Bavaria's representatives at Münster, Georg Christoph Freiherr von Haslang and Dr. Johann Adolf Krebs.[147] Longueville wrote to Mazarin that "I find the Bavarian ambassadors very good people and quite faithful, but not as intelligent as one could wish." He also found them too frank and claimed that they did not know things that were going on at the conference that were detrimental to them, having to find out from the French. Mazarin responded that he was disappointed to hear this, "but since they are well-intentioned, it is necessary to take the trouble to instruct them."[148] The French had reason to change their mind in 1646, when they saw how effectively Bavarian threats convinced the emperor to give in to France's demand for Alsace. Outside of Münster, France and Bavaria had no official means of communication. They nevertheless managed to arrange several extra conferences through means such as secret envoys or captured officers; in addition, the papal nuncio in Paris, Bagno, served as a constant intermediary, although the messages that were sent through him sometimes got distorted (see above). In spite of the difficulties, France and Bavaria came to support each other's interests at the conference, and their repeated attempts at a separate treaty were finally rewarded at Ulm in 1647.

3
The Military Tool, Part I: Limitations and Effectiveness of Strategy

> *I confess, continued the king [of Spain], that when I hear talk of the prodigious armies that the Orient vomits from its body, and of their stunning magnificence, and when I compare them to our small corps of twenty to thirty thousand soldiers, which are so difficult to cloth and to feed, I am tempted to believe that the Orient was created a long time before the West.*
> —from "The Princess of Babylon," by Voltaire[1]

RECENTLY, THE FRENCH MILITARY EFFORT IN THE 1640S HAS BEEN singled out for attack: first, by David Parrott's excellent critique of French military administration under Cardinal Richelieu (the conclusions of which he extends to the end of the Thirty Years' War); and second, by Jeremy Black, in his book criticizing the "Military Revolution." "After 1643," writes Black, "it was less a question of French defeats than of a failure to make much progress."[2] Moreover, historians have marked the Imperial front as a particular weak point. It is, on the one hand, considered secondary by the likes of S. H. Steinberg, who writes that "the campaigns in Germany were of importance only so far as they assisted in interrupting the supply-line to the Spanish Netherlands." But others go further and claim that the French effort in Germany was especially unfruitful: for example Parrott, who writes that "French forces in Germany and Italy were hugely expensive to maintain, and produced the most limited results," and John Gagliardo, who claims that the Bavarians "inflicted one defeat after another on French forces" until the battle of Alerheim.[3]

Yet it is not just the French who are presumed to have been strategically inept; instead, all early modern armies—and especially those of the last stage of the Thirty Years' War—are considered clumsy and ineffective. Whatever the feelings toward a "Military Revolution" in other aspects, Michael Roberts stands almost alone in believing in a revolution in strategy. But even he limits the revolution to Gustavus Adolphus, calling strategy both before and after the Swedish king "sterile."[4]

In his book *Supplying War*, Martin van Creveld wrote that in the latter period of the Thirty Years' War "it looked as if military art was about to make a return to the middle ages"—which, for the modern military historian, is the ultimate insult. In van Creveld's estimation, strategy had "degenerated into a series of more or less deep cavalry raids against enemy towns." The publication of Geoffrey Parker's 1976 article, "The 'Military Revolution', 1560–1660—a Myth?," and his 1988 book, *The Military Revolution*, added new fuel to the debate over strategy. In a critique of the "Military Revolution" that draws heavily upon van Creveld's negative assessment, David Parrott asserts that armies became so concerned with occupying fortresses, which they needed in order to control the land and hence to supply themselves, that they became useless for offensive operations. Parrott's criticism has been echoed by Jeremy Black, who claims that "in general, . . . campaigns were inconclusive," and calls the fighting of the period "inchoate." And Parker himself, who helped revive the notion of a "Military Revolution," identified a problem in early modern strategy, claiming that "strategic thinking had become crushed between the sustained growth in army size and the relative scarcity of money, equipment and food."[5]

Parker's comment focuses on the essential element of contemporary criticism of early modern strategy: that states were incapable of dealing with supply problems. It is useful to group historians of this question into two categories: the "fluid" critiques and the "static" critiques. The best representative of the "fluid" critiques is van Creveld. He calls Thirty Years' War armies "probably the worst supplied in history; marauding bands of armed ruffians, devastating the countryside they crossed." Drawing their provisions from contributions extracted from the populace, "lines of communication were of little moment in determining the directions of their movements." Far from being restrained on a supply tether, he says, armies "were forced to keep on the move in order to stay alive." Since they had no bases, it was "strategically impossible to cut seventeenth-century armies off from anything." But rather than contributing to offensives, according to van Creveld, "this kind of warfare did not even make for a sustained and purposeful advance in any well-defined direction."[6] In his interpretation, then, armies could move virtually at will, but lacked the ability to defend their territorial gains and thereby make cumulative progress. This assessment is similar to that of Clausewitz, who asserted that "armies, particularly in the Thirty Years' War, moved about sporadically," and echoes Roberts's statement about "the bland indifference of most generals during the Thirty Years' War to any threat to their line of communications."[7]

A second school of criticism of Thirty Years' War strategy focuses not on the excessive mobility of the armies, but on the lack of it. Historians of this school emphasize the territorial nature of wars. This is sometimes, for example in Roberts, contrasted with a "strategy of annihilation" in conscious reference to Clausewitz. Others, such as Parrott, merely deride "attempts . . . to dignify what had degenerated into a struggle almost exclusively concerned with control of territory."[8] Parrott begins his critique of strategy with supply problems, or, as he puts it, "the vice of logistical constraints" and "its grip upon the formulation and execution of strategy." Like van Creveld, Parrott notes that

> the central feature of seventeenth-century warfare was the relative ease with which states could raise large numbers of troops, but in circumstances where it proved impossible to match these forces with adequate or reliable administrative mechanisms.[9]

However, Parrott draws the opposite conclusion from van Creveld: far from causing armies to wander about more, supply problems "reduced strategy to a crude concern with territorial occupation or its denial to the enemy." He sees an "obsession" with fortresses, which were necessary to secure the territory off of which armies were fed. Rather than moving around at will, as in van Creveld's model, armies in Parrott's model had little mobility. The only way they could avoid disastrous attrition was "by not outrunning the supply facilities (however inadequate) established in the frontier provinces, and by imposing the most rigorous constraints upon military action." And this was when things were going well. As the war progressed, supply and strategy regressed as armies "abandoned systematic Contributions in favor of direct extortion and a *guerre des courses* devoid of strategic significance." "While it might be too sweeping to suggest that commanders in the Thirty Years' War were entirely uninfluenced by strategic considerations," he concludes, "their freedom to act in accordance with any overall strategy was almost completely curtailed."[10] Though Parrott offers the most recent and comprehensive critique of early modern strategy, his emphasis on territoriality and limited mobility are shared by many others.[11]

Van Creveld and Parrott therefore come to the same essential conclusion—that strategy was stagnant, and that armies were incapable of making substantial, sustained progress—but in two very different ways: van Creveld posits an extremely fluid model of military operations, Parrott an extremely static one. Something is obviously amiss; both cannot be the case, and one is hesitant to accept either extreme view when its opposite is defended by an eminent historian. The problem is that although van Creveld and Parrott are correct to point to supply as the most importance hindrance to effective military action, they err in arguing that supply *determined* strategy.[12] To say that strategic decisions took place within the context of supply limitations is not the same as to say that leaders ignored other strategic factors when making decisions. Once one looks beyond the difficulties faced by armies of the period, it becomes clear that the armies were indeed capable of capturing significant amounts of enemy territory. They did not achieve Napoleonic rates of advance; but that is inevitable in a pre-Napoleonic period.[13] On the other hand, their progress was by no means so slow as to be trivial.

This chapter aims to correct the overemphasis of previous historiography on supply in particular, and the limitations on strategy in general. While acknowledging that supply was the most important consideration of armies in the 1640s, it will examine the possibilities as well as the constraints of strategy in order to show, not only that armies could and did make substantial progress, but also that statesmen—at least in the cases of Mazarin and Maximilian—were aware of the limitations on military campaigns, and capable of using the military instrument within their overall diplomatic strategy.

The Parameters of War

The most important military imperative of the early modern period was keeping an army in being. The problem was not raising troops in the first place, for there were always men ready to serve, and governments could usually scrape together the money to recruit them.[14] Maintaining the armies, however, was another matter. As a contemporary observer of the French army put it, "the ease of raising [troops] is balanced by negligence in keeping them."[15] Supplying an army of fifteen thousand was a problem akin to providing food for a moving town, and one that proved all but beyond the capacity of early modern governments.[16] It was common for soldiers to go for several days at a time without food; but while veterans might tolerate this, new recruits deserted at an alarming rate.[17] Even more difficult than feeding the soldiers was providing the massive amount of fodder needed for the horses. And though horses rarely deserted, insufficient food combined with overwork killed many of them, leaving expensive cavalry troopers dismounted and depriving the army of its mobility.[18]

The preferred method of feeding troops was to provide supply trains: it was relatively secure, and helped maintain discipline by keeping the troops from wandering off in search of sustenance.[19] But the massive supply trains necessary to carry grain, handmills, and oven parts required advanced planning and ready cash, two quantities in short supply in seventeenth-century governments.[20] In addition, an army with up to one thousand wagons moved slowly and was vulnerable to enemy raids; in some cases, virtually the entire supply column was lost at a single engagement.[21] Another method was to set up fixed magazines from which food could be distributed; but even assuming a commander had the foresight to do so, which was not always the case, such magazines imposed even more severe restraints upon mobility than did a supply train, for an army could never stray from its base.[22]

The traditional alternative to these two relatively sophisticated means of supply was to let troops find their food from the surrounding populace. In the best circumstances, soldiers were given money with which to buy food[23]; in the worst, they simply took what they could. Yet this haphazard practice was a last resort, since it made desertion an easy alternative for hungry troops, alienated the population, and exhausted even wealthy areas rapidly as troops took more than they needed and often burned the rest. It was Wallenstein's innovation to replace plunder by collecting fixed contributions from towns; the money was then used to feed the troops, who were prevented from taking anything from the civilians.[24]

But the most certain means of supplying an army in the 1640s was neither plunder nor contributions, but sending the troops into quarters.[25] This represented a sort of compromise: the troops were sent out directly into towns and collected their food and other needs from the families with which they stayed. Ideally, this avoided the worst abuses of plunder, but required less organization than contributions, where the money had to be collected and food bought and distributed to the troops by the army staff. The disadvantage was that an army in quarters could not fight; it was thus a posture usually adopted only in the winter, far from the enemy and in relatively safe areas.[26]

States came to depend on contributions and quarters to keep their military establishment going. One study shows that over ninety percent of the money received by Imperial troops in the Westphalian Circle came from contributions.[27] That was higher than for the French army, but it, too, required contributions to maintain its size. Mazarin wrote to Turenne in 1644 complaining that he sometimes had trouble in the council because Turenne made such high financial demands for the *Armée d'Allemagne;* under Guébriant, by contrast, it would sometimes go a whole year without funds, and even return some to the king's treasury.[28] Indeed, generals such as Wallenstein and Melander were hired as much for their ability to provide for their troops and to prevent desertion as for their tactical and strategic insight.[29]

Strategy itself had to operate within the restrictions imposed by supply problems. Since armies were usually supplied at least in part from the surrounding countryside, war was extremely territorial. Because an army collected money and supplies based on the area it controlled, the more it held, the bigger it got; and the bigger it got, the more it controlled. Mazarin echoed Wallenstein when he noted to Turenne that it was easier to supply an army of twenty-five thousand than one of ten thousand, because the army of twenty-five thousand could safely control enough territory to supply itself, whereas that of ten thousand could not.[30]

Capturing territory therefore became even more important than usual, since, besides the strategic advantages it offered, it also provided a means of wearing down one's opponent and enhancing one's own strength. Winter quarters being the most important means of supplying an army, commanders grappled during the year in order to be in a position to occupy fresh quarters during the winter. As Turenne explained in his memoirs,

> The fruit that one gets from [battles is] to gain a country in order to have quarters, and thus to augment one's army and diminish that of the enemy by the means which one takes from him, which with a little patience sends him to his ruin.[31]

In the struggle between France and Bavaria in the 1640s, the territory in the Swabian Circle (now roughly the area covered by Baden-Württemberg) was the most sought-after prize. At least from 1642 on, each French campaign aimed at security quarters in Swabia, while the Bavarians strove to prevent French encroachment.[32]

The French court was convinced that to assure themselves of quarters in Swabia they needed to capture Heilbronn, the best fortress in the region. Possession of Heilbronn would certainly have given the army strong security in case of an enemy attack, and, if the army were forced to retreat back across the Rhine, could have held out against a siege long enough for the French to muster reinforcements and relieve it. However, it proved too difficult a target; and by 1646, Turenne was arguing that it would have been inadequate anyway. "Such a narrow country [around Heilbronn] would not have given us nearly enough on which to subsist during the whole winter," he said in explaining his decision not to besiege it.[33] He occupied several other towns instead, but still requested reinforcements during September and October; "I hold rather considerable areas now," he wrote, "but nothing provides quarters in Germany except an army as strong as that of the enemy."[34]

Supply also dictated the temporal parameters of the campaign. Since it was almost impossible to feed horses before grass grew, few campaigns began before May. Even that was pushing the limit; it was because of foraging problems that Turenne sent his troops into quarters in May 1645, leading to the disastrous battle of Herbsthausen.[35] Big battles tended to occur in August: Freiburg, Alerheim, and the allied breakthrough in 1646 all happened in that month. By that time, grain was ripening, permitting a large army to operate with more freedom.[36] The last few months of the campaign saw most armies weakened from desertion and casualties, and one of Turenne's cardinal principles was to preserve his strength until late in the campaign, preferably with the addition of reinforcements from France, in order to make good progress against a diminished opponent.[37] The end of the campaign was also particularly important because armies needed to position themselves for winter quarters. Campaigns often ran into November, but rarely beyond. Some small actions usually occurred throughout the winter, but Turenne considered it a minor miracle that he could keep together just one thousand infantry and six hundred cavalry for the siege of the castle of Kreuznach in December 1644.[38] On rare occasions, campaigns continued virtually throughout the winter: the battle of Jankov, for example, which saw fifteen thousand troops on each side, was fought in early March; and the French won a major victory at Kempner Heide in January 1642 as Guébriant's army fought its way back to France. But such operations were inevitably accompanied by great attrition, and hence were avoided; the French never conducted a major mid-winter campaign from 1643 to 1646.

Supply also influenced the spatial parameters of the campaign. An army that tried to maintain the precarious supply link to its home territory necessarily remained limited in mobility. Armies attempted, where possible, to operate along rivers. The waterways not only provided an easy method of transporting fodder and grain, but the flat valleys along their sides were also easy march routes with good roads, and usually contained the richest lands.[39] But the armies of the Thirty Years' War period were not tied to their lines of communication as were those of Marlborough over fifty years later. For one thing, they were smaller, and therefore easier to supply off the land[40]; for another, states in the 1640s simply did not have the same administrative capacity that they did in the 1700s, and consequently armies had little choice but to live off the land to some extent. This meant that, in some cases, far from being tied to a particular area, they were actually forced to move around to avoid remaining in an exhausted country where supplies could no longer be found.[41] Worst of all was the fate of armies hemmed in by their opponents; with a limited foraging range, they were likely to suffer starvation, disease, and desertion that would reduce their numbers rapidly. This was the cause of Gallas's 1644 disaster, and of the dramatic depletion of Leopold Wilhelm's forces in 1646.[42] At Freiburg, Mercy reported that his army had suffered terribly because it had been in a battle line for eight days opposite the French.[43] But lack of supplies in the area saved the town from French reconquest: Mercy's army had been in the area for so long that there were no supplies left to support the French in case of a long siege.[44]

Yet army mobility was not shaped by supply alone; the geography of the Rhineland and southwest Germany also played an important role. The most dominant feature of the area was the Rhine itself. Already thought of as a natural political boundary by some, it was also an effective military barrier.[45] France's only bridge over it remained Breisach. Not that it was difficult to cross the Rhine at any point using pontoon bridges; the problem came when an army needed to retreat quickly in the face of overwhelming enemy strength.[46] To this end, the capture of Philippsburg was crucial in providing a safe refuge. It saved the French army from annihilation at the end of 1645, and its location further down the Rhine from Breisach gave the French a second and more convenient invasion route. The Rhine also served as a barrier to the

Bavarians, and Maximilian's failure to capture Breisach in 1644 helped convince him that the war was not winnable (see chapter 6). But if his troops could not get west of the Rhine, Maximilian intended that no French troops would remain east of it; "it must finally be made clear to the French," he said while formulating a counterattack in late 1645, "that they will not reach the right bank of the Rhine."[47]

Besides the Rhine, the Black Forest was the most important geographical feature of the campaigns in the southwest. Its mountains, stretching east of the Rhine from the Swiss border to Stuttgart, formed a difficult barrier to invasion from the upper Rhine. Armies could and did cross the Black Forest, most notably the French under Guébriant in 1643. But it was much easier to traverse the mountains in the summer; in the winter they were covered with snow, and supply became a major problem. This was one of the major complications that led to the French debacle at Tuttlingen (see part II, introduction). Since France's only fortified position east of the Rhine from 1638 to 1644 was Breisach, her only invasion routes lay across the Black Forest, making a successful attack difficult. Once Philippsburg was captured, all French invasions began much further downriver in order to avoid this obstacle.

After the Rhine and the Black Forest, few physical obstacles hindered the advance of an army until one came to Bavaria proper, but there, a double line aided the defense: first, the mountains of the Swabian and Franconian Alps; and second, the Danube. The one break in the mountains came at the open plain known as the Ries, the site where a meteorite had once landed. Invaders tended to follow this natural gap, marching down the Wörnitz River toward Donauwörth. It was here that the battle of Nördlingen was fought in 1634, and in 1645 the second battle of Nördlingen (as it is known to the French) or Alerheim; and in 1646 the Swedes invaded Bavaria along the same path. Crossing the Danube above Donauwörth posed little problem, but invaders then had to cross the Lech to get into Bavaria proper.[48]

Terrain, however, was only one aspect of military geography; even more important were fortified towns—the anchors by which an army secured its quarters and the hinges on which swung the gates of invasion.[49] Recent historians such as John Lynn and David Parrott have emphasized the role of fortresses in war financing.[50] This role had two aspects: first, fortresses served as bases for collecting contributions or for conducting *courses* against surrounding territory, thereby contributing to the king's treasury and helping to offset the costs of war; second, by providing a secure place for troops to quarter in the winter, fortresses contributed directly to the size of the army a state could afford to maintain.

However, fortresses also performed two important strategic functions unrelated to finances. First, fortresses constituted the basis for friendly supply lines and the main impediment to enemy ones. Magazines were constructed in the safe confines of their walls, from which bread and other necessities could be shuttled forward to the troops. Conversely, enemy supply columns passing near friendly fortresses were likely to be ambushed if not heavily guarded.[51] Second, fortresses provided material impediments to enemy advances and protected friendly armies. This is the most frequently overlooked, albeit in some ways most obvious, function of fortified towns in military campaigns. While recent historians have emphasized the financial function of fortresses and sometimes recognized their supply function, few have paid any attention to the more basic fact that it was difficult for an army to advance through an area containing major enemy fortifications.[52] Usually historians will acknowledge this function only at geographical chokepoints, such as bridgeheads over a river (as at Breisach) or covering mountain passes. Yet even if a fortress was located in a place where it could easily be bypassed, the advancing army had to be on guard for raids by the garrisons it left in its rear. They might not only interdict inadequately protected supply columns, but also attack detachments sent on scouting or foraging missions; in extreme cases, several garrisons might combine and form an entire army in the rear of the attacker.[53] By the same token, a fortress was the most secure place for a friendly army to retreat. Not that a whole army would ever retire inside a fortress; in that case, it would be shut up and quickly starved out, for fortresses held supplies for only small amounts of men.[54] By retreating under the walls (and guns) of a fort, however, a force became almost invulnerable to enemy attack; even a few regiments were safe from a whole enemy army.[55] Besides this direct support, forts were ideal gathering places for the retreating remnants of a defeated army.[56]

Siege warfare was notoriously slow, and it is true that the longest sieges of the Thirty Years' war went on for six months or more (for example, Brünn in 1645 and Lerida in 1646). Although any walled town could hold up an attacker without artillery, however, all but a few of the strongest would fall very quickly to an enemy army, and most were vulnerable even to relatively small detachments.[57] This was particularly true in the Empire, where the density of really strong fortresses was normally very low compared to Flanders or northern Italy. The vast majority of sieges, therefore, were small affairs, over in a week to ten days; and even major sieges typically lasted only about a month.

Sieges would have lasted much longer if garrisons had had to be starved into submission, but this was rarely the case. Instead, the attackers usually battered down a wall, ran a trench up to it, and assaulted through the breach.[58] This process might take some time, but defenders had strong incentive not to wait until the last moment, since the surrender terms got worse the further the siege progressed. The attacker would call on the defender to surrender before the siege started, sometimes without even having a force ready to begin the siege.[59] Talks began as the attack advanced; the besieger might even show the defenders the advanced state of the siege works, or might give them a certain amount of time to await a relieving army before surrendering.[60] The attacker also had reason to compromise, since he wished to avoid spending too much time on just one town when there were so many to capture, and also to avoid taking unnecessary casualties. The result was usually a compromise in which the defending force left the town unmolested and the attacker entered in his place. The details varied depending on the exact state of the siege: the garrison might be permitted to carry out its own arms but not its baggage or artillery, or it might have free choice of where to go instead of having it specified in the capitulation. But a garrison that waited too long could be forced to surrender itself as prisoners; or, worse, to surrender to the mercy of the captor—who might choose to put the defenders to death. There was also the possibility that the attackers would storm the town and capture it, in which case the defenders—civilian as well as military—would be automatically at their mercy.[61]

Because of this bargaining process, a siege was really a tense war of nerves that depended at least as much on the morale of the defenders as on the quality of their walls.[62] The key factor was usually whether there was hope of being relieved. Often friendly commanders would encourage towns to hold out by promising them relief within a short period.[63] After a battle, however, the towns defended by the losing side often lost hope quickly, for example, those in South Germany after the battle of Nördlingen.[64] Mazarin expected that Freiburg would surrender quickly for this reason if the French besieged it after the battle fought under its walls. On another occasion, he criticized a commander for not following up a victorious battle with an offensive against enemy towns. "It seems to me," he wrote,

> that in the heat of the victory and in the fright that it has doubtless caused throughout the country, you would have been able to achieve what we wanted you to undertake, even with few troops, while you will not be able to do so when you have been reinforced with twice the troops, but the enemy has had the leisure to reassure himself.[65]

Towns might sometimes feel that resistance was useless even without a battle. This was a particular problem for Bavaria, and was compounded by their inadequate garrisons (see chapter 6). During Turenne's advance to the Danube in April 1645, Mercy repeatedly complained to Maximilian that towns were unwilling to fight. He asked the leaders of Rothenburg three times whether they would defend themselves, and they promised to do so all three times, but nevertheless gave up at Turenne's approach. And he promised Hall that he was sending assistance and hence they should not give up on any account, but, he reported, "they brought the keys to the enemy themselves."[66] Several towns, such as Mainz in 1644, rejected Bavarian assistance in order to surrender; the troops that Mercy sent had to return to the army (see below, chapter 6). The town of Mergentheim, on the other hand, actually had a sizeable garrison of one hundred dragoons and one hundred cavalry, but the soldiers fled when, at the appearance of the French, the townsmen announced that they would not defend themselves.[67] Mazarin was careful to preserve this advantageous situation, writing to Enghien that "above all you should be careful to treat the towns that surrender well, because this may lead others to do the same, and the opposite could cause them to think of changing their master."[68]

Under these circumstances, it was possible for an army to make great progress over the course of a campaign. The French, for example, were able to march from the Rhine to the Danube twice in a single year (1645), capturing nearly every important town along the way; and twice they were pushed back, and the Bavarians recaptured everything the French had taken. The French gains were insecure because all of the towns they took were small, with weak fortifications; they had no major fortress that could hold up the Bavarian counterattacks long enough for Turenne to muster a relieving force. That is why campaigns usually centered around the one or two major fortresses capable of withstanding enemy attacks for a long time.[69]

The prize stronghold in southwest Germany was undoubtedly Breisach, which not only guarded the only Rhine bridge, but was also one of the best fortresses in the Empire. After its capture by Bernhard in 1638, it was securely in French hands, and was never seriously threatened; certainly the Bavarian offensive of 1644 never came close even to besieging it, much less capturing it.

Just across the valley a little over ten miles from Breisach, at the foot of the Black Forest, lay Freiburg. The French mistakenly believed that it would always be dominated by the owner of Breisach, but in fact it remained Bavarian until the end of the war, and served to check French incursions into the region.[70] Across the Black Forest, the isolated but virtually impregnable fortress of Hohentwiel, held by the Duke of Württemberg, provided a constant thorn in the side of Bavarian and Imperial forces in the Black Forest region.[71] The other towns in the area, such as Rottweil and Tuttlingen, were simply not strong enough to serve as bases, as the fate of the *Armée d'Allemagne* in November 1643 shows.[72]

After Breisach, the most important fortification on the Rhine was Philippsburg. It had several design faults and did not control a bridge, but it was nevertheless the strongest fort on the right bank, especially after French improvements in the winter of 1644 (see chapter 6). Mannheim, by contrast, traded hands so often that the Bavarian Mercy had it razed late in 1644 so that he would not have to defend it.[73] Mainz, on the left bank at the confluence of the Rhine and Main rivers, was important because it gave France a means of linking up easily with Hesse. It had enormous fortifications—so enormous, in fact, that it was virtually indefensible because it required a garrison of seven thousand men. Instead of defending the town, therefore, the French concentrated on building up the citadel.[74] The one fortress that eluded the French in this region was Frankenthal, held by the Spanish. It tied down French garrisons in Speyer, Worms, and other neighboring towns, and raided French supply columns. But with fortifications as strong as any in the Netherlands, it was "a piece of food that would be difficult to digest," and Mazarin discouraged Turenne from expending the effort to capture it.[75]

Outside of the Rhine valley, most operations centered on Heilbronn, an Imperial Free City located in the center of modern Baden-Württemberg along the Neckar River. By 1645, the French were convinced that it was the key to holding the area, but it was so strong that they did not dare attack it in two campaigns; eventually they managed to get it as security in the Truce of

Ulm.[76] Often mentioned in the same breath, but playing a surprisingly secondary role, was Heidelberg, the great fortress of the Lower Palatinate also on the Neckar. In 1646, Turenne suddenly announced that Schorndorf, which the French had not so much as mentioned during their offensives in 1645, was second only to Heilbronn in the region. However, even it lasted only a single week against Turenne's siege.[77] No other town between the Rhine and the Danube—Schwäbisch Hall, Rothenburg, Dinkelsbühl, or Nördlingen—was likely to offer more than a few days' resistance to attackers; in fact, such towns could actually make the attacker stronger because of the stores he captured (see below on offensives).[78]

It did not prove difficult for the French and Swedes to invade Bavaria once they crossed the Danube. Augsburg was a strong fortress guarding the Lech, but it could not keep the allies west of the river because it was flanked above and below by two much weaker towns, Rain and Landsberg. The Swedes captured Rain in 1646 as easily as they had in 1632, while Landsberg fell quickly to a Franco-Swedish attack in the same year. Though Maximilian abandoned Munich in both 1646 and 1648, it was heavily fortified and was not captured in either year. Nevertheless, the Bavarians did not even try to defend the Isar line in 1648; if the allies got past the Lech, all of Bavaria lay at their feet.[79]

Because of the importance of fortresses, sieges were the most fundamental aspect of warfare. Defeating the enemy's army in battle was rarely an end in itself, but instead served to accomplish some other goal, as the French court acknowledged when it announced the need "to get solid advantages from the victory" at the battle of Freiburg.[80] But although battles were secondary, they nevertheless formed an important part of war. Since it was difficult to capture a town in the face of an enemy army, a commander might decide to fight a battle to force the enemy to retreat; alternatively, the defender might want to fight to relieve a besieged town. Battle was also the only way to prevent the enemy from continuing to advance, occupying (and plundering) more territory. Mercy retreated across Swabia twice in 1645, yielding to superior French armies under Turenne and Enghien until he could find a suitable occasion for combat; he finally fought battles at Herbsthausen and Alerheim because any further retreat would have permitted the French to cross the Danube and enter Bavaria proper.

Battles were risky affairs.[81] The typical set-piece battle saw each army divided into three parts: infantry in the middle, and cavalry on either wing (where it could maneuver better and keep the army from being outflanked). Because cavalry was strong in attack but relatively weak in defense, the side that charged first on a given flank usually won. Once its cavalry was defeated, infantry was relatively helpless, especially in the open. If it was in a strong defensive position, as the Bavarians were at Alerheim, it could protect itself from the enemy cavalry, but could not defeat the enemy by itself. Since victory hinged on risky cavalry charges, therefore, no commander could initiate battle without considerable hazard. At Alerheim, for example, the French were numerically superior, but von Werth's successful charge on their right flank very nearly caused the total destruction of the army; only a series of blunders by von Werth after the charge gave Turenne a chance to save the day (see chapter 7 for an analysis of the battle). Nor was a good defensive position a guarantee of victory. Enghien attacked an almost equally strong enemy at Freiburg in prepared positions in the mountains, yet he managed to carry the entrenchments on the first day, and only a mistimed attack prevented further success when the battle was renewed. Similarly, the French infantry was thrown out of their position in the woods at Herbsthausen.

No one was more aware of the dangers of battle than Maximilian, and he ordered his armies to avoid combat except when absolutely necessary, and usually (especially under Mercy) only when they enjoyed an excellent defensive or offensive position. The only two battles the Bavarians initiated, Tuttlingen and Herbsthausen, were both surprise attacks virtually guaranteed to succeed. Mazarin, too, considered combat hazardous; but his commanders, Turenne and Enghien, happened to be two of the most aggressive, battle-oriented generals of the war. Enghien alone fought four major battles in just six years—Rocroi, Freiburg, Alerheim, and Lens; while Turenne's philosophy of war consciously favored battles over sieges.[82]

A successful battle almost always led to the capture of at least the nearby towns—Tuttlingen gained the Bavarians Rottweil, and Alerheim won the French Nördlingen. But the victorious army still had to go through the laborious procedure of besieging enemy strongholds, and at a much-reduced strength; thus, after Alerheim, the French were unable to achieve their objective of taking Heilbronn.[83] That is why battles were sometimes avoided, such as at the allied breakthrough on the Main in 1646. A skillful attacker could out-maneuver his opponents and capture fortresses without having to risk a battle; this was the secret to Turenne's successful invasion of Bavaria in 1646.

Under the circumstances outlined here, could Thirty Years' War armies make substantial, sustained progress? The conditions of war favored neither offensive nor defensive, but instead provided for a dialectic that balanced both. As an army advanced, it could gain strength from capturing supplies in enemy towns or from the enemy army, and its strength could actually swell by the enlistment of enemy prisoners.[84] At the same time, it would lose a certain number of troops in sieges, and more in the towns that it captured and had to garrison along the way.[85] The attacker was also likely to suffer greater desertion as he pushed his troops harder and advanced away from his supply lines[86]; the defender was granted natural breathing pauses every so often as the attacker stopped to rest and resupply his men. Ultimately, capturing enemy territory was financially beneficial; in the short run, however, the new land was usually ruined[87] and almost always required more troops to defend than it could supply.[88] It was only as the new gains were consolidated that a state could reduce garrisons in the rear and improve the financial situation in the areas that were formerly in the front line, but now safely behind it.[89]

Sometimes offensives were stalled or reversed by unexpected events, such as the resistance of Brünn against Torstensson in 1645 or Turenne's defeat at Herbsthausen in the same year. This additional factor gave the defender a slight edge, and made an attacker's job difficult. But the side that kept the strategic initiative was nevertheless an almost certain victor in the long run. It would probably capture some fortresses more quickly than expected (such as the French at Philippsburg in 1644) and perhaps win some battles more decisively than one would have thought; the major reason, however, was that the economic pressure of operating in an enemy's territory and even seizing some of it for oneself was a long-range benefit that outweighed all the short-range disadvantages by far.[90] We now turn to the question of how well Mazarin understood this consideration and shaped his strategy around it.

4
The Military Tool, Part II: The French Army, its Allies, and its Enemies

The Making and Execution of Strategy

WAS THERE SUCH A THING AS STRATEGY IN THE THIRTY YEARS' WAR? While some critics have noted that the word "strategy" was only created in the nineteenth century and have questioned whether any such thing existed before Napoleon, a short overview of French command methods will demonstrate that Mazarin did think about strategy as such, had an overall plan for the progress of the war, and consulted regularly with military officials.[1]

France's plan for each campaign was decided in a special Council of War, which had been organized soon after Richelieu's death by Gaston d'Orléans.[2] It consisted of all marshals, the secretaries of state, and a *commissaire général des troupes*, along with the king, Mazarin, previous *lieutenants généraux*, and the *ministres d'État*. The exact working of the council is unknown; however, since it was created at a time of crisis, as the new regime was just ascending to power, one may surmise that over time Mazarin established his overall control just as he did in the *Conseil d'en Haut*.[3] In any case, it is clear that Mazarin himself was making all of the important strategic decisions.

Mazarin's only direct military experience had come almost twenty years previously when he had raised his own company. Nevertheless, he was an acute observer of military affairs, and must have learned a great deal during the last few years with Richelieu: right from the beginning he showed that he understood strategy as well as his generals. He relied very little on Michel Le Tellier, the secretary of state for war. Though Le Tellier corresponded frequently with Turenne, d'Erlach, d'Oysonville, and the other commanders in the theater, his orders were usually restricted to matters of organization, pay, supply, and the like; as with diplomatic affairs, Mazarin reserved major military decisions for himself.[4]

One of the starting points for Mazarin's ideas about strategy that he shared with virtually every other French minister was that war was very risky. "The prosperity of arms is never continual," he wrote to his plenipotentiaries late in 1643, perhaps chastened by the recent defeat at Tuttlingen; and on another occasion he commented that "certainty . . . is not at all to be found in the pursuit of war, which is always subject to great changes."[5] This was particularly true in Germany, where, according to Turenne, war was "subject to such great revolutions that one makes propositions that appear ridiculous fifteen days later."[6]

Probably this emphasis on insecurity was considerably exaggerated. It is true that fortresses were less common in the Empire, and that attacks were correspondingly less secure; hence Turenne's emphasis on having the superior army as the only guarantee of quarters (see chapter 3). With fewer fortresses, there were fewer sieges and more battles; and battles, as we have seen, involved considerable chance. But it is still difficult to agree with the frantic assessment of Servien that "we are running the risk of losing everything in an instant" by continuing the war in 1646, or to feel that d'Avaux was justified in saying that they had had "three great alarms" in less than six weeks over military matters in July 1646.[7] The French might have lost a battle or been forced west of the Rhine, as in 1645; but at the time Servien made his statement, the French army was already limited to the west bank. The chance that a Bavarian army would have been able to capture Breisach or Philippsburg or Mainz—virtually the only way they would have been able to make the French position any worse—was extremely slim. Nor can this pessimism be attributed merely to excessive caution, because the French were consistent in believing that the Habsburgs were running similar risks. "One single accident of the kind that occurs every day in military affairs is capable of ruining his grandeur forever and putting him in a state from which he will not be able to recover," wrote Mazarin of the emperor; "for this reason, he does not want to hazard the success of the next campaign."[8]

An attritional strategy aimed at a slow but certain strangulation of the enemy suited Mazarin's conception of war, in which uncertainty was the most important factor. His orders repeatedly stressed the need to besiege Heilbronn and thereby secure quarters in the Empire. He almost certainly would have agreed with Turenne's assessment that "maintaining ourselves powerfully in this territory, [the enemy] must inevitably make peace or succumb."[9] It was, one might complain, a ponderous, almost pedestrian method of attack; but what alternative was there? In 1632 Gustavus had invaded Bavaria quickly, won a decisive battle at Rain, and captured Munich; but he had not won the war. Only by occupying the enemy's territory, and thereby removing his means of waging war, could victory be achieved. The Weimarian cavalry argued this forcefully in a 1643 memorandum: "In conclusion, it is necessary to make all possible efforts to recross the Rhine and to subsist there, because this will end the war, and all other designs will only serve to continue it."[10]

Mazarin's overall military strategy was therefore a strategy of attrition. This applied only to the aim of getting quarters, however; there was not a conscious attempt to "bleed the enemy white" by fighting battles where both sides suffered heavy casualties. This may seem odd, considering that that is precisely what the French did at Freiburg and Alerheim, two of the bloodiest battles of the war, both of which ended in practical draws. But both the logic of war and the actual French reasoning at the time show that they were not directly part of an attritional strategy. First, wearing down an opposing army did not have the same permanent effect in the Thirty Years' War that it does today. States fought with only a fraction of the available population, and new recruits were almost always available, even in depleted areas.[11] It is true that there was an additional cost involved in recruiting, but it was minimal compared to the ongoing cost of supplying the men already in the army. The main purpose of depleting the enemy army was to enable one's own army to capture towns, and therefore territory.[12] Both Freiburg and Alerheim were part of French attempts to capture towns, and thus contributed indirectly to Mazarin's attritional strategy. But they were not themselves attritional in purpose.

Freiburg and Alerheim had an additional, more direct goal for Mazarin than simply contributing to the capture of enemy towns: they demonstrated to Bavaria that France was serious about the war. They were a sort of public display in which honor was as much at stake as strategic gains. As Mazarin wrote to Turenne shortly before the battle of Freiburg, Enghien's army was not being sent "to be a spectator of the capture of that place, and render it more glorious for the enemy and more shameful for us."[13] After the battle of Freiburg, Mazarin pushed for the recapture of the town because the battle simply did not seem like a victory if the French could not get it (see chapter 6). Similarly, in 1645 Mazarin commanded Enghien to bring Mercy to battle even if the Bavarians were entrenched because he felt that Maximilian would become more pliable if he lost a battle. Maximilian was inconsistent, he later noted to Longueville, but now he will probably take up the same conciliatory language "that the accident of Herbsthausen interrupted."[14] Alerheim was thus a way of showing that France would not be put off by a single loss—as Brienne put it, "France cannot be conquered by small defeats"—and that Bavaria could not win; and indeed it affected Maximilian just as Mazarin had hoped.[15] Besides mortifying Maximilian, the court recognized that a show of force in Germany would help tie France's allies to her more strongly.[16]

Within the framework of Mazarin's overall strategy of attrition, the most important annual decision was to determine which front would receive the most men and funds for the upcoming campaign. At times, it seems like Germany was the most important front. After all, in 1644, the plenipotentiaries Servien and d'Avaux had written to Mazarin that

> it is very certain, Monseigneur, that all public affairs are moved by and depend in some way on those of Germany . . . Our enemies testify that they do not mind all the losses that they suffer elsewhere, so long as their designs prosper in the Empire. They hold it as assured that if the divided members of this great body can be once reunited to act together under one leader, there will be few powers capable of resisting it. It is from a similar hope that they . . . claim to be content that France make its greatest efforts in other places, which according to their opinion are only accessories and where they say that one single fortress is the fruit of a year of war and the only prize of a prodigious expense that consumes insensibly the forces of the State, whereas they gain whole provinces to their cause and render themselves masters of the forces of an entire great country, with which they promise themselves one day, carrying the war into the heart of the Kingdom, to recapture all at once the conquests of many years . . . That is why, Monseigneur, Your Eminence would not know how to take a more useful resolution to the Queen according to our feeble opinion than to have the affairs of Germany particularly at heart and possibly to make the greatest efforts of the war there from now on.[17]

It was a strong argument, and Mazarin responded with wholehearted agreement, saying that he had been "very persuaded for a long time that we have nothing to fear except from that front."[18]

Yet one finds the same plenipotentiaries four months later writing to Mazarin of Catalonia that

> certainly, Monsieur, whether one considered the length of the war or the advancement of the peace, nothing appears so important as to support affairs strongly in this country.[19]

Mazarin appeared to incorporate this into his strategic plans, writing later that "it is certain that German affairs and those of Catalonia are the only ones that can reduce the enemies to reason," while the Italian conflict was a waste of time.[20]

But all of these accounts ignore Flanders; and it was in Flanders that the French continued to put most of their resources year after year.[21] Nor can it be said that the plenipotentiaries were simply taking the greater effort there for granted, since their mentioning the slowness of conquest on other fronts is almost certainly a reference to Flanders. Yet even as Mazarin was writing to assure Servien and d'Avaux of his commitment to the German front, he told them that Enghien was to operate on the Moselle because of a gap in the French lines there. This was on 17 July 1644, just twelve days before the fall of Freiburg.

The fact is that the plenipotentiaries tended to react to circumstances: when they pushed for Germany as the main front, Freiburg was besieged; when they pushed for Catalonia, French affairs were going poorly there due to the fall of Lerida and the failure of the French counteroffensive. Mazarin sought to reassure his plenipotentiaries, and his generals, that what they saw as French interests were supported to the utmost. As one historian has noted, "Mazarin was a skilled dissimulator, and the innumerable letters drawn up for him by his secretaries are not always an expression of the truth, but of what the Cardinal wanted his correspondents to believe."[22] But he himself kept the larger picture in focus, and never let a momentary setback avert him from his overall purpose. Mazarin did commit larger resources to Germany in response to the Bavarian offensive of 1644, and he followed this up when the battle of Freiburg created an opening that could be exploited. But the next year, Enghien was back operating in the Low Countries, and Turenne, with about ten thousand men, was the main French force in the Empire. And though Mazarin committed substantial reinforcements to Catalonia in 1645 in an effort to reverse the defeat at Lerida, Flanders continued to draw the most French resources and the largest armies.[23]

Clearly, however, Italy was indeed the absolute last priority for resources. Mazarin became so frustrated with the great expense and slow progress of the Italian front that, in December 1644, he proposed the idea of a truce there to his plenipotentiaries. He noted that

> it is next to impossible that the arms of the King can make any considerable progress in Italy . . . The next campaign will be the tenth since the declaration of war, yet we are still starting on the State of Milan, the places of which are so well fortified . . . that even supposing all prosperity for our arms, it would be a great deal to capture one every year, with enormous expense.

The savings from a truce could be split between Catalonia and Germany, where the money would be more useful. True, the Spanish would also save, but they would need to maintain their garrisons at a certain level to guard against revolt anyway. This plan should put to rest the suggestion that Mazarin was obsessed with Italian affairs; if he launched major invasions in 1646 and 1648, it was because the opportunity presented itself, not because he felt somehow drawn to his native land.[24]

A typical year therefore saw two armies in Flanders totalling up to thirty thousand men, another in Luxembourg, and one army each in Catalonia, Germany, and Italy, with priority usually going in that order. Since the French almost always took the offensive on every front, the court set goals for the armies, usually the capture of a particular town. Lerida was a frequent goal in Catalonia; Dunkirk was the long-range goal in the Low Countries up until its capture in 1646; and the main goal in the Empire was to secure winter quarters by taking Heilbronn and Heidelberg.

As with diplomatic information, there was rarely a truly secret campaign plan; both were formulated in the same or similar decision-making bodies, and both were therefore vulnerable to the same sorts of enemy spying.[25] This is probably how Turenne learned of the Imperial plans for the 1644 campaign as early as February, even as they were still being formulated[26]; similarly, the French knew of Imperial aid being sent to Bavaria in 1645 long before it actually went.[27] The French were somewhat more successful at hiding their intentions, perhaps because Mazarin sent out so many conflicting signals as to which front had primary importance for the upcoming year (see chapter 6). Maximilian, for example, remained convinced in 1644 that Mazarin was going to mount a major effort to avenge Tuttlingen, whereas in fact the cardinal intended to remain solely defensive on the German front. As always in intelligence matters, the interpretation of evidence is as important as the gathering of it. If, for example, Mazarin underestimated the strength of the Bavarian offensive on the Rhine that year, it was because he ignored warnings, not because he was unaware of them. Likewise, in August and September 1645, the French court persisted in believing that the emperor would be too occupied by the Swedes to send aid to Bavaria, in spite of warnings to the contrary.

Movements of large bodies of troops also rarely stayed secret for long.[28] Both sides had correspondents in various cities who reported specifically on military matters.[29] Often this information went first to the central government, and only then to the commander in the field. In August 1644, Mercy learned from Maximilian of the Hessians' attempt to link up with Turenne, while in that same month, Mazarin was able to provide Enghien with more information on the strength of the Philippsburg garrison than the duke had been able to gather himself.[30] Generals could also have their own correspondents; Mercy, for example, was kept informed of French reinforcements in 1644 by an informant in Strasbourg.[31] If all of these methods proved insufficient, the numerous newspapers circulating in the Empire usually reported major events in a timely fashion; indeed, one contemporary commented ironically that "a young woman from Leipzig or from Halle knows where the armies are in Germany, Hungary, and other countries better than the politicians."[32] It was common for commanders to rely on newspapers for general information, yet Gronsfeld, the Bavarian commander in 1648, did not even do that: Maximilian complained that he could have gotten better information if he would only bother to read newspapers regularly, and sent him a copy of one from Nuremberg to prove the point.[33] Of course, sometimes even relatively good sources yielded bad information, but intelligence on this level was generally sound.[34]

As happens so frequently in modern warfare, communication with one's base was as often an intelligence liability as a benefit. Unlike diplomatic correspondence, military correspondence did not enjoy legal protection,[35] and the rapidly changing positions of the armies made secure transmission of information difficult.[36] In addition, military letters, if intercepted, were unlikely to be returned; sometimes the code key itself was stolen.[37] Interception of Mercy's letters helped the French locate his position in both 1644 and 1645, and possibly aided the French flank march after the battle of Freiburg.[38] Turenne's correspondence was no safer:

he once made the extraordinary claim that all of his letters to the plenipotentiaries from 10 September to 29 December 1644 had been intercepted, and on another occasion he said that "of four letters that one writes in this country, three are lost."[39] Where possible, therefore, military messages were communicated orally rather than in writing. Though this might have slowed the hemorrhaging of information to the enemy, it could not prevent couriers from being captured or killed, thereby keeping the information from reaching its intended recipient.[40]

Maximilian generally demanded more complete and more frequent reports from his commanders than did Mazarin, which was consistent with their overall management styles. Admittedly, it was easier for Maximilian to correspond with his commanders, because the distance between them was much shorter, particularly as the French approached and then crossed the Danube in 1645 and 1646. By that time, Maximilian was getting reports and sending orders every single day, sometimes more than once a day.[41] He was also quick to chide his commanders when he did not feel they were writing often enough (see below). Mazarin, by contrast, seemed to be happy with occasional, very sketchy reports, which is what he generally got from Turenne. On one occasion, he actually wrote to Enghien not to send couriers when there was no news to report, "because you cannot believe what a bad effect [it] has in Paris, where everyone is curious, and everyone makes conjectures." If he makes another report without substantial news, Mazarin continued, "they will think that everything is lost, and they will take this silence for a sign that some misfortune has occurred."[42]

Under these circumstances, it is not surprising that Mazarin had less information about his armies than did Maximilian, and that he consequently could not micromanage them in the same way.[43] Crucial decisions were often taken in the field long before Mazarin even knew what was going on.[44] Mazarin recognized the problems of trying to direct a campaign from Paris, however, saying on one occasion that "I write this to you from afar, and on the foundation that the notices we receive provide us. You who are on the spot and closer to the events can be informed both better and sooner than we"; and at another time he even noted that "since I am not on the spot, I could be mistaken in my plans and my hopes."[45] Typically his letters contained what amounted to suggestions rather than orders. In recommending that Enghien besiege Freiburg in August 1644, for example, he added that "we nevertheless leave it entirely to you to do what you think is best for the affairs of the King, after having weighed the alternatives carefully."[46] And on at least one occasion, Mazarin deliberately avoided putting the king's name on a letter "so that you would remain in greater liberty to make your resolutions."[47]

Thus, while the broad outline of French strategy was in Mazarin's control, major operational decisions were taken by Turenne and Enghien, often against Mazarin's advice. In 1644, the commanders decided not to attack Freiburg, even though it was a high priority for Mazarin; in 1646, Turenne chose to besiege Schorndorf because Heilbronn, which Mazarin wanted, had been too heavily reinforced. There was the potential that such initiative at the front could get out of hand, especially with the political tensions existing between Mazarin and his commanders. Enghien, a prince of the blood and consequently much more powerful than Turenne, was actually less of a problem in this regard: although a member of the pro-Spanish peace party, he was so anxious to gain personal glory that Mazarin had no difficulty convincing him to attack the enemy with abandon. The only real point of contention was that Enghien was unhappy when he was not in command of the army in Flanders, the most important French force; but this was more due to his power struggle with Gaston d'Orléans than to his quarrels with Mazarin.[48] Turenne, on the other hand, had significant political differences with the régime. His brother, the duc de Bouillon, had participated in the Soissons rebellion of 1641 and illegally left the country afterward, and Turenne frequently petitioned Mazarin on behalf of his brother's interests.[49] In contrast to Enghien, Turenne was a Protestant and a hawk who wanted to destroy the emperor, and, if necessary, Bavaria.[50] This led to some problems in 1646, when Turenne's troops—never very disciplined anyway—did not go out of their way to spare Bavaria, as Mazarin wished. Turenne was also reluctant to leave the Empire after the Truce of Ulm, and opposed the peace in 1648 because he favored delivering a deathblow to Habsburg power by invading the Hereditary Lands.[51]

In spite of these problems, however, Turenne remained a loyal commander until after the Peace of Westphalia. Most significantly, in 1646 Turenne scrupulously refrained from joining forces with the Swedish army in spite of his ardent desire to do so, instead remaining west of the Rhine and insisting on further orders from court (see chapter 8). He was so punctilious, in fact, that his hesitation caused a substantial delay in the junction, and strained relations with Sweden. In lamenting the misunderstanding, Mazarin noted that "what touches me even more in this is that I know that your passion to do everything that you think I want is in part responsible for the confusion."[52] Nor was Mazarin's operational advice always ignored. He managed to talk Turenne out of besieging Frankenthal in both 1645 and 1646, even though Turenne was convinced that it was the best option.[53]

In general, Mazarin recognized Turenne's importance, and did everything he could to caress his ego. He downplayed their political and religious differences, once saying that

> I write you this not as a person of a different religion from ours, but as a general in the King's army, who acts according to his intentions in a war that is not at all a war of religion, and in a country where, in truth, practically only Lutheranism—which is not your religion—is involved.[54]

In accordance with his laissez faire management style, Mazarin was tolerant of errors, hardly ever having a harsh word for his commanders (though admittedly there was little to criticize in the conduct of the German campaigns during the last five years of the war).[55] Overall, the relationship between Mazarin and Turenne was not perfect, but it worked as smoothly as one could have hoped during the war.[56]

The Armies

"This army is not at all constituted like the others," Turenne wrote of the *Armée d'Allemagne,* the French army in the Empire, upon first taking command.[57] It was a hybrid force, consisting partly of French government troops (mostly Frenchmen, but sometimes Irish, Italian, or from some other foreign land), and partly of the remnants of the German army of Bernhard of Saxe-Weimar, known as the Weimarians.

In spite of a changing makeup, accelerated by the heavy casualties they suffered at the battles of Tuttlingen, Freiburg, and Alerheim, the Weimarians retained a sense of corporate identity—German, Protestant, and Bernardine—that prevented the French from contravening the terms of their 1639 treaty.[58] This meant that the Weimarians chose all of their own leaders and handled all internal disciplinary matters; only the overall commander of the *Armée d'Allemagne* could issue them orders.[59] The continued survival of Bernhard's subordinates in important roles enhanced

Weimarian independence. The most important such officer was Hans Ludwig von Erlach (or d'Erlach), who held the governorship of Breisach by virtue of the treaty. He was an able soldier and an effective administrator, but sometimes difficult to get along with.[60]

The loyalty of the Weimarian army could never be taken for granted. Mazarin always feared their desertion to Sweden, which felt betrayed by Richelieu's acquisition of Bernhard's forces.[61] His fears were realized in 1647 with a full-scale mutiny in which the Weimarians refused to go to the Low Countries and demanded back pay. They fled halfway across the Empire before Turenne caught and defeated one contingent; the remainder escaped to the Swedes.[62] In normal times, the French could control the Weimarians by treading softly and flattering the leaders as much as possible; however, the continued existence of the Weimarians as a corporate entity—what one historian has called "a literal soldier republic"—and the command of the most important fortress on the Rhine by d'Erlach served as constant reminders of the shaky basis for French authority in the Empire.[63]

In spite of this, the French continued to recruit German troops year after year, instead of allowing the Weimarian corps to dwindle and be replaced by French troops. This was necessary because French troops were almost invincibly resistant to serving in Germany, where the weather was bad and the land considered poor.[64] Time after time, individually or in whole regiments, they refused to cross the Rhine. Even the knowledge that they were going to Germany could cause a unit many miles away to mutiny, so the French took precautions not to give advance warning, even going so far as to send a unit by a roundabout march route.[65] Sometimes soldiers were lured across the Rhine by means of bonus pay[66]; but wherever possible the French just avoided sending native units at all.[67] Mazarin's rule of thumb was that one had to send twelve hundred troops into Germany for every five hundred one needed there.[68] At such a desertion rate, it was easier to send foreign troops, or, better still, to recruit Germans directly.[69] Nominally, German troops cost more than French ones; but, Mazarin noted, "in effect, they cost us less, because the soldiers desert less and do not disperse so easily." One particularly egregious case of desertion among French units caused Mazarin to despair that "we should decide once and for all not to send any more infantry into Germany."[70] And, indeed, it appears that the proportion of German troops in the *Armée d'Allemagne* was increasing, not decreasing, in the last years of the war.[71]

The problem of desertion was worsened by the peculiarities of French military administration. Most states used private enterprise to enhance their own limited administrative capacities. Paying colonels to raise and maintain regiments eased the burden on the state; in exchange, the colonels were permitted to profit from the war by what they could gain in plunder and legally extorted contributions. But in order to maintain its authority, the French crown preferred to have its nobility raise and maintain troops as part of their voluntary service to the crown. The officers were indeed willing and even anxious to participate in the system; but, being deprived of any legal means of recouping the money that they sank into their units, they had no incentive to maintain them at full strength. Instead, they would deliberately allow troops to desert, then attempt to pad their payroll when it came time to collect their pay—and pocket the difference. So surely did this lead to the diminution of troops that the French automatically discounted newly raised forces on a "vingt pour douze" basis—that is, for every twenty troops paid for, they assumed that only twelve would be effectively recruited.[72]

The French recognized the inadequacy of their administrative apparatus. The plenipotentiaries in Münster (including Servien, a former secretary of state for war, and Longueville, a former commander of the *Armée d'Allemagne*), complained that France put too much effort into raising troops and not enough into maintaining them, and specifically urged Mazarin to pay particular attention to supply.[73] And Lionne, Mazarin's secretary, lamented that "whatever immense expenditures we make to have big armies, it is afterward impossible to make them follow the plans that we want."[74] Some progress toward reform was apparently made under Le Tellier, but desertion remained a major problem.[75]

Compared to the armies of Wallenstein and Gustavus, those of the 1640s were generally smaller and contained a larger proportion of cavalry.[76] On campaign, cavalry served as scouts, defended foraging parties, and attacked enemy supply columns and any small groups that got too far from the main force. Infantry did not dare to go from one town to another without a cavalry escort.[77] The commander with superior cavalry was "master of the countryside" in Mercy's words: he knew where his opponent was while keeping his own movements hidden, forced his opponent to keep his army close together, denied it forage, and could get to any location first.[78] Both after Freiburg and again before Herbsthausen, Mercy lamented that Turenne could force him back to the Danube because of his cavalry superiority; similarly, Turenne was forced to recross the Rhine in October 1645 because of Bavaria's ascendency in mounted troops.[79] In battle, too, a victory by one side's cavalry usually carried the day (see chapter 3 for a discussion of the dynamics of battle).[80]

In spite of the crucial importance of cavalry, however, Mazarin repeatedly insisted that infantry would be the primary need of the *Armée d'Allemagne*. This was not because he thought infantry were better troops in general, but for two other reasons. First, Mazarin's main goal for the army was to capture quarters by besieging Heilbronn; and in a siege, infantry's defensive capabilities could be exploited to the utmost.[81] Once entrenched in lines of circumvallation and contravallation around a town, an army was almost as hard to attack as the town itself would be. Cavalry performed important roles in a siege, but they could not man the siege lines that were its essence.[82] Moreover, with the infantry desertion rate the French faced, it was always a struggle to keep adequate numbers in the army; and recruiting more could sometimes be difficult, as the French found in 1645 and 1646, when every contractor who approached them wanted to raise a certain amount of cavalry in exchange for recruiting infantry. Mazarin lamented that "it is a strange situation that with all the difficulties there are to raise infantry in Germany, if the King wanted to raise ten thousand cavalry there, I would be able to do so in six weeks."[83]

The *Armée d'Allemagne* rarely reached a strength of ten thousand, as much as half of which could be cavalry.[84] Though there are some complaints about the quality of French cavalry in Germany, in general they performed more than adequately, in contrast to the infantry.[85] The Weimarian cavalry mirrored the qualities of their commander, Reinhold von Rosen—brave, but undisciplined. This manifested itself in very practical ways: their successful charge was largely responsible for the French victory at Alerheim, but their failure to keep an adequate watch contributed greatly to the French defeats at Tuttlingen and Herbsthausen.

The commander of the *Armée d'Allemagne* after the battle of Tuttlingen was Henri de la Tour d'Auvergne, vicomte Turenne. He had served under Bernhard of Saxe-Weimar in the 1630s and participated in the successful siege of Breisach. After the disaster at Tuttlingen, he was recalled from the army in Italy, promoted to marshal, and put in charge of rebuilding the shattered *Armée d'Allemagne*. According to the French plenipotentiary Servien, Turenne was brave enough, but careless and lacking in foresight. "Perhaps with a little warning he will remedy these faults, which prevent him from passing for a great man," Servien concluded.[86] Nowadays, Turenne is considered the greatest French commander of the seventeenth century. His reputation is based mostly on his performance in later wars, but even in the 1640s, Mazarin did not share Servien's low opinion of him.[87] It is true that Turenne was not a particularly careful commander; Mazarin once urged him to profit from a lost battle to "punish the disorder that has always reigned in your army."[88] Nevertheless, Turenne was an excellent leader—aggressive, clever, and original. The 1646 and 1648 campaigns were masterpieces of maneuver that contributed materially to the ending of the war. Turenne had the added advantages of being Protestant and speaking fluent German—no small matters considering that he had to make himself respected by the Weimarians, and probably important factors in his appointment as commander (see part II, introduction). Because of the reinforcements he needed in 1644 and 1645 and the link-up with Sweden in 1646 and 1648, Turenne never actually commanded an independently operating army in Germany during the war. However, in spite of certain, practically inevitable difficulties, he cooperated extremely well with both Enghien and Wrangel.

Turenne's only rival as greatest French commander of the century, the duc d'Enghien (known to history as the Great Condé), also served in the German theater in the 1640s: in both 1644 and 1645, Mazarin sent him and his army to reinforce Turenne. Though only in his twenties, Enghien had already established his fame with his victory at Rocroi in 1643. Being a prince of the blood, he outranked the much older Turenne; thus, he commanded the combined armies and received credit for the battles of Freiburg and Alerheim. Enghien had a well-deserved reputation, even in the 1640s, of being almost recklessly aggressive.[89] He attacked Mercy's entrenched mountain position at Freiburg against all the rules of warfare, and again in the following year he engaged the Bavarians head-on in their fortifications at Alerheim.[90] It is to his credit, however, that he managed at least to secure a draw in both battles; and the costly fighting probably helped bring Maximilian to the conference table faster than any other method would have.[91]

Turenne's most important subordinate was Alexandre de Prouville, marquis de Tracy, *commissaire général* in the *Armée d'Allemagne* under Guébriant as well as Turenne. Tracy was praised by Turenne and Mazarin alike for his excellent work in keeping the army supplied.[92] It is difficult to disagree with the assessment of one contemporary observer that French commanders, at least in

Germany, were "the most glorious and the most valorous in the world," helping turn the awkward mélange of troops into a first-rate fighting force.[93]

The French would have had a much more difficult time in the Empire had they not been aided by Sweden and Hesse-Cassel, their two most important allies. Sweden, assisted by an annual French subsidy, fielded probably the best army of any state in the war. They were led by Lennart Torstensson until worsening gout forced his retirement at the end of 1645, at which time Karl Gustav Wrangel took command.[94] The Swedes occupied Imperial forces, and, in 1646, combined with the French for a joint campaign. Military cooperation was organized through the plenipotentiaries in Münster and Osnabrück; in addition, the French maintained an attaché, the Baron d'Avaugour, with the Swedish army.[95] Turenne and Wrangel preserved their armies as separate units when they campaigned together, but coordinated their plans and operated near one another. There were undoubtedly great tensions between them—over the status of the Weimarians, operational goals, and other issues—but on the whole they got along at least as well as their opponents.

Hesse maintained a small army, no larger than ten thousand troops including garrisons. They nevertheless played an important military role because their troops were among the best in the Empire.[96] Hesse had been closely allied with Sweden earlier in the war, and continued to cooperate with the Swedes militarily because of their proximity to one another. They had, however, shifted the focus of their alliance to the French, who provided Amalie Elisabeth with a substantial annual subsidy, without which she could not have maintained her military establishment.[97] At times, there was considerable tension between the French and Swedes over who would get the assistance of Hessian troops. In general, the Swedes campaigned with them more, if only because they had a common frontier and it was easy for them to do. The Hessians did cooperate with the French in 1645 and played an important role at the battle of Alerheim.[98] However, Amalie had her own agenda, and only agreed to stray so far from her own territory because Mazarin was paying an additional subsidy that year. Afterward, she recalled her troops to Hesse; similarly, in 1646, the Hessian general Geyso did not continue with the allies south of the Main. One of the reasons Hesse was more willing to conduct joint military operations with Sweden than France is that the Swedes helped Hesse capture a number of fortresses, while the French showed little willingness to participate in Amalie Elisabeth's war in central Germany.[99]

Opposing the French was what may arguably be termed the Bavarian army. Technically, however, there was no such thing: after 1635, all forces fighting for the emperor were under his supreme command. But in order to induce Saxony to accept the Peace of Prague, Ferdinand II had been forced to agree to appoint Johann Georg commander of one part of the Imperial army; and, in order to mollify the claims of Maximilian, the same right was granted to him. The Imperial forces were thus divided into three "Reichsarmaden": one under Johann Georg of Saxony; one under Maximilian of Bavaria; and one under the Emperor himself. The two armies not under the emperor's direct control were, in all but name, independent forces that were recruited, administered, and commanded by the electors. In addition, the troops in the Westphalian Circle, which were largely cut off from main action elsewhere in the Empire, gradually fell under the sway of the Archbishop of Cologne. He never gained the same legal status as his fellow electors, but by the end of the war he exercised sufficient control to prevent the emperor from drawing troops from the circle if the archbishop judged that he needed them for his own defense.[100]

The army headed by Maximilian was essentially the old army of the Catholic League with a new name. But already by 1635, the once-heterogeneous force had shed its multinational and polyglot character and become an essentially Bavarian army. Many of the non-Bavarians had left to join Wallenstein's massive armies, while Maximilian had simultaneously embarked upon a deliberate campaign to recruit more soldiers from Bavaria in particular, and southwest Germany in general. Marching under standards with pictures of Mary and Jesus, and increasingly in blue and white (the Wittelsbach colors), the troops who fought for Maximilian in the 1640s were fiercely loyal to him. It is true that some of Bavaria's highest commanders were not of Bavarian origin; Mercy, for example, was from Lorraine, and von Werth came from the Low Countries.[101] And it is also true that, in the 1645 armistice negotiations with France, Maximilian himself pointed out that his troops were his only under the command of the emperor. But Maximilian was playing a diplomatic card here rather than speaking entirely in earnest; certainly the French concluded that he had sufficient control of his own army.[102] More significant, however, was what happened when Maximilian's control was put to the ultimate test: recalled by Ferdinand III in 1647 by virtue of their oath to him, the soldiers mutinied and refused to follow von Werth, instead returning to the only leader to whom they felt faithful. The Bavarian army had become a fact.[103]

With about one million inhabitants, Bavaria was comparable to Sweden, one of the dominant powers of the war, in population and wealth. Why did Bavaria not field as powerful an army as Sweden?[104] To begin with, Maximilian did not have the benefit of a large annual foreign subsidy (although the emperor did provide some assistance) or Baltic port tolls as did Sweden. But neither Bavaria nor Sweden could finance the war out of their own coffers, no matter how carefully Maximilian and Axel Oxenstierna managed their budgets. Instead, both states relied upon the quarters system to maintain their armies; and Sweden simply controlled more extensive areas on which to quarter her troops. Maximilian dominated three Imperial Circles—Swabia, Franconia, and Bavaria—that he could use for quarters.[105] But Franconia was often infringed upon by the Imperials, and Maximilian tried to spare his beloved duchy the economic disaster of having an army spend the winter in it.[106] This left Swabia as the main area for Bavarian quarters year after year. Thus, while Swabian quarters were an enticing prospect for French arms, mainly as a means of relieving the exhausted areas of Alsace and Lorraine, they were absolutely essential if Bavaria was to continue to field a sizeable army. It is therefore not surprising that Maximilian concentrated his effort on keeping the French out of Swabia at all costs. He was willing to compromise on almost everything else, but he had to save his quarters if he was to remain a major player in the war.

In response to the complaint of one of his commanders that there were not enough troops, Maximilian once responded, "what we lack in quantity must be made up for in quality."[107] It is true that Bavarian troops were considered excellent, even by their enemies; they were particularly highly regarded for their steadfastness in the face of food shortages.[108] Bavaria's military was tightly organized, and does not seem to have suffered from the worst faults of French military administration. Furthermore, Maximilian worked hard to keep his armies supplied, especially with remounts for the cavalry.[109] And when Bavaria threatened to fall too far behind France in number of soldiers, he appealed to the emperor for assistance. As a result, Bavaria was not usually so shorthanded against France in the field.[110]

Nevertheless, their shortage of troops did have two significant consequences for the course of the war. First, Bavarian cities were almost always inadequately garrisoned because the troops were needed to fill out the main army. In 1644, for example, the French were able to take a whole series of cities along the Rhine because the city garrisons were too small and the Bavarians were unable to reinforce them in time.[111] In April 1645, the Bavarian field marshal Mercy complained to Maximilian that Rothenburg had surrendered to Turenne without defending itself. Maximilian wrote back criticizing Mercy for only leaving twenty-five dragoons for the defense of the town, and ordering him to put more troops into Windsheim to prevent the same thing from happening there.[112] Even the most important Bavarian garrisons rarely contained three hundred men; by contrast, the French maintained over fifteen hundred in Breisach, and over a thousand in Philippsburg; even Sélestat, located in Alsace and therefore almost guaranteed safe from enemy attacks, contained three hundred men.[113] The small Bavarian garrisons provided little resistance during the French invasions of 1645 and 1646.

The second important consequence of Bavaria's manpower shortage was that Maximilian was cautious with his army almost to the point of obsession. He knew that he remained a vital player in the diplomatic game only so long as he retained an army in the field, and his orders to his generals were filled with instructions not to let the enemy force them to a battle. Maximilian was not always defensive-minded; he tried to attack the French after the battle of Alerheim, and in 1644 he proposed an offensive campaign that called for his forces to lead a major attack on France. Yet even in 1644, Maximilian's caution may have cost him the decisive victory that he needed to turn the tide of the war. Mercy had an opportunity—brief, to be sure, but still an opportunity—to attack Turenne in the last days of July at overwhelming odds, but refrained from doing so in the absence of specific orders from Maximilian permitting it.[114] Criticism of Maximilian's unwillingness to fight aggressively, however, must be tempered by recognition of the fact that he was very successful in obtaining his war aims. Bavaria had few dramatic victories, but neither did it lose any battles as decisively as the French did at Tuttlingen, the Spaniards at Rocroi, or the Imperials at Jankov. Less caution might have permitted even greater success, but it might also have jeopardized the great amount of success that he did have while fighting for the losing side.

Maximilian was the prototype absolute ruler prior to Louis XIV. Unlike the emperor, he appointed no "Generalissimo" to command his forces, for Maximilian was his own Generalissimo. And unlike both Mazarin and the emperor, he kept his generals on a tight string.[115] He expected them to report to him frequently—daily, if possible—and he issued orders with similar regularity.[116] Though he often left decisions up to his commanders' "military experience,"[117] he was not above interfering in minutiae, such as telling them to put extra troops in a particular garrison or recommending a certain defensive position.[118] Above all, Bavarian generals did not dare commit their army to an attack without prior approval from Maximilian. The decision to fight, whether offensively or defensively, was also almost always preceded by a formal council of war of the highest officers, the result of which was duly reported to Munich.

Not all Bavarian commanders adapted to Maximilian's tight control and cautious approach with equal skill. Leopold Wilhelm (not a Bavarian, but receiving orders from Maximilian nevertheless) overreacted in 1646, refusing to fight even when the road to Munich was opened as a consequence.[119] But Franz Freiherr von Mercy, Bavarian commander from 1643 until his death at the battle of Alerheim in 1645, thrived under Maximilian. He fought two brilliant defensive campaigns in 1645, giving ground slowly before the French, but keeping his army between them and the Danube. At the battles of Freiburg and Alerheim, he showed an excellent eye for defensive positions, while at Tuttlingen and Herbsthausen, he led surprise attacks that twice destroyed French armies. He has been criticized for lacking aggressiveness, but Mercy recognized that Maximilian did not want to fight an offensive battle that was not heavily weighted in his favor. Not quite of the stature of Gustavus or Torstensson, Mercy nevertheless deserves to be counted among the greatest commanders of the war.[120]

Serving with Mercy was the dashing cavalier, Johann Freiherr von Werth. Captured at the battle of Rheinfelden in 1638, he was exchanged for the Swede Gustav Horn in 1642 and resumed his duties as commander of Bavarian cavalry. He was a popular hero renowned for his invasion of France in 1636, but lacked Mercy's attention to detail; Maximilian also seems to have thought that his abilities were declining as the war continued (see chapter 7). Twice bypassed for promotion when the position of field marshal came open, von Werth defected to the Imperials in 1647. He probably would not have been as good a commander as Mercy or even

Geleen (who took over after Mercy's death at Alerheim), but as second in command he was a formidable opponent, both on the battlefield and in operations.[121]

On the whole, then, despite certain problems, Bavaria was a worthy opponent to France: Maximilian managed, for the most part, to compensate for his smaller economic base with better organization and leadership. Yet while Bavaria could field an army to match France's most of the time, it lacked both the reserves necessary to rebuild an army quickly, and the extra room that would have provided breathing space in case of a French victory.[122] It was fortunate for Maximilian, then, that he could easily call upon the assistance of his brother-in-law, Ferdinand III, when in desperate need. In spite of almost constant friction between Bavaria and the Austrian Habsburgs—in part because of different political goals, in part because of disagreement over methods—the two allies cooperated about as effectively as could have been hoped. Imperial troops were present at Tuttlingen, and reinforced Maximilian for his 1644 offensive against France both before and after the battle of Freiburg. At the beginning of 1645, Maximilian lent Ferdinand a contingent in time for the battle of Jankov, while at the end of the year he called upon Ferdinand's assistance to push the French back across the Rhine after the battle of Alerheim.

This last maneuver was particularly daring—coming as it did at a time when the Swedes were threatening to invade Lower Austria—and particularly successful. It seems to have inspired the joining of French and Swedish armies in 1646 and 1648, which, for several reasons, resulted in a total disaster for Maximilian. First, the whole weight of the war shifted onto Bavaria, the target of the Franco-Swedish invasion. Second, the advantage of interior lines was nullified, depriving Maximilian of anywhere to appeal for last-ditch assistance. Third, it created enormous new tension with the Habsburgs. Maximilian did manage to wrest effective control of the Imperial army while it was in Bavaria, but he still complained bitterly about its lack of discipline and inability to refrain from plundering the populace. Fourth, and perhaps most disastrously, it saddled Bavaria with incompetent Imperial commanders who had a proven inability to manage a military campaign.[123] First Leopold Wilhelm, then Peter Melander bumbled their way to defeat, leaving Bavaria twice exposed to the ravages of French and Swedish armies. This, more than the weaknesses of the Bavarian army itself, was the decisive factor leading to the Truce of Ulm and thence to the Peace of Westphalia.

The Brutality of War

The Thirty Years' War is a byword for rapacious troops and oppressed civilians, not without some reason. Lorraine, under the iron hand of La Ferté-Senneterre, suffered from being a frequent site of quarters. "War and pity do not go together," he once wrote. He turned aside the complaints of some inhabitants, declaring simply that "the soldiers must eat."[124] And, indeed, it was the financial pressures of military needs that created such a burden on the populace. Alsace fared little better than Lorraine.[125] Mazarin's repeated efforts to spare it by gaining quarters in the Empire did not succeed until 1646. If its governors were notoriously corrupt and its finances pathetic, at least by 1644 it was no longer subject to enemy raids like Lorraine.[126] But this did not prevent things from degenerating to such a point that Turenne feared quartering his troops there because the population had begun to retaliate by attacking them.[127]

The situation was worse for those territories in southwest Germany held by Bavaria. In the south, Hohentwiel was a constant thorn in the side, raiding with such impunity that its garrison once actually captured Überlingen.[128] It received occasional support from Breisach, France's only fortress east of the Rhine until 1644. From that point on, however, Philippsburg—closer to the population centers—was the main origin of French raids. They became so debilitating that Bavarian administration broke down; with food unable to reach the soldiers in nearby garrisons, her starving troops began deserting by the end of the war.[129]

Even the ordinary task of gathering supplies from the countryside, which was unpleasant for the inhabitants in the best of times, could become a nightmare if the troops were given too much license. The Bavarians kept a tight rein on their troops, if only because they were operating on the defensive and Maximilian did not want to ruin his own lands. Mazarin, too, wished to avoid destroying Bavaria; but his commander, Turenne, had no such compunctions. His troops were notoriously undisciplined, for which he was rebuked on many occasions; Mazarin once complained that their friends feared them as much as their enemies.[130] The cardinal urged Tracy to take care to build magazines for the army's subsistence, which would "convince the spirit of the people to receive us with the least repugnance." However, Mazarin's concern for occupied territories also had its limits. "It is the custom of people," he wrote in response to complaints from Mainz, "however little they suffer, to amplify their grievances beyond measure."[131]

Bernhard Kroener has noted that the responsibility for the violence of the "soldateska," a derogatory term for soldiers, rests with the governments who recruited more troops than they could feed and left them to get by as best they could.[132] But the harshness of the war was not just a product of criminal neglect and extortion used to feed the war machine; instead, cruelty was a deliberate policy on the part of the participants. Bavaria, fighting tenaciously to hold onto its territory in the face of its giant neighbor, brutally threw back several French attempts to cross the Rhine. The Bavarian commander, Mercy, made a deliberate policy of showing no clemency to French garrisons east of the Rhine. At one siege, rather than offer terms, he pressed the attack until the troops surrendered unconditionally. He contemplated massacring them, but concluded that it would be more useful to recruit them into Bavarian service.[133] Nor were civilians spared; when Mercy recaptured Mannheim in 1645, he razed the town and deported the inhabitants to Heidelberg to live by begging because he felt that they had not put up stiff enough resistance against the French. Pitifully, they applied to Maximilian for the right to move elsewhere and earn a living.[134]

French brutality appears, in its way, even greater, if only because their offensive operations gave it greater scope. "We hold their retreat for a victory because we can go into Bavaria without resistance and spread terror everywhere," wrote Tracy gleefully after the breakthrough in 1646.[135] When reoccupying Rothenburg in 1645, Turenne put the small garrison to death, apparently out of anger that the townsmen had attacked French stragglers after the battle of Herbsthausen.[136] But the worst came in his two invasions of Bavaria, in 1646 and 1648.[137] The French, too, took out their anger on the population in a way perhaps not so different from U.S. behavior in Vietnam. At La Mothe, for instance, the enemy garrison signed a capitulation by which the population was allowed to keep its goods and the clergy could remain in town if they swore an oath to France. Upon being received at court, however, these terms were seen as too lenient. Contrary to the agreement, La Mothe was evacuated, its people dispersed, and fifteen hundred nearby peasants forcibly recruited to aid in the demolition of its houses.[138]

When reading about the French negotiations with Bavaria and their eventual *rapprochement*, it is too easy to fall into the trap of believing them to be natural allies who carried no particular ill will toward one another. The fact that the two states often seemed to be in a state of *de facto* truce, or at least not to cause too much damage to each other, makes the military campaigns suspect to some scholars. But however much Mazarin and Maximilian might have preferred to be allied, their armies fought the conflict with a desperation that belied the common interests of their states. Whatever the situation in Münster, on the battlefield the fight was serious.

Part II
The Road to Peace

5
Introduction: From *Guerre couverte* to the Conference Table, 1630–1644

THE FRENCH FIRST BECAME INVOLVED IN THEIR EASTERN BORDER-lands in the early 1630s. Charles IV of Lorraine had been a source of trouble to Richelieu for several years because of his intrigues with Gaston d'Orléans. In January 1632, he seemed to put these concerns to rest in signing the Treaty of Vic, which forced him to give up all foreign alliances, permit the French free passage through his duchy, and hand over the town of Marsal as security.[1] But three days before this treaty had even been signed, Gaston secretly married Charles's sister in Nancy. Gaston then invaded France in an attempt to topple Richelieu, but he failed completely and his main supporter, Montmorency, was executed. By June, Charles was again forced to sign a treaty with France, but continued his contacts with Gaston and the Imperials. Richelieu was less conciliatory this time; with the Swedes advancing on the Rhine, he was anxious to secure a French presence there, and pressed hard terms on Charles. The duke of Lorraine eventually permitted the French to take Nancy in September 1633, beginning a twenty-five-year occupation of Lorraine.[2]

Full success escaped Richelieu, because Charles himself fled with his army to join the Imperials, and would continue to be a thorn in the French side for many years. Nevertheless, the occupation of Lorraine was crucial, because it opened up the route to Alsace and hence to the Rhine. The real treasure was not Alsace itself, but Breisach, the important fortress on the west bank of the Rhine. But when the Maréchal de La Force[3] advanced to the border of Alsace with an army, several Alsatian towns requested French protection against the Swedes. To accept these requests was dangerous because it meant that France was acting against its own allies, but La Force successfully inserted French garrisons into several towns without exciting too much enmity in the Swedes. Swedish power along the Rhine collapsed after their defeat at Nördlingen in 1634, and Axel Oxenstierna drew back his forces and consolidated what was left of the Swedish position in the Empire. As part of his withdrawal, he agreed to hand over seventeen Swedish-occupied Alsatian towns to France, keeping only Benfeld, the strongest fortress and the only one that could defend itself. Richelieu also gained the Swedish-occupied town of Philippsburg on the right bank of the Rhine, but lost it again the very next year. It was not the lack of Benfeld and Philippsburg that bothered Richelieu so much as Breisach, which had escaped Swedish and French occupation altogether.[4]

The French had occupied Alsace by treaty, not by conquest, so they had no right to it by the laws of war. Indeed, they had assured all the towns taken over from the Swedes that their occupation was only to extend to the end of the war, and that these towns would not be separated from the Empire. But Richelieu later sent a *"Revers"* stating that the status of the towns would indeed be determined by the peace treaty, thereby overturning his previous promises and opening up the way for French annexation.[5] French rights in other towns were even less certain. Those that had requested protection from the Swedes had their own guarantees of independence that were not specifically overturned. Colmar, the largest and most important town outside of Strasbourg, arranged a separate treaty with France that contained explicit guarantees which were renewed in 1644.[6] Strasbourg itself, by far the dominant town in the region and one that controlled a bridge over the Rhine, remained independent and neutral in the war.

Because of the different ways the French had gained Alsace and Lorraine, the new administration they set up was also different in each province. Lorraine had an intendant, but it also had a governor—from 1643, de La Ferté-Senneterre—who exercised extensive powers.[7] The administration of Alsace was less unified. Since the French first became involved in it through a series of protection relationships with separate towns, the governors installed in those towns were the strongest authorities. As the French tried to meet the costs of their garrisons, their control spread over the countryside surrounding the towns and led to conflicts between governors. Even after the appointment of the first intendant, M. de Bélesbat, in 1639, some governors retained a strong hand in administration. The most important of these, d'Erlach, took over the governorship of Breisach after the death of Bernhard of Saxe-Weimar (see below), dividing the Alsatian intendancy into two non-contiguous parts. The baron d'Oysonville was created a *lieutenant de Roi* to serve under him for military purposes, and carved out his own area of competence partly independent from d'Erlach. Furthermore, when Philibert de Baussan replaced Bélesbat as intendant in Alsace in 1645, François de Vautorte was appointed as the first intendant over the recently conquered areas in the Lower Palatinate, which included a series of fortresses stretching along the Rhine around Alsace.[8] There was thus no central authority, and relations between d'Erlach, d'Oysonville, and the local intendant or intendants remained uncomfortable at best, and hostile at worst, until the end of the war.[9]

Over time, the French gradually began to think of Alsace more and more as their own possession, and not just as a trust to be held until the end of the war. Bélesbat's 1639 instructions, for example, already spoke of the areas "under our obedience" rather than "in our protection"; he also administered an oath of fidelity.[10] Six years later, in 1645, the orders to Baussan were to "facilitate the task of the negotiators in Münster," including respecting local customs so as not to make the Alsatians object to being transferred to France.[11] Baussan was also authorized to raise taxes for supporting the garrisons in Alsace, something that had been formerly prohibited by the king.[12] By that time, Mazarin's interest in the province was explicit, and he wrote to Turenne a little later that he expected him to consider Alsace "as much a French province as Champagne."[13] After d'Erlach captured and demolished the fortress of Wildenstein in April 1646, Alsace was entirely safe from enemy incursions.[14]

When the French entered the war against the emperor in 1636, they quickly found that they had too few troops to defend all their fronts. To cover this weakness, they hired Bernhard of Saxe-Weimar and his entire army, formerly in Swedish service, to wage war for them in the Empire, chiefly along the Upper Rhine. With his victory at Rheinfelden in 1638 and capture of Breisach later that year, Bernhard cut Spanish communications with the Low Countries, provided the French with a bridgehead into the Empire, and laid the basis for France's territorial demands at the Congress of Westphalia; but it also enhanced his own ambition to create an independent state for himself based in Alsace. His sudden death of the plague in 1639 saved Richelieu from this grandiose scheme. Richelieu signed a treaty with the officers of Bernhard's army, keeping it in French service and guaranteeing it certain rights (such as German officers), but with a Frenchman now as its leader.

In 1640 and 1641, Longueville and Guébriant led the *Armée d'Allemagne,* as it was known after Bernhard's death, deep into the Empire in cooperation with the Swedish commander, Johan Banér. It was present at the siege of Regensburg, and participated in the victory at Wolfenbüttel in 1641. But then Banér and Guébriant separated, leaving the French army in the middle of the Empire with winter fast approaching.[15] Guébriant retreated to the west, winning a brilliant victory at Kempner Heide, in the Electorate of Cologne, in January 1642. For the next two years, he tried unsuccessfully to establish his army in southwest Germany.

Meanwhile, on 19 May 1643, the young duc d'Enghien won a crushing victory over the Spanish at Rocroi; and Mazarin, newly installed in power, decided to use this opportunity to shift more French strength to the east. Enghien marched quickly southeast and laid siege to Thionville, which he captured on 10 August. But at that point Enghien suddenly decided to return to the court at Paris, leaving his army at the height of the campaigning season. After a delay of some weeks, Mazarin managed to convince Enghien to return to the field for long enough to send some eight thousand reinforcements, under the command of the comte de Rantzau, to Guébriant's army.[16]

Guébriant had thus far been unsuccessful in securing quarters east of the Rhine. He had besieged Rottweil from 24 to 28 July 1643, but the Bavarian von Werth forced him to lift the siege just before the town was ready to capitulate. Guébriant therefore retreated across the Rhine, where the Bavarians followed him, plundering Alsace. But when Rantzau's reinforcements finally reached him on 23 October, Guébriant resumed the offensive. This was all the easier since the Lorrainer troops that had been cooperating with the Bavarians had returned to fight the French troops in their home duchy. With an army of some eighteen thousand troops, therefore, Guébriant had a considerable numerical superiority and an excellent chance of securing quarters.[17] He crossed the Rhine on 2 November and was at Rottweil by the 7th despite heavy rains that made the roads impassable for a few days. Ominously, a Bavarian detachment surprised the Weimarian cavalry in Geislingen on the night of 7–8 November and massacred them. Nevertheless, Guébriant pressed ahead with the siege of Rottweil, and the garrison surrendered on 19 November. With the winter snows already beginning, it appeared that the French had achieved their goal.[18]

However, three things soon led to a dramatic peripeteia. Guébriant had been wounded in the siege of Rottweil on 17 November, and died on 24 November, thus leaving the French army in the far less capable hands of Rantzau.[19] The troops were also cut off from their supplies when it snowed and the mountains became impassable; Tracy tried to bring some around via the Rhine Valley to the south, but he did not reach them.[20] This dangerous conjuncture occurred precisely when the Bavarians were secretly preparing a strike aimed at sending the French back over the Rhine, out of the precious Swabian quarters. Charles IV returned from Lorraine with his force, and, combined with the Bavarians and some Imperial reinforcements, quietly approached Tuttlingen on the night of 24 November.[21] The Weimarians under Rosen had completely failed to post a guard, and the town surrendered immediately. Mercy sent ahead two thousand troops to Rottweil and followed them on 27 November with the rest of the army. After refusing for a while to offer terms, the Imperial forces eventually permitted the duke of Württemberg to exit the town with his baggage on 2 December, but the remaining French troops were enlisted in the Bavarian army. Rantzau tried to compensate for his failure to keep an adequate watch by recklessly marching to save one contingent, and was captured in the attempt. The remnants of the French army, shattered and leaderless, fled across the snow-covered mountains toward Breisach.[22]

All told, the French lost 7,000 prisoners and 4,000 killed at the battle of Tuttlingen and the subsequent engagements and sieges. At first, the magnitude of the disaster was not apparent to the French, even those close to the situation. Tracy considered French losses no more than 1,400 to 1,600 captured and 200 dead. He noted Rosen's success in retreating with six cavalry regiments and three infantry brigades, and felt that the losses suffered at Tuttlingen would be trivial if they could only hold Rottweil.[23] Even after it fell, though—and real as the French losses were—the same snow that had prevented supplies from reaching the French also made Bavarian pursuit impossible; instead, Mercy settled down in the newly conquered quarters.[24]

In spite of the court's equally utopian view of affairs—they declared on 8 December that the battle "had not noticeably weakened" the army and spoke of recrossing the Rhine at the first opportunity—they still took the occasion for a major reform of the *Armée d'Allemagne*.[25] The principal concern was a new commander, and the court chose Turenne, then commanding in Italy and only made a marshal that same November. The choice seemed appropriate: Turenne spoke German and was a Protestant like the Weimarians; he was favored by Tracy; and he proved an excellent commander eventually, though there was not so much evidence of it as yet.[26]

Besides appointing Turenne, the court also undertook to reform and strengthen the army. The infantry in particular was judged substandard, and the Italian and Liège regiments were sent back, along with any other weak units. To replace them, the court was recruiting 2,000 Irish; in addition, Turenne was urged to pull 1,200 to 1,500 troops from the Alsace garrisons. All regiments were to be reformed to a minimum strength of 500 soldiers, the cavalry remounted, and Turenne sent some artillery, all of the previous cannon having been captured in the Tuttlingen disaster. Negotiations for the repatriation of prisoners were also begun. Finally, the court urged Turenne to think of forming a small, separate corps to cover Alsace and Breisach in case he should operate elsewhere. Throughout all this, Mazarin asserted and reasserted his great passion for German affairs, no doubt in order to allay fears that the Weimarians would be abandoned after the latest debacle.[27]

While the court strained its resources and reestablished the *Armée d'Allemagne* materially, its efforts to reform the command structure were less successful. They proposed making the officer structure in the Weimarian army the same as that in the French army, but nothing came of this. Turenne objected to the appointment of d'Aumont as *lieutenant général*, arguing that the Weimarians would not accept him as their superior, since by their treaty they were only to take orders from the supreme commander; the court eventually caved in, granting d'Aumont the salary of a *lieutenant général* without the title. Finally, Mazarin was concerned about the loyalty of the Weimarians, and attempted to break their contacts with fortress governors, in particular by giving d'Erlach a post in the army. However, this plan failed before it even began, because d'Erlach was already unhappy with Turenne's appointment (a post he had wanted for himself) and had withdrawn from Breisach in protest. The court managed to coax him back, but his discontent continued, eventually manifesting itself in a serious conflict with his French counterpart in Breisach (see below).[28]

Such were the military conditions in the Empire as the peace negotiations began. The Treaty of Hamburg, which laid out the conditions for the Congress of Westphalia, had been signed on Christmas Day, 1641. According to its provisions, negotiations were supposed to begin in Münster and Osnabrück just three months later, on 25 March 1642. But both sides delayed sending representatives, and by the autumn of 1643 only the Danes, the Imperials, one Spaniard, and the Venetian mediator Contarini had appeared, with the Swedes waiting some distance away so as not to arrive before the French.[29] But Servien and d'Avaux did not even depart from France until the end of October, and stopped in The Hague to negotiate a new treaty with the Dutch, renewing their agreement of 1635. Since these negotiations proved more difficult than expected, they were held up in the Netherlands until the following spring, further delaying the beginning of the talks at Westphalia.[30]

The powers of the French plenipotentiaries were regulated by a 20 September 1643 instruction from the king. All three were mentioned—Servien, d'Avaux, and Longueville—but two of them had the power to negotiate in the absence of the third. This was a practical matter, since Longueville did not leave for the congress until 1645, and then mainly because Servien and d'Avaux were quarrelling. They were only permitted to conclude a "general and universal peace"—that is to say, no separate peace with the Empire, to the exclusion of Spain, was being contemplated at this time.[31]

Ten days after sending the plenipotentiaries' powers, the court sent a much longer document giving them their basic instructions. Early in this text, the court declared the necessity to tell "all sorts of people, Catholic and Protestant, that Her Majesty does not seek to enlarge her possessions in Germany and in Italy at the expense of anyone." Nevertheless, two paragraphs later it noted that "it is important that Her Majesty not be separated from Germany, in order that she be in a position not to tolerate the oppression of the princes who possess estates there," and followed this with a justification that France, unlike the Habsburgs, was not dominated by self-interest in its demands.[32] The ground was thus gently laid for a more explicit delimitation of French demands. The general principle behind these demands was to be "never to make any treaty except *à la hollandaise*, that is to say, in not returning anything that one has conquered by arms." This was in part intended to justify French demands to their allies, but was also partly a reaction against what the French saw as the usual Habsburg way of proceeding.[33]

Far from leaving it at this, however, the court provided explicit instructions for each area where France was engaged in the war. The demands in Lorraine, which followed immediately upon those in Italy, were obviously very important.[34] Nothing in this section indicates possible compromises, but only a long series of reasons why France was entitled to complete possession of Lorraine. The "Three Bishoprics" of Metz, Toul, and Verdun, occupied since 1552, are mentioned only as an afterthought, because the crown preferred not to see them discussed at all at the conference. France had occupied them for so long that the court felt that bringing the issue up could only damage French interests, since their rights there were so firmly established by tradition.

The section on Lorraine was followed by one on the Spanish possessions in the Low Countries and Franche-Comté and then on Alsace. Since Alsace was by no means a unified province in a legal sense, having evolved over the years a complex mix of rights and freedoms that varied from one part to the next, a brief discussion of its administration is essential to understanding the negotiations. To oversimplify somewhat, the Habsburgs exercised extensive rights in the southern half of the province, known as "Upper Alsace," in their quality as "landgrave." In the northern half of the province, "Lower Alsace," there was also a landgrave—the bishop of Strasbourg—but the title was an almost completely empty one. Instead, Lower Alsace was dominated by the *Reichsritterschaft*, the personal holdings of the bishop of Strasbourg, and the possessions of Strasbourg itself, a free Imperial city not considered part of the province. A group of ten Imperial cities, known as the "Decapolis," comprised five members each in Upper and Lower Alsace. The Imperials also controlled the Prefectorate of Haguenau, which not only gave them extensive rights over numerous villages, but also some vague protection rights over the Decapolis.[35]

The French occupied most of the towns in Alsace outside of Strasbourg itself; and although they did not control Benfeld, which was garrisoned by the Swedes, they did possess Breisach. Breisach was surrounded by a territory known as "the Breisgau," which the French claimed on some occasions, although they never occupied much more than Breisach itself and some of the surrounding countryside after the Bavarians recaptured Freiburg in 1644. "The Sundgau," another territory the French sometimes mentioned, was actually a part of Alsace that they occupied, and hence was eventually subsumed under the title of the whole province (see chapter 6 for a more complete discussion of the French understanding of the Sundgau). Finally, the French made some effort to gain what were known as the "Forest Towns"—Waldshut, Rheinfelden (the site of Bernhard's 1638 victory over the Bavarian-Imperial army), Säckingen, and Laufenburg. These four towns lay along the right bank of the Rhine just north of Switzerland; control of them would help the French dominate the entire Upper Rhine. The town of Basel and the surrounding bishopric sat uncomfortably between the Forest Towns and Alsace at the point where the Rhine bent toward the north. Neither was yet considered a part of Switzerland, but both managed to stay neutral and, for the most part, out of the area of French influence.[36]

The section of the plenipotentiaries' instructions dealing with Alsace proposed that, although it would be difficult, there was reason to believe that the emperor would give France Breisach, the Forest Towns, Colmar, Sélestat, Belfort, Saverne, Haguenau, "and the other places we possess between Lorraine and the Rhine"—that is to say, in essence, all of Alsace. In order to show that they were not being unreasonable, France would agree to return Haguenau; in addition, one of these places could be given to Bavaria to encourage Maximilian to support the settlement. The instructions then reminded the plenipotentiaries of the need to maintain a line of communications to Breisach, including Saverne and Sélestat, and, if possible, Benfeld (occupied by Sweden).[37]

This is simple and direct, but it is complicated by a supplementary instruction that was probably attached.[38] Noting that "it is impossible to predict and to prescribe the conditions by which we can conclude the peace treaty, because this depends on the advantages that we will be able to gain by arms," the memo outlined six alternatives of a peace settlement. In the first of these, France would retain everything that she had occupied from the Habsburgs. In the second, third, and fourth alternatives, France would retain from the emperor Saverne, Sélestat, Benfeld, Breisach; "another passage close to the Rhine"; and the territory necessary for the subsistence of these places and the passage of troops to them. In the fifth alternative, France would return Breisach and "all of Alsace" to an allied family: either the Habsburg archdukes (whose alliance, the memo recognizes, could only be imaginary), or to Bavaria. Finally, the sixth alternative was a twenty-year truce in which France would retain all of its conquests. The memo closed by noting that all possible settlements were "chimerical" now, because the military situation was not yet good enough that the Habsburgs would agree to the kind of territorial sacrifices necessary that would prevent them from unjust endeavors, and thus assure the peace.

These additional instructions present two main difficulties. In the first place, they were clearly not sent to Servien and d'Avaux as written. The only copy still extant dates from 1642, and at the end it mentions attaching two royal memos that were written by Louis XIII. But once the possibility of a different version is admitted, it becomes impossible to say with any certainty what other parts might or might not have been changed. While it is clear that Mazarin made few changes in the main instructions, he certainly did make some, and we cannot know what subtle but potentially important changes he made in the supplement. In the second place, it is impossible to know how strongly Mazarin favored one or another of the alternatives. Though arranged in descending order of preference, there may have been some points that Richelieu had intended to concede more readily than others (especially the first alternative, which is extremely harsh). What, after all, is one to make of the fact that the main instructions argue for the likelihood of achieving all the demands "although there may be great difficulty"? Third, the fact that the demands themselves were predicated on further military success means that Richelieu had been looking ahead when designing the demands in the first place, and it is difficult to guess what state he expected the war to be in when he wrote that he thought the emperor would agree to surrender the French-held towns in Alsace. Fourth, and finally, the fact that the alternatives were composed by Richelieu leaves a further lacuna between the text and Mazarin's intentions.[39]

The French conception of Alsace would play a considerable role in the negotiations and in subsequent historiography; but their conception is hard to gauge from the preliminary instructions. On one hand, these instructions named the towns under French control, and they emphasized the need for a line of communication to Breisach; thus, the French would seem to have thought of the area more as a series of fortified points than as a unified province.[40] On the other hand, the instructions also refer to "all of Alsace" at one point; and this is not the first such usage by the French court. The original treaty with Bernhard, for example, promised him "the landgraviate of Alsace," and in 1640 the court wrote to d'Avaux that there was evidence that the Germans would be willing to let France have "Alsace."[41] Thus the French court seems, appropriately, to have had an ambiguous view of the territory that would be the source of so much dispute in the ensuing centuries.

The plenipotentiaries' instructions therefore included several options, the choice of which was not yet decided. In the ensuing years, the precision of the demands would be increased without having their essential nature altered. There was plenty of time for this, because the negotiations got off to a slow start.

6
1644: France Alone

THE FRENCH POSITION IN THE EMPIRE WAS PARTICULARLY WEAK AT the beginning of 1644. The king, Louis XIII, had recently followed his chief minister, Richelieu, to the grave, and the new regency remained still insecure. The disaster at Tuttlingen in late November 1643 was compounded when, on 22 December, the main Swedish army under Lennart Torstensson invaded Denmark's Jutland peninsula, leaving the French without support in their war against the emperor. It was hardly a propitious stance from which to begin negotiations.

A pessimistic January letter giving further instructions to Servien and d'Avaux reflected the poor French position. It noted that France wanted peace, but that many experts considered it impossible because of the complex issues involved. Moreover, the Dutch—with whom Servien and d'Avaux were negotiating a renewed alliance before going to Münster—did not want peace, and France could not go against their wishes. Anne, the French queen and regent for her son Louis XIV, was therefore ready to consent to a truce. She noted with regret that "our intention is completely contrary, and only the necessity of not being able to do better persuades us to a truce." As the secretary of state, Brienne, remarked in a separate letter, "Presently, the only thing we can all desire is to conserve the kingdom in its entirety and also the alliances that the late king [Louis XIII] has contracted"; only when Louis XIV had reached his majority could France think of "giving the law to its neighbors."[1]

In these circumstances, it was fortunate for France that no substantive issues were actually discussed at the conference in 1644.[2] The issues addressed were only preliminary ones, such as questions of precedence among the various ambassadors; whether the powers delegated to a state's ambassadors were adequate to negotiate peace; and whether the German estates should be present at the negotiations. Not until the end of the year were these resolved even in principle, and the question of the admission of the German estates continued to be debated throughout most of 1645.

The emperor was chiefly to blame for the delays. He was elated at the Swedish invasion of Denmark, which game him a new *de facto* ally. Hoping to court Denmark into a full alliance, the emperor tried to avoid entering into substantial negotiations as long as Christian IV was not represented at the conference. In Osnabrück, the Imperial plenipotentiaries refused to begin talks with Sweden on the grounds that there was no mediator (the Danes having been excluded by virtue of their war with Sweden). In Münster, they seized on alleged defects in the powers delegated to the French plenipotentiaries as a delaying tactic. Their main complaint was that the prologue to the French powers excoriated the emperor and blamed him exclusively for the war. They also objected that the French powers only allowed them to negotiate with their allies, and that the powers were signed by the minor king, not his regent mother or any members of council. The French met these criticisms with some of their own. They argued that the Imperial powers spoke only of negotiating the means to peace, but not of peace itself; they were also particularly concerned that the Imperial powers said nothing about the right to conclude with France's allies. The French raised further objections over Spanish powers.[3]

Some historians have viewed these discussions merely as a delaying tactic; in particular, Mazarin has often been blamed for deliberately stalling the negotiations in 1644 in order to conquer more territory and to exclude Spain.[4] In fact, however, at no time in these opening years did he show himself anxious to delay negotiations; to the contrary, everything he did indicates that he wanted the negotiations to progress faster. In mid-June, for example, he became so frustrated with the failure of the plenipotentiaries of either branch of the Habsburgs to produce adequate delegated powers that he told his own representatives that it would be worthwhile to threaten to withdraw from the conference. This was elevated to an order in his letter of 17 July.[5]

It must be emphasized that this threat was intended to remain simply a threat; Mazarin was not looking for an excuse to break off talks, but rather wanted to use the threat of breaking them off to produce movement in the negotiations.[6] His policy toward Sweden further demonstrates his desire to see the talks progress. The Swedes, growing impatient over the refusal of the Imperial plenipotentiaries to begin negotiations, threatened to withdraw from the negotiations, but were much more serious about this than the French. Brienne made it clear that this would hurt the allied cause, since it would give the enemy the moral high ground.[7] In a July meeting with Salvius, Servien and d'Avaux were able to convince the Swedish ambassadors to remain in Osnabrück; however, it remained a sensitive issue until the emperor finally began to negotiate with Sweden in September.[8]

These are not the actions of a power trying to stall negotiations. Thus, one must see in the vexing questions of precedence and full powers something more than a delaying tactic. In fact, the purpose of the French complaints was twofold: first, they were a counterattack against Imperial objections to French powers; and second, the French were fighting for something that they felt was important. The precedence questions are perhaps the most difficult to understand from the point of view of the advantage to be gained from them. However, though the issue might itself be of minor significance, to surrender on it would have been seen as a concession of weakness, and thus have led to more serious consequences.[9] That the French considered this a serious matter is evident from the fact that they also contested precedence matters with the Dutch, at the great risk of alienating their own allies.[10] Moreover, there can be no question that Mazarin deliberately planned a precedence quarrel to stall the negotiations, since the issue was actually dealt with in the original instructions to the plenipotentiaries (which, as we have seen, were largely drawn up by Richelieu).[11] In the sharply hierarchical world of early modern Europe, precedence questions were real issues, and the states had a responsibility to uphold their rights, if not for the sake of their own prestige, then for that of their representatives.[12]

The struggle over the wording of the plenipotentiaries' powers is less difficult to understand. Ever since Richelieu had renounced the Treaty of Regensburg, negotiated by his ambassadors in 1630 to end the Mantuan War with the Emperor, statesmen had been forced to examine the powers of the opposing plenipotentiaries more carefully.[13] In inspecting the powers of the Spanish ambassadors, the French plenipotentiaries—and not Mazarin—detected what they viewed to be faults. It is true that Mazarin seemed to share their concerns, but wrote that,

> nevertheless, the extreme passion that Her Majesty has to see the treaty advance . . . obliges Her Majesty to offer from her side all possible facilities to surmount the obstacles that would retard the

peace. For this effect, she has found it a good idea that you continue to put up with the matters and pass ahead in the negotiation,

on the condition that the Spanish obtain revised powers within six to eight weeks.[14] This again proves that Mazarin was in no way trying to stall the negotiations by haggling over the enemy ambassadors' powers; to the contrary, he was anxious to advance the negotiations even as the dispute over powers was being resolved. On the other hand, France's insistence on the Imperial delegates having power to negotiate both with France and with her allies demonstrates just how thoroughly Mazarin's strategy emphasized—and depended on—cooperation with his allies. But especially during this year, cooperation would prove hard to achieve.

The French plenipotentiaries did not arrive in Münster—"this filthy town of Münster, as wet and muddy as it could possibly be," as one of d'Avaux's secretaries put it—until the spring: d'Avaux on 17 March, Servien on 5 April. On their way to the conference, they had visited The Hague to negotiate a new treaty with the Dutch. The French were already concerned about the possibility of the Dutch signing a separate treaty with Spain, and Brienne wrote to the plenipotentiaries warning them of this on 19 March.[15] By their new treaty with France, the Dutch were specifically permitted to talk to Spanish ambassadors separately; Brienne admonished the plenipotentiaries, however, always to have a secretary on hand during these talks. The plenipotentiaries responded that they would try, but this precaution would not be adequate if the Dutch had already made up their minds to sign a separate treaty.[16] Later in the year, Servien would write to the French resident at The Hague that it was in France's interests to keep the Dutch away from the conference as long as possible. "Their [i.e., Dutch] interests with the Spanish envoys," he wrote, "can be solved in four days, and ours, which are composed of very important different points, are not even sketched out."[17] Fear of Dutch desertion would become a French obsession later, as it became increasingly obvious that the Dutch were indeed working out their differences with Spain and had no intention of remaining in the war to support French interests.

Relations with Sweden were better, if still strained. Mazarin was not so much worried about having Sweden desert France, but wished Sweden would conclude its war with Denmark and get back to the main task of defeating the Habsburgs. "We have nothing more to desire at present," wrote Mazarin to his plenipotentiaries, "than the end of this Danish war." To help end it, the French dispatched the sieur de La Thuillerie to mediate the conflict. But he was subject to endless delays because the Imperialists would not grant him a passport to get to Denmark overland.[18] The plenipotentiaries debated sending him by ship, but felt that they would need to clear this with Sweden first. He finally got underway in June, but was unable to find King Christian IV of Denmark. Servien wrote a frustrated letter to Brienne complaining, "The general treaty depends entirely from now on the good or bad humor of the King of Denmark, who, however, traipses about at sea with his fleet, without Monsieur de La Thuillerie knowing where to look for him."[19]

If communication with the Danes was difficult, that with the Swedes was hardly better. While the Swedes maintained first Hugo Grotius and then Marc Duncan Cérisantes as a representative in Paris, the French had no resident in Stockholm. By the end of the year, Servien was arguing that the lack of such a representative was a serious mistake, and repeatedly pressed the court to take action.[20] But it was not until 19 December that Mazarin finally decided to act on his suggestions, and even then, it would be some time until an ambassador was actually sent.[21] Nor was the situation much better in Westphalia, where the French and Swedish plenipotentiaries should, in theory, have been able to meet easily to resolve their difficulties. In fact, the two sets of plenipotentiaries did not meet, at least as a group, for the whole year.[22] First they could not agree who would make the first visit (and hence concede priority); then they could not decide on an appropriate location, equidistant from Osnabrück and Münster; when that was settled, d'Avaux fell sick.[23] The Swedes finally gave up on trying to arrange a public meeting, and instead sent Salvius to Münster in June, *incognito* so that Swedish honor would not be at stake.[24] This meeting, and the constant communication maintained between the French delegation and the Swedish resident Rosenhane, enabled the alliance to function adequately. Nevertheless, d'Avaux was moved to ask in October "how is it that we have now been here eight months and Lord Oxenstierna and I have yet to see one another?"[25] But even this query, accompanied by several means for accommodating Swedish pride, was not enough to get the two delegations together. Oxenstierna finally did visit Münster in December, but again *incognito*, and mostly "for pleasure and curiosity," he said.[26]

Meanwhile, France had been approached by another potential ally, Bavaria. This was not the first time the two powers had engaged in talks, but it was the first time during Anne's regency; and Maximilian's approach was taken as a very good sign by Mazarin. In reporting the news on 9 April, he gushed to his plenipotentiaries of "this advance, made by a Prince [Maximilian] whose credit you know, of such a proven prudence, who, acting according to the maxims that he has witnessed up to this point, cannot have other interests in Germany than the same ones that we have." In the same letter, he twice commented that "the person of the said Duke of Bavaria, well managed, is the best piece to lead the negotiation of the peace to its conclusion to the advantage of this crown." His reason for believing that Maximilian was so important: the Spanish "deferred" to Maximilian and feared upsetting him, since he could conceivably convince the emperor to make a separate treaty with France. This the Spanish wished to avoid at all costs, "knowing well what prejudice their affairs would receive if we only had to deal with them alone." Their fear of a separate peace by the Empire would make them more pliant "and more reasonable in the conditions of a general peace."[27]

Bavaria was thus the centerpiece of Mazarin's evolving strategy against Spain. If Maximilian insisted on peace, the emperor would have to follow; and Spain must follow the emperor, for it could not afford to fight on alone against France. It is important to note that Mazarin did not wish—nor did he ever wish—to exclude Spain from the peace and thereby split the House of Austria in two. Instead, he hoped to use the *threat* of this split to gain advantages at the peace table, without having to go through the military strain of wrenching them from his enemies at great expense and over a long period of time. It was a policy aimed, in short, at striking at the weakest link in the enemy alliance. But it depended on two important, yet uncertain, correlations: the emperor must be unwilling to see Bavaria desert, and Spain must be unwilling to let the emperor desert. If one or both of these links did not hold, Mazarin's policy could cause him to lose control of the negotiations, as in fact happened to him later.

The French plenipotentiaries, while agreeing that Maximilian was the best hope for French success, were decidedly less sanguine about the degree to which Bavarian and French interests coincided. They argued that Maximilian did not particularly like France, and (far worse) did not wish France to retain her conquests in the Empire. They believed that Maximilian's interest in France lay mainly in the fact that he would like to see the treaty concluded as soon as possible. He was old, and his children were young; the succession was thus uncertain. If he died while the war was still going on, the emperor would take over his troops and his position as head of the Catholic party. It was from this more pessimistic—and more accurate—basis that the French plenipotentiaries felt there was hope for an accord with Bavaria.[28]

As with Denmark and Sweden, the problem with the Bavarian negotiations in 1644 was the lack of anyone with whom to negotiate. The plenipotentiaries mentioned in their letter of 23 April that they would talk to the Bavarian plenipotentiaries at the first opportunity; but Bavaria had as yet sent none. On 11 June, Mazarin proposed that the plenipotentiaries send a secret message to Maximilian to indicate their willingness to advance Bavarian interests to the extent that Bavaria supported French interests.[29] But on 2 July, the plenipotentiaries wrote back complaining that there was still no one with whom to talk.[30] Why was Maximilian being so stubborn?

The Franco-Bavarian talks had stalled because of a larger issue about which Maximilian was firm. France and Sweden had made it a central part of their plank that the negotiations, to be valid, must have the participation of all the German estates and princes; the emperor by himself, they claimed, had no authority to negotiate. This was part of their larger plan to weaken Habsburg authority, making it impossible for the emperor to declare war on France or Sweden in the future without the consent of the Imperial Diet.[31] It was also assumed that having the estates participate in the negotiating process would make it easier for the "two crowns" (as France and Sweden called themselves) to achieve their territorial aims.[32]

It may seem that Maximilian would also have wished to limit the Emperor's authority in this way; after all, it would have given Bavaria a chance to send representatives to the conference. But Bavaria was in a privileged position. In the first place, it had been elevated to the Electoral College, and the electors preferred to limit the participation of other princes and estates so as to strengthen their own influence with the emperor. Moreover, Maximilian himself had by far the most influence with the emperor by virtue of their familial ties (Maximilian had married the emperor's sister) and their close cooperation since 1618 (both Ferdinand II and Ferdinand III leaned heavily on Bavarian arms and money in their military effort). The French plenipotentiaries referred to him as the "soul" of the emperor's council; this may be an exaggeration, but there is no doubt that Maximilian and the emperor worked closely together, and the emperor could scarcely afford to take a major diplomatic step without Bavarian approval.³³ Maximilian therefore saw cooperation with the Emperor as the best way to achieve his goals, and took a hard line against the German estates and princes being able to send representatives to the conference.³⁴

Rather than negotiate the right of German princes to come to the conference, the French plenipotentiaries decided to write a circular letter directly to the princes inviting them to send representatives.³⁵ The letter was sent out on 6 April, but the estates responded only slowly. No one had arrived by 12 May, and d'Avaux wrote a concerned letter to Mazarin saying that the princes were weaker than he had imagined, and hence unwilling to send deputies against the emperor's will; he hoped that they could be aroused to come to the conference by the upcoming campaign.³⁶ Part of the problem may have been the tone used in the letter: d'Avaux and Servien did not shrink from calling the emperor a "tyrant," for which they were rebuked by Mazarin.³⁷ Many Germans might have wished to see the emperor's power limited, but they still looked on him as their sovereign.³⁸

Another problem was the tactics used by the enemy to scare off the princes. Mazarin complained to his plenipotentiaries that their opponents constantly characterized French arms as "partial, and that, under the pretext of protecting and assisting the Germans, we have only had the design of usurping and of establishing ourselves in Germany." Naturally, he rejected this as completely false, and said it should be easy to rebut; after all, there was the example of Italy to the contrary, where France had always proven her disinterestedness.³⁹ Whatever the merits of this reasoning, some states did start to send representatives eventually. The Hessians arrived on 15 June, and the representative of Brunswick on 15 July; Frankfurt, the Hanse towns, and possibly the rest of Lower Saxony were expected to follow.⁴⁰ This was still, however, far below French expectations, and the court ordered the plenipotentiaries to send a second circular letter on 6 August.⁴¹

It appeared that much would depend on the outcome of the military campaign. Here, the French were severely handicapped by the absence of the main Swedish army from the Empire, but they had a strong bargaining tool to get it back: they paid an annual subsidy that Sweden needed in order to keep its army operating. At first, the court sent off a haughty letter to its plenipotentiaries, informing them that France would pay none of the subsidy, because she had extra expenses now that the emperor could oppose her with all of his forces.⁴² But, in a memo of 3 June, Servien indicated the problems with not paying the subsidy:

first, Sweden might say that France was violating the treaty, and make a separate agreement with the emperor; and second, that Swedish affairs, which were stretched thin at this moment because of the extra effort of the Danish war, might degenerate into an even worse state—which would hardly be to the advantage of France. On the other hand, paying the subsidy presented two disadvantages: it would undermine the French position of neutrality in mediating the Swedish-Danish war (and hence might cause it to drag on longer), and Sweden might look on payment as a sign that France would underwrite the costs of the Danish war, which would make them even less anxious to leave Jutland. To escape this dilemma, Servien proposed two expedients. First, they could tell Torstensson that the subsidy money was available for him in Hamburg, as soon as he started marching back to Germany; or, if this proved too harsh, they could pay the subsidy under the condition that Sweden only use the money to support troops within the Empire.[43]

Mazarin, who had already come to the idea of adopting a less harsh line and using the subsidy money as a bargaining chip to get the Swedes back into Germany, adopted Servien's ideas wholesale.[44] The plenipotentiaries met with Salvius in early July and quickly worked out an agreement by which France would pay part of the subsidy immediately, and the rest once Torstensson began his return to Germany.[45] But on 17 August, they wrote to the Swedish plenipotentiaries complaining at length about Sweden's lack of action against the emperor, announcing that France was going to withhold part of the subsidy. It was not until 3 September that the plenipotentiaries finally wrote to Brienne that they had agreed to pay the remainder of the subsidy. Finally Torstensson left Denmark and began pursuing the weakened army of Gallas, the Imperial commander.[46]

The absence of the Swedes from the Empire in 1644 did indeed leave the way open for the Imperial forces to shift more of their weight against France. At a February 1644 meeting at Passau—the last attempt by the Habsburg forces to coordinate a military campaign—Maximilian adamantly urged a strong offensive against the French. The Imperials, he pointed out, were losing the war, and the longer it went on, the less inclination the enemy seemed to have for peace. Thus, they must attempt to inflict a major defeat on one of their opponents: the army must "not simply operate to recover one or another fortress, but with God's help can inflict a major disaster [Haubtabbruch] on the enemy in the field."[47] The enemy chosen to attack could only be France, because French money kept all of the other allied states in the war. By delivering a crushing blow to the French, they would cause the opposing alliance to disintegrate, and they could make an honorable peace.[48] As Maximilian summarized the situation in the instructions to his delegates going to the conference, "We have no more quarters. We must hurt France."[49]

Maximilian proposed to deliver this blow himself with his beloved Reichsarmada, but he would require assistance from the emperor and from Spain. The emperor would have to remain on the defensive against Sweden (which was tied down in Denmark) in order to allow him to send money to Bavaria with which to bulk up the Reichsarmada. For their part, the Spanish were to conduct a diversionary offensive against France, in order to keep them from shifting more forces against Bavaria.[50]

This bold plan fell apart for several reasons. In the first place, the emperor refused to remain defensive on the Swedish front, since, for political reasons, he needed to support his new Danish ally. In the second place, Spain was in no position, in the year following Rocroi, to launch anything like an offensive; it was all they could do to defend that part of Flanders that remained to them.[51] However, even if everything had gone smoothly with his allies, it is doubtful whether Maximilian's "Haubtabbruch" would really have been able to knock France out of the war. France had suffered a great defeat at Tuttlingen without flinching, and would suffer two more at Lerida in coming years; more than a single battle would have been required to shake Mazarin's hold on power and force him to make peace.

Despite the difficulties, Maximilian's plan was approved. The Spanish governor-general of the Low Countries, Melo, voiced his consent to a Spanish diversionary offensive, despite knowing that there was no way he could fulfill his obligation. The emperor scraped up enough troops to reinforce the Bavarian army, while at the same time building an Imperial force strong enough to march against Torstensson. A reserve corps under Melchior von Hatzfeld was formed in Franconia, causing some controversy because it impinged on Bavarian quarters. And thus the Bavarian commander, Mercy—fresh from his victory at Tuttlingen the winter before—set out on 15 April with an eye to recrossing the Black Forest and recapturing the important fortress of Freiburg.

Maximilian must have expected a major battle, for he was convinced that the French would send a large force to avenge Tuttlingen. Girolamo Giustiniani, the Venetian ambassador to Paris, also expected the French to go on the offensive in Germany. He wrote to his master that French plans,

> (if they do not change them, which would be a miracle in France) are to hold on the defensive in Flanders and in Champagne, at least unless they have an opportunity to conquer some place with certainty. In Italy, they will not make any great efforts, and they will push their advantages as much as possible in Catalonia and in Germany.[52]

But to speak of "pushing advantages" in Germany was absurd after the French defeat at Tuttlingen; Giustiniani must have been neither very well informed, nor an acute observer of military affairs. The main French effort would actually be made in Flanders, as it was nearly every year. This was the front where the French had the most to gain—and the most to lose.[53] The "first and foremost" ("première et principale") French army, under Gaston d'Orléans, would attack Gravelingen in Flanders, seconded by an army under Gassion.[54] The Duke of Enghien, victor of Rocroi, would command a third army in Champagne.[55] Undoubtedly he would have liked to have undertaken an offensive of his own; however, Mazarin, "having esteemed it neither appropriate nor possible to undertake attacks on the enemies at the same time in different places," instead ordered Enghien to cover the siege of Gravelingen, and not to tie himself down in any major offensive.[56] Besides these forces, there would be the usual armies operating in Catalonia and Italy. Finally, an army was created in the center of the kingdom (Saintonge and Angoumois) "which can prevent the effect of the bad intentions of those who in our [Louis XIV's] young age might attempt to stir up troubles in our provinces."[57]

Where did this leave Turenne's battered but heavily reinforced army in Alsace? Though Turenne wrote that he hoped to campaign on the other side of the Rhine in order to preserve Alsace, it is clear that no major offensive was planned.[58] He already knew by 5 February 1644, that Bavaria was going to enter the campaign with an army twice the size of his own; it would have been all he could do to defend the French-occupied towns east of the Rhine without assistance.[59] It is true that Mazarin intended Turenne and Enghien to link up after the capture of Gravelingen, but the plans called for Turenne to march north to help Enghien, rather than the other way around.[60]

It appears from this that Mazarin underestimated the size and importance of the Bavarian offensive.[61] He was leaving Turenne with too few forces, while urging him to operate across the Rhine so as to spare Alsace. He even, as we have seen, planned to strip the Upper Rhine of even more troops, and wrote to Turenne in April telling him to form a small corps under a trusted subordinate to cover Breisach and Alsace.[62] Perhaps he was swayed in these plans by Enghien's understandable desire to lead another offensive. Even in the previous year, after his great victory at Rocroi, Enghien had been forced to end his offensive in order to bring reinforcements to the German front, and now he was anxious for another chance at glory.[63] But Enghien could just as well have attacked on the Upper Rhine; the fact was that the French—and not just Mazarin—saw their interests lying elsewhere. The Black Forest was a very difficult area to attack; and, as the previous year had shown, even successful advances were nearly impossible to supply in the winter. Servien wrote a strongly worded letter on 1 April arguing that it was necessary to drive the enemy away from Münster in order to negotiate more freely; "it would be more advantageous to us in the present conjuncture and perhaps easier to make a great effort in Westphalia than toward the Upper Rhine."[64]

Fortunately for Mazarin, Mercy's offensive was long delayed while he besieged Überlingen, a town on Lake Constance that the French had captured in the winter of 1642 and which lay astride his line of advance. Turenne made the most of the opportunity.[65] While most of his troops were in quarters, he took a small force and made a lightning attack into Franche-Comté. He captured some towns, including Vesoul, but found the territory so devastated that it was hardly worth his trouble.[66] On news that Charles IV of Lorraine had crossed the Moselle, Turenne retreated quickly northward in an attempt to surprise him. But it proved to be a mere raid, and Turenne dispersed his troops back into quarters in mid-April. Rosen, whom he had dispatched across the Rhine, returned at the same time for want of forage. Turenne complained that the peasants of Alsace were so ruined that it was becoming unsafe for his troops to quarter there[67]; at the same time, he noted his shortage of infantry. There was also a more ominous portent: a regiment in Breisach had revolted and shot its officers.[68]

The revolt was suppressed immediately by d'Erlach, co-commander of Breisach, at the same time that the Bavarians were entering the campaign (15 April).[69] The court at first attempted to attribute the revolt to the rivalry between d'Erlach and d'Oysonville, but soon a second revolt broke out.[70] The plenipotentiaries, apparently unaware of the actual events going on in Brei-

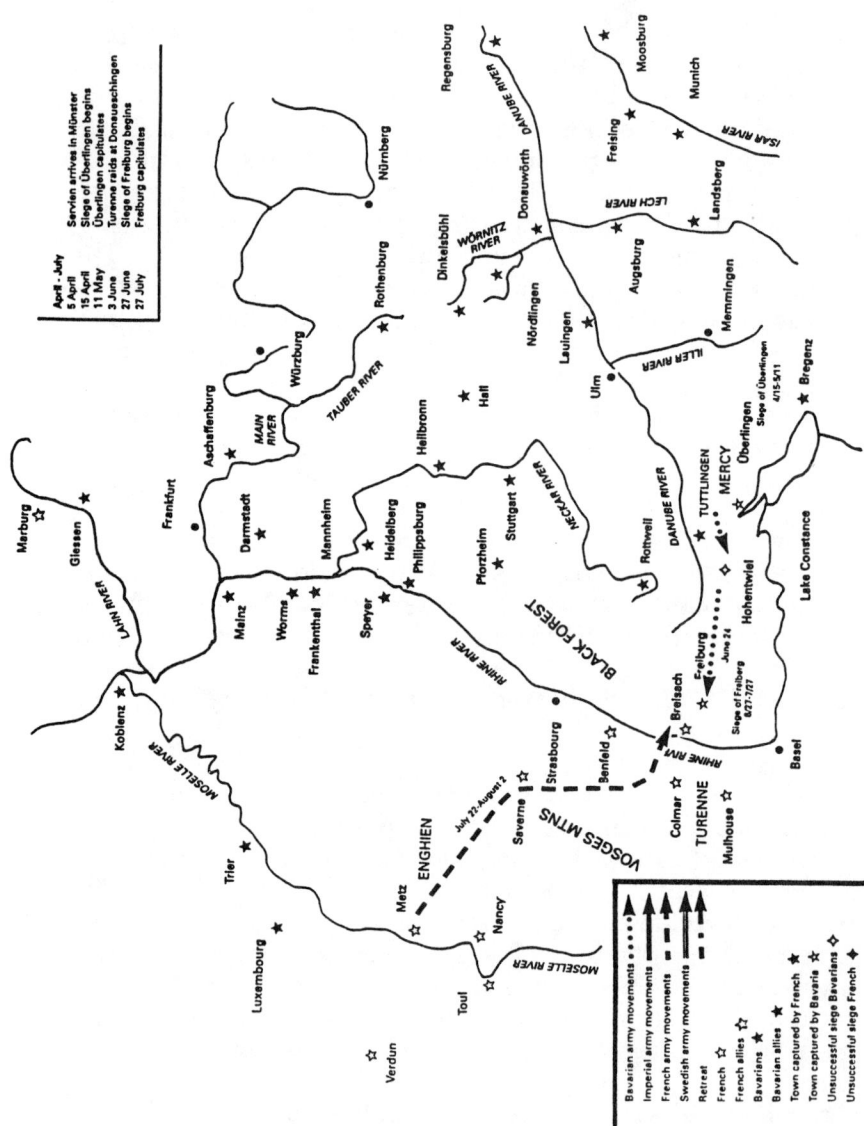

1644, April–July

sach, simultaneously reported that they had information that Maximilian

> has made all sorts of efforts to render his army more powerful than usual, that he has designs against Breisach, that he has secret contacts in the town, and that he intends to enter it by the gilded door [i.e., through bribery].[71]

The court persisted (correctly, as it turned out) in laying the blame on the d'Erlach-d'Oysonville rivalry, and ordered the replacement of the latter. Fortunately for the French, Überlingen held out longer than anyone expected. The garrison was admittedly weak, but the commander was excellent. It was not until 12 May that the town finally surrendered.[72]

By this time, the French were finally getting their forces into the field. Orders had gone out to the generals on 22 April, but these (apart from Turenne) did not actually go to their armies until the middle of May. Yet, rather than press his advantage, Mercy dawdled. Instead of marching directly against the French, he besieged Hohentwiel—a fortress of only local concern, garrisoned by troops from Württemberg and located on a mountain that could not be assaulted, but only starved out.[73]

Turenne again made use of the delay. Learning from a prisoner that Mercy had left his troops spread out in quarters, Turenne led a force of cavalry and infantry across the Rhine on 4 June, surprised a Bavarian cavalry outpost near Donaueschingen, and defeated it decisively; he then retreated quickly back across the Rhine before Mercy could react. This raid of more than forty miles was an effective morale-booster for the Weimarian cavalry, still demoralized after Tuttlingen; it did not, however, significantly alter the balance of forces in the theater. Turenne wrote to Mazarin on 25 June that it would be pointless for him to join Enghien, since he would be recalled immediately by enemy action. Yet Mercy remained strangely inactive. Turenne could not understand why the Bavarians wanted to besiege Hohentwiel, and had to assume that they were merely conserving their forces. He urged Enghien to do the same so that the French would still be strong at the end of the campaign.[74]

Suddenly, Mercy appeared before Freiburg on 26 June. Turenne had written that same day to court that he did not believe the rumors of their advance. But, after a failed attempt to buy off the commander of Hohentwiel, Mercy had in fact left a few thousand men to cover the fortress and moved out on 20 June. By the 28th, the bulk of his forces were before Freiburg, and he began to besiege the town. Turenne crossed the Rhine, but discovered that the enemy had already occupied the post he wanted. He found the Bavarians extremely well equipped, mostly with items captured the previous year at Tuttlingen. Their numerical superiority was so great that he feared "an accident could happen to us"; at least he needed more infantry to garrison the Alsatian towns, which he had stripped to provide men for his own army.[75]

Why were the French so weak relative to the Bavarians? First, the absence of the Swedes had left the emperor free to fortify the Bavarian "Reichsarmada" far beyond its usual strength. But France had been deserted by her other allies, too. In the first place, there was the hope of winning over the troops of Duke Charles IV of Lorraine. The vacillating policies of the duke irritated the French perhaps more than any other aspect of the Thirty Years' War. At the peace conference, they made Habsburg abandonment of Charles a *sine qua non*. The French plenipotentiaries repeatedly called attention to the Treaty of Paris (1641), by which Charles had agreed to abandon all other alliances and join with France—or forfeit his entire duchy.[76] But when Charles reopened peace feelers with France in January 1644, Mazarin entertained the offers in the hope of winning him over by a negotiated treaty, and attempted to detach him from the Habsburg alliance by secret negotiations. This would not only remove a persistent thorn in France's side; it would also achieve positive military advantages in the form of his battle-hardened (if scant) troops, and, more importantly, additional Rhine crossings.[77]

The negotiations dragged on throughout the first part of the year, then the two sides seemed to reach an agreement. Brienne wrote to the plenipotentiaries on 2 July that France was "practically assured of the Duke of Lorraine," and reiterated this on 9 July. And, indeed, the French ambassador left on 10 July for Worms to sign the treaty. But when he arrived, he found Charles not there; and, a week later, the ambassador gave up and left. Mazarin still wrote of the advantages that would accrue to France from the treaty, especially the gaining of Rhine crossings to permit further invasions of Germany. But on 23 July, Lionne wrote to Servien to say that the court had just received news that Charles had joined his forces with the enemy. The plenipotentiaries at first refused to believe the rumors they heard in Münster and hoped that Charles could join with Turenne in time to relieve Freiburg; but on 15 August, Mazarin wrote to say that the affair was, indeed, finished. He drew solace from the fact that France had kept Charles's troops inactive for most of the campaign, but remained bitter about the failed talks: in September, he wrote a lengthy complaint about Charles's actions to his plenipotentiaries, and requested a list of all the reasons why France should not negotiate with him in the future.[78]

There remained France's steady ally in the Empire, Hesse-Cassel. Mazarin had begun the year with the hope that Hesse could help make up for the absence of the Swedes. He increased the Hessian subsidy, and formed a special corps of twenty-four hundred men in the Bishopric of Liège to join with the Hessians.[79] However, Mazarin really hoped to unite this corps with the French armies, and tried to sound out whether the Hessians would accept more money instead of the troops. When Amalie-Elisabeth insisted on the men, Mazarin found an excuse—the hostility of the Liège-recruited men to Hesse—to keep them anyway; Amalie-Elisabeth was granted thirty thousand additional Reichstalers to keep her satisfied.[80]

This was not enough to sour relations with Hesse, nor did a Cologne-inspired Westphalian defense league ever amount to anything. But on 2 July, the plenipotentiaries first reported to the French court the ominous news that the Count of Emden had been raising some troops in East Frisia. This was a grave threat to Amalie-Elisabeth, who needed East Frisia as a base for her troops and a place to raise contributions. She sent Hessian forces to clear the territory, threatening the French plenipotentiaries that she would have to withdraw from the war if the situation were not soon resolved. The plenipotentiaries, for their part, complained that "if Freiburg is lost, we will be in part obligated to those who gave the Count of Emden the desire to raise troops so much out of season."[81]

It was thus just as the campaign was reaching its peak, in the middle of July, that it became clear that the French would have to fight alone. Mazarin, however, was slow to realize this and to react to it. On 12 July, he informed Enghien that, since the siege of Gravelingen was now so far advanced, he was free to undertake an offensive against the enemy commander in his area, Beck. Mazarin even said that Turenne could support such an attack by a diversion of his own, suggesting that the cardinal did not even realize yet that Freiburg was under siege.[82]

Meanwhile, the city's plight worsened. Mercy had to give up on the idea of a direct assault because of the proximity of Turenne's army, but a flanking manoeuvre by Turenne failed completely when the attacking infantry broke under fire. Afterward, the two armies faced each other in fortified camps while Mercy pushed ahead with the siege. The French were in desperate need of a *montre* (pay for the soldiers), and Tracy had to borrow money on his own credit to pay the cavalry; they were also short of infantry, and the money they poured into strengthening it was largely wasted because of corrupt officers.[83] Yet the Bavarians, too, were suffering. Tracy reported that so many of their soldiers had deserted that one could form two of the best regiments in France from them. In addition, Turenne dispatched Rosen on a cavalry raid that caused six hundred enemy losses. Turenne saw that Freiburg was going to fall soon, but felt that the campaign would still be a French victory: the Bavarians, after their heavy losses, would be forced to retreat back across the mountains, while Freiburg itself was untenable unless its owner also occupied Breisach. Then, on the 24 July, Turenne—in fear of being attacked should the Bavarians take Freiburg, which he knew to be near capitulation—pulled back further from the town.[84]

The race was on. On 20 July, Mazarin had finally written to inform Turenne that, in light of the failure of the negotiations with Charles, he was sending Enghien's army to relieve Freiburg. But would he arrive in time? Mazarin was emphatic that Freiburg must be relieved; the troops were coming only on condition "that there is certitude . . . that one can defeat the enemy in his entrenchments, or that he will retire of his own accord from before Freiburg."[85] But Freiburg fell on 28 July; Enghien learned of the defeat on the 31st, while still across the Rhine at Benfeld.[86] Mazarin's gamble had failed.

Turenne, however, wrote anxiously to Enghien to press on and attack Mercy, whom he mistakenly believed not to know of Enghien's arrival in Alsace. In fact, Mercy was well aware of his situation; however, in a conference with his officers, it was decided that it would be better to stand and fight than to surrender Freiburg after the difficult siege. The worst problem was not so much the French army as the lack of supply the Bavarians faced, after having been confined to the same small area for such a long time.[87]

With Mercy strongly entrenched in the mountains, then, there was nothing for the French to do, if they were to do anything at all, but to make a frontal attack.[88] This they did, throwing their infantry against the Bavarian entrenchments first on 3 August, and again on 5 August. Although they appeared at times close to a breakthrough, decisive victory eluded them. Enghien pulled back, and the French and Bavarian armies camped next to each

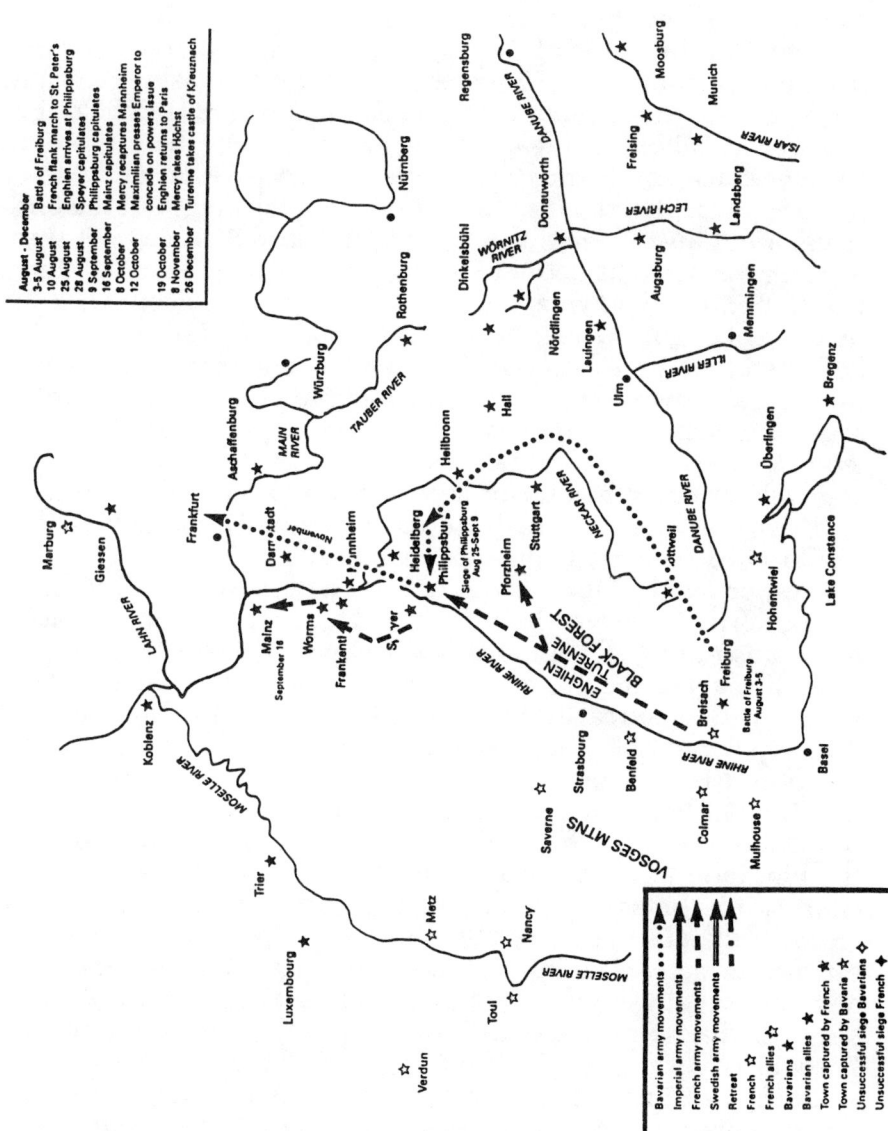

1644, August–December

other for three days without further combat. The bloody action had cost each army about half of its effectives, perhaps seventy-five hundred men per side.[89]

Victory at the Battle of Freiburg has been alternately bestowed on the French or on the Bavarians, according to taste. Tactically, it was a clear draw, since both armies remained on the field. Enghien had failed to break through, but Mercy had failed to counterattack the French and achieve a decisive victory. Mercy has been sharply criticized for not counterattacking, but the criticisms are unjust.[90] First, it is clear that Maximilian did not want to risk a battle; in his letter of 5 August (which, to be sure, Mercy would not have known about, but which was consistent with the duke's policy), he wrote, "you will not want to allow yourself to be forced to fight, but to remain defensive, and allow the enemy's fury to cool down." Moreover, even had Mercy wanted to counterattack, he lacked the means. As he pointed out in his 7 August letter to the Imperial general Piccolomini, "if the enemy were not so much stronger than us in cavalry, it would certainly have come to a decisive engagement [Hauptaction], and hopefully an end would have been made of such an enemy."[91]

In other words, Mercy could not win a decisive victory without a superiority in cavalry. Infantry could blunt the enemy's attacks, but it was not in itself an offensive weapon. Mercy's weakness in cavalry enabled the French, several days after the battle, to raid his army in its retreat and force him to abandon his baggage; and it was to this problem that Mercy returned again and again in his letters to Maximilian in subsequent weeks. On the 9th, he said that he had been forced to break off contact because of his lack of cavalry; on the 15th, he gave the same reason for abandoning the blockade of Hohentwiel, since "the enemy is master of the countryside [meister der campagna] and in particular is much stronger than us in cavalry." On the 23rd, Mercy made his strongest plea to date, claiming that the enemy cavalry, "although . . . also somewhat weakened by fatigue, all the same . . . is still much stronger than ours"; should Enghien again press the Bavarians, "he will drive us where he wants, indeed all the way Donauwörth . . . and I will not be able to resist him." These warnings were accompanied by repeated appeals to remount the Bavarian cavalry as quickly as possible.[92]

How did Maximilian view the Battle of Freiburg? In spite of his warning to Mercy not to allow himself to be forced to battle, Maximilian did not berate his general for actually having fought one. It seems clear that he intended his order to mean that Mercy should not fight an unnecessary battle that would lead to excessive casualties; Maximilian was far too intelligent to believe that a general could fight a campaign without ever allowing the enemy to attack him, even in favorable defensive terrain. It is true that Maximilian became less pleased once he learned of the extent of the Bavarian casualties, but he never condemned Mercy for having fought.[93]

However, Maximilian immediately recognized that the French were on the offensive, and reported to Mercy that the Bavarian army was now responsible for "the salvation of the Holy Roman Empire." He began rushing artillery and remounts to the army, and convinced the emperor to send four regiments, in addition to a reserve corps under the Count of Hatzfeld, as reinforcements. Maximilian's immediate concern was the defense of Swabia, without whose quarters Bavaria could not maintain its armies. He urged Mercy above all to prevent "the enemy, through the capture of one or another important place, to set a firm foot in Swabia," and in particular to strengthen the garrisons of Mannheim, Heidelberg, and Heilbronn.[94]

The two French commanders, on the other hand, saw Freiburg as a victory, and nearly a decisive one. Enghien wrote to Mazarin that "if the Bavarian army has not been absolutely defeated, at least it has been ruined to a point where it will have trouble recovering"; Turenne claimed that the French had been close to breaking through, but said that in any case the Bavarians had lost half of their effective strength. Perhaps most insightfully, one of the *maréchaux de camp*, d'Aumont, wrote that "the enemies have absolutely lost their infantry and are unable to oppose us during this campaign. It is true that our forces are a little diminished, but men are more rare in Bavaria."[95]

But how were the French to use their victory? We know that Mazarin had not intended the battle simply to wear down the Bavarians, and he reinforced this now in a letter to Turenne urging him "to use the victory well, and not to lose its fruit."[96] But what kind of "fruit" did he expect to gain? In a retrospective analysis from late August, Turenne wrote that there had been three possibilities for exploiting the battle: first, to recapture Freiburg; second, to pursue the Bavarians; and third, to move down the Rhine and besiege Philippsburg.[97]

At first, the court hoped to do all three. The first dispatches expressed the hope that Freiburg would surrender immediately, since there was no chance of its being relieved.[98] Later, when the commanders had made it clear that the area around Freiburg had been too depleted to be able to sustain a besieging army, Mazarin continued to cling to the hope of its recapture, urging it as a secondary option that could be undertaken by a small force while the rest of the army moved on.

The reason for this stubbornness was not Mazarin's lack of strategic insight, but rather public pressure to show some tangible gain after the great battle. One must remember that it was still only Mazarin's second full year as first minister, and the possibility that a new *Cabale des Importants* would arise to challenge his power was still alive. Mazarin insisted to Turenne that

> the people demand the recovery of Freiburg, and we something more solid—above all, the establishment of quarters for your army across the Rhine,[99]

while at the same time urging some action against the town. It is entirely credible that Mazarin meant what he said, because his policy toward the *Armée d'Allemagne,* from 1643 onward, aimed consistently at one thing: the establishment of winter quarters east of the Rhine. But his insistent statements from July that Enghien must either save or recapture Freiburg and not merely witness its fall indicate that Mazarin was sensitive to public opinion. It was not a matter of military strategy, but of political necessity, that led Mazarin to insist on some concrete gain from the battle. Ultimately, however, Mazarin conceded to his generals' logic that the recapture of Freiburg would be too difficult for the minimum strategic gain that it provided.[100]

The court also urged Enghien to push ahead with the pursuit of the Bavarian army. Mazarin felt that, while the infantry and a part of the cavalry was used in a siege, the bulk of the cavalry could be sent against the retreating Bavarians. This would deny the Bavarians their excellent quarters in Württemberg and force them back into Bavaria, where they would be forced to "consume their own country." But these optimistic plans fell apart, like the siege of Freiburg, for want of supplies: to pursue the Bavarians would have been to follow them along a path that had already been foraged, and the pursuing troops would have been ruined.[101] They also underestimated the strength remaining in the Bavarian army, which had not been so weakened by the battle that the French could pursue them through the mountains with only a part of their force and hope to inflict much damage.

The last option, and the one that was ultimately adopted, was to march down the Rhine and besiege Philippsburg. This important fortress on the right bank of the Rhine in the bishopric of Speyer would provide the French with a second secure point from which to invade the Empire, and one much better sited than Breisach. Though attacking Philippsburg was not the only option the court considered, neither was it a mere opportunistic reaction to the situation. Plans for capturing Philippsburg and towns in the Lower Palatinate went back at least to 1642, when Guébriant had commanded the *Armée d'Allemagne*. But that was not all. Turenne had proposed this plan anew on 29 February 1644, and had received approval just two days prior to the Battle of Freiburg. In fact, in the court's decision to send Enghien to join Turenne, one of Mazarin's major reasons for supporting it was his belief that, after the battle had been won, Enghien and Turenne could turn northward and conquer the Palatinate.[102]

Thus, the court knew and had well considered the advantages to be gained from this campaign; the battle of Freiburg merely provided an unlooked-for opportunity to execute it. It would not be easy, however, to take an army badly battered in battle and besiege a modern fortress like Philippsburg. Turenne complained on 12 August that "the fatigue here is without comparison greater than that of any of the other French armies" and that expenses were enormous. He argued that, if the French could pass over to the defensive in Picardy, it would be good to send a corps to Metz under Enghien's command to strengthen his depleted army.[103] Mazarin responded that

> although the progress being made in Flanders, where all appearances are that the people are about to revolt, make everyone here complain about the great prejudice the affairs of the King would receive if his army were diminished there . . . , His Majesty [has nevertheless determined] to send a corps of 2000 effectives and 12–1500 cavalry from [Flanders and] does not doubt that this will be done in three or four days at the latest.[104]

In addition, he recommended taking twelve to fifteen hundred men from Breisach and the Alsace fortresses, since they had no need to fear an attack from the Bavarians at the moment. The artillery and baggage from the army were shipped down the Rhine, while the men marched through Baden; the siege lines at Philippsburg were opened on 24 August.[105]

Mercy knew of the French threat to the Palatinate. In fact, as early as March Maximilian knew of, or at least suspected, French plans to attack it. At the meeting to decide whether to fight at Freiburg, several officers expected the French not to fight at all, but instead to march for the Palatinate. A letter of 18 August shows that Mercy knew the French were already near Philippsburg, and he ordered the commander of Heilbronn to give aid to the Palatinate towns if they needed it. On 21 August, Maximilian wrote to Mercy to reinforce the Philippsburg garrison with a dragoon regiment, or at least with a few companies. But the town's commander, Bamberg, ignored Mercy's timely warnings; by the time he requested an engineer and three hundred additional troops, the siege lines had been closed.[106]

Nor could Mercy himself intervene directly to disrupt the siege. Shortly after the battle of Freiburg he had written that

> the cavalry as well as the infantry is so fatigued because of the constant [stetigen] work and fighting that they are pitiable, which is why it would be nice if the enemy would leave us a little in peace.[107]

He seemed discouraged when he learned of the strong reinforcements going to the French army while he still awaited the slow-moving Imperial troops, and the interrogation of prisoners gave him vastly inflated figures of enemy strength. Even Maximilian, rather than urging Mercy to do everything possible to save Philippsburg, merely told him to notify the commander that reinforcements were coming, so as to encourage him to hold on longer.[108]

In fact, Maximilian seemed more concerned with Heilbronn than he did with Philippsburg. Mercy's report of 18 August, that the winter quarter situation was good because the enemy had not attacked any place in Württemberg, seems to have been in line with the thinking of his master. While Maximilian certainly would have preferred to save the Rhine crossing, it was essential that he not let the enemy occupy Bavarian quarters in Württemberg. In any event, he recognized that Mercy could do little without reinforcements, which were slow arriving; on 6 September, he approved Mercy's defensive stance, writing that "we find the decision that the Armada take up a post near Heilbronn until reinforcements arrive not unwise." On that same day, two regiments from Hatzfeld's reserve corps—which had sat idle during the crucial campaigning months of July and August—reached Mercy's camp.[109]

But it was too late, for Philippsburg fell on 9 September. The French had achieved a stunning coup, capturing a modern fortress more quickly than anyone had expected, in the face of an enemy army nearly as strong as their own. The reasons for this success fall into two categories: first, those that prevented Bavaria from interfering; and second, those that led the fortress to fall so quickly. In the first category lie Maximilian's emphasis on the defense of Württemberg, and especially Heilbronn, over that of Philippsburg. Mercy's cavalry inferiority, caused by the grave supply difficulties he experienced in conducting the month-long siege of Freiburg, also played a large role. In the second category, the incompetence of the Imperial commander stands out: his refusal of Mercy's offer of assistance until it was too late; his failure to garrison a small fortress that guarded the Rhine approach; and his inattention to the town's defenses, all played important roles in the speed of the siege of Philippsburg.[110]

But another consideration is the weakness of the Philippsburg defenses themselves. Though relatively modern (finished only in the 1620s) and considered strong, after-action improvements by the French make it clear that there was much to be desired in them. One French commander suggested some changes "to put this fort in the state of defense that it should be, in view of its advantageous position"; these changes included the creation of a counterscarp and demi-lunes. Turenne noted that it was essential to build an outlying fort near the Rhine, or else "the enemy, when he is stronger, will be able to establish himself between the Rhine and the fortress as we did." These specific changes were accompanied by repeated requests for money to strengthen Philippsburg; by October, it had been so improved that it was being called "the Casale of Germany," thus confirming the improvements made by the French.[111]

If Philippsburg was unable to resist the French for long, other towns were not even going to try. Speyer had already answered a French summons on 28 August.[112] Turenne then marched immediately after the fall of Philippsburg to Worms, which sent him the keys before he even arrived. Pressing on to Mainz, he began treating with the town when eight hundred Bavarian dragoons appeared on the other side of the Rhine, asking for boats to cross the river into the town and defend it. Like Ulysses Grant before Fort Donelson over two hundred years later, Turenne threatened an immediate attack, informing them

> if they did not order the Bavarian troops to retire immediately that he would no longer continue treating, and that if he saw the smallest boat cross the water . . . he would attack the place from all sides.[113]

Mainz refused the garrison and welcomed the French in, on the condition that Enghien come take possession of it in person.[114]

This campaign indicates an aspect of early modern warfare that is often overlooked. Sieges were difficult against a determined enemy, but the enemy was most determined when there was some hope of an army coming to relieve him. After Freiburg, there was little chance that Mercy was going to interfere with the French as long as they were operating in the area around the Lower Palatinate; and Philippsburg proved this. The other towns, which should have provided much stiffer resistance than they did, fell as a matter of course.[115] The battle of Freiburg thus helped the French not only materially, by weakening the Bavarian army, but also morally, by weakening the will of the then-isolated garrisons.

Another problem, however, was that the garrisons were considerably understrength: Worms held three hundred troops, Mainz and Philippsburg only six hundred though both were major fortresses.[116] This was in part attributable to the divided command of the enemy, and in part to the poor financial state to which he had been reduced. The Rhenish towns were mostly garrisoned by Imperial or Lorrainer troops, and neither gave adequate attention to this theater. Because of this, Maximilian had ordered the Bavarian *Statthalter* in the Lower Palatinate, Horst, to garrison Speyer in March. But when Charles IV promised sufficient garrisons for the towns, Maximilian withdrew his order, and the Bavarian troops returned east of the Rhine. Yet even had they wanted to, the Bavarians could probably not have garrisoned the towns adequately before the French attack, because their forces in the area had been reduced by two-thirds in the previous campaign in order to provide troops for Mercy. Mercy tried to garrison the towns himself, but his troops invariably arrived too late, as at Mainz.[117]

The effect of the campaign on Maximilian was profound. His offensive had not only failed; France had counterattacked and captured important towns. The French could now easily invade Germany, but the Imperial forces controlled no bridge over the Rhine by which to invade France. The war was henceforth going to be fought solely on German soil, so all the Imperials could hope for was a war of attrition. But this they could not hope to win; as Maximilian wrote in his instructions to a representative going to explain the situation to the emperor, France "can outlast us." Maximilian's response was to send his representatives, at last, to Münster, and to send an apologetic letter to Servien and d'Avaux explaining his long delay and asking for reconciliation. The French plenipotentiaries correctly surmised that this letter was a direct result of the war. Maximilian further urged the emperor, on 12 October and again on the 22nd, to give in on the question of the powers of the French plenipotentiaries to get the negotiations moving.[118]

Ironically, Mazarin ordered his plenipotentiaries to compromise on the powers issue at the same time. This concession may seem paradoxical, given France's military success, but in fact it was that very success that made such a move possible: now, it could not be perceived by the enemy as a sign of weakness, and it was worth conceding in order to advance the negotiations. As Mazarin wrote,

> in the flourishing state of the affairs of this kingdom, where nothing that the Queen does could ever be attributed to baseness but to a veritable desire for peace, she should not make difficulties about giving in on that which will not bring her any prejudice.[119]

While part of his reason for conceding this point was to throw the blame for the stalled negotiations on the Habsburgs, this statement clearly shows that Mazarin was not interested in impeding the negotiations at this point.

Mazarin's concession, however, now proved unnecessary: the emperor, impelled by Maximilian's urgings, had already agreed to a compromise solution that in fact conceded the key points to France. On 20 November, an agreement was arranged obligating France and the emperor to produce revised powers within two months, but allowing the negotiations to continue in the meantime. The related disputes with Spain were also solved. First, Spain refused to grant its plenipotentiaries the title of "ambassador," while a precedence issue of listing France and Spain together as "the two crowns" was resolved by a complicated compromise that involved creating several different versions of the same text.[120] The way was now clear for the next stage of the negotiations to begin: each side was to submit a proposal on the terms of the peace.

After the capture of so many enemy towns in the summer, the French military position in the Empire necessarily weakened. Not only had the sieges and small engagements caused a certain amount of attrition; more importantly, large numbers of infantry were siphoned off as garrisons for the newly conquered towns. Turenne wrote that "Your Eminence judges well that in putting the infantry necessary in the fortresses there will not remain any for the campaign." His army had been reduced to under three thousand effectives; when asked how to assure the Rhenish conquests, his response was to recruit more German infantry. On 4 October, moreover, Enghien—who had remained at Philippsburg to work on the fortifications and to distract the enemy—returned to Champagne with his army. He left a large garrison in Philippsburg (at least one thousand troops) and additional infantry for Turenne, but he took most of the cavalry with him. Turenne protested, but Mazarin said that the cavalry was needed more in Champagne than in Germany.[121] In essence, Mazarin had been concerned about the gap created in French lines ever since Enghien marched to Freiburg in late July. While the enemy had not been able to muster enough strength for a full-scale invasion, Enghien's absence had left Champagne to be ravaged by enemy cavalry forces. Now that the campaign had been a success, Enghien was to return to defend French territory, and for that, he needed the cavalry.[122] Turenne was to be compensated partially by new reinforcements brought by Magalotti from Lorraine, but these troops would not nearly equal the ones he was losing.

Mazarin kept his eyes fixed on the goal of establishing Turenne in quarters across the Rhine. On 16 September, Le Tellier wrote to Enghien of the campaign that "we are seeing [German affairs] lead to a solid establishment for the subsistence of our army, which is all that can be desired," and Mazarin continued to emphasize this point to Turenne right up until 3 November. Turenne's lieutenant, Tracy, told Mazarin that "my opinion . . . is that, Magalotti having come and the Hessians having joined the army, that we should go to Heilbronn and establish ourselves on the Neckar." He had heard that Turenne was planning to go into quarters west of the Rhine, but added that "I cannot believe it yet, unless Monsieur de Turenne is constrained to do so by reasons unknown to me . . . My opinion will always be to leave the conquests free and to go into the enemy's country if it is possible."[123]

The reasons constraining Turenne, however, were overwhelming. In the first place, Magalotti did not ultimately join him; he remained in place to join with Enghien. In the second place, the hoped-for link-up with the Hessians never took place. Tracy had been to Cassel in early September to sound out Hessian plans, and Turenne hoped that, if Enghien left him sufficient infantry and cavalry, he would be able to link up with the Hessians and capture some quarters in Württemberg. Mazarin was confident that the Hessians could join the *Armée d'Allemagne* with four thousand infantry and two thoudand cavalry soon. But when the Hessians appeared north of the Main with only fifteen hundred cavalry and one thousand infantry, Turenne had to order them to retreat to safety, for he had no bridge over the Main (though he had captured Mainz, it had no bridge) and was afraid that the enemy would fall on the Hessians and destroy them. Without the Hessians, Turenne's offensive at the end of September petered out after only a few days, and the French forces were sent reeling by a Bavarian counteroffensive. Mercy recaptured Pforzheim and Mannheim, thus clearing the right bank of the Rhine of French strongholds outside of Philippsburg, but the French army was able to escape across the Rhine before Mercy could attack their pontoon bridge.[124]

Mazarin did his best to send reinforcements to Turenne. Even considering each company's strength to have been much less than it was on paper, the reinforcement could have amounted to well over five thousand troops. Mazarin used the occasion of this substantial aid to reassure Turenne of the importance of the *Armée d'Allemagne*, arguing that "you will judge by the reinforcement that is being prepared for you . . . whether German affairs are dear to us."[125] But Germany did not get as high a priority as Mazarin made it seem; and, even with the reinforcements, Turenne still found himself weaker than his opponents. His German cavalry regiments contained fewer than one hundred horses each, and his French ones were entirely dismounted. An attempt to advance on Frankfurt collapsed due to lack of supply. Mazarin finally conceded in November that there was no way for Turenne to secure quarters in Württemberg, and gave him permission, once again, to quarter in Alsace and Lorraine.[126]

The Swedish army, however, had finally returned to the Empire (a truce having been concluded with Denmark in November), and Torstensson had a bold plan. Having defeated the Imperial general, Gallas, and ruined his army, Torstensson proposed to continue the campaign into the winter to press the Imperials while he had the advantage. In December, he requested from the French plenipotentiaries advance payment of the winter subsidy, the loan of Hessian troops, and the promise of a diversion from Turenne should the Bavarians move to aid the Imperial army. The plenipotentiaries approved this plan so fully that they not only wrote in strong terms to the court supporting it, they even borrowed one hundred thousand Reichstalers on their own credit to give to Torstensson right away.

Mazarin had already gotten word of the march of the Hessians, and admitted to Turenne that the fate of Gallas's army was the most important military consideration in Germany at the moment. He urged Turenne to make a diversion in favor of Torstensson if the Bavarians moved away, adding, however, that in this case it would be advantageous if Turenne could use the opportunity to gain quarters in Württemberg. Even before Turenne had received this notice, he launched a diversion. But the Bavarians had lain in ambush, and Turenne had been forced to retreat with the loss of some artillery.[127] For the moment, then, Mazarin was supporting the Swedish thrust. However, he was already planning for the upcoming campaign, and he was determined not to be deprived of Hessian support for a second year. He had thus secured a promise of two thousand infantry from Amalie-Elisabeth.

The front lines had shifted forward in the Empire, and with the new conquests, it was decided that Alsace was safer; the garrisons there were consequently reduced to provide troops for Turenne's army. But the enemy retained one important fortress west of the Rhine, Frankenthal, that made all of the other French conquests unsafe. Turenne put a high priority on capturing it, but he lacked the strength during the winter. He managed to win the castle of Kreuznach in December, but the main town was too much for him. In part because Frankenthal forced the French to maintain larger garrisons than they might otherwise have, and in part simply because it had been so ruined during the campaign, the Lower Palatinate could not even support its own garrisons; as Turenne complained to Mazarin, he had "a large territory to guard that cannot, until it has recovered, furnish one-fourth of the men necessary to defend it."[128]

Yet, in spite of the relative poverty and indefensibility of the Palatinate, it was a major gain for France. As Tracy noted, "the enemies will regret its loss in the future, because the way into their country is open." Breisach provided France a bridge, but it was too far to the south; few advances could be expected if they had to originate and draw their supplies from a point near the Black Forest. In the coming years, French offensives into the Empire generally originated from Philippsburg, and it was at Philippsburg that they returned back across the Rhine in case of trouble. Mainz, too, was an important gain. It was essential to have a secure crossing north of the Main so as to be able to link up with Hesse, and also to break communications between Charles IV's Lorrainer army and the Bavarians. That is why the French put so much effort into strengthening the fortifications of these cities, which Turenne described as "two posts of incredible importance."[129] Summing up Enghien's accomplishments during the year, the court wrote that "he took Philippsburg, Mainz, Speyer, Worms, Landau, and the other fortresses that assure us the Rhine and give our forces an entrance into the heart of Germany to gain new advantages there, and to support those of our allies."[130]

Mazarin had not planned to invade the Lower Palatinate at the start of the year. As late as mid-July, he was still thinking of an offensive toward Trier or Luxembourg.[131] Such an offensive would have helped to guard the French frontier from enemy raids, and would have supported the main French offensives in the Low Countries. But Mazarin did recognize the value of the Lower Palatinate. He had deliberately held Enghien's army in reserve until Gravelingen was captured, intending all along to have it operate in conjunction with the *Armée d'Allemagne*. By the time Gravelingen was captured, the situation at Freiburg had become clear, and Mazarin was flexible enough to change his plans.

It was one of the crucial decisions of the war. By blocking the Bavarian offensive, he had convinced Maximilian that the Imperials could not win the war, and thus set him down a path that would lead to cooperation with France at the negotiations. Mazarin further yielded to his commanders' decision that Freiburg was not worth recapturing, and instead allowed them to take Philippsburg and the towns of the Lower Palatinate. These were strategic fortresses, but they did not ease the burden on the French treasury, and in fact probably increased it. What Mazarin had failed to achieve by negotiations with Charles IV, he had obtained by military force.

If anything, Mazarin became even more flexible in the negotiations after the campaign. He further demonstrated his already strong desire to push ahead with the talks by instructing his plenipotentiaries to give in on the *"conjunctim cum confoederatis"* issue. The question of Spanish powers ended in a Spanish victory, though this point was raised and settled entirely in Münster, without orders from the French court. Otherwise, the French negotiating position hardly altered at all during the year, though admittedly there was little to alter. The admission of the German estates, which was the *sine qua non* of Swedish and French participation in the conference, remained unresolved at the end of the year. Mazarin was not going to concede, and he had no reason to do so given his military success. The first months of 1645 would demonstrate that his patience had born fruit.

7
1645: Mazarin Gains Confidence

By the winter of 1644, all plenipotentiaries except for the Spanish had adequate authority to negotiate, and there was pressure for France and Sweden to submit their propositions for peace. But the starting point for the discussion of French terms hardly seemed to accord with the military successes that France had gained in the previous campaign. Instead of making bold demands, Servien conceived the idea of beginning with a proposal to withdraw French arms from the Empire if Ferdinand would agree to restore the Empire to its 1618 state. This would be a propaganda coup for France: it would demonstrate that France really was fighting to restore German liberty, and there was no danger that the emperor would agree, since it would mean relinquishing the crown of Bohemia.[1]

The problem was that France was not fighting just to restore German liberty; it wanted material gain as well. Paris responded skeptically to Servien's first proposal, then, later, rejected it absolutely. Mazarin gave four reasons why the proposal was unacceptable. First, it would alienate Maximilian, who would never agree to turn over the Upper Palatinate and Electoral title, and who would not want to see this proposed by the French. Second, it would alienate the Swedes, who also wanted territorial gain. Third, if the emperor feigned to accept this proposal, it would leave the French in a very difficult situation. Fourth, and finally, such a proposal would leave the German estates feeling abandoned, since it would give France no point of entry into the Empire should the emperor revive his attempt to impose his authority over the whole Empire.[2] This letter should end doubt, if any still existed, that Mazarin was fighting this war for reasons other than those of power politics. He was interested in German liberties, but only insofar as they weakened Habsburg power; and he was not interested in fighting a war that did not include territorial gain for France.

The proposal that the French finally did give the mediators on 4 December included no substantial suggestions on how peace was to be made. Instead, it merely insisted on the presence of the German estates as an essential precondition for the negotiations to begin; as a corollary, the Archbishop of Trier, a French ally, had to be released from Imperial captivity.[3] The enemy immediately pounced on the proposal, claiming that the French were stalling. After all, they had issued several circular letters inviting the estates to the conference, yet very few had shown up; how much longer were they willing to wait? Even the mediators felt that time was being wasted, and proposed a deadline after which negotiations would automatically start, regardless of whether all the estates were present.[4]

Were the French trying to delay bringing up their demands as long as possible in order to avoid the unpleasant task of presenting them to the congress? This is the argument of Fritz Dickmann in his book, *Der Westfälische Frieden*.[5] It is true that Servien wrote that the Swedish plenipotentiary Johann Oxenstierna had agreed that the joint demands of France and Sweden might frighten off some of the estates from sending representatives;

> that is why they [the Swedes] judge, as we do, that we must not propose any substantial matter [*ne rien proposer d'essentiel*] before the arrival [of the estates], in order not to give them a reason not to come at all.[6]

But this agreement was not made until *after* the French proposition of 4 December had already been submitted. In the dispatch from 26 November, concerning the discussions the French had had with the Swedish plenipotentiary Salvius before the French proposition, it was phrased in quite different terms:

> Until the said Princes and Estates or their deputies have come, neither side will open up any matter, in order not to prejudice our demand [not to negotiate without the estates] and the right to make and conclude peace, for which we have such a great interest to associate them with the emperor.[7]

This letter also points out the need not to enter into any substantial matter before the arrival of the estates, so as to demonstrate the sincerity of the two crowns in including them. In other words, while the French and Swedes were clearly delaying the negotiations until the estates arrived, the reason had at least as much to do with the importance that the allies attached to the participation of the estates in the negotiations as it did with safeguarding French and Swedish satisfaction. The presence of the estates was not merely an aid in helping the French gain their territorial objectives, but was an end in itself. By assuring that the German estates had the *jus belli et pacis* (right of making war and peace), the French were hindering the emperor from seeking revenge on France at a later date.[8] This was a form of *assecuratio*, or security, for the peace. *Assecuratio* had always been the first French priority for peace: Richelieu had decided on this principle; it was in the French instructions; and Mazarin had reiterated it to the plenipotentiaries in his letters.[9] Since the idea of a league of German princes to secure the peace had foundered on Sweden's lack of support, the presence of the estates—and hence their gaining of the *jus belli et pacis*—was the best security France could manage.[10]

While on this issue the French remained firm about settling one point before moving on to another (because moving on to other points would have interfered materially with the first point), on other issues Mazarin was flexible and showed his anxiousness to see the talks progress. He continued to reject the idea of discussing Spanish issues first, but finally let himself be convinced that German affairs could be laid on the table at the same time as Italian ones, which he had previously insisted must come first.[11] He felt that French demands there were so moderate that the plenipotentiaries "need not fear not being well seconded"; "it is unquestionable that the enemies will not know how to avoid either giving in to our pretensions, or that the Princes who have the same interest do not gather on our side to force him to do so."[12]

Servien also raised the question of whether the assembly at Westphalia should be made into an Imperial Diet in order to make its decisions official. This, however, ran into serious difficulties.[13] In the end, the French court and the Swedish plenipotentiaries independently rejected the idea on the grounds that it would take too long, and they wanted to get on with the negotiations. If necessary, the decisions of the assembly could be approved by a Diet called later.[14] This suited the mediators, since they had themselves proposed the same thing.[15] Once again, Mazarin showed himself not to be interested in stalling, but rather in advancing the talks. Indeed, he strongly objected to the inclusion of a demand for the freedom of the Elector of Trier, Philip von Sötern, in the French proposal. He reasoned that the question of von Sötern's freedom was not a matter for preliminaries—which is how the French proposal of 4 December was viewed—but rather for the peace talks themselves; it was thus too harsh of the plenipotentiaries to say they would not negotiate until this condition had been fulfilled.[16]

Mazarin found two other aspects of the French proposition about which to be unhappy. First, he objected to their decision to submit the proposition in writing, "without even having notified him." Second, he complained that the plenipotentiaries should not have implied that the Congress would be invalid if not all the German princes and estates sent delegates. Mazarin wanted the estates to participate in principle, but he did not want to slow the negotiations for the sake of the stragglers. "After all," he wrote in a memo of 1 January 1645, "if other considerations retain them, is it necessary to wait with one's arms crossed because of their inconvenience or fear and to reject all negotiations?" He went one step further and said that the negotiations could be settled by the plenipotentiaries of the emperor, France, Spain, Sweden, and the Netherlands—that is, without the German estates—provided adequate security was obtained.[17]

Mazarin felt so strongly about what he saw as mistakes in the first French proposition that he prepared a second version for the plenipotentiaries to deliver to the mediators.[18] Servien and d'Avaux tried to defend themselves, but each was intent on justifying his own role in the proposition while attacking his colleague. Both, however, felt that their orders had been confusing, especially regarding von Sötern, and Servien specifically blamed the confusing and contradictory letters from Brienne.[19] In the end, Mazarin's upbraiding would have significant consequences on the plenipotentiaries as they began working on the second French proposition: the next time around, they would be much more careful about getting prior approval and negotiating the conflicts between the demands of court and allies.

Torstensson's winter campaign (see above, chapter 6) kept military considerations at the forefront during the first months of 1645, and especially the need to provide a diversion to assist the Swedish advance. Already on 6 January, Brienne wrote to the plenipotentiaries that the court was prepared to order Turenne to follow the Bavarian army "so closely that it dare not go to aid Gallas, for fear of leaving the Duchy of Bavaria prey to our forces." In any case, he added, "there is reason to promise to put the army in the field before the grass has grown, if Bavaria abandons the Rhine to approach the Danube, and if it passes the river to go to Bohemia to oppose Torstensson." The court rejected a proposal by Turenne that he attack Frankenthal, arguing that it would cost him most of his infantry "at the beginning of a campaign, which is the time when the weakness of the enemy seems to give occasion for considerable progress across the Rhine." Instead, they accepted Turenne's alternate proposal to cross the Rhine and relieve Alsace of the burden of supporting an army, a burden that much greater since France had signed a neutrality agreement with Franche-Comté, which denied Turenne some of the quarters that he had used the previous year.[20] Turenne received considerable reinforcements, especially cavalry, and a separate corps of thirty-five hundred troops was formed to cover the Rhine while the *Armée d'Allemagne* was away. Meanwhile, an alternate plan to attack Frankenthal with Enghien's army, supported by troops taken from nearby garrisons, was formulated. Mazarin wrote confidently to the plenipotentiaries on 7 April of the chances for military success in Germany during the coming campaign, citing the progress made in 1644; the end of the Danish war; Sweden's victory at Jankov; the participation of Transylvania, which had entered the war against the emperor; and the fact that Turenne had already crossed the Rhine.[21]

In the meantime, several important developments in the negotiations had sharpened the importance of the military campaigns. By agreement with the Swedes, the question of the presence of the estates had been pushed off at least until January; by that time, the newly agreed-upon powers of the plenipotentiaries would have arrived from their governments, and no substantive negotiations could take place until then anyway. But this only delayed the problems. On 7 January, the plenipotentiaries wrote to Brienne that they were caught among three forces: the German estates, who were slow to come to the conference; the mediators and the enemies, who wanted to advance the negotiations; and the Swedes, who absolutely refused to take another step until all the estates had arrived. Again on 31 January they noted that "we find ourselves, on one hand, prevented from satisfying the court's orders, and on the other from not contravening the precedents that oblige us to do nothing without Sweden."[22] On his trip to Osnabrück at the beginning of February, d'Avaux was unable to convince Sweden and Hesse that the French should be permitted to submit their revised proposition before the estates arrived, though he was able to get them to agree that the presence of Mainz, Brandenburg, and the Franconian Circle would be sufficient.[23] The French court, however, had already added its weight on the side of advancing the talks, stating flatly that "one does not consider here that it is necessary to wait longer for the deputies of the princes and estates of the Empire." The result was that, when the French submitted their revised proposition at the end of February, the Swedes were furious with d'Avaux for having misled them, since he had told them that France would wait for the arrival of the estates. Servien blamed d'Avaux for not having represented the French position more strongly in Osnabrück; for his part, d'Avaux was so shaken that he requested his recall.[24]

In spite of this development, it appeared for a while that it was Servien who would be disgraced. Not only had he had the greater role in the shaping of the French proposition denounced by Mazarin; he had compounded his problems by agreeing to send one of d'Avaux's *créatures* to court to defend the proposition, who naturally put the defense in a manner favorable to d'Avaux. Furthermore, Servien had written an acerbic letter to the *Deputationstag* at Frankfurt that did not help French popularity in the Empire. "Is it possible," Mazarin had asked his secretary, Lionne, regarding the letter, "that Servien has made such a great error?" The ambassador committed yet another error in judgement in the hard line he took on matters of protocol. First, there was the issue of the title of "Excellence," usually reserved for sovereign princes, that the Imperial Electors had demanded; Servien argued that France should not give the title to Saxony and Brandenburg unless they wrote to the king and requested it, as the other electors had done. Second, he complained about the behavior of the Hanse delegates. When they made their obligatory first visit to the French plenipotentiaries, Servien was not present. Rather than following up their visit to d'Avaux with a separate one to Servien, the delegates visited the Spanish next. This, said Servien, was detrimental to French dignity, and he requested orders on how to proceed.[25]

The court spurned both of Servien's arguments. For the Excellence title, Brienne noted that it would be advantageous for France to strengthen the independence of the Electors and thereby to weaken the emperor. Since the emperor had already conceded to the electors on this point, Brienne added that the plenipotentiaries should make it seem as though he had been forced to by French pressure, so it would not appear that the French were being compelled to follow his lead. As for the Hanse delegates, Lionne wrote to his uncle that Mazarin "does not want the king's affairs to be delayed for the sake of trifles." Brienne did issue a command that, in the future, all first visits were to be received by both plenipotentiaries together; but he also criticized Servien's pettiness.[26]

But Servien was fortunate to have an ally, his nephew Lionne, by Mazarin's side. At the end of one of his letters, Servien requested his recall; Lionne, however, struck out this line before giving the letter to Mazarin, arguing that it was unnecessary and could produce no benefit. Meanwhile, d'Avaux had stubbornly persisted in his recall request, which had been withheld for him by Brienne. It appears that d'Avaux was trying to force Mazarin to choose between him and Servien—an ill-advised move, since Servien was a protégé of Mazarin's. Although the cardinal softened the queen's anger against d'Avaux, he did not refuse d'Avaux's recall request, thus demonstrating that he did not feel d'Avaux's presence at the conference to be necessary; as he noted somewhat sarcastically to Longueville, "In the end, Monsieur, very few people are necessary."[27] At this precise moment, as the problems between Servien and d'Avaux had reached their worst point, Longueville was finally sent to Münster to lead the French delegation. His presence had been planned for some time, but it was judged more necessary than ever to heal the divisions between the other two plenipotentiaries. Upon seeing that his plan of forcing Servien's recall had faltered, d'Avaux hesitated, then wrote that he had decided to stay in Münster because of Mazarin's pleading. This was clearly an exaggertion and d'Avaux lost much of his credit by his failed brinksmanship and his irresolution. Though he and Servien had both been strongly chastened in the first part of 1645, Servien emerged by far the better off of the two.[28]

In spite of their differences, the plenipotentiaries did manage to agree on one point: their opposition to Mazarin's new Spanish policy. At the beginning of 1645, Mazarin stepped up his efforts to frighten Spain about the possibility of concluding peace without her. "It will seem to many, perhaps," he wrote in a royal memorandum,

> a paradox to believe that the emperor will ever take the resolution to reach an agreement with France and her allies without the king of Spain. But besides the many notices we have to the contrary, there is reason to believe that the Germans, seeing their affairs deteriorate more every day without hope of improving their condition by arms, will not want to permit themselves to be sacrificed any longer to the passions of the king of Spain.

Spain, he noted, would like to negotiate several different points at once, to insure that they are not left out once German affairs are resolved. But even if France were to agree, Mazarin noted,

Spain could not prevent "us from proposing easier expedients for the accommodation [with the Empire], and that we persist in wanting to retain everything that we have acquired [from them] during this war"; in that case, the German estates would surely insist on concluding the peace with France first if that with Spain seemed a long way off.[29]

The plenipotentiaries, however, were of a different opinion. They noted that

> we see that the court is inclined to separate the interests of the emperor from those of Spain, which we do not consider very good if it is with the intention of making a treaty with the emperor without including the king of Spain, or if it is simply to make a demonstration in order to light a fire under the Spanish feet and make them more pliant.[30]

Despite their disagreement, the plenipotentiaries followed orders, finding some small matters in the Spanish powers that they demanded be fixed. At the same time, they assured the mediators that this would not delay negotiations with the emperor. Although they hoped that this would encourage the Spanish to adjust their powers sooner, they added in their report to Paris that the "principal motive of our resolution comes from the orders that were sent to us to do something with the Imperials in order to offend the [Spanish]."[31]

Ironically, the mediators approached Servien in February with proposals that seemed to further Mazarin's goal of frightening the Spanish. First, the papal mediator Chigi asked Servien whether it would not be easier to make peace just with the emperor; then, in a separate meeting, the Venetian Contarini suggested to Servien that France make a peace with the emperor but only a truce with Spain. This, he pointed out, would make an early accommodation easier, since France had more problems to resolve with Spain. But Servien felt that he had to reject both advances. The problem was that Mazarin's policy of delaying the negotiations with Spain without really intending to make a separate peace with the emperor seemed to confuse his plenipotentiaries throughout the year. At the same time that he was delaying the talks with Spain through the actions of Servien and d'Avaux, Mazarin was complaining to the nuncio in Paris that Spain seemed not to want peace, noting that, though Philip IV had designated important men as representatives, none of them had gone to Münster yet. This accusation produced the response that Mazarin had hoped for: the Spanish dispatched their main negotiator, Peñaranda, shortly thereafter. Servien felt unsure of the exact stance that he should adopt in his meetings with the mediators, and wrote to Lionne, "I pray you to tell this to His Eminence to know his intentions, because if we always reject these propositions when they are made to us by people either knowledgeable or disinterested, it will be difficult ever to get affairs going in that direction."[32]

Nevertheless, the idea of excluding Spain soon received further impetus from another source: Bavaria. At the start of the year, French relations with Bavaria seemed to have stalled right as they had been showing signs of promise. While Mazarin had long argued that Bavaria was the best means for France to obtain satisfaction in the Empire, it was not until 14 December 1644 that Brienne first mentioned the advantages of separating Bavaria from the emperor. And, with the Bavarian representatives on their way to Münster, the time seemed propitious for talks on this subject to begin.[33]

But it was to be over a month before Georg Haslang and Dr. Johann Krebs, the Bavarian representatives, actually entered Münster. The problem was one of protocol: the French plenipotentiaries had not decided on the form by which they were to address the Bavarians, so the latter remained outside of town until it was settled. In the first talks between the French and Bavarian representatives, both sides engaged in compliments without saying anything substantial. Each was deliberately trying to sound out the other; the result was a total lack of communication.[34]

Maximilian, however, already had other plans for opening talks with France: since 1643 he had been contemplating sending his confessor, the Frenchman Vervaux, on a secret mission to Paris. Mazarin issued an invitation at the beginning of 1644 through the mediation of the papal nuncio in Paris, but he hesitated for a long time to send the necessary passport. Only after the Bavarian legation reached Münster did he finally issue the requisite papers, in February 1645; and Vervaux set out, in disguise, in March.[35]

Maximilian and Mazarin had very different plans for the meeting. Maximilian had been trying for some time to form a bloc of Imperial Electors who could set themselves up as mediators between France and Sweden on one side, and the Empire on the other. When this plan failed, he instead tried to make Bavaria into a "neutral" mediator. The Vervaux mission was designed to further this new plan. Maximilian hoped to convince Mazarin to make a short-term truce, during which time the peace could be negotiated without the ambassadors constantly having to keep one eye on the military campaigns. Then, he hoped that Mazarin would put forth France's territorial demands, so that Maximilian could take them to the emperor and convince him to accept them. Maximilian felt that peace could be obtained much sooner by this method than by the cautious public negotiations in Münster.[36]

It is not clear specifically what Mazarin hoped to gain from the conference, but it is clear that his general goals were diametrically opposed to those of Maximilian. First, Mazarin was against any short-term truce, which he felt would only delay peace because it would remove pressure from the emperor and Spain. Instead, Mazarin was thinking of a long-term truce, which Maximilian opposed because he wanted the war settled once and for all. Second, there was no chance that Mazarin would agree to settle French demands by secret Bavarian mediation with the emperor. France's position in the Empire was heavily dependent on Sweden, and Mazarin would do nothing that would seriously risk their alliance.

In fact, Mazarin was so concerned about the effect that secret talks with Bavaria would have on Sweden should they become known that he almost backed out at the last moment. Already in November 1644, his plenipotentiaries had warned him that many delegates thought that France and Bavaria were engaged in secret talks, and that it would be better to limit all negotiations to Münster. Indeed, the Swedish plenipotentiary Salvius approached Servien and d'Avaux complaining about a supposed Bavarian representative in Paris, but the French denied any such thing. The French plenipotentiaries again warned Mazarin that rumors of Franco-Bavarian negotiations via the papal nuncio were current in Münster and had prompted comments from the mediators. They went on to argue that

> certainly, Monseigneur, France's situation seems to be so good in this war that we need only continue as we have while it lasts, and to keep all things in the state where they have been up until now. It could be dangerous to admit the slightest change.

The plenipotentiaries maintained that it would be good to woo Bavaria, but only if they could get Swedish support. It was probably because of these warnings that, in February, Mazarin sent a note to Maximilian that he had changed his mind and decided not to go through with the talks. In the end, he yielded to Maximilian's pleas and agreed to receive Vervaux, but his hesitation was not a propitious sign for the Bavarians.[37]

Vervaux's first meeting with Mazarin, on 3 April, got off to a bad start when Mazarin presented him a letter from Frankfurt saying that Maximilian had sent a representative to Paris for secret talks. Since the talks were no longer secret, Mazarin said, Vervaux would not be able to stay long. Vervaux tried to draw out French demands from Mazarin, without success. He also suggested that the emperor would be willing to make peace without Spain, and Maximilian was even willing to guarantee that the emperor would not be able to give aid to Spain in such a case, not only in his quality as emperor, but even in his quality as king of Hungary (a key point, since the emperor's advisors argued that he could only be restricted *qua* emperor, leaving him free to support Spain in his capacity as ruler of Hungary). The first meeting ended without any agreement.[38]

Vervaux was not able to meet with Mazarin again for over a week. In the meantime, he received new orders from Maximilian that changed the character of his mission dramatically: for on 5 March, the Imperial army, including a large Bavarian contingent, had been destroyed at the battle of Jankov by Swedish forces under Torstensson. Reacting to the news, Maximilian hastily sent Vervaux additional instructions. He hoped to use this defeat to his advantage by convincing Mazarin that Swedish power was growing too strong in the Empire. Vervaux was still to propose a short-term, general truce as a starting point; however, if this did not succeed, he was to go on to suggest a separate truce between Bavaria and France only. As a last resort, he was to request that France take Bavaria, together with the Swabian and Franconian Circles, into its protection. It was a striking demonstration of Maximilian's fear of his worsening military situation, since at the same time that the Swedes were advancing rapidly toward Vienna, Turenne was pressing Mercy back toward the Danube from the west.[39]

At the next meeting, on 8 April, Vervaux introduced Maximilian's proposals one at a time; Mazarin, however, received them all coldly. Though inwardly ecstatic at the Bavarian offers, he was too concerned about Swedish opinion to allow the talks to go further, at least in Paris. Instead, he told Vervaux that France would be happy to discuss the matter further in Münster, after proper consultation with her allies. When Vervaux finally brought up the possibility of France's taking Bavaria under her protection, Mazarin asked under what conditions this was to take place. Vervaux responded that he did not know the conditions; and that was the end of the talks. Mazarin rejected one last request by Vervaux at least to order Turenne not to attack, replying that Turenne was only across the Rhine to get quarters, and had nowhere else to go. Vervaux's repeated requests to be allowed to stay longer were coolly rebuffed; he returned to Munich empty-handed.[40] Mazarin then carefully leaked a report of the talks to Cérisantes, the Swedish resident, to avoid all possibility of scandal should the Swedes find out on their own.[41]

The meaning of the Vervaux mission has received intense scrutiny in the last thirty years. The exponent of the most extreme view, Andreas Kraus, has argued that Maximilian was not sincere in his request for French protection, but instead hoped to reveal the secret talks to drive a wedge between France and Sweden. Gerhard Immler, while cautiously opposed to this view, suggests that it cannot be known with final certainty. That may be, but the evidence suggests strongly that Maximilian was quite sincere in his request. First, had he been more interested in deceiving the French than in getting French protection, it seems unlikely that he would have made the request for French protection the last of three proposals, to be brought up only if the first two were rejected. Second, there is evidence from the Bavarian council's subsequent vote for an attack on Turenne's advancing army. One council member was concerned that an attack so shortly after the talks might be seen as duplicitous. However, another councillor argued that France did not want a truce, but sought only to separate Bavaria from the emperor. Still another councillor stated forcefully that Bavarian offers had gone too far, and said that they would have to fight a battle in order to regain French respect. If Bavaria did not mean the offers sincerely, however, why the concern about their having gone too far? There is no reason to posit duplicity, moreover, since a simpler reason is near at hand: the battle of Jankov, to which the protection request was a direct response. News of the battle sent the Bavarian council, and Maximilian in particular, into deep consternation. The updated orders to Vervaux reflected their real concern about the state of the duchy; once the talks had clearly failed, however, they returned to arms as the only means possible to save them from invasion.[42]

Kraus has also argued that Mazarin only agreed to receive Vervaux in order to put pressure on the emperor and Spain through the appearance of separate talks with Bavaria, while at the same time to isolate Bavaria from the emperor. We are less well informed of Mazarin's intentions than of Maximilian's, but it seems certain, for two reasons, that he was not using the talks as a means of isolating Bavaria. First, the court assumed that Maximilian had already informed the emperor of Vervaux's mission in advance (as in fact he had), so there could be little to be gained from that angle.[43] Second, and more important, France simply had more to lose than did Bavaria: Bavaria was in the advantageous position of being indispensable to the emperor, but France herself needed Swedish military support and felt herself in constant danger of Swedish defection. Mazarin's hesitant acceptance of the talks demonstrates that he was aware of these facts, and it seems most unlikely that he would have willingly agreed to receive Vervaux only as a means of isolating his enemy when he realized that he himself was the more vulnerable party.

A more serious question is what effect the talks with Vervaux had on the diplomatic situation. For Maximilian, it seems clear that they had been a total failure. He had gotten neither French protection, nor a truce, nor even knowledge of French demands; everything had simply been referred to Münster. The Bavarians' disappointment can be measured by their military response upon hearing of the result of Vervaux's second audience (see below). Both Kraus and Immler, by contrast, point to the Vervaux mission as a turning point in French policy toward Bavaria. They argue that, after Vervaux, Mazarin felt he could demand more from Bavaria, and claim that he both adopted a tougher negotiating stance (in particular, in that he was no longer willing to grant Bavaria the Electorate for nothing) and applied increased military pressure to get what he wanted.[44]

Of increased military pressure there can be little question. Mazarin had been urging Turenne to cross the Rhine in order to prevent Bavaria from aiding the emperor since the end of 1644; these orders had been reiterated at the beginning of 1645; and Turenne's plan to attack Frankenthal had been specifically rejected in February in order to speed his invasion of the Empire. It is true that the plenipotentiaries adopted a stronger line in favor of military force than did the court. They wrote in January that "the most certain means to bring this prince [viz. Maximilian] to reason is to press him strongly by arms and in the negotiation." He was so tied to the emperor, they continued, that he could not voluntarily change his alliance; however, "he should not think it wrong that we furnish him an honest pretext [to change alliances], and that we give him the means to demonstrate how, in order to avoid perishing, he will have been forced by necessity to make that choice." When they finally began having discussions with the Bavarian plenipotentiaries, and as it became clear at the beginning of April that these were going nowhere, Servien and d'Avaux again recommended military force as the solution. Since the Bavarians seemed to respond to military pressure, they wrote, "perhaps they will hasten to speak more clearly if monsieur le maréchal de Turenne is in a position to second Swedish arms in a timely manner."[45]

Servien was particularly critical of Turenne's inaction. At the end of March, the plenipotentiaries noted in their common dispatch that Maximilian was hastening to send troops to aid the emperor after his defeat at Jankov, and urged that Turenne be sent to the Danube to distract the Bavarians. Servien added in his own letter that "intelligent people believe that Turenne should cross the Rhine if he wants to remount his cavalry and remake his army, after the retreat of the Bavarians has left him the way open"; this should be done soon, however, before the situation changes. Toward the end of April, he complained further that "it is necessary that we appear a little stronger across the Rhine than Turenne's army is . . . it will be a sort of embarrassment for us if, at the point of a peace treaty, we have so little part in the fruits of this victory."[46]

But if Servien took a hard line on the use of military force, it would be wrong to conclude that Mazarin took a soft one. On 7 April, he wrote to the plenipotentiaries of the advances that France promised to make in the coming campaign, adding that "all this makes me conclude, it seems to me, that we and our allies will be masters of the negotiation, and that the others will be happy at any price to find in us some disposition for an accommodation." This letter demonstrates not only Mazarin's seriousness about the use of military force, but also that he tied the military advance directly to diplomatic success. Moreover, it was written after his first meeting with Vervaux, but before the second; hence, Vervaux's unusually extravagant offers of the second meeting cannot be held to have induced Mazarin to adopt a hard line, as Kraus and Immler have claimed.

Mazarin's outright rejection of a truce in either meeting with Vervaux, but especially in the second, is indicative of his bargaining principles, according to which a truce could only delay an agreement and not accelerate it. The policy of applying military pressure, expressed clearly in the royal memo of 13 May, thus in no way originated with Servien. The continuity in Mazarin's policy is further evident from the memo itself, which noted that the emperor's affairs were in a terrible state, and that his only hope of salvation was for the Bavarians to send him significant aid. This gave Sweden even more reason to agree to separating Bavaria from the emperor, since if France and Sweden "continue to act with the same vigor from their side and from ours, the complete decay of their affairs seems inevitable." The same general tenor had been expressed over a month earlier in a letter to d'Avaugour, the French attaché with the Swedish army. The one major difference is that, in the d'Avaugour letter, Mazarin indicated that Turenne's army would not be at full strength until the beginning of summer; otherwise, the plan of crossing the Rhine and seconding Sweden remained the same. The pivotal aspect of the campaign to Mazarin, then, was the emperor's poor military situation after the battle of Jankov. It was thus Jankov, and not Vervaux, that exercised the crucial influence on French strategy, as is evident in the statements that France and Sweden are to *continue* their military pressure, and that Sweden should be *even more* willing to detach Bavaria from the emperor.[47]

With Mazarin's continued urging, Turenne began pressing the Bavarian army hard toward the Danube. Mercy reported to Maximilian on 17 April that Turenne was taking one town after another, as they all refused to defend themselves, instead opening their doors upon Turenne's approach. Drawing food and horses from the towns, Turenne was getting stronger all the time; soon he would be able to throw Mercy back across the Danube. Once again, it was cavalry that proved the decisive factor; as Turenne was gaining remounts for his cavalry, the Bavarians were only getting weaker. Mercy argued that the only solution was to attack Turenne now, before he got too powerful.[48]

The changing balance of forces puzzled and disturbed Maximilian, who wrote repeatedly to Mercy that he could not understand how the Bavarians could be getting weaker relative to the French even as he sent the army fresh horses for remounts and Turenne weakened himself by leaving garrisons in the conquered towns. Already on 21 April, Maximilian told Mercy to keep his eyes open for a good opportunity to attack the enemy, but wanted him to wait for further remounts so that the balance would be more in Bavaria's favor; and on 28 April, he told Mercy to take a vote in a council of war (comprising the leading officers in the army) on the best way to stop Turenne. But on 30 April, Maximilian finally accepted Mercy's logic. "We remember, it is true," he wrote, "that we gave you orders on 23 April that you were not to engage in any battle. However," he continued, he had changed his mind; now he ordered that Mercy "should defeat Turenne by any possi-

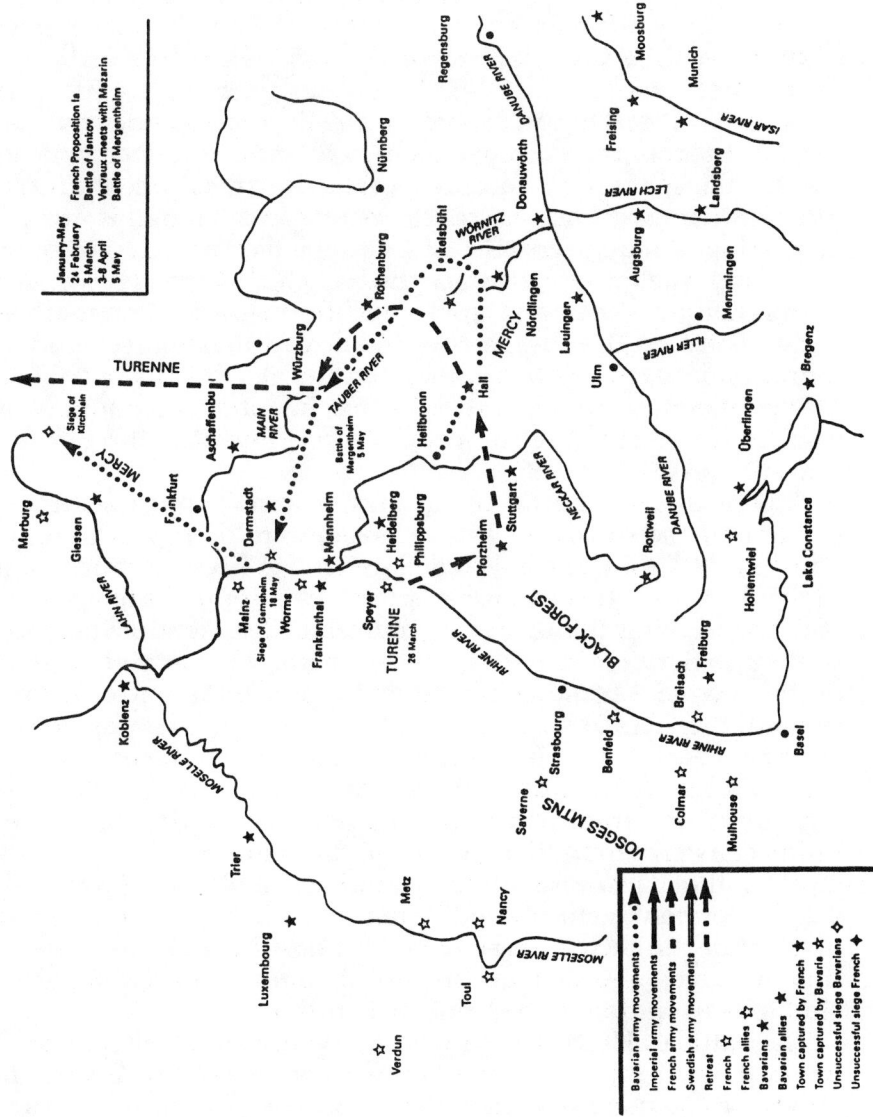

1645, January–May

ble and workable way and means that is available by the nature and reason of war."[49]

Mercy took advantage of the opportunity. The French, too, were having supply difficulties because of the season. Tracy, writing to Mazarin on 29 April, claimed in glowing terms that affairs "are in the best possible state," and spoke of pushing the Bavarians back across the Danube; however, he also noted somewhat ominously that the troops were all fatigued, and requested reinforcements. Thus, even as Turenne was occupying Rothenburg and Mergentheim without resistance, he was weakening his army by dispersing it in quarters. On 30 April, the Bavarian council of war voted overwhelmingly to attack the French.[50] Mercy received final permission on 4 May, and infiltrated Turenne's position that very night. The next day, he decisively defeated those forces that Turenne had been able to gather hastily at Herbsthausen, near Mergentheim. Turenne lost all of his infantry and most of his cavalry; the remnant of his army fled northward to the safe confines of Hesse.[51]

This result seemed to justify Servien's more pessimistic view of the military situation, which caused him to appear more of a hard-liner than Mazarin. While Servien had been writing toward the end of April that France was too weak in the Empire, Lionne had been giving the different, more positive view of the court, writing to Servien that Turenne had made considerable progress on his own and could expect to make even more once he linked up with the Hessians. However, Bavarian council records indicate that the view from Paris was more in line with the actual situation than was Servien's: Turenne's rapid advance across Württemberg and approach toward the Danube had caused Maximilian even more consternation than Mazarin thought. But when, in response, the Bavarians attacked and defeated the *Armée d'Allemagne,* Servien again blasted Turenne for letting German affairs deteriorate to such a terrible state. Mazarin, however, rejected this negative view sharply, instead planning for a renewed invasion that would be even stronger than the first.[52]

The battle of Herbsthausen (or Mergentheim) came at a crucial juncture not only in regard to the secret talks with Bavaria, but also in the general negotiations at Münster. To understand how it affected the French position, it is necessary to step back and consider it within the context of France's relations with her allies, Sweden and the Netherlands, in the first part of the year.

France's frustration with the slow progress of the talks—and also her dependence on allies—is evident in the plenipotentiaries' dispatch of 31 January, in which they note with chagrin that "of the two principal allies of France, we lack the presence of the one and the consent of the other" to advance the negotiation. The Dutch, still debating over which representatives to send and their mode of negotiating, had not yet even appeared at the conference. Servien and d'Avaux judged that it would be unwise to advance the talks too far without the Dutch present, for fear of giving them cause to feel abandoned. While not agreeing that the talks should be slowed because of the Dutch, the court did believe that it was essential to treat them well, for three reasons: first, they needed the Dutch to provide a strong military diversion during the campaign; second, they needed Dutch aid to resolve the East Frisian affair (involving Hessian quarters; see chapter 6); and third, they were concerned lest Spain lure the Dutch into a separate treaty.[53]

The military commitment of the Dutch had become questionable because Sweden tried to convince them to send a naval force against the Danes. This idea was especially popular in Holland, where the merchants resented the tolls charged by the Danes on ships passing into the Baltic, but was opposed by the Stadholder Frederik Hendrik. The plenipotentiaries were concerned that such a diversion would prevent the Dutch from upholding their end of the war in the Low Countries, in which case France would be pressed on that front and "it will be difficult for us to act in Germany with the vigor that we have used up till now, and for which we had prepared for this campaign." The Dutch did ultimately enter the war against Denmark, but placated the French by promising not to diminish their military strength on land.[54]

French and Dutch interests also ran foul of one another in the East Frisian affair, which continued to drag out in spite of the optimistic letters sent out from Paris. Servien warned that Amalie Elisabeth might not send the promised two brigades to France if she did not get her way in this matter. The problem was papered over yet again when the temporary agreement between the Netherlands, Hesse, and East Frisia was extended on 24 April for another ten months; but the tensions remained.[55]

The most serious threat to Franco-Dutch relations, however, was the possibility of a separate peace between Spain and the Dutch Republic. Mazarin had already been aware of this possibility in 1644, but his concerns deepened at the beginning of 1645. He wrote to Servien and d'Avaux in January that Josèphe Bergaine, one of the Spanish plenipotentiaries, had always been used for negotiations with the Dutch, and he feared that Bergaine's appointment was part of an attempt by the Spanish to separate the Dutch from their French alliance. Yet the Netherlands's representatives continued to remain away from the conference, confirming French suspicions that they were not interested in making peace at all. By July, Brienne wrote in a frustrated tone that Spain had a right to complain about the absence of the Dutch negotiators; it was absurd that they had not yet appeared.[56]

It was to placate the Dutch, and to alleviate their own fears of being abandoned, that the French court ordered the plenipotentiaries on 21 January to give in to the Dutch in all matters of precedence, and particularly to give them the title of "Excellence" that had been conceded to the Imperial Electors; the order was repeated on 18 February. Though the aforementioned problems continued to vex relations between France and the Netherlands, at least the Dutch did participate in the upcoming military campaign.[57]

Sweden's activity at the start of 1645, too, caused concern for the French court. Rumors in Münster during January indicated that Sweden had signed a treaty with the English Parliament, or at least that they were carrying on negotiations. This shocked Mazarin, who not only felt French interests threatened, but who was concerned that Sweden had no right to make such alliances without notifying France first.[58] He was finally moved to respond to Servien's repeated requests of the previous year and to appoint an ambassador to Sweden, in order to be better informed about Sweden's future moves, and to have a means of countering them, if necessary, in a timely fashion. The Swedish embassy to England also awakened him to the different interests that France and Sweden had in Germany, especially in religious matters. "There is nothing," he wrote in the royal memo of 21 January, "that Her Majesty would not do to conserve a perfect and indissoluble union with the Swedish crown . . . , but it is necessary to be aware that we might have a particular interest in Germany different from theirs which it will be necessary to manage in all cases with great care." Not only was he speaking of the English embassy here, but also of Sweden's jealousy over French relations with Bavaria. He rejected their concerns that France was trying to form a new alliance and separate from Sweden, instead affirming that Catholics as well as Protestants were needed to limit the emperor's authority.[59]

But it was in the actual negotiations that the problems in Franco-Swedish relations became most evident. At first, Sweden sought to delay the negotiations until all the German estates had arrived at the conference, which caused considerable tension when the French presented their modified proposition at the end of February (see above). But at the end of March, a deputation of representatives of German estates visited the Swedish plenipotentiaries to request that the negotiations be begun in earnest. Under this pressure, the Swedes concluded that they had fulfilled their responsibility to wait for the German estates to assemble. They reversed their position from one of waiting to one of pressing ahead, and began urging the French to come to a rapid agreement on a second peace proposition.[60] Servien and d'Avaux were caught completely off guard; they pleaded for more time because they needed further orders, at the same time urging the court to respond as quickly as possible for fear of alienating Sweden.[61]

The broad outlines of the second proposition had already been agreed to in a December meeting with Oxenstierna. Most of the points were obvious and uncontentious: cessation of hostilities, reestablishment of trade, and the return of prisoners, for example. Several issues would require further elaboration in the coming negotiations; these included the restoration of the Empire to its 1618 state, the promulgation of a general amnesty, provisions for the security of the peace, and satisfaction for the two crowns. These controversial points formed what Servien and d'Avaux later referred to as the "four-sided stone" that served as the foundation of the negotiations.[62]

The main point of contention between France and Sweden was the proposal to return the Empire to its 1618 state.[63] Although Servien's 1644 proposal to offer to withdraw French arms from the Empire if the emperor acceded to this demand had been decisively rejected both by Sweden and by the French court, he and d'Avaux were united in feeling that France had to leave in the demand to return to the 1618 situation, since they had repeatedly stated it as the goal of French arms and had led Germans to believe that they were fighting for it. The court was concerned, however, that Sweden was using this demand to further the religious interests of the Lutherans. Mazarin particularly worried about the effect such a demand might have on Maximilian, since a return to the 1618 situation meant that he would not only lose the Palatinate, but the Electorate as well. Yet the court nevertheless gave tacit approval to the plenipotentiaries' position, saying that, if necessary, they could let Maximilian know secretly that it would not prevent France from supporting Bavarian interests regarding the Electorate. In an 15 April memo, Servien argued in favor of 1618 as the "normative" year for Imperial affairs on the grounds that France was obligated to it by its treaty with Sweden. True, it might offend Maximilian, but he "is our declared enemy, and, whatever appearance he makes to the contrary, he has little good will for us." He concluded by supporting the court's expedient of letting Maximilian know secretly that the clause was not aimed at him.[64]

The other issue on which France and Sweden differed was the question of how the peace was to be secured. While Mazarin wanted to create a league of signatories who would guarantee the treaty against all transgressors, Sweden argued that the true security of the peace lay in the continuing Franco-Swedish alliance, friendship with the German estates, and the territory that the two crowns would annex in Pomerania and along the Rhine. Servien and d'Avaux did get the Swedes to agree to a league in principle, but only with the addition of the phrase "if it is possible"—a substantial modifier that would allow Sweden, if it desired, to point to any difficulties in its negotiation as a sign that it was not possible. But while Brienne complained, correctly, that Sweden really wanted to establish security through a balance between Protestants and Catholics in the Empire, he concurred that the best security would indeed be the conquered territory.[65]

In an 7 April meeting with Oxenstierna, the French plenipotentiaries agreed to present a new peace proposition, on the condition that they be allowed to send it back to court for approval. They also agreed, upon Swedish insistence, to a new departure in the style of the proposition: instead of introducing one item at a time, the proposition would include all aspects of the treaty. It would also "be conceived in the most general terms possible"; this would permit them to insert other things later without appearing to stall the treaty by introducing new demands, and would also save them from the insistent demands of the other deputies at the congress, each of whom wanted his own demands included the proposition. Furthermore, by not specifying their territorial claims, the French would have the freedom to increase or decrease them as necessary, and to trade them off for other items. This was a major change in the method of negotiating, as Servien recognized, that went explicitly contrary to Mazarin's insistence that they negotiate only one item at a time. Yet, surprisingly, the change went unremarked in the royal response. Evidently Mazarin must have been persuaded by the compelling reasons presented by Servien in favor of it.[66]

Servien and d'Avaux met with the Swedish plenipotentiaries in Osnabrück at the beginning of May to straighten out further details of the proposition. The French negotiators raised the possibility of signing a truce rather than a peace, to which the Swedes objected, arguing that they would work for a peace and consider a truce later if a peace proved unobtainable. The French also met with a rebuff when they tried to get the Swedes to promise to remain in the war in case peace were made with the emperor but not with Spain. The Swedes did, however, assure the French that they would never make peace unless there were a clause in the treaty guaranteeing that the emperor could not assist Spain—an assurance that later proved very valuable to France.

What effect did the defeat at Herbsthausen have on the French proposition? Interestingly, though the French plenipotentiaries remarked on the inconvenient timing of the defeat, they were not particularly concerned about its effect on French demands; indeed, these were formulated so vaguely that there is little they could have done to trim them, and the plenipotentiaries certainly did not shrink from demanding satisfaction and the other points that had been agreed upon in January. Instead, the battle had the effect of weakening France's position in its negotiations with Sweden, especially on the sensitive question of the role of religion. The French court was principally concerned to prevent Sweden from unduly strengthening the Protestant party in the Empire, and forbad the plenipotentiaries to mention religion in the proposition. Servien, however, was concerned that not referring to Protestant interests at all might cause them all to abandon France and throw their support behind Sweden. He carefully constructed the phrasing of the clause demanding the restoration of the 1618 situation so that it referred only to temporal matters (or at least so that it could be interpreted that way), but could not avoid a separate clause supporting the Protestants in their religious rights, and could not keep Sweden from including more references to religion in their proposition than the French would have liked. As he wrote to Brienne on 20 May,

> the accident that occurred recently [i.e., Herbsthausen] . . . forcing us to reunite ourselves more tightly with our old friends and to assure ourselves of their affection by new indulgences, does not permit us to dispute with them everything that we would have been able to dispute before.[67]

While the French plenipotentiaries sent the revised proposition back to court for approval, the Swedes grew increasingly impatient, and threatened to hand in their proposition without the

French if action were not taken by the agreed-upon deadline of Pentecost. For his part, Mazarin was very upset with Servien for having sent the proposition back, already having had adequate approval. Servien's later apology that he thought he would have been accused of "too much boldness" had he not gotten additional approval probably indicates that his humiliation over the first French proposition was still fresh in his mind. Mazarin further criticized Servien for allowing the Swedes to insert religious clauses in their proposition; when Lionne tried to defend Servien by arguing that he had wheedled down the exorbitant Swedish pretensions, Mazarin commented "that if one demands ten thousand *écus* from a man who owes nothing, if he pays one thousand to close the affair, he has still made a very bad deal."[68]

In a third meeting at the beginning of June, the French plenipotentiaries got the Swedes to remove a word from their preface that suggested that they were fighting the war at least in part for the sake of religion; they could not, however, convince the Swedes to change a clause calling for the restoration of Karl Ludwig of the Palatinate, which the French had hoped to leave vague. After the Swedes attempted, unsuccessfully, to move up the deadline for submitting the proposition to 7 June, the final versions were handed over on Sunday, 11 June. The propositions were not identical, and the Swedes complained about some alterations in the French version, but overall the two states had been successful in reconciling their diverse aims into a common form.[69]

Soon after the crowns' second proposition had been submitted, the Habsburgs, the mediators, and the German estates alike began insisting that they elaborate their territorial demands so that negotiation could begin in earnest. The French, however, were not yet entirely clear on what they wanted. The plenipotentiaries' main instructions from 1643 offered three alternatives: either all French conquests in Alsace; a sizeable proportion of them; or turning over all conquests to a French ally (see chapter 5). This still left considerable room for choosing and narrowing, however, and there is little evidence of this being done prior to 1645. Although the 1644 French campaign in the Empire would be an ideal opportunity to study how French territorial demands changed in response to military action, since it was fought entirely in and around Alsace, the sources are surprisingly silent. Neither Mazarin, nor Brienne, nor the plenipotentiaries responded to the Bavarian advance, the battle of Freiburg, or the subsequent series of successful French sieges with any reference to how they would affect their negotiating stance. Undoubtedly this is attributable to the fact that the negotiations themselves had not advanced to such a point as to make their discussion necessary; only when they did, toward the end of the year, did the plenipotentiaries begin floating possibilities.[70]

It has been argued that the French only decided after the battle of Freiburg to demand all of Alsace. While it is true that the plenipotentiaries spoke of "the conservation of Alsace" in October, 1644, this is too temporally removed from the battle, and their previous statements are too vague, to permit one to draw conclusions about the effect of the campaign on French demands. Indeed, the French were generally quite careless about how they stated their demands to each other, a point that renders meaningless attempts to make sense of changes in their position with great precision.[71]

One new demand can, however, safely be attributed to the 1644 campaign—that of Philippsburg, a town that France had not occupied beforehand, and that played no part in the main instructions. In a letter to the queen on 9 December, d'Avaux explained how he had convinced Servien not to demand the restoration of the Elector of Trier to all his estates, since this would be tacitly to include Philippsburg. D'Avaux was thus assuming that Mazarin would want to include this new French demand, although there had been no word of it from court. This was the first explicit mention of French demands as such during 1644. Servien soon joined in, mentioning French demands several times in his last few letters of the year. He wrote to Brienne on 17 December that he thought the court's intention was "to conserve Lorraine, Alsace, and all the towns on the Rhine," adding, "as I think one should," and again on 31 December he said that, if the court had resolved to keep "Breisach and all of Alsace," they should negotiate with the Swedes for Benfeld. He also mentioned Philippsburg on several occasions (see below).[72]

These presumptions turned out, however, to be premature; Brienne responded that they would discuss Benfeld "from the moment when Their Majesties will have determined not only to keep Breisach, but all Alsace, Upper and Lower." It was not until 7 April 1645, that Mazarin, noting the defeat of the Imperials at Jankov, the initial approach of Vervaux, and the positive outlook for the upcoming campaign, judged the time right to come to a firmer position on French demands. He asked Servien and d'Avaux for their opinions on what France might be able to get, adding, "I well know that the conquests are the most important, but I cannot well judge which would be the easiest to retain."

Servien was the first to respond with a special memo on 22 April. He argued that it was necessary for France to demand more than she expected to get, because if the military situation worsened, she would have to surrender certain demands. He suggested Alsace, Lorraine, and everything that France held across the Rhine up to Philippsburg, plus French protection over a line of communication to Philippsburg. At this time, he was still thinking of France's acquiring these territories as fiefs of the Empire. The key points were Breisach and Philippsburg, possession of which would enable the crown "to hold all the neighboring territories in devotion to France." Lionne noted Mazarin's favorable response, without referring to specific points.[73]

The plenipotentiaries did not produce a common response until the middle of June. Their suggestions were essentially the same as Servien's, but a little more detailed: Philippsburg, Breisach and its neighboring towns, and Upper and Lower Alsace, with the same rights then possessed by the emperor. No mention was made of a line of communication to Philippsburg; of greater significance, they also totally left Lorraine out of their letter. The court approved this outline in a 1 July memo, adding the path to Philippsburg, and noting that French pretensions to Lorraine would not be affected by their demands. Presumably the French policy of excluding all issues relating to the duke of Lorraine from the conference was responsible for their failure to include the duchy as one of their demands, but it is striking how casually this decision was apparently made, without any explicit discussion whatsoever in the surviving correspondence.[74]

Much has been made of the French demands for "Alsace" as a province, as opposed to the various component parts of which it was composed (insofar as it can be said to have existed as an entity at all).[75] Again, however, careless terminology on the part of the French seems to be more responsible for the confusion than their actual understanding, incomplete as it may have been. For if the plenipotentiaries never referred to the territory as anything other than "Alsace" in 1644, the fact that they spoke of "Upper and Lower Alsace" in their memo of 17 June 1645 shows that they knew at least that it was not a unified province. While it is possible that they had learned the distinction in the meantime, it seems unlikely. Certainly in July they requested information from the court on the exact judicial makeup of the land, so they would not have received anything like it earlier.[76] And Brienne's use of the term "all Alsace, Upper and Lower" seems only like a more detailed version of Servien's previous use of "all

Alsace." Most important, however, is the fact that the French, both at court and in Münster, continued to use the term "Alsace" even after they had made it abundantly clear that they knew that it consisted of at least two parts.[77]

This lax usage is all the more obvious when one looks at other, more substantial differences that appear in French demands from one letter to the next, and sometimes even within the same letter. In his last letter of 1644, for example, Servien repeatedly mentioned Breisach and Philippsburg as the two main French conquests in the Empire, indeed, speaking of them as though France would keep them and nothing else. This was on the same day that, in another letter, he spoke of French demands as Alsace and Breisach, without a word of Philippsburg.[78] Similarly, in 15 April memo, he said that he believed the court's intention to be to retain Alsace and Philippsburg; yet in the very same paragraph he cites one of the obstructions to be a treaty preventing France from acquiring Breisach, and later in the same letter notes the importance of gaining Benfeld to secure Breisach.[79] Such important omissions and additions indicate nothing other than that Servien (and the rest of the French statesmen) were very imprecise. And, though it is true that in some cases the omissions were understood by the reader, in other cases they caused confusion.[80]

A case in point is the royal response to the plenipotentiaries' memorandum on French satisfaction, in which the court had cavalierly approved of the plenipotentiaries' plan to "be content with" the list of demands, whereas in fact the plenipotentiaries had simply meant them to be a starting point that might be whittled down. Servien and d'Avaux responded rather anxiously on 22 July that their proposal had been "more to say their sentiments on what they could demand than [in] the hope that they had to obtain all of it." They specifically noted the difficulty of obtaining Philippsburg, and requested more information from court to sort out the tangled jurisdictional questions in French-occupied Germany.[81]

The French plenipotentiaries were certainly concerned about the effect that their demands would have on the German estates. As far back as January, Servien and d'Avaux had dampened the court's optimism by noting that Germans were unlike Italians in that they were "touched much more by the love of their country and cannot accept that foreigners dismember the Empire."[82] On 15 July, they noted that "we will attempt to conduct ourselves with the greatest restraint possible," and Longueville himself added on 22 July that they were letting the estates know their demands a little at a time, and thus "accustom[ing] them to hear that we do not want to return anything." Yet this does not mean that the French were somehow afraid of laying their demands on the table and avoided doing so until the last moment. To the contrary, they were doing everything they could to advance the negotiations and to enter into details as soon as possible, but were delayed by three problems. First, they had to deal with all the estates rather than a single ruler, and they pleaded with the court to let them mention all of their demands at once or "we will have no hope of ever completing this treaty." Second, the Swedes were intent on waiting until they had received the Imperial response before formulating their demands; d'Avaux did his best to convince them that it was essential not to delay too long thereafter, for fear that the emperor would resolve his differences with the estates and then unite with them against the satisfaction of the two crowns. Finally, Longueville noted on 26 August that the situation was perfect to enter into substantive negotiations, but they were prevented by the tedious negotiations of the estates over their mode of consulting with the emperor. "We press as much as we can," he added with regret, "but it is with little effect."[83]

If concern over the opinion of the German estates had little influence on French demands, the battle of Herbsthausen did not register at all. The demands expressed in the 1643 instructions were taken over wholesale in Servien's April 1645 memo, with the addition of Philippsburg and the absence of the Breisgau. Both of these changes no doubt reflected the military developments of 1644, in which France lost Überlingen and Freiburg, but gained Philippsburg and other towns along the Rhine; however, it is impossible to trace the exact cause of the changes, because no one ever seems to have discussed them. Servien's list of demands was, in turn, incorporated into the plenipotentiaries' letter of 17 June without significant changes, and were later approved by the court. Clearly, the loss of a single battle was not enough to deter the French from their long-term goals—a claim that they themselves repeated often enough. Interestingly, the French court noted on 13 May—before news of Herbsthausen had arrived—that "one accident alone has already many times changed the face of German affairs in a single day." However, they behaved with considerably more steadfastness than this statement would indicate. The fact that Herbsthausen was a small battle, and that Enghien was readily available to reinforce Turenne, no doubt lessened the effect of the defeat considerably.[84]

Neither, on the other hand, did the battle of Jankov seem to influence the French position, contrary to what others expected. Vervaux, for example, reported to Maximilian that "the Bohemian disgrace seems to have changed their designs significantly, and will probably ensure that the peace will cost much more than it would have if this blow had not been so rude for us."[85] But this does not correspond to the surviving information on French policy. One of the questions included in an 15 April memo by Servien read, "Whether it is necessary to advance or to slow an accommodation after the recent good successes." He concluded that France should push forward militarily, but not to gain new demands; rather, he hoped that the newly occupied territory would both force the emperor to accede to existing French demands, and serve, via its restitution at the peace, as a means to justify those demands. All of the demands taken up by Servien and d'Avaux and approved by the court, moreover, had already been mentioned in 1644.[86]

No progress could be made on the negotiations, however, until the emperor delivered his response, and he could deliver no response until the estates had resolved the method by which they were to advise him.[87] As these debates continued, military events developed further and changed the face of affairs once again. While Mercy was exploiting his victory at Herbsthausen by capturing Gernsheim on the Rhine and then invading Hesse, Mazarin reacted quickly. As soon as the extent of Turenne's defeat had become clear, he sent out orders to Enghien to march directly to the Rhine without delay, and wrote to Turenne that "we will forget nothing in the future . . . to remove the counterweight that Bavarian forces provide to ours."[88] Marsin, then at Metz, was to provide immediate reinforcements to Turenne by taking one thousand cavalry into Germany, and troops were hastily gathered from excessively large garrisons in Alsace and in the towns along the Rhine to provide additional troops. But after learning that Turenne had retreated safely into Hesse, Mazarin instructed Enghien to march to Germany slowly; this would keep his troops from becoming fatigued, and, more importantly, would help cover the nearby siege of La Mothe. As usual, however, Mazarin left a great deal of leeway to his commander, and could only approve when he learned that Enghien had advanced quickly to the Rhine in spite of the delays in the siege of La Mothe, which only fell on 7 July.[89]

Meanwhile, Mazarin and the plenipotentiaries were also busy trying to get aid from Hesse and Sweden. Amalie Elisabeth had

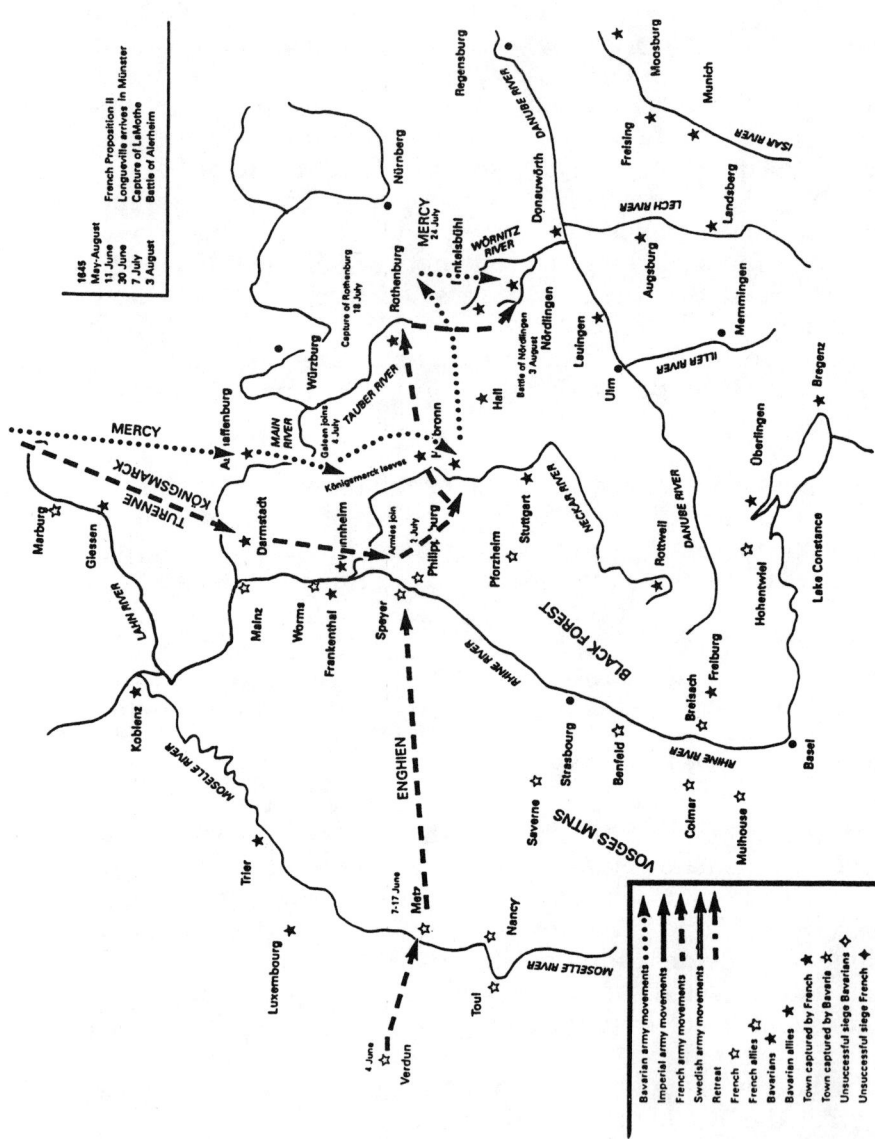

1645, May–August

been promising to send two brigades since late in 1644, and these were the first to link up with Turenne's battered army. The Swedes, too, agreed to send reinforcements: Königsmarck and his four thousand troops joined Turenne near Warburg on 29 May. His army now numerically inferior to the allies, Mercy was forced to raise the siege of Kirchhain, in Hesse, and retreat to Aschaffenburg. The allied army moved south, crossing the Main near Frankfurt and descending the *Bergstraße* (a strip of territory south of Frankfurt), stopping to plunder Darmstadt on the way. They linked up with Enghien near Heidelberg on 2 July and discussed plans for the campaign.[90]

To secure quarters east of the Rhine, the French judged that they needed to capture Heilbronn, so they marched for it quickly in the hope of getting there before Mercy. But the Bavarian commander, who had joined with Geleen's four thousand Westphalian troops on 4 July, anticipated this move and arrived just in time. The two armies, now swollen to around twenty thousand men each—extremely large by the standards of the theater—faced each other across the Neckar. Mercy, encamped in a strong position on a mountain, had effectively placed himself to block any attempt to besiege Heilbronn, while also preventing the French from engaging him on advantageous terms. The obvious solution for the allied army was to cross the Neckar above Heilbronn and approach Mercy from the south; however, this was not feasible because to do so would have been to put the Bavarians between the allied army and northern Germany, and neither the Hessians nor the Swedes would allow themselves to be cut off from their bases. Therefore, Enghien had to settle for an alternate plan: they would cross the Neckar below Heilbronn and march to the Danube; then, with the Bavarians pushed deep back in their own territory, the allies would return quickly to Heilbronn and attempt to besiege it before the Bavarians could save it.[91]

The allies easily seized a Neckar crossing at Wimpfen (the site of the 1622 battle between Tilly and Georg Friedrich of Baden-Durlach) and advanced to Rothenburg-ob-der-Tauber, whose small garrison surrendered almost immediately and was put to death.[92] But now the Hessians and Swedes again raised difficulties. Königsmarck insisted that he was needed elsewhere, and departed on a successful campaign in Saxony, much to the chagrin of the French.[93] The Hessians agreed to remain with the French if Amalie Elisabeth instructed them to, so the two armies camped in the vicinity of Rothenburg while waiting for a response to Enghien's letter pleading with the Landgrave to let the Hessians stay with the French for a little longer. Good news finally arrived, and the allied force marched south on 30 July with the intention of besieging Dinkelsbühl. There, however, they found the Bavarians just two hours away on the other side of a wood, in a position to interfere with the siege. Enghien quickly abandoned the idea of attacking Dinkelsbühl, and instead turned east in an attempt to engage Mercy. His orders were clear: Mazarin had written to him on 11 July that

> I imagine either that you will force the enemy in his entrenchments, or, if reason of war does not permit that you attempt it, that you will attack them in a place so sensitive that they will be obliged to come relieve it, and give you, consequently, occasion to attack them without their advantages.[94]

But Mercy's position at Dinkelsbühl proved to be too strong: the field separating the two armies was crisscrossed by ponds and bogs that left only a single, vulnerable passage between them. After exchanging cannon fire for a whole day, causing several hundred casualties on each side, Enghien again marched south, toward Nördlingen. Assuming that the Bavarians had crossed the Danube, he had already given orders for the march back to Heilbronn when a scouting party arrived saying that the Bavarian army was camped nearby. Enghien, overjoyed to have the occasion to attack Mercy, was not deterred by the strong position the Bavarians had taken up on two hills flanking the town of Alerheim. He sent his infantry against the Bavarian infantry in the town, only to be repulsed after a bloody engagement in which Mercy was killed. Then, von Werth's cavalry charged off the hill on the Bavarian left and broke the French right flank. The day seemed lost for France, and probably would have been, had von Werth not made the same mistake that commanders of the era made over and over again: he permitted his troops to plunder the French baggage train rather than turning them against the undefeated French left. This remaining force, under Turenne, reversed the situation by charging and breaking the Bavarian right, after which some of the Bavarian infantry in the center surrendered. Von Werth returned to the field to find the battle already decided. As at Freiburg, both sides camped on the field, so tactical victory can be accorded to neither. Yet it was the Bavarians who withdrew the next day, while Enghien used his army to capture Nördlingen—a sure sign that the effect of the battle was more to France's advantage.[95]

As with many other major battles, it is not easy to distinguish the differences in a state's policy beforehand and afterward. Already before the battle, in mid-July, Servien and d'Avaux had both been thanked by the Bavarian plenipotentiaries for France's continuing good will after the battle of Herbsthausen, and they attributed "this redoubling of civility" to the fear that the French advance had induced. The Bavarians also reassured the French of Maximilian's willingness to help them obtain reasonable satisfaction; and when they reacted strongly against d'Avaux's outline of French demands, Maximilian rebuked them, saying that they should offer to co-operate with the French and not oppose them. Maximilian further wrote to his brother, the Archbishop of Cologne, of the need to give the French territorial satisfaction. The 2 August meeting of the Bavarian council shows the extent to which they were concerned about the situation: several councillors voiced the need to cover the Danube at all costs, and Maximilian himself asked whether he should abandon Munich. In some ways, the battle of Alerheim seems to have been an anticlimax. The main concern of the council in their 5 August meeting was finding a new leader, not finding a new army; indeed, one of the councillors concluded that the Bavarian army was in better shape than the French.[96]

But if the battle had not proven a disaster for Bavaria, the military situation was still precarious. The council agreed to request immediate reinforcements of two to three thousand cavalry from the emperor, and to urge him to advance the negotiations, including ceding Alsace. It is difficult to determine whether the decision to press the emperor to agree to relinquish Alsace was a direct result of the battle of Alerheim, since the general direction of Bavarian policy—at least since Vervaux's mission, if not since the 1644 campaign—had been toward helping France obtain satisfaction. However, it does seem significant that it should have been decided precisely at this moment, and in the context of a discussion of the actions to be taken after the battle.[97]

What is less disputable is the impetus the battle gave the talks about a separate armistice between Bavaria and France. During the July meeting with the Bavarian plenipotentiaries, d'Avaux had raised the question of a separate truce that Vervaux had first suggested. The Bavarian council showed itself concerned enough about the military situation to consider the offer seriously, but rejected it on three grounds: first, it would turn the other German estates against Bavaria; second, they were not yet desperate enough for such a measure; and third, they felt that they could not trust France. Immediately after the battle, however, the situation was very different. This time, Maximilian's query to his council whether they should begin talks with France met with an affirmative response. These negotiations were not only to cover a potential truce, but, acting on an apparently independent proposal by the Parisian nuncio Bagno, the Bavarians decided to offer to join their army with France's in order to fight any state that showed itself uninterested in peace.

Maximilian initiated the talks in two different ways. First, seeking a more direct route to the French court, he met with the comte de Gramont, a French commander captured at the battle of Alerheim.[98] Maximilian arranged to exchange Gramont for his own commander, Geleen; but before he sent Gramont on his way, he invited him to Munich, entertained him lavishly, and proposed an armistice with France. Gramont, however, parried Maximilian's proposals with the skill of a diplomat, citing the same reasons as Mazarin for why Bavaria should want peace, and referring all concrete negotiations to Münster.[99]

With this route closed, Maximilian had little choice but to send orders to Haslang and Krebs to approach d'Avaux secretly, which he did on 9 August. They were to reiterate Bavaria's willingness to help France obtain satisfaction; however, "so that our resolution and declaration does not remain fruitless . . . , before all else it is necessary that the French . . . not . . . damage our troops through real [würklicher] attacks." If d'Avaux responded that the Bavarians were suddenly becoming more cooperative in light of the recent battle, the Bavarians were to answer him that "the engagement fell out in such a way that neither side gained a particular advantage or victory . . . , and therefore things remained in the same situation that they were in before the battle." It is difficult, however, to believe that Maximilian honestly believed the battle to have resulted in no "particular advantage," not only because his approach to France contradicts this view of the battle, but because later in the same letter Maximilian himself informed his plenipotentiaries that they were to claim that "things in the Empire are in a much better state than you in fact know them to be."[100]

On 20 August, acting on Maximilian's orders from 2 August (that is, before Alerheim), the Bavarian plenipotentiaries approached d'Avaux secretly and affirmed that they were willing to intervene in favor of French satisfaction in exchange for French support for the Electorate for Maximilian and his posterity. When asked what satisfaction the French should get, the Bavarians responded that it should be "proportional to the advantages that [France] has in Germany." D'Avaux then raised some possibilities, which the Bavarian plenipotentiaries explained in their letter of 21 August in great detail: only the rights possessed by the Habsburgs, which they clarified to include Breisach; the Breisgau; the Sundgau (further refined to mean the land from Breisach to Switzerland, and running between the Rhine and the Vosges); and the Landvogtei and protection ("Schirmgerechtigkeit") over the Decapolis. In addition, France was to have garrison rights in Saverne (owned by the Bishopric of Strasbourg) and Philippsburg (owned by the Electorate of Trier). Explicitly excluded from d'Avaux's demands were the other immediate estates in Alsace. D'Avaux himself, however, only said in the plenipotentiaries' common dispatch that he spoke of Alsace, Breisach, and Philippsburg "in general terms," wanting to wait until he had talked with his colleagues before going into more detail. Since he would not have wanted to offend his colleagues by negotiating too much without them, it is reasonable to wonder whether d'Avaux understated the detail of his meeting with the Bavarians. On the other hand, when the plenipotentiaries were outlining their much more detailed demands later in the same letter (see below), they also called them "somewhat general." In any case, the demands proposed by d'Avaux on the 20th, and again by all the French envoys on the 23rd, were so similar as to make any subterfuge on d'Avaux's part inconsequential for the progress and meaning of the talks.[101]

The French next mentioned their demands, at Bavarian prompting, three days later, with Servien, Longueville, and d'Avaux all present. After saying that they could justly claim to retain all of their German conquests, the French restricted themselves to "Upper- and Lower-Alsace, with Breisach and Philippsburg and the surrounding territory . . . , as well as the four Forest Towns." The Bavarians reacted strongly, arguing that, even if they could get the emperor to agree to give up his rights (which would be difficult), it would be completely unfair to demand other territories that had never raised arms against France. The French then said that they believed that the king would be content to have only those territories that belonged to the Habsburgs: Breisach, the Breisgau, the Sundgau,

> and the other lands and sovereign rights that [the House of Habsburg] had in Upper and Lower Alsace, and protection of the ten Imperial cities, with garrisons in the places where the King will judge neces-

sary. And, last, that the estates immediate to the Empire and that were under the protection of the [Habsburgs] will remain in the Empire and will be under the protection of the King, and the mediate estates will be controlled by His Majesty as Landgrave of Alsace.[102]

This exchange raises at least two questions. First, why did the Bavarians object so strongly to the French demands of 23 August, when they knew from their 20 August meeting that the French were demanding nothing more than Habsburg rights? The most likely possibility seems to be that they wanted to force the French to specify their demands more clearly, but this must remain conjecture.[103]

Second, what is one to make of the accretion of the Breisgau to French demands? This territory, which lay across the Rhine in what is now Baden-Württemberg, had never been mentioned before, and was not mentioned again in 1645. The original instructions to the plenipotentiaries from 1643 specified the territory "between Lorraine and the Rhine" (although it had included the Forest Towns, which are also in modern Baden-Württemberg). Now, suddenly, this new territory was being included, along with other details such as the Sundgau, which also do not reappear in the correspondence. Alfred Overmann has made the case that the French were extending their demands because they had learned that the Habsburg rights in Alsace were not as extensive as they had thought, and wanted additional land as compensation. While possible, it seems unlikely that the plenipotentiaries would have increased their demands deliberately without explaining their reasons to the court; by the same logic, it seems likely that the court would have responded had it recognized the Breisgau as a new demand. In later correspondence, after they had received the report on the legal situation in Alsace that they had requested in July, the plenipotentiaries dismissed both the Breisgau and Sundgau, saying they did not belong to the Habsburgs. In these talks in August, however, they seem to equate Habsburg control precisely with those territories. This corresponds strikingly closely to a memorandum prepared by Théodore de Godefroy, who happened to be present with the plenipotentiaries as an historiographical and juridical assistant. It seems, therefore, that the French were not extending their demands, but rather clarifying them to the best of their knowledge as it stood at that time. Moreover, being aware that they still had much to learn, they claimed to have left their discussion with the Bavarians in general terms, "so that when we get the information for which we are waiting, we will only have to clarify our demands, and not augment them."[104]

According to Andreas Kraus, Maximilian could have obtained these terms for France, and hence hastened the end of the war, had Mazarin's primary goal been territorial conquest. "But," he writes, "already in August 1645, after Alerheim and the talks with the Bavarian delegation, it was clear that Mazarin for a long time had not wanted to settle for mere conquests." Instead, continues Kraus, Mazarin aimed to separate Bavaria from the emperor, who, thus weakened, would be prey to France's military might. He would only have been content with the "ruin of the House of Austria"—"France's original war aim"—and not just territory.[105]

These strong claims, however, rest on an unstable foundation. Kraus's main piece of evidence is a citation from a royal memo of 1 September, which notes that, if Bavaria were to be separated from the emperor, "there would follow the ruin of the House of Austria in Germany, or the conclusion of a peace such as we and our allies desire." It seems clear from this very statement that Mazarin preferred and expected the latter alternative. Nowhere else does he talk about ruining the Habsburgs, suggesting that its one mention was just a means to emphasize the advantageous position in which Bavaria's separation from the emperor would put France, and not policy. Mazarin's real strategy was to build up military superiority in order to force the enemy to accept French terms, not to destroy him entirely. As Brienne wrote to the plenipotentiaries, "The only way to stop the run [of French military successes] is to consent to a just peace."[106]

That Mazarin aimed to separate Bavaria from the emperor is not in question; the idea of a separate truce was taken up enthusiastically by Mazarin after having been proposed by Maximilian. This does not mean, however, that Mazarin was trying to delay the peace talks in the meantime. To the contrary, France was anxious to get them moving in August and September, while her military situation was so favorable. Mazarin wrote of Alerheim that it permitted the plenipotentiaries not only to speak with authority, but to "lay down the law just as you like to our opponents, and they will be forced to acquiesce to everything that we demand from them." The problem was that the public negotiations remained stalled while the German estates continued to debate their method of advising the emperor, and there was little about this that the French could do; as Longueville lamented, "we press as much as we can, but it is with little effect." They could not even get Sweden to begin discussing the satisfaction of the two crowns, since Oxenstierna preferred to wait until the Imperials gave their response. Far from trying to slow the talks, then, France was trying to do just the opposite.[107]

To criticize France for not trying to use Bavaria to mediate secretly with the emperor to achieve her demands is hardly fair. Mazarin had good reasons for wanting to negotiate above the table, even though he knew it would be slower. Not that he was uninterested in using Bavaria to assist him; in fact, he had written to his plenipotentiaries on 12 August (and therefore before the news of Alerheim had arrived in Paris) that they should inform Bavaria confidentially of everything they told the mediators concerning the peace. Since Maximilian was so anxious for peace, he noted, the Bavarians "will themselves become the mediators to make our enemies consent to what we want in order to achieve peace."[108]

But beyond this informal arrangement Mazarin was not willing to go, because he so greatly feared the effect that secret talks with Bavaria would have on Sweden. Although he himself expressed great discontent at the separate Swedish truce with Saxony at Kötzschenbroda (6 September), he refused to return one secretly arranged agreement for another: not because he was particularly concerned about keeping his word, but because France had more to lose. In a 9 September letter, he sought to explain this paradox, in which "it is up to the superior to tolerate the weaker." For France, he avowed, was more glorious and more powerful than Sweden. On the other side, however, "all of the Habsburgs' hate is against us. There is nothing that they would not sacrifice happily to avenge themselves against this crown." France was therefore obliged to do everything possible to keep Sweden from accepting the great offers of the Habsburgs, and this included honoring the treaty forbidding secret negotiations. This would slow down the talks, admittedly; but it was worth it, because the risks of negotiating without notifying Sweden were "infinitely greater" than those of negotiating with Swedish cognizance.[109]

In light of this consideration, it is unreasonable to criticize Mazarin for not agreeing to use secret Bavarian intervention with the emperor. Even if Maximilian could have expedited French satisfaction, this would have done little in itself to hasten the end of the war, since French satisfaction was only one small piece of the puzzle. Such a move would almost certainly have alienated the Swedes, who, seeing their allies achieve full satisfaction surreptitiously, might well have bound themselves closer to the Protestant estates and sought to lengthen the war. The fault is much more Maximilian's for not recognizing the strength of the Franco-Swedish alliance, and the need to work through it, rather than around it.[110]

The French anticipated that Sweden might accept the notion of a truce with Bavaria, but would probably not want to agree to support Maximilian in the retention of the Electorate (a matter that touched the most sensitive difference between France and Sweden, since the disowned Elector Palatine had been a Protestant). In order to obtain a truce, however, Mazarin was willing to guarantee French support for Bavaria in the matter of the Electorate, if necessary via a secret treaty.[111]

But neither Mazarin nor the French ambassadors trusted Maximilian. Mazarin said that "there is great reason to be wary of this prince . . . [who is] cunning and deceitful to the core." They were particularly leery of Bavaria's offer to turn its army against any side not interested in peace. The problem, as the plenipotentiaries pointed out, was the difficulty of determining "which of the two parties did not want peace." Servien noted, with characteristic acumen, that "everyone wants peace; the only difference is in the conditions." The only way to clarify this situation would have been to agree on precise peace terms, but this would have been difficult, especially since Bavaria had so many differences with the Swedes and the Protestants. To accept the offer without firm conditions, however, would have meant leaving Maximilian the arbiter of the peace, an impossible condition. Mazarin agreed with the plenipotentiaries' assessment, saying that they would not accept the offer "even supposing that he was the most ingenuous and the most sincere of all men, whereas he is in fact one of the most deceitful and the most adroit."[112]

Furthermore, the French suspected Maximilian of altering his plans according to the military situation—or, as Mazarin elegantly put it, "the duke of Bavaria always makes his decisions according to circumstances." This was a damning comment, because it implied that Maximilian was not true to his word. Mazarin correctly guessed that Bavaria would become more pliant after the battle of Alerheim; but it was precisely this inconstancy that made Mazarin and his plenipotentiaries also anticipate that he would withdraw his generous post-Alerheim offers if the military situation improved. Longueville berated Krebs on this point at the beginning of September, saying that if Maximilian was not more constant in regard to France in the future, he could expect no further assistance from her.[113]

In spite of the virtual certainty that Maximilian would change his terms, and possibly even break the treaty altogether, Mazarin persisted in the negotiations. In part, he reasoned that France would gain even if Maximilian did intend to break the treaty at a later date: first, because France would have a chance to refresh her army in the meantime; and second, because the mere fact of his having signed a separate treaty would make the emperor fear being abandoned, and would consequently lead him to make peace at the first possible moment. But Mazarin did not just rest on this logic: he insisted that Bavaria guarantee the treaty by disarming all or part of its army and handing over to France fortified towns.[114]

The Bavarian army proved the least difficult issue to resolve. In the first place, the plenipotentiaries' strong objections to disarming Maximilian, since it would hurt the French and Catholic positions in the Empire, led to its being dropped before it was even mentioned to the Bavarians. Maximilian later claimed that he could not guarantee what would happen to his troops in case of a truce, since his army was not his to dispose of—a statement that, while technically true, was misleading in the extreme (see chapter 4). The French court, knowing the reality of the situation, assured the plenipotentiaries that Maximilian had firm control over his army. Longueville asked the Bavarian representatives point-blank "with whom we are treating, an absolute prince with an army who can do what he promises, or a subject prince who disposes of nothing, and who, in case of a contravention of the treaty, would pay us only excuses?" This pointed question shamed the Bavarians into changing their manner of talking.[115]

Maximilian's hedge concerning his control of his army, however, only increased the importance of the second issue: the question of Bavaria's handing over fortified towns as security. The Bavarians felt that France should trust them, just as Bavaria was trusting France. But, as the French pointed out, it was not France that had been reduced to requesting protection. There was no way the French were going to accept a neutrality treaty from a leader whom they regarded as so inconstant; the only question was with what fortress or fortresses they would be content. The plenipotentiaries initially proposed Ehrenbreitstein as the best option. An extremely powerful stronghold located near Koblenz at the confluence of the Rhine and Moselle rivers, Ehrenbreitstein would have strengthened French control of the Rhine immeasurably; given them an additional Rhine crossing; and cut off the Imperial garrisons along the Moselle. Yet it did not belong to

Maximilian, but rather to his brother, the Archbishop of Cologne. For the French even to have suggested such excessive security indicates that they overestimated their position. The Bavarians naturally refused, deflecting criticism by saying that it was not theirs of which to dispose. The plenipotentiaries suggested to Mazarin a number of other possible alternatives, including Heidelberg, Heilbronn, Mannheim, Freiburg, and Offenburg. They considered Freiburg particularly desirable, both because of its proximity to Breisach, and because it might be left to France at the peace. The court did approve and even encouraged substitutions in case Ehrenbreitstein was unobtainable. On 14 October, they favored accepting Heilbronn, Heidelberg, and Freiburg, or, if necessary, two of the three. They felt that this would be more acceptable to Maximilian than Ehrenbreitstein, which was incomparably better than even all three other fortresses. But such a demand was completely out of touch with reality, because Bavaria was not about to surrender three, two, or even one of the major fortresses that France was requesting. Comparing this demand with what France actually got (Heilbronn and the minor town of Lauingen) at the Truce of Ulm in 1647, when France's military situation was incomparably better, demonstrates just how absurd it was.[116]

Even had Mazarin given in completely on the security issue, however, the talks would still have been futile, because both Bavaria and France had the same goal, quarters in Württemberg; and it was a goal not subject to compromise. Admittedly, from early on, the French decided to accept dividing the quarters with the Bavarian army. Maximilian, however, wanted a truce precisely so that he would not have to share his armies' quarters with the French, so any division, no matter how favorable, would have been unacceptable. At first, Mazarin felt confident that Enghien would capture Heidelberg and Heilbronn on his own, but preferred to negotiate for quarters rather than to go through with the heavy expenditures of a military operation. But when Enghien fell ill and was forced to return to France, Mazarin's confidence sank. By the end of September, he felt that France could only gain the quarters militarily with Swedish aid, and impressed upon the plenipotentiaries that it was more necessary than ever to get them through negotiation, since it seemed unlikely through military means.[117]

The French situation had seemed so promising in the immediate aftermath of Alerheim. Enghien turned immediately against Nördlingen, which had been left in poor defensive shape, and whose citizens wanted to surrender immediately. The commander rebutted Enghien's offer of terms with a sharp note that "I am awaiting the duke with bullets and the sword point"; but when the French opened a breach on 6 August, the garrison surrendered to discretion the next day.[118] Meanwhile, Maximilian was struggling with the question of who should replace Mercy. As General of the Cavalry, von Werth was the highest ranking officer, and could have been expected to get the position. However, Maximilian seems to have questioned von Werth's ability to command an entire army. Though dashing, popular, and brave, he was given to indiscipline and rash decisions. Maximilian had begun even to question his aggressiveness: late in 1644, he demanded that von Werth explain his failure to defeat a French detachment that he had outnumbered, wondering whether he was no longer "the old Werth," and giving Mercy permission to remove him if he felt it desirable. At Alerheim, von Werth's failure to bring his victorious troops back to the field on time had cost Bavaria a major victory, and probably lowered him further in Maximilian's eyes. According to Gramont, Maximilian would have preferred to promote Ruischenberg, the Master of Artillery. However, since this would have placed an inferior over the head of von Werth, he instead chose Geleen, a competent but unspectacular officer who had been in charge of the Imperial war effort in the Northwest. Since Geleen had been captured in the battle, Maximilian quickly arranged for his exchange for Gramont.[119] Bavaria also had difficulty getting reinforcements for its battered army. Though the emperor had promised three thousand cavalry immediately after the battle, only fifteen hundred had arrived over a month later.[120]

However, France was unable to capitalize on these advantages for several reasons. Losses at Alerheim had been so heavy that, a few days after the battle, fewer than fifteen hundred infantry had been gathered. The army remained at Nördlingen until 18 August, then marched north to besiege Dinkelsbühl. The trenches were opened on 20 August, and the town fell on the 24th. But the day before it surrendered, Enghien became ill with a fever. He had to be carried back to Philippsburg, his life in danger, and was unable to take further part in the campaign. Mazarin was despondent about this turn of events, since he put great faith in Enghien's abilities.[121] The French carried on the campaign with a split command: Turenne in charge of the *Armée d'Allemagne*, Gramont in charge of Enghien's army. The goal of the campaign, Heilbronn, had not been forgotten. It was essential

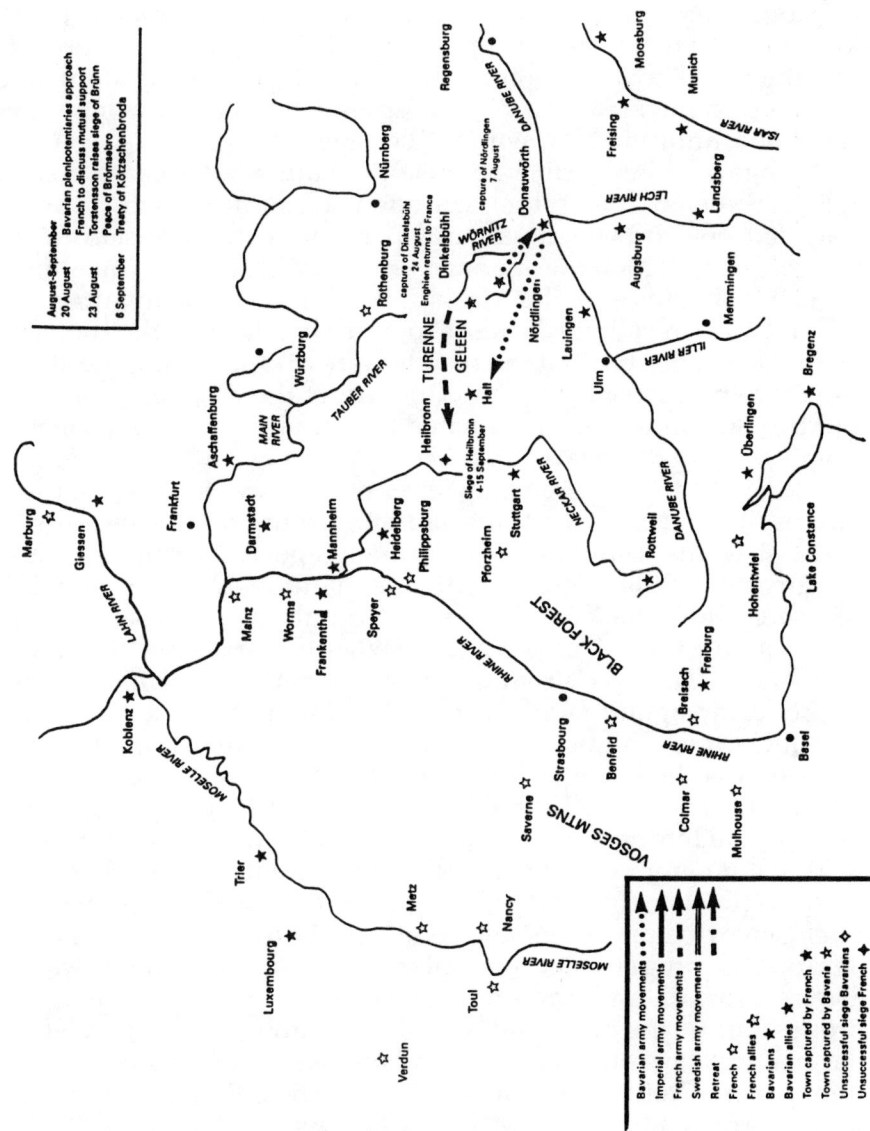

1645, August–September

to "gain solid advantages from the battle" that Enghien had won; this meant quarters in Swabia, "without which all the conquests that one makes in Germany would remain at the expense of the kingdom in such a fashion that it would be impossible to provide for them." The army therefore broke from Dinkelsbühl and marched to the area near Heilbronn on 4 September, where they remained until the 15th without besieging the city.[122]

A siege was impossible because the battle had taken a greater toll on the French than their confident accounts of victory would have led one to believe. Mazarin is reported to have said to the elated queen, "Madame, so many men are dead that you should almost not rejoice at the victory."[123] The need for infantry was immediately recognized. Mazarin and Le Tellier worked to send as much as possible, but the results were disappointing. Le Tellier hoped to pull nearly two thousand out of the Alsatian garrisons, but he considerably overestimated the number of troops available. Some Irish that Mazarin had been gathering revolted at Pont-à-Mousson, so there were many fewer of them available. Even those troops that did cross the Rhine at Philippsburg did not necessarily make it to the army; one commander reported groups of thirty to forty men deserting camp one night because of the bad weather. The same commander found only two thousand troops "in a state to fight" at the armies when he arrived.[124] Food was also short. The area around Heilbronn had been ruined by the earlier campaigning, and the French were unable to get adequate supplies from Philippsburg. Tracy, the indomitable quartermaster, said that he knew where to get enough supplies that the army could subsist for free for three more months; but this entailed leaving Heilbronn.[125] Moreover, the Bavarians had advanced to within four hours of the French and entrenched themselves in such a position that they could interfere with the siege without themselves being vulnerable to attack. Without even having attempted a proper siege of Heilbronn, then, Turenne advanced back eastward and captured Schwäbisch Hall. He spread his troops out in the surrounding villages (though not so widely as he had earlier in the year, at Herbsthausen) and waited, hoping the Imperial reinforcements would return to Bohemia and leave him in a position to secure winter quarters within six weeks.[126]

It turned out to be a vain hope. Far from pulling his troops out of Bavaria, the emperor was actually plotting a bold stroke: sending more reinforcements—half of his army—against the French, with the intention of throwing them back across the Rhine. This resolution came at a time when Torstensson was threatening to cross the Danube, but Maximilian's pleas left Ferdinand no choice: without Imperial aid, and quickly, Bavaria might have pulled out of the war. The French were ill-prepared for this new threat, for, while they had finally accumulated sufficient infantry, they were desperately short of cavalry. After Alerheim, Turenne had felt that remounting the existing cavalry would be adequate; there was no need to recruit new companies. A month later, facing the first Imperial reinforcements and a Bavarian army that had remounted its cavalry faster than he had counted on, he regretted his earlier statement.[127]

While Turenne waited near Hall, unable to attack the Bavarians, the emperor's reinforcements arrived under the command of Leopold Wilhelm. Turenne, now vastly outnumbered, immediately retreated west. Breaking camp on 3 October, he marched to Wimpfen without stopping, arriving on 5 October. Because of heavy rains, the river was too swollen to throw a pontoon bridge across the Neckar. Consequently, Turenne sent the baggage and some of the infantry across in boats. The cavalry swam across, with the remainder of the infantry doubling up on the horses. The French did not stop on the west bank of the Neckar, but, leaving the artillery and some baggage in Wimpfen, kept going straight back to Philippsburg, arriving on 10 October. Hoping to secure quarters east of the Rhine, Turenne did not cross the river, but instead marched to the town of Graben, two hours to the southeast. The Bavarian and Imperial forces, however, crossed the Neckar at Heilbronn and continued straight for Philippsburg. The French learned of this just in time to march back without their baggage, arriving only three hours before their opponents. Turenne had narrowly averted a major disaster, for if the Imperials had arrived first, his army would have been cut off east of the river in the face of a much superior enemy. He camped between the town and the river, sending over the cavalry and artillery once some boats arrived from Speyer. When Leopold Wilhelm retired to besiege Wimpfen, Turenne tried a surprise march to save his artillery there, but the German cavalry refused to recross the Rhine. Turenne could only look on helplessly as the Imperials recaptured one town after another; Wimpfen, with its prize of French baggage and artillery, fell on 26 October.[128]

Meanwhile, Maximilian continued to spin out the truce talks. He resisted handing over a town as a pledge for his sincerity, but offered hopeful insinuations concerning quarters. On 10 October, the plenipotentiaries reported that he was sending someone else to Münster with special powers to negotiate the treaty, but they

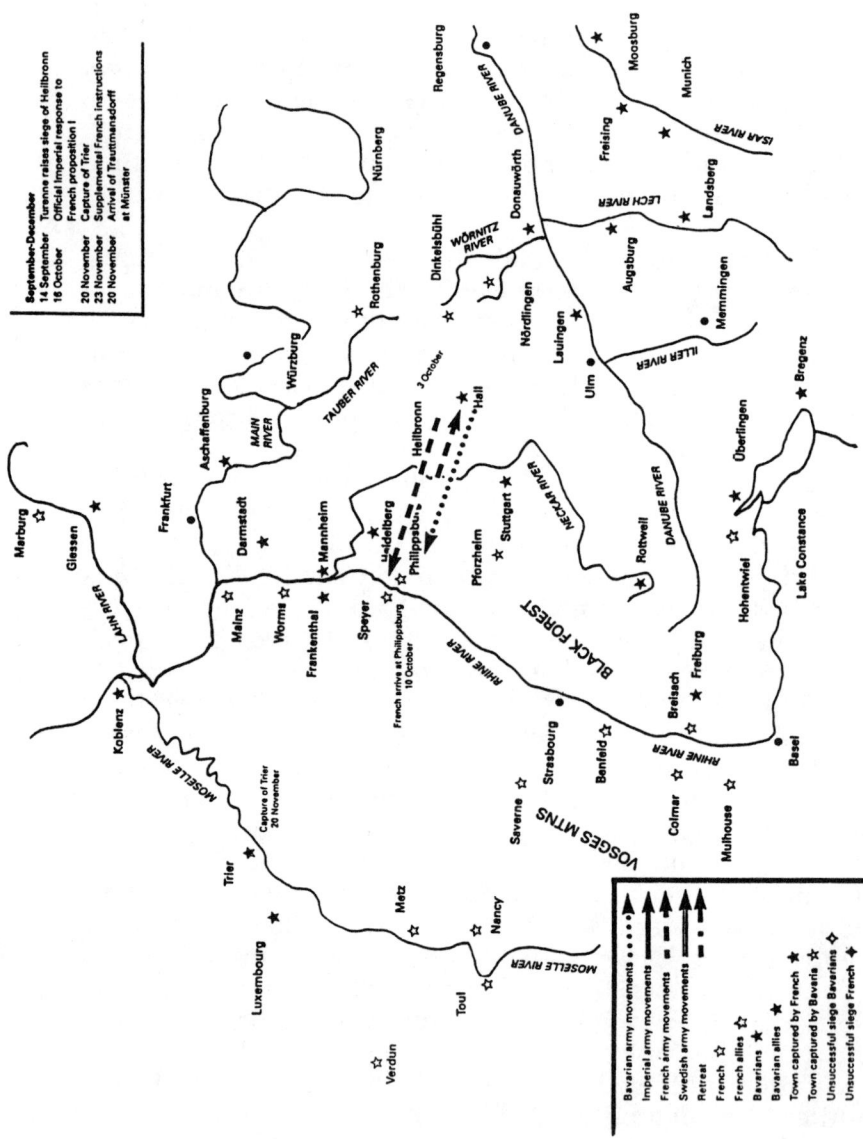

1645, September–December

learned a few days later that it was just a young councillor carrying the orders for Krebs. In any case, this new representative did not leave Munich until 22 October, and did not arrive in Münster until 1 December. The French plenipotentiaries realized that Maximilian was deliberately stalling until his military situation improved, at which point he would break off the talks altogether. They felt betrayed, and Servien in particular complained bitterly. Mazarin, however, excused Maximilian's carrying on an offensive campaign and peace talks at the same time. "It would not be prudent for him to act otherwise," the cardinal wrote; they should not expect Bavaria to stop fighting "until such a point as an accord has been concluded." He approved a mild scolding of the Bavarian plenipotentiaries, but noted that they should not be too harsh, and thus drive Maximilian to more extreme measures, "either in abandoning himself entirely in the emperor's arms, or in resolving to unite himself more closely with the Spanish." Yet even once it was clear to the French plenipotentiaries that Maximilian was stalling, they stated flatly to Brienne that they were not going to make any treaty without quarters, regardless of the military situation. Nor was this a policy conceived of in Münster, as Mazarin's repeated emphasis on quarters shows. Instead, it was clear from the beginning of September that quarters were a primary reason for the talks, and not an unnecessary appendix.[129]

When the Bavarian-Imperial army threw Turenne back across the Rhine, then, it was clear that French chances for gaining quarters east of the Rhine had been lost. By the time they had gotten Sweden to agree to a truce, the plenipotentiaries complained, Bavaria had lost interest.[130] True, they had fouled the talks themselves by not giving the Bavarians the "categorical" guarantee of the Electorate that they demanded, an action that drew a sharp rebuke from Brienne.[131] But by then, it was already too late; the affair had been settled on the battlefield. Mazarin still held out faint hope of a Swedish invasion of the Upper Palatinate that would force the recall of Imperial troops in time to save the situation, but he realized that time was short: if the Bavarians once recaptured the towns that Enghien had gained in Swabia, there would not be enough of the campaigning season left to capture them again. As this seemed unlikely, Mazarin bitterly complained of the lack of Swedish assistance, comparing the heavy losses of French infantry necessitated by the recrossing of the Rhine to the advantage Sweden had gained by the Imperial troops sent to reinforce Bavaria.[132]

The talks with Bavaria had, despite Mazarin's complaints, been foreordained to fail. Maximilian had only begun them because of his precarious military situation, and continued only until that situation had improved. Most of his councillors disapproved of signing a separate truce with France; while Maximilian himself was not so opposed, he was reluctant to abandon the emperor. He wanted to be assured from the start that France would not aid Sweden if Bavaria pulled out of the war, using as a bargaining tool the fact that the Bavarian army technically belonged to the emperor and could be thus used by Ferdinand even if Bavaria was under truce. Maximilian also rejected handing over security. But by far the most important difficulty was the quarters question: Maximilian simply was not going to surrender his quarters, which, for his small state, were absolutely essential to the maintenance of his army. Unless France could gain the quarters militarily (and this was unlikely, given the substantial aid sent by the emperor), she was not going to get them at all, because Bavaria was not going to give in through simple negotiations.[133]

In the Franco-Bavarian talks of 1645, who was the initiator and who the receptor? Recent revisionist scholarship by Bavarian historians has shifted the onus of activity onto the French, claiming that they were seeking out the Bavarians to obtain their war aims, rather than it having been the Bavarians seeking out the French to escape further destruction. There is, in a sense, a grain of truth to the revisionist argument: after all, it had been Mazarin who had invited Vervaux at the end of 1644; it had been the French plenipotentiaries who had approached the Bavarians after the Vervaux mission; it had been d'Avaux and Servien who had brought up the idea of a separate truce in July; and it had been the French who had aggressively approached the Bavarians in September and October in an attempt to separate them from the emperor. It is also true that the French needed a truce more than the Bavarians at the end of the year, since the balance of the military equation had turned against them, and they wished to obtain winter quarters east of the Rhine via other methods, as they themselves stated. However, it seems odd to attribute the diplomatic initiative to the French in all these cases when they were, in fact, merely responding to Bavarian proposals. Maximilian had originally suggested the Vervaux mission, and if the French attempted to carry the talk of a separate truce proposed by Vervaux into Münster, this was because it had been mooted by the Bavarians, not because it was a French idea. It was also to Vervaux's ideas that Servien and d'Avaux were referring in July when they mentioned a separate truce; moreover, they only raised the possibility after they had been approached by the Bavarians and profusely thanked for their assistance. In August, it was plainly the Bavarians who brought the idea up again on their own, after they had flatly rejected it before Alerheim. As the court wrote to the plenipotentiaries on 1 September,

> It is not one of the least fruits of the victory at Nördlingen [i.e., Alerheim] to have obliged the duke of Bavaria to seek anew with great desire the protection of France.[134]

The French pressed the Bavarians on this issue because they thought the Bavarians were serious about their offer. This may have been true at first, but the Bavarians increasingly lost interest as their military situation improved. There is, after all, considerable truth to the continual complaints from all French statesmen that Bavaria reacted more strongly to military events, making generous offers when things were going poorly, and retracting them quickly when things began to look up. No doubt the French had an interest in detaching Bavaria that they were willing to pursue, even in the face of Bavarian resistance; but it should not be forgotten that it was Bavaria that brought up the idea twice during the year, and one should not marvel at the fact that it took the French a while to adjust to the rapid shifts in Bavarian policy.[135]

Yet if Maximilian had withdrawn (again) from his generous offers of August, the campaign had convinced him more than ever of the need for peace. And in September, the emperor, too, began to feel the effects of French military pressure on Bavaria. The mere fact that Bavaria had been carrying on secret talks with the French (talks that had become known to Habsburg ministers) forced the emperor to consider the Bavarian situation more carefully. But Maximilian went further: in a series of September conferences with the emperor, his representative made it clear that Bavaria could not support the war effort much longer, and pressed new policies on the Habsburgs. In the first place, Maximilian insisted on increased military assistance against France, including extended quarters and more money. Above all, however, he demanded that the emperor begin negotiations with France in earnest, including a willingness to surrender Alsace. Nor did these demands remain without effect: in direct response to Bavarian pressure, the November orders issued to Trauttmansdorff, the emperor's chief negotiator, were to give in on Alsace if necessary. The very sending of Trauttmansdorff, which indicated the emperor's seriousness about advancing the talks, was considered by statesmen in both Paris and Madrid to be a sign of Bavarian influence with the emperor. Indeed, Maximilian's influence would prove crucial right through the 1646 negotiations and the signing of the preliminary treaty. These thoughts helped to cool French ire at the failure to reach an agreement in 1645.[136]

Moreover, in spite of the failure of the Franco-Bavarian truce talks in October, Mazarin seemed more confident than ever. Already, earlier in the year, he had decided definitively against concluding peace with the emperor without Spain. The war was going so well that there seemed no point in it. In Flanders, the capture of Bourbourg and other towns along the Lys had opened the way to Dunkirk, the Spanish privateering stronghold. In Catalonia, the capture of the crucial port of Rosas and Harcourt's victory at Llorens seemed to open the way to further conquests. The capture of La Mothe, the last enemy stronghold in Lorraine, secured the frontier of Champagne from enemy raids. And if the German campaign had not yielded all the results that it had promised, it had still convinced Maximilian of France's seriousness, and shown that he would work for French satisfaction at the conference. The internal situation, too, seemed promising. After a dispute over the *toisé*, an old tax revived to prop up the sagging royal finances, the regency held a *lit de justice* on 7 September. Such a move was extremely rare in a king's minority, but it achieved its end: the *toisé* was abandoned, in exchange for which the *Parlement* approved a series of new taxes that put the monarchy on a sounder financial footing, at least for the moment.[137]

With everything going so well, Mazarin judged that France could get a peace on the same terms that she had been considering for a truce: namely, "to retain all of our conquests, or at least the most considerable parts, and with solid right and title." A truce was easier to obtain, but a peace was preferable because it was "more secure [and] less exposed to changes."[138] Indeed, in order to gain "the right and the greater security that peace would give us in the preservation of our conquests . . . and to exit once and for all gloriously and advantageously from all our affairs," France would "sacrifice something that [it] would be able to retain in a truce." Moreover, there was no need to make peace without Spain, as they had thought, because the military situation was so favorable that Spain, too, would be forced to accede to French demands.[139] Indeed, Mazarin now expected to be able to conclude with Spain before the emperor, a stark reversal of policy.

This change had come about suddenly in August. In July, Mazarin requested the plenipotentiaries' opinion on the advisability of a separate peace with the emperor that would exclude Spain. Meanwhile, he was staying with his policy of frightening Spain by the threat of a separate peace, suggesting to Longueville that he give the appearance of having orders to conclude with the emperor, "not to do so, but to gain the effect that we are trying to produce on the Spanish ministers."[140] The plenipotentiaries, confused, asked for clarification on whether they would be allowed to make peace with the emperor. "We do not recall having written you that we want to make peace with the emperor without having concluded with Spain," responded Brienne somewhat acerbically, "but to make them afraid of this possibility so that they will hasten to offer" us what we want.[141]

At the beginning of August, Mazarin's policy appeared to have paid off. During the week of 12 August, Contarini approached the plenipotentiaries and discussed the possibility of a long truce with Spain, which the French rejected vigorously. They divined that Contarini's proposals must have had a Spanish origin, and wrote concerning the meeting,

> After having examined everything among ourselves and conferred on what was said separately to each of us, we believe that the Spanish fear nothing so much as that which has been told us, which is to see us make peace with the emperor without them, . . . and that they have the intention to pre-empt it and to conclude a treaty with us while we are still at war with the emperor.[142]

Why they drew such a conclusion at precisely this time is difficult to say; after all, Contarini had been making similar proposals at least since February. But whatever the reason, it appears to have convinced Mazarin. His very next letter claimed that "Spanish affairs are going in the direction of being able to be concluded in little time by the absolute necessity that our enemies have of [peace]"; soon his plenipotentiaries, too, were talking as though the Spanish treaty were close to being achieved. The mediators were pushing the notion, and Longueville asked for orders on whether they could make peace with Spain while excluding the emperor. Longueville even noted that "there is a means that seems to us a powerful aid in making us the masters of German affairs: being in a state to be able to conclude with Spain." Thus, the French policy had swung 180 degrees, from trying to frighten Spain by the threat of a separate peace with the emperor, to trying to frighten the emperor by the threat of a separate peace with Spain.[143] Clearly, Contarini had had a large role in the change, for he had been pushing a rapid accommodation with Spain, either through a truce or through a peace with a marriage alliance, since the beginning of the year. His reason for wanting a speedy end to the conflict is not hard to find: war had broken out between Venice and the Ottoman Empire, and the Republic needed assistance badly. Nor was Contarini particularly secretive about this, for at the end of October, he pleaded with the French to say that they would make a separate truce with Spain at least in case it came to an all-out attack by the Turks (an offer deftly sidestepped by the French). Besides this desperate need for peace, Mazarin felt that Venice was acting "by reason of the equilibrium in Christianity, which is one of [their] chief maxims, siding with our enemies and favoring them since they are the weaker party."[144]

However, it is also significant that Contarini's overtures fit well into Mazarin's image of the war, for it is clear that he viewed Spain as a defeated power. He was writing in this vein well before the encouraging note from the plenipotentiaries in August, and even after they had ceased to speak of the Spanish truce as imminent, Mazarin still claimed that it "depends upon us" to make the truce when they wanted.[145] As the talks dragged on, however, Mazarin became increasingly puzzled by Spain's tenacity, for he could not understand why they would continue to fight a losing war. The first real signs of his frustration came in an 12 August letter, in which he wrote that

> one can see with reason that on the same day that France signs the peace, she will give the Spanish the greater part of their estates, which she could easily have conquered in the continuation of the war . . . I do not see the motive of their blindness, and why they do not rush to this peace which is the only means by which they can stop their entire ruin.[146]

Thrown back on all fronts; their military situation growing steadily worse; their realms near or already in rebellion; and with the Turks threatening war—despite all these problems, the Spanish persisted in resisting French terms, and Mazarin could not understand how they could be so unreasonable. As the emperor became more forthcoming and the Spanish remained stubborn, French policy shaped itself more and more around the Spanish side of the equation. Indeed, it was because of Spain, and not Austria, that Mazarin had been so anxious to conclude a separate truce with Bavaria: a memo from the fall indicates that he intended to send Turenne's army to the Low Countries in case Bavaria pulled out of the war.[147]

There were other discouraging developments as well. In particular, by the end of the year, France's relations with its allies and neutrals seemed to be reaching a nadir. The court was so concerned about papal hostility that they wrote to the plenipotentiaries to ask whether the pope could reasonably continue as a mediator; Chigi, the representative in Münster, was especially suspect. Eventually, the idea of expelling the pope as a mediator was rejected on the grounds that it would just be used by the enemies to claim that France did not want peace; however, the plenipotentiaries did suggest that punishing him in some matter "that touches his purse" would be appropriate in order to make him change his conduct.[148]

Of perhaps greater moment, Transylvania shocked the French by breaking their treaty and making a separate peace with the emperor. News of the preliminary agreement, signed in August, was greeted with skepticism; the plenipotentiaries wrote that the talks were only "feints and amusements to gain time."[149] The truth, however, was that the French had been out-maneuvered by the emperor. He understood the political situation better, and thus realized that the key was to bypass Rackóczy and negotiate in Constantinople. By this method, he had successfully convinced the Ottoman sultan to force Transylvania to make peace. As Brienne wrote despondently at the end of October, "Before, I did not believe that the Porte's commandments were so pressing that they would force Transylvania to make peace. The vizier talked in this way to Monsieur de La Haye." The French briefly considered sending a special envoy to Constantinople to remedy the situation, but abandoned the idea; and on 16 December, Rackóczy signed the Peace of Linz, formally pulling out of the war.[150]

France's relations with the Netherlands also took a turn for the worse. At the beginning of August, Servien was still thinking of threatening to exclude Spain; if Spain would not accept their terms, he wrote, they should tell the mediators that the Dutch might as well stay home, since France had nothing more to say about the Spanish treaty. But by the end of the month, the positive military developments—in particular the battle of Alerheim—led to a reversal of this policy, and Mazarin wrote that it was time to press the Dutch to arrive as soon as possible so that negotiations could progress.[151] While the Dutch continued to be dilatory in coming—they did not even leave the Netherlands until January

1646—new concerns arose about Dutch fidelity: fresh rumors of separate negotiations between Spanish and Dutch representatives concerning a separate truce reached Paris and Münster almost simultaneously toward the end of September. Since the French hoped to avoid this at all costs, the court immediately rejected any further talk of acquiring the Low Countries from Spain. "Would not the offer of the Low Countries as dowry throw the Estates into great jealousy," the royal memo read, "and in the fear that it would be effected?" No French promises, it noted, would be able to allay Dutch fears adequately. But while the French were becoming suspicious, and Servien in particular wrote a long, violent diatribe against the Dutch, Mazarin remained essentially upbeat. He felt that the possibility of a separate truce with the Netherlands, or of a revolt within France, were Spain's last hopes; if neither was realized soon, Spain would make peace on France's terms.[152]

Franco-Swedish relations, which had reached a high point at the beginning of August, deteriorated steadily after that. The first *faux pas* was the Truce of Kötzschenbroda, signed by Saxony and Sweden, without French knowledge, on 6 September. Though an allied victory, the truce irritated Mazarin, since, by their alliance, neither France nor Sweden was supposed to sign an agreement without the consent of the other. The fact that France was scrupulously avoiding making a similar treaty with Bavaria at the same time only made matters worse.[153] Then, as France's hopes of gaining quarters in Swabia withered away, Mazarin's mistrust of Sweden increased. By the end of September, he was regarding the Swedish military buildup with suspicion. Their attempts to hire discharged Danish and Dutch troops was seen as an attempt to build three large army corps and thus "to render themselves arbiters of all Imperial affairs." Interestingly, the plenipotentiaries reached the same conclusion independently at the same time, and for the same reason (the hiring of Dutch troops). "To this extent they judge it important to be strong in Germany at the time of the treaty," they wrote to Brienne, "and we believe that they do it no less to make themselves considerable to their allies and to have authority in the negotiations, than to make themselves feared by their enemies." But the French were already acting in the same fashion, making their army as strong as possible, "it not being at all less necessary, perhaps, to render ourselves powerful in that country in order to be considerable to our friends, than to do ill to our enemies."[154]

Complaints of Swedish military inactivity, which flowed steadily from Mazarin's pen in October, transformed into fears that Sweden had struck a secret deal with the emperor and was deliberately leaving the *Armée d'Allemagne* in the lurch. Rumors were current, and at least credible, the court noted, for how else could the emperor have sent such a large reinforcement at a time when his own estates were threatened? In late October, the court tended to reject the reports, and the plenipotentiaries concurred, noting that the siege of Brünn had reduced the Swedes to such a point that they could not pursue an effective offensive anyway. But at the end of November, Mazarin did give credence to new rumors that Rosenhane, the Swedish resident in Münster, had approached Peñaranda (the chief Spanish negotiator), complained of French infidelities (most notably the secret negotiations with Bavaria), and suggested that the emperor approach Sweden for separate talks. Since it seemed unlikely that a subordinate such as Rosenhane would undertake something of this sort on his own initiative "if he has even a little common sense," Mazarin speculated that a court faction contrary to Axel Oxenstierna had sent orders to Salvius, who had conveyed them to Rosenhane. But Mazarin also admitted that he did not know on whom Rosenhane "depended," and was generally ignorant of Swedish court politics. Therefore, he gave the plenipotentiaries broad orders to handle the affair as they best saw fit. In any case, he was taking the threat very seriously; if the plenipotentiaries could not achieve anything in Münster to prevent Swedish defection, they were to send someone "to the very source"—Stockholm—to deal with it.[155] In fact, the source was not Swedish at all but Spanish, since it had been Saavedra who had approached Oxenstierna. Oxenstierna had, in turn, asked Rosenhane to procure a copy of Saavedra's new book, *Idea de un principe politico-christiano,* in preparation for talking to Saavedra during a trip to Münster. Saavedra had then continued this contact by visiting Rosenhane again in November, thus sparking the rumors.[156]

Despite all of the negative developments, however, Mazarin remained optimistic. If his allies were a source of concern, at least they remained faithful. The misgivings about Sweden had been at least partially offset by the marriage alliance between Wladislaw IV of Poland and Marie de Gonzague-Nevers on 5 November, which helped assure Poland's continued neutrality vis-à-vis their Vasa cousins to the north.[157] Furthermore, France appeared to be on the verge of gaining a new *de facto* ally in the Turks, since it was expected that their war against Venice would soon widen to include Spain or Austria. True, the letters from court spoke of how France wanted peace all the more so that she could turn her arms against the enemy of Christendom. However, Servien remarked on several occasions the advantages that accrued to France from the Turkish threat, and even noted that "it would be extremely perilous to let an agreement be made [with the Ottomans] before ours is completed." Mazarin certainly showed no concrete signs of being more accommodating in light of the Turks, as he said he would, except for his gracious offer to Spain that they might use fighting the heathens as an excuse if they wished to save face in giving in to French demands.[158]

And, finally, the German campaign ended with a French coup: Turenne turned his army northward and captured Trier. Mazarin had been considering an attack on Trier earlier in the year, before Enghien had to be sent to stabilize the Bavarian front. Then, on 12 April, the emperor had suddenly released the Elector, Philipp Christoph von Sötern, held prisoner since 1635. Coming right after the French had removed their demand for his immediate liberation, it was a surprising move. In essence, however, Sötern had signed a treaty giving the emperor everything he wanted; this included recognition of the Peace of Prague, and promising to help win Philippsburg back from the French. The French were understandably suspicious of the Elector, who had originally been imprisoned because of his protection treaty with France. Could he be trusted now that he had committed to a new agreement with the emperor?[159]

As it became increasingly clear that Turenne would probably not be able to get quarters east of the Rhine, the idea of capturing Trier came to the fore again. It was problematic, since the Elector claimed neutrality, and the French did not want to antagonize an ally, even if they were as yet uncertain of his loyalty. Sötern, however, wanted the Spanish garrison out of his capital, and cleverly worked to arrange this with the French. First, he invited Turenne to liberate Trier, arguing that the garrison was so small that it would easily capitulate. Then he convinced the commander of the Spanish garrison that he would not permit a French garrison to remain in the town if it were handed over, and tried to show that the siege would inevitably be successful anyway. Thus, when Turenne arrived with only a portion of his army on 18 November, the Spanish commander withdrew without a fight. Sötern then signed a treaty with the French that left no French troops in the garrison, but which promised him aid in the case of attack. Moreover, in a secret article, France was granted free access over the important Moselle bridge in the city, while this was denied to the Spanish. Sötern had managed to free Trier without the ravages of a siege, and at the same time to preserve at least some appearance of neutrality. The French, on the other hand, had gained a strategically located area that isolated Spanish-held Luxembourg without having had to fight for it. It was a useful arrangement for both parties, even if the French were prevented from quartering on his territory, which they had desperately wanted.[160]

Thus, the French position at the end of 1645 was immeasurably stronger than it had been just two years earlier, in the aftermath of Tuttlingen. This came just as the negotiations were reaching what Servien described as their "crisis." The arrival of Trauttmansdorff at Münster on 29 November signalled a new stage, since, as one of the emperor's closest advisors, it was clear that he had full power to make peace.[161] Moreover, the emperor had delivered his response to the French proposition on 25 September. One opposition delegate described it as "the Peace of Prague well illuminated and gilded," noting wryly that "the Imperials expressly chose a dry, serene time to bring it out, for fear that the colors would be spoiled."[162] It made extensive concessions to the Imperial estates, but categorically rejected satisfaction for France and Sweden.[163] It was now again the turn of the two crowns, and France would soon have to present its third proposition specifying what territory it was demanding; for this purpose, the court issued a set of supplemental instructions at the end of November.[164]

The supplementary instructions began by noting that the king expected a treaty to be achieved soon. The advent of Trauttmansdorff, the expected arrival of the Dutch, and the Spanish desperation for peace (as viewed from Paris) demonstrated that an agreement could not be long in coming. The king also wanted peace. Besides his concern for his subjects, fear of a Huguenot rebellion, and desire to turn against the Turks, the memo also mentioned that "the more the prosperity of this crown increases, the more it excites envy even among its friends, and jealousy and fear among those who are indifferent." It was therefore desirable to make peace before they took some resolution prejudicial to France. Moreover, the plenipotentiaries were encouraged to conclude an agreement promptly if possible, so as "to spare a part of the excessive expenditures that we are already making for the preparations of the next campaign"; the money saved could be "converted to the relief of the people."

The instructions noted from the outset that the king would much prefer a general peace with all his opponents, to such an extent that he granted the plenipotentiaries the right to give in on any point if necessary to arrive at one. However, recognizing that this might not be feasible, the bulk of the letter was devoted to possible solutions other than a general peace. The most desirable of these would be to conclude a peace with the emperor and either a truce with Spain, or a truce with Spain in Catalonia and Portugal and a peace on the other fronts. Such an arrangement would give France solid gains in the Empire, while the court felt that France could use its allies to keep the emperor from aiding Spain. A second solution would be to conclude a long truce with Spain and a short, six-month armistice with the emperor, during which time the Imperial peace would be negotiated. Third, and finally, they would accept a general truce, provided it was for at least ten years.

French territorial demands in the Empire were explicitly stated as Philippsburg, Breisach, and Upper and Lower Alsace in the form suggested by the plenipotentiaries in their June memorandum. In short, these demands had not altered over the course of the campaign, in spite of the French victory at Alerheim and the imminent capture of Trier. The instructions noted that the emperor would doubtless consent to French demands. In the first place, the Bavarians did not find them "exorbitant" when they were informed of them. In the second place, the emperor knew about the demands, via the Bavarians, before he sent Trauttmansdorff, and he would not likely have sent his advisor without orders to conclude. This was very astute, and entirely accurate.[165]

It is clear from these supplementary instructions that Mazarin was very confident of success, and expected a rapid settlement. A considerable portion of the royal memorandum was devoted to explaining why the French were certain that Spain had determined to make peace "at any price" if they could not separate France from her allies. Among the reasons were that France had already secured its finances for the upcoming military campaign, while Spain was having difficulty doing the same; similarly, "France will easily have all the soldiers that she needs, and it is practically impossible for Spain to recover hers, especially infantry." The memo also recounts the defeat of the Spanish army in Catalonia, the progress of the French in Milan, and says of Flanders that it "is in such a state that it will be practically a miracle in the upcoming campaign if we do not chase the Spanish from it."

In spite of the fact that Mazarin knew the Spanish were resting their hopes on detaching France's allies, however, he reversed his policy from late September and declared that France would be willing to accept the Low Countries as a dowry from Spain in making a marriage alliance part of the treaty of peace. The memo even noted that "as soon as the Spanish see that we have even consented to listen to the proposal, they will be impatient to inform the Dutch if they believe that they can make them jealous and divide us by this means." Nevertheless, the court judged that they could counter such a move adequately by notifying the Dutch of the proposal and discussing it with them beforehand.

French success had, it seemed, gone to Mazarin's head. The cautious statesman of the beginning of the year, who warned repeatedly of the dangers even of a marriage alliance by itself, had become convinced that France was on the verge of victory. He was less willing to accept a truce, and more willing to discuss the acquisition of the Spanish Low Countries. This came at a time when France was less certain than ever of the loyalty of its allies, particularly the two most important ones: the Dutch Republic and Sweden. Whereas at the start of the year, a break with the Swedes was unthinkable, by the end of the year both Mazarin and Servien remarked that France could continue the war without them.[166] This was by no means their preference, but it demonstrates just how far French thinking had changed over the course of the year. While his negotiating stance regarding the Empire had changed minimally if at all, Mazarin's evolving policy toward Spain would have a major effect on the German negotiations in the subsequent years.[167]

8
1646: Triumph and Continued War

ON JANUARY 7, THE FRENCH ISSUED THEIR THIRD PEACE PROPOSAL (hereafter referred to as Proposition III). At last yielding to Mazarin's insistence, the plenipotentiaries refused to submit a written document, giving their demands orally instead; these were then written down by the mediators and submitted to the Imperial delegates. France was to gain greater security, as well as satisfaction for the expenses of the war, through the following territorial acquisitions: Upper and Lower Alsace; the Sundgau; the Breisgau; Breisach; the Forest Towns; and the right to maintain a garrison in Philippsburg.[1] These demands extended considerably beyond those made in the supplementary instructions of November 1645. The excess was intended to be used as bargaining chips, although the French, as we shall see, were not above attempting to obtain them where they thought they saw an opening.

Nevertheless, it became clear in the weeks and months following the supplementary French instructions that Mazarin was more confident of obtaining Alsace and Breisach than were the plenipotentiaries.[2] It is thus not surprising that the plenipotentiaries seemed more ready to propose ways to accommodate the emperor's objections. D'Avaux, for example, was favorable to a marriage alliance between Louis XIV and the emperor's eldest daughter, noting that "this alliance, treated in its time, could serve to facilitate the retention, and to assure the possession, of Alsace and the fortresses on the Rhine." At first, Mazarin agreed. But in a subsequent letter, he noted a preference for a Spanish alliance; best of all, however, would be to wait until France could get other advantages, since French satisfaction in the Empire was already assured.[3]

In a memorandum from 16 December, Servien proposed offering the archdukes (the branch of the Habsburgs that ruled Alsace) an annual subsidy equal to the cash income from Alsace.[4] Since this ultimately became part of the treaty terms, in a modified form, it is interesting to trace its evolution in the ensuing months. Mazarin initially agreed to Servien's idea in principle, but felt that the emperor was in such a poor position that it would not be necessary. The official orders from court permitted granting a subsidy only as a last resort, after the archdukes "will have completely despaired of being able to obtain our entire demand." The payment could either be made completely within five or six years, or could be an annual subsidy. In either case, it would be beneficial if it were stipulated that the archdukes must use the money to buy other sovereign lands.[5] At the beginning of February, Brienne reemphasized that the payment was only to be made if unavoidable, and limited it to fifty thousand *écus*.[6]

To a man, however, the plenipotentiaries came out in favor of the indemnity. On 17 February, they wrote that it would "render much more plausible the design that we have to retain Alsace." They even declared that it would be better to pay it than not, since it would make the French title to Alsace more solid.[7] Then the indemnity fell to the background for a while, only to return in greater force in April, as the negotiations began to make substantial progress. Servien, looking ahead as usual, pointed out that paying an indemnity could serve as an excuse for revoking alienations that had been made in the Habsburg domains. Less than a week later, he again emphasized that it was better to pay compensation than not to pay it; just as it was good to stand firm on big issues, one should be accommodating in small ones. However, he preferred to pay an annual subsidy (the better to bind the archdukes to France), whereas the Habsburgs wanted a lump-sum payment.[8] Longueville added that "I do not believe, whatever one gives, that one could pay too much." The higher the indemnity, the less jealousy would remain on the opposing side; they could compensate for the extra payment by reducing the amount of the subsidy against the Turks. D'Avaux proposed that France could defend its reputation against claims that it had been forced to buy Alsace by countering that the archdukes had been forced to sell their domain.[9] These persistent arguments had their effect on Mazarin, who eventually agreed that it was a good idea to pay the indemnity.[10]

Two other compromises proposed by the plenipotentiaries were accepted by Mazarin. First, it was agreed that France would, if necessary, assume the debts that the archdukes had contracted for Alsace.[11] Second, the French ministers agreed that France should offer to provide support for the Habsburgs against the

Ottomans. Since the French felt that the Ottomans presented a serious danger to the Habsburgs, they considered assistance against this threat a good way to soothe the Habsburgs for their loss of Alsace. Moreover, such an offer was in keeping with Mazarin's rhetoric about desiring to fight the Turks. But he did not want to help the Habsburgs build up their own military forces, especially at a time when France would presumably be at peace and thus remain vulnerably unarmed. Instead of sending money, therefore, Mazarin wanted to send French troops against the Ottomans. The mediators were right, he admitted, that sending troops would be less efficient than sending cash. But, besides keeping France militarily prepared, sending troops also permitted France to provide an occupation for its soldiers after the end of the war. When the mediators finally asked whether France would provide money, the preference for sending men instead of money crystallized into a fixed rule.[12]

Part of the reason that the plenipotentiaries were more willing to compromise was that they were more exposed to the opposition of other delegates at the Congress to French demands: everyone, it seemed, was against them.[13] And while Servien, at least, felt that France was strong enough to hold Alsace and Breisach regardless of the opposition of the Imperial estates, all French ministers would certainly have preferred to get it with their consent.[14] This issue became particularly pertinent when foreign satisfaction was put up for a vote by the Imperial estates.

The basis of Trauttmansdorff's strategy at the conference was to unite with the estates by making compromises with the Protestants; then, once the Empire had solved its internal problems, to turn and put up a strong front against foreign satisfaction. However, France and Sweden were aware of this plan and forced him to put the question of foreign satisfaction to a vote of the estates before the *gravamina*, or religious complaints, were resolved (see below for d'Avaux's mission to Osnabrück). The result was, if not an overwhelming triumph for the two crowns, at least a victory. In the Princes' College, Bavarian support helped carry the day. The Electors' College voted against foreign satisfaction, but the significance of the vote was softened by the strong objections of Bavaria and Cologne to the majority opinion. It was clear that the emperor would have no choice but to give satisfaction to France and Sweden.[15]

Nevertheless, the plenipotentiaries were still careful not to offend the estates, who, if they had voted in favor of satisfaction, did so only in the interests of peace, and not because they were happy to see foreigners seizing territory in the Empire. One point of concern was the line of communication to Philippsburg, which excited jealousy among the nearby German states, especially the Protestants.[16] Strasbourg, a powerful Imperial city, was even more troublesome. She not only maintained a representative at the conference to keep an eye on French demands, but also complained about the French raising contributions on her territory, and sent a representative to Paris to complain. Although the court felt that it had a strong case, it was decided to withdraw from all disputed territory because of the plenipotentiaries' opinion "that it is necessary always to give a good impression of our moderation to our Alsatian neighbors."[17]

The French particularly desired to remain on good terms with their immediate neighbors in and around their conquests. Colmar, the strongest fortress in French-controlled Alsace, was a special concern. Upon the accession of Louis XIV, it had requested and been granted a renewal of its protection treaty, which guaranteed its rights. It is true that Servien reported to court in November 1645 that Johann Balthasar Schneider, Colmar's representative at the congress, told him that "it was indifferent to him whether his sovereign was called Louis or Ferdinand."[18] If Schneider said this, however, it was against the general tenor of his efforts at the conference. He was at first incredulous that the French would demand Colmar and other Alsatian territory after they had issued repeated affirmations that all of the occupied lands would be returned at the conclusion of peace. Once he realized that the French demands were real, he sought to limit their extent and to assure a continuation of the freedom that Colmar and the other immediate estates had enjoyed under the Empire. The French tried to soothe him on several occasions by claiming that they were only interested in rights held by the Habsburgs, and that under French government they would be equally free.[19] He was not convinced, however, and appealed to the other Imperial estates and to Sweden to intervene on their behalf. These attempts were not entirely useless (see below on the ambiguous wording of the treaty), but they fell far short of attaining his goal of a clear statement of Colmar's rights. "You see, therefore," wrote a Colmar magistrate to d'Erlach, "to what these promises of restitution that were made prodigiously to us ultimately come: to nothing but to separate us from the Empire, to despoil us of our liberties that it secures for us, to reduce us to the condition of subjects of another power, all in spite of the assurances of ministers and of treaties!"[20]

The confusing legal situation in Alsace made France's demands there all the more problematic. As Servien wrote at the end of January,

> We will need to be much better instructed on the true situation in Alsace by some intelligent person. Because, having to negotiate the King's satisfaction with the estates of the Empire, it is equally harmful to demand things that one cannot obtain as to omit those things that could be useful to us. There are many principalities in that territory that are immediate to the Empire, and we could not reasonably demand them without irritating the other German princes, although we have declared that we only want to put them under the protection of the King.[21]

Three conclusions may be drawn from this statement. First, the French ministers (for this sentiment was shared by the others in varying degrees) were highly concerned about German opinion. Second, they only intended to demand control over Habsburg territory. They wanted protection over the immediate estates, but seemed prepared to live without it if the Germans resisted. Third, they were by no means fully informed on the status of Alsace.

It is noteworthy that Servien asked for further instructions on Alsace only after the French had made their official territorial demands. Perhaps he had only just been made aware of the difficulties he faced by the response of German delegates; or perhaps it was only now that the negotiations began to enter into details that he felt a fuller knowledge was necessary. In either case, the plenipotentiaries' incomplete knowledge must be considered when evaluating their demands of 7 January 1646. As it happened, the court had already asked Vautorte, the intendant of the French Rhine territories, to gather more detailed information on Alsace, and Brienne wrote on 3 February that the intendant's secretary would arrive in a day or two with a description of the province. It was not, however, until 8 March that he announced the sending of information, including a map of the province with Habsburg rights delineated; even then he confessed that "for myself, I don't understand it."[22] The plenipotentiaries acknowledged receipt of the map at the end of March, but still awaited further information. In mid-April, on the same day that the Imperials made their official offer of Alsace, Brienne wrote that he was sending a new memorandum on Alsace since the previous one was full of errors.[23] The plenipotentiaries thus had a map by the end of March, but still had many gaps in their knowledge during the heart of the negotiations. Nor were the French alone in their ignorance; the mediators also made mistakes, and even those at the Imperial court in Vienna did not understand the situation fully. In truth, there seems to have been only one person who knew the actual legal situation in Alsace well: Isaac Volmar, the delegate who drafted the Imperial offer.[24]

While the plenipotentiaries worried about the fate of French demands, Mazarin seemed to know that they would be accepted. As early as 12 January, he wrote that he had certain news that the emperor would give in on Alsace. As the negotiations went on, he received further reports, and used his knowledge to apply pressure on Trauttmansdorff to make concessions that he was known to have the authority to make. Some of Mazarin's information came to him from a spy at the Imperial court; other information from the Bavarians. Not all of it turned out to be correct, but it all confirmed Mazarin's conviction that the emperor would be forced to give in, and thus led Mazarin to avoid making concessions.[25]

In spite of his belief that France would ultimately win its demands, Mazarin knew that the emperor would not give in easily. To counteract the enemy's stubbornness, Mazarin insisted on the utmost steadfastness in negotiating. As he put it, "it is indisputable that they will accommodate themselves little by little to what we desire in the measure that they become accustomed to seeing us demand it with firmness." The plenipotentiaries followed orders, claiming that they were speaking so firmly about Alsace that it shocked even the mediators.[26] Predictably, Mazarin attributed advances in the negotiations to France's resolute stance, and, in turn, interpreted these advances as justifications for further firmness.[27]

This tough stance, which was adopted in regard to Spain as well as to the emperor, was more extreme than simple unwillingness to compromise, because it involved projecting the image that France was indifferent to peace. As Servien put it, nothing was more advantageous for France than the opinion of the enemy that they were not at all serious about making peace. And Longueville noted on another occasion that France's open desire for peace was taken by Spain as a sign of weakness.[28] France may well have been militarily ascendent, but the weakness of a regency was known to all, even if it appeared stable at the moment. Not only was Spain basing its hopes on dissension within France, but many of France's own ministers were convinced that a rebellion was a serious possibility, if not a certainty: D'Avaux expected a revolt after the war, while Longueville predicted one would break out in two or three years.[29]

Projecting indifference to peace was not easy, even though the plenipotentiaries agreed with Mazarin and Brienne that it was important.[30] France was caught between the need to appease public opinion, both at home and in Germany, by emphasizing its desire for peace, as it did in all of its public proclamations; and the need to wring satisfaction from the emperor by projecting an indifference to peace, as it did in private talks with the enemy. Mazarin was not blind to this contradiction, and noted that some attacked him for the continuation of the war and indifference to the suffering of the people. He defended himself by pointing out that he wanted peace, but only with glory. As he wrote to the plenipotentiaries at the end of 1645,

> For myself, although there is nothing in this world that I wish more ardently than to see this crown established in peace with glory and advantage in Christianity, nevertheless, so as not to prejudice affairs and the advancement of your negotiations, I avoid as much as possible to reveal myself to the world, and I submit myself sooner to be blamed by those who want to see me preach endlessly in the streets that France wants to do anything to have peace, hoping that events will soon show, by the conclusion of the peace, what intention I have had in my conduct.[31]

In order to present a united front, Mazarin insisted that others in the council stop announcing France's need for peace (see chapter 2).

Mere firmness, Mazarin recognized, would be hollow without military pressure. As the court wrote to the plenipotentiaries in December 1645,

> [You] can rest assured that we are doing everything necessary in order to have greater forces next year on all fronts than we have had up until now, without regard to any peace negotiation, it being certain that the strongest reason that we can give to our enemies to lead them to a fair accommodation . . . is to make them realize that we are in such a state that we cannot fail to make more progress if the war continues.

The letter continued that it was the policy of the mediators to try to make both sides fear the military threat of the other. Yet the enemy was in better shape last year, and nothing had come of it. Instead of adopting the enemy's method, which was to trumpet their military preparations, the court suggested that the plenipotentiaries would "give the enemy more to think about in not saying a word, and in holding firm in demanding great advantages for the conclusion of the peace."[32] It is difficult to tell if Mazarin really believed that de-emphasizing French military preparations would be more effective, or whether he was more concerned of the jealousy that French arms were causing; certainly he was aware that many felt France was becoming too strong.[33]

In either case, Mazarin clearly believed that little progress would be made until the campaign got underway. Although he did not criticize the Habsburgs for stalling while the armies were still in winter quarters, he did seek to push French forces into the field as quickly as possible. This applied equally to Spain, where he had already sent Harcourt in March, as to the Empire, where Turenne began early preparations. "Nothing," he wrote to Longueville, "is so important for the advancement of the peace as putting Marshal Turenne's army in a state to act."[34] As the talks progressed, Mazarin eschewed the idea of slowing down military preparations, instead arguing that they should be redoubled; only this threat would keep the enemy from delaying the talks. The military card held even more value because the emperor had not, Mazarin believed, made adequate preparations for the campaign; "one single accident, of the kind that occurs every day in military affairs, is capable of ruining his grandeur forever and putting him in a state from which he will not be able to recover."[35]

French military pressure was not aimed directly at the emperor, however, but at Bavaria. The experience of the truce negotiations in 1645 convinced the plenipotentiaries more than ever that nothing was to be hoped for from Bavaria unless Maximilian were facing a direct military threat. They therefore led the way in insisting that Turenne's army cross the Rhine as soon as possible; but they were preaching to the choir, because Mazarin had already concluded that "it will always be useless to speak of a separate treaty with [Maximilian] while our army is west of the Rhine and there is hope that he can get out of his situation with more reputation and certainty by the means of a general peace in the Empire." The plenipotentiaries' sentiments not only fell on sympathetic ears at court, but also proved to be accurate in practice.[36]

In spite of French disillusionment with Bavaria after the 1645 truce talks, the two sides continued informal discussions over mutual assistance in the negotiations, France supporting Bavarian desire for the Electorate, and Bavaria supporting French satisfaction in Alsace. Both Mazarin and Brienne seem to have remained convinced that it was in Maximilian's interests to see France secure a passage into the Empire in order to assist him in case of attack by either Spain or the emperor. Their persistence is striking in light of the repeated insistence of the plenipotentiaries, dating back to the very beginning of the negotiations in 1644, that this simply was not the case. Maximilian needed France, it was true, but he had no desire to see her established in the Empire. In March, the Bavarian plenipotentiaries even stated flatly that "what causes the most trouble and jealousy is Alsace, which puts France in a position to trouble and invade the Empire anytime she wishes," and that "if we wanted to take the king's satisfaction in some other place, we would perhaps not encounter such difficulty."[37] It may have been a growing realization that Bavaria was not as happy to see France established in the Empire as Mazarin had thought that led him to drop the idea of transferring some Imperial territory in southwestern Germany, such as the Breisgau and the Forest Towns, to Bavaria.[38]

If Maximilian was not such a natural French ally as the court had supposed, the French could still attempt to exploit his dislike of Spain. The Bavarians had long since agreed that they would not permit the war in the Empire to be continued just because Spain had not made peace; and, to a certain extent, some diplomatic gains could be made out of their distrust of the emperor. For example, when the emperor proposed having the Electorate alternate between Bavaria and the Palatinate, the French gleefully reported the news to Haslang and Krebs, who were very disturbed by it.[39] But such a tack could only take them so far, because, as Servien recognized, Maximilian was firmly attached to the emperor; he would separate from the alliance only unwillingly, and would never permit Bavaria to get involved in the war against Ferdinand.[40] The French were on far sounder ground when they emphasized more realistic common interests with Bavaria, most notably the Electorate. As Longueville wrote, "they can be well assured that if our interests lag behind, theirs will fare even worse."[41]

This strategy worked exactly as the French had hoped. While Maximilian had rejected a separate treaty with France, he realized that the war could not be won, and therefore supported French satisfaction as the only means of making peace. At the same time, he hoped to win his own demands—the Upper Palatinate and the Electorate—by cooperation with France.[42] In December, he even proposed a written treaty to this effect. True, Mazarin rejected it out of concern for how French allies (especially Sweden) would react; and, for the same reason, the court also continued to refuse an open French declaration in support of Bavaria for the Electorate.[43] Nevertheless, Bavarian-French cooperation continued and intensified at the beginning of 1646. In fact, Bavaria's ceaseless, open support for French satisfaction made it difficult for the plenipotentiaries to delay a public statement in support of Bavarian demands. The plenipotentiaries did, however, assure Haslang and Krebs that French and Bavarian satisfaction were inseparable war aims.[44]

Maximilian eventually grew impatient with the emperor's stalling on the issue of French satisfaction. In mid-February, he sent one of his advisors to Linz to press the emperor, under the threat of separate Bavarian talks with France, to begin negotiating in earnest. The emperor took the threat seriously: Trauttmansdorff's orders, which were sent on 2 March and arrived on 15 March, were to make peace before the start of the campaign, by surrendering Alsace if necessary. It was thought by Maximilian, and hence by the emperor, that the French would give in on the other demands (Breisach, Philippsburg, etc.) if they received Alsace.[45]

But Ferdinand's orders met with resistance in Münster, where Trauttmansdorff still hoped to find a way around surrendering Alsace. He was supported in this by the Spanish, who strongly opposed the cession of Alsace because it would formally cut the Spanish Road, already blocked *de facto* since the French occupation of Alsace in 1634. Alsace was of such importance to the Spanish military situation that they had negotiated for it in the Oñate treaty of 1617, the terms of which were never carried out.[46] Now they threw their weight against the French demands, urging Trauttmansdorff to stall. On 21 March, they proposed, in the name of the whole Habsburg house, Pinerolo and a few towns in the Low Countries as French satisfaction. The Spanish hoped that, by offering France compensation elsewhere, they could avoid the surrender of Alsace. This view was not without foundation; as Mazarin had written to the plenipotentiaries in December, "It is good in finishing this war to gain advantages on all sides. But if it is necessary to give in somewhere, my opinion is that it should be done sooner in the Empire than in Spain." But Mazarin was now too assured of Alsace to want to give in anywhere; and, moreover, he wished to keep the Imperial and Spanish negotiations separate, so as to increase pressure on both. The Spanish offer was therefore emphatically rejected.[47]

Though the attempt at a common Habsburg negotiating position had therefore failed, Peñaranda, the leading Spanish plenipotentiary, continued urge Trauttmansdorff to stall on Alsace. The Spanish had one trump card left: separate negotiations with the Netherlands. It was no secret that Spain had been attempting to lure the Dutch into a separate peace since the beginning of the conference. But while the Mazarin had been extremely concerned about the possibility of Dutch desertion in 1644, by the end of 1645 he had become confident that it was not very likely.[48] He therefore finally ordered the plenipotentiaries to lend a favorable ear to the proposal of a marriage alliance with Spain, coupled with an exchange of Catalonia for the Low Countries, that he had been resisting up until that point.

The idea of the exchange, which would undoubtedly have been a very great gain for France, caught Mazarin's interest, and he pursued it with a controlled passion. "May it please God that this venture succeed," he wrote to the plenipotentiaries on 13 January. Ignoring the warnings of his plenipotentiaries, who argued that the project shocked not only the Dutch, but the English, Portuguese, and Catalans as well, Mazarin pushed them to enter into substantial discussion of the matter with Contarini at the first opportunity. He felt that, as long as it was proposed by the mediator, there was little danger.[49]

The Dutch had arrived in Münster on 11 January 1646, and were immediately visited by the Spanish representatives, who made no difficulty over granting them the titles they desired. At first, their talks with Spain advanced slowly; they claimed to find a fault in Spanish powers, and suspended negotiations.[50] Meanwhile, the mediator Contarini met with Longueville and d'Avaux at the end of January and brought up the possibility of a marriage alliance. The French plenipotentiaries were afraid to say too much—they were later berated by Mazarin for not saying enough—but Contarini did gather that it would be permissible for him to mention the idea to the Spanish. It was at this time that Peñaranda received orders from Philip IV to propose a marriage alliance with France—that is, the same proposal that the French were interested in accepting. But Peñaranda opposed the move, and therefore greeted Contarini's overture coolly; he said that he would need a formal offer, and would have to write to court for further instructions. Already he hoped that the marriage alliance might be used against France in the Dutch negotiations.

Superimposed on this negotiation was a Spanish offer, officially made to Longueville by Chigi and Contarini on 20 February, to have the French queen, Anne, mediate an end to the Franco-Spanish conflict. Things came to a head when the Dutch plenipotentiaries Pauw and Knuyt left Münster on 23 February and arrived in The Hague on the 26th, the same day that another French envoy, d'Estrades, was sounding out the Stadtholder Frederik Hendrik on whether he would approve the marriage alliance. All three points—the mediators' proposal of a marriage alliance and territorial exchange, the French discussion with Frederik Hendrik on the same matter, and the Spanish offer to let Anne mediate their war with France—were brought before the Estates General of the United Provinces on 27 February. An immediate uproar against France ensued. Speeches were made, pamphlets were printed, and pro-Spanish sentiment in the Dutch Republic soared.[51]

Probably the most damaging revelation was France's secret negotiations with Frederik Hendrik, which seemed to challenge the supremacy of the Estates General, as well as advancing a territorial change that the Dutch flatly opposed. For, if the Dutch were French allies of long standing, they had no desire to replace a weak Spanish state on their southern border with a strong French one. As the contemporary dictum had it, "Gallus amicus sed non vicinus" (France, our friend but not our neighbor). But even the Spanish offer to let Anne mediate an end to their war with France made the Dutch suspect a plot to hand over the Spanish Low Countries to France, even if the French foresaw the consequences and turned down the offer on the grounds that it was a simple courtesy.[52] Mazarin realized that the Spanish were attempting to manoeuvre the Dutch into a separate peace by letting it be known that they were close to an agreement with France, but were willing to listen to Dutch proposals; yet he seemed powerless to overcome it.[53]

While recognizing that the exchange was no longer likely, the court still clung to some hope of it.[54] But the dramatic deterioration in the French diplomatic position carried with it potential military consequences: if the Dutch decided to make a truce with Spain, France would be forced to carry the burden of the war in the Low Countries alone. And a truce was a real possibility: not only were the Dutch outraged over the revelations of 27 February, but they were also inherently concerned about growing French strength, and had no desire to contribute to it through the continuation of the war. Mazarin moved to repair the damage by a new treaty that offered the Dutch an additional subsidy of one hundred thousand *écus*. By the beginning of April, this agreement had been signed, but concerns that the Dutch would not participate in the upcoming campaign—at least, not in earnest—remained.[55]

The approach of the campaigning season therefore lent new urgency to the negotiations. Bavaria, and consequently the emperor, hoped to conclude peace in time to avoid another invasion; but France also had reason to want at least a truce in the Empire. The idea of a truce with Bavaria was originally proposed in by February Servien. He noted that the major argument against a truce had been that Bavaria would no longer continue to support French satisfaction once military pressure against the duchy was removed. But Bavaria was doing everything that France could hope for at the beginning of 1646, and the French position was so good that a further campaign could only be harmful. It was not just that France did not want to ruin Bavaria; French ministers, from Mazarin and Brienne down to the plenipotentiaries, were united in agreeing that all possible military results would be harmful to the negotiations. As Servien outlined it,

> If Bavaria is defeated, we will lose a great deal. If the Imperials are defeated, the Swedes will become insufferable. If the Swedish army is ruined, it will be even worse: the emperor will speak more highly, and Bavaria will no longer be as favorable toward us.[56]

Servien managed to convince the other plenipotentiaries of this, and Mazarin took up his ideas almost word for word in his response on 16 February.[57]

The French believed, somewhat irrationally, that a single battle could change the entire face of the negotiations. The mutability of affairs was used equally as an argument for why the Habsburgs should make peace before the upcoming campaign (in order to prevent a great disaster) as for why the French should also want peace (in order to prevent a reversal of fortune).[58] Though the French, by this reasoning, potentially stood to make great gains, the unanimous sentiment was that it was not worth the risk. Servien wrote to Lionne on 19 April that

> I beseech you to represent to His Eminence how necessary it is to risk nothing on any front this year. We are at the point of gathering the fruits of all our labors, provided only that we are patient and firm. If our generals do not all carry out these orders exactly . . . , we run the risk of losing everything in an instant.[59]

A similar message had already been sent by Longueville on 6 April. Mazarin not only agreed in principle, but said that he had already come to the same conclusion, and had sent orders to Harcourt, Turenne, and the commanders in the Low Countries to that effect.[60] (Ironically, this extreme caution came at a time when the court was expressing the utmost confidence in French military preparations. The *Armée d'Allemagne* was considered in its best shape ever, and Brienne even spoke of being in a position to cross the Danube.[61])

Because of concern over a potentially harmful military reversal, therefore, the court was willing to listen to Bavarian requests for a truce. While Mazarin remained firm about wanting French satisfaction resolved before a truce was made, he favored making a truce after the resolution of satisfaction while the remaining treaty issues were adjusted. It is clear that he did not anticipate the need for a long truce, since he expected the Imperial treaty, at least, to be settled before the upcoming campaign.[62]

But while France was anxious for a truce, Sweden preferred to continue the conflict. The queen and her ministers had two concerns. First, they felt that a pause in fighting would put them out of their strong military situation and give the emperor a chance to recover. Second, and more important, they saw an armistice as a serious danger to Sweden because of her soldiers, who demanded considerable compensation before they would disband. As long as the war continued, they would continue to fight, but a pause in the struggle could result in discontent and possibly mutiny, damaging Sweden's position in the negotiations. Therefore, Christina urged her plenipotentiaries "to carry on with the negotiations, no less than the general with arms at his side, until God grants a good end to the war." She also called upon France to send Turenne across the Rhine as soon as possible to provide a diversion in favor of the Swedish army, which continued to campaign throughout the winter.[63]

This was just one difficulty in the Franco-Swedish alliance. Relations between the two crowns, which had degenerated rapidly at the end of 1645, continued to go downhill in the first weeks of 1646. The French feared two different possibilities: first, that Sweden would abandon the alliance and leave them to fight the emperor alone; and second, that Sweden would unite more closely with the Protestants and make exorbitant demands against the Catholics in the Empire, possibly with the intention of continuing the war without France. French fears of being abandoned were serious enough that they considered contingency plans for continuing the war without Sweden: Longueville wrote that France could successfully retain her conquests even if abandoned by her allies; Servien even suggested that, in case of extreme need, the French could ally with Bavaria and the emperor against Sweden.[64] Their concern was exacerbated by the refusal of the Swedes to let the French resident in Osnabrück, Jean de La Barde, sit in their meetings with the Imperials. This contravened a specific provision of the Franco-Swedish treaty of alliance, and led the French plenipotentiaries to suspect that the Swedes were carrying on negotiations for a separate peace.[65]

But the French were perhaps even more worried about the possibility of Sweden carrying on a religious war in close alliance with the Protestants—a concern so real that Servien went so far as to speak of using the Spanish to counterbalance the Swedish and Protestant bloc in the Empire if the latter became too haughty in their demands. Three issues caused apprehension on the part of France. The court and Servien both complained about the Swedes' slowness in negotiating, which seemed incompatible with a genuine desire for peace.[66] At the same time, the Swedes protested that French demands were too high—complaints forcefully denounced by the French.[67] Most troubling of all was the question of the order of the negotiations. In broadest terms, the two issues to be resolved were satisfaction for France and Sweden, and the *gravamina* of the estates against the emperor and each other (in part religious in nature, in part political). France felt strongly that their satisfaction should be resolved first, for fear that, if the *gravamina* were dealt with first, the German estates would no longer need France and Sweden, and hence would cease to support their satisfaction. And this was precisely Trauttmansdorff's strategy. Sweden, however, supported the Protestants in their desire to have the *gravamina* resolved first, leaving France puzzled over whether Sweden simply did not want peace, or perhaps whether she had already reached a secret agreement with the emperor on her satisfaction.[68]

For their part, the Swedes had no intention of abandoning the French alliance, and certainly not of leading a Protestant crusade, although their ministers were shrewd enough to recognize the value of courting Protestant support. Instead, the Swedes were in a constant state of vexation over real or imagined French breaches of faith, such as Turenne's long delay in opening the campaign, supposed secret truce negotiations with Bavaria, and the possibility of a French-Imperial accord that excluded Sweden.[69] The Swedish plenipotentiaries voiced their concerns about specific French acts of disloyalty, and the chancellor, Axel Oxenstierna, always seemed to find space in his brief letters to his son for at least one sentence to complain about the general faithlessness of France.[70] The alliance of the "two crowns" therefore stumbled forward, both sides mistrusting the other, but both too afraid of being abandoned to risk offending its untrusted ally.

One of the most important strains on the alliance in the early months of 1646 was a treaty of friendship signed by France and Denmark on 5 November 1645.[71] France had taken advantage of her mediation of the peace between Denmark and Sweden to negotiate a pact with Christian IV by which France gained the same favorable toll rates as the Netherlands, and both states pledged not to aid the other's enemies. Sweden regarded this agreement with enormous suspicion, since Denmark was her archenemy and France an essential ally. To calm Swedish fears, Mazarin had sent La Thuillerie on a special mission to Stockholm in December 1645, and had sent Pierre Chanut to Stockholm at the same to serve as resident ambassador.[72]

Unbeknownst to the court, however, the French plenipotentiaries also sent a representative, St. Romain, to Stockholm, in part to address specific French complaints, and in part to find out whether the Swedish plenipotentiaries were acting in response to orders or on their own initiative. The court disapproved of the mission, judging it unlikely that St. Romain could achieve any more than Chanut, and fearing that the Swedes would get the impression that they were in control of the negotiations, with so many embassies being sent by France.[73] In fact, St. Romain arrived in March had only a brief discussion with Axel Oxenstierna before being brushed off on the excuse that the chancellor was ill. It was only in April that he was finally able to have a long discussion with Christina. By that time, however, the issue had long since been handled by Chanut, who discussed a catalogue of French grievances with Oxenstierna. On the issue of the exclusion of de La Barde from Swedish meetings, Oxenstierna responded that the Swedes were only reacting to a similar affront to the Swedish resident in Münster, Rosenhane. Although Rosenhane participated in French meetings in their own quarters and at those of the Imperial delegates, the papal mediator Chigi excluded the Swede from meetings at his residence. So long as the French accepted this state of affairs, the Swedish representatives would retaliate in kind, excluding de La Barde from their meetings.[74] Furthermore, he denied categorically that Sweden had called French demands excessive; to the contrary, he argued that

France had the right to demand whatever it wanted, but had no right to question Swedish demands, which the French had been trying to moderate.[75]

The plenipotentiaries had more success with a second mission, that of d'Avaux to Osnabrück in mid-February. Although d'Avaux became convinced, in the course of his talks with the Swedes, that they did not want peace, he did manage to convince them and the Protestant estates that the *gravamina* should be resolved at the same time as, and not before, the crowns' satisfaction. Oxenstierna also outlined his three-step plan for a successful peace: continued firm alliance between France and Sweden; continuation of the war until the treaty was signed; and uniformity in the negotiating stances of the two crowns.[76] By this time, Mazarin had already received assurance from La Thuillerie that the Swedes were not going to separate from France; and at the end of March, the plenipotentiaries saw a definite improvement in the attitude of the Swedes. Indeed, Christina told St. Romain shortly thereafter that she had rebuked Johann Oxenstierna for his disagreeable behavior.[77]

At the same time that he was reassuring his plenipotentiaries of Swedish sincerity, however, Mazarin wrote that "we must constantly keep our eyes open." For if Franco-Swedish relations were warming, Mazarin still feared that Trauttmansdorff's great offers to Sweden would prove too tempting to resist. Interestingly, Mazarin did not criticize the Imperials for trying to separate France from her allies, but he did take steps to prevent the design from succeeding.[78]

The most important step in this direction was to keep the two crowns' negotiations at the same pace. Both powers feared the consequences of the other achieving its satisfaction first. At the extreme, there was the possibility of being abandoned altogether. Failing that, however, the power more advanced in its negotiations might still pressure the other to conclude without achieving its full demands, or might advance new demands that were undesirable for its ally. Sweden seemed most concerned that France would make peace with Spain and shift all its weight against the Empire, thus gaining an unacceptable preeminence. But it was France that felt it was falling behind in the Imperial negotiations, especially by the beginning of April. In a discussion with Salvius over the status of Swedish satisfaction, Longueville reversed French policy and did not try to press the Swedes to lower their demands, apprehensive that they would achieve them too quickly if they did.[79]

8: 1646: TRIUMPH AND CONTINUED WAR

A combination of factors therefore led France to want a settlement: fear of Sweden reaching a settlement first; fear of Dutch abandonment, and, more immediately, of Dutch nonparticipation in the upcoming campaign; desire to avoid another campaign, which would be risky and could only detract from the strong French position; and desire to aid Charles I in England.[80] If peace could not be made, Mazarin preferred at least to achieve an armistice, which would avoid many possible dangers. Something clearly had to be done soon, for Swedish calls for a link-up with Turenne were increasing in urgency. Yet Sweden's firm policy against a general armistice meant that the only possibility was a separate truce with Bavaria. Maximilian, on the other hand, preferred a general armistice; but above all, he wanted to avoid another campaign—which, if it did not seem to offer France any advantages, promised to be even worse for Bavaria. Since all talk of a general armistice foundered on Swedish resistance, Maximilian finally began, in mid-March, to entertain talks on a separate truce proposed by Servien.[81] At the same time, he stepped up pressure on the Imperials to make concessions to France.

Trauttmansdorff had returned from Osnabrück on 26 February, unable to make a separate peace with Sweden. After the estates voted to give the two crowns satisfaction, Trauttmansdorff approved the 21 March Spanish offer of Pinerolo and some towns in the Low Countries that was made in the name of the Habsburg house (and which was rejected out of hand by the French). Since Peñaranda was unwilling to make further offers, Trauttmansdorff had little choice but to make a substantial offer of his own. By his instructions, he was to offer first part of Alsace, then the whole province. Accordingly, on 28 March he submitted to the mediators a document drawn up by Volmar in which the French would receive Habsburg rights in Lower Alsace: protection over the Lower Alsatian part of the Landvogtei Haguenau and other scattered titles. He anticipated that this minimal offer would be rejected, but he expected at least to buy some time while the French considered it; meanwhile, he hoped that progress in the Spanish-Dutch talks would weaken the French bargaining position. But he was disillusioned on both points. The Spanish-Dutch talks continued to stall, while the French rejected the offer of Habsburg rights in Lower Alsace out of hand.[82] Trauttmansdorff made one last attempt to stall on 4 April, when, in discussions with Longueville, the Frenchman proposed taking Strasbourg along with Upper and Lower Alsace. Longueville agreed to request further orders from court on this matter, but the Bavarians were not so patient. Their plenipotentiaries, acting under orders from Maximilian, issued Trauttmansdorff an ultimatum on 7 April: either he would offer the French Alsace within eight days, or Bavaria would begin making arrangements for a separate truce. Trauttmansdorff, whose orders were already to surrender Alsace before the upcoming campaign, caved in: on 14 April, the Imperials officially offered France Alsace.[83]

But this offer, too, was rejected by the French, who insisted on Breisach as well as Alsace. The French were not going to stand firm on their entire Proposition III demand, but neither were they going to accept Alsace without Breisach. As Longueville rebuked Contarini, who had told him that France would never get the Rhine fortress, "France will not take for its satisfaction things that could be taken from her in four days."[84] The supplementary French instructions from November 1645, which went back to the memorandum from Servien and d'Avaux the previous June, remained the basis for France's negotiating position. There had been very little discussion of French demands since that time, except for the proposing of potential areas of compromise (such as the indemnity to the archdukes; see above). Mazarin had given the plenipotentiaries the authority to give in on part of Alsace if they deemed it necessary; and, on 3 March, Servien wrote an extraordinary letter in which he said that the plenipotentiaries had agreed that there was "some appearance" that France could retain Upper Alsace (only), provided that they made the compromises that they had discussed with Mazarin.[85]

But when it came to the actual negotiations in the crucial period from 28 March (the Imperial offer of the Landvogtei Haguenau) to 14 April (the Imperial offer of all of Alsace), the plenipotentiaries—whatever their concerns—remained true to Mazarin's policy of firmness. Indeed, Longueville wrote on 7 April that Contarini had upbraided him "against our firmness and our manner of proceeding in always saying no, never proposing anything, and never giving in on anything."[86] The French were insistent on Upper and Lower Alsace and Breisach, precisely as their orders instructed them; but on the other areas—Philippsburg, the Sundgau, the Breisgau, and the Forest Towns—there was some disagreement. Philippsburg, the most important, will be discussed below. D'Avaux made a firm stand in favor of keeping the Sundgau, a Habsburg-controlled territory in Upper Alsace whose ambiguous relationship to the rest of Upper Alsace is evident in d'Avaux's dispatches. In one letter from 6 April, he argued that the Sundgau was automatically included with Upper Alsace; in another letter from the next day, he said that it is "so mixed and enclaved" with Upper Alsace that to leave the two in different hands would be to invite future conflict. Mazarin agreed that the Sundgau was part of Upper Alsace; and, furthermore, Servien agreed that France should retain it. Only Longueville was willing to give it up.[87]

Longueville was the most pessimistic of the French plenipotentiaries. He believed that the best France could hope for was Upper and Lower Alsace and Breisach. In order to avoid future conflict with the archdukes, however, he hoped that the Breisgau, Sundgau, and Forest Towns could be left to Bavaria, in compensation for which the archdukes would receive part of the Upper Palatinate. Longueville also believed that the Imperials would more easily accept French demands if non-Habsburg territory were demanded. Perhaps this influenced his decision to request, in an 4 April meeting with Trauttmansdorff, the Bishopric of Strasbourg instead of Breisach. True, the current Bishop of Strasbourg was a Habsburg; but this was a recent (post-1600) development, unlike Breisach, which was an old Habsburg patrimony. Servien also attributed to Longueville a desire for Philippsburg, which could arguably be traced to the same desire to seek non-Habsburg compensation. Yet, in spite of these exploratory thoughts, Longueville remained relatively firmly fixed on the basic demand of Upper and Lower Alsace and Breisach; his one major departure from the court and the other plenipotentiaries was that he did not insist on the Sundgau.[88]

Servien was the only plenipotentiary to feel that the Forest Towns were worth fighting for. He considered them, together with the Sundgau,

> absolutely necessary to assure the whole right flank going from France to Breisach, to conserve the freedom of the Rhine, communication with the Swiss, interrupt that between Franche-Comté and the other [Habsburg] hereditary lands, put out of questioning and jealousy all that will remain to us across the Rhine, and secure our means of putting a relief force into Breisach by way of the river in case it comes to be besieged one day.[89]

Servien was therefore primarily interested in keeping the path to Breisach open, not in territorial annexation in itself. On the other hand, d'Avaux was interested in the Sundgau, which he called "some of the best country in the world," for its own sake. But d'Avaux was also interested in securing the Rhine, and therefore pressed for the annexation of the small fortress of Neuenburg, which was incorporated into French demands.[90]

On 6 April, d'Avaux met with the Bavarian plenipotentiaries to discuss French satisfaction. He originally demanded Upper and Lower Alsace, the Sundgau, Breisgau, Forest Towns, and Breisach—the entire French Proposition III demands with the exception of Philippsburg. However, the Bavarians objected that they had heard from Bagno that Mazarin would give in on the Breisgau and Forest Towns. D'Avaux responded that he would talk with Longueville and the two together would force Servien to accept this arrangement, although Servien felt strongly about the Forest Towns and would not want to give in. He added that France would have to have, besides Breisach, Neuenburg. Two days later, on 8 April, the Bavarian and French plenipotentiaries gathered for another discussion. This time the French said they wanted Upper and Lower Alsace, the Sundgau, Breisach, Philippsburg, Benfeld, and Saverne. However, it is clear that their core demands included only the first three items, because they specifically said that they would be willing to negotiate further over Philippsburg, Benfeld, and Saverne; and, moreover, that they would be willing to sign an armistice as soon as the Imperials offered Alsace, the Sundgau, and Breisach.[91] Additional demands, such as d'Avaux's of 6 April for the Breisgau and Forest Towns, merely represent the persistent French attempts to test how far their opponents were willing to go; they were, in short, purely tactical expedients. It was in just this vein that the French tried to convince the Bavarians on the 8th that the Breisgau and Forest Towns were included in their understanding of "Alsace," before being rebuked that this could not be true or they would not have mentioned them separately in their Proposition III. Similarly, the day after that meeting, the French insisted to Wartenberg, the Bishop of Osnabrück, that they would not make peace without the Breisgau and Forest towns; when Wartenberg objected that the news from Paris suggested otherwise, the French retorted that it must have come from Bagno, who either did not know the real French position, or was including all Habsburg territory in "Alsace." In explaining their demands, they also included Neuenburg as one of the Forest Towns—an attempt to justify a new demand that did not fool Trauttmansdorff.[92] Such temporary probes aside, therefore, it was on the basis of their 1645 instructions that the plenipotentiaries continued to negotiate. The only two real departures were the Sundgau, considered the same as Upper Alsace or mixed in with it, and Neuenburg; and it was d'Avaux who insisted upon both.

The approach of the campaign—and Turenne's army—had had a crucial effect in forcing Trauttmansdorff to offer Alsace. Trauttmansdorff himself was not so concerned about the campaign, but the Bavarians were; and it was their pressure that finally got him to act. On the day of their ultimatum, they told Trauttmansdorff that they had received news that Turenne had moved out; since it was clear that the Imperial forces could not resist him, they wanted at least to conclude an armistice. Two days later, they said that they had certain news that Turenne had already begun marching with eight thousand men, giving them all the more reason to engage in separate talks with France if Trauttmansdorff did not offer Alsace and Breisach immediately.[93] But he could not offer Breisach for the simple reason that he did not have orders to give up anything east of the Rhine. The French agreed, however, to a three-week truce while Trauttmansdorff waited for further orders on Breisach and the French waited for orders on the Breisgau and Forest towns; and the Bavarians agreed that they would not pursue separate talks during this time.[94] The French insisted, however, that the truce remain unwritten.[95]

This short truce was an exception to Mazarin's general conviction that France should not let up on military pressure until a treaty had actually been signed. He had consistently rejected a truce during the negotiations. As he told Vervaux early in 1645, "Her Majesty and her allies are not thinking of diminishing the fire of war by a suspension of arms, but of extinguishing it altogether by a good peace."[96] Thus, he had undertaken massive new levies in the winter in the hope of bringing the French *Armée d'Allemagne* to its greatest strength ever. Contracts were issued for the raising of sixty-seven hundred infantry and eight hundred cavalry, and he explored the possibility of recruiting even more. Almost all of these troops were actually raised in Germany, and, for the first time, most of them were levied in the north and northwest. One captain, who was supposed to have raised troops in 1645, finally carried through his contracts, while Meulles, the French resident in Hamburg, took charge of recruiting in that city.[97] Overall, Mazarin expected to enter the campaign with eight to nine thousand infantry and seven thousand cavalry in Turenne's army. This, he said, would make Turenne as strong alone as he had been in the past year with Enghien's reinforcements. Mazarin was so confident of his military preparations in the German theater that he sent Enghien, for lack of a better place to employ him, to the Low Countries as second in command to Gaston.[98]

But the *Armée d'Allemagne* would not act alone in the coming year. Surveying the results of the 1645 campaign, Torstensson concluded that the allies had been defeated by superior cooperation on the part of the Habsburg and Bavarian armies. Bavarian troops had been present at Jankov (without altering the course of it, to be sure); more decisively, the emperor's reinforcement of Maximilian with several thousand troops in the fall had prevented the French from taking advantage of their victory at Alerheim. Torstensson therefore proposed that the French and Swedes link up in 1646, advancing on a single front in Germany, and thereby preventing either one of them from being fallen upon by two enemies.

Mazarin was fundamentally amenable to this plan of action. "Experience has shown," he wrote to d'Avaugour, the French attaché with the Swedish army,

> that the method of diversions is very uncertain, and that it is a remedy whose operation is not sufficiently prompt on certain occasions, when one of the two confederate armies could be repulsed or defeated by both enemy armies, which join together when they please, and in little time.[99]

Arguing that the union of the Swedish and French armies was "absolutely necessary," Mazarin promised that Turenne would enter the campaign by 1 May at the latest. In fact, though Turenne left court in mid-March, he remained in Lorraine for some time, partly to inspect the troops who had quartered there, and partly to help destroy a fort the Habsburgs were building on the Moselle.[100] He did not arrive in Alsace until mid-April. By the time he had gathered his troops at Mainz toward the beginning of May, three further considerations hindered his crossing the Rhine. First, he needed money for artillery and supplies, and felt that it would also be advisable to pay the troops a *montre* before asking them to cross into Germany.[101] Second, the truce had been concluded with Bavaria, delaying the linkup for at least three weeks. And third, Mazarin had become increasingly squeamish about the planned junction and sought to delay it as long as possible.

The history of Franco-Swedish military cooperation in the Thirty Years' War had been spotty at best. Mazarin was still bitter about Königsmarck's desertion of the allied army in 1645 just before the battle of Alerheim, but he could also cite Guébriant's linkup with Banér in 1640–41, after which Guébriant had been

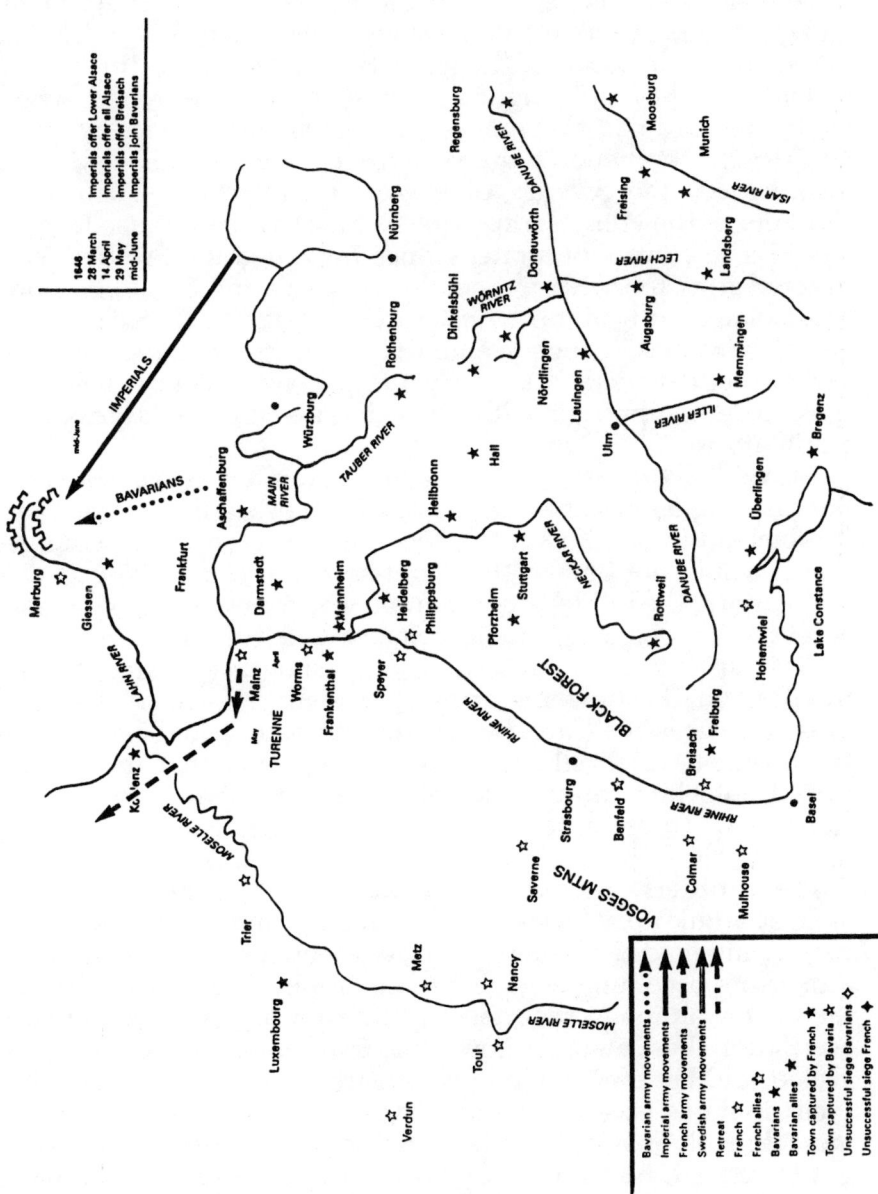

1646, March–June

forced to retreat alone back to the Rhine in the middle of the winter, and probably would have been destroyed completely had he not won the battle of Kempner Heide. Moreover, the Swedes still felt that they had a right to France's Weimarian troops, whose leader Bernard had been enticed out of Swedish service by Richelieu's money. Whenever the two armies were together, Mazarin complained, the Swedes practically recruited the Weimarians right out of the French army. Finally, Mazarin feared that Turenne would lose control of strategy once he joined the Swedes. With his own army too weak to fight the Imperials and Bavarians alone, and isolated far from his bases, Turenne could be forced to follow Swedish wishes, which seemed to point in the direction of an invasion of Bavaria and possibly a major battle, in which France's most ardent supporter within the Empire could be destroyed as a military force.

To avoid all these difficulties, Mazarin wanted to delay the junction as long as possible, preferably until peace was made. Since it promised to be difficult to effect the linkup anyway, he judged that it would not be hard for Turenne to avoid it while plausibly maintaining the polite fiction that he was trying his best. If, however, the negotiations should collapse and Turenne were forced to link up, Mazarin ordered that he should operate near the Swedes, but keeping his army as a distinct force. If, by some pressing necessity, Turenne felt that he had to join his army to the Swedes, he should first extract a promise that the Swedes would help him capture Heidelberg and Heilbronn; only afterward was Turenne to help Sweden attack an area of their choosing.[102]

These orders, issued on 18 May, emphasized the reasons against a link-up. However, Mazarin had another design whose development added a more positive reason for keeping Turenne's army from becoming engaged in the Empire. The basic cause was the Dutch: although their talks with Spain had proceeded slowly even after the Catalonia-Low Countries exchange had been revealed, in May they made rapid progress, resolving almost all of their disputes except for those over the Indies (admittedly the most difficult ones).[103] As Mazarin pondered fighting Spain without Dutch aid, he became convinced that the best solution would be to use Turenne's army, combined with the troops that La Ferté-Senneterre could gather in Lorraine, to attack Luxembourg. Sweden could hardly object, he argued, if Turenne left a force of seven to eight thousand troops on the Rhine, which would be as strong as Guébriant's had been when he died in 1643.[104] Moreover, it was excusable if France wished to withdraw some forces to use against "the greatest enemy that we have." If the Swedes proved difficult, Mazarin suggested that at worst Turenne could get Torstensson to allow him to campaign in Luxembourg for six weeks, if necessary by bribing him under the pretense of paying a subsidy to the Swedish army. Mazarin confessed his "great passion" for the plan to attack Luxembourg, adding that "I desire it with all the more ardor since I see that the Dutch have not yet entered the campaign, and they do not seem to be in a hurry to enter it soon." By attacks in both Flanders and Luxembourg—the success of which Mazarin did not doubt—France would show the world that Spain was not better off when fighting France alone than when fighting France and the Dutch Republic; at the same time, they would show the Dutch that they were not as necessary to France as they believed they were.[105]

Mazarin sounded out his plenipotentiaries on the possibility of sending Turenne to Luxembourg during the oral truce while they waited for the emperor's final word on Breisach. The plenipotentiaries, however, resisted, arguing that it would appear that France was abandoning German affairs; and, moreover, a month was simply not enough time for an operation, even a small one. They therefore ordered Turenne to remain on the Rhine until the negotiations became clearer.[106] But this turned into an uncomfortable position, since Turenne's supply situation quickly became precarious as he exhausted the region around Mainz. Moreover, Mazarin's desire to turn Turenne's army against Luxembourg increased over the last weeks of May and the first week of June, even though it became clear that the Dutch were not going to make peace with Spain, at least not in time for the current campaign. Far from being fearful of the war in the Low Countries, Mazarin thought he had struck upon the means to achieve a decisive breakthrough. He correctly surmised that Spain had been partly responsible for Trauttmansdorff's unwillingness to compromise (although he overestimated their influence), and he therefore became convinced that the quickest way to win the war in Germany was to attack Spain. As he wrote to the plenipotentiaries,

> Since the difficulties in concluding peace in the Empire are certainly caused by the Spanish, who fear being left alone in the war, the true means to obtain all that the allied crowns desire from the Imperials is to attack Spain more forcefully, using Turenne's army. In that case

they will presumably resolve themselves to peace soon and will become accommodating in all affairs.[107]

Yet Mazarin's strategy in this regard was somewhat paradoxical, for while he was trying to achieve peace in the Empire by sending Turenne against Spain, he was also trying to send Turenne against Spain by achieving peace in the Empire. By the reasoning of the first strategy, having Turenne attack Spain would bring peace to the Empire; but the second strategy had this exactly reversed, hoping that a peace already obtained in the Empire would free up Turenne to campaign against Spain. The compelling reasons to avoid another campaign in Germany had not diminished, and Mazarin became increasingly willing to compromise in order to avoid one. This willingness was encouraged by his plenipotentiaries, who feared that Sweden would get their satisfaction first and force France to settle quickly, on unfavorable terms if necessary. After the Imperial offer of 14 April, they therefore urgently requested that Mazarin inform them of his final intentions on "how far we can give in rather than break off the treaty."[108]

Essentially, the plenipotentiaries agreed that France should settle for Alsace, the Sundgau, and Breisach, but they were not above fishing for other advantages if they could get them. Their response to the Imperial offer of 14 April insisted on Neuenburg as well as Breisach, and offered either to return the Breisgau or to pay an indemnity, but not both.[109] Yet as Servien noted in his letter of 19 April, these stipulations were included only to fatten French demands; they had no intention of insisting on them. To begin with, they were only a bargaining position designed to get one or two Forest Towns, Servien's old demand. Even at that, however, Servien wrote of the Forest Towns that "they do not, in my opinion, merit breaking a peace in which we find the King's profit so advantageously elsewhere." Similarly, he felt that it was better to pay the subsidy than not to pay it, since "to obtain great things, in which it is good to be firm, it is useful to be easy and accommodating in small ones." Servien also noted that he saw little hope for obtaining Benfeld, and felt that they could settle for the destruction of the fortifications at Saverne, an important small fortress at the entrance of Alsace north of the Vosges.[110]

The court sanctioned the plenipotentiaries' approach. In an official memorandum of 26 April giving them power to conclude peace, the court permitted either returning the Breisgau or paying an indemnity, but not both. However, a separate, secret memorandum gave them power to give in on both, and Neuenburg as well, which d'Erlach, the governor of Breisach, reported to be of minimal military significance. The plenipotentiaries were also authorized to make peace with the emperor even if Spain did not conclude at the same time. In that case, noted the letter, Spain would be isolated and thus forced to make peace; and, moreover, the French could use Turenne's army against the Low Countries.[111]

At the same time, Mazarin noted that he had secret information that the emperor would give in on Breisach. He reported on 21 April that his informant in Vienna had revealed to him that the emperor would surrender Breisach eventually, though he would first propose to destroy its fortifications; this was then confirmed on 26 April and again on 5 May.[112] In fact, the emperor had made the decision to allow Trauttmansdorff to give in on Breisach on 22 April; Mazarin's informer must therefore have been an astute observer of court politics, but he could not have betrayed the official decision at such an early date.[113] Nevertheless, it was essentially accurate information, and Mazarin received further confirmation—this time perhaps from the actual secret council meeting—at the end of May.[114] This makes it all the more striking that it was precisely at the end of May that he softened his policy, permitting the plenipotentiaries to surrender Breisach if they could get its fortifications destroyed and acquire Philippsburg instead. Though he wrote that he believed Philippsburg to be "a better acquisition even than Breisach," this is hardly credible. Not only was Breisach one of the strongest fortifications in Germany, it also controlled a bridge over the Rhine, whereas there was none at Philippsburg. That he considered Breisach superior is evident from a letter of 2 June in which he made the more reasonable judgement that Philippsburg would be just as good if they could get Benfeld, Saverne, and possibly two of the Forest Towns with it.[115]

Mazarin's willingness to forego Breisach for Philippsburg was obviously a tactical retreat designed to end the negotiations as soon as possible. For Mazarin had another bit of inside information: that, although Trauttmansdorff had orders to surrender Breisach, Peñaranda hoped to delay the offer until he could make a truce with the Dutch, thereby forcing France to settle on unfavorable terms with the emperor. Though Mazarin professed that the military situation was just as good as last year's even without the Dutch, it was evidently this concern that led him to be so accommodating in the negotiations. By the end of May, he was willing to accept Philippsburg instead of Breisach; and, if the plenipotentiaries managed to get Breisach anyway, the question of Philippsburg "should not prevent making peace with the emperor."[116]

It is therefore surprising to find that when Trauttmansdorff did finally offer Breisach on 29 May, the plenipotentiaries rejected the Imperial proposal because it did not include Philippsburg. The Imperials were shocked by the French action, but the Bavarians, who had enticed the emperor into giving up Breisach with the assurance that France would make peace, felt particularly betrayed.[117] It was already generally known by the end of March that the French intended to give in on Philippsburg, a decision reached by the court over a month earlier. The plenipotentiaries had initiated the retreat on Philippsburg, noting in mid-February their concern over "the jealousy [of] the neighboring princes." The problem was greatly magnified by the line of communications on which the French insisted; as Longueville explained, "Philippsburg [is] difficult to keep without including a large territory in which many estates have interests." Relations with Protestants were particularly affected.[118]

Mazarin was immediately sympathetic to the plenipotentiaries' concerns, but did not want to give up Philippsburg for nothing. He permitted the plenipotentiaries to give in on Philippsburg once they had obtained Alsace and Breisach, but only if they held firm on other issues such as the indemnity; in addition, he preferred that it be razed if possible.[119] It became increasingly difficult for the plenipotentiaries to put on a bold face regarding Philippsburg, however, because rumors at Münster said that the French court had already decided to give in, and it was only the plenipotentiaries themselves who were causing difficulties. Mazarin encouraged them by saying that if the Imperials said that France had decided to give in, "it is something that they guess, but about which they must have doubts, the affair having been resolved . . . only in the presence of Monsieur le Duc d'Orléans [Gaston], of Monsieur le Prince [Henri de Condé], and of Monsieur de Brienne."[120]

Nevertheless, Mazarin's essentially hard line on Philippsburg weakened considerably in April; by the 14th, he wrote that it was up to the plenipotentiaries to do whatever they saw fit, whether to stand firm, exchange it for some other point, or give in completely. Mazarin obviously wished to retain it, but he did not want to alienate French support among the estates. Hence his instructions to the plenipotentiaries on 21 April to consider whether they should renounce the claim to Philippsburg immediately, "in order to gain by this concession applause in the Empire and particularly among the princes and estates who had wanted to demolish this fortress, or whether it would be expedient to wait a little longer in order to bring the Imperials to our position."[121]

Less than a week later, Mazarin appeared to have second thoughts about the policy of willingly surrendering Philippsburg. He felt that it could safely be returned to its present owner—Philipp von Sötern, Elector of Trier—but, Sötern "already having one foot in the grave," Mazarin preferred to retain the fortress until he could be assured of Sötern's successor. If it appeared that this would prevent peace being made, the plenipotentiaries could return it immediately, provided that it be razed. In spite of these new conditions, however, he continued to insist that, if even this demand would cause too much scandal in Germany, Philippsburg could be returned without conditions.[122] By the end of May, he was proposing to keep Philippsburg instead of Breisach, and even arguing that it would be better.

It may seem understandable how, based on these orders, the plenipotentiaries continued to insist on Philippsburg after the Imperial offer of 29 May. But while it is true that the desirability of retaining Philippsburg shifted several times in Mazarin's instructions over the course of April and May, the common thread—even more on Philippsburg than on most items—was that it was up to the plenipotentiaries to decide the best course of action.[123] Moreover, Mazarin had stated in unequivocal terms that Philippsburg was not to hold up the peace.[124] How, then, could the plenipotentiaries have refused an offer that met all of Mazarin's other demands?

To begin with, the Imperial offer of 29 May, although it included Breisach, was not everything the French could have hoped it to be. Attached to it were several unacceptable conditions: France was to support the Catholics in the matter of religious *gravamina*, and Bavaria in the Upper Palatinate question; to guarantee the inclusion of Spain and Lorraine in the peace; and to pay an indemnity of four million Reichstalers for its conquests. The indemnity was too high; France would, under no circumstances, permit Lorraine to attend the conference; and, though she supported Bavaria and the Catholics generally, she would not bind herself to them by treaty for fear of offending the Swedes and Protestant estates of the Empire. As Servien noted, "they added to Breisach so many restrictions that the affair cannot yet be considered resolved"; in their common dispatch, the plenipotentiaries said that the Imperials "seem to have had the idea of laying us a trap to discredit us in the assembly and to put us into bad relations with our allies." They reported that they had countered with new demands of their own,

> not so much in the hope of obtaining them as with the intention of arming ourselves against their demands, having judged that in order to bring affairs to the point where one wants them, it would be advantageous to hold firm on those things on which one might give in, to oblige them to do the same on their side.[125]

But even if the conditions had been adequate, the French would still not have accepted them, for on 24 May La Barde, the French resident in Osnabrück, wrote them a letter informing the plenipotentiaries that Swedish satisfaction was, in fact, advancing much slower than they had thought. Whereas the French had been working to conclude their satisfaction as soon as possible in order not to finish after Sweden, now they suddenly became concerned not to finish before Sweden so as not to make their allies jealous. While they had very real concerns about the conditions in the Imperial offer, they would have dropped them quickly if Sweden were to have resolved its satisfaction; but since Sweden was still a long way from this goal (her satisfaction was not, in fact, to be settled until February 1647), the French plenipotentiaries felt that they might as well use the time in between to get even better terms for France. Servien recognized that it would have been preferable to make peace immediately, but justified their actions by noting that "our conduct is perpetually constrained, and . . . we are forced to act like doctors, who, in prescribing medicine to cure the stomach, must be careful not to damage the liver."[126]

In fact, the French concern not to sign any agreement before Sweden was based on an exaggerated idea of how Sweden would react to such a situation. It is true that Oxenstierna wrote to his father on 19 March that "we begin more and more to fear French progress," and on 28 May he and Salvius wrote with perplexity that they did not know "what the French want, either in the negotiations or in fighting."[127] The Swedes did, however, believe that their negotiations were further from a conclusion than the French ones, since they thought Trauttmansdorff did not have the authority to meet their demands, as he did the French.[128] Their references to the speed of French negotiations show only a cool concern, nothing like the panic that the French had expected, nor the obsession with timing the negotiations that the French had. They made no contingency plans and did not change the pace of their own talks, but merely noted that it was a concern.

If the French overestimated Sweden's fear of an early French agreement with the emperor, however, they were correct in their judgement that the impending military campaign made it impossible for France to withdraw from the Empire even if they did reach an accord. Two major reasons had impelled France to desire "satisfaction" quickly: the fear of being forced to settle for less if Sweden achieved theirs first, and the desire to avoid the junction of Turenne with the Swedes. With the first reason out of the way, the only reason impelling a quick settlement was to keep Turenne out of Germany, both because of the harmful effects it could have within the Empire, and because his forces could be better employed against Spain. However, avoiding the junction of French and Swedish troops would be the most blatant way of snubbing Sweden, and to do so at a time when French satisfaction had already been concluded would be even worse, since obviously self-interested. Ideally, the need for a military campaign in the Empire could be completely avoided by a truce, but Sweden understandably rejected this so long as her own satisfaction remained unsettled. The other alternative was a separate truce with Bavaria; but, however much Maximilian wished to avoid the upcoming campaign, he would not agree to separate from the emperor. There therefore remained no choice but to consent to Turenne's linkup and to the fighting of another campaign.[129]

The French plenipotentiaries were surprisingly unanimous in the decision not to conclude with the Imperials. D'Avaux wrote that "we have already obtained good conditions. I see, however, something yet more, and I dare hope everything from the prudent conduct of Monsieur le Duc de Longueville and of Monsieur de Servien, who can truly never be praised enough for the vigilance and the skill that they use." He was especially anxious to retain Philippsburg. Longueville was also firmly behind the increased French demands. He noted that Maximilian had written to Mazarin to get the French to give in, but urged that "it is very important that he believe that we will not [give in], so that he will support us in getting what we demand." Servien, who is normally considered the main impetus behind a policy of aggressive annexation, certainly supported the decision not to make peace and may even have originated it; nevertheless, he began his report to Lionne by noting that "it is very disappointing that we are not yet in a position to be able to give any certainty about the conclusion of the treaty with the emperor."[130]

At the time of Servien's letter—June 5—it was still expected that the remaining issues would be resolved relatively quickly; Servien estimated eight to ten days. On 7 June, Trauttmansdorff gave up on the French negotiations and went to Osnabrück to work out the religious *gravamina* and Swedish satisfaction; but even on 18 June, the plenipotentiaries thought that he would be returning shortly, probably to conclude the treaty.[131] By that time, however, they had been forced to approve the linkup of French and Swedish troops.

The plenipotentiaries were understandably uncertain about whether the court would approve their actions.[132] They need not have been; Brienne was enthusiastic, and Mazarin also agreed that their course was best. However, Mazarin added that

> at the same time that I am delighted to see this crown's satisfaction assured with so much glory and utility, I am extremely concerned about the junction that it seems that the Swedes want to press between our army and theirs, because they are advancing to the Rhine, according to what one hears, with great speed.[133]

In other words, as late as this letter, written on 15 June, Mazarin still hoped to avoid Turenne's linkup with Sweden. But by that time, the plenipotentiaries had already given the order to Turenne to carry through with it; and it was missed communications and the problems of time and distance that almost led to a military disaster in the Empire.

The usually simple chain of command running from Mazarin to Turenne (and with much of the decision-making authority in Turenne's hands) was complicated by the problem of linking up with Sweden, which was as much a political as a military question. In order to ensure that Turenne could respond as quickly as possible to political events, Mazarin instructed him to follow the orders sent by the plenipotentiaries in Münster. That way, Turenne could take advantage of a truce to turn against Luxembourg; or, contrariwise, he could link up with Sweden if their political pressure made it necessary.[134]

Turenne strongly favored the junction. Politically, Turenne was a hawk who wanted to crush the emperor decisively.[135] Moreover, as a Calvinist, he had none of the *dévot* sympathy for Catholics in the Empire, and hence had no desire to spare Bavaria, as Mazarin did. He also argued that his army was not strong enough to operate across the Rhine without cooperating with the Swedes.[136] Whether this opinion was influenced by his political views or not, it is true that the *Armée d'Allemagne* was weaker than expected in the early months of 1646. Various French estimates put its strength at not more than about eight thousand troops.[137] Substantial reinforcements were being raised in northern Germany, but these were prevented from reaching the army by the advance of the Imperial and Bavarian armies into Hesse. Moreover, a series of problems delayed the recruits in Lower Saxony much longer than expected. The plenipotentiaries had contracted with a German soldier formerly in Imperial service, Lothar von Bönninghausen, to raise twenty-three hundred troops in 1645. Because of a series of difficulties, these troops were still unavailable at the beginning of 1646. In letter after letter, Mazarin complained of Bönninghausen and told the plenipotentiaries to hurry his recruits along.[138] Other troops being raised by Meulles du Tartre, the French resident in Hamburg, were also slow in appearing because of miscommunications. To make matters worse, the French could not make contracts solely for infantry, which Mazarin judged to be their chief need, but instead had to accept a certain proportion of cavalry along with the footsoldiers.[139] As late as 4 May, Turenne did not even have any news about the progress of the recruiting in the North. His own army suffered from a lack of money—deliberately withheld by Mazarin, Turenne believed, because the peace was near—which prevented adequate preparation of supplies and artillery. As the clear, confident predictions of winter yielded to the muddy reality of spring, Mazarin was forced to see Turenne's expected date to begin operations pushed back from the beginning of to May its end; and even with such a substantial delay, there was still a rush to get everything ready on time.[140]

While Mazarin strongly opposed the linkup and Turenne strongly favored it, the plenipotentiaries held a middle position: they feared the consequences of the junction of French and Swedish troops, but they were also sensitive to the political danger of not supporting Sweden militarily. They would have supported sending him across the Rhine by himself, but they agreed with him that he was not strong enough to operate safely alone. On the other hand, they disagreed with Turenne's desire to join with Sweden, and Servien complained to Mazarin that "he is the only royal minister who finds this junction advantageous for His Majesty." Throughout May, the plenipotentiaries adopted a policy of anxious waiting, hoping to conclude an armistice in the Empire at any moment and thereby to free Turenne for the Luxembourg venture. Even after the Imperial Breisach offer of 29 May, they continued to tell Turenne to wait until the negotiating situation became clearer.[141]

By mid-June, however, military events in the Empire had overtaken them. Their origin lay in yet another dispute that had been added to the already multifaceted problems in the Empire, the eruption of the Hessian War late in 1645. At his death in 1604, Landgrave Ludwig had divided his portion of Hesse between the two remaining branches: a Calvinist branch based at Cassel; and the other, staunchly Lutheran, at Darmstadt. The prize, however, the town of Marburg with its university, had gone to Cassel. Since Cassel introduced Calvinism into Marburg against the terms of the will, the leaders of Darmstadt argued that the town should revert to them. They failed at first, but later won a favorable ruling from the Habsburgs during the 1620s.

When Sweden invaded the Empire in 1630, Hesse-Cassel was one of their earliest and firmest adherents. However, Hesse-Darmstadt, which had been reconciled to the emperor because of his support in the Marburg succession dispute, remained neutral; and Sweden, which did not want to attack a fellow Lutheran state, supported her in this. The two Hesses therefore remained at peace for more than a decade. In 1644, however, Amalie Elisabeth denounced the 1627 agreement surrendering Marburg, and tensions began to mount, with military raids occurring between the two states. Finally, after the 1645 campaign and Hesse-Cassel's successful participation in the battle of Alerheim, Amalie Elisabeth withdrew her troops back to Hesse and began attacking her southern neighbor in earnest. Her army captured Marburg on 3 November and Marburg Castle on 15 January 1646, giving her a strong negotiating position from which to win the town back for good.[142]

Darmstadt was in a poor state to respond to these attacks: although its army was nominally over ten thousand men, in actuality it contained more like three thousand.[143] At the beginning of 1646, therefore, Landgrave Georg repeatedly appealed to the emperor to send reinforcements. Ferdinand was responsive, but his own army was weak, and so he continually pressed Maximilian to join forces. Yet as part of the truce Maximilian had agreed with France that, so long as the French army did not join the Swedish, the Bavarian army would remain separate from the Imperial one. In mid-May, Maximilian did permit part of his forces to join the Imperial army under the Archduke Leopold Wilhelm, while both the Imperial army, strengthened by Bavarian troops, and the remainder of the Bavarian army, operating separately under Geleen, moved into Hesse along the Main. Their advance, however, was countered by Wrangel, who had replaced Torstensson in command of the Swedish army. With the conclusion of the Truce of Eilenburg with Saxony on 10 April, he was freed to move west.[144] After successfully capturing Höxter and Paderborn, two more bargaining chips for Amalie Elisabeth, he joined with Königsmarck in mid-June and marched south, occupying Amöneburg on 25 June. With the approach of the Swedes, Maximilian finally yielded to Imperial pressure and permitted the remainder of his army to link up with that of Leopold Wilhelm.[145]

Opinion among the Bavarian and Imperial forces was divided on the best action to take. In a military council at the end of April, Leopold Wilhelm argued that they should attack and defeat the French and Swedes in turn. The Bavarians felt that this plan had little hope; they argued that enemy troop strength had been deliberately underestimated, and felt that there was no way to prevent the enemy from breaking through. They had no counterproposal, however; in fact, they argued that military plans were pointless and that the best option was to make peace immediately.[146] Leopold Wilhelm therefore idled in a position south of Marburg, first retreating before the threat of an allied linkup, then advancing again by the end of June when it became apparent that such a junction was not imminent.[147] There was talk of invading the Westphalian Circle or of attacking Marburg, but Maximilian discouraged both ventures.[148] Indeed, he continued to behave as though the truce were in effect until late June, urging Leopold Wilhelm not "to give any reason to fight or [to take] offense . . . so as not to break the peace treaty that we hope will be achieved soon."[149] That, and Maximilian's typically extreme caution with his army, prevented Leopold Wilhelm from taking advantage of the window of opportunity between the end of the truce and the time it took Turenne to join Wrangel, during which Wrangel's forces were considerably outnumbered. Instead of attacking, the Imperial-Bavarian and Swedish armies merely eyed each other cautiously across fortified lines in Lower Hesse.[150]

It was a letter from Turenne to Wrangel that had caused the Swedish commander to approach the Rhine in preparation for a linkup; and it was the apparently imminent Franco-Swedish junction that had caused Maximilian to permit his troops to join with the Imperials on 11 June and to advance with their superior army toward Wrangel. Consequently, it appeared to the plenipotentiaries by mid-June that to avoid sending Turenne to Wrangel's aid would confirm the Swedes' suspicions of French disloyalty, and would, moreover, in case of defeat risk the entire treaty, which the French continued to believe was just around the corner.[151] To avoid this danger, they wrote to Turenne on 13 June "leaving him in full liberty to act according to his orders and to what he judged best."[152] It therefore came as a shock to Mazarin when, on 22 June, Turenne's secretary arrived to inform the court that Turenne was more determined than ever to await further orders before crossing the Rhine. Mazarin rushed out two couriers to Turenne, each travelling a separate route, ordering him to link up immediately. "You can imagine the anxiety I am in," he wrote,

> being assailed by two fears: either that, if the junction is not made, all the enemy's forces fall on the Swedes and defeat them; or that the Swedes, imagining that our behavior is a consequence of the satisfaction proposed to us by the emperor, decide to anticipate our actions in making a separate treaty.

The plenipotentiaries found out about the delay independently and sent similar orders on 25 June.[153]

They need not have worried. After gathering his troops at Mainz and feinting a siege of Frankenthal, the still-unreduced Spanish fortress west of the Rhine, Turenne had camped at Bacharat in June and built a pontoon bridge there in anticipation of crossing the Rhine and joining Wrangel. Not only did he personally feel that the junction was the best policy, but his troops were suffering from lack of forage, a common problem when an army was forced to remain in the same place for an extended period. On 22 June, he requested from Mazarin "a prompt resolution, this country being so ruined that we cannot avoid starving" unless he received fifty thousand Reichstalers.[154]

It was at this juncture that letters got crossed in the mail, creating confusion in Paris and at Münster. The plenipotentiaries' letter of 14 June had reached Mazarin on the 22nd, faster than usual, while their letter to Turenne from 13 June only arrived in his camp on the 24th. During the time in between, Turenne received a message, originally from the plenipotentiaries to d'Avaugour (the French representative with the Swedish army) but which had somehow ended up in Wrangel's hands and had been passed along to him, that said to delay the junction. It was in reaction to this message that Turenne had sent his secretary to court on 17 June; but before the secretary had returned, the orders from the plenipotentiaries to link up with Wrangel arrived. Turenne, in favor of the junction and concerned about the supply situation of his army, did not hesitate to act without further instructions from court.[155]

By that time, however, the advance of the Bavarian and Imperial armies had hindered the junction; and though Turenne wrote asking Wrangel to hold his position for another week while Turenne sought a means to reach him, the Swedish commander retreated, giving the Imperial and Bavarian forces the opportunity to position themselves so that it was impossible for Turenne to join Wrangel from where he was. Turenne therefore judged that only three options were available. First, he could remain near Mainz and harass the enemy's rear; however, they could counter such a move by approaching the Main. Second, he could go south and cross the Rhine at Breisach. But this, too, was inadequate, since, although he could capture a fortress or two, he would be forced to recross the Rhine in the end. The last possibility was to march down the Rhine and cross somewhere in the vicinity of Cologne, thereby allowing him to reapproach Wrangel from the rear, unimpeded by the enemy. This was the course of action that Turenne finally adopted, sending an emissary to the Hague to get permission to cross the Rhine at the Dutch fortress of Wesel.[156]

Wesel was located near the confluence of the Rhine and the Lippe in Kleve, near the Dutch border. To reach the Swedes via Wesel would therefore mean a march of over 120 miles downriver, through the hostile Archbishopric of Cologne, and back upriver toward Hesse. Such a long maneuver was not without risk. First, Turenne judged that the enemy could block his path near Bonn. Second, there was a possibility that the enemy would attack the French Rhine towns during Turenne's absence. (This was not why he left nearly two thousand men on the Rhine, however. Instead, these extra troops were still planned for use against Luxembourg, the attack on which Mazarin had not yet abandoned.[157]) Third, and most important, there was the problem of leaving Wrangel alone in the meantime. Not only would the Swedes complain during Turenne's march (as in fact they did), but there was the danger that Wrangel would be attacked and defeated before Turenne could reach him.[158] Because of this last danger, the plenipotentiaries decided in mid-July that Tracy, who was still with the newly gathered recruits near Hamburg, should join Wrangel immediately. Undertaking a forced march with his flank exposed to the enemy, Tracy was able to bring nearly four thousand troops to reinforce Wrangel even after the losses he suffered en route.[159]

The pressure of military events, coupled with France's alliance with Sweden, had, therefore, prolonged the negotiations to the point that the French no longer had much incentive to make peace. When Trauttmansdorff stormed off to Osnabrück, the French part of the treaty stalled; but even after he returned to Münster on 26 June, there was little progress. The Imperials not only refused to give in on any of the remaining problem points, but created two new ones by refusing to sign any treaty without the inclusion of Spain and Lorraine. With the delay in Turenne's linkup with Sweden, the military situation was a stalemate; the French would have to wait for the effects of the campaign if they were to expect further concessions.[160]

Meanwhile, the French tried to speed Sweden along to peace. Although their stated policy was to avoid concluding their treaty until the Swedes were almost done with theirs, the plenipotentiaries—somewhat paradoxically—spoke of applying pressure to the Swedes to make peace sooner by means of a quick end to their own treaty. That the French were trying to carry out two diametrically opposed plans at the same time may be attributed in part to the dilemma in which they felt themselves. On one hand, they could not afford to be abandoned by Sweden; on the other hand, none of the French plenipotentiaries liked Sweden or supported their territorial demands, which seemed to grow greater as the negotiations progressed. D'Avaux was particularly outraged. "What would you say, Monseigneur," he wrote,

> when you hear that, besides the bishoprics of Minden and Osnabrück, they are now demanding that of Münster, where they do not own an inch of land? . . . I am no longer making a case of conscience; I say as a good politician that it is necessary to assist the Swedes when they are in a bad state, and to pull back our hand a little when they become so strong.[161]

The plenipotentiaries even wrote that Trauttmansdorff was right to complain about Sweden's "excessive and unjust" demands. Mazarin felt similarly, and complained that Trauttmansdorff's conciliatory attitude toward Sweden only delayed peace, since it led the Swedes to feel that they could obtain anything by increasing their demands. He even argued that it would be good if Trauttmansdorff broke off the negotiations as he had threatened, since this would undoubtedly bring the Swedes to reason when they saw the security of their gains being sacrificed. Nevertheless, Mazarin felt that Trauttmansdorff's appeasing behavior was "an evil that has no remedy, because we would not dare tell Trauttmansdorff how he should conduct himself regarding the Swedes; it would be very dangerous in case they used the same method against us."[162]

There were, on the other hand, several indications that Sweden was becoming more inclined toward peace. Both St. Romain, just returned from Stockholm, and Chanut, the new French ambassador, indicated that Sweden wanted peace. This seemed to be confirmed by the behavior of Oxenstierna, whose greater flexibility corresponded, the plenipotentiaries felt certain, to new orders from Queen Christina.[163] It was also rumored that Oxenstierna wanted to return to Stockholm to replace his ailing father as Chancellor, and that he therefore hoped to conclude peace as quickly as possible.[164]

If there was a softening of the Swedish position, however, it was more apparent than real. Axel Oxenstierna urged patience and fortitude for his plenipotentiaries even more strongly than Mazarin did for his. The chancellor's occasional letters to his son were short but almost invariably emphasized the need not to push things too quickly, no less in July than they had in March. "Such a difficult thing does not fall with one blow," he wrote once, with characteristic harshness.[165] Nor was Christina appreciably more yielding on the question of Swedish satisfaction. She sent no orders at all from 26 January to 21 March, and when she did finally dispatch a letter, it instructed the plenipotentiaries to remain firm.[166] The approaching conclusion of French negotiations left her unmoved, contrary to French expectations. When Salvius reported anxiously on 7 May that "final orders are suddenly entirely necessary" on Swedish satisfaction, the queen replied casually that she was considering the possibility of retracting her demands somewhat, but was currently too busy with a Russian legation to make a final decision.[167] In the meantime, the plenipotentiaries were not to retreat an inch. This hard line was repeated in July and August; if there was an increasing desire for peace, it was still far beneath the surface.[168]

The French were correct, at least, that Johann Oxenstierna wanted to return to Sweden, but had adduced the wrong reason. Far from pushing aggressively for more political power, the younger Oxenstierna was pulled by family concerns. His wife fell ill toward the end of June and eventually died at the beginning of August. Johann was so upset by this that he asked his father permission to return home, but the chancellor replied that, however much he wanted to grant a leave of absence, he could not do so in such a critical political situation.[169]

Oxenstierna's visit to Münster at the beginning of July helped solve some problems with the French, but the meeting "did not produce everything that [they] had hoped for the advancement of the peace."[170] Oxenstierna agreed, with difficulty, to allow Bavaria to retain the Electorate and to create an eighth one for the Palatinate. When he complained about the delay in Turenne's junction with Wrangel, the French said that Turenne "never had orders from court not to cross the Rhine"—which was a plain lie. Nevertheless, Oxenstierna seemed to be satisfied with it, as well as with the French claim that they never had a truce with Bavaria (a somewhat less blatant lie). Furthermore, he assured the French that Sweden would take no action against Poland for its continuing armament, relieving French fears that Sweden would again launch an aggressive war outside of the Empire.[171] On the issue of Swedish demands, however, he was less compromising: the Swedes continued to insist on both parts of Pomerania, Wismar, Bremen, and Verden. The French tried to demonstrate the need for moderation by pointing to their own example in paying an indemnity for Alsace, but Oxenstierna remained firm.[172] The plenipotentiaries therefore urged that Magnus Gabriel de La Gardie, Christina's favorite and a special Swedish envoy to Paris, be received with "all the caresses, honors, and demonstrations possible," since the continued goodwill of the queen (perceived to be the head of the peace party in Sweden) was considered essential if Axel Oxenstierna's warlike tendencies were to be reined in and Sweden were to make peace on reasonable terms.[173]

It was, remarked Longueville, a bad time to make peace. With the military situation unfavorable and the enemy therefore hopeful, there was little to do but to be patient.[174] But it was difficult for Mazarin to be patient when the Dutch were threatening to defect and French satisfaction seemed so assured. "It is no small skill," he wrote to d'Avaux, "to quit the game when one is winning, because one secures one's gain and one can count that which remains among one's possessions. In the name of God," he continued, "work for this with all your ability." Mazarin noted that he was ready to make peace immediately, in the middle of the campaign, and "to sacrifice not only our hopes for future conquest, but even to cede a part of what we already have."[175] This declaration was accompanied by a letter from Lionne to Servien with the brief and somewhat cryptic instruction to "make peace as soon as you are able." A week later, Lionne clarified his message by explaining that France was in such financial need that it could not make the military progress that it wanted.[176] The plenipotentiaries therefore devoted themselves to advancing the peace as best they could under the circumstances.

They had raised three difficulties with the Imperial offer of 29 May: first, the size of the indemnity for the archdukes and the amount of the debt of the Alsatian administration that the French would assume; second, the fate of the immediate estates in Alsace; and third, garrison rights in Philippsburg.[177] The indemnity was the least important. The emperor had insisted on four million Reichstalers in the 29 May offer. The French were offering three million, but they had the authority to go all the way to six million, and at times they told Mazarin that it would be better to offer more rather than less (see above). The Imperials also wanted the French to assume the entire debt in the province, while the French wanted only to take over half of it.[178]

The question of the immediate estates was more problematic. France had claimed all along that it would accept Alsace as a fief of the Empire. Doing so would not only placate the Imperial estates, which did not wish to see the Empire dismembered, but also offered several potential advantages over acquisition of the territory in sovereignty. By becoming a member of the Empire, France would be better able to negotiate treaties with German estates, and would be able to attend the Imperial Diet; ultimately, too, it opened the possibility of a French king becoming emperor. But the Imperials, in part because they were aware of the disadvantages that would accrue to them should France become a member of the Empire, and in part to increase the apparent size of their offer, proposed to give France Alsace in sovereignty. Yet if the emperor did not want France to hold Alsace as a fief of the Empire, was this not, Servien argued, a good reason for France to want to?

The chief contrary argument was that holding Alsace in sovereignty was more dignified: "there is no advantage," wrote Servien, "that equals that of not depending on anyone, and of being an absolute sovereign." Most of the advantages of taking Alsace as a fief, it could be argued, were small or nonexistent. Diets were rare and usually only dealt with taxes, and in any case France could send ambassadors if they wanted to view the proceedings. The German estates might prefer that Alsace not be removed from the Empire, but "one is obliged in great matters to consider what is convenient, advantageous, and honorable, rather than what is agreeable to foreigners." And if both the emperor and France found it advantageous that France get Alsace in sovereignty, it would not be the first time that "the same thing has made both sides happy."[179]

The plenipotentiaries debated the issue at great length, but eventually decided that taking Alsace in sovereignty would be "more proper to the dignity and grandeur of the crown." Actually, Servien and Longueville supported taking Alsace in sovereignty, while d'Avaux preferred acquiring it as a fief. At court, both Brienne and Mazarin felt that it would be best to accept Alsace as a fief; yet they delayed so long in making a firm decision that ultimately it was the plenipotentiaries who made the choice. As late as 7 September, less than a week before a preliminary agreement on French satisfaction was signed, Mazarin rather casually wrote to d'Avaux that there was time to examine the matter further, and requested d'Avaux's opinion. With no instructions from Paris, Servien and Longueville carried the day, and Alsace was taken in sovereignty. Perhaps ultimately the most decisive argument was that the Imperials insisted that if France took it as a fief, it would only be for the rest of the Bourbon line; the chance that Alsace might escheat back to the Habsburgs outweighed all other reasons.[180]

Since both the emperor and the majority of the French plenipotentiaries favored France taking Habsburg territory in sovereignty, there was no further dispute on this point. The real difficulty was the question of what was to happen to non-Habsburg territory in Alsace, i.e., the "immediate" estates that were part of the Empire, but lacked a direct overlord. Since the terms of the final treaty on this matter were ambiguous, and since their interpretation led to disputes that were not resolved until the 1680s with the final annexation of all of what is now known as "Alsace" to the French crown, this has been the most heavily contested and thoroughly analyzed question of the Peace of Westphalia. In 1848, the Count de Garden felt that, after two centuries of debate, the issue had calmed down sufficiently to permit an objective assessment. But the German annexation of Alsace and Lorraine after the Franco-Prussian War, followed by their recovery by France after World War I, reopened the debate with a new urgency. Far from fading away, it has received new, intensive treatment since World War II.[181]

The problem can be said to have originated in the hopelessly complex legal situation in Alsace, and the ambiguous meaning and problematic usage of the term "Alsace"; but the first practical difficulty came with the Imperial offer of Alsace on 14 April. At that time, the Imperials were under great pressure from Bavaria to conclude peace as soon as possible. They therefore phrased the Alsace offer in such a way as to make it seem as great as possible, saying they would cede "Upper and Lower Alsace with the Sundgau, under the title of the Landgraviate of Alsace." This, however, was a problematic formulation, since there was no such thing as the Landgraviate of Alsace. It is true that there were Landgraviates of Upper Alsace and Lower Alsace, and in Upper Alsace the title still meant considerable authority, and was possessed by the Habsburgs. In Lower Alsace, however, the Landgraviate was held by the Bishop of Strasbourg, and had practically no value outside of the mere title. The Habsburgs possessed some rights in Lower Alsace, mainly the Prefectorate of Haguenau, but these rights were extremely limited both geographically and in quality. The offer of Lower Alsace under the fictitious title of the "Landgraviate of Alsace" therefore created the impression that the Habsburgs had many more rights than they actually did.

This worked to their advantage in the short run, since the French were indeed elated over the concession. However, when the Imperials issued their *Postrema Declaratio*, or "Final Declaration," on 29 May, they attempted to clarify the legal situation in Alsace. Instead of the "landgraviatus Alsatiae," they specified the Landgraviate of Upper Alsace and the Prefectorate of Haguenau. In addition, they added a clause demanding that France not interfere with the rights of the immediate estates in either part of Alsace.[182]

This offer was probably not meant to retract anything granted in the 14 April offer, but only to clarify the legal situation so as to deny the French any grounds for extending their authority beyond what was given. To the French, however, who did not fully understand the extent of Habsburg rights, it seemed like a step backward. Why had they been offered all Habsburg rights in Lower Alsace on 14 April, but only the Prefectorate of Haguenau on 29 May? And why had the rights of the immediate estates been exempted? To counter what they saw as changes, therefore, in their 1 June response the French demanded Alsace "in complete propriety and sovereignty," including "all kinds of subjected territories and dependencies . . . without any reserve or exception."[183]

Was this, as some have claimed, a new demand on the part of the French? Or was it, as others maintain, the result of their misunderstanding of Habsburg rights in Lower Alsace? In one sense, it was certainly a new demand: the original French demands issued on 7 January called for Alsace as a fief of the Empire, not in sovereignty. But it had been the Imperials who had raised the issue of surrendering Alsace in sovereignty in the first place. In insisting on sovereignty "without any reserve or exception," the French saw themselves as counterattacking the Imperials for the conditions they had insisted upon in their offer. They were particularly concerned with the declarations that the Imperials demanded that the French make limiting Swedish and Hessian satisfaction, since "they seem to have had the intention of offering a trap in order to discredit us in the assembly and to cause ill feelings between us and our allies." "Since this procedure took from us the means to conclude as we had hoped," they continued in a letter to the king, "we judged that we should defend ourselves by the same arms by which we were attacked."[184] Because the new French demands were only intended to soften Imperial terms, they were not firm, and the plenipotentiaries even recognized a certain danger in them. "As for the pretension of sovereignty over the immediate estates," wrote Longueville, "seeing that it shocks the Imperial estates, we will not insist upon it, but will only use it to advance our other pretensions."[185]

Yet if the French response was a widening of their demands, it is still true that they did not really understand what rights the Habsburgs possessed in Lower Alsace. In noting that they brought the question of sovereignty over Lower Alsace to the fore, the French plenipotentiaries said that they demanded "cession of sovereign rights over all of it, just as they were offered over one part." But that one part—the Prefectorate of Haguenau—was the only substantial part over which the Imperials exercised significant rights. Even the Imperial Council was confused on this point, since they responded to the French demand by agreeing that the Imperials should not have limited the offer to the Prefectorate of Haguenau, but should have surrendered all Habsburg rights in Lower Alsace. The French misunderstanding went still deeper, however, for if the Imperial Council was willing to concede Imperial rights in Lower Alsace of which they were not aware, the French were quite clear in thinking that the Habsburg exercised rights over the immediate estates in Lower Alsace just as they did in Upper Alsace—which was not the case. This misunderstanding would return to cause further difficulties in September and beyond.[186]

While the form of the Alsace cession turned out to be more important to future generations, at the time the French were far more concerned about the acquisition of Philippsburg. Like the other French demands, it was not a point that they would insist upon if it were the sole remaining obstacle to peace. As d'Avaux explained, even all the advantages it offered

> do not blind our eyes. We are only pursuing them while waiting until our allies are almost in agreement on their affairs, without which the peace cannot be concluded, and we are resolved not to delay peace by a single day when it is only held up by this interest.[187]

Nevertheless, Mazarin and the plenipotentiaries were more intent upon winning this demand than upon regulating the size of the indemnity or acquiring Alsace in sovereignty. Philippsburg helped to defend Alsace and to secure a stretch of the Rhine, and the French were anxious to obtain these advantages while waiting for Sweden to conclude.[188]

D'Avaux was the most actively engaged in the Philippsburg negotiations. Already in mid-June, his discussions with the Bavarian plenipotentiaries led him to believe that the French could obtain the fortress, and Mazarin responded enthusiastically.[189] When Trauttmansdorff returned, d'Avaux discussed the issue with him immediately. Trauttmansdorff offered the demolition of the fortress, or that it remain with France until Sötern's death; "but according to what I could judge from his words and his face," d'Avaux wrote to Mazarin, "he will go further, and after all these gradations he will give in on Philippsburg as he did on Breisach."[190] On 16 July, d'Avaux noted that he had a report from "a person from whom I have sometimes received good information" that France was assured of Philippsburg; and two weeks later, he recounted another meeting with Trauttmansdorff that supported his optimism. While Trauttmansdorff did not promise the fortress, he did say

> that at the first opportunity he will propose it to the Imperial estates, and that if they approve it, he will also consent in the name of the emperor. And when I said that it would be useless to propose the affair to the estates if he did not have the intention of making it succeed, he responded that he understood it so.[191]

While things appeared hopeful from the Imperial standpoint, however, there was a further difficulty in winning over Philippsburg's owner, Philipp von Sötern, the Elector of Trier. The French felt that his support would be decisive in securing a garrison right in the fortress, and in fact the Swedish resident, Rosenhane, had suspected ever since the middle of June that they already had such an agreement, else they would not have held so firm in this demand.[192] Sötern wanted to retain Philippsburg, a defensive bulwark against Protestantism to which he had devoted much of his life; already in December 1645, he had sent a representative to Paris to try to get the French to agree to have the garrison swear an oath to him as well as to Louis XIV, but had been rebuffed. He felt, however, that he was adequately protected from French demands by the terms of his 1632 treaty with them; moreover, he needed French protection against Protestant encroachment, and was therefore afraid of offending them.[193]

Sötern's plenipotentiaries were less concerned about offending the French and more forthright in their defense of Philippsburg than was the Elector. They rejected French assurances that France only wanted a garrison right in the fortress, and refused to support French territorial demands even in the Empire. The French were shocked at this; Brienne, conflating the actions of Sötern's plenipotentiaries with the opinions of the Elector, complained that "he seems so strongly German that I fear his affection for his country makes him forget what he owes a neighboring king." Sötern reacted in mid-April by sending his representatives a stern command to support all French demands except for Philippsburg. At the same time, he drafted a treaty that would have provided for French protection of the Bishopric of Speyer. Again, however, his advance was turned away; the French refused to accept a new burden without any corresponding benefits.[194]

Sötern's request for protection may have contributed to a hardening of the French demand for Philippsburg in May. In the French response to the *Postrema Declaratio*, they denied that the emperor had the right to interfere in their negotiations with Sötern for the right to garrison Philippsburg. Over the ensuing month, they pressed the Elector on this issue, threatening him with the restoration of Karl Ludwig in the Palatinate, and professing that they would obtain their demand with or without his consent. At the beginning of July, the French plenipotentiaries sent a special envoy, the Sieur d'Anctoville, armed with the ability to promise up to fifty thousand Reichstalers indemnity, to negotiate with Sötern in person.[195] Sötern at first refused to see d'Anctoville, and broke off their meeting with a feigned illness. But d'Anctoville was persistent, and his efforts met with surprising success: on 19 July, Sötern signed a treaty granting France the right to garrison Philippsburg. Sötern was not able to convince the French to let the garrison swear an oath to him, nor did he win a single one of the fifty thousand Reichstalers d'Anctoville could have offered him (but prudently avoided doing). He did, however, get French protection for Speyer, as well as a guarantee that he would retain all sovereignty over Philippsburg. He also obtained French support for his personal goods and his family, a clause that he kept secret for as long as possible.[196]

Rather than publishing this treaty immediately, the French plenipotentiaries kept it secret and urged the court to do the same. In their estimation, it would have a greater effect if it were saved and revealed at the proper time.[197] Meanwhile, their letters displayed an increasing impatience with the campaign and confidence that it would solve their remaining problems.[198] There was another lull in the negotiations at the beginning of August while everyone waited for the unfolding campaign. D'Avaux spoke of the "coldness and silence of our opponents," and Longueville wrote that "peace will either be made in the month of September, or there will be no reason to hope for it for a long time." The plenipotentiaries generally agreed that "the Imperials and Spanish retreat rather than advance" in the negotiations.[199] However, this was the quiet before the storm. Turenne crossed the Rhine on 20 July and joined Wrangel on 10 August, and their operations soon put an entirely different face on the negotiations.[200]

The French had been unnecessarily worried about Wrangel's fate at the start of Turenne's march; far from being overwhelmed by the Imperials, he held his ground firmly while the Imperial forces were decimated by disease and starvation. The only action was an indecisive cavalry engagement on 7 July.[201] In mid-July, Leopold Wilhelm announced to Maximilian his intention of engaging the enemy in a battle if possible; however, this was to be preceded by a withdrawal of ten to fourteen days in order to refresh his army. By the time this had been accomplished, Turenne was across the Rhine, and Leopold Wilhelm settled on a purely defensive stance against the allies.[202] But this arrangement also had problems, since the Swedes were better supplied—largely thanks to the Hessians—than were the Imperials. It was difficult for armies of the 1640s to remain in one place for a long time, and the two-month sojourn along the Main had left the area devastated and both armies weakened from hunger. Maximilian lamented that "the army is unfailingly weakened over time, and everything works to the advantage of the enemy's superior forces . . . not to mention that the peace talks are likely to be set back."[203]

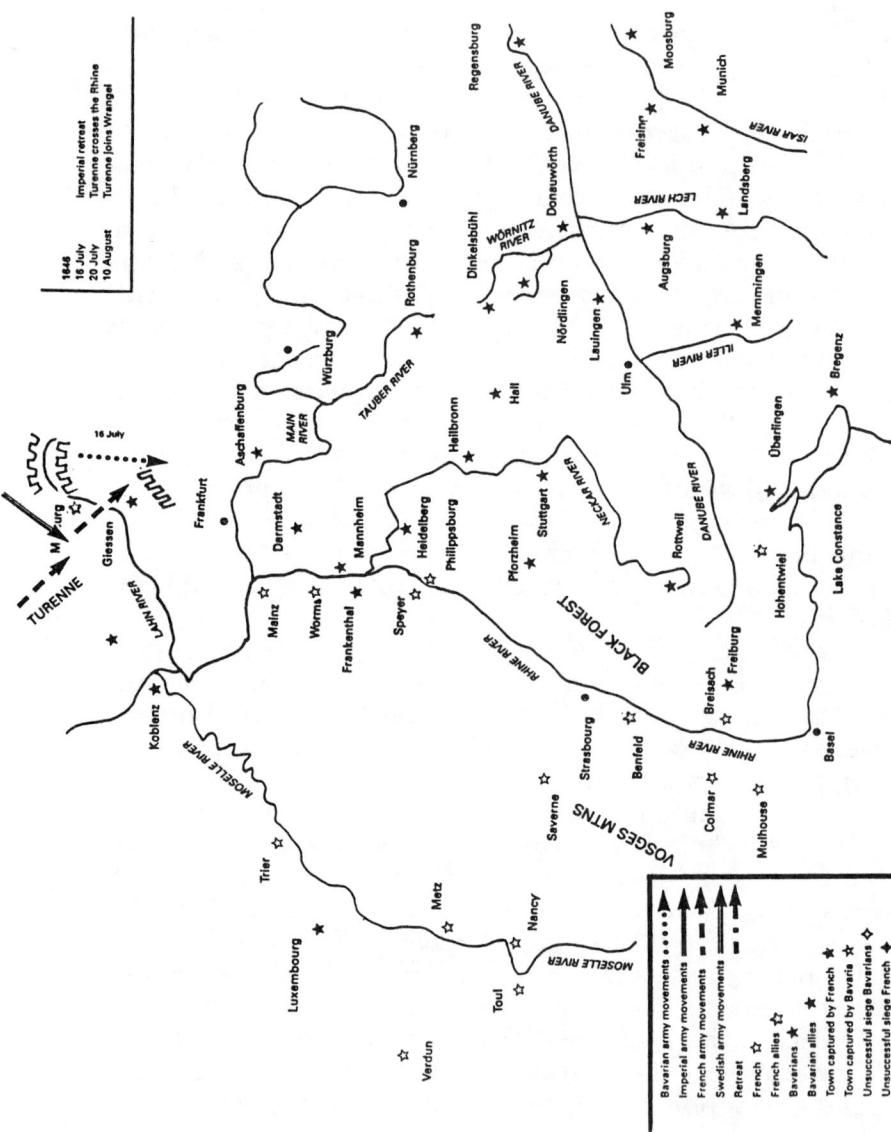

1646, July–August

In spite of his difficulties, Leopold Wilhelm felt that he had a strong defensive position which the allies could not attack except at a severe disadvantage. His plan was simple: "to await the enemy in our advantage [i.e., entrenchments]."[204] His letters to Maximilian are full of statements that he was concerned "above all with the conservation of Imperial arms."[205] This defensive-mindedness was reinforced by Maximilian's usual instructions not to let the enemy force him into battle. On 16 July, Maximilian claimed that the Protestants were being so difficult that they would only be brought to reason by a military defeat; on 31 July, however, he said that the negotiations seemed to be going better, with the caveat that this "will continue only as long as our arms suffer no special defeat."[206]

Leopold Wilhelm's excessive caution was a major factor in the disaster that followed.[207] In contrast to him, Turenne and Wrangel were commanders of conspicuous energy and aggressiveness: Turenne arrived in the Swedish camp on 10 August; the allies advanced to Friedberg on the 12th; and they attacked Leopold Wilhelm on the 14th. They considered the possibility of trying to beat Leopold Wilhelm to Heilbronn, just as Turenne and Enghien had tried to beat Mercy there the previous year, but concluded that this plan had little chance of success. Instead, Turenne sent an advanced guard to Bonamös, a small town guarding a crossing of the Nidda on the Imperial left flank. The French seized the crossing and repulsed the Bavarians sent to reinforce the garrison; shortly thereafter, Königsmarck effected a parallel *coup de main* on the Imperial right. Leopold Wilhelm remained safely in his entrenchments—but with his communications to the south cut off by the allied pincers.[208]

Turenne and Wrangel had achieved one of the most startling victories of the war. In a matter of just two days, they had bypassed an enemy army and cut off its retreat. The tables had been completely turned: now it was the Imperial-Bavarian army that could not go south without attacking at a disadvantage. In response to this situation, Leopold Wilhelm decided, in consultation with his officers, to take the extraordinary step of moving north. They could then, he pointed out, link up with Lamboy and Melander, the Imperial commanders in Westphalia; if the enemy followed, the burden of the war would be carried further into Hesse.[209] Turenne and Wrangel indeed considered following Leopold Wilhelm, figuring that they could push him across the Rhine and destroy his army in the process. However, in doing so they would lose their unparalleled opportunity to invade Bavaria,

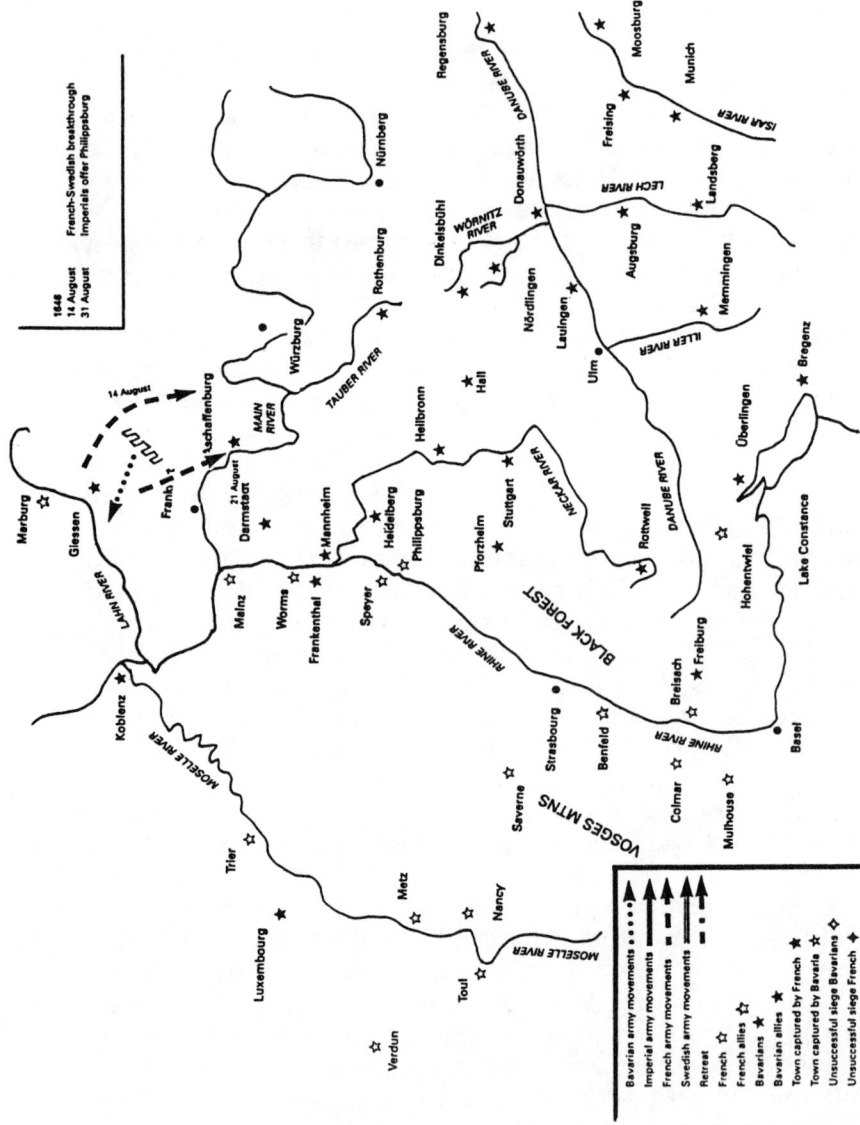

1646, August

which lay completely open to them. "We hold their retreat to be a victory, because we can go right into Bavaria without resistance and spread terror everywhere," wrote one French officer to Mazarin. Instead of giving Maximilian a chance to raise a new army to oppose them, therefore, they decided on an immediate and rapid advance to the south.[210]

Leaving garrisons in Steinheim and Aschaffenburg, which had a bridge over the Main, Turenne invaded the Swabian Circle. He intended to attack Heilbronn, the crucial fortress that he had failed to capture in 1645, but Leopold Wilhelm had reinforced the garrison with two thousand troops. It would take a long time to besiege such a strong fortress, and it would probably require Swedish assistance. In addition, Turenne feared that he would be so weakened in infantry by the end of the campaign that he would once again be forced to leave the Empire and take quarters west of the Rhine. The manoeuvre to get around Leopold Wilhelm had already fatigued the troops, who had had little rest since they began marching to join the Swedes at the end of June. Already on 22 August, Turenne was pleading for reinforcements before the end of the campaign so as to avoid the disastrous retreat of the previous year. "I hold fairly considerable posts at this time," he wrote to Mazarin in September, "but nothing provides quarters in Germany except an army as strong as the enemy's."[211]

Bypassing Heilbronn, therefore, Turenne instead besieged Schorndorf, taking it on 9 September after a weeklong siege. He judged it the second best place in Württemberg and Swabia behind Heilbronn, and felt it was necessary to assure his communications between the Danube and the Rhine. He then advanced further south and captured the town of Lauingen on the Danube. The bridge had been destroyed, but the town had been left ungarrisoned. Turenne quickly rebuilt the bridge and moved east toward Augsburg, at which point he was called to Rain by Wrangel. Just as in 1632, the Swedes had used massed artillery to force their way across the Lech and besiege the town. Turenne arrived at the siege on 20 September, just a day before Rain capitulated.[212]

Meanwhile, the Imperial forces had helped Darmstadt gain an advantage over Hesse-Cassel. The general of Hesse-Cassel's forces, Geyso, separated from the allies at Aschaffenburg and returned to Ziegenhain. The Darmstadter general, Eberstein, caught Geyso in the open on 18 September and routed his forces, forcing him to retreat under the guns of the fortress. But this victory was to be short-lived, for Darmstadt success depended

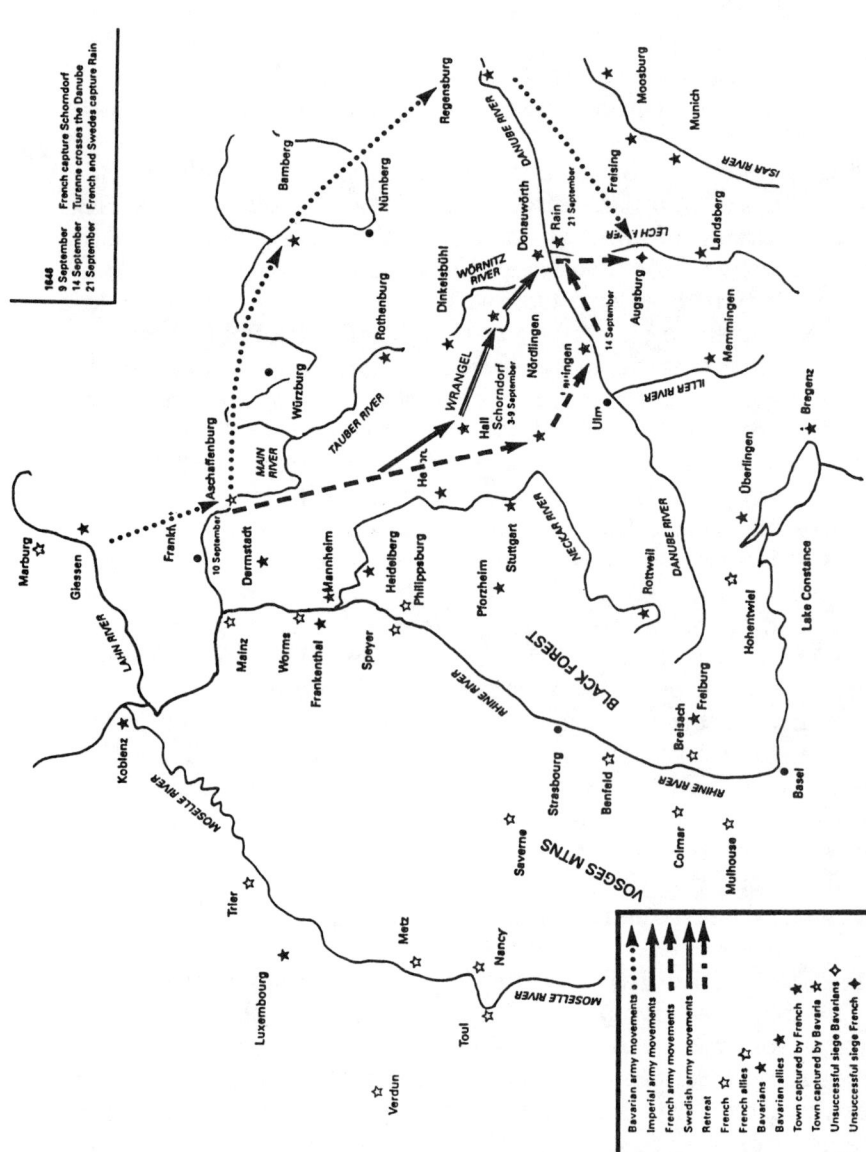

upon Imperial and Bavarian troops that were desperately needed elsewhere.[213]

Maximilian learned of the allied breakthrough on 19 August, and correctly guessed that Turenne would march straight for the Danube. Rejecting Leopold Wilhelm's attempt to draw the allies northward, he ordered an immediate return to defend Bavaria, failing which he threatened the emperor with pulling out of the war. Leopold Wilhelm complied on 4 September, recapturing Aschaffenburg and returning to Bavaria via Regensburg on 19 September. By that time, however, Maximilian had already fled Munich and the allies occupied all of Bavaria except Munich, Ingolstadt, and Rain, and Rain would fall in the next two days.[214]

The allied military breakthrough had an immediate impact on the peace negotiations. After their pessimistic letters of 13 August, the plenipotentiaries were already writing of significant progress by 20 August; d'Avaux even said that he expected affairs to be resolved within eight days.[215] The first and most pressing issue remained Philippsburg. Contarini upbraided the French, complaining that they had always said they would make peace if they received Breisach; this new demand had "ruined everything" and caused the Imperials to adopt a tougher stance. The French responded that they were now willing to drop their demand for sovereignty in Alsace and convince the Swedes to make peace on reasonable terms if they were given Philippsburg. A week later, Contarini again objected to the Philippsburg demand, arguing that the Imperials could not offer it without first submitting the issue to a vote of the estates. He also pointed out the difficulty of getting the estates to approve the transfer when Sötern, its owner, was vehemently opposed. At that moment, the French revealed the 19 July treaty with Sötern, completely undermining Contarini's line of reasoning. Bavarian and Imperial resistance to the surrender of Philippsburg collapsed. The question was put to a vote, but only of the Electors, who approved it without dissent on 23 August.[216] France had achieved the major objective of her summer negotiations.

The Imperials formally offered Philippsburg in their *Ultima generalis declaratio* of 31 August. As in their *Postrema declaratio* of 29 May, they attached many unacceptable conditions to the new concession. The most difficult of these was the question of French sovereignty over the immediate estates in Alsace and the three bishoprics of Metz, Toul, and Verdun. But with their important demand resolved, the French became more stubborn on this question as well. "Since we are assured of Philippsburg," Servien wrote, "it is necessary, it seems to me, to think strongly about the other side of the river."[217] There thus followed two weeks of intense negotiations over the details of the legal form of the surrender of Alsace and the three bishoprics—minutiae in one sense, but minutiae that had significant consequences for the amount of territory France acquired and her rights over it.

The Imperial cession of Alsace was changed from "Landgraviatus Alsatiae," the form used in the 14 April offer, to "Landgraviatus Superioris et Inferioris Alsatiae." The clearer formulation of the 29 May offer, in which the French were to get the Landvogtei Haguenau and the Landgraviate of Upper Alsace, was therefore abandoned, under pressure from the French, in favor of a return to the ambiguous "Landgraviate of Alsace," tempered only by the addition of "Upper and Lower," but with "Landgraviate" remaining in the singular. In addition, the Imperials incorporated a special clause reserving the rights of the immediate estates, which had, in the time since the 29 May offer of Alsace in sovereignty, clamored for exemption. The French were unable to resist this exemption without offending the German estates, but insisted on inserting an additional clause (beginning "ita tamen") afterward saying that the exemptions would not be understood to detract from French sovereignty accorded before.[218]

The exact meaning of the provisions for the transfer of Alsace to France has been debated endlessly: some maintain that France acquired all of Alsace in sovereignty; others, that it acquired only Habsburg rights; others have occupied varying positions in the middle ground. There seems no disputing that the terms were ambiguous; everyone involved, including the French, the Imperials, and the Alsatians, agreed on this point. "I believe it is necessary that everyone remains with his pretensions and explains the treaty as he understands it," wrote Servien in explaining it. Volmar, the Imperial legist, was more realistic. "The stronger will interpret them [i.e., the treaty clauses] to his advantage," he said.[219] The problem lies in explaining exactly which parts of the cession are paradoxical and which are clear.

The root of the ambiguity goes back to the Imperial offer of 14 April and the use of the term "Landgraviate of Alsace," or, as it finally made it into the treaty, "Landgraviate of Upper and Lower Alsace." Since the Landgraviate of Lower Alsace was essentially meaningless—and there was certainly no unified Landgraviate over the whole province—there was bound to be difficulty in interpreting it. The Imperials managed to insert a clause leaving the immediate estates "in that liberty and possession of immediacy towards the Roman Empire" that they have hitherto experienced, such that the French king "cannot pretend any royal superiority over them, but shall rest contended with the rights which appertained to the House of Austria." This seems clear enough, but then the "ita tamen" clause adds, "In such a manner, nevertheless, that by the present declaration, nothing is intended that shall derogate from the right of dominion already hereabove agreed to."[220]

As Georges Bardot has pointed out, the real contradiction lies in the last two clauses, not the first two. It was not a contradiction to grant France Alsace and then reserve the rights of the immediate estates, but it was a contradiction to say that the rights of the immediate estates—which includes the provision that France cannot claim "royal superiority"—should not detract from the "right of dominion" of France. What can be the meaning of the "immediacy" of the estates toward the Empire if France is to have "dominion"? If France were taking the territory as a fief, this would make sense, but it was not; the territory it acquired was being removed from the Empire altogether. Even Brienne wondered back in May how it made sense to exempt the immediate estates:

> There remain, and I am surprised that the Imperials did not notice it, new causes for debates between France and the Empire, since the latter reserves for itself the immediate estates that are enclaved in Alsace, the sovereignty of which they must renounce if France accepts that of the province.[221]

The matter is further complicated by the fact that the reserve clause specifically mentions a number of legal entities, some of which were being transferred to France (such as the Decapolis) and some of which were not (such as Strasbourg and the Lower Alsatian nobility). The Decapolis presented a particular problem, since the French were taking over the protection rights of the Habsburgs, yet the Decapolis itself remained immediate to the Empire. D'Avaux seemed to indicate the fuzziness in the French understanding of "immediacy," since he assured representatives from the Decapolis that he wanted them to remain "free states" as there were in France, citing Languedoc as an example. In other words, d'Avaux saw the acquisition of the Decapolis as yielding definite French authority, something the Decapolis disputed vigorously, but without success. The French continued to be unsure of the details of Alsatian administration for years afterward: Mazarin was urging Baussan to get matters straightened out in 1650 so the government could send a commission to take it over, and as late as 1664 the French requested permission to use Strasbourg's archives to figure out precisely what authority they had![222] With this sort of uncertainty in French thought, it is fruitless to search for a precise meaning to the contradictory treaty clauses. Everyone knew they were ambiguous, but few understood precisely why. No amount of research can unravel the contradictions; it was a matter to be resolved by the sword, not the pen.[223]

Similar difficulties arose with respect to the three bishoprics, with additional linguistic and legal complications. German distinguishes between *Stift*, the possessions of a bishopric, and *Diözese*, the area that it oversees as spiritual leader. Such a distinction did not exist in French (or English) because bishops in that land were not territorial lords. The Imperials tried to make an offer clearly limited to the temporal lands of the bishoprics (which also happened to be the lands effectively occupied by the French since 1552), but the French rejected their attempts; the final treaty therefore mentioned only the ambiguous term "districtus," which could be interpreted either way. The French were aware of the ambiguity, but calculated that it could help them extend their authority in the long run. Moreover, unlike in Alsace, the French completely deleted a clause reserving the rights of immediate estates in the bishoprics.[224]

One potential sticking point in the negotiations was the status of Spain and Lorraine, without whom the emperor did not wish to make peace. The question of Lorraine had already been discussed extensively by the French in the preceding weeks, especially since it also touched the Spanish negotiations. At one point the Portuguese representatives, not officially recognized at the congress, told the French plenipotentiaries in the first week of August that Mazarin had said he would permit Charles IV to send ambassadors to Münster if Spain would permit the Portuguese to do the same. This, however, was forcefully rebutted by the French, and Mazarin denied ever having made such an offer.[225] Nevertheless, the French did continue to consider possible ways of reaching an accommodation with Charles. Their position had always been that he could send representatives to Paris, but that his quarrel with France was unrelated to the talks at Münster and he was therefore not welcome there. From d'Avaux's discussions with others at the conference, he gathered that France could probably achieve its goal of excluding Lorraine from the congress; the emperor did not want to abandon Lorraine, but would not necessarily insist on his full participation, nor on a full restoration of his lands. D'Avaux, however, felt that France would be better off resolving their dispute with Lorraine in Münster. Mazarin, surprisingly, reacted positively to this suggestion.[226] But the court remained undecided on the best course, and again it was left to the plenipotentiaries to choose. Again a combination of Longueville and Servien overruled d'Avaux; they insisted that Charles not be permitted to carry on negotiations in Münster.[227] Since the emperor would not agree to this, the point remained in contention.

Even if the Lorraine issue had been resolved, however, the more difficult problem of what to do with Spain would have remained. It was unlikely that the emperor would abandon his cousin, yet France was insistent that this was precisely what he must do. Fortunately for the progress of the negotiations, Contarini suggested a compromise solution that was acceptable to both parties. Since this was just a preliminary treaty that would not end the war, he proposed that the emperor insert a clause saying that he would not make peace without his allies, Spain and Lorraine; and that the French put in a clause objecting. The plenipotentiaries wrote to Mazarin that they could have insisted on striking the emperor's clause entirely,

> but it seemed that we could not reasonably require the emperor to stop making [such assertions] until the end of the treaty, since his honor is engaged in them, and it should appear to the whole assembly that when he gives them up that he was constrained and forced for the good of the peace.[228]

With the resolution of this problem, the French and Imperials had reached an accommodation, and signed a preliminary treaty on 13 September. The final provisions included an indemnity of three million livres, as well as payment of two-thirds of the debts of the Alsatian administration.

The court praised the plenipotentiaries and celebrated a major triumph, while the plenipotentiaries went to Osnabrück in an attempt to convince Sweden to make peace.[229] The Swedes, who had suspected a French-Imperial treaty to be in the works for some weeks, immediately recognized the significance of the agreement.[230] They exhibited no bitterness or feelings of betrayal, as the French had feared in May, and in fact they welcomed French mediation to help them resolve their own satisfaction. Before September was over Christina had agreed to sacrifice half of Pomerania if necessary.[231] Somewhat ominously, d'Avaux saw a Swedish proposal for resolution of the *gravamina* and judged that it would take two years to resolve. The French court, on the other hand, entertained illusions of a quick end to hostilities. Upon hearing news of the treaty, they wrote that "the Spanish, seeing themselves pressed at the end of a campaign more than they had expected, have resolved to extricate themselves at any price, and to give us a *carte blanche*."[232] Mazarin's redoubled confidence ill prepared him for the disappointments of the coming year.

But the preliminary treaty, which would be taken up in the final instrument of peace almost word for word, represented a major accomplishment of French arms and French diplomacy. French territorial demands, first stated at the beginning of the year, had been resolved within nine months; Sweden, by contrast, continued negotiations for nearly fourteen months. Mazarin's strategy of using Bavaria to apply pressure on the emperor had worked brilliantly; and French military pressure was the decisive element in winning Bavarian support. The approaching campaign accelerated the negotiations in April and May, leading up to the *Postrema Declaratio* of 29 May, in which France was offered Alsace and Breisach.[233]

But the French had gone further. Afraid of achieving their treaty before Sweden, they used the time while they were waiting for Sweden to conclude in order to obtain Philippsburg and enhanced rights in Alsace and the three bishoprics. It may seem paradoxical that the French would not complete a treaty in May but would in September, considering that Sweden appeared just as far away in both cases. It is true that French logic changed somewhat; by September, they were growing increasingly impatient of Sweden's demands, and the threatening defection of the Dutch made the French desire a peace more than they had earlier. But the situations in May and September also had the great difference that one was at the beginning of a campaign, while the other was at its conclusion. In May, Sweden was being pressed by superior Imperial and Bavarian arms, and France could not have avoided sending Turenne to join Wrangel. By September, the campaign was winding down. Signing a treaty then seemed more reasonable, especially as the French expected Sweden's negotiations to be concluded well before the next campaign. In 1647, they could and did argue that they needed their troops more in the Low Countries; with both crowns' satisfaction achieved, and Bavaria out of the war, Sweden could no longer object. Moreover, the restrictions that the Imperials had attached to their offer of

29 May made French acceptance impossible; and without the help of military pressure, it seems most unlikely that the French would have been able to obtain their revocation.

In short, Philippsburg had been in no sense the cause of the continuation of the war by France. Even in September, when its acquisition seemed assured, the plenipotentiaries wrote of it as "that for which we wished more than we hoped."[234] These same plenipotentiaries were united in fearing the results of another campaign, which, to their way of thinking, could only work to France's disadvantage. They wanted peace before the campaign, not because they favored peace over war generally, but because they saw it was in France's best (diplomatic) interests. When it became clear to them that another campaign was inevitable, they yielded to it reluctantly; but they used it to their advantage once they had accepted it.

There is no obvious case of French demands being increased because of the military campaign in 1646. The increased demands in their response of 1 June were a reaction to the conditions attached to the Imperial offer, and were intended to be bargained away. At no time did they speak of using France's military advantages gained during the campaign to achieve anything other than the dropping of the Imperial conditions and the acquisition of Philippsburg. Nevertheless, it was precisely French military success that enabled the plenipotentiaries to achieve their demands so casually added on 1 June. Military affairs may therefore be said to have had an incidental role in the increasing of the terms France achieved in the preliminary treaty of 13 September.

Part III
Conclusion

9
Mazarin as Negotiator and Strategist

THE PRELIMINARY TREATY BETWEEN FRANCE AND THE EMPIRE DID not end the war. Although the French expected a general treaty to be just around the corner, negotiations dragged on for more than two years until the peace was finally signed on 24 October 1648. First, d'Avaux went to Osnabrück to help secure Swedish satisfaction. This was settled by February 1647, but, in the middle of the subsequent negotiations over Hessian satisfaction and the Palatinate question, the religious *gravamina* flared up again and caused the negotiations to stall.

France also had a part in the failure to make peace in 1647. Mazarin hoped to delay the Imperial peace until he could force Spain to accede to his demands, thereby removing all of France's enemies and preventing the possibility of the Austrian Habsburgs either reentering the war after Sweden had withdrawn, or secretly aiding Spain against France.[1] With Bavaria finally signing a separate truce at Ulm in March, Mazarin was able to send Turenne's army to the Low Countries to help deliver the coup de grâce to Spain.

Though the French situation appeared favorable, however, everything went wrong. First, the Weimarian army rebelled, part of it going to Sweden and Turenne losing valuable time pursuing the remainder. Rather than making rapid progress, France's military situation in the Low Countries stagnated without the Dutch, who refused to enter the campaign while carrying on negotiations with the Spanish. Then, in September, Maximilian grew frustrated with the pace of the talks and reentered the war.[2] Sweden's military situation, so promising the previous year, disintegrated, and Mazarin was forced to send Turenne back to the Empire to assist Wrangel.[3]

Meanwhile, Trauttmansdorff's June 1647 peace proposal included some retrenchments that detracted from France's gains in the preliminary treaty. The French quickly proposed a new treaty that was more in their favor. Only in November did the two sides at last agree to go back to the ambiguous formula used in the 1646 agreement.[4]

By the beginning of 1648, Mazarin had all but given up on the hope of including Spain in the peace; instead, he became increasingly fearful that Sweden would abandon France.[5] He therefore ordered his plenipotentiaries to conclude the negotiations as quickly as possible, but only under the condition that the emperor be barred from aiding Spain in any fashion.[6] Turenne and Wrangel's successful 1648 campaign, which paralleled their victories in 1646, forced the emperor to give in at last.[7] But although defeated handily at Lens, the Spanish continued to hold out, aware of the beginnings of the Fronde and the shaky position of the French leadership. It was thus that, much against his will, Mazarin consented to the Peace of Westphalia on 24 October 1648, ending the Imperial phase of the war.[8]

Almost immediately upon the signing of the Peace of Westphalia, Mazarin was criticized by Frenchmen for not making peace with Spain at the same time. Some accused him of not being interested in peace and thus demanding too difficult terms, while others felt that he was leaving France vulnerable to intervention from the Austrian Habsburgs in her continuing war with Spain.[9] Later, along with the rehabilitation of Mazarin's historical image, came a corresponding reassessment of the Peace of Westphalia: most historians began seeing it as a major accomplishment rather than a defeat.[10] But unlike other aspects of Mazarin's policies, his success at Westphalia has been questioned recently, in part by historians who are otherwise favorable to Mazarin, and in part by military historians who have nothing positive to say about the strategy of any early 17th century state (see the introduction to part I).

> *Because statesmen hazarded their reputation in foreign policy, later historians have judged them by it.*
> —Henry Kamen[11]

Evaluating a state's gains at the end of a war is extremely difficult, but it is essential if we are to make any sense of the war's outcome. Previous historians have usually summarized French gains and evaluated them all in the same breath, without any attempt to put them within the context of the time. Johannes Burkhardt, for example, asserts that the French did not gain much from the war because it brought "neither any recognized precedence, nor materially a singularly preferable standing in Europe."

Even more strongly, Stephen Lee speaks of France's "limited gains" at the Congress, since "Mazarin, as a pupil of Richelieu, certainly intended to push France's frontiers deep into Germany."[12] Given preconceptions like these, it is no wonder that French policy is often seen as a failure. Yet neither Richelieu, nor Mazarin, nor any other French minister sought these goals from the war; they were certainly not why the war was begun, and French demands at the conference never extended so wide that France would have achieved success on Burkhardt's or Lee's terms. Nor, it seems, would this have been a reasonable expectation based on the military and political situations. It would therefore be more logical to evaluate French gains in terms that would have made sense to contemporaries: by determining what France demanded at the beginning of the negotiations; how the French, their allies, and their opponents reacted to French gains; and what one might have expected the French to get, based on their military situation and the territory they actually occupied. By any of these standards, French gains—the acquisition of Alsace, Breisach, a garrison right in Philippsburg, and formal recognition of the Three Bishoprics—represent a major achievement.

The original French instructions in 1643 had called only for the acquisition of Breisach and the French-occupied towns in Alsace; as late as 1645, the French were still uncertain whether they would demand all of Alsace, and Philippsburg remained an expendable demand right up until the Imperials acquiesced in September 1646. This background puts French acquisitions in a much more positive light, demonstrating that their actual acquisitions in the treaty were lofty compared to their lowest expectations, and were close to their highest hopes. One common tactic for minimizing French gains, especially popular in recent years, is to elaborate on the specific territory conceded to France to show that she did not get all of Alsace. This approach usually results in a confused summary of the treaty terms, with the Sundgau emerging as France's main territorial acquisition in Alsace.[13]

Though preferable in many ways to the old textbook simplification of France getting Alsace, this approach leads to its own errors which can distort the historical picture even more. Stephen Lee, for example, concludes after summarizing the treaty terms that "there is no doubt that Mazarin had hoped for more." This is true to an extent—who does not hope for more in a negotiation?—but his evidence shows that Lee has fundamentally misunderstood the situation: he notes Mazarin's letter to Turenne in December 1647 saying "to consider Alsace a country which belongs to the King no less than Champagne does," as though this were an expectation of the future.[14] In fact, as the previous chapters have shown, Mazarin's understanding was that the treaty *did* give France Alsace. It is true that Mazarin's definition of "Alsace" included only Habsburg rights, but the important thing is that this was all that he was striving for. Moreover, the details of Alsatian administration being what they are, historians are unwilling to go into the very complicated details of the question of whether France received Alsace in sovereignty. The simplification they choose, however, usually gives weight more to the limitations that were placed on French authority than to the possession of the territory that was equally well, and in some ways more firmly, granted. For example, listing the Sundgau as France's main territorial acquisition ignores the fact that the treaty clearly grants France the Sundgau *in addition to,* and not instead of, Alsace.[15]

France's acquisitions in Alsace stand out even more strongly when compared to Richelieu's goals there. Richelieu's original ambitions in Alsace had included only a few fortified towns, not the entirety of Habsburg rights that was eventually conceded.[16] Moreover, every indication suggests that contemporaries felt that the French were getting more than Richelieu would have. D'Avaux, for example, wrote that "if the late cardinal Richelieu returned to the world, he would hardly be able to believe that since his death, Your Eminence [i.e., Mazarin] had carried our affairs to such a high point," while a royal memorandum declared that "the advantages that France and her allies have gained since the death of [cardinal Richelieu] give us reason to hope for greater satisfaction in Germany than one would have hoped for at that time."[17] Servien once told Mazarin that he would have the glory "to have acquired for the King that which most people would not even have dared to demand." It seems likely that he was not just flattering Mazarin on this point, because he had already earlier argued that France was doing so well in the treaty that they should not risk breaking it off to gain the Forest Towns; surely if he did not believe that France was doing well, he would not have said this.[18]

French success in the negotiations should be contrasted with the failure of the emperor, who was forced by stages to surrender almost every point that the French demanded—first all of Alsace, then Breisach, and finally Philippsburg. Whereas the French acquired more than they had originally hoped, the emperor lost more than he had expected. Nor was it only the French who felt themselves successful: upon being told that Mazarin thought highly of him, Trauttmansdorff responded by saying that "cardinal Mazarin . . . has done more against us and negotiates now with more rigor than cardinal Richelieu or any other French subject."[19] French gains were recognized to be even greater because they were accomplished under a regency; as the plenipotentiaries wrote to the queen, "Your Majesty will have this glory, that during a royal minority, when all concerns have always been on keeping the State whole, you will have not only extended French borders to their oldest limits, but also to have acquired two very important fortresses on the Rhine."[20]

Louis XIV's ministers were not simply deluding themselves into believing that they had accomplished a great deal in the negotiations, because France's acquisitions were great in proportion to her military position. The French occupied Lorraine, Alsace and other territory along the middle Rhine, and considerable land in Swabia at the time of the peace. Lorraine was deliberately excluded from the negotiations because France wished to deal with it separately, so it should not be considered in these calculations. Swedish territorial gains were comparable: part of one province (Pomerania) and two secularized bishoprics (Bremen and Verden). Although Bremen was much wealthier than Breisach or Philippsburg, Swedish rights to it were unclear, and Alsace was wealthier than Pomerania. The single major difference appears to be the indemnity: whereas the French paid the Imperials compensation for Alsace, the Swedes received money from the Imperial Circles. Yet the French consciously chose to pay an indemnity that they might well have avoided because they wished to mollify the Habsburgs and keep them from trying to reclaim Alsace. This strategy was only a partial success, but it compares favorably with Sweden's harsher terms, since Sweden became locked in a struggle with the Great Elector over the possession of West Pomerania in the years immediately following the war. Moreover, one must also consider that Sweden occupied considerably more territory than France in 1648: most of Northern Germany, passage rights in Brandenburg and Saxony, large parts of Silesia, Moravia, and Bohemia. With more to exchange, Swedish bargaining power was correspondingly greater. Undoubtedly Sweden received more than France did, but the difference is not as great as one might expect given their military success in the war.[21]

But is this not in itself an indictment of France? How could a state of nearly twenty million people not conquer more than Sweden, which had a population around one-tenth of that? The obvious reason is that the Empire was only a secondary theater for the French, who were preoccupied with fighting Spain in the Low Countries, Italy, Catalonia, and the Mediterranean. It is not merely that France had fewer resources to devote to the German theater, but that Mazarin deliberately kept his commitment there as low as possible so as to concentrate most of his effort against Spain. This strategy became even more important after the Dutch defection, and it explains Mazarin's decision to send Turenne to Luxembourg in 1647 rather than marching for the Habsburg hereditary lands in Bohemia. This move may have been a bad decision, but one must evaluate French gains at the Congress of Westphalia based on their own priorities. Considering the military realities of the day, and the fact that the French devoted very limited resources to the Empire, it is difficult to see how they could have achieved more.[22]

Military campaigns of the 1640s did not generally conform to the impressions of present historians: offensives were not especially hampered, and armies were not so encumbered by logistical concerns that their sole purpose became their own survival. Since southwestern Germany, the chief battleground, contained few strong fortresses, cavalry was the most important element on the campaign and in battle. So far from being a matter of slowly grinding attacks, the battles that shaped the course of the campaigns each year were often the result of one side surprising and overwhelming the other, as at Tuttlingen, Herbsthausen, and Zusmarshausen. French officials, from Mazarin down to Turenne, viewed this uncertainty as the central aspect of the war and shaped their actions accordingly.

Mazarin applied his understanding of war skillfully. By adopting an attritional strategy based on occupying Bavaria's winter quarters, he made effective use of France's material leverage while seeking to minimize the potential dangers inherent in deep invasions such as those that had been carried out by Guébriant in the years from 1640–1643. Mazarin also carefully coordinated his military strategy with his diplomatic aims; in particular, he was anxious not to cause too much damage to Bavaria, a potential partner, but instead preferred to use military pressure only when the Bavarians failed to support French aims at the peace conference. He used the minimum strength necessary against Bavaria, twice holding Enghien's army in reserve and only sending it to reinforce Turenne when it became clear that there was no other way to prevent a Bavarian offensive. Furthermore, Mazarin was capable of using military force for different purposes and in different strengths: blunting a Bavarian offensive in 1644; showing

France's seriousness after the defeat at Herbsthausen in 1645; applying pressure to Bavaria in 1646, but without engaging the Bavarian army and thus weakening a potential ally.

Mazarin did not try to micromanage the campaigns or the negotiations. True, he delegated little authority to Brienne or Le Tellier, but he used his central control only to issue broad policy directives and not specific commands, such as when and where to fight. This management style permitted his generals and plenipotentiaries to adapt to local circumstances rapidly. In 1645, for example, Mazarin urged Enghien to engage the enemy in late July, but, unlike Maximilian before the battle of Herbsthausen, he did not try to weigh the strengths of the two armies to decide for himself when would be the best time to strike. Similarly, in 1646, Mazarin told Turenne to linkup with Wrangel, and gave him general instructions to keep as much independence as possible from the Swedish army (although, significantly, he provided several choices depending on how firmly Wrangel demanded that Turenne remain nearby). The negotiations functioned in much the same way: Mazarin issued orders in 1643 and again at the end of 1645 describing French demands in several steps, so that the plenipotentiaries could choose the appropriate course based on circumstances at the conference. He managed the negotiations more closely than the military campaigns, but he still allowed the plenipotentiaries considerable leeway.

Mazarin's flexibility meant that some decisions of which he did not approve would inevitably be taken by those on the scene, but this was relatively rare. Moreover, his commanders never acted on their own against his orders, as is sometimes claimed in the secondary literature. The only possible case of insubordination was Turenne's linkup with Wrangel in 1646, but a close examination of the correspondence shows that Turenne had already received orders from the plenipotentiaries to execute the junction, and in fact was being unusually punctilious in waiting for direct orders from court. Unlike Richelieu, Mazarin was not vindictive, and never punished a subordinate for disobeying orders (though he did sometimes rebuke one). He was fortunate that Turenne, Enghien, d'Avaux, Servien, and Longueville were so talented, but part of the credit for this must go to Mazarin. He chose Turenne and Servien personally, and retained his subordinates more conscientiously than Richelieu, in spite of occasional political differences. In addition, Mazarin wisely bypassed the less competent Brienne as much as possible. Maximilian's management style was very different: he insisted on close control over all affairs, diplomatic and military. This proved as successful, in its own way, as Mazarin's style; Maximilian was often unhappy with his subordinates, but almost always because they were incompetent, not because they were disobedient.

While Mazarin allowed his generals and plenipotentiaries freedom of action, he himself remained focused on his goals and pursued them with great patience. Historians have long recognized Mazarin's tenacity, but it is often forgotten among talk of the grandiose, "Italian" plans that are usually attributed to him.[23] If patience is not considered a particularly Italian characteristic, neither was it considered very French, at least not in the seventeenth century. In his tract "De l'intérêt des princes et des états de la chrétienté," published in 1637 and reprinted many times in the 1640s, Henri de Rohan commented that the French had to be careful to choose as negotiators "phlegmatic people who have no trace of the impatient humor."[24] Mazarin was aware that he was going against the prevailing view of the French national character, and he remarked to d'Avaux, on the subject of the arrival of Longueville's wife in Münster, that "the bad opinion that people have of our patience, and that a long assembly makes you afraid, has made them judge that the news of this voyage is an artifice and a vain show of our firmness." He continued, however, by noting that some ministers in Brussels were convinced

> that the French have changed their nature . . . It appears by the resolution that [Longueville] has made to bring his wife to live with him that he is putting himself in a state to pass his life at Münster sooner than to cede anything by impatience of the things that concern the honor of Her Majesty and the advantages of her crown.[25]

Georg Heyner, who has written specifically on Mazarin's German policy, portrays a very different view of Mazarin, one in which patience and consistency have little role:

> Fundamentally, Mazarin's German policy up to 1648 shows a peculiar weakness and indecision. The lack of a firm line and the frequent fluctuations are attributable above all to the effect of the military events, which influenced the negotiations in Münster and France's relations with individual German states to the utmost.[26]

It is true that Mazarin sanctioned the continuing of military operations while negotiating: when Servien loudly complained that Maximilian was being deceitful to conduct secret talks with France while carrying on a military offensive in April and again in October of 1645, Mazarin explicitly excused the Bavarian practice, saying it would be imprudent for them to act otherwise (see chapter 7). Besides, Mazarin believed that the fastest way to peace lay through continued military pressure. As he wrote to Turenne after Vervaux's visit in 1645,

> to heat up this negotiation . . . the best means . . . is for you to act vigorously, such that neither the duke [Maximilian] . . . nor the others see any possibility to improve their situation except through an accommodation.[27]

It often seemed that Mazarin was equally happy to allow the military campaigns to push his own demands higher or lower according to French success or failure on the battlefield. "It would be very just," read an official memorandum, "that, if the allied armies make considerable progress, France and Sweden demand new advantages in the peace in proportion to those that we have conquered in the war and that we would be in a state to increase even more if it continues."[28] Similar references could be multiplied, but the most striking one of all is found in a letter from Mazarin to d'Avaux, in which he writes that "France will always regulate its pretensions according to its affairs, and she will speak differently according to them, as she did when she appeared to claim that she did not demand anything in Germany, and now she is demanding some satisfaction."[29] In other words, Mazarin was justifying France's *volte-face* regarding satisfaction in the Empire by saying simply that her military situation had gotten better. He also wrote deceptively that France "appeared to claim" no satisfaction before, whereas in fact Richelieu had been very explicit on this point in the early days of the war. A more blatantly dishonest and self-justifying statement would be hard to find.

This makes it all the more surprising to find Mazarin complaining on other occasions about the inconstancy of France's allies and enemies, who changed their conduct according to the actual state of affairs. Maximilian was a particular target for the French, who claimed that he "always makes his decisions according to circumstances."[30] The Elector of Trier was upbraided for his "ordinary lightness of spirit," and even France's close allies, the Swedes, were criticized because they were "not as easy to please as we . . . after having been accorded everything, they make new demands."[31] This last statement was particularly ironic given that, just eight days later, the French would reject an Imperial offer of

Alsace and Breisach, precisely what the French had demanded, and insist upon obtaining Philippsburg as well (see chapter 8).

In some cases the French deliberately used the inconstancy of other states as a justification for their own changing terms. As Mazarin once wrote to the plenipotentiaries, "But since in this change in affairs for which the Imperials hoped, they changed their conduct and raised their voices, it would also be appropriate, the situation having again become favorable to us, that you imitate them and speak more firmly than ever."[32] These and similar statements are contrasted with images of France, and Mazarin in particular, as steadfast in the face of changes, whether for better or for worse. Longueville, for example, wrote to Mazarin that

> prosperity never led you to refuse reasonable conditions, and in the same fashion, adversity redoubles in you, by your natural generosity, the firmness and the cares by which you have so advantageously remedied all failures that have occurred up until now;

and Mazarin himself wrote that "the passion that I have for peace is always the same, and does not suffer any increase."[33]

The perplexing thing is the way that both tendencies in French thought—the willingness to take advantage of changing circumstances by changing policies, and the feeling that steadfastness in the face of adversity was the only honorable course—could be combined in one statement, as though it made perfect sense to be both changeable and unchangeable at the same time. One royal letter spoke of the conduct of the plenipotentiaries,

> which certainly could not have been more prudent *nor more proportioned to the present state of affairs,* and to the constant passion that Their Majesties always have to see Christianity's repose well established, *without this constancy being in any fashion shaken by the successes of their arms* and by the appearances that they will be able to increase them more and more in the continuation of the war.[34] [italics added]

In light of these contradictory statements, the only way to judge the French is by their actual behavior. By this standard, Mazarin's policy was anything but indecisive, and military events had few perceivable repercussions at all. France's territorial acquisitions by the preliminary treaty of September 1646 differed little from the original instructions sent to the plenipotentiaries in 1643. It is true that Mazarin had increased his demands in some ways: he did not concede any part of Alsace, as envisaged in the instructions, and added Philippsburg to his other demands. No doubt these changes reflected the successful 1644 campaign in which France's control of Alsace was assured and Philippsburg was conquered, but it is impossible to trace the exact moment when they became incorporated into French demands.

The difficulty in speaking of "French demands" before they were made public in January 1646 is that they remained extremely flexible; indeed, to the extent that they can be traced in the surviving correspondence, there can hardly be said to have been a French negotiating position at all before that time. The court did not even discuss demands with the plenipotentiaries until the middle of 1645, and did not issue formal orders until November of the same year. By that time, French ministers generally agreed that France should get Alsace, Breisach, and Philippsburg, but most of the details were left unclear, especially since the ministers themselves were unsure of the exact legal status of the territory they were demanding.

Even after the French made their demands public in January 1646, however, the imprecise and sloppy use of terminology by the plenipotentiaries and the court in their internal correspondence makes nonsense of any attempt to follow French demands very closely. If they were to be traced exactly, French demands would change with practically every mention, since no one made an effort to state what he meant with any precision.[35]

In addition, the French plenipotentiaries made numerous informal proposals designed to test their opponents. These exploratory demands, which did not reflect the true orders sent out from the court, were sometimes rejected outright (as the Bavarians rejected the French proposal in August 1645), and sometimes grudgingly accepted (as the Imperials eventually accepted the demand for Philippsburg). The plenipotentiaries had little to lose by such measures: made in private, they could easily retreat from them if rejected; but if the enemy accepted them, it was so much the better for France. Given the decentralized nature of the talks, with the plenipotentiaries carrying on negotiations and receiving orders only after a two-week time lag, the opportunistic nature of these French probes is essential for understanding the evolution of French demands. The plenipotentiaries would not have departed from the main line of Mazarin's policy, but they were willing to try almost anything within this broad context, such as Longueville's request for Strasbourg in a discussion with Trauttmansdorff. "Since we are trying to gain things over and above our instructions, we are only attempting this as long as we can do so without breaking off or retarding the negotiations,"

Longueville explained to Mazarin.[36] This kept pressure on the Imperials and, sometimes (as in the case of Philippsburg), materially altered the course of the talks. All of the plenipotentiaries also showed a surprising willingness to distort prior statements, misinterpret the legal situation, and feign ignorance if these ruses could help them gain more territory.[37]

It is only with these strong reservations, therefore, that it is possible to speak of the French negotiating position at all. Within these limits, the surprising conclusion is that the military campaigns had little effect on French demands.[38] Neither Freiburg, nor Jankov, nor Alerheim led the French to increase their demands in any immediate sense, nor did Mazarin lower his demands after their defeats at Tuttlingen or Herbsthausen. Undoubtedly the conquest of Philippsburg led, in the long run, to its incorporation in French demands, but neither Mazarin nor his plenipotentiaries made any comment to this effect until months afterward, and never in connection with the military campaign itself.

France's official demands were firm and consistent. Mazarin insisted, from the end of 1645, on Alsace and Breisach. The official demands of January 1646 included these plus Philippsburg, which he hoped for, and several other items, which were intended only as padding, to be given away under the guise of concessions. The end result was that France obtained precisely what Mazarin had insisted upon.[39]

Why was the French negotiating position virtually impervious to military success or defeat, contrary to what almost all historians have argued? One explanation that dovetails with some recent scholars' reinterpretation of Mazarin is that he was an internationalist interested in creating peace in the *Res publica Christiana*; if this is true, then Mazarin deliberately sacrificed French interests in order to make peace sooner. For example, Charlie Sheen claims that the idea of Christendom "acted to counter the concern of individual rulers and statesmen for the particular good of their own lands . . . statesmen generally accepted the obligations that it imposed on their activity," and, more specifically, he argues that "Mazarin's attitude toward the papacy continued to reflect a sense of order in Christendom." Other historians, looking at the negotiations at the Congress of Westphalia in light of Mazarin's inferred interest in the *Res publica Christiana*, have argued that Mazarin was fundamentally moderate and even pacifistic.[40] It is easy enough to find statements by Mazarin indicating his ardent support for religion and his passionate devotion to peace, but this is not the same as demonstrating his actual beliefs. Abraham de Wicquefort, a contemporary of Mazarin's, once wrote that "the cardinal wanted everyone to believe that peace was not only his inclination, but also his interest; and he talked about it so much and with such strong expressions that he almost persuaded himself that he wanted something [peace] to which he was in fact averse."[41] Whether or not one agrees with Wicquefort's assessment, his statement makes it clear that one has to look beyond Mazarin's professions of his desire for peace. The real question is not what he said, but what he did.

One important aspect of this question is whether French territorial demands were aggressive or defensive. Most recent historians have opted for the latter view. The most extreme among them claim that he saved France, "a Catholic monarchy threatened with death"; but even a more moderate historian such as Laurain-Portemer has written that "in the East, in making of the Rhine a natural frontier all along Alsace . . . , Mazarin had no other goal than to make the capital safe from invasion."[42] Lossky argues that France's borders were more secure at Mazarin's death than any other time, adding that "moderation was the secret of his success in bringing the gift of security to his adopted country."[43]

Numerous statements by Mazarin and his ministers support the idea that defense was the major goal of their negotiations in the 1640s. Mazarin, for example, wrote that the Flemish conquests would form a "second line of defense" for Picardy.[44] Brienne once commented that Picardy was necessary for the defense of Paris, and Servien made the oft-quoted statement that the acquisition of Cambrai and Cambrésis "would render our frontier impregnable from that side, which would make Paris very secure."[45] Alsace, too, can arguably be seen as a defensive demand, since it interdicted the Spanish road: "this dangerous communication of the forces of the House of Austria, which our fathers feared," wrote the plenipotentiaries, "is now broken and discontinued by the efforts and the prudent conduct of Your Majesty."[46]

But if part of the reason for France's acquisitions was defensive, which it undoubtedly was, it still seems hard to argue that they were not partially based on aggressive expansionism.[47] Breisach, the basis of French demands, was intended primarily to give France an invasion route into the Empire. It was therefore a fundamentally offensive demand; Alsace without Breisach would serve France "like an arm without a hand," wrote one French representative.[48] Of course, all such demands were wrapped in the defensive rhetoric by the French, who spoke of their need to preempt

Habsburg aggression. Another Frenchman, de La Force, once described Alsace as a "defensive wall for the security of Lorraine"; Breisach, in turn, served to block the Habsburg invasion route into Alsace, as Mazarin explicitly noted in rejecting the Imperial offer of Alsace without Breisach.[49] Such a "defensive" policy, however, would never end, since each new territory would require further conquests for its own security.[50] This line of reasoning is supported by the fact that Trauttmansdorff had offered to destroy Breisach and to allow the French to build a new fortress west of the Rhine—and he been emphatically rebuffed. Moreover, even if Breisach was essential for defending the Rhine, what was the purpose of Alsace? The mostly successful attempt to stretch out French control beyond the major fortresses in the province can only have been an endeavor to gain additional territory for France in the pursuit of national aggrandizement, and not to create an easily defensible border along the Rhine.[51] Indeed, with its territorial enclaves jutting out far from French territory, on the other side of Lorraine, Alsace was more of a defensive hindrance than a benefit.[52]

Another way of testing Mazarin's commitment to peace in Christendom and the defense of the *Res publica Christiana* is through his policy toward the Ottoman Empire, especially since some historians have used this case to defend the idea of Mazarin as a Christian internationalist. Andrew Lossky, for example, notes that Mazarin bequeathed a large sum for a war against the Ottomans, and Maurice Schumann claims that "throughout his whole ministry . . . we have always seen him conduct himself and curb himself as though he felt that a menace continued to press upon a divided Europe."[53]

Based on his actions in the 1640s, however, there is little evidence that Mazarin put forth special efforts to fight the Turks. It is true that he provided Venice, the one state under direct attack from the Ottomans, with more sailors than did Spain; however, this is hardly saying much, considering that the French were in a dominant position in the Mediterranean naval war.[54] Mazarin's one bold, self-sacrificing initiative in fighting Turks was his proposal of a naval truce in 1645 to allow Spain a free hand against them; yet this was, by his own admission, a blatant ruse that would actually help France rather than hurt her.[55] Otherwise, Mazarin was not even willing to make apparent concessions in order to aid other states against the Turks. For example, his diplomats deftly sidestepped a request by the Venetian mediator Contarini to get them to agree to a truce with Spain in case the Turks launched a full-scale attack.[56] Mazarin did agree to assist the emperor against the Turks after the war was over, but repeatedly insisted on sending men rather than money. He admitted that this would be less efficient, but did not wish to see the Habsburgs maintain an army during peacetime. Mazarin spoke of this venture not with the zeal of a crusader, but with the cold calculation of a statesman; after all, he noted, what else would France do with all those discharged soldiers after the war?[57]

If Mazarin did little to help fight the Turks while the Thirty Years' War continued, neither did he do much to end the "European Civil War" so that Christendom could unite against the common enemy. Naturally, official letters spoke openly of the sacrifices France was making by not raising its demands; in private, however, Mazarin and the other French ministers were more open about the advantage provided by the Turkish threat.[58] Servien, for example, wrote that "all that conscience requires of us in this occasion is that we do not demand new conditions because of it," and in another letter he wrote that France's last offer to Spain "is very reasonable, especially since they have become afraid of being attacked by the Turks. If they were in our place, they are not such good Christians that they would want to give up conquests they had already made."[59] Servien even indicated that France should try to delay an agreement between the Ottomans and their enemies before France had made peace with the Habsburgs.[60] Mazarin did not personally make such bold statements, but neither did he show any inclination to lessen his terms in order to conclude peace sooner. The only expedient he proposed for making peace was to offer Spain the excuse of the Turkish threat if they needed to save face in giving in to all of France's demands—hardly a sacrifice on Mazarin's part.[61]

These are not the actions of a leader surrendering the interests of his own state for the sake of peace. The Venetian ambassador Nani, the observer with the most at stake in France's participation in the conflict against the Ottomans, told the Senate not to expect anything from Mazarin, even after the war. He said that Mazarin was really trying to use the Turks as a balance against the Austrians, and that "it is easy to promise from afar because time always brings changes and accidents."[62] One of Mazarin's own statements indicates that the promise of aid against the Turks was just another diplomatic tool for him: in 1645 he wrote to the plenipotentiaries that

> it would be useful not to lose any occasion to keep talking to the mediators and always assure them more that France will take marvel-

lous action for the good of Christendom [against the Turks] provided that peace is made. It appears that this motive will cause them to put all of their effort into getting our enemies to concede the conditions that we desire.[63]

Such forthrightness about deceptive means is not surprising in light of other statements by Mazarin. Most strikingly, he once wrote that "I support [the king's interests] with more firmness and courage, when it comes down to it, than Monsieur le Cardinal-Duc [i.e., Richelieu] ever did. I dissimulate, I equivocate, I soothe, I accommodate as much as I can."[64] In other words, he admitted that he adapted himself to the circumstances. It therefore seems reasonable to assume that he would have adopted the garb of a *dévot* in order to quiet internal dissent and to satisfy Catholics abroad, rather than admit that he was promoting French interests at any cost. The fact remains that, although Mazarin may well have been a religious man, Christianity impinged little upon his political decisions; Osiander's assertion that "neither the French prime minister Mazarin nor his protégé at the congress Servien hesitated to sacrifice religion to raison d'état" seems accurate.[65]

It would be a mistake, however, to discard the modern idea of Mazarin as an internationalist peacemaker only to return to the equally exaggerated seventeenth century view of Mazarin as a deceitful, self-interested Italian.[66] As Saint-Aulaire notes, Mazarin was merely playing by the rules of the game, and those rules included clothing self-interest in religious costume where necessary.[67] Undoubtedly some statesmen put religion even before interest of state, but the voices proclaiming a community of Christian nations were so loud in part precisely because rulers were promoting their individual states more than ever.[68] Moreover, people who believed in the unity of Christendom often felt that unity only in a religious sense, or as a feeling of European civilization as united against heathens and infidels; it did not necessarily imply a Christian commonwealth, as André Corvisier has pointed out.[69]

If Mazarin was neither a flatly immoral leader intent on preserving his own power, nor a pacifist, what was he? Saint-Aulaire's portrait of Mazarin as a French nationalist is probably an exaggeration, but closer to the truth than either of the alternatives.[70] Mazarin was certainly interested in keeping power and enriching himself, but he was just as obviously interested in promoting France's international position. As he once wrote to d'Avaux,

> I am not at all unhappy that the Spanish accuse me of having an aversion to peace. It means, to judge it soundly, that I know their weakness and the good state of our affairs, and that I do not want to lose the great advantages that France can gain in such a conjuncture; and consequently they declare me by this accusation to be a very good Frenchman, as I effectively am.[71]

In other words, Mazarin was willing to pursue French aggrandizement through whatever means necessary. Most historians, even some of Mazarin's staunchest defenders, have been willing to admit that Mazarin practiced what Georges Livet calls "a marvelous demonstration of political realism of the fashion that is customarily designated under the name of Machiavellianism"[72]; Paul Guth speaks of Mazarin's "pitiless realism," whereas Saint-Aulaire prefers to distinguish between Mazarin's realism and the less savory term, opportunism (with only marginal success).[73] In order to understand why Mazarin's negotiating terms were very stable, then, it would be better to look for an answer in diplomatic and military realities than in Mazarin's supposed Christian idealism.

To begin with, Mazarin conceived of the military situation in fluid terms, believing that it could be completely reversed within a short time. As he noted on several occasions, "the prosperity of arms is never continual."[74] His fears were probably overstated, but it is true that surprise attacks were common and that superiority in number of troops was even less of a guarantee of success than at other times in history. Because of this, Mazarin was anxious to take advantage of France's superiority while he could, rather than risking a defeat that would undo years of success. At the same time, however, caution on the military front did not lead Mazarin to hasty withdrawals on the diplomatic front. He knew that France had massive resources, and was prepared to ride out short-term military defeats. As Brienne wrote after the disaster at Herbsthausen, "France has resources which other states simply do not, and when she manages them with care she lacks neither men nor money . . . for defending herself and for carrying the war into the enemy's country."[75] Mazarin's entire strategy was aimed at converting this material superiority into a battlefield victory in the safest way possible. Instead of being shaken by temporary defeats, therefore, he waited until France's resources could turn the war to his advantage again.

Mazarin's caution had another, purely diplomatic side. He realized that, beyond a certain point, France was too dependent on the goodwill of the German estates and on the faithfulness of Sweden to follow up military victories with increased terms in Münster.[76] The demands for all of Alsace and for Philippsburg created enough anxiety among the French because of this dependence; to have insisted on Mainz as well, for example, would have been diplomatic suicide. Mazarin in effect acknowledged this when he sought to assure the Prince of Orange that "even if the King of Spain were to offer Her Majesty all of his kingdoms to have peace, we would never accept it except jointly and with the consent and satisfaction of the United Provinces and of all the allies of this crown."[77] Moreover, once France's demands were made public in 1646, there could be no more question of increasing them, since this would be seen by all as negotiating in bad faith. Although Mazarin occasionally protested that France had a right to increase its demands when she conquered more territory, he was too astute ever to do this in practice.[78] What sometimes appear to be new demands are almost always mere clarifications, which were inevitable given the ambiguous legal situation in Alsace. (The sole exception is the small town of Neuenburg, which the French demanded briefly during 1646 but then dropped.)

Mazarin once wrote that fear of Sweden making a separate peace "should always prevail over all other considerations."[79] There are good reasons for this apparently excessive concern with one of France's allies. First, Mazarin was always more interested in Spain than in the emperor, in spite of occasional statements to the contrary. This meant that he wanted to put as few resources as possible into the German war, which, in turn, meant a maximum reliance on Sweden (and, to a lesser extent, Hesse-Cassel). Second, Mazarin felt that the Habsburgs hated France more, and hence were anxious to avenge themselves on France, even at the expense of making heavy concessions to get Sweden out of the war.[80] This was, in fact, the essence of Trauttmansdorff's strategy. "Now it has become crystal clear," he wrote to the emperor on 30 March 1646,

> that if we want to have peace, it must be obtained through the reconciliation of the Imperial estates, Sweden, and the Dutch, and by withdrawing their assistance to force France to make peace. All the plans that one hears here and there that we should first give France satisfac-

tion, and then make peace with the other enemies through their help, are without any foundation.[81]

Though the Habsburgs may have aimed at isolating France, however, their hatred of France was not as extreme as Mazarin believed. After all, though Ferdinand did try to make a separate peace with Sweden first, he then tried the same game with France, only to be rebuffed. Nor can Servien's explanation be accepted that Sweden was simply too difficult to invade;

> the rude climate, the frightening forests, the inaccessible rocks of Sweden, her severity and her poverty make soldiers fear being sent there as much as the softness of the air, the fertility, and the richness of the provinces of France make them desire to be brought here.[82]

The real reason France was a particular target of the Habsburgs, as well as many other states, was simply that it was getting too strong. As Mazarin himself acknowledged, "the greater this crown's prosperity becomes and the more it increases, the more it excites envy even in our friends, and jealousy and fear in those who are indifferent."[83] Fear of Spanish hegemony was slowly being replaced by fear of French hegemony, as the Dutch acknowledged *de facto* when they made a separate peace with Spain in 1648. The balance of power principle was operating in practice, if not consciously.[84]

Some historians, especially Laurain-Portemer, have praised Mazarin for being a faithful ally.[85] However, it is difficult to find any cases where Mazarin was faithful on principle instead of merely out of self-interest.[86] John O'Connor's assessment is more reasonable: that Mazarin, in contrast to Louis XIV, was particularly good at keeping his schemes in line with the interests of his allies.[87] As Gaston Zeller has pointed out, Mazarin had no compunction about abandoning England and Portugal in 1659.[88] Moreover, it is clear that he was ready to abandon Portugal and Catalonia in the 1640s if Spain had been willing to abandon Lorraine. It is therefore more accurate to say that Mazarin was a faithful ally because he was a good diplomat than to say that he was a faithful ally because he was inherently loyal.

Most books on negotiating theory would be entirely unable to predict Mazarin's stable bargaining position in the face of a sometimes rapidly changing military situation. Admittedly, the best of such books, Paul Pillar's *Negotiating Peace*, has moved beyond the simple stimulus-response model in which military victory or defeat leads directly to greater or lesser demands, a model so often found in works of political theory that narrate the developments at several peace conferences, and even in history books devoted specifically to the Congress of Westphalia.[89] Pillar recognizes that a state's negotiating position responds to *anticipated* changes in the military situation, which can lead to seemingly paradoxical concessions on the part of a victorious power, as in the Russo-Japanese War of 1904–5. But Pillar also admits that he is considering negotiation only from the perspective of two bargainers. The same bilateral perspective is shared by Michael Handel's *War Termination—A Critical Survey;* and while Robert Randle acknowledges that allies did play a part in the fashioning of the Peace of Westphalia, he declines to incorporate them into his discussion on the grounds that they render the situation too complex to analyze.[90]

The results of this book suggest that the role of allies is too important to be left out of negotiating theory.[91] Allies can moderate demands, as the French acknowledged when they were hesitant to ask for too much in Alsace for fear of offending the German estates; or increase them, a surprising effect of the Swedish alliance on France's new demand for Philippsburg in May 1646. In either case, allies proved as important as the military campaigns themselves in determining the French negotiating position. In a sense, France's military conquests provided the framework for her demands, while her allies established the amount of the conquests that she would demand and whether she would increase or decrease them over the course of the negotiations. Bilateral bargaining dynamics did, of course, occur, but they make little sense if considered in isolation from the entire diplomatic milieu in which the negotiations took place.

This study also helps provide a better explanation of why the negotiations continued for so long. Their length is often blamed on the fact that there was no truce during the talks, but this hypothesis does not hold up in light of the evidence. Far from delaying the negotiations while waiting for more military successes, France was in fact usually hastening the negotiations in the hope of making peace while her favorable military situation lasted (particularly in the negotiations with Bavaria in the fall of 1645 and with the emperor in the spring of 1646). It is true that on occasion the Bavarians or the Imperials delayed the negotiations in the hope of gaining a stronger military position, most notably Bavaria in the fall of 1645. However, the most crucial delaying tactic occurred in the spring of 1646, when Trauttmansdorff tried to stall French satisfaction until the Spanish concluded a separate truce with the Dutch—a delay attributable to purely diplomatic factors. By contrast, the approach of the next campaign actually hastened the Imperial concessions of Alsace and Breisach. The French and Swedes continued to believe throughout the talks—and with good reason—that their enemies would be more likely to make the necessary concession for peace if they were under constant military pressure. Since the French did not increase their demands in response to military success, and since the military campaigns were successful in getting Bavaria and the emperor to make the hoped-for concessions, it appears on the balance that the failure to conclude a truce actually decreased the length of the talks rather than increased them.

Why, then, did the negotiations continue to drag on for five years? One possibility is that the Swedes did not behave with the same restraint as the French, instead increasing their demands as the war continued. If one believes the French ministers, this sounds like a valid hypothesis; certainly Sweden's original demands, which included Silesia as well as Pomerania, were absurdly high. This question must remain uncertain until further primary research can be done, but the secondary literature suggests that the Swedes were no more interested in continuing the war than the French. Like Mazarin, Axel Oxenstierna believed in adopting high demands and remaining firm until they were conceded. If anything, the Swedes actually ended up conceding more than the French, since they only received half of Pomerania.

But the close alliance between the French and Swedes (and the French and Dutch for a time) did hinder the progress of the negotiations in one respect. Since the two crowns were careful not to advance the negotiations without each other (although they were not always successful in this), the talks were delayed repeatedly while France and Sweden waited to confer with one another. This shows up in the presentation of each successive proposal, and is even more obvious in the refusal of the French to sign a preliminary agreement in May 1646, without the Swedes having done the same thing. Had the French simply signed it, the Imperials would have been able to put more effort into the Swedish negotiations, and the Swedes would have been more likely to concede half of Pomerania at an earlier date. The French were similarly forced to wait on the Dutch literally for years before beginning serious negotiations with the Spanish; they even encouraged this at first because they feared the consequences of the

Dutch and Spanish talking together (obviously with good reason). This, again, is a problem related purely to the diplomatic constellation.[92]

Another crucial factor in the slow progress of the talks relates to a peculiarity of the Congress of Westphalia: the decision to negotiate issues one at a time. Studies have shown that negotiations in which issues are resolved serially progress slower than if package proposals are made.[93] But serial negotiations were in part inevitable because of the types of issues involved. First, no other negotiations could be conducted until the matter of the participation of the German estates in the conference had been resolved, as the French repeatedly emphasized. Since this was really a preliminary issue, one might argue that the congress did not truly begin until the first substantial Swedish and French propositions in January 1646. After that, it is true that French and Swedish satisfaction and the religious gravamina were negotiated simultaneously, at least in theory. However, in practice this did not work out as effectively, especially since the congress took place in two different cities: Trauttmansdorff had to spend time shuttling back and forth between Münster and Osnabrück, so he could only carry on serious talks with one opponent at a time. Moreover, Hessian satisfaction, an essential part of the allied program, was pushed entirely to the background, only to be resolved, under allied pressure, after the French and Swedes had received their own satisfaction. The indemnity for the Swedish army was deliberately reserved for last, creating another issue that dominated negotiations in the first half of 1648. Finally, there remained the delicate question of Austrian assistance for Spain, which the French had agreed to leave on the back burner until all other issues were resolved.

The result, if not the intention, was that issues were resolved one at a time. Even worse, while other things were being debated, previously resolved matters such as French satisfaction sprouted up again with new complications. These were not new demands per se, but clarifications that resulted from further debate of the treaty terms by the German estates. Even when a simple solution was found—the French and Imperials agreed to leave the treaty as it had been originally worded in September, 1646—valuable negotiating time was lost in the meantime, leaving the way open for still other problems, such as Bavaria's reentry into the war.

The influence of "public opinion" on the negotiations is interesting but still unresolved. Parker indicates that there was a strong desire for peace in all major states by 1643, and that this influenced governments to begin negotiations.[94] No doubt Mazarin and Oxenstierna were aware of opposition to the war, and would have been happy to conclude peace to silence it. Nevertheless, the striking thing is that both ministers pressed ahead with tough demands over the objections of moderates. Where "public opinion" did play a role, however, was in the Empire. There, where the brunt of the cost of the war was borne, leaders of states of all sizes were tired of supporting the conflict, and pushed all powers concerned—France and Sweden no less than the emperor—to make peace. By 1648, the negotiations had developed a sort of momentum of their own that made it impossible for any state to withhold agreement without risking having the entire Empire turn against it. It was thus that the emperor was forced to separate from Spain, and that Mazarin was forced to accept peace rather than bringing the Habsburgs to their knees.

Mazarin can no longer be blamed for the length of the German war, because it is now clear that he was anxious to make peace there at the earliest opportunity in order to fight Spain. He did not increase his demands, and the decision to negotiate and fight simultaneously did not cause the talks to go slower, and may even have helped speed them up. Instead, the length of the negotiations at the Congress of Westphalia is attributable primarily to the structure of the peace conference. It was carried on in two separate cities, and communication with home governments was extremely slow, especially for Sweden and Spain. Even more troublesome, the sheer number of different interests to be resolved made it impossible to negotiate block solutions, and forced states to advance at the pace of their slowest ally. Furthermore, no substantive negotiations could take place until the question of the participation of the Imperial estates had been resolved, since to begin without them would have been for France and Sweden to concede the point to the emperor. Thus, the heart of the negotiations only began with the French and Swedish propositions of January 1646. By this reckoning, the conference lasted less than three years. That is still a long time, but not so long considering the difficulties that had to be overcome.

Notes

Preface

1. Peter Evans, Dietrich Rueschemeyer, and Theda Skocpol, eds., *Bringing the State Back In* (New York, 1985).
2. Bruce D. Porter, *War and the Rise of the State: The Mlitary Foundations of Modern Politics* (New York, 1994), ix.
3. See, for example, Lucien Bély, *Les relations internationales en Europe (XVIIe–XVIIIe siècles)* (Paris, 1992) and *Espions et ambassadeurs au temps de Louis XIV* (Paris, 1990). But it is not only Bély who is now interested in these questions, as the new volumes that he has written with Jean Bérenger and André Corvisier, *Guerre et paix dans l'Europe du XVIIe siècle*, 2d edition, 2 vols. (Paris, 1991), indicate.
4. John H. Elliott, "A Europe of Composite Monarchies," *Past and Present* 137 (1992): 48–71; Mark Greengrass, ed., *Conquest and Coalescence: The Shaping of the State in Early Modern Europe* (New York, 1991); Peter Sahlins, *Boundaries: The Making of France and Spain in the Pyrenees* (Berkeley, 1989).
5. For some interesting, if unsystematic, thoughts on this subject, see Andrew Lossky, *Louis XIV and the French Monarchy* (New Brunswick, New Jersey, 1994), 40–41, and Perry Anderson, *Lineages of the Absolutist State* (London, 1974), 57–58.
6. Wolfgang Hans Stein, *Protection Royale: Eine Untersuchung zu den Protektionverhältnissen im Elsaß zur Zeit Richelieus, 1622–1643*, Schriftenreihe der Vereinigung zur Erforschung der Neueren Geschichte, v. 9 (Münster, 1978), 528–29, notes that "French protection in Alsace in Richelieu's time had left no direct legal consequences and had been forgotten" by the eighteenth century, because the Peace of Westphalia overruled all of the protection treaties and created an entirely new legal situation. The present study can also, thankfully, dispense with the origins of the main instructions for the French plenipotentiaries in 1643, and concentrate on how they got from those instructions to the final treaty terms. The issue of the origins of the instructions, and of Richelieu's policy toward the Empire in general, has been dealt with in enormous depth by Fritz Dickmann, *Der Westfälische Frieden*, 2d ed. (Münster, 1965), and Hermann Weber, "Richelieu et le Rhin," *Revue Historique* 239 (1968): 265–80, inter alia.
7. On the role of France in Alsatian religion, see Rodolphe Reuss, *L'Alsace au Dix-Septième Siècle*, Bibliothèque de l'École des Hautes Études, fasc.116 (Paris, 1897), v. 2, 534–74; on language, ibid., 185–201.
8. See the examples of the futility of Alsatian appeals in Reuss, *L'Alsace au Dix-Septième Siècle*, v. 1, 151, 155, 158, and below, chapter 8.
9. Reuss, *L'Alsace au Dix-Septième Siècle*, v. 1, 139. Stein also specifically notes the apparent paradox of the French encouraging the Alsatian towns to send representatives to the peace conference as part of their insistence that the em-

peror could not negotiate without the consent of the Empire's constituent members, while at the same time bargaining to obtain possession of Alsace without the participation of those very representatives (Stein, *Protection Royale*, 528–29).

Chapter 1. Introduction: Negotiating While Fighting

1. Paul Pillar, *Negotiating Peace* (Princeton, 1983), 16–17.
2. Indeed, the term "negotiating while fighting" was given as a title to the published version of Admiral Turner Joy's diary of the Korean peace talks; Allan E. Goodman, *Negotiating While Fighting: The Diary of Admiral C. Turner Joy at the Korean Armistice Conference* (Stanford, 1978).
3. André Corvisier, *La France de Louis XIV: ordre intérieur et place en Europe*, 3d edition (Paris, 1990), 87; "'Modernité' de la guerre de Trente Ans," in *Destins et enjeux du XVIIe siècle*, ed. Yves-Marie Bercé et al., (Paris, 1985), 96–101, contains the standard Cold-War era assumption that negotiated wars have gone out of style. Pillar, 30–36, notes that negotiations since the Russo-Japanese war have been increasingly carried out before an armistice has been arranged, contrary to prior practice. He attributes the change to technological improvements, since before the invention of rapid communications, governments either had to designated army commanders as proconsuls, or else move themselves closer to the military action, to be able to react fast enough to events. What he does not seem to realize is that, at the Congress of Westphalia, governments did neither: they simply lived with the inconveniences of slow communications. See below, chapter 2.
4. The numbers for some of the most important studies are: Ritter, 92%; Pagès, 76%; Wedgwood, 77%; Polisensky, 78% (figures calculated on the basis of the page numbers in Geoffrey Parker, *The Thirty Years' War* (Boston, 1984), xiv, footnote 7). The percentage for Parker's book, the most recent comprehensive survey, is 75% (not including the first section on the origins of the war). See also Hubert Salm, *Armeefinanzierung im Dreißigjährigen Krieg: Der Niederrheinisch-Westfälische Reichskreis 1635–1650*, v. 16 of Schriftenreihe der Vereinigung zur Erforschung der Neueren Geschichte (Münster, 1990), 1–9.
5. Parker, *The Thirty Years' War*, xiv.
6. See below, chapter 6, footnote 86.
7. In a typical comment, Josef Engel, "Von der spätmittelalterlichen respublica christiana zum Mächte-Europa der Neuzeit," in *Die Entstehung des neuzeitlichen Europa*, ed. Josef Engel, Handbuch der europäischen Geschichte, v. 3 (Stuttgart, 1971), 351, calls the later campaigns "of subordinate importance." See the discussion of the effect of the campaigns on the negotiations below, and also chapter 3. At least in the field of financing, an excellent start has been made with the recent works of Salm and David Parrott, "The Administration of the French Army During the Ministry of cardinal Richelieu," D. Phil. diss. (Oxford, 1985).
8. For more on this subject, see conclusion, footnote 84.
9. In his *Frankreich, Deutschland und Europa im 17. und 18. Jahrhundert: Beiträge zum Einfluß französischer politischer Theorie, Verfassung und Außenpolitik in der Frühen Neuzeit*, Marburger Studien zur Neueren Geschichte, v. 4 (Marburg, 1994), for example, Klaus Malettke completely skips over Mazarin, jumping from Richelieu to Louis XIV. On the crucial influence of Mazarin and the Peace of Westphalia on Louis XIV's reign, see Ragnhild Hatton, "Louis XIV and His

Fellow Monarchs," in *Louis XIV and Europe*, ed. Ragnhild Hatton (Columbus, Ohio, 1976), 30, 41. See also Peter Jonathan Berger, "Military and Financial Government in France, 1648–1661," Ph. D. Diss. (University of Chicago, 1979), 11.

10. Karl Federn, *Mazarin* (Munich, 1922); Paul Guth, *Mazarin*, (Paris, 1972); Georges Mongrédien, ed., *Mazarin* (N.p., 1959); Geoffrey Treasure, *Mazarin: The Crisis of Absolutism in France* (New York, 1995). Pierre Goubert, *Mazarin* (Paris, 1990); Goubert himself admits in his conclusion that "it was not Mazarin who led me to Mazarin. It was the attentive study . . . of the condition and of the life of the people . . ." (503). He also focuses on the Fronde (9–10). The best existing coverage of Mazarin for the 1640s is still that of Adolphe Chéruel, *Histoire de France pendant la minorité de Louis XIV*, v. 1 (Paris, 1879).

11. See, for example, Claude Dulong, *La Fortune du Mazarin* (Paris, 1990), and the discussion of Mazarin historiography below.

12. Joseph Bergin, *The Rise of Richelieu*, and in particular his article "Richelieu: A Prelate's Progress," *History Today* 41 (January 1991): 14–20; he concludes on p. 20 by stating that "The secular political actor and thinker is proving increasingly difficult to recognise behind the red robes." William F. Church, *Richelieu and Reason of State* (Princeton, New Jersey, 1972); Malettke, 287. See Hermann Weber, "Une Bonne Paix': Richelieu's Foreign Policy and the Peace of Christendom," in *Richelieu and his Age*, ed. Joseph Bergin and Laurence Brockliss (Oxford, 1992), 67, footnote 69, for further references. For the critiques of Black and Parrott, see chapter 3.

13. Georges Dethan, *Mazarin: Un homme de paix à l'âge baroque, 1602–1661* (Paris, 1981).

14. Comte Auguste de Saint-Aulaire, *Mazarin* (Paris, 1946), 304.

15. Saint-Aulaire, 240–41, 310; Maurice Schumann, "Mazarin Européen," in Georges Mongrédien, ed., *Mazarin* (N.p., 1959), 185, 194, et al.

16. Andrew Lossky, *Louis XIV and the French Monarchy* (New Brunswick, New Jersey, 1994); Madeleine Laurain-Portemer, "Questions Européennes et Diplomatie Mazarine," *XVIIe siècle* 42 (1990); Treasure, *Mazarin*, 242. For a more complete discussion of Mazarin's historiographical fate, see Dethan, *Mazarin*, 275–312.

17. Lossky, 49, 60–61; Dethan, *Mazarin*, 258.

18. Saint-Aulaire, 315; Guth, 402, 407, 415. The quotation is from Saint-Aulaire; Guth calls Mazarin "a single God in three persons," "Christ to the outrages of politics," and cites the Book of John about Jesus not being recognized by his people in reference to Mazarin.

19. See below, chapter 3.

20. Orest Ranum, *The Fronde: A French Revolution 1648–1652* (New York, 1993), 82–83. Similarly, Kalevi Holsti writes that "The war came to an end not because of any great commitment to peace in the abstract or because of decisive military victories and defeats. Rather, the parties exhausted themselves. Their treasuries were depleted, the mercenaries who constituted the bulk of the military forces refused to fight without pay, and since the huge armies and their hordes of camp followers had to live off the land, inflicting great cruelties among the peasantry, they began to run out of the means of survival" (29).

21. Lossky, 50–51.

22. Cited in René Kerviler, "Abel Servien," *Revue Historique et Archéologique du Maine* 3 (1878): 62.

NOTES TO CHAPTER 2   285

23. In addition to the historians cited below, one may add Birger Steckzén's comment (*Karl Gustaf Wrangels Fälttåg 1646–1647 till och med fördraget i Ulm* (Uppsala, 1920), v) that "the last phase of the Thirty Years' War offers a pregnant picture of the connection between politics and war."

24. Peter Englund, *Ofredsår: Om den svenska stormaktstiden och en man i dess mitt* (Stockholm, 1993), 382.

25. Goubert, 178.

26. R. R. Palmer, *A History of the Modern World*, 2d ed. (New York, 1961), 126. See also Georg Heyner, *Mazarin's Bündnispolitik in Deutschland (1643–1648)* (Marburg, 1946), 5: military events "were of decisive importance for the course of the peace negotiations and for Mazarin's attitude toward the German estates"; and the passage from Cousin at the beginning of this section.

27. Carl von Clausewitz, *On War*, ed. and trans. Michael Howard and Peter Peret (Princeton, 1976), 111–12.

28. Gaston Zeller, *L'Organisation défensive des Frontières du Nord et de l'Est au XVIIe siècle* (Paris, 1928), 45–46; see also p. 47, where he speaks of Mazarin's "military preoccupations" at the Treaty of Vincennes. Also Georges Livet, *Guerre et Paix de Machiavel à Hobbes* (Paris, 1972), 80, where he speaks of "l'alliance de la force et de la diplomatie" in the negotiations.

29. Georges Livet, "International Relations and the Role of France 1648–1660," in *The Decline of Spain and the Thirty Years War 1609–48/59*, ed. J. P. Cooper, v. 4 of *The New Cambridge Modern History* (Cambridge, 1970), 416. Also Laurain-Portemer, 11, and Guth, 411.

30. Franz Bosbach, et al., eds., *Die Französischen Korrespondenzen: 1645*, series II, section B, v. 2 of *Acta Pacis Westphalicae* (Münster, 1986), Mazarin to Longueville, 9 September 1645, 208. (Hereafter cited as *APW II B 2*.)

31. Treasure, *Mazarin*, 241.

Chapter 2. The Decision Makers

1. Treasure, *Mazarin*, 57.

2. Chéruel, *Histoire de France*, v. 1, 54–69; Ranum, *The Fronde*, 46–48; Richard Bonney, *Political Change in France Under Richelieu and Mazarin* (Oxford, 1978), 25, points out that this did not mean that the government was prepared to accept more Parlementary interference in royal affairs, but rather was an exception. See Sarah Hanley, *The Lit de Justice of the Kings of France: Constitutional Ideology in Legend, Ritual, and Discourse*, Studies Presented to the International Commission for the History of Representative and Parliamentary Institutions, v. 65 (Princeton, 1983), 295–315, for a unique perspective on what she terms "inaugural" *lits de justice*; she sees it as an unqualified royal success.

3. Ruth Kleinman, *Anne of Austria, Queen of France* (Columbus, Ohio, 1985), 147–50 and 229–32.

4. Kleinman, introduction and 172; Bonney, *Political Change*, 5–6; Nicolò Barozzi and Guglielmo Berchet, eds., *Relazioni degli stati europei lette al senato dagli ambasciatori veneti nel secolo decimosettimo*, Series 2, Francia, v. 2 (Venice, 1859), 440–41.

5. Anuschka Tischer, ed., *Die Französischen Korrespondenzen: 1646*, series II, section B, v. 4 of *Acta Pacis Westphalicae* (work in progress), Mazarin to d'Avaux, 14 September 1646, 156. (Hereafter cited as *APW II B 4*.) On the régime's early troubles, see the extensive coverage in Chéruel, *Histoire de France*, v. 1, 119–220.

6. Bonney, *Political Change*, 8, 10. On the structure of the council, see Roland Mousnier, "Le Conseil du Roi de la mort de Henri IV au gouvernment personnel de Louis XIV," in *La Plume, la Faucille, et le Marteau* (Paris, 1970), 141–173.

7. Barozzi and Berchet, 441–46; for the role of Gaston d'Orléans, see Georges Dethan, *La Vie de Gaston d'Orléans* (Paris, 1992), especially pp. 247–51. For Condé and Enghien, see Duc d'Aumale, *Histoire des princes de Condé pendant les XVIe et XVIIe siècles*, v. 4 (Paris, 1886) (subsequent references will all refer to v. 4); *NBG*, v. 11, 402–19.

8. Chavigny had been disgraced in 1643 and replaced as foreign secretary by Brienne. He reentered the council later in the same year, but was forced to dissimulate his hatred for Mazarin in order to retain his position. See Orest Ranum, *Richelieu and the Councillors of Louis XIII: A Study of the Secretaries of State and Superintendants of Finance in the Ministry of Richelieu, 1635–1642* (Oxford, 1963), 166–80 for Claude le Bouthillier and 77–99 for Chavigny; also Fauvelet Du Toc, *Histoire des secrétaires d'estat, contenant l'origine, le progrès, et l'établissement de leurs charges, avec les éloges, les armes, blasons, et généalogies de tous ceux qui les ont possédées jusqu'à present* (Paris, 1668), 259–62 for Bouthillier and 283–89 for Chavigny. The Prince de Conti, Enghien's younger brother, was permitted to sit on the council, but never did. The four secretaries of state also participated on a rotating basis, but did not have a vote. Ranum, *Richelieu*, 61–63; Amédée Outrey, "Histoire et Principes de l'Administration Française des Affaires Etrangères," *Revue Française de Science Politique* 3 (1953): 309.

9. Ranum, *The Fronde*, 118.

10. Jean Le Clerc, *Négociations secrètes touchant la paix de Munster et d'Osnabrug*, v. 3 (Amsterdam, 1726), Mazarin to plenipotentiaries, 20 January 1646, 26–27. Condé's desire for an immediate peace consistently troubled Mazarin; see, e.g., Elka Jarnut, ed., *Die Französischen Korrespondenzen: 1645–1646*, series II, section B, v. 3 of *Acta Pacis Westphalicae* (work in progress), Mazarin to Longueville, 9 February 1646, 107, p. 278. (Hereafter cited as *APW II B 3*.)

11. Mazarin to d'Avaux, 20 July 1646, *APW II B 4*, 80. See also Condé's public opposition to Mazarin's relations with the pope in Mazarin to d'Avaux, 20 July 1646, *APW II B 4*, 80.

12. Mazarin to plenipotentiaries, 20 January 1646, Le Clerc, v. 3, 26–27. Note also Servien's statement in his memorandum to Lionne, 17 September 1646, *APW II B 4*, 161 that, if he had to voice his opinion in council, he would agree with Mazarin; but, since Mazarin was requesting Servien's personal opinion, he will say something different.

13. Gaston d'Orléans to Longueville, 7 March 1646, Le Clerc, v. 3, 107, and Condé to plenipotentiaries, 8 March 1646, 112. Mazarin similarly berated Omer Talon for his excessively critical speech in the 15 January 1648 *lit de justice* because of its effect on the French diplomatic situation; clearly the question of whether internal dissent affected the French diplomatic position was an important factor in Mazarin's decision to repress it. Ranum, *The Fronde*, 92. As for other council members, the Venetian Nani also commented that Longueville was present "solely to adore the propositions and the opinions of the prime minister . . . in the fashion of the others" (Barozzi and Berchet, 444–45).

14. For instance, Brienne says in his memoirs that the question of whether to take Alsace in sovereignty was heavily disputed, but that Mazarin forced it through in the end. Henri de Loménie, Comte de Brienne, *Mémoires du Comte de Brienne*, v. 36 of *Collection des mémoires relatifs à l'histoire de France depuis l'avènement de Henri IV jusqu'à la Paix de Paris conclue en 1763*, ed. M. Petitot (Paris,

1824), 119–21. See also below on how Mazarin's personal letters and those from the council never differed substantially. Laurain-Portemer, 26–27, gives the impression that Mazarin was more restricted in his control than was in fact the case. The mere fact that he submitted all matters to the council does not mean that that body had any great influence on the actions he took, any more than did the fact that he scrupulously asked the queen's opinion on important matters—and had them confirmed without hesitation.

15. On Le Tellier and Brienne, see Du Toc, 303–9 and 223–29. On the administrative, as opposed to policy-making, role of the *secrétaires d'État*, see Outrey, 307–9. See below, chapter 4, footnote 43, on Mazarin's increasingly close management of military affairs.

16. Barozzi and Berchet, 449, 454.

17. Mazarin to d'Avaux, 26 April 1646, *APW II B 3*, 245. Trauttmansdorff also recognized that Mazarin was spurred by his desire to appear faithful to French interests, but argued that he actually went too far in this; d'Avaux to Mazarin, 18 April 1646, *APW II B 3*, 224.

18. This point is missed by Pillar (51–52), who says that using negotiations to manipulate public opinion is a twentieth-century phenomenon. He also claims that governments tend to strike a harder line with their citizens to convince them of the need to fight (65–66); Mazarin, by contrast, was forced to emphasize his reasonableness and desire to compromise in order to keep the pro-Spanish party content. See also William Beik, *Absolutism and Society in Seventeenth-Century France: State Power and Provincial Aristocracy in Languedoc* (New York, 1985), 186, for the effects of military defeats abroad on popular opinion and government at home.

19. D'Avaux to Mazarin, 7 April 1646, *APW II B 3*, 208; Servien to Lionne, 20 April 1646, 230.

20. Chéruel, *Histoire de France*, v. 2, 64.

21. Servien to Lionne, 16 January 1645, *APW II B 3*, 64, p. 174. However, see the supplementary instructions for a desire to save money from the army to relieve the people (end of chapter 7). On the lack of popular influence on Mazarin's peace policy, see Roland Mousnier, "Les mouvements populaires en France avant les traités de Westphalie et leur incidence sur ces traités," in *Forschungen und Studien zur Geschichte des Westfälischen Friedens. Vorträge bei dem Colloquium französischer und deutscher Historiker vom. April 28–30. April 1963 in Münster* (Münster, 1965), 33–48, and "Les crises intérieures françaises de 1610 à 1659 et leur influence sur la politique extérieure française, surtout de 1618 à 1648," in *Krieg und Politik 1618–1648: Europäische Probleme und Perspektiven*, ed. Konrad Repgen (Munich, 1988), 169–83, as well as René Pillorget, "Die Bauernaufstände im Frankreich des 17. Jahrhunderts," in *Soziale und Politische Konflikte im Frankreich des Ancien Régime*, ed. Klaus Malettke (Berlin, 1982), 71.

22. Mazarin to plenipotentiaries, 6 February 1646 [probably 16 February in reality], Le Clerc, v. 3, 52–53.

23. Mazarin to Longueville, 7 October 1645, *APW II B 2*, 232

24. Bonney, *Political Change*, 441. Cp. Saint-Aulaire, 223–24.

25. Cp. Gaston Zeller, *La Guerre de Trente Ans et les relations internationales en Occident de 1610 à 1660* (Paris, 1947), 155–56.

26. Fred Charles Iklé, *Every War Must End* (New York, 1971), 14–16, on rational actors vs. sub groups. See below for qualifications on Mazarin's control. It may be added that Iklé's argument that governments do not act rationally in continuing a war long after costs have exceeded benefits has been shown to be

inaccurate by Pillar, 172–73, because earlier costs are sunk costs and only marginal costs need be considered. See also Berenice A. Carroll, "War Termination and Conflict Theory: Value Premises, Theories, and Policies," *Annals of the American Academy of Political and Social Science* 392 (November 1970): 18–23 on gamelike vs. fightlike wars; whatever the situation at the front, this was clearly a "game-like" war from the perspective of policy makers.

27. Kerviler, 33–35.

28. See Dennis H. O'Brien, "Mazarin's Diplomatic Corps, 1648–1661," *North Dakota Quarterly* 45 no.1 (Winter 1977): 31–42.

29. Servien to Lionne, 14/19 April 1646, *APW II B 3*, 228. Servien also once advised Mazarin to stay out of the English civil war until France had finished with her own war (Servien to Lionne, 10 March 1646, *APW II B 3*, 166, p. 467).

30. Bougeant called him "quick and penetrating . . . prompt and firm to the point of stubbornness." Even his apologist, Kerviler, admits that he was "proud, irascible, haughty, very vulnerable on the subject of his personal importance and dignity" (v. 3, pp. 30–31 and 37).

31. Ursula Irsigler and Kriemhild Goronzy, eds., *Die französischen Korrespondenzen: 1644*, series II, section B, v. 1 of *Acta Pacis Westphalicae* (Münster, 1986), p. 4, footnote 2. (Hereafter cited as *APW II B 1*.) Ursula Irsigler, "Einleitung," in ibid., lxvii-lxix; *Nouvelle Biographie Générale . . . , depuis les temps les plus reculés jusqu'à nos jours*, v. 43 (Paris, 1862–66), pp. 814–17 (hereafter *NBG*); René Kerviler, as above plus v. 2 (1877): 593–649 and 3 (1878): 29–96, 167–245; Tallemant des Réaux, *Historiettes*, ed. Antoine Adam, v. 2 (N.p., 1961), 192–97; Du Toc, 271–80. Carl Ekberg, "Abel Servien, cardinal Mazarin, and the Formulation of French Foreign Policy, 1653–1659," *International History Review* 3 (1981): 329, argues that Servien's hard realism was an appropriate balance for Mazarin's almost dreamy optimism, while Kerviler (36–37) praises him as the perfect compliment to d'Avaux. Servien has also been treated extensively by Anne-Marie Enaux-Moret, "Abel Servien, négociateur des traités de Westphalie: du parlement de Grenoble à la surintendance des finances, 1593–1659," Ph. D. Diss. (Paris, 1968), and M. A. Helly, *Deux Diplomates Dauphinois au XVIIème Siècle: Abel Servien—Hugues de Lionne* (Grenoble, 1924). Unfortunately, I have been unable to obtain these works.

32. Chéruel, "De la Court," 460–62, 466.

33. *APW II B 1*, p. 23, footnote 6; *NBG*, v. 3, pp. 816–17; Irsigler, lxvi-lxvii, lxxxi; Tallemant des Réaux, 197–201.

34. Servien to Lionne, 6 August 1646, *APW II B 4*, 104.

35. Dickmann, *Der Westfälische Frieden*, 269; see also Dethan, *Mazarin*, 269–70. Servien did have a reputation for not wanting peace; see the comments of Contarini in Servien to Lionne, 11 September 1646, *APW II B 4*, 152.

36. It is true that Servien once wrote to Lionne of the acquisition of Alsace that "before conquering the enemies on this subject it was necessary to fight my colleagues for a long time," but this referred to only one particular aspect of the annexation, and not to the principle (Servien to Lionne, 17 September 1646, *APW II B 4*, 161). See the interesting article by Hermann Weber, "Friede und Gewissen," in *Forschungen und Studien zur Geschichte des Westfälischen Friedens: Vorträge bei dem Colloquium französischer und deutscher Historiker vom. April 28–30. April 1963 in Münster* (Münster, 1965), 85–108, especially 102–8. On Servien's bellicosity, Dethan, *Mazarin*, 259–60.

37. See Irsigler, lxxxi-lxxxii; Kerviler, v. 3, 39–58.

38. Kerviler, 41–42.

39. Servien to Lionne, 28 August 1646, *APW II B 4*, 133.
40. Kerviler, 46.
41. Servien to Lionne, 17 September 1646, *APW II B 4*, 161.
42. Lionne to Servien, 16 February 1646, *APW II B 3*, 119; 24 February 1646, 130, p. 359; 24 March 1646, 185; 31 March 1646, 197, p. 527; 14 April 1646, 217; 20 May 1646, 278; Irsigler, lxiii. See also Ekberg, 317–29, in which he argues that Servien had a strong influence on Mazarin's policy in the 1650s. Such an influence was by no means new; although Servien grew in Mazarin's confidence over the years, Mazarin was already making liberal use of Servien's ideas in the 1640s.
43. Mazarin to Longueville, 21 September 1646, *APW II B 4*, 164. On the basis of this evidence, it seems that Laurain-Portemer does not do justice to Servien's special status. He clearly received better treatment and had a larger influence on Mazarin than either d'Avaux or Longueville, though Mazarin did not follow his advice blindly (for example, he accepted d'Avaux's plan for dealing with Catalonia over Servien's, Mazarin to d'Avaux, 26 April 1646, *APW II B 3*, 245).
44. Mazarin to d'Avaux, 20 July 1646, *APW II B 4*, 80.
45. Du Toc, 321; *NBG*, v. 31, 310–14.
46. Lionne to Servien, 15 June 1646, *APW II B 4*, 16.
47. Lionne to Servien, 2 July 1646, *APW II B 4*, 47, et al.
48. See also Irsigler, lxxvii-lxxviii.
49. *APW II B 1*, 5, 14: Mazarin to d'Avaux, 19 March 1644, and Lionne to Servien, 26 March 1644 (cited in Anuschka Tischer, untitled and unpublished preliminary paper, 1994, p. 13).
50. On d'Avaux's relationship with Brienne, see Brienne to d'Avaux, 31 August 1646, *APW II B 4*, 136.
51. Bavarian support for d'Avaux: Servien to Lionne, 10 July 1646, *APW II B 4*, 64. Swedish plenipotentiaries to d'Avaux, 16 March 1645, Le Clerc, v. 1, 337–39.
52. Lionne to Servien, 6 July 1646, *APW II B 4*, 56; Servien to Lionne, 21 August 1646, 123; Servien to Lionne, 17 September 1646, 161.
53. Brienne to d'Avaux, 31 August 1646, *APW II B 4*, 136; d'Avaux to Brienne, 10 September 1646, 150.
54. See *APW II B 2*, p. 72, footnote 6, and *NBG*, v. 31, pp. 586–87.
55. Barozzi and Berchet, 444–45.
56. Mazarin to Longueville, 20 July 1646, *APW II B 4*, 79; Lionne to Servien, 20 July 1646, 81.
57. For example, see Dickmann, *Der Westfälische Frieden*, 196; Guth, 401.
58. This follows from Mazarin to Longueville, 9 September 1645, *APW II B 2*, 209, p. 668, as demonstrated by Tischer, 16.
59. See Malettke, 191–219.
60. De La Court accused St. Romain of collecting pay while serving no useful purpose; exactly what he did in between missions is unknown. Chéruel, "De La Court," 456–57.
61. See d'Avaux to Rorté, 6 December 1644, *APW II B 1*, 316; *APW II B 2*, xxxi–xxxiv, and p. 366, footnote 3; and ibid., Servien to Lionne, 21 October 1645, 244. On de La Barde, who was Chavigny's cousin and one-time secretary, see also Outrey, 311, and Ranum, 91.
62. De La Court to Servien, 6 July 1646, *APW II B 4*, 57; Chéruel, "De La Court," 456–57, on how de La Court did not get along with d'Avaux.
63. For this section, see Irsigler, lxii-lxv.

64. Ibid. Additional information is provided in Franz Bosbach, *Die Kosten des Westfälischen Friedenskongresses: Eine strukturgeschichtliche Untersuchung*, v. 13 of Schriftenreihe der Vereinigung zur Erforschung der Neueren Geschichte (Münster, 1984), 22–26; however, Bosbach does not try to estimate the size of all of the Imperial delegations, so it is impossible to make a more firm statement.

65. Servien to de La Court, 7 July 1646, *APW II B 4*, 58.

66. Plenipotentiaries to Brienne, 9 July 1646, *APW II B 4*, 59; 16 July 1646, 70; 20 August 1646, 120; 3 September 1646, 139.

67. D. P. O'Connell, "A *cause célèbre* in the History of Treaty-Making: The Refusal to Ratify the Peace Treaty of Regensburg in 1630," *The British Yearbook of International Law* (1967), 71–90.

68. Anne to plenipotentiaries, 29 September 1646, *APW II B 4*, 178. See also Laurain-Portemer, 26–27.

69. Brienne to plenipotentiaries, 17 March 1646, Le Clerc, v. 3, 126; Lionne to Servien, 24 February 1646, *APW II B 3*, 130, p. 359.

70. See the introduction to *APW II B 2*, and chapters 6 and 7.

71. Mazarin to plenipotentiaries, 22 November 1645, *APW II B 2*, 266, p. 868.

72. Mazarin to Longueville, 14 April 1646, *APW II B 3*, 215; 21 April 1646, 233.

73. Plenipotentiaries to Anne, 17 September 1646, *APW II B 4*, 159. Also Louis XIV to plenipotentiaries, 30 May 1645, *APW II B 2*, 114, pp. 392–93; Mazarin to Longueville, 14 April 1646, *APW II B 3*, 215; Louis XIV to plenipotentiaries, 21 April 1646, *APW II B 3*, 232; and countless others.

74. Lionne to Servien, 24 February 1646, *APW II B 3*, 130, p. 359.

75. Longueville to Mazarin, 7 April 1646, *APW II B 3*, 207; Mazarin to Longueville, 14 April 1646, 215.

76. Lionne to Servien, 25 August 1646, *APW II B 4*, 128.

77. On some occasions, orders were oral rather than written, e.g., as reported in Mazarin to plenipotentiaries, 26 April 1646, *APW II B 3*, 243, and plenipotentiaries to Brienne, 10 February 1646, Le Clerc, v. 3, 57–60.

78. Mazarin to plenipotentiaries, 3 February 1646, Le Clerc, v. 3, 44.

79. Mazarin to Longueville, 13 July 1646, *APW II B 4*, 69.

80. Mazarin to plenipotentiaries, 9 December 1645, *APW II B 3*, 18, p. 49. In still another letter, Mazarin wrote to Longueville that "I charge myself with telling you the substance of the queen's sentiments," contrasting this with Brienne's letters; *APW II B 3*, 183.

81. On the plenipotentiaries' problems with Brienne's letters, see chapter 7, and specifically plenipotentiaries to Brienne, 7 January 1645, *APW II B 2*, 7; Servien to Lionne, 15 January 1645, 14; d'Avaux to Brienne, 21 January 1645, 20; and Servien to Lionne, 20 May 1645, 106, p. 359.

82. Plenipotentiaries to Mazarin, 30 December 1645, *APW II B 3*, 46, p. 139; Dethan, *Mazarin*, 306–9.

83. This striking piece of information is found in *APW II B 3*, 183, cited by Tischer, 17. On Brienne's role, see Irsigler, lxxix-lxxx, and Bosbach, xxxiv.

84. For example, Richelieu (Ranum, 96–97).

85. Mazarin to d'Avaux, 21 September 1646, *APW II B 4*, 165.

86. Georges Dethan, "Wicquefort et Callières à l'ombre de Mazarin?," in *Guerre et Pouvoir en Europe au XVIIe siècle*, ed. Viviane Barrie-Curien (Paris, 1991), 100.

87. On the practice of sending *ordinaires*, established no later than the reign of Louis XIII, see Ranum, 92. On the custom of writing every week, which the

plenipotentiaries refused to break even when they had nothing to say: Brienne to plenipotentiaries, 3 August 1646, *APW II B 4*, 94. See also Bernhard Kroener, *Les Routes et les Étapes: Die Versorgung der französischen Armeen in Nordostfrankreich (1635–1661). Ein Beitrag zur Verwaltungsgeschichte des Ancien Régime*, v. 11 of Schriftenreihe der Vereinigung zur Erforschung der Neueren Geschichte (Münster, 1980), 34–35, on the need to repeat orders frequently.

88. Though this was not unique to the 1640s; see Geoffrey Parker, "The Worst-Kept Secret in Europe? The European Intelligence Community and the Spanish Armada of 1588," in *Go Spy the Land: Military Intelligence in History*, ed. Keith Neilson and B. J. C. McKercher (Westport, Connecticut, 1992), 55–56. The most detailed work on early modern spies is Lucien Bély's *Espions et Ambassadeurs au Temps de Louis XIV*, (Paris, 1990). Note from John Rule's review, 745–47, that a "new generation" had recently sprung up in the 1690s that was more consciously concerned with diplomatic service. John Rule, "Review Article: Gathering Intelligence in the Age of Louis XIV," *International History Review* 14 (1992), 732–52. Also the rather more unsatisfying article by Eckhard Opitz, "Diplomacy and Secret Communication in the Seventeenth Century: Some Remarks on the Method of Gaining News in the Age of Absolutism," in *Clio Goes Spying: Eight Essays on the History of Intelligence*, ed. Wilhelm Agrell and Bo Huldt (Malmö, 1983), 64–84.

89. Karl Schweinesbein, *Die Frankreich Politik Maximilian I. von Bayern, 1639–1645* (Munich, 1967), 195–98; plenipotentiaries to Brienne, 12 November 1644, *APW II B 1*, 292, pp. 626–27, and 26 November 1644, 303, pp. 681–82.

90. Karsten Ruppert, *Die Kaiserliche Politik auf dem Westfälischen Friedenskongreß (1643–1648)*, Schriftenreihe der Vereinigung zur Erforschung der Neueren Geschichte, v. 20 (Münster, 1979), 126–38.

91. Sigmund Riezler, "Bayern und Frankreich während des Waffenstillstands von 1647," *Sitzungsberichte der philosophisch-philologischen und der historischen Classe der k.b. Akademie der Wissenschaften zu München* 2 (1898): 514–15, 525.

92. Wilhelm Fleitmann, "Postverbindungen für den Westfälischen Friedenskongreß 1643 bis 1648," *Archiv für deutsche Postgeschichte* 1 (1972), 8–9. Irsigler, lxxxiv–lxxxv, mistakenly says that the letters went out on Friday.

93. See Irsigler, lxxxv; but also note further intercepted letters reported in Louis XIV to plenipotentiaries, 14 April 1646, Le Clerc, 150–51; Servien to Lionne, 24 July 1646, *APW II B 4*, 85. E. John B. Allen, *Post and Courier Service in the Diplomacy of Early Modern Europe* (The Hague, 1972), 23–24, provides numerous examples of intercepted letters in the latter half of the sixteenth century, and argues that little was usually done in response besides the obvious: intercepting one's opponents' letters.

94. Fleitmann, 17–20. Cases of intercepted letters: Mazarin to plenipotentiaries, 1 July 1646, *APW II B 4*, 45; Longueville to Mazarin, 2 July 1646, 49; plenipotentiaries to Louis XIV, 9 July 1646, 60.

95. As was d'Artagnan, who was in Mazarin's personal service. Geoffrey F. Hall and Joan Sanders *D'Artagnan: The Ultimate Musketeer* (Boston, 1964), 49–54; Cyrano de Bergerac to Mazarin, 26 September 1645, CP All., v. 48, fol. 369r; Mazarin to Gramont, 2 October 1645, *Lettres*, v. 2, 94, p. 229.

96. It also, oddly, took longer, since the couriers stopped for too long in Brussels; Fleitmann, 44. See also Mazarin to Longueville, 20 May 1646, *APW II B 3*, 277; Louis XIV to plenipotentiaries, 22 June 1646, *APW II B 4*, 23; William James Roosen, *The Age of Louis XIV: The Rise of Modern Diplomacy* (Cambridge, Massachusetts, 1976), 130; Allen, *Post and Courier*, 39.

97. There are numerous examples of encoding or decoding taking so long that they slowed correspondence: Mazarin to Longueville, 9 September 1645, *APW II B 2*, 209, indicates that he has only had time to decipher the plenipotentiaries' letters, not read them; Mazarin to Longueville, 15 June 1646, *APW II B 4*, 15; Lionne to Servien, 6 July 1646, *APW II B 4*, 56; Lionne to Servien, 20 July 1646, *APW II B 4*, 81: "Of your three memoranda from July 10th, we have only had time to decipher the one that you wrote me via the abbot Mondin"; Lionne to Servien, 3 August 1646, *APW II B 4*, 97: "Your last memorandum has only been half deciphered"; also Louis XIV to plenipotentiaries, 22 June 1646, *APW II B 4*, 23, in which the court announces that it is sending a copy of a letter from Maximilian to Bagno, "which we risk this time without code because we lack the time to encode it." Leaving formulaic parts of letters *en clair* also protected the integrity of the code, since such parts were easier to decipher. See Roosen, 137–38, and especially Corvisier, *La France de Louis XIV*, 297. At least there seem to have been none of the problems that the Spanish experienced under Ferdinand and Isabella: many letters lie in the archives undeciphered, with marginalia such as "Nonsense," "Impossible," or "Order the ambassador to send another despatch." James Westfall Thompson and Saul K. Padover, *Secret Diplomacy: Espionage and Cryptography, 1500–1815*, rev. ed. (New York, 1963), 258.

98. I would like to thank Anuschka Tischer, editor of two forthcoming volumes of the *Acta Pacis Westphalicae*, for sharing with me her work on deciphering the French codes. See also Irsigler, lxxxii; M. S. Anderson, *The Rise of Modern Diplomacy, 1450–1919* (New York, 1993), 21–23.

99. Often the attackers were merely interested in the courier's horse; see Fleitmann, 14–15. Roosen, 137–41. He concludes that codes were easy to break, but the evidence is ambiguous: there were few profession code-breakers (France did not establish a separate *Bureau des Chiffres* until 1749; Outrey, 314), and some codes were not successfully deciphered until the nineteenth century (Thompson and Padover, 256–61). Volmar had great difficulty deciphering a letter from his own master without a key in October 1648: extract from the protocol of the Imperial Chancellery in Mainz, 8 October 1646, Archives du Ministère des Affaires Étrangères (hereafter omitted), Correspondance politique (hereafter CP) Allemagne (hereafter All) v. 110, fols. 47r–50v, and Dickmann, *Der Westfälische Frieden*, 489–90. See also three essays in *Go Spy the Land: Military Intelligence in History*, ed. Keith Neilson and B. J. C. McKercher (Westport, Connecticut, 1992): Gerhard F. Strasser, "Diplomatic Cryptology and Universal Languages in the Sixteenth and Seventeenth Centuries," 73–98; Gunther Rothenberg, "Military Intelligence Gathering in the Second Half of the Eighteenth Century, 1740–1792," 101 (however, in spite of Rothenberg's claim that intelligence methods had changed little, the seventeenth century was certainly less sophisticated at breaking codes than the eighteenth); and, more relevant, Parker, "The Worst-Kept Secret in Europe?," 54, where he notes that—in spite of the apparent existence of several permanent officials hired to break codes—remarkably few deciphered letters survive. It must also be remembered that England had the most advanced intelligence network in Europe in the late sixteenth century; see Stevan Dedijer, "The Rainbow Scheme: British Secret Service and Pax Britannica," in *Clio Goes Spying: Eight Essays on the History of Intelligence*, ed. Wilhelm Agrell and Bo Huldt (Malmö, 1983), 12–13.

100. On intelligence networks in general, see Arne Losman, "The European Communications Network of Carl Gustaf Wrangel and Magnus Gabriel de la Gardie," in *Europe and Scandinavia: Aspects of the Process of Integration in the seven-*

teenth Century, ed. Göran Rystad, (Lund, 1983): 195–200; C.-G. Picavet, *La diplomatie française au temps de Louis XIV (1661–1715): Institutions, moeurs, et coutumes* (Paris, 1930), 182–89. Roosen's assertion that spying was of limited value (pp. 154–57) is hard to accept based on the evidence from the Congress of Westphalia. The French gained innumerable pieces of information that materially affected decisions, including their negotiating stance. The most important was Mazarin's advance warning that the emperor would give in on Breisach in May 1646, which led him to keep a firm line longer than he might otherwise have done in light of the Dutch situation (see chapter 8).

101. Mazarin's Imperial spies are indicated in Mazarin to plenipotentiaries, 22 November 1645, *APW II B 2*, 266, pp. 861–63; also Mazarin to Longueville, 21 April 1646, *APW II B 3*, 233, and Mazarin to plenipotentiaries, 12 January 1646, Le Clerc, v. 3, 11 (unclear whether it is referring to the same spy). The latter reference also shows that Mazarin was getting news from Brussels. Mazarin to plenipotentiaries, 10 February 1646, Le Clerc, v. 3, 60 reports Spanish news "from a very good place" ("d'un fort bon lieu"). Servien's spy: Servien to Lionne, 28 August 1646, *APW II B 4*, 133.

102. On the Dutch inability to keep secrets, Servien to Lionne, 11 November 1645, *APW II B 2*, 260, pp. 841–43. Venice also provided the French with information; see Gerhard Immler, *Kurfürst Maximilian I. und der Westfälische Friedenskongreß*, Schriftenreihe der Vereinigung zur Erforschung der Neueren Geschichte, v. 20 (Münster, 1992), 247.

103. Mazarin to Longueville, 9 September 1645, *APW II B 2*, 209.

104. Brienne to plenipotentiaries, 20 July 1646, *APW II B 4*, 76, and 27 July 1646, 86. Writing on the period of Louis XIV's personal rule, Bruno Neveu argues that foreign diplomats had little trouble gathering information at the French court. After explaining some of their methods, he writes that "From a distance of three centuries, one has the impression that Louis XIV's contemporaries were well aware of the progress of diplomatic affairs and military operations: the substance of the meetings between the King and his secretary of state spread rather easily and quickly among his courtiers, who spent most of their time commenting on news about which they had heard." "Correspondances diplomatiques et information," *XVIIe siècle*, no. 178 (1993): 51.

105. Picavet, 225–26.

106. Immler, *Kurfürst Maximilian I.*, 104–5, on the offer of Bagno that was eventually rejected by Mazarin; also Louis XIV to plenipotentiaries, 26 April 1646, *APW II B 3*, 241, indicates that Bagno said that France would settle for "Alsace," in spite of the fact that the French have never said they would give in on Philippsburg.

107. The press was also used freely by both sides to publish things they wished people to know, or believe. Mazarin complained to the plenipotentiaries on 17 March 1646 (Le Clerc, v. 3, 127–28) that the Spanish had insisted that France not put anything of the talks in their press, but then published it everywhere themselves; and on 12 July of the same year (*Mémoires du Maréchal de Turenne*, ed. Paul Marichal (Paris, 1909), *pièces justificatives*, 281) he told Turenne that the Imperials had published some of Turenne's intercepted correspondence in order to sow discord with Sweden, adding that he hoped Turenne knew which of Mazarin's words could be passed on.

108. See Marie-Noële Grand-Mesnil, *Mazarin, la Fronde et la Presse* (Paris, 1967), in general; Mazarin to Longueville, 4 November 1645, *APW II B 2*, 250, p. 811 for one instance of Mazarin's irritation: "I have said fifty times that the

secretaries of state of foreign affairs and of war should be careful of the Gazette . . . , and nevertheless, you see what happens." Servien also complained, that it talked too much of Sötern's dependence on France. Servien to Lionne, 16/21 December 1645, *APW II B 3*, 30, p. 86.

109. Servien to Lionne, 10 July 1646, *APW II B 4*, 64.

110. D'Avaux to Mazarin, 30 July 1646, *APW II B 4*, 92. See also plenipotentiaries to Mazarin, 24 March 1646, *APW II B 3*, 187; Servien to Lionne, 8 April 1646, *APW II B 3*, 211; Servien to Lionne, 24 July 1646, *APW II B 4*, 85; and plenipotentiaries to Louis XIV, 13 August 1646, *APW II B 4*, 111 for other complaints. The two conjectured sources of the leak were either a foreign ambassador (most likely the Venetian Nani), or an internal spy. Brienne also suspected that Nani was the source of the leaks. This would seem to contradict the impression give by Charles Carter ("The Ambassadors of Early Modern Europe: Patterns of Diplomatic Representation in the Early Seventeenth Century," in *From the Renaissance to the Counter-Reformation: Essays in Honor of Garrett Mattingly*, ed. Charles H. Carter [New York, 1965], 279–80) that Venetian ambassadors were not particularly well informed.

111. Brienne to plenipotentiaries, 17 February 1646, Le Clerc, v. 3, 72–73; Mazarin to Longueville, 21 November 1645, *APW II B 2*, 265. See also Mazarin to plenipotentiaries, 26 April 1646, *APW II B 3*, 243, and Mazarin to Longueville, 26 April 1646, *APW II B 3*, 244.

112. Louis XIV to plenipotentiaries, 7 April 1646, Le Clerc, v. 3, 146–47; Lionne to Servien, 27 July 1646, *APW II B 4*, 89.

113. Mazarin to d'Avaux, 10 August 1646, *APW II B 4*, 108; Lionne's ideas: Lionne to Servien, 3 August 1646, *APW II B 4*, 97.

114. Lionne to Servien, 10 August 1646, *APW II B 4*, 109. See also Louis XIV to plenipotentiaries, 27 July 1646, *APW II B 4*, 87 and Mazarin to d'Avaux, 24 August 1646, 127.

115. For example, see Longueville to Mazarin, 25 June 1646, *APW II B 4*, 30.

116. Longueville to Mazarin, 13 June 1646, *APW II B 4*, 7.

117. Longueville to Mazarin, 16 July 1646, *APW II B 4*, 73.

118. D'Avaux to Mazarin, 16 July 1646, *APW II B 4*, 74, and 27 August 1646, 132. The plenipotentiaries also found out about Rosenhane's secret talks with the Spanish: *APW II B 3*, 233.

119. Mazarin to Longueville, 21 April 1646, *APW II B 3*, 233; Mazarin to plenipotentiaries, 26 April 1646, 243; ibid., 31 May 1646, 297. See also Ruppert, 166–67, footnote 149, on how Mazarin might have learned of Trauttmansdorff's orders.

120. Longueville to Mazarin, 25 June 1646, *APW II B 4*, 30; see also plenipotentiaries to Brienne, 2 July 1646, 48.

121. Plenipotentiaries to Brienne, 13 August 1646, *APW II B 4*, 110.

122. Mazarin to d'Avaux, 20 July 1646, *APW II B 4*, 80; see also Louis XIV to plenipotentiaries, 24 August 1646, 125.

123. Mazarin to Longueville, 6 July 1646, *APW II B 4*, 54.

124. Turenne, *Mémoires*, 298; see also chapter 8, for the passage of information between the *Armée d'Allemagne* and Münster.

125. Plenipotentiaries to Brienne, 2 July 1646, *APW II B 4*, 48.

126. Plenipotentiaries to Louis XIV, 9 July 1646, *APW II B 4*, 60. D'Avaux also complained that the plenipotentiaries were accused of not having orders to send the circular letter to the estates in 1644: d'Avaux to Brienne, 16 July 1644, *APW II B 1*, 175.

127. See Brienne to plenipotentiaries, 10 August 1646, *APW II B 4*, 105, and Mazarin to d'Avaux, 10 August 1646, 108 on the Catalonia exchange project; plenipotentiaries to Louis XIV, 13 August 1646, *APW II B 4*, 111 on a truce in Portugal; and d'Avaux to Mazarin, 27 August 1646, *APW II B 4*, 132, on Lorraine. See also Pillar, 67–69, on unwillingness to take the first step in negotiations.

128. Parker, *Thirty Years' War*, 179.

129. Barozzi and Berchet, 458–59.

130. Interestingly, the Papal mediator Chigi spoke in almost exactly the same terms; see Alphonse Dupront, "De la Chrétienté à l'Europe: La passion westphalienne du Nonce Fabio Chigi," in *Forschungen und Studien zur Geschichte des Westfälischen Friedens: Vorträge bei dem Colloquium französischer und deutscher Historiker vom. April 28–30. April 1963 in Münster* (Münster, 1965), 63.

131. Parker, *The Thirty Years' War*, 158–61.

132. See Sigmund Goetze, *Die Politik des schwedischen Reichskanzlers Axel Oxenstierna gegenüber Kaiser und Reich*, v. 3 of *Beiträge zur Sozial-und Wirtschaftsgeschichte*, ed. Wilhelm Koppe (Kiel, 1971).

133. Jürgen Steiner, *Die pfälzische Kurwürde während des Dreißigjährigen Krieges (1618–1648)*, Veröffentlichung der Pfälzischen Gesellschaft zur Förderung der Wissenschaften in Speyer, bd. 76 (Speyer, 1985), 152–88, covers the entire length of the negotiations concerning the Palatinate. Steiner claims (152–62) to find a change in the French position on the Palatinate question from October 1643 to March 1645, during which time the French favored full restoration. One must, however, separate the public French position from their ultimate aims; see especially the debate over insisting on a normal year of 1618 (chapter 7) as an example of this and the French awareness of the distinction. Steiner emphasizes the importance of the French in securing the Upper Palatinate and the electorate for Maximilian.

134. See Sune Lundgren, *Johan Adler Salvius: Problem Kring Freden, Krigsekonomien och Maktkampen* (Lund, 1945), 216–306; Sven Lundkvist, "Die schwedischen Kriegs-und Friedensziele 1632–1648," in *Krieg und Politik 1618–1648: Europäische Probleme und Perspektiven*, ed. Konrad Repgen, Schriften des Historischen Kollegs, Kolloquien, v. 8. (Munich, 1988), 238–39. Although Lundgren and Lundkvist go to pains to show that there was no "peace party-war party" distinction in Sweden, the French were surely right to see Salvius as the queen's ally and the best chance for getting Sweden to compromise on Pomerania.

135. Lionne to Servien, 10 June 1645, *APW II B 2*, 125.

136. Plenipotentiaries to Rorté, 15 April 1644, *APW II B 1*, 44; also plenipotentiaries to Brienne, 13 May 1644, *APW II B 1*, 98; plenipotentiaries to Brienne, 10 September 1644, *APW II B 1*, 243; et al.

137. See Chéruel, "De La Court," 457; d'Avaux to Mazarin, 13 August 1646, *APW II B 4*, 113; Longueville to Mazarin, 24 September 1646, *APW II B 4*, 169; Mazarin to d'Avaux, 14 October 1646, *APW II B 4*, 200.

138. Servien to Lionne, 3 October 1646, *APW II B 4*, 183.

139. *APW II B 1*, 52, footnote 3; *APW II B 2*, p. 157, footnote 16.

140. Jonathan Israel, *The Dutch Republic and the Hispanic World, 1606–1661*, (New York, 1982), 361 and 365; Jan Joseph Poelhekke, *De Vrede van Munster* (The Hague, 1948), 1–4.

141. Jean Dumont, *Corps Universel du Droit des Gens*, v. 6 (Amsterdam, 1726–31), 178.

142. Kurt Beck, *Der Hessische Bruderzwist zwischen Hessen-Kassel und Hessen-Darmstadt in den Verhandlungen zum Westfälischen Frieden von 1644 bis 1648* (Frank-

furt, 1978), 18; Erwin Bettenhäuser, *Die Landgrafschaft Hessen-Kassel auf dem Westfälischen Friedenskongress 1644–1648* (Wiesbaden, 1983), 16, 27.

143. For example, see plenipotentiaries to Louis XIV, 9 July 1646, *APW II B 4*, 60.

144. *Correspondance authentique de Godefroi comte d'Estrades de 1637 à 1660*, ed. A. de Saint-Léger and L. Lemaire, v. 1 (Paris, 1924), Mazarin to d'Estrades, 27 May 1645, 115, p. 256; Dickmann, *Der Westfälische Frieden*, 184.

145. See Peter Claus Hartmann, "Bayern als Faktor der französischen Politik während des Dreißigjährigen Krieges," in *Um Glauben und Reich: Kurfürst Maximilian I. Beiträge zur Bayerischen Geschichte und Kunst, 1573–1657* (Munich, 1980), 448–55, and Schweinesbein, 86–91.

146. Hartmann, 448–50. See also Robert Bireley, "Antimachiavellism, the Baroque and Maximilian of Bavaria," *Archivum Historicum Societatis Jesu* 53 (1984): 137–59, for an interesting view of Machiavellianism as seen at Maximilian's court.

147. On the Bavarian plenipotentiaries, see Immler, *Kurfürst Maximilian I.*, 17–20.

148. Plenipotentiaries to Louis XIV, 14/19 April 1646, *APW II B 3*, 87, p. 226; Mazarin to Longueville, 9 February 1646, 107, p. 278.

Chapter 3. The Military Tool, Part I

1. Voltaire, "La princesse de Babylone," in *L'Ingénu et autres contes* (Paris, 1993).

2. Parrott, "The Administration of the French Army," 15; Jeremy Black, *A Military Revolution? Military Change and European Society, 1550–1800* (London, 1991), 15–16. See also Corvisier, *La France de Louis XIV*, 90–91, where he compares military operations to Sisyphus, and particularly mentions 1646–48; and R. A. Stradling, "Seventeenth-Century Spain: Decline or Survival?," in *Spain's Struggle for Europe, 1598–1668* (London, 1994), 26–28.

3. S. H. Steinberg, *The "Thirty Years War" and the Conflict for European Hegemony, 1600–1660* (London, 1966), 73; Parrott, "The Administration of the French Army," 348–49; John G. Gagliardo, *Germany under the Old Regime, 1600–1790* (New York, 1991), 68.

4. Michael Roberts, "The Military Revolution," in *Essays in Swedish History* (London, 1967), 202, 215; "Gustav Adolf and the Art of War," in *Essays in Swedish History* (London, 1967), 60, 74. The sole exception to this rule, so far as I can tell, is Per Sörensson in his old but not outdated article, "Das Kriegswesen während der letzten Periode des Dreißigjährigen Krieges," in *Der Dreißigjährige Krieg: Perspektiven und Strukturen*, ed. Hans Ulrich Rudolf (Darmstadt, 1977), 454–57 (originally published in 1932).

5. Isaak Bernays, "Die Diplomatie um 1500," *Historische Zeitschrift* 138 (1928): 1–23; G. Perjés, "Army Provisioning, Logistics and Strategy in the Second Half of the seventeenth Century," *Acta Historica Academiae Scientiarum Hungaricae* 16 (1970): 35–38; Martin van Creveld, *Supplying War* (New York, 1977), 17; Geoffrey Parker, "The 'Military Revolution', 1560–1660—a Myth?," *Journal of Modern History* 48 (1976), 195–214, and *The Military Revolution: Military Innovation and the Rise of the West, 1500–1800* (New York, 1988), 43–44; David Parrott, "The Military Revolution in Early Modern Europe," *History Today* 42 (December, 1992), 21–27, and "Strategy and Tactics in the Thirty Years' War: The "Military Revolution," *Militärgeschichtliches Mitteilungen* 38 (1985), 19–22; Black, 13–17 (and cast-

ing particular aspersions on the second half of the Thirty Years' War). Parrott's general judgement that the increase in army size outstripped the ability of states to supply their troops, as well as his specific critique of Roberts' favorable assessment of Gustavus's 1632 campaign plan, repeats van Creveld's argument (7–8, 16–17). In his "Maurice of Nassau, Gustavus Adolphus, Raimondo Montecuccoli, and the Military Revolution' of the Seventeenth Century," in *Makers of Modern Strategy from Machiavelli to the Nuclear Age*, ed. Peter Paret (Princeton, 1986), Gunther Rothenberg also wrote of how warfare "had become increasingly static and indecisive" (32–33). Although he was speaking of the period before the Military Revolution, he does not seem to believe that any major improvement occurred afterward. He calls Maurice and Montecuccoli mediocre strategists, and says that even Gustavus "could not escape the limitations of his time"; indeed, he says that Gustavus points toward the limited, positional warfare of the eighteenth century (37, 46, 54–55). Steinberg writes that "the majority of the campaigns were little more than large-scale raids with limited tactical objectives" (101–2). Andreas Kraus, *Maximilian I.: Bayerns Großer Kurfürst* (Graz, 1990), 155, sees a "transition to a strategy of diversions and raids" after 1635.

Other, more general accounts also typically see seventeenth century strategy in a negative light, e.g., B. H. Liddell Hart, *Strategy*, 2d revised edition (New York, 1967); Engel, 351; J. C. Allmayer-Beck, and E. Lessing, *Die Kaiserliche Kriegsvölker von Maximilian I bis Prinz Eugen 1479–1718* (Munich, 1978), 119–20. Michael Howard (*War in European History* [New York, 1976], 37) writes that "In the Thirty Years War warfare reached the nadir of brutality and pointlessness . . . Armies were in a continual state of deliquescence, . . . their movements governed not by strategic calculation but by the search for unplundered territory. It was a period in which warfare seemed to escape from rational control; to cease indeed to be 'war' in the sense of politically-motivated use of force by generally recognized authorities, and to degenerate instead into universal, anarchic, and self-perpetuating violence." Russell F. Weigley, *The Age of Battles: The Quest for Decisive Warfare from Breitenfeld to Waterloo* (Indianapolis, 1991), makes numerous comparable statements, e.g., "Gustavus's strategy of annihilation remained susceptible to the tyranny of military logistics over military strategy" (p. 35). See also pp. 28, 36, 537. Robert L. O'Connell, *Of Arms and Men: A History of War, Weapons, and Aggression* (New York, 1989), 147: "Armies increasingly devoid of intelligible political objectives, to say nothing of regular logistics, tended to degenerate into traveling mobs living in a symbiotic relationship with the countryside." Finally, E. A. Beller makes further disparaging comments in "The Thirty Years War," in *The Decline of Spain and the Thirty Years War 1609–48/59*, edited by J. P. Cooper, v. 4 of *The New Cambridge Modern History* (Cambridge, 1970), 351.

6. Van Creveld, 8–10. For a critique of *Supplying War*, see John Lynn "The History of Logistics and *Supplying War*" in *Feeding Mars: Logistics in Western Warfare from the Middle Ages to the Present*, edited by John A. Lynn (Boulder, 1993), 9–27, and "Food, Funds, and Fortresses: Resource Mobilization and Positional Warfare in the Campaigns of Louis XIV," ibid., 140.

7. Clausewitz, 330, 553; Roberts, "The Military Revolution," 215.

8. Roberts, "Gustav Adolf," 59 and 73; Parrott, "Strategy and Tactics," 21.

9. Parrott, "Strategy and Tactics," 21.

10. Parrott, "Strategy and Tactics," 19–22.

11. Zeller, *L'Organisation défensive des frontières*, 124–26, speaks of the need to renew strategy to get away from sieges; J. W. Wijn, "Military Forces and

Warfare 1610–48," in *The Decline of Spain and the Thirty Years War 1609–48/59*, ed. J. P. Cooper, *The New Cambridge Modern History*, v. 4 (Cambridge, 1970), 224: "War was more territorial in character"; Geoffrey Parker, *The Army of Flanders and the Spanish Road, 1567–1659: The Logistics of Spanish Victory and Defeat in the Low Countries' Wars* (New York, 1972), 6–10; M. S. Anderson, *War and Society in Europe of the Old Regime, 1618–1789* (Leicester, 1988), 42; Roberts, as footnote 6. Somewhat paradoxically, Roberts' critique of strategy falls into both "static" and "fluid" camps.

12. This is the root error of almost all critiques of early modern strategy; see also Steckzén, vi–viii; Georges Livet, *La Guerre de Trente Ans*, Que Sais-Je, v. 1083 (Paris, 1966), 80.

13. Armies in the seventeenth century were slower than their Napoleonic counterparts for a wide range of reasons: a weaker administrative apparatus, mistrust of soldiers and hence inability to forage freely, and lack of roads, among others. (My thanks to Geoffrey Parker for pointing out the dearth of adequate roads.)

14. Salm, 165; Geoffrey and Angela Parker, *European Soldiers 1550–1650* (New York, 1977), 22–26. On the background of soldiers, see Robert Chaboche, "Les soldats français de la guerre de Trente Ans, une tentative d'approche," *Revue d'histoire moderne et contemporaine* 20 (1973), 10–24.

15. Barozzi and Berchet, 433.

16. Perjés says that an army was "not only a war machine, but an immense milling, baking, foraging and transportation device at the same time, a device with a particular mechanism that operated according to rules all its own" (26).

17. The value of veteran soldiers was widely recognized. Turenne, for example, reported in 1644 that Bavaria's experienced soldiers could go for three to four days without bread, which would ruin the French army (Turenne to Mazarin, 2 July 1644, CP All. 23, fols. 254r–55r). On another occasion, Mazarin urged Turenne to give the new troops, "at least at the beginning, little work and a few conveniences so that they will come to like serving" (Mazarin to Turenne, 17 August 1644, *Lettres du cardinal Mazarin*, ed. Adolphe Chéruel, v. 2 (Paris, 1872), 17 (this and all subsequent references refer to the number of the letter rather than the page)). Overall rates of attrition are difficult to come by, but two examples demonstrate how severe it could be: in 1645, a French officer reported troops deserting in bands of thirty to forty one night (CP All. 45, fols. 276r–77r), while Tracy claimed to lose five hundred men out of thirty-three hundred, or fifteen percent, in a single day during a forced march (Turenne, *Mémoires [pièces justificatives]*, 283–84). The fate of the Bavarian army in April 1645 is an object lesson in desertion (see Maximilian to Mercy, 17 April 1645, Bayerisches Hauptstaatsarchiv (hereafter omitted), Kurbayern, Äußeres Archiv (hereafter KAA) v. 2818, fols. 473r–77r; 15 April 1645, 455r–59r; and Mercy to Maximilian, 20 April 1645, 492r–96r), but it is hardly unique. Perjés, 12–13, notes that even when they received their rations, soldiers were likely to be undernourished and hence more vulnerable to disease. See also Bernhard Kroener, "Soldat oder Soldateska? Programmatischer Aufriß einer Sozialgeschichte militärischer unterschichten in der ersten Hälfte des 17. Jahrhunderts," in *Militärgeschichte: Probleme—Thesen—Wege*, ed. Manfred Messerschmidt et al., (Stuttgart, 1982), 114–15. See Parker, *The Army of Flanders*, 207–21, on wastage; his chart on p. 208 makes the interesting point that almost as many soldiers deserted in peacetime as during a war.

18. Probably the single most common complaint of Bavarian army commanders was the need to remount the cavalry (see, e.g., Mercy to Maximilian,

23 August 1644, KAA v. 2795; Aumale, p. 608; and so forth). Since Turenne managed the army funds himself, he did not write to ask for remounts; nevertheless, he did report the need for them on several occasions. For cases of campaigns ruined by supply problems, see Kroener, *Les Routes et les Étapes*, 83–94, and Salm, 30–46.

19. See Perjés, 25, on the disadvantages of having troops find food on their own.

20. Perjés (7–8 and 10–11) notes that even in the best of times, armies only carried three to four days provisions; to have carried a month would have required an impossibly long supply train that was two days by courier from head to tail. However, note that Turenne did carry eight days of bread on his raid in June 1644 (Tracy to Mazarin, 8 June 1644, CP All. 23, fols. 233r–233v), and Guébriant ten days worth in his second invasion of the Empire in 1643 (Amblard de Noailles, *Le Maréchal de Guébriant [1602 à 1643]* [Paris, 1913], 377). On the organization of supply trains in the French army, see Louis André, *Michel Le Tellier et l'organisation de l'armée monarchique* (Paris, 1906), 451–54.

21. For example, the French at Tuttlingen (Turenne to Mazarin, 2 July 1644, CP All. 23, fols. 254r–55r). During their August 1646 breakthrough the French captured four hundred wagons ([Tracy?] to Mazarin, 18 August 1646, CP All. 66, fols. 258r–59r), not even counting the ones the Imperials burned deliberately so that they would have a chance of catching up to the French (Turenne, *Mémoires [pièces justificatives]*, 298). The Imperials also lost nine hundred wagons at Zusmarshausen (reports from Zusmarshausen, 18 May 1648, CP All. 108, fols. 103r–103v). Sörensson's puzzling statement that there were no real baggage trains is contradicted by his own evidence, which shows that the emperor contracted to provide a wagon for every company in one case (443–44).

22. There are numerous examples of the use of magazines, e.g., Le Tellier to Tracy, 20 December 1643, Bibliothèque Nationale (hereafter BN), Manuscrits français (hereafter Mf), v. 4199, fols. 24r–27r, and Le Tellier to d'Erlach, 11 October 1644, fols. 120r–24r; Turenne to Mazarin, 13 September 1644, CP All. 24, fols. 263r–64r and 269r–269v; Maximilian to Leopold Wilhelm, 11 May 1646, KAA v. 2846, fols. 439r–42r. But they required careful foresight; for example, Tracy was already buying grain for the 1645 campaign in August 1644, at the height of the campaign (Le Tellier to Tracy, 6 August 1644, BN Mf v. 4198, fols. 140r–140v). Maximilian ordered the construction of magazines in 1646, and supposedly the army had food for fifty days in May 1646, but well before that time they had run out and desertion became a serious problem (Maximilian to Leopold Wilhelm, 22 May 1646, KAA v. 2846, fols. 457r–58r; KAA v. 2901, fols. 3r–4r). For the organization of French magazines, see André, 455–66; Kroener, *Les Routes et les Étapes*, 85.

23. See, for example, Turenne to Mazarin, 23 November 1644, CP All. 25, fols. 111r–15v.

24. Fritz Redlich, "Contributions in the Thirty Years' War," *Economic History Review* 12 (1959–60), 247–54. Parker, *The Army of Flanders*, 142–44, notes that Don Luis de Requesens was the first to raise contributions, and they had also been used by Spìnola and Mansfeld; I cite Wallenstein because he is generally recognized as having introduced systematic contributions on a vast scale, but this is not to say that his accomplishments were without precedents.

25. See Kraus, *Maximilian I.*, 149–55, on the development of the quarters system. Most accounts, e.g., Redlich (see particularly pp. 252 and 253), do not distinguish between contributions and quarters. However, collecting money

from surrounding areas, often where an army was not even present, to use to pay troops, seems fundamentally different from having troops take food directly from the hosts on whom they are quartered, even though both systems are based on supplying armies off the country.

26. There are exceptions, however. In 1644, the French used only a small portion of their troops to besiege Philippsburg, sending the others into quarters nearby; they had learned that the enemy was more than twenty hours away, and hence presented no threat (Turenne, *Mémoires*, 27). In 1645, Turenne put his troops in the villages surrounding Hall, but deliberately kept them close together to avoid a repeat of the Herbsthausen disaster (Gramont to Mazarin, 20 September 1646, CP All. 48, fols. 283r–84r). For a general (and somewhat superficial) overview of quarters, see Hans Schmidt, "Der Einfluss der Winterquartiere auf Strategie und Kriegführung des Ancien Régime," *Historisches Jahrbuch* 92 (1972), 77–91. The absurd idea of S. H. Steinberg, 102, that winter quarters were created only for the comfort of officers, need hardly be discussed here.

27. Salm, 165 and 168. These totals are, however, inflated by the fact that most of the troops in the Westphalian Circle were in garrisons.

28. Mazarin to Turenne, 16 July 1645, CP All. 47, fols. 402r–3r. Jean-Baptiste Budes, comte de Guébriant, b. 1602, d.1643, led the *Armée d'Allemagne* from 1639 until his death in 1643. *Dictionnaire des Maréchaux*, 211–12; Noailles, *Le Maréchal de Guébriant*. See also the introduction to part II.

29. Nevertheless, organizational and financial ability were only one factor, and probably not the most important one, in determining a commander's success (*pace* Herbert Langer, *The Thirty Years' War*, trans. C. S. V. Salt (Dorset, 1978), 159, and André Corvisier, *La France de Louis XIV*, 90–91).

30. Mazarin to Turenne, 22 June 1648, Bibliothèque Mazarine manuscrits (hereafter BM), v. 2215, fols. 267v–71r. Wallenstein had said that it was easier to supply an army of fifty thousand than one of twenty thousand (cited in Parrott, "The Military Revolution," 27). It is impossible to tell whether Mazarin was echoing what had by 1648 become the conventional wisdom, or whether it was an original thought of his. In either case, the different numbers used by Wallenstein indicate the different scale of armies in the 1620s and the 1640s. Also significantly, in spite of Mazarin's statement, Turenne's army never approached twenty-five thousand, even when reinforced by Enghien.

31. Turenne, *Mémoires*, 79.

32. There are practically innumerable statements by Turenne and the French court to this effect, but some of the most interesting may be found in Mazarin to Enghien, 22 September 1644, *Lettres*, v. 2, 40; Turenne to Mazarin, 13 May 1644, CP All. 23, fols. 201r–201v; Le Tellier to Tracy, 12 November 1644, BN Mf v. 4170, fols. 274v–75r; and Le Tellier to Enghien, 19 August 1645, Archives de Guerre, Correspondance (hereafter AG), v. 94, fols. 105v–10v.

33. Turenne to Mazarin, 25 September 1646, CP All. 66, fols. 455r–57r.

34. Turenne to Mazarin, 9 September 1646, CP All. 66, fol. 380r. He also noted (Turenne, *Mémoires [pièces justificatives]*, 303) that "whatever advantage I have at this moment, if I am ruined during winter, it will be necessary to recross the Rhine."

35. See also Turenne to Mazarin, 13 May 1644, CP All. 23, fols. 201r–201v, in which Turenne excuses Bavaria's failure to advance in May 1644 on the lack of grass, and excuses his own failure to relieve Überlingen on the same grounds; Mercy to Maximilian, 20 April 1645, KAA v. 2818, fol. 496v, noting the lack of

grass; Mazarin to plenipotentiaries, 3 March 1646, *APW II B 3*, 139, p. 397, indicating May was the starting time for the 1646 campaign; and Perjés, 15–16.

36. Guébriant to Mazarin, 1 July 1643, CP All. 23, fols. 44r–46v.

37. Turenne to Mazarin, 25 June 1644, CP All. 23, fols. 236r–236v, 302r–3r; Mazarin to Enghien, 21 June 1645, BM, v. 2215, fols. 64r–65r.

38. Turenne to Mazarin, 29 December 1644, CP All. 25, fols. 364r–65r.

39. The extent of reliance on river valleys is demonstrated by Kroener, *Les Routes et les Étapes*, 93, 99–100, and 170, and also noted by Luitpold Luz, *Die Bayerische Artillerie von ihren ersten Anfängen bis zur Gegenwart* (Munich, 1894), 9. Some examples from the 1640s: the French shipping artillery down the Rhine after the battle of Freiburg in 1644 (Aumale, p. 312, 365–66; however, he errs in saying that it was "a new idea to use a great river as a line of operations"); Le Tellier to Enghien, 12 July 1645, AG v. 89, fols. 112r–17r, in which Le Tellier says that the possibility of sending supplies down the Moselle would make it easier to besiege Trier; Sörensson, 443–44, on the Imperial campaign along the Elbe in 1641; and Frankfurt news, 12 April 1644, CP All. 26, fols. 369r–369v on the Imperials in Hungary being afraid to leave the Danube because they would starve. Rothenberg, "Maurice of Nassau . . . ," 50, also notes that Gustavus was tied to river lines during his invasion of the Empire.

40. See Perjés, 38–39.

41. See, for example, d'Erlach's complaints about how the army made it impossible for him to feed his garrison troops (Le Tellier to Tracy, d'Erlach, and d'Oysonville, 23 August 1644, BN Mf v. 4199, fols. 88r–92v), and Turenne's insistence in 1646 that a political decision had to be made on where to send his army because he could not continue to supply it if he remained in the same place (Turenne to Mazarin, 22 June 1646, CP All. 66, fol. 82r). Disease was another consideration; see chapter 8, for Imperial problems in 1646, and Colin Jones, "The Welfare of the French Foot-Soldier," *History* 65 (1980), 196.

42. Salm, 30–46; Turenne, *Mémoires*, 291–93. An even more famous example, though considerably earlier, was Gustavus's unhappy sojourn at the Alte Veste in 1632.

43. Mercy to Maximilian, 15 August 1644, KAA v. 2795, fols. 509r–13r.

44. Mazarin argued that a siege was possible because the infantry did not need to live off the land; however, he was overruled by Enghien (Mazarin to Enghien, 21 August 1644, *Lettres*, v. 2, 22, and chapter 4 for details on the decision.) Supply certainly influenced the strategic decision to invade the Lower Palatinate in this case, but it would not be fair to say that it dictated it, because it was a plan that had been in the offing for at least a year, and Mazarin favored both the invasion and a siege of Freiburg. In fact, the Palatinate was also ruined, and according to some sources this was the main hope the Imperials had that the French attack would be unsuccessful (Mazarin to Turenne, 17 September 1644, *Lettres*, v. 2, 34). It is therefore at least as correct to say that the French overruled supply considerations in invading as it would be to say that supply was decisive.

45. Plenipotentiaries to Anne, 17 September 1646, *APW II B 4*, 159, the queen has "extended France's borders to its most ancient limits" ("estendu les limites de la France jusques à ses plus anciennes bornes"); Konrad Repgen, "Über den Zusammenhang von Verhandlungstechnik und Vertragsbegriffen," in *Historische Klopfsignale für die Gegenwart* (Münster, 1974), 69, footnote 18, from Contarini. See also Peter Sahlins, "Natural Frontiers Revisited: France's Boundaries since the Seventeenth Century," *American Historical Review* 95 (1990): 1425–33,

and *Boundaries*, 35–37. On the distant origins of the Rhine as part of the French border, see the fascinating study by Fritz Kern, *Die Anfänge der französischen Ausdehnungspolitik bis zum Jahr 1308* (Tübingen, 1910), 15–21.

46. On bridging methods, see Eduard Wagner, *European Weapons and Warfare, 1618–1648* (Prague, 1979), 231–35, and John Lynn, *Giant of the "Grand Siècle": The French Army, 1610–1715* (Cambridge, 1997), 536–37. See also below, chapter 6 for an example of a Bavarian attempt to destroy the French pontoon bridge.

47. Immler, *Kurfürst Maximilian I.*, 120–21. Ultimately, of course, this failed, but the tactics used to achieve this goal could be vicious (see below).

48. This, however, did not usually prove difficult; see Heinrich Heilmann, *Kriegsgeschichte von Bayern, Franken, Pfalz und Schwaben von 1506 bis 1651* (Munich, 1868), 765, for the problems with the Lech as a line of defense.

49. They were actually described as such in contemporary discourse; see Lynn, "A Quest for Glory: The Formation of Strategy under Louis XIV, 1661–1715," in *The Making of Strategy: Rulers, States, and War*, ed. Williamson Murray, MacGregor Knox, and Alvin Bernstein (New York, 1994), 194. As background for the following discussion, see the excellent article by John Lynn, "Food, Funds, and Fortresses," (in *Feeding Mars*.).

50. Lynn, "Food, Funds, and Fortresses," 145–50; Parrott, "The Military Revolution," 21–27.

51. In just one interesting case, the garrison of Frankenthal captured a French convoy in 1646, seizing seven thousand pistolles and over thirty prisoners; Turenne, *Mémoires [pièces justificatives]*, 278. See also Perjés, 45.

52. Although see Parker, "In Defense of *The Military Revolution*," in *The Military Revolution Debate: Readings on the Military Transformation of Early Modern Europe*, ed. Cliff Rogers (Boulder, 1995), 350–51.

53. This never seems to have happened in the period covered by this study, but it was a danger of which commanders were aware; Turenne, for example, noted his concern as he marched through the Archbishopric of Cologne in 1646 (Turenne, *Mémoires [pièces justificatives]*, 285–87). It was less of a problem in the southwest because there were simply fewer fortresses. The French disaster in the Gravelingen campaign of 1558, however, demonstrates the danger of leaving garrisoned fortresses in one's rear. Sir Charles Oman, *A History of the Art of War in the Sixteenth Century* (New York, 1937), 280.

54. Putting just one extra cavalry company into Gießen caused the Darmstadt fortress major supply problems (Hans H. Weber, *Der Hessenkrieg* (Gießen, 1935), 50). See also Napoleon, *Précis des guerres de Napoléon Ier* (Paris, 1965), 140–43, and the interesting example in Simon Pepper and Nicholas Adams, *Firearms and Fortifications: Military Architecture and Siege Warfare in Sixteenth-Century Siena* (Chicago, 1986), 129.

55. There are many instances of this, most notably Turenne's harboring of his army near Philippsburg at the end of 1645, and the Imperial-Bavarian retreat under the guns of Augsburg after the battle of Zusmarshausen. There is an actual case of four Imperial regiments saving themselves from Wrangel's army by retreating under the guns of Gießen (Hans H. Weber, 102). Ziegenhain twice served this purpose for the allies: once for Turenne after the battle of Herbsthausen (Heinrich Heilmann, *Die Feldzüge der Bayern in den Jahren 1643, 1644 und 1645* [Munich, 1851], 219), and once for Hesse-Cassel's army after an attack by Darmstadt (Hans H. Weber, 108–9). At the battle of Freiburg, Gramont notes that the cavalry guarding the Bavarian right remained under the walls of the town, "where it could not be attacked without temerity and complete madness"

(*Mémoires du Maréchal de Gramont, duc et pair de France*, ed. Michaud and Poujoulat, v. 7 of *Nouvelle collection des mémoires pour servir à l'histoire de France, depuis le XIIIe siècle jusqu'à la fin du XVIIIe* [Paris, 1839], 257). Condé also saved his army under the guns of the Bastille after its defeat by Turenne in July 1652.

56. The French court issued specific orders to fortress commanders after the battle of Herbsthausen (Le Tellier to de Beauvais-Plesian, BN Mf v. 4171, fols. 278r–83r), but it was almost certainly common practice.

57. The French had little trouble taking numerous small forts on their two advances to the Danube in 1645, for example, nor in their 1644 attack on the middle Rhine (Mazarin to Enghien, 4 September 1644, *Lettres*, v. 2, 29; Mercy to Maximilian, 17 April 1645, KAA v. 2818, 482–482v). The garrison of Hohentwiel itself managed to take both Überlingen and Rottweil (Walther Ernst Heydendorff, "Vorderösterreich im Dreißigjährigen Kriege: Der Verlust der Vorlande am Rhein und die Versuche zu deren Rückgewinnung, Part 2, 1639–1648," *Mitteilungen des Österreichischen Staatsarchivs* 13 (1960): 182–83 and 190). Often commanders would not even bother to garrison a town they did not feel was strong enough to defend itself (e.g., Turenne at Vesoul in 1644 (Turenne to Mazarin, 31 March 1644, CP All. 23, fols. 171r–72r), and Wrangel at Bregenz in 1647 (Peter Broucek, *Die Eroberung von Bregenz am 4. Jänner 1647*, v. 18 of Militärhistorische Schriftenreihe, Vienna, 1971). But there was a whole range of forts, running from large and virtually impregnable down to small, vulnerable chateaux, and even the latter could get a small garrison if it was felt it could delay the enemy; a list of Bavarian garrisons in the Lower Palatinate, for example, shows some as small as five or seven men (Franz Maier, *Die bayerische Unterpfalz im Dreißigjährigen Krieg: Besetzung, Verwaltung und Rekatholisierung der rechtrheinischen Pfalz durch Bayern 1621 bis 1649* [New York, 1990], 394).

58. Israel, *Dutch Republic*, 318–19 and 320–21, also makes the point that garrisons were rarely starved out.

59. For example, in the French offensive of 1644, Eichelsheim was called upon to surrender, but it refused and was never attacked (Maier, 384). By contrast, Speyer rejected the first summons, but accepted the second once Turenne had arrived with his army; Worms did not even wait that long, but handed over the keys before Turenne arrived (BN Mf v. 6180, map 22).

60. On showing the defender the siegeworks, see Mazarin to Longueville, 8 March 1646, *APW II B 3*, 157, p. 436, and Michel de Montaigne, *Essais*, ed. Jean Plattard, v. 1 (Paris, 1959), 31.

61. Few garrisons, of course, surrendered to mercy, since it was little better than fighting to the death. One garrison, for example, rejected a call to surrender to mercy, and instead was taken prisoner (Sieur de Pontis, *Mémoires du Sieur de Pontis*, v. 32 of *Collection des mémoires relatifs à l'histoire de France depuis l'avènement de Henri IV jusqu'à la Paix de Paris conclue en 1763*, ed. M. Petitot (Paris, 1824), 386–87). But others did accept these terms; some, such as that in Rothenburg that surrendered to the French in July 1645, were put to death (allegedly for killing French stragglers after the battle of Herbsthausen), while others, such as one French garrison that surrendered to the Bavarians, were taken into enemy service (Heilmann, *Feldzüge*, 223; Maier, 393). The terms for the surrender of Philippsburg to the French are found in CP All. 24, fols. 232r–33r. Numerous copies of surrender terms are printed in J. P. Lotichium, *Theatri Europaei oder Historische Beschreibung aller Vornembsten und Denwürdigsten Geschichten, so sich hin und wieder in Europa sonderlich im Reich Teütscher Nation von A. 1642 biß A. 1647 zugetragen* (Frankfurt, 1647). On rules of sieges, see Jean-François Pernot,

"Guerre de sièges et places fortes," in *Guerre et Pouvoir en Europe au XVIIe siècle,* ed. Viviane Barrie-Curien (Paris, 1991), 140–43.

62. See Parker, "If the Armada Had Landed," in *Spain and the Netherlands, 1559–1659: Ten Studies* (Glasgow, 1979), 140. See also d'Erlach to [?], 1 May 1645, CP All. 46, fol. 422r, in which d'Erlach says that he would not be able to take Wildenstein "if those inside simply have the courage to defend themselves." The negotiating character of sieges is the true reason for the occasional practice of allowing the defenders to exit unharmed, and not, as some have maintained, that war was somehow gentlemanly.

63. For example, at Philippsburg, Maximilian to Mercy, 29 August 1644, KAA v. 2795, fols. 575r–76v. See also chapter 6 for other Bavarian attempts (mostly futile).

64. See Parker, "In Defense of *The Military Revolution,*" 348–49.

65. Chéruel, *Histoire de France,* v. 3, 41; on Freiburg, Le Tellier to Enghien, 17 August 1644, BN Mf v. 4169, fols. 131r–36v.

66. Mercy to Maximilian, 17 April 1645, KAA v. 2818, fols. 481r–481v, and 25 April 1645, fols. 526r–526v.

67. Mercy to Maximilian, 28 April 1645, KAA v. 2818, fols. 545r–46r.

68. Mazarin to Turenne, 22 September 1644, *Lettres,* v. 2, 38.

69. See Fritz Textor, *Entfestigungen und Zerstörungen im Rheingebiet während des 17. Jahrhunderts als Mittel der französischen Rheinpolitik,* v. 31 of *Rheinisches Archiv,* ed. A Bach and Fr. Steinbach (Bonn, 1937), 11, on the inability of numerous small fortresses to stop a determined advance.

70. Turenne to Mazarin, 26 July, CP All v. 23, fols. 298r–298v; Mazarin to Turenne, 22 June 1648, fols. 267v–71r; August von Gonzenbach, *Der General Hans Ludwig von Erlach von Castelen: Ein Lebens- und Charakterbild aus den Zeiten des dreißigjährigen Kriegs,* v. 2 (Bern, 1880), 470.

71. For an excellent account of the raids out of Hohentwiel, see Heydendorff, "Vorderösterreich im Dreißigjährigen Kriege."

72. One French officer did judge that Rottweil was essential if the French were to have a way to invade Württemberg and Swabia. His analysis was correct, but Rottweil proved too weak a basis for French arms in the Black Forest. Rocqueservieres to Mazarin, 4 December 1643, CP All. 23, fols. 106r–7r.

73. Maier, 388–90.

74. Turenne to Mazarin, 3 September 1644, CP All. 24, fols. 156r–58r; 13 September 1644, 263–64; 30 September 1644, 349–50; and Enghien to Mazarin, 18 September 1644, 306r–6v; Hermann-Dieter Müller, *Der schwedische Staat in Mainz, 1631–1636: Einnahme, Verwaltung, Absichten, Restitution,* v. 24 of *Beiträge zur Geschichte der Stadt Mainz* (Mainz, 1979), 52–60, 220–22, 228–35.

75. Turenne to Mazarin, 23 November 1644, CP All. 25, fols. 111r–15v, and 8 December 1644, 281r–84v. The quotation is from MD v. 855, fols. 155r–56v. See also above, footnote 51.

76. French interest in Heilbronn is repeated over and over in the sources, Champlastreux to Mazarin, 3 [September, misdated to August] 1644, CP All. 48, fols. 29r–30v, being just once instance. Interestingly, Mercy indicated some key faults in the design of the fortress in April 1645, but apparently had them repaired before the French offensive in July (Mercy to Maximilian, 30 April 1645, KAA v. 2818, fol. 555v).

77. Tracy to Mazarin, 9 September 1646, CP All. 66, fols. 376r–376v, and Turenne to Mazarin, 9 September 1646, 378–80; see also Turenne, *Mémoires,* 91, footnote 1.

78. See Mercy to Maximilian, 17 April 1645, KAA v. 2818, 482-', and Enghien's undated after-action report on the Alerheim campaign, CP All. 48, fols. 9r–9v, in which he actually says that they are capturing enemy towns deliberately in order to "refresh" themselves.

79. Göran Rystad, "Die Schweden in Bayern während des Dreißigjährigen Krieges," in *Um Glauben und Reich: Kurfürst Maximilian I. Beiträge zur Bayerischen Geschichte und Kunst, 1573–1657*, v. 2, part 1 of *Wittelsbach und Bayern* (Munich, 1980), 433–34. In Turenne to Mazarin, 25 September 1646, CP All. 66, fols. 455r–57r, Turenne says that Rain is not a good fortress, and calls both Donauwörth and Lauingen (the French bridge over the Danube) "very bad forts."

80. Le Tellier to d'Uxelles, 18 August 1645, AG, v. 94, fols. 103v–5v. See also the quotation from Turenne (footnote 31 above) about the "fruit" to be gained from battle.

81. Cp. Weigley, 34. It was because of this, and the fundamental importance of sieges, that there were relatively few battles; rather than, as some claim, the economic losses caused by battles (Langer, 158).

82. Turenne once explained his strategy as "undertake few sieges and many combats . . ." Curtis Cate, "The Making of a Marshal," *MHQ* v. 5 no.3 (Spring 1993), 26. See also Lynn, "A Quest for Glory," 193, and *Giant of the "Grand Siècle,"* 530–32.

83. See also Perjés, 43–44, for a (somewhat too pessimistic) assessment of the difficulties of following up a victory.

84. See Turenne to Mazarin, 13 February 1644, CP All. 23, fols. 159r–159v. However, troops enlisted in this way were unlikely to remain for long; see Le Tellier to Turenne, 2 September 1645, BN Mf v. 4200, fols. 189v–90r. See above for armies increasing in strength as they attacked.

85. Maximilian to Mercy, 28 April 1645, KAA v. 2818, fols. 538r–41r.

86. See the court's order to Enghien to advance slowly so as not to fatigue the troops; Le Tellier to Enghien, 21 May 1645, BN Mf v. 4171, fol. 327v. Turenne also suffered from this problem in 1646; see chapter 8.

87. Turenne to Mazarin, 30 September 1644, CP All. 24, fols. 349r–50v.

88. For example, at the end of 1643, the French considered Alsace a valuable province "because it furnishes a good part of the support of the garrisons of the country" (Le Tellier to Turenne, 8 December 1643, BN Mf v. 4169, fols. 59r–59v)—that is to say, it was exceptional in that it was able to support much of its own garrisons. Maier, 359, also notes that Bavaria was happy enough to have their part of the Lower Palatinate support its own garrisons, even though it occupied the territory for virtually the whole war.

89. For an interesting case study, see chapter 6 below on the French occupation of the Lower Palatinate in 1644. Their financial problems continued into 1645; shortly before the battle of Herbsthausen, the court issued orders for a major reform designed to turn the king's conquests to his advantage (rather than working to his disadvantage, as they had been doing). They ordered dramatic reductions in garrison strengths in Alsace and lesser reductions in other towns, although the Alsatian garrisons were still probably too high (see Georges Livet, *L'intendance d'Alsace sous Louis XIV, 1648–1715* (Strasbourg, 1956), 105). Louis XIV to de Beauvais-Plesian, 11 May 1645, BN Mf v. 4171, fols. 271r–78r.

90. See also Lynn, "A Quest for Glory," 190–91, which notes the advantages of limited offensives even in an overall defensive campaign. (However, this was

not the case for the French in the 1640s: they were on the offensive on all fronts almost every year.)

Chapter 4. The Military Tool, Part II

1. Martin van Creveld is one of the most famous critics of early modern strategy; see his *Command in War* (Cambridge, Massachusetts, 1985), 18. The idea that strategy did not exist before the development of special institutions and terminology, however, has been brilliantly exploded in Everett L. Wheeler's "Methodological Limits and the Mirage of Romand Strategy," *Journal of Military History* 57 (1993): 7–41 and 215–40. I have been unable to take into account the new study by Ernst Höfer, *Das Ende des Dreißigjahrigen Krieges: Strategie und Kriegsbild* (1997).

2. Mousnier, "Le Conseil du Roi," 162.

3. There is one interesting reference in Mazarin to Longueville, 14 April 1646, *APW II B 3*, 215 in which Mazarin says that "We were at Liancourt this week to talk with Marshal Gassion, who came to discuss plans for the next campaign." If this was a council of war, why was Gaston not mentioned? And if it was not a council of war, why was it discussing campaign plans? If he was following later practice, Mazarin was discussing with a trusted marshal a plan that had already been formulated in a council meeting (see Lynn, "A Quest for Glory," 182–83). But in that case, the plans would not have been decided in a Council of War, because all marshals were present at such a meeting; instead, they would have been made in the *Conseil d'en Haut*. Because of this evidence, and in the absence of any clear references to the council of war from 1644 to 1648 in my research, I am skeptical whether it met after 1643.

4. See André, *Michel Le Tellier*. Appointed on a provisionary basis on 11 April 1643 with the disgrace of the former war secretary Sublet de Noyers, Le Tellier was confirmed in that post on 22 October 1645 after Noyers's death.

5. Mazarin to Longueville, 19 August 1645, *Lettres*, v. 2, 87; Mazarin to plenipotentiaries, 3 December 1643, *Lettres*, v. 1, 344.

6. Turenne to Mazarin, 4 October 1644, CP All. 24, fols. 373r–74r.

7. Servien to Lionne, 14/19 April 1646, *APW II B 3*, 228; d'Avaux to Mazarin, 30 July 1646, *APW II B 4*, 92.

8. Mazarin to plenipotentiaries, 24 March 1646, *APW II B 3*, 182, p. 494; see also Mazarin to Longueville, 21 April 1646, *APW II B 3*, 233.

9. Turenne, *Mémoires [pièces justificatives]*, 303.

10. C.P. All 23, Mémoire touchant l'Allemagne, au tems de Maréchal de Guébriant, 127v. The document also urges crossing the Lech and invading Bavaria, because Maximilian is old and loves his duchy and would sooner separate from the Habsburgs than see it ruined. These were the exact lines that Mazarin's strategy would follow in the ensuing five years. See also Le Tellier to Marsin, 15 January 1644, AG v. 89, fols. 67v–74r: "recognizing more and more that to arrive [at a good peace] . . . there is no better means than to attack them in their country."

11. See above, chapter 3, on recruiting. New troops could be ready in a few months, e.g., Le Tellier to Courval, 19 August 1645, AG v. 94, fols. 100v–102r, although in the worst cases it took more than a year.

12. It is clear that Mazarin was aware of some advantages to eroding enemy strength in the long term. After the capture of Bourbourg, he wrote that the

capture of enemy infantry would be as great a loss to them as the town (Mazarin to Longueville, 12 August 1645, *Lettres*, v. 2, 85); and after Freiburg, a French officer wrote back that it was advantageous to France in spite of the relatively equal losses because "men are more rare in Bavaria" (d'Aumont to Le Tellier, 8 August 1644 [falsely given as 4 at August the top of the letter, but correctly as 8 August at the end], AG, v. 98, #61 (refers to letter numbers because the folios in AG v. 98 are not paginated)). But when the court wrote after Alerheim that Bavaria would have more difficulty raising a new army than France, it was in the context of Bavaria being unable to "put itself in safety" from the threat of new French attacks—that is, the battle was, again, a means to an end (Louis XIV to plenipotentiaries, 1 September 1645, *APW II B 2*, 201).

13. Mazarin to Turenne, 20 July 1644, BM, v. 2214, fols. 217r–217v.

14. Mazarin to Longueville, 19 August 1645, *Lettres*, v. 2, 87. For a full discussion of the events surrounding the battle of Alerheim, see chapter 7.

15. Brienne to Servien, 31 May 1645, *APW II B 3*, 116, pp. 397–98; court to plenipotentiaries, 30 May 1645, *APW II B 3*, 114.

16. Court to Turenne, 8 December 1643, AG v. 89, fols. 42r–55v. See also Servien's comment in April 1645 that "it is necessary for us to appear a little stronger across the Rhine than Turenne's army is now . . . it would be a sort of embarrassment for us at the point of concluding a peace treaty to have so little part of the fruits of this victory, and for the Bavarians to be still in a state to prevent Turenne from advancing in spite of their recent losses. It is a matter in which reputation must be handled carefully, even when there is no other advantage to be gained." Servien to Lionne, 22 April 1645, *APW II B 2*, 89.

17. Plenipotentiaries to Mazarin, 2 July 1644, *APW II B 1*, 157, pp. 313–14.

18. Mazarin to plenipotentiaries, 17 July 1644, *APW II B 1*, 177, p. 368. That Mazarin felt that Germany was the main front has become the standard view, e.g., Dickmann, *Der Westfälische Frieden*, 117–18, and de Garden, 97–98: "Cardinal Mazarin was himself persuaded of this maxim, that the success of the treaty depended uniquely on the success of the war in Germany" ("le cardinal Mazarin était lui-même persuadé de cette maxime, que le succès du traité de paix dépendait uniquement du succès de la guerre en Allemagne").

19. Plenipotentiaries to Brienne, 5 November 1644, *APW II B 1*, 283, p. 601.

20. Mazarin to plenipotentiaries, 21 December 1644, *APW II B 1*, 333, p. 794.

21. For example, Le Tellier to Enghien, 1 May 1644, BN Mf v. 4169, fols. 101r–3v. Certainly in 1646 as well: see Mazarin to Longueville, 8 March 1646, *APW II B 3*, 157. See also the list of French armies in 1644 in Le Clerc, v. 1, 281–82: Flanders is the only one with multiple armies; others are located in Catalonia, Italy, under Enghien, and near Breisach. Also see Mazarin to Longueville, 14 April 1646, *APW II B 3*, 215, in which Mazarin concentrates heavily on the Flanders front when describing the upcoming campaign. Also at the end of the same letter, he discusses how much Enghien wanted to be on the Flemish front; since Enghien sought the most prestigious armies, he must have considered the ones in Flanders to be the most important. It is also interesting to compare the memoirs of Madame de Motteville (*Mémoires de Madame de Motteville*, Collection des mémoires relatifs à l'histoire de France depuis l'avènement de Henri IV jusqu'à la Paix de Paris conclue en 1763, ed. M. Petitot, vols. 36 and 37) and of Mademoiselle (*Mémoires de Mademoiselle de Montpensier, Fille de Gaston d'Orléans, Frère de Louis XIII*, Collection des mémoires relatifs à l'histoire de France depuis l'avènement de Henri IV jusqu'à la Paix de Paris conclue en 1763, ed. M. Petitot, v. 40), both of which concentrate far more heavily on the

Flanders front than anywhere else (understandable in the case of Mademoiselle, but not for Motteville). They both ignore Germany completely when Enghien is not there (neither even mentions Turenne), and do not even mention the preliminary treaty with the emperor in September 1646. One of the reasons historians have been quick to overrate the importance of the German front in 1644 and 1645 is the two major battles fought in those years (see, for example, André, 147); but battles were not necessarily signs that the war was going well, or that the French were making their greatest efforts there.

22. Grand-Mesnil, 9. This ability apparently also extended to Mazarin's subordinates. Consider two letters from Le Tellier to Turenne, in BN Mf v. 4198, fols. 12r–14r, 26 February 1644, and BN Mf v. 4199, fols. 27r–29v, 21 December 1643: in the former, he protests that "we want to support German affairs, preferably, the same as all the others," while in the latter he notes that Mazarin "is particularly concerned about Germany . . . you can be assured that there is absolutely no other army better supported, nor in a better state to make considerable progress, than yours." These statements were clearly made to convince Turenne that his interests were not being neglected, and do not reflect the true situation; besides the other evidence presented above, it is clear that not all fronts were the same, as the first letter claims.

23. See also Le Tellier to Enghien, 21 May 1645, BN Mf v. 4171, fols. 325r–26r, in which the court urges Enghien to seize quarters in the Empire, noting that money spent on French troops quartered within France are not available against Spain. In other words, by getting quarters in the Empire, the *Armée d'Allemagne* was not improving its own financial situation, but instead freeing up money for use against Spain—which was therefore clearly the main enemy. The historiography on Spanish priorities is contradictory. Robert Stradling, "Conclusion: Second Thoughts," in *Spain's Struggle for Europe, 1598–1668* (London, 1994), 293, argues that Spain chose Catalonia over the Low Countries beginning in 1644; but Jonathan Israel, "Olivares, the cardinal-Infante and Spain's Strategy in the Low Countries (1635–1643): the Road to Rocroy," in *Spain, Europe and the Atlantic world: Essays in honour of John H. Elliott*, ed. Richard Kagan and Geoffrey Parker (Cambridge, 1995), 270, claims that "there was never, at any stage, the slightest possibility that Spain's main army would be stationed anywhere other than in the south Netherlands," and further asserts (295) that this policy continued after 1643, and indeed until the end of the war in 1659. Whatever the truth of the matter, it is clear that the Low Countries were of crucial importance both to France and Spain; as Israel notes, Spain's reason for concentrating on the Low Countries was not that it was the most important territory to them, but precisely because it was where France was the most vulnerable (292–93).

The plenipotentiaries' inability to realize the limited resources of the crown and consequently to decide that one front simply had to be privileged over the others is reminiscent of the strategic myopia of Philip II (Parker, "The Making of Strategy in Habsburg Spain: Philip II's 'bid for mastery,' 1556–1598," in *The Making of Strategy: Rulers, States, and War*, ed. Williamson Murray, MacGregor Knox, and Alvin Bernstein [New York, 1994], 115–50) and Philip III (see Paul Allen, "The Strategy of Peace: Spanish Foreign Policy and the *"Pax Hispanica,"* 1598–1609," Ph. D. diss., Yale, 1995); however, it was not shared by Mazarin. Compare the orders to Enghien in 1644: the court "having esteemed it neither *a propos* nor possible to undertake to attack the enemies at the same time in different places," decided to put Gaston in a state to undertake "some great design" while Enghien covered Champagne (Le Tellier to Enghien, 1 May 1644,

BN Mf v. 4169, fols. 101r–3v). This clearly shows an ability to recognize limitations and assign priorities.

24. *APW II B 1*, 333; Gaston Zeller, *De Christophe Colomb à Cromwell*, part 1 of *Les temps modernes*, v. 2 of *Histoire des relations internationales*, ed. Pierre Renouvin (Paris, 1953), 258. Engel, 354, argues that Mazarin turned to Germany because he could not successfully shake Spanish control of Italy. While it is clearly true that his interest in the Milanese front was minimal from 1644, certainly his activity in 1646–1648 indicates that he had not given up on Italy altogether. Also, it is a mistake to see the progress of the German treaty as a consequence of France's failure to make progress against Spain; the efforts against the Austrian and Spanish Habsburgs were concurrent and complementary. Moreover, the French effort against the Habsburgs was hardly restricted to Italy.

25. Richard Wilmer Rowan's estimate *(The Story of Secret Service* [New York, 1939], 94) that military espionage was far behind diplomatic espionage may be true to an extent, but the fact is that the two overlapped to such a great extent that, especially at the grand strategic level, they were virtually indistinguishable.

26. Tracy to Mazarin, 5 February 1644, CP All. 23, fol. 155r.

27. Plenipotentiaries-Brienne, 5 August 1645, CP All. 48, fols. 40r–45v; the news came from Bönninghausen, a former Imperial colonel who had entered French service.

28. There is a fairly good survey of intelligence sources in van Creveld, *Command in War*, 19–20 and 22–23; however, he is too pessimistic about their usefulness, especially newspapers.

29. See also Rowan, 100.

30. Mazarin to Enghien, 4 September 1644, *Lettres*, v. 2, 29; Maximilian to Mercy, 5 August 1644, KAA v. 2795, fol. 463v. See also Maximilian to Mercy, 18 May 1645, KAA v. 2818, fols. 637r–39v, and 27 April 1645, fols. 521r–22v for other examples of the leader giving his general information; these could be multiplied, but especially for the Bavarians, since Maximilian was closer to the action and was able to gather information from many friends and allies. In another interesting case, the French plenipotentiary Servien apparently used his diplomatic immunity as a guise for gathering intelligence on Lamboy's army, which was very close to Münster. Rainer Babel, "Der Westfälischer Friedenskongreß in französischer Sicht: Ein Tagebuchfragment Nicolas Doulceurs aus den Jahren 1647 und 1648," *Francia* 16 part 2 (1989): 24.

31. Maximilian to Mercy, 22 August 1644, KAA v. 2795, fols. 548r–49v.

32. Livet, *La Guerre de Trente Ans*, 107.

33. Maximilian to Gronsfeld, 18 April 1648, KAA v. 2961, fols. 220r–23v; on another commander who did use newspapers, see Leopold Wilhelm to Maximilian, 7 July 1646, KAA v. 2902, fols. 5r–5v.

34. See Frankfurt news, 2 October 1644, CP All. 24, fols. 367r–68r for a rare instance of an army making a movement because of a false rumor. It was less likely that a general would be actively misled by such information; instead, he would often freeze his forces in anticipation of an enemy advance that never came.

35. As the Swedes once had to remind the Imperials: Fleitmann, 39.

36. In a rare direct reference to this, Leopold Wilhelm reported in 1646 that "because of the insecurity of the roads, I am not able to write" to other Imperial commanders (Leopold Wilhelm to Maximilian, 17 August 1646, KAA v. 2902, fols. 63r–63v).

37. Turenne to plenipotentiaries, 16 August 1645, CP All. 48, fols. 87r–87v; Mazarin to Longueville, 6 July 1646, *APW II B 4*, 54: hard to communicate military news because "until now most couriers have been killed or taken prisoner by the garrisons of la Bassée and of Aire, which the enemy has reinforced strongly."

38. Mercy to Max, 11 August 1644, KAA v. 2795, fols. 490r–92v; Turenne to Mazarin, 6 August 1645, CP All. 48, fol. 63r.

39. Turenne to plenipotentiaries, 29 December 1644, CP All. 25, fol. 363r; Turenne to Mlle. de Bouillon, [no date], *Lettres de Turenne extraites des archives Rohan-Bouillon*, ed. Suzanne d'Huart (Paris, 1971), 413.

40. Turenne, *Mémoires [pièces justificatives]*, 20 (Mazarin to Turenne, 26–30 August 1646); Mazarin to Turenne, 17 January 1648, CP 107 fols. 61r–62r, indicate Mazarin's explicit fear that Turenne would not get a message and the need to send a second courier. Naturally, the use of oral messages also makes it more difficult for the historian to recreate the military situation than the diplomatic one.

41. In the 1648 invasion, for comparative purposes, a letter from Paris took eighteen days to reach Turenne (Turenne to Mazarin, 5 May 1648, CP All. 108, fols. 24r–24v).

42. Mazarin to Enghien, 11 July 1645, *Lettres*, v. 2, 79.

43. He left his military commanders even more leeway than he left his plenipotentiaries. This seems to have been in contrast to Richelieu, who, according to Parrott, gave his commanders only the appearance of autonomy, in actuality driving them into aggressive and fruitless campaigns, especially after 1638 (Parrott, "The Administration of the French Army," 71–72). As the following discussion will show, Mazarin not only told his commanders that they had independence, but tolerated a large amount of deviation from his own campaign ideas. Mazarin may have been more willing to leave commanders considerable freedom because his ministry was relatively new; there is some evidence to suggest that he became more involved in micromanaging military campaigns in the 1650s, e.g. Treasure, *Mazarin*, 369–70, footnote 2. See also André, 124, footnote 2, and Lynn, "A Quest for Glory," 183. On communication problems and their influence on supplies, see Kroener, *Les Routes et les Étapes*, 34–35.

44. For example, in 1645, Turenne made the decision to retreat into Hesse rather than to recross the Rhine after Herbsthausen at a time when Mazarin was not even sure that Turenne was still alive. See below, chapter 7.

45. Mazarin to Turenne, 2 December 1644, *Lettres*, v. 2, 47, and to Enghien, 21 August 1644, 22.

46. Mazarin to Enghien, 21 August 1644, *Lettres*, v. 2, 22.

47. Mazarin to Enghien, 21 July 1644, *Lettres*, v. 2, 4. References to Mazarin leaving decisions to his commanders could be repeated indefinitely; see also Mazarin to Enghien, 21 July 1644, BM, v. 2214, fols. 218v–19r; Anne to Enghien, 17 August 1644, AG, v. 98, #69; Le Tellier to Turenne, 27 April 1646, AG, v. 99, fols. 199v–201r; Mazarin to Turenne, 22 September 1644, *Lettres*, v. 2, 38, and Turenne, *Mémoires [pièces justificatives]*, 261, 272, and 281.

48. For example, when Mazarin granted Gaston command of the Flanders army in 1644, the year after Enghien had won the battle of Rocroi. Chéruel, *Histoire de France*, v. 1, 276–78.

49. See Jean Bérenger, *Turenne* (Paris, 1987), part II, chapters 2 and 3.

50. Bérenger, *Turenne*, 231, cites evidence that shows that even the Bavarians thought Turenne was the main obstacle to peace; also 265. Turenne's political

opinions are not surprising when one realizes that his mother was William of Orange's daughter, and his aunt was wife to Friedrich V of the Palatinate, the Winter King (Riezler, 507, footnote 2).

51. Bérenger, 265; Turenne, *Mémoires*, 102–3.

52. Turenne, *Mémoires [pièces justificatives]*, 273–74.

53. The same applies to Enghien; in 1645, he urged Enghien to attack Mercy at all costs, which led directly to the battle of Alerheim (see chapter 7). Turenne was clearly concerned about what the court thought of his actions, as demonstrated by his relief at the capture of Philippsburg in 1644 (Turenne to Mlle. de Bouillon, 10 September 1644, *Lettres de Turenne*, 406) and his justification of his retreat across the Rhine in the autumn of 1645 (ibid., 17 October 1645, 422).

54. Turenne, *Mémoires [pièces justificatives]*, 258.

55. This seems to have been in contrast to Richelieu, who took out military failures on his commanders, sometimes going so far as to have them executed (see Parrott, "The Administration of the French Army," 327–31, and Jean Chagniot, "Ethique et pratique de la 'profession des armes' chez les officiers français au XVIIe siècle," in *Guerre et Pouvoir en Europe au XVIIe siècle*, ed. Viviane Barrie-Curien (Paris, 1991), 85–86). It seems that the only incidence of Mazarin being anywhere nearly as harsh was in his trial of De La Mothe-Houdancourt after the incompetent Catalonian campaign of 1644. Even there, the Catalans initiated the complaints (Chéruel, *Histoire de France*, 66–72; and, according to André, 321–26, it was mostly Le Tellier's affair anyway); and in 1646, when Harcourt tried to starve out Lérida against Mazarin's advice and ended up ignominiously retreating, Mazarin did not attempt to punish him. See also Aumale, 314, for an opinion that Mazarin's treatment of the commander surrendering Freiburg was more lenient that Richelieu's would have been.

56. Bérenger, 192, calls Turenne one of Mazarin's clients; it may be an exaggeration, but it is true that they did get along well overall. (Cp. Ranum, *The Fronde*, 314–15.)

57. Turenne to Mlle. de Bouillon [his sister], 22 January 1644, *Lettres de Turenne extraites des archives Rohan-Bouillon*, ed. Suzanne d'Huart (Paris, 1971), 393.

58. Mazarin noted as late as 1646 that "they have not lost the name of Weimarians" (Turenne, *Mémoires [pièces justificatives]*, 257–58). Turenne was chosen as their commander partly because of his Protestantism, an example of the need to compromise with their interests. Note Turenne's concerns to get a Lutheran pastor for the army in 1644 (*Lettres de Turenne*, 403, 407–8).

59. André, 146–48. Upon taking control of the army, Turenne noted to Mazarin (18 December 1643, CP All 23, fols. 116–116v) that "the old cavalry will never suffer a lieutenant general." The court evidently accepted his reasoning, because it later gave d'Aumont the salary of a lieutenant-general, but not the title (Le Tellier to Tracy, 13 April 1644, AG 89, fols. 90v–94r).

60. For example, he sulked when Turenne was appointed commander of the *Armée d'Allemagne* (Le Tellier to d'Erlach, 25 February 1644, BN Mf v. 4198, fols. 10v–11v). A complete history of d'Erlach has been published by Gonzenbach, *Der General Hans Ludwig von Erlach von Castelen*.

61. Turenne, *Mémoires [pièces justificatives]*, 257–58.

62. The Swedes continued to believe that the Weimarians had been taken from them illegally, and hence readily accepted those who returned; Goetze, 207.

63. The more so when a commander like d'Erlach could interfere with French administration in the Empire, for example when he vetoed the appoint-

ment of an intendant to handle finances in Breisach, and quarrelled with d'Oysonville, his French counterpart in Breisach, until the government was forced to remove d'Oysonville to another post. The government took this latter action specifically because they feared that not giving in might spark a mutiny among the Weimarians. Livet, *L'Intendance d'Alsace*, 80–81 and 90–91; André, 225–27. See also the introduction to part II, for failed attempts to integrate the Weimarians better into the French command structure.

64. Barozzi and Berchet, 431; ? to ? [probably from Le Tellier], 18 August 1644, AG, v. 98, #70. Turenne felt it necessary to ask Mazarin to provide coats for new recruits going into Germany (Turenne to Mazarin, 9 September 1646, CP All. 66, fols. 378r–80r). Turenne also wrote in 1644 that troops desert at four times the usual rate in Germany because "the fatigue is greater" there (Turenne to Mazarin, 12 August 1644, CP All. 24, fols. 50r–51v). The dislike of French soldiers for serving in Germany continued at least until the end of the seventeenth century; see Perjés, 38, for some assessments of later commanders (which, however, understate the problems of the Thirty Years' War period considerably). On this issue, see also André, 210–11.

65. Turenne to Mazarin, 3 June 1644, CP All. 23, fols. 219r–20r; Le Tellier to Turenne, 18 November 1645, BN Mf v. 4200, fol. 248 ff.

66. Le Tellier to Arnaud, 16 August 1644, AG, v. 90, fols. 91r–93v; Le Tellier to Turenne, 19 July 1646, BN Mf v. 4174, fols. 36v–37v. It is unclear in the latter case whether the money is going to the troops, or to the commanders for getting the troops across the Rhine.

67. Le Tellier to Enghien, 6 September 1644, BN Mf v. 4198, fols. 166r–68r; Le Tellier to Turenne, 3 November 1644, BN Mf v. 4199, fols. 136r–38r; Mazarin to Enghien, 11 July 1645, *Lettres*, v. 2, 79.

68. Mazarin to Turenne, 2 December 1644, *Lettres*, v. 2, 47. At another time, he estimated that two-thirds of the troops desert; Mazarin to Turenne, 4 September 1644, BM, v. 2215, fols. 171v–73v.

69. Louis XIV to plenipotentiaries, 14 October 1645, *APW II B 2*, 237, p. 750.

70. Mazarin to Turenne, 2 December 1644, *Lettres*, v. 2, 47.

71. Most of these references are taken from the period prior to the Weimarian mutiny, at which point the number of German troops undoubted decreased, at least temporarily. It does seem, however, that the French were recruiting more in Germany, particularly with the levy of nearly five thousand soldiers in Lower Saxony in 1646, France's first recruitment in the Northwest.

Though French troops were reluctant to enter Germany, there is some evidence that they did not desert much once there. Tracy was surprised to discover this in 1646 (Tracy to Mazarin, 7 September 1646, CP All. 66, fols. 367r–367v), and Turenne remarked in his memoirs that "soldiers do not desert much in Germany" (86; however, this is contradicted by a statement he made in 1644, see above, footnote 64). It may be that the troops were afraid of being in the German countryside, which helped keep the army together.

72. Barozzi and Berchet, 433; Parrott, "The Administration of the French Army," 111, 160–61, 218–21. The idea that French army administration was flawed prior to Le Tellier was stated eloquently by André and expanded on by Parrott in his dissertation. But, as the following quotations show, the French themselves were aware of the problem, and the Venetian ambassador, Nani, painted a picture of the French army that would not be out of place in the historiography of the 1990s. (However, contrary to Parrott's argument that

French officers were apathetic and mediocre, Nani calls them the backbone of the French army.)

73. Servien to Lionne, 7 April 1646, *APW II B 3*, 209; plenipotentiaries to Brienne, 14 April 1646, 218; plenipotentiaries to Mazarin, 14 April 1646, 220.

74. Longueville to Mazarin, 24 July 1646, *APW II B 4*, 89.

75. André, especially 657–61; on the struggle against desertion, see Bernard Masson, "Un Aspect de la Discipline dans les Armées de Louis XIII: La lutte contre la désertion du soldat, 1635–1643," *Revue historique des armées* 162 (1986), 12–23. However, as one historian has pointed out, the lack of great mutinies in the French army as occurred in the Spanish, English, and Swedish armies indicates that the crown must have been doing something right; Bonney, *Political Change*, 260–61.

76. Kraus, *Maximilian I.*, 149; Parrott, "Strategy and Tactics," 19–22. The increase in cavalry is generally attributed to their ability to help an army insure supplies from the countryside. However, this ignores the fact that cavalry was actually more difficult to supply than infantry: not only was there an additional beast or more to supply for every man, but feeding horses was more difficult than feeding men. A better explanation for the increasing proportion of cavalry is simply its evident effectiveness in combat and operations. See Allmayer-Beck, 108–9, and Stradling, "Spain's Military Failure and the Supply of Horses, 1600–60," in *Spain's Struggle for Europe, 1598–1668* (London, 1994), 238–40.

77. This is one of the more surprising discoveries of my research, but the sources are full of references to commanders ensuring that infantry had adequate cavalry escorts (not even to mention cavalry escorts for supply trains). See Le Tellier to Arnaud, 16 August 1644, AG, v. 90, fols. 191r–93v; 223v–24v; Gramont to Mazarin, 20 September 1645, CP All. 48, fols. 283r–84r; Turenne, *Mémoires [pièces justificatives]*, 288; plenipotentiaries to Brienne, 27 January 1646, Le Clerc, v. 3, pp. 34–36; Oman, 266. Also Kroener, *Les Routes et les Étapes*, 90, notes that cavalry covered the front, rear, and both sides of an army on the march—a clear indication that they were seen as necessary guards to the infantry in the middle.

78. The word he uses for "countryside" in this case is the Italian "campagna," so the phrase could also be translated as "master of the campaign." In either case, the meaning is essentially the same.

79. Mercy's quotation is from Mercy to Maximilian, 7 August 1644, KAA v. 2795, fols. 470v–73v. Turenne attributed his retreat to his cavalry inferiority; Turenne to Mazarin, 23 October 1645, CP All. 48, fols. 525r–525v; Mercy claimed that Turenne would be able to push him back to the Danube in 1645 in a memorandum from Mercy to Maximilian, KAA v. 2818, fols. 482r–482v, 17 April 1645. See chapter 6 for details of Mercy's comments after Freiburg. Cavalry continued to be the crucial arm in operations down to the eighteenth century (e.g., Pradeep Barua, "Military Developments in India, 1750–1850," *Journal of Military History* 58 (1994): 600–604); its importance is often overlooked.

80. Cp. Weigley, xiv, 16, 36. Note also the chapter of *Simplicissimus* in which the title hero, fighting on foot, slays a mounted opponent in a duel; he describes the engagement in the table of contents as "Ein ungleicher Kampf, in welchem der Schwächste obsieget" ("An unequal battle, in which the weaker party wins"). Hans Jacob Christoph von Grimmelshausen, *Der aberteuerliche Simplicissimus Teutsch* (Stuttgart, 1985), 264, 298–302.

81. André, 554, cites a royal edict from 1658 stating that infantry "is the most necessary for the attack and defense of fortresses, as well as for war in

the countryside [la guerre de la campagne]"; and in the same vein, Raimondo Montecuccoli later clarified the roles of the different types of infantry, writing that "an army has twice as many musketeers as pikemen—because of siegemaking and other military tasks which require such arms quite frequently—and the former drop out of action almost too often on the day of battle" (Thomas M. Barker, *The Military Intellectual and Battle: Raimondo Montecuccoli and the Thirty Years War* [Albany, 1975], 106).

82. See, for example, Courval to Le Tellier, 11 November 1644, AG, v. 98, #79, in which the governor of Mainz requests one hundred cavalry, both to prevent being surprised by the enemy, and as part of the actual defense where the ditch is dry. See also Parker, "In Defense of *The Military Revolution*," 348–51.

83. Mazarin to plenipotentiaries, 10 February 1646, Le Clerc, v. 3, 63; see also Mazarin to Tracy, 28 April 1646, CP All. 64, fol. 304r; Mazarin to Meulles, 24 April 1646, CP Suède 6, fols. 410r–410v (which insists on a 5:1 ratio of infantry to cavalry for new recruits as the minimum); Rocqueservieres to Mazarin, 4 December 1643, CP All v. 23, fols. 106r–7r: it is absolutely necessary to work to put the army in good order again, "and especially the infantry, without which we will never be able to recross the Rhine." Recruiting in Germany was notoriously difficult (Turenne to Mazarin, 23 November 1644, CP All. 25, fols. 111r–15v; CP All. 46, fols. 6r–7r; and the series of letters to Meulles in CP Suède 6, fols. 410r–13v), which is one of the reasons Mazarin continued to use large numbers of Frenchmen in spite of their high desertion rate. The contract with Freiherr von Bönninghausen is an object lesson in the perils of subcontracting recruitment: originally signed early in 1645, he only produced the troops in mid-1646, and with less infantry and more cavalry—and four times the cost per head—than originally called for. The problems with Bönninghausen are extremely well-documented; see, e.g., plenipotentiaries to Brienne, 27 January 1646, Le Clerc, v. 3, 34–36, and 17 February 1646, 66; Le Tellier to Tracy, 19 April 1646, BN Mf v. 4201, fols. 142r–43r; Le Tellier to plenipotentiaries, 23 May 1646, AG, v. 99, fols. 256r–58v, and Helmut Lahrkamp, "Lothar Dietrich Freiherr von Bönninghausen: Ein westfälischer Söldnerführer des Dreißigjährigen Krieges," *Westfälische Zeitschrift* 108 (1958): 336–47. The plenipotentiaries were generally in charge of German recruiting, but Meulles and Tracy were also involved in 1646 (Le Tellier to Tracy, 13 February 1646, AG, v. 99, fols. 55v–63v), and they seem to have had more success; in any case, Tracy was able to recruit over four thousand troops, a very substantial amount (plenipotentiaries to Brienne, 16 July 1646, *APW II B 4*, 70, and chapter 8 below). See also Bonney, *Political Change*, 269.

Unfortunately, as John Lynn notes, "It seems that *contrôles* and *états* for the entire army are rare or nonexistent during the Mazarin regime" (John. A. Lynn, "Recalculating French Army Growth during the *Grand Siècle*, 1610–1715," *French Historical Studies* 18 (1994): 891–92). The best we have to go on are the reports from Turenne and Tracy, along with Mazarin's (probably optimistic) estimates; and even for these, figures are rare.

84. The French always seemed to be trying to rebuild the confidence of their cavalry, e.g., after Tuttlingen (Hans-Helmut Schaufler, *Die Schlacht bei Freiburg im Breisgau, 1644* (Freiburg, 1979), 46–47) and Alerheim (Mazarin to Gramont, 2 October 1645, BM, v. 225, fols. 370r–72v). However, Turenne also praised his French cavalry and said they would be hard to replace (Turenne, *Mémoires [pièces justificatives]*, 285–87).

85. There is also evidence that Turenne considered Germans better soldiers; Turenne to Mazarin, 4 October 1644, CP All. 24, fols. 373r–74r. See also André, 217, and Barozzi, 433.
86. Servien to Lionne, 7 April 1646, *APW II B 3*, 209.
87. Lionne to Servien, 17 April 1646, *APW II B 3*, 217. Turenne has attracted numerous biographers. The most recent is Jean Bérenger; his work is useful, but contains numerous factual errors. The very old biography by Andrew Ramsay, *Histoire du vicomte de Turenne*, 4 vols. (La Haye, 1736), remains the standard.
88. Mazarin to Turenne, *Lettres*, v. 2, 21 May 1645, 67. See also Mazarin to Turenne, *Lettres*, v. 2, 2 December 1644, 47, and 27 March 1645, 57; 16 July 1645, CP All. 47, fols. 402r–3r; and Pierre Braun, "La Lorraine pendant le gouvernement de La Ferté-Sénectère (1643–1661)," *Mémoires de la Société d'Archéologie lorraine et du Musée Historique lorrain* 56 (4th ser., v. 6) (1906): 192–96. One could multiply such evidence indefinitely.
89. Maximilian hoped to use Enghien's aggressiveness against him after the battle of Alerheim. He requested reinforcements from the emperor, not doubting that he could use them to force an engagement, since experience showed that Enghien "is always easily resolved to give battle." Immler, *Kurfürst Maximilian I.*, 117.
90. See Napoleon's comments on Enghien's attacks at Freiburg and Alerheim, 133–34 and 140–43.
91. The best history of Enghien is in Aumale, *Histoire des princes de Condé*. For contemporary praise of Enghien, see Barozzi and Berchet, 443–44.
92. Mazarin to plenipotentiaries, 10 February 1646, Le Clerc, v. 3, 63; Le Tellier to Tracy, 13 February 1646, AG, v. 99, fols. 55v–63v; Turenne, *Mémoires*, 286. Tracy got along particularly well with Turenne, whom he had suggested as a replacement for Guébriant (Tracy to Mazarin, 2 December 1643, CP All. 23, fols. 101r–2r). On the creation and function of *commissaires généraux*, see André, 449–55, and Kroener, *Les Routes et les Étapes*, 28–32.
93. Barozzi and Berchet, 433.
94. Karl Gustav Wrangel, 1613–1676, irascible but highly effective Swedish general. He not only served in numerous land campaigns, but, in 1644, led the Swedish fleet to victory against the Danes. When gout forced Torstensson to give up command in January 1646, Wrangel was chosen to take his place. Steckzén, *Karl Gustal Wrangels Fälttåg*; on Torstensson's replacement by Wrangel, Lars Tingsten, *De Tre Sista Åren av det Trettioåriga Kriget jämte den Västfaliska Freden* (Stockholm, 1934), 5, and Johann Oxenstierna to Axel Oxenstierna, 9 January 1646, *APW II C 2*, 16.
95. Adolphe Chéruel, "Le Baron Charles d'Avaugour, ambassadeur de France en Suède 1654–1657," *Revue d'histoire diplomatique* 3 (1889): 523–34. D'Avaugour had been participating in diplomatic missions to Sweden since 1629, and would lay the foundations of the Peace of Oliva before his death.
96. At least, according to Mazarin (Mazarin to Enghien, 4 September 1644, *Lettres*, v. 2, 29) and Servien (Servien to Lionne, 14/19 April 1646, *APW II B 3*, 228).
97. Hessisches Staatsarchiv Marburg, Archiv Johann Caspar I, Bestand 340 v. Dörnberg, 4125, Amalie Elisabeth to Mazarin, 18 May 1645: "I would not be able to subsist if the queen withdrew her helping hand" ("je ne pourrois subsister si la Reine retire sa main auxiliaire").
98. The decisive role, if the report of one Hessian officer is to be believed: Herzog August Bibliothek, Augustei, 11.8, fols. 245r–245v, 4 August 1645; also Lotichium, 632.

99. That, and the fact that she felt her troops were ill-treated by France. She had originally planned to secure quarters along the Main and Tauber in 1645 (Hessisches Staatsarchiv Marburg, Archiv Johann Caspar I, Bestand 340 v. Dörnberg, 4125, Amalie Elisabeth to Geyso, 10 July 1645), but recalled her troops after Alerheim because, among other things, their baggage train had been plundered by French cavalry (ibid., 4118, Amalie Elisabeth to Mazarin, 27 August 1645).

100. Salm, 75, 119, 166–68; for limitations on Cologne's control, see Joachim Foerster, *Kurfürst Ferdinand von Köln: Die Politik seiner Stifter in den Jahren 1634–1650,* Schriftenreihe der Vereinigung zur Erforschung der Neueren Geschichte, v. 6 (Münster, 1976), 285–96, especially 290–93.

101. In fact, so many of Maximilian's ministers came from the Rhineland that one historian has recognized a Rhenish bloc in Bavarian service. Karl Stommel, *J. A. Freiherr Wolff gen. Metternich zur Gracht* (Rheinland Köln, 1986), cited in Willi Osterbrauck, *Johann Reichsfreiherr von Werth, 1591–1652: Chronik eines umstrittenen Volkshelden* (Cologne, 1992), 94.

102. See below, chapter 7; Brienne to plenipotentiaries, 4 November 1645, *APW II B 2,* 249, p. 805; 261, pp. 844–45.

103. See Franz Weber, "Gliederung und Einsatz des bayerischen Heeres im Dreißigjährigen Krieg," in *Um Glauben und Reich: Kurfürst Maximilian I. Beiträge zur Bayerischen Geschichte und Kunst, 1573–1657,* v. 2, part 1 of *Wittelsbach und Bayern* (Munich, 1980), 400–401. Kraus, *Maximilian I.,* 151, claims that the Bavarian army remained multinational, citing one regiment raised in 1644 that contained 534 Germans, 218 Italians, 43 Burgundians, 54 Poles, 26 Greeks, 24 Lorrainers, 15 Turks (!), and 15 French, along with Spanish, Hungarians, Bohemians, Dalmatians, and others. It is certainly true that Italy remained an important recruiting ground for Bavaria, but the regiment cited by Kraus was probably atypical; in 1644, for example, Mercy reported that the regiment he was leaving to defend Freiburg consisted mostly of soldiers from Alsace and the Breisgau, so it would be easier for it to recruit (Mercy to Maximilian, 15 August 1644, KAA v. 2795, fols. 509r–13r). It seems likely that Bavarian soldiers were not only mostly German, but largely from the three Imperial Circles of Swabia, Franconia, and Bavaria—their primary recruiting grounds. The in-depth study by Cordula Kapser, *Die bayerische Kriegsorganisation in der zweiten Hälfte des Dreißigjährigen Krieges, 1635–1648/49,* Schriftenreihe der Vereinigung zur Erforschung der Neueren Geschichte, vol. 25 (Münster, 1997), appeared too late to be incorporated into this work. Fortunately, its conclusions generally confirm rather than contradict the present analysis on the constitution, legal status, and financing of the Bavarian army.

104. This fascinating question is raised by Kraus (*Maximilian I.,* 154–55). His answer, that it was risky to use quarters to build an army, is interesting but not entirely adequate; for as he later admits (327), Maximilian did rely on quarters after 1635.

105. Salm, 66.

106. Not only was this entirely understandable, since every other state had more or less untouchable areas not used for quarters, but Maximilian had also faced a rebellion in 1632 when, forced onto his last reserves by the Swedish invasion, he tried to quarter his army in Upper Bavaria.

107. Heilmann, *Kriegsgeschichte,* 702.

108. Tracy to Le Tellier, 22 July 1644, AG, v. 98, #56; Turenne to Mazarin, 21 August 1645, CP All. 48, fols. 151r–52v; Turenne to Mazarin, 2 July 1644, CP All. 23, fols. 254r–55r; Mazarin to Turenne, 11 April 1645, *Lettres,* v. 2, 59.

109. The plea for remounts was the most constant theme in the letters of all Bavarian commanders; Turenne also seemed to think Maximilian was effective at keeping the cavalry with adequate numbers of horses. Turenne, *Mémoires [pièces justificatives]*, 250–51 and 254. The exact number of troops in the French and Bavarian armies remains unknown, although that of Bavaria could probably be calculated with considerable accuracy from the surviving documents. Georg Tessin (*Die Regimenter der europäischen Staaten im Ancien Régime des XVI. bis XVIII. Jahrhunderts*, Part 1, *Die Stammlisten* (Osnabrück, 1986)) gives figures for the total number of regiments raised by both states. Of course, France had troops on at least four different fronts, which makes an overall comparison of limited value. Significantly, however, Bavaria raised only one regiment after 1645, while France continued to raise a fairly constant amount throughout the end of the war. (Actually, the more detailed list found in Franz Weber, 406–7, says that Bavaria raised no new units at all after 1645 and only five after 1640.)

110. See Eugen von Frauenholz, *Die Landesdefension*, v. 3, part 2 of *Entwicklungsgeschichte des deutschen Heerwesens*, ed. Eugen von Frauenholz (Munich, 1939), for a discussion of the failure of Bavaria and other German states to develop a popular militia (in spite of their best efforts).

111. Part of the blame for this must lie on the Imperials and Lorrainers, whose responsibility it was the garrison the towns in normal times. However, the Bavarians expected and feared a French attack in that direction, yet they failed to reinforce them before it was too late. See Maximilian to Mercy, 12 August 1644, KAA v. 2795, fols. 477r–82r, in which Maximilian notes that "Mannheim and Heidelberg will be weakly garrisoned, but we do not doubt that you will keep a careful eye on them, and if necessary, think of strengthening them so that the enemy not have an opportunity to storm them." He also warned about the inadequate garrison in Heilbronn, which was Bavaria's responsibility. See also chapter 6.

112. Maximilian to Mercy, 28 April 1645, KAA v. 2818, fols. 538r–41r.

113. Maier, 394, puts the garrison of Heidelberg—probably the best fortress in Bavarian hands—at just 250 at the end of 1644. The garrisons in Breisach and Philippsburg are given in Turenne to Mazarin, 27 April 1646, CP All. 64, fols. 302r–3r and Enghien to Mazarin, 14 September 1644, CP All. 24, fols. 265r–67r, and of Sélestat in Livet, *L'Intendance d'Alsace*, 105. (One must calculate the Philippsburg garrison based on the units given: eight companies at forty men each, one infantry and one cavalry regiment, plus some additional recruits. This seems likely to total at least one thousand, but even that would understate the garrison somewhat, since Philippsburg was usually occupied by several additional regiments on their way to or from the front (in the reference here, for example, it contained a regiment destined for Turenne's army; in 1646, Turenne noted that he left a regiment of three hundred men in addition to the garrison (Turenne, *Mémoires [pièces justificatives]*, 278–79)). By contrast, the Imperial garrison during the French siege was only 600 (CP All. 24, fols. 265r–67r, *op. cit.*).)

On some occasions, Bavaria was capable of putting together extremely large garrisons; for example, when it became clear in 1646 that Leopold Wilhelm would be unable to defend Swabia, he and Maximilian reinforced the garrison of Heilbronn to two thousand men (Curtius to Mazarin, 23 August 1646, CP All. 66, fols. 296r–97r; Turenne to Mazarin, 4 September 1646, CP All. 66, fols. 362r–63v; Leopold Wilhelm to Maximilian, 17 August 1646, KAA v. 2902, fols. 63r–63v. However, this merely led Turenne to attack Schorndorf, which held only two hundred men; once captured, he left a force of four hundred to defend it (Heilmann, *Kriegsgeschichte*, 706).

114. For a discussion of the decision not to attack Turenne, see chapter 6. Kraus, *Maximilian I.*, 154–55 and 328–29, also notes Maximilian's cautious approach to strategy. The campaign of 1635 was very similar to that of 1644: Maximilian urged a combined offensive against France, but refused to let von Werth cross the Rhine for the invasion.

115. Kraus, *Maximilian I.*, 153–54, 328.

116. See Maximilian to Leopold Wilhelm, 3 August 1646, KAA v. 2902, fols. 24r–24v, in which Maximilian complains that Leopold Wilhelm is not writing enough; his other generals send reports at least twice a week. This is far more than Turenne or Enghien wrote to Mazarin.

117. See for example, Maximilian to Mercy, 19 April 1645, KAA v. 2818, fols. 485r–485v. Note also, however, that Maximilian expected his commanders to consult with the other officers before taking important decisions, and there are records of such meetings before major battles such as Freiburg and Herbsthausen.

118. For example, see Maximilian to Mercy, 27 April 1645, KAA v. 2818, fols. 521r–22v, telling Mercy to send fifty cavalry to Freiburg; Mercy to Maximilian, 9 August 1644, KAA v. 2795, fols. 474r–474v, requesting permission to leave a regiment in Freiburg; and Maximilian to Mercy, 12 August 1644, KAA v. 2795, fols. 477r–82v, arguing against Pforzheim as a defensive position (which Mercy accepted). It is particularly difficult to imagine Turenne even informing Mazarin that he was leaving a regiment to garrison a town, much less actually asking permission to do so.

119. This may be compared to Mercy's willingness to fight at Freiburg in spite of Maximilian's warning not to let himself be forced into a battle (Maximilian to Mercy, 5 August 1644, KAA v. 2795, fols. 461r–65v); significantly, Maximilian never complained afterward. Contrast this with his reaction to Gronsfeld, who let the enemy occupy Bavaria without a fight and was put on trial (Heilmann, *Kriegsgeschichte*, 764–65). Ottavio Piccolomini also chafed under Maximilian's interference; Thomas Barker, "Ottavio Piccolomini (1599–1659): A Fair Historical Judgement?," in *Army, Aristocracy, Monarchy: Essays on War, Society, and Government in Austria, 1618–1780* (New York, 1979), 107.

120. A steady commander rather than a romantic hero like von Werth, Mercy has never attracted a biographer. Nevertheless, he has received his due as a commander, at least among those who have studied the campaigns of the 1640s. See the works by Heilmann, particularly *Die Feldzüge der Bayern*, for more on Mercy. Enghien is supposed to have erected a memorial on the spot of his death with the inscription, "STA VIATOR HEROEM CALCAS" (Stand, traveller, you tread on a hero). Karlheinz Scheible, "Die Schlacht von Alerheim, 3 August 1645," *Rieser Kulturtage* 4, 1982 (1983): 270, footnote 46.

121. Osterbrauck, *Johann Reichsfreiherr von Werth*, Helmut Lahrkamp, *Jan von Werth: Sein Leben nach archivalischen Quellenzeugnissen*, v. 24 of Veröffentlichungen des kölnischen Geschichtsvereins (Cologne, 1962).

122. I would like to thank Frau Doktor Kathrin Bierther for bringing this point to my attention.

123. Leopold Wilhelm, Ferdinand's brother and one of the archdukes, was refined, brave, and talented—but completely incompetent as a military commander. He had already been responsible for the catastrophic defeat at Breitenfeld in 1642 when he was appointed to lead the Imperial armies in 1644 upon

Gallas's dismissal. After his inept performance in 1646, he was again sacked, only to be named Governor General of the Spanish Netherlands in 1647. The next year, his superior army was defeated by the French at Lens, probably delaying the worst effects of the Fronde for another six months and ending any chance that Spain would be included in the Peace of Westphalia. The decision to place him in command of the Imperial army in 1645 was largely due to his position as the emperor's brother rather than to his military ability; see Peter Broucek, "Erzherzog Leopold-Wilhelm und der Oberbefehl über das kaiserliche Heer im Jahre 1645," in *Aus drei Jahrhunderten: Beiträge zur osterreichischen Heeres- und Kriegsgeschichte* (Vienna, 1969), 8–38.

124. Pierre Braun, "La Lorraine pendant le gouvernement de La Ferté-Sénectère (1643–1661)," 175–86.

125. For a discussion of the "misères et tribulations" of Alsace, see Reuss, *L'Alsace au Dix-Septième Siècle*, v. 1, 109–32.

126. Livet, *L'Intendance d'Alsace*, 83–9. The orders of Baussan, sent as intendant in 1645, give his mission specifically as seeing to "the relief of the inhabitants"— a mission only possible in an already-pacified territory (Livet, 103). Kroener, *Les Routes et les Étapes*, 113, footnote 157, notes that Alsace was spared the worst of what Champagne got.

127. Turenne to Mazarin, 20 February 1644, CP All., v. 23, fols. 160r–61r, and 17 April 1644, fols. 183r–4v.

128. See the Heydendorff article, especially p. 90.

129. See Maier, 401–2, 408–9, 411, and 421–30.

130. Mazarin to Turenne, 16 July 1645, CP All., v. 47, fols. 402r–3r. Tracy admitted that it was impossible to keep the troops from plundering, which not only hurt the population, but also (and more important to him) used up supplies faster (Turenne, *Mémoires [pièces justificatives]*, 304).

131. Mazarin to Tracy, 10 April 1645, CP Suède 6, fols. 239r–239v; Mazarin to Agelo Ottaviani, 17 December 1644, CP Suède 6, fol. 215r.

132. Kroener, *Les Routes et les Étapes*, 171–73; "Soldat oder Soldateska?," 122.

133. Maier, 393.

134. Maier, 388–90.

135. [Tracy?] to Mazarin, 18 August 1646, CP All., v. 66, fol. 257v.

136. Barthold, 515; Heilmann, *Feldzüge*, 223.

137. See Maximilian's complaints in Maximilian to Bavarian plenipotentiaries, 7 September 1646, KAA 3058, fol. 204r, and plenipotentiaries to Louis XIV, 6 August 1646, APW II B 4, 99, among many others.

138. Braun, 142–3. See also Charvériat, 550, and Foerster, 284, for the similar fate of Ahrweiler: contrary to an agreement, the French pillaged the town, killed the burgermeister, magistrates, and curate, and raped the women, including those in convents; after two full days of plunder, the town was burned.

Chapter 5. Introduction: From *Guerre couverte* to the Conference Table, 1630–1644

1. Walter Mohr, *Das Herzogtum Lothringen zwischen Frankreich und Deutschland (14.–17. Jahrhundert)*, part 4 of *Geschichte des Herzogtums Lothringen* (Trier, 1986), 292–302.

2. Mohr, 302–16.

3. Jacques Nompar de Caumont, marquis and later duc de La Force, b.1558, created marshal 1622, d.1652. See *Dictionnaire des Maréchaux de France*, 245–46.

4. On the French occupation of Alsace, see Stein, *Protection Royale*, 160–360.

5. Stein, *Protection Royale*, 328–29.

6. Livet, *L'Intendance d'Alsace*, 109–10; Stein, *Protection Royale*, 324–26.

7. Pierre Braun, "La Lorraine pendant le gouvernement de La Ferté-Sénectère (1643–1661)," 109–266.

8. Le Tellier to Vautorte, 21 January 1645, AG v. 93, fols. 67r–71v.

9. Stein, *Protection Royale*, 389–514; Livet, *L'Intendance d'Alsace*, 78–113. The court, in fact, explicitly rejected an attempt by d'Erlach to set up a commission of the authorities already in the region to control administration more efficiently, presumably out of fear that it would concentrate power too dangerously in the frontier area (ibid., 108).

10. Livet, *L'Intendance d'Alsace*, 67–76.

11. Livet, *L'Intendance d'Alsace*, 101–2.

12. Reuss, *L'Alsace au Dix-Septième Siècle*, v. 1, 105.

13. Cited in Stephen J. Lee, *The Thirty Years War* (New York, 1991), 66. On the extension of French control in Alsace, see also Stein, *Protection Royale*, 486–514, and Louis Batiffol, "Richelieu et la question de l'Alsace," *Revue Historique* 138 (1921): 161–200.

14. Reuss, *L'Alsace au Dix-Septième Siècle*, v. 1, 105.

15. While Mazarin always blamed the Swedes for abandoning Guébriant, the Swedes looked at it quite the opposite way; see Pufendorf's essay in M. Rousset, *Recherches sur les alliances et les intérêts entre la France et la Suède, rélativement aux circonstances présentes des affaires du nord et de l'Empire* (Amsterdam, 1745), 42–47.

16. Josias, comte de Rantzau, 1619–1650. His family originated in Holstein, and Rantzau served under Sweden, Holland, and the emperor before entering French service. He was made a marshal in 1645 and, at the time of his death, was missing an eye, an ear, an arm, and a leg. *Dictionnaire des Maréchaux de France*, 365–66; Jean Dupaquier, *Le Maréchal de Rantzau, 1609–1650: . . . son sang fut en cent lieux le prix de la victoire et Mars ne lui laissa rien d'entier que le coeur* (N.p., 1985), 31–32. Conceivably, had he led the French to victory at Tuttlingen, he could have received command of the army instead of Turenne; like Turenne, he was a German and a Protestant, and would have seemed a logical choice.

17. Heilmann, *Feldzüge*, 17–18; Le Tellier to Guébriant, 10 November 1643, BN Mf v. 4169, fols. 38r–41r; Noailles, 369. However, Turenne, *Mémoires [pièces justificatives]*, 267, has Guébriant with only seven to eight thousand troops at the time of his death.

18. Heilmann, *Feldzüge*, 19–21; Noailles, 376–85.

19. While brave, Rantzau spent most of his time drunk; Dupaquier, 27, 29, 33. His inattention probably contributed to the army being surprised.

20. Tracy to court, 23 November 1643, CP All. 23, fols. 95r–95v.

21. In "Catastrophe and Recovery: The Defeat of Spain, 1639–43," (in *Spain's Struggle for Europe, 1598–1668*, [London, 1994], 209–10), Robert Stradling appears to misread a passage from Matías de Nova's *Historia de Felipe IV, Rey de España* (printed in *Coleccion de Documentos Inéditos para la Historia de España*, v. 86, ed. José Sancho Rayon and Francisco de Zabalburu [Madrid, 1886], 156) as saying that Spanish units were present at Tuttlingen. In fact, the reference clearly indicates that it was French units sent to the Rhine after the battle of Rocroi who fought at Tuttlingen, not Spanish. However, Noailles, 394, does claim that

Charles IV had some Spanish troops under Don Juan de Vivero (though only a fraction of them—also his own, Truckmuller's, and Lamboy's).

22. Heilmann, *Feldzüge*, 20–70; Noailles, 392–400; Sieur de Pontis, 377–91 (however, many question the authenticity of Pontis's memoirs, or even whether such a person existed at all). In his otherwise excellent study, *Protection Royale*, Stein twice refers to the "battle of Überlingen" (487 and 489) when he clearly means Tuttlingen.

23. Tracy to court, 2 December 1643, CP All. 23, fols. 101r–2r, and 6 December 1643, CP All. 23, fol. 108r.

24. Bérenger, 194, is among those to criticize Mercy for not following up the victory at Tuttlingen. However, as Noailles, 402, has pointed out, the bad weather made further pursuit nearly impossibly ruinous.

25. Court to Turenne, 8 December 1643, BN Mf v. 4169, fols. 50r–62v.

26. Tracy implied that Turenne would be the best commander without stating so directly: Tracy to court, 2 December 1643, CP All. 23, fols. 101r–2r. See also Noailles, 404–8.

27. Le Tellier to du Plessis-Besançon, 4 December 1643, AG, v. 89, fols. 38r–42r; Le Tellier to Turenne, 1 January 1644, BN Mf v. 4198, fols. 1r–2v; Le Tellier to Turenne, 1 January 1644, BN Mf v. 4199, fols. 32r–34v; Le Tellier to Turenne, 26 February 1644, BN Mf v. 4198, fols. 12r–14r.

28. On reforming the command structure: Le Tellier to Turenne, 8 December 1643, BN Mf v. 4169, fols. 50r–62v; d'Aumont: Court to Turenne, 4 January 1644, CP All. 23 139–41v; Turenne to Mazarin, 18 January 1644, CP All. 23, fols. 144–144v; Turenne to Mazarin, 9 April 1644, CP All. 23, fols. 180r–81r; Le Tellier to d'Aumont, 22 April 1644, AG, v. 89, fols. 179r–81v; Turenne to Mazarin, 29 June 1644, CP All. 23, fols. 249r–249v; d'Erlach's retreat: Le Tellier to Turenne, 1 January 1644, BN Mf v. 4198, fol. 2v; Le Tellier to d'Erlach, 25 February 1644, BN Mf v. 4198, fols. 10v–11v; early problems with d'Oysonville: Le Tellier to d'Erlach, 20 December 1643, BN Mf v. 4199, fols. 21v–22v.

29. Dickmann, *Der Westfälische Frieden*, 104–5, 120.

30. For their mission in the Hague, see Irsigler, xxxii-lvi.

31. French powers, 20 September 1643, Le Clerc, v. 1, 151–52.

32. Fritz Dickmann, et al., eds., *Instruktionen: Frankreich, Schweden, Kaiser*, series I, v. 1 of *Acta Pacis Westphalicae* (Münster, 1962), 62–63. (Hereafter cited as *APW I 1*.)

33. *APW I 1*, 69, 93–94.

34. *APW I 1*, 88–97.

35. See Alfred Overmann, "Die Abtretung des Elsass an Frankreich im Westfälischen Frieden," *Zeitschrift für die Geschichte des Oberrheins* 58 (= N. F.19) (1904), 83–111, and, somewhat more simply, Repgen ("Über den Zusammenhang," 64–69), Reuss (*L'Alsace au Dix-Septième Siècle*, v. 1, 447–57), and Georges Livet (*L'intendance d'Alsace*, 116–19) for further details. Georges Bardot, *La question des six villes impériales d'Alsace depuis la paix de Westphalie jusqu'aux arrêts de "réunion" du conseil souverain de Brisach, 1648–1680* (Paris, 1899), 18–27.

36. Dickmann, *Der Westfälische Frieden*, 294; Stein, 175–78, 181–82, 218–20, 317–19, et al. Although Basel itself was untouched by France at the peace, some of the territory of the bishopric, which extended into Alsace, became a matter of contention.

37. *APW I 1*, 100–101.

38. *APW I 1*, 150–58

39. Treasure, *Mazarin*, 56, claims that Mazarin drafted the original peace instructions to d'Avaux, but does not provide a source. Based on Dickmann's more extensive research in the original sources, I have accepted his opinion from the introduction to *APW I 1*, pp. 1–2. See also p. 5 and footnote 1 for the validity of the supplement.

40. Livet, *L'intendance d'Alsace*, 116.

41. Rodolphe Reuss, *Histoire d'Alsace*, 11th edition (Paris, 1916), 103, 110–11.

Chapter 6. 1644: France Alone

1. See *APW II B 1*, appendices 1 and 2.

2. Irsigler, lvi.

3. Dickmann, *Der Westfälische Frieden*, 169. French fears were not unfounded. In 1596–98, for example, Spain had tried to make separate treaties with each of its enemies (France, England, and the Dutch Republic) in order to break up the opposition alliance. Even though they intended to make peace with all of their enemies, it made a difference whether this came through one treaty or three. See Paul Allen, "The Strategy of Peace," chapter 1. For a list of complaints over powers, see Le Clerc, v. 1, 294–95.

4. C. V. Wedgwood, *The Thirty Years War* (London, 1938), 471, 476; David Maland, *Europe at War, 1600–1650* (New York, 1980), 171, 179; Treasure, *Mazarin*, 239–40. James Breck Perkins, *France Under Mazarin, with a review of the Administration of Richelieu*, v. 1 (Paris, 1902), 468, calls the negotiations over powers "a long huckstering," without assigning specific blame to Mazarin. For more on this issue, see chapter 7.

5. The Austrian Habsburgs were themselves stalling, because they did not want to negotiate without their ally, Denmark; Ruppert, 51–52. Mazarin to plenipotentiaries, 16 April 1644, *APW II B 1*, 46, pp. 281–82. The idea of threatening to withdraw had been previously suggested by Servien: Servien to Mazarin, 3 June 1644, *APW II B 1*, 127, pp. 241–42. Mazarin to plenipotentiaries, 16 July 1644, *APW II B 1*, 177, p. 371.

6. Plenipotentiaries to Mazarin, 30 July 1644, *APW II B 1*, 187, p. 407.

7. Brienne to plenipotentiaries, 15 October 1644, *APW II B 1*, 268, pp. 546–47.

8. Rorté to plenipotentiaries, 7 July 1644, *APW II B 1*, 159, pp. 328–29. Ernst Manfred Wermter, ed., *Die Schwedischen Korrespondenzen: 1643–1645*, series II, section C, v. 1 of *Acta Pacis Westphalicae* (Münster, 1965), Salvius to Christina, 8 July 1644, 190, p. 266. (Hereafter referred to as *APW II C 1*.) Ruppert, 61–63.

9. Cf. Dickmann, *Der Westfälische Frieden*, 209–10, and, on the theory behind how concessions are interpreted, Pillar, 91–100.

10. Dickmann, *Der Westfälische Frieden*, 207; Abraham de Wicquefort, *Mémoires touchant les ambassadeurs et les ministres publics*, (Cologne, 1676), 348–49, 412–13.

11. *APW 1.1*, 64–67. The precedence struggle between France and Spain dated back over a hundred years, and continued after the Congress of Westphalia; Wicquefort, 321–24, and *infra*, footnote 12. Moreover, see the introduction to *APW II B 2*, xxxvi: "For all the significance of the niceties of protocol and ceremonial demands, in Paris they did not hesitate to fall back in such questions if they could thereby avoid disadvantages or make progress in the negotiations."

12. In 1661, for instance, there was a clash between French and Spanish diplomats in London over whose carriage would go first: it left one person dead and several wounded. It was not until the Congress of Vienna that precedence matters were established according to a fixed rule. Diplomats were divided by the rank accorded them by their governments; within each rank, first precedence was given to the diplomats who submitted their credentials first. This method was adopted by the Convention of Vienna in 1961. But the fact that diplomats today must follow carefully regulated protocol, including such delicate questions as the order of seating around a table, indicates that precedence matters have not been eliminated; they have merely been regulated. Andreas Osiander, *The States System of Europe, 1640–1990: Peacemaking and the Conditions of International Stability* (Oxford, 1994), 85 and 88, attributes France's particular concern with precedence matters to its status as a rising power, and compares it to nineteenth century Germany. This may be valid to an extent, but it does not explain why every other power—Spain, the Dutch Republic, Sweden—was equally concerned with precedence (indeed, the precedence struggles between the two allies, France and Sweden, were among the most bitter of the conference). See William Roosen, "Early Modern Diplomatic Ceremonial: A Systems Approach," *Journal of Modern History* 52 (1980): 452–76; Heinz L. Krekeler, *Die Diplomatie, Geschichte und Staat*, v. 110–111 (Munich, 1965), 28–29, 110–20; Roosen, 178–84; Anderson, *The Rise of Modern Diplomacy*, 17–20; John T. O'Connor, "The Diplomatic History of the Reign," in *The Reign of Louis XIV: Essays in Celebration of Andrew Lossky*, ed. Paul Sonnino (Atlantic Highlands, N. J., 1990), 147; Englund, 380–81; Kenneth Colegrove, "Diplomatic Procedure Preliminary to the Congress of Westphalia," *American Journal of International Law* 13 (1919): 451; Hermann Weber, "Une Bonne Paix," 55–57.

13. O'Connell. Richelieu also refused to ratify the treaty with Sweden handing over the Alsatian garrisons in 1634; Gaston Zeller, *Comment s'est faite la réunion de l'Alsace à la France* (Paris, 1948), 92–93. Ironically, however, Richelieu himself deeply mistrusted the Spanish and insisted on the precise formulation of their orders; Hermann Weber, "Une Bonne Paix," 63–65. See also the interesting analysis by J. Eugene Harley, "The Obligation to Ratify Treaties: Is Ratification Necessary for the Validity of a Treaty?," *American Journal of International Law* 13 (1919): 389–405, especially 389, 404–5. Suspicion of the other side's insincerity continues to be an important problem in modern treaty-making as well. Rosemary Foot writes of the Korean armistice talks that "it could also be argued that the U. S. distrust of negotiation encouraged a more generally remarked proneness to emphasize details, the technicalities, the fine print, and the need to close all loopholes." Rosemary Foot, *A Substitute for Victory: The Politics of Peacemaking at the Korean Armistice Talks* (Ithaca, New York, 1990), 16.

14. Mazarin to plenipotentiaries, 30 April 1644, *APW II B 1*, 79, p. 155.

15. Brienne to plenipotentiaries, 19 March 1644, *APW II B 1*, 3, pp. 6–7. The quotation is from 17 March 1644, Le Clerc, v. 1, 243.

16. Servien to Brienne, 1 April 1644, *APW II B 1*, 21, p. 39.

17. Servien to Brasset, 18 December 1644, *APW II B 1*, 330, pp. 781–82.

18. Rorté to plenipotentiaries, 9 May 1644 and 11 May 1644; and plenipotentiaries to Brienne, 13 May 1644, *APW II B 1*, 94, 95; and 98, pp. 179–80.

19. Servien to Brienne, 9 April 1644 and 11 June 1644, *APW II B 1*, 37 and 138, p. 264; plenipotentiaries to Brienne, 23 April 1644, *APW II B 1*, 65.

20. Servien to Lionne, 15 October, 12 November, and 29 November 1644, *APW II B 1*, 272, p. 565; 293; and 305.

21. Lionne to Servien, 19 December 1644, *APW II B 1*, 332.
22. Plenipotentiaries to Mazarin, 2 July 1644, *APW II B 1*, 157, pp. 309–12.
23. Plenipotentiaries to Rorté, 15 April 1644, *APW II B 1*, 44; plenipotentiaries to Brienne, 23 April 1644, *APW II B 1*, 65, pp. 126–27; Servien to Swedish plenipotentiaries, 6 June 1644, *APW II B 1*, 134; plenipotentiaries to Brienne, 25 June 1644, *APW II B 1*, 150, pp. 290–91; and many others. From the Swedish side, see Oxenstierna to Christina, 29 April 1644, *APW II C 1*, 157; Rosenhane to Oxenstierna and Salvius, 18 May 1644, 158; and Oxenstierna and Salvius to Christina, 3 June 1644, 164.
24. Oxenstierna to Christina, 1 July 1644, *APW II C 1*, 187.
25. Rosenhane to Oxenstierna and Salvius, 27 October 1644, *APW II C 1*, 238, p. 374.
26. Oxenstierna and Salvius to Christina, 30 December 1644, *APW II C 1*, 264, p. 445.
27. Mazarin to plenipotentiaries, 9 April 1644, *APW II B 1*, 31, pp. 57–59. The idea for separating the Spanish and Austrian Habsburgs goes at least back to Salvius c. 1640 (Ernst Manfred Wermter, ed., *Die Schwedischen Korrespondenzen, 1643–1645*, series II, section C, v. 1 of *Acta Pacis Westphalicae* [Münster, 1965], xxv).
28. Plenipotentiaries to Mazarin, 23 April 1644, *APW II B 1*, 67, pp. 130–31.
29. Mazarin to plenipotentiaries, 14 June 1644, *APW II B 1*, 140, pp. 268–69.
30. Plenipotentiaries to Mazarin, 2 July 1644, *APW II B 1*, 157, pp. 314–15.
31. Plenipotentiaries to Brienne, 26 November 1644, *APW II B 1*, 303, pp. 679–81.
32. Dickmann, *Der Westfälische Frieden*, 163–69.
33. Plenipotentiaries to Brienne, 12 November 1644, *APW II B 1*, 292, pp. 626–27.
34. Immler, *Kurfürst Maximilian I.*, 151–52.
35. As reported in Anne to plenipotentiaries, 9 April 1644, *APW II B 1*, 30; for a copy of the letter, see Le Clerc, v. 1, 247–50.
36. Plenipotentiaries to Mazarin, 12 May 1644, *APW II B 1*, 96; d'Avaux to Mazarin, *APW II B 1*, 52, pp. 99–100.
37. Servien to Swedish plenipotentiaries, 16 April 1644, *APW II B 1*, 154, p. 304.
38. Dickmann, *Der Westfälische Frieden*, 233–34; Le Clerc, v. 1, contains two responses to the French letter from Frankfurt (pp. 244–46 and 250–69).
39. Mazarin to d'Avaux, 30 April 1644, *APW II B 1*, 80.
40. Plenipotentiaries to Anne, 28 May 1644, *APW II B 1*, 119; plenipotentiaries to Brienne, 25 June 1644, and 23 July 1644, *APW II B 1*, 150, p. 293, footnote, and 182.
41. Louis XIV to plenipotentiaries, 6 August 1644, *APW II B 1*, 192; second circular from 4 September 1644, Le Clerc, v. 1, 289–93; the letter was actually mailed on 4 September.
42. Anne to plenipotentiaries, 28 May 1644, *APW II B 1*, 118.
43. Servien to Mazarin, 3 June 1644, *APW II B 1*, 127, pp. 242–43.
44. Mazarin to plenipotentiaries, 14 June 1644, and 18 June 1644, *APW II B 1*, 140, pp. 266–67, and 142, pp. 271–72.
45. Plenipotentiaries to Mazarin, 2 July 1644, *APW II B 1*, 157, pp. 309–12.
46. Plenipotentiaries to Swedish plenipotentiaries, 17 August 1644, *APW II B 1*, 213, pp. 461–64; F. W. Barthold, *Geschichte des großen deutschen Krieges vom Tode Gustav Adolfs ab mit besonderer Rücksicht auf Frankreich*, part 2, "Von der

Wahl Ferdinands III. zum römischen Könige bis zum Schluße des westfälischen Friedens" (Stuttgart, 1843), 498–99; Hermann Kellenbrenz, "Hamburg und die französisch-schwedische Zusammenarbeit im 30jährigen Krieg," in *Der Dreissigjährige Krieg: Perspektiven und Strukturen*, ed. Hans Ulrich Rudolf (Darmstadt, 1977), 284–85.

47. Immler, *Kurfürst Maximilian I.*, 501.

48. Immler, *Kurfürst Maximilian I.*, 498–507 transcribes the whole document.

49. Notes of Adelzreitter, 23 October 1644, Bayerisches Hauptstaatsarchiv (hereafter omitted), Kurbayern, Geheimer Rat (hereafter KGR), v. 198, fasc.3, fol. 45r.

50. Immler, *Kurfürst Maximilian I.*, 30–32.

51. Gerhard Immler, "Bayerisch-Spanische Beziehungen während des Dreissigjährigen Krieges, insbesondere in den Jahren 1643–1645," in *Aus Bayerns Geschichte: Forschungen als Festgabe zum 70. Geburtstag von Andreas Kraus*, ed. Johannes Greipl, Alois Schmid, and Walter Ziegler (St. Ottilien, 1992), 321–23; Immler, *Kurfürst Maximilian I.*, 31–36; and Israel, 295.

52. Jean Bérenger, Ph. Loupès, and J.-P. Kintz, eds., *Guerre et Paix dans l'Europe du XVIIe siècle: Textes et documents* (Paris, 1991), 202–5. Modern authors also commonly make the mistake of assuming that Mazarin was out to avenge Tuttlingen in 1644; see, e.g., Henri Sacchi, *La guerre des cardinaux*, v. 3 of *La Guerre de Trente Ans* (Paris, 1991), 317–18; Heyner, 34.

53. It is true that earlier in the document Giustiniani says that "the most visible effort will be in Picardy," but contrasts this with the "real" offensive in Catalonia. In fact, the main effort—apparent and real—was in Flanders. Brienne mentions 3 armies operating in Flanders (though one is actually Enghien), compared to one on each of the other fronts; Brienne to d'Avaux, 2 April 1644, *APW* II B 1, 23, pp. 46–47. See Chéruel, *Histoire de France*, v. 1, 274–79, and Aumale, 262–66. Aumale, however, understates the size of Enghien's army, which was actually as large as Turenne's. Though Bérenger, *Turenne*, 194–95, does not provide a source when he says that the main French efforts will be in the Low Countries and Catalonia, he is probably using Giustiniani's letter. See also Jonathan I. Israel, "Olivares, the Cardinal-Infante and Spain's Strategy in the Low Countries (1635–1643)," cited in chapter 4, footnote 23.

54. The expression "première et principale" army was not just a descriptive term, but referred formally to the most important army; see Ranum, 53. Jean, comte de Gassion, 1609–1647: a Protestant, he served for five years under Gustavus Adolphus, played a glorious part at the battle of Rocroi (for which he received the marshalate in November 1643), and died on 2 October 1647 of a musket shot to the head received while reconnoitering at the siege of Lens. He commanded an army in Flanders each year from 1644 to 1647, and was considered an excellent soldier, though Mazarin did not like him. *Dictionnaire des Maréchaux*, 199–201. Louis XIV to Gassion, 22 April 1644, AG, v. 89, fols. 166v–70v.

55. Louis XIV to Enghien, 22 April 1644, AG, v. 89, fols. 170v–73v.

56. Instruction to Enghien on taking over the army in Champagne, 1 May 1644, BN Mf v. 4169, fols. 101r–3v. This seems like rather a better reason for the French limit to one offensive than the pessimistic view of Chéruel, *Histoire de France*, v. 1, 244–45 and 273–74, and Aumale, 262–66, that Mazarin hoped to add to the feud between Orléans and Enghien. First, it seems likely that putting Enghien under Orléans would have led to more problems that it would have solved, and would probably have impaired the efficiency of the army. Second, had Mazarin really been trying to deny any role to Enghien, he would not have

busily plotted offensives for him all spring, and would not have eventually given him the command over an army of twenty thousand men aimed at attacking the Bavarians.

57. Le Tellier to Villeroy, 22 April 1644, AG v. 89, fols. 176v–179r.

58. Turenne to Mazarin, 24 March 1644, CP All v. 23, fols. 167r–167v.

59. Tracy to Mazarin, 5 February 1644, CP All v. 23, fol. 155r. Where they got this extraordinary intelligence is unknown, but it is likely that the coalition conference at Passau had been infiltrated; Mazarin is known to have had a spy in the Habsburg court in Vienna. See above, chapter 2.

60. Louis XIV to Turenne, 13 June 1644, AG, v. 89, 108–12; Le Tellier to Enghien, 6 June 1644, BN Mf v. 4170 fols. 131v–38v; Mazarin to Enghien, 9 July 1644, CP All v. 23, fols. 262r–63v (though the letter is unsigned, it seems likely to have been from Mazarin). These plans almost certainly originated with Turenne; see Memorandum to Turenne, 20 May 1644, BN, Mf, v. 4198, fols. 44r–48r.

61. We know for certain that he mistakenly thought Bavaria to have pushed to keep Denmark in the war at the Passau conference; Mazarin to plenipotentiaries, 19 March 1644, *APW II B 1*, 4.

62. Louis XIV to Tracy, 13 April 1644, AG, v. 89, fols. 90v–94r.

63. See *supra*, footnote 54.

64. Servien to Brienne, 1 April 1644, *APW II B 1*, 21, p. 40.

65. Schaufler, 44; Immler, *Kurfürst Maximilian I.*, 39–40. On the siege of Überlingen, see Heydendorff, 185–86.

66. Turenne to Mazarin, 24 and 31 March, CP All v. 23, fols. 167r–167v and 171r–72r.

67. Inhabitants would sometimes resist quarters by attacking the troops; surprisingly, the French crown actually sanctioned this in the case of troops who strayed from their assigned quarters in an ordnance from April 1644. See Kroener, *Les Routes et les Étapes*, 114–15.

68. Turenne to Mazarin, 9 and 17 April 1644, CP All v. 23, fols. 180r–81r and 183–84v.

69. Schaufler, 44.

70. Instruction to Turenne concerning the mutiny of the regiment in Breisach, 1 May 1644, BN Mf v. 4169, fols. 98r–101r; Tracy to Mazarin, 6 May 1644, CP All v. 23, fols. 194r–194v.

71. Plenipotentiaries to Anne, 13 May 1644, *APW II B 1*, 99, p. 191. D'Oysonville (admittedly, not an unbiased source) similarly attributed the revolt to enemy spies; D'Oysonville to [probably Le Tellier], 3 June 1644, CP All v. 23, fols. 223r–223v.

72. Turenne to Mazarin, 7, 8, and 13 May 1644, CP All v. 23, fols. 195r–91v, 199, 201-'; Schaufler, 44. D'Oysonville's position was weak after the disgrace of his uncle, Sublet de Noyers, the former secretary of state for war; Reuss, *L'Alsace au Dix-Septième Siècle*, v. 1, 104.

73. Mazarin to plenipotentiaries, 14 May 1644, *APW II B 1*, 104, p. 202; Louis XIV to Gassion, Enghien, etc., 22 April 1644, AG, v. 89, 166v–70v, 170v–73v, etc.; Lionne to Servien, 21 May 1644, *APW II B 1*, 111, p. 206; Schaufler, 45. Hohentwiel successfully defeated five siege attempts during the Thirty Years' War; Fritz Fezer and Uwe Muuß, *Luftbildatlas Baden-Württemberg: Eine Landeskunde in 72 farbigen Luftaufnahmen* (Munich, 1971), 154–55. See the same book for a striking view of Hohentwiel rising sharply in the middle of a plain; one can see why it was so hard to capture.

74. Turenne to Mazarin, 3 and 25 June 1644 and Tracy to Mazarin, 8 June 1644, CP All v. 23, fols. 219r–20r, 236r–236v, and 233r–233v; Schaufler, 46–47. Schaufler gives the figure of ten thousand men for the raid. The *Gazette* mentions four thousand cavalry and as much infantry, but the advance guard under Rosen—which did the actual fighting—was only four to five regiments. Schaufler's dates (he says the raid began on 1 June and ended 4 June) also seem to be off. Turenne wrote in the above letter of 3 June that he was leaving the next day, and he wrote to his sister on 8 June that he had returned the previous day. See Turenne, *Mémoires,* 8; Turenne to Mlle. de Bouillon, 8 June 1644, *Lettres de Turenne,* 401; Bérenger, *Turenne,* 200. (Bérenger, however, misreads Turenne's memoirs to say that the offensive was held up by Hohentwiel, whereas in fact Hohentwiel was being besieged by the Bavarians at the time.) The success of Turenne's raid was no doubt aided by the fact that Mercy was lying ill in Stühlingen at the time; Heydendorff, 188.

75. Turenne to Mazarin, 29 June and 2 July 1644, CP All v. 23, fols. 248r–248v and 254r–55r; Le Tellier to Turenne, 13 June 1644, BN, Mf, v. 4170, fols. 138v–40v; Immler, *Kurfürst Maximilian I.*, 41–42; Schaufler, 50. On the operations surrounding Hohentwiel, see Heydendorff, 186–89.

76. See Mohr, 336–37; the treaty is printed in Du Mont, v. 6, 211–12.

77. Mohr, 343–44. On the French opinion of Lorraine, see *APW 1.1,* 88, footnote 1. On the fact that the talks were secret, Brienne to plenipotentiaries, 9 July 1644, *APW II B 1,* 161, p. 334. Louis XIV to Turenne, 13 June 1644, AG, v. 89 fols. 108r–12r; Mazarin to plenipotentiaries, 17 July 1644, *APW II B 1,* 177, pp. 368–70. The origin of the statement of military advantages is clearly Turenne's letter of 17 in April CP All v. 23, fols. 183r–84v.

78. Mohr, 344–47; Brienne to plenipotentiaries, 2 July 1644, and 9 July 1644, *APW II B 1,* 153, p. 302, and 161, p. 334; Lionne to Servien, 23 July 1644, 181, p. 387; plenipotentiaries to Mazarin, 30 July 1644, 187, p. 404; plenipotentiaries to Brienne, 23 July 1644, 182, p. 396; Mazarin to plenipotentiaries, 15 August 1644, 208, pp. 451–52; Mazarin to plenipotentiaries, 24 November 1644, 254, pp. 520–21. For a detailed account of the negotiations, see Ferdinand Des Robert, *Charles IV et Mazarin (1643–1661)* (Nancy, 1899), chs. 1 and 2.

79. Louis XIV to Marsin, 15 January 1644, AG, v. 89, fols. 66v–74r; Mazarin to plenipotentiaries, 9 April 1644, *APW II B 1,* 31, p. 60. The discrepancy in the early figures, which are for four thousand troops, and the latter, for twenty-four hundred, are probably attributable to the normal attrition rate of "vingt pour douze"; see Parrott, "The Administration of the French Army," 111.

80. Servien to Mazarin, 23 March 1644, *APW II B 1,* 10; 21, p. 40; Mazarin to plenipotentiaries, 16 April 1644, 46, p. 89; Brienne to plenipotentiaries, 30 April 1644, 78, p. 153. This is not to say that the decision was necessarily a poor one; Liège-Hesse relations were indeed bad because of Hessian contribution-raising within the bishopric, and Mazarin also noted the difficulty of supplying the additional troops in Hesse (see Brienne to plenipotentiaries, 23 April 1644, *APW II B 1,* 61, p. 119; plenipotentiaries to Brienne, 13 May 1644, 98, p. 180; and Mazarin to plenipotentiaries, 30 April 1644, 79, p. 157).

81. Plenipotentiaries to Brienne, 18 June 1644, *APW II B 1,* 146, p. 282, etc. See plenipotentiaries to Mazarin, 16 July 1644, *APW II B 1,* 174, pp. 363–64 on the Westphalian defense league. Plenipotentiaries to Mazarin, 2 July 1644, *APW II B 1,* 157, pp. 315–16; d'Avaux to Mazarin, 8 July 1644, 160, p. 331; plenipotentiaries to Mazarin, 16 July 1644, 174, pp. 363–64. The quotation is from plenipotentiaries to Brienne, 23 July 1644, *APW II B 1,* 182, p. 394. On the East Frisian

affair, which was settled in October, see Heyner, 36–39. On the Westphalian defense league, see Foerster, 225–65.

82. Louis XIV to Enghien, 12 July 1644, AG, v. 89, fols. 112r–17r; [presumably Mazarin] to Enghien, 9 July 1644, CP All v. 23, fols. 262r–63v.

83. Schaufler, 51, 58; Tracy to Mazarin, 11 July 1644, CP All v. 23, fols. 270r–270v; Le Tellier to Turenne, 19 July 1644, BN, Mf, v. 4198, fols. 122v–25r.

84. Tracy to Le Tellier, 22 July 1644, AG, v. 98, #56. (The folios in this volume are not paginated, but the letters are numbered.) On the Bavarian supply situation, cf. also the 1 August officers' meeting below, footnote 84. Turenne to Mazarin, 26 July, CP All v. 23, fols. 298r–298v; Schaufler, 62. Tracy actually estimated that Freiburg would hold out to the end of the month (Tracy to Mazarin, 22 July 1644, AG, v. 98, #56).

85. Mazarin to Turenne, 20 July 1644, BM, v. 2214, fols. 217r–217v. *Pace* Aumale (v. 4, 309–11), Mazarin was certain of his decision once he took it; there is no evidence that he reconsidered.

86. Aumale, 312. It is sometimes possible to read in secondary sources that France *captured* Freiburg in 1644, evidently by authors who have been misled by the French victory in the ensuing battle: Douglas Clark Baxter, *Servants of the Sword: French Intendants of the Army, 1630–70* (Urbana, 1976), 104; Goubert, 168; V.-L. Tapié, *La Guerre de Trente Ans* (Paris, 1989), 392. Brienne even commits this error in his memoirs (p. 111).

87. Aumale, *pièces justificatives*, 602–3; Mercy to Maximilian, 31 July 1644, KAA v. 2975, fol. 434r. Minutes of officers' meeting, 1 August 1644, KAA v. 2795, fols. 439r–41r.

88. Aumale, 317–20, demonstrates that a flank assault, contrary to what is sometimes written, was not an option because of the difficulty of maneuver in the mountains. For the opposite opinion, see Napoleon, 133–34.

89. Of course, casualty figures are very difficult to come by. If one takes the figures that Schaufler gives for the four stages of the battle—for which, however, he does not always provide a source—the total comes to seventy-six hundred French and twenty-four hundred Bavarians. Considering the Bavarian reaction after the battle, however, this must far underestimate their casualties. Unfortunately, they do not provide us with figures themselves. Turenne estimated that the enemy had lost nine thousand out of eighteen thousand men; this is to put initial Bavarian strength a bit high, but I agree in principle that the losses totalled about half their strength. The sources for French casualties are equally scanty, but they apparently had only about three thousand infantry in the ensuing campaign, which would put their losses at about seven thousand. Casualties would have been much higher among the infantry, since the cavalry had hardly any role in the battle except in the few cases where they dismounted. Schaufler, 82, 84, 97, 100; Turenne to Mazarin, 9 August 1644, CP All v. 24, fols. 40r–41v. See also Général Hardy de Périni, *Turenne et Condé, 1643–1671*, vol. 4 of *Batailles Françaises* (Paris, n.d), 57–67.

90. For a general discussion of the criticism of Mercy, see Schaufler, 100–103. Schaufler points up Mercy's difficulties, but ultimately comes down against him.

91. Aumale, *pièces justificatives*, 607–8. That the French cavalry was in excellent shape, see Aumale, *pièces justificatives*, 641. Maximilian to Mercy, 12 August 1644, KAA v. 2795, fols. 465r–465v.

92. Schaufler, 104–12; Mercy to Maximilian, 9, 15, and 23 August, KAA v. 2795, fols. 474r–474v, 509r–13r, and 550r–53v. Mercy did not, as Aumale would have it, march to Rothenburg-ob-der-Tauber after the battle (which would have

been a prodigious marching feat indeed), but rather to Rottenburg, on the other side of the Black Forest. Aumale, 351.

93. Maximilian to Mercy, 12 and 15 August, KAA v. 2795, 477–83v and 498–98v.

94. Maximilian to Mercy, 12, 13, 15, and 22 August, KAA v. 2795, fols. 477r–83v, 485r, 498r–98v, and 538r–538v.

95. Aumale, *pièces justificatives*, 609; Turenne to Mazarin, 9 August 1644, CP All v. 24, fols. 40r–41v; Aumont to Le Tellier, 8 August 1644, AG, v. 98, #61.

96. Mazarin to Turenne, 17 August 1644, *Lettres*, v. 2, 17.

97. Turenne to Mazarin, 27 August, CP All v. 24, fols. 126r–26v.

98. Instruction to Enghien following the battle of Freiburg, 17 August 1644, BN, Mf, v. 4169, fols. 131r–31v.

99. Mazarin to Turenne, 21 August 1644, *Lettres*, v. 2, 21, and Mazarin to Enghien, 21 August 1644, 22. Cf. also a letter from Condé to Enghien (his son) on 27 August, in which he complains that Enghien's friends, and the rest of Paris, are unhappy with Enghien for failing to do three things: first, capture Freiburg; second, return to capture a place west (not east) of the Rhine; and third, bring back the troops that he took with him to Germany (Aumale, *pièces justificatives*, 616–17).

100. Also La Serre-Aubeterre to Enghien, 27 August 1644, quoted in Aumale, 364–65. [Enghien to Mazarin], no date, CP All v. 25, fols. 377r–377v. (The author and recipient of this letter are a bit problematic. It is labelled M. le Prince, but the handwriting and content suggest strongly that it is actually Enghien who wrote it. Since it is included in the *Archives du Ministère des Affaires Étrangères* rather than the *Archives de Guerre*, presumably it was sent to Mazarin.) The chief problem lay in the supply situation: having already been the site of a major siege, the surrounding area had very little left with which to support an army. This contention of Turenne, mentioned in his memoirs, is confirmed by a letter of Le Tellier from 23 August (BN, Mf, v. 4199, fols. 88r–92v). Turenne's argument that one could not control Freiburg without Breisach turned out, however, to have been false; Bavaria held Freiburg to the end of the war. Chéruel (*Histoire de France*, v. 1, 325) is therefore wrong to adopt the (yet again) false news of Nani that d'Erlach took Freiburg at the end of 1644; see, e.g., Mazarin to Condé, 6 May 1645, *Lettres*, v. 2, 62.

101. Anne to Enghien, 17 August 1644, AG, v. 98, #69.

102. Aumale, 363; Mazarin to Turenne, 1 August 1644, *Lettres*, v. 2, 8 and the footnote; Chéruel, *Histoire de France*, v. 1, 299–300 and 325–27. However, Turenne was relieved when the capture of Philippsburg vindicated his strategy; otherwise, he thought, the court might have complained about the failure to besiege Freiburg (Turenne to Mlle. de Bouillon, 10 September 1644, *Lettres de Turenne*, 406).

103. Turenne to Mazarin, 12 August 1644, CP All v. 24, fols. 50r–51v.

104. Anne to Enghien, 17 August 1644, AG, v. 98, #69.

105. Contrary to Bérenger, *Turenne*, 206, the soldiers did not cover the entire ground from Freiburg to Philippsburg in 5–6 days; this error evidently results from an ambiguous passage in Turenne's memoirs. Cp. Aumale, 372–74, and Turenne, *Mémoires*, 27 and the footnotes.

106. Officers' meeting, 1 August 1644; Maximilian to Mercy, 21, 22, and 25 August 1644; Mercy to Maximilian, 18 August 1644, KAA v. 2975, fols. 439r–41r, 534r–534v, 548r–48v, 578r–78v and 595r–96r, and 540r–42v and 544r; Maier, 381.

107. Mercy to Maximilian, 11 August 1644, KAA v. 2795, 490–92v, 496.

108. Maximilian to Mercy, 22 and 29 August 1644, KAA v. 2795, 548–48v and 575–71v.
109. Mercy to Maximilian, 18 August 1644, and Maximilian to Mercy, 29 August 1644, KAA v. 2795, fols. 540r–42v and 544r, and 598r–98v; Maximilian to Mercy, 2 and 6 September, KAA v. 2796; Immler, *Kurfürst Maximilian I.*, 45–46.
110. The performance of Bamberg, the garrison commander, was so bad that the Imperials thought of putting him on trial. Enghien to Mazarin, 10 September 1644, CP All v. 24, fols. 240r–42r; Aumale, 375–76, 379.
111. Turenne to Mazarin, 10 and 13 September 1644; Lamot to Mazarin, 10 September 1644, CP All v. 24, fols. 234r–35v, 263r–64r, and 238r–39r. News from Frankfurt, 2 October 1644, CP All v. 24, fols. 367r–68r. On Hatzfeld's corps, Salm, 33–34. Rudolf Schott, "Die Kämpfe vor Freiburg, die Eroberung von Philippsburg und die Belagerung mehrerer Städte am Rhein im Jahre 1644," *Militärgeschichtliche Mitteilungen* (24 February 1978), 15–16, gives an exhaustive analysis of the physical layout of the town.
112. Military news, August and September 1644, CP All v. 24, fols. 142r–43r; BN, Mf, v. 6180, map 22. This contradicts Aumale's account that the city asked for French protection on its own (Aumale, 375–76, 379).
113. Turenne, *Mémoires*, 32–33.
114. BN, Mf, v. 6180, map 22. Turenne to Mazarin, 13 September 1644, CP All v. 24, fols. 263r–64r.
115. See also Mazarin to Enghien, 17 September 1644, BM v. 2215, fols. 46v–47v.
116. Enghien to Mazarin, 14 and 18 September, CP All v. 24, fols. 265r–67r and 306–6v. Mainz was a gigantic fortress that required at least seven thousand troops for its defense; its capture in 1631 and 1635 had resulted largely from inadequate garrisons. See Müller, 52–60, 156–66, 220–22, 228–35.
117. Maier, 381–84, 394. Besides the example of Mainz, the 350 troops Mercy tried to put into Pforzheim were defeated by a French force of 2,000 before they could enter the town; similarly, Wolf arrived at Philippsburg with 300 dragoons just as it was surrendering. Even the main Bavarian-held towns had relatively small garrisons: Heidelberg, by far the most important, had 330; Mannheim was second with only 200. Compare this to the size of French garrisons at Philippsburg and Breisach (both over 1000).
118. Notes of Adelzreitter, 23 October 1644, KGR, v. 198, fasc.3, fol. 45r; plenipotentiaries to Brienne, 22 October 1644, *APW II B 1*, 274, pp. 575–76; Immler, *Kurfürst Maximilian I.*, 48–50. The assessment of Siegfried Niklaus ("Der Frühjahrsfeldzug 1645 in Süddeutschland (Schlacht bei Herbsthausen)," *Württembergisch Franken* 60 (1976): 129) that the 1644 French campaign in Germany gained "relativ geringen Erfolge" ("relatively small results") is not tenable in the light of either Maximilian's reaction to the campaign, or the campaign considered from a purely strategic standpoint. Had the 1645 French campaign had equal success, the Truce of Ulm would not have had to wait until 1647.
119. Mazarin to plenipotentiaries, 12 November 1644, *APW II B 1*, 290, p. 620. The decision to concede the point at a time of military success is predictable in the light of negotiation theory; see Pillar, 48–49.
120. Dickmann, *Der Westfälische Frieden*, 169; d'Avaux to Brienne, 23 November 1644, *APW II B 1*, 296; Servien to Brienne, 25 November 1644, 300; Ruppert, 61–63.
121. Turenne to Mazarin, 3 and 10 September 1644; Lamot to Mazarin, 10 September 1644; Enghien to Mazarin, 14 September 1644, CP All v. 24, fols.

156r–58r, 234r–35v, 238r–39r, and 265r–67r; Aumale, 305–6; Mazarin to Turenne, 22 September 1644, *Lettres,* v. 2, 38.

122. Mazarin to Enghien, 27 July 1644, *Lettres,* v. 2, 6, on how Enghien's absence had left Champagne open to Beck, which created unrest in Paris (!).

123. Le Tellier to Enghien, 16 September 1644, BN, Mf v. 4198, fols. 170v–71v; Le Tellier to Turenne, 12 November 1644, BN, Mf v. 4170, fols. 274v–75r; Tracy to Mazarin, 20 September 1644, CP All v. 24, fols. 315r–16r.

124. Turenne to Mazarin, 3 and 13 September and 4 October 1644, CP All v. 24, fols. 156r–58r, 263r–64r, and 373r–74r; Maier, 385–90.

125. Le Tellier to Turenne, 16 September 1644, BN, Mf v. 4198, fols. 171v–72v; Mazarin to Turenne, 22 September 1644, *Lettres,* v. 2, 38, and Mazarin to Enghien, 22 September 1644, 40. On French troop strength, see Bernhard Kroener, "Die Entwicklung der Truppenstärken in den französischen Armeen zwischen 1635 und 1661," in *Forschungen und Quellen zur Geschichte des dreißigjährigen Krieges,* v. 12 of the Schriftenreihe der Vereinigung zur Erforschung der Neueren Geschichte (Münster, 1981), 172–77, 192. Even at twenty-five men per company, the reinforcement would have been over five thousand; however, there is good reason to believe that the attrition for troops going to Germany, especially at this time, was even greater. See Anne to Enghien, 17 August 1644, AG, v. 98, 69, and Mazarin to Turenne, 12 September and 17 September 1644, *Lettres,* v. 2, 33 and 34.

126. Turenne to Mazarin, 23 November 1644, CP All v. 25, fols. 111r–15v); Le Tellier to Turenne, 12 November 1644, BN, Mf, v. 4170, fols. 274v–75r.

127. Servien to Mazarin, 22 December 1644, *APW II B 1,* 335; Mazarin to Turenne, 2 December 1644, *Lettres,* v. 2, 47; Turenne to Mazarin, 8 December 1644, CP All v. 25, fols. 281r–84v.

128. Turenne to Mazarin, 30 September, 4 October, 23 November, and 29 December 1644, CP All v. 24, fols. 349r–50v and 373r–74r, and v. 25, fols. 111r–15v and 364r–65r. Louis XIV to d'Oysonville, 25 November 1644, AG, v. 90, 299–300. Tracy (Tracy to Mazarin, 20 September 1644, CP All v. 24, fols. 315r–16r) claimed that it could support the garrisons for 18 months, but this is contradicted by Turenne's later comment (Turenne to Mazarin, 8 December 1644, CP All v. 25, fols. 281r–84v). Charles IV of Lorraine had gone so far as to claim that the occupation of the Palatinate was disadvantageous to its owner; Des Robert, 37.

129. Turenne to Mazarin, 3 and 30 September; Tracy to Mazarin, 14 September; Enghien to Mazarin, 18 September 1644, CP All v. 24, fols. 156r–58r, 349r–50v, 269r–269v, and 306r–6v. On the long-term importance of Philippsburg, there is this quotation from Bossuet's 1686 eulogy to Condé: "Philisbourg, qui tint si longtemps le Rhin captif sous nos lois" ("Philippsburg, which held the Rhine captive under our laws for such a long time"). Textor, 24.

130. Louis XIV to Enghien, 25 April 1645, BN, Mf, v. 4171, fols. 220v.

131. Louis XIV to Enghien, 12 July 1644, AG, v. 89, 112–17.

Chapter 7. 1645: Mazarin Gains Confidence

1. Plenipotentiaries to Brienne, 12 November 1644, *APW II B 1,* 292, pp. 628–30. Though the memorandum is from both plenipotentiaries, it is clear from later actions that the idea was Servien's.

2. Mazarin to plenipotentiaries, 19 December 1644, *APW II B 1,* 331, pp. 783–84.

3. Dickmann, *Der Westfälische Frieden,* 171; a copy of the proposal is in Le Clerc, v. 1, 318.

4. Plenipotentiaries to Rorté, 9 December 1644, *APW II B 1,* 319, pp. 726–27; 321, pp. 744–45; the Imperial proposition is in Le Clerc, v. 1, 321. Goetze, 223 and 225, notes that the Swedes had favored admitting the Imperial estates *qua* allies, but had given into the French demand.

5. Dickmann, *Der Westfälische Frieden,* 169–71.

6. Servien to Brienne, 31 December 1644, *APW II B 1,* 343, pp. 824–25.

7. Plenipotentiaries to Brienne, 26 November 1644, *APW II B 1,* 303, p. 679.

8. Dickmann, *Der Westfälische Frieden,* 171–72.

9. For example, see Mazarin to plenipotentiaries, 16 April 1644, *APW II B 1,* 46, pp. 85–86.

10. Dickmann, *Der Westfälische Frieden,* 169–74. *Assecuratio* was also Sweden's main goal, but they differed in how they hoped to achieve it; see footnote 65.

11. Brienne to plenipotentiaries, 26 November 1644, *APW II B 1,* 302, p. 671; 331, p. 786.

12. Ibid.

13. Servien to Brienne, 10 December 1644, *APW II B 1,* 321, pp. 742–43.

14. Brienne to plenipotentiaries, 27 December 1644, *APW II B 1,* 340, pp. 812–13. The Swedes privately opposed a Diet because they feared that France would gain control of its Catholic majority and dominate the assembly; Goetze, 223–24.

15. Dickmann, *Der Westfälische Frieden,* 172; Servien to Brienne, 10 December 1644, *APW II B 1,* 321, pp. 744–45.

16. Lionne to Servien, 24 December 1644, *APW II B 1,* 337, 340.

17. Louis XIV to plenipotentiaries, 1 January 1645, *APW II B 2,* 1, pp. 2–3.

18. See the copy in Le Clerc, v. 1, 328–30.

19. The plenipotentiaries' defense: Plenipotentiaries to Brienne, 7 January 1645, *APW II B 2,* 7; Servien's specifically: Servien to Lionne, 15 January 1645, *APW II B 2,* 14; d'Avaux's: d'Avaux to Brienne, 21 January 1645, *APW II B 2,* 20.

20. Brienne: Brienne to plenipotentiaries, 6 January 1645, *APW II B 2,* 6, pp. 22–23; rejection of Turenne's proposal: BN Mf v. 4200, fols. 8v–10r; Turenne-Mazarin, 4 Feb 1644, CP All v. 46, fols. 94r–94v, and 19 Feb 1644, fol. 116r. On the truce with Franche-Comté, Léonce de Piépape, *Histoire de la Réunion de la Franche-Comté à la France: Événements Diplomatiques et Militaires (1279 à 1678),* v. 2 (Paris, 1881), 175–77; Jean-François Solnon, *Quand la Franche-Comté était Espagnole* (N.p., 1983), 277–81; Frieda Gallati, "Die Eidgenössische Politik zur Zeit des Dreißigjährigen Krieges," *Jahrbuch fur Schweizer Geschichte* 41 (1919): 219–25; and Stein, *Protection Royale,* 510–13.

21. Mazarin-Turenne, 9 Mar 1644, CP All v. 46, fols. 197r–99r; Enghien: Aumale, 414–15 and BN Mf v. 4200, fols. 73r–75v; attacking Frankenthal: Le Tellier-Tracy, 6 February 1645, AG v. 93, fols. 126v–28v; reinforcements for Turenne: Le Tellier-Turenne, 28 February 1645, AG v. 93, fols. 137r–38r, and Le Tellier-Turenne, 9 March 1645, AG v. 93, fols. 154r–57r; separate corps for the Rhine: Le Tellier to Bellenave, 6 March 1645, AG v. 93, fols. 152r–53v. French treaty with Transylvania: 22 April 1645, Le Clerc, v. 1, 359–65.

22. Plenipotentiaries to Brienne, 7 January 1645, *APW II B 2,* 7, pp. 27–30, and 31 January 1645, 28, pp. 100–101; the December agreement with the Swedes: Rorté to plenipotentiaries, 15 December 1644, *APW II B 1,* 325, p. 764.

23. D'Avaux to Servien, 8 February 1645, *APW II B 2,* 37; Oxenstierna and Salvius to Christina, 22 February 1645, *APW II C 1,* 285, p. 499; Oxenstierna and Salvius to Rosenhan, 23 February 1645, 286.

24. Court's insistence on submitting: Louis XIV to plenipotentiaries, 21 January 1645, *APW II B 2*, 17, p. 75; d'Avaux's letter: d'Avaux to Mazarin, 27 February 1645, *APW II B 2*, 48, and defense to the Swedes: d'Avaux to Swedish plenipotentiaries, 8 March 1645, Le Clerc, v. 1, 335–36; Servien's letter: Servien to Lionne, 11 February 1645, *APW II B 2*, 39, and 25 February 1645, 47. The Swedish critique is found in Oxenstierna and Salvius to Rosenhan, 24 February 1645, *APW II C 1*, 288, and Oxenstierna and Salvius to Christina, 10 March 1645, 293.

25. On d'Avaux's smaller role in the first French proposition: d'Avaux to Brienne, 21 January 1645, *APW II B 2*, 20; St. Romain (the subordinate sent to court to defend the plenipotentiaries): Lionne to Servien, 4 February 1645, *APW II B 2*, 33; Frankfurt letter: Lionne to Servien, 5 January 1645, *APW II B 2*, 5, p. 21; Excellence title: Servien to Lionne, 15 January 1645, *APW II B 2*, 14, pp. 63–64, and 22; Hanse delegates: Servien to Brienne, 29 and 30 January 1645, *APW II B 2*, 26 and 27.

26. Excellence title: Brienne to plenipotentiaries, 28 January 1645, *APW II B 2*, 23; Hanse towns: Lionne to Servien, 25 February 1645, *APW II B 2*, 46; Brienne to plenipotentiaries, 4 March 1645, *APW II B 2*, 52. A response by the Hanse delegates to Servien's charges may be found in Le Clerc, v. 1, 354–56. See also Wicquefort, 345–47, who also criticizes Servien.

27. Mazarin to Longueville, 25 June 1645, *APW II B 2*, 153; Lionne withholds Servien's recall request: Lionne to Servien, 7 April 1645, *APW II B 2*, 76.

28. D'Avaux's waffling over his recall: d'Avaux to Louis XIV, 22 April 1645, *APW II B 2*, 88; Brienne to d'Avaux, 27 May 1645, 109; and d'Avaux to Mazarin, 31 May 1645, 117. Lost credit, Lionne to Servien, 17 June 1645, *APW II B 2*, 137. Interestingly, however, the Swedes did support d'Avaux and insisted that he remain in Münster: Swedish plenipotentiaries to d'Avaux, 16 March 1645, Le Clerc, v. 1, 337–39. An account of Longueville's entry into Münster is found in Le Clerc, v. 1, 374–75.

29. Louis XIV to plenipotentiaries, 1 January 1645, *APW II B 2*, 1.

30. Plenipotentiaries to Brienne, 31 January 1645, *APW II B 2*, 28, p. 99.

31. Plenipotentiaries to Brienne, 3 March 1645, *APW II B 2*, 49, pp. 158–61.

32. Mazarin: Louis XIV to plenipotentiaries, 21 January 1645, *APW II B 2*, 17, and Mazarin to plenipotentiaries, 21 January 1645, 18; Servien to Lionne, 6 February 1645, *APW II B 2*, 36, pp. 121–22.

33. Brienne to plenipotentiaries, 14 December 1644, *APW II B 1*, 323, pp. 757–58.

34. Bavarian address: Servien to Lionne, 11 February 1645, *APW II B 2*, 39; first meeting: plenipotentiaries to Brienne, 11 March 1645, *APW II B 2*, 55; Immler, *Kurfürst Maximilian I.*, 59–61 and 83–86.

35. Schweinesbein, 183–86.

36. Schweinesbein, 192–95.

37. Schweinesbein, 187; plenipotentiaries to Brienne, 12 November 1644, *APW II B 1*, 292, pp. 626–27, and 26 November 1644, 303, pp. 681–82; plenipotentiaries to Mazarin, 14 January 1645, *APW II B 2*, 13, pp. 49–51.

38. Schweinesbein, 192–95, 207–10.

39. Schweinesbein, 199–207; Immler, *Kurfürst Maximilian I.*, 69–71.

40. Schweinesbein, 210–14.

41. Cérisantes to Oxenstierna and Salvius, 29 April 1645, *APW II C 1*, 324.

42. Andreas Kraus, "Kurfürst Maximilian I. von Bayern und die französische Satisfaktion (1644–1646): Neue Quellen zu einem alten Problem," in *Frühe Neu-*

zeit, v. 2 of *Land und Reich—Stamm und Nation: Probleme und Perspektiven bayerischer Geschichte. Festgabe für Max Spindler zum 90. Geburtstag,* ed. Andreas Kraus (Munich, 1984), 28–29; Immler, *Kurfürst Maximilian I.,* 77–78 and 82–83. Kraus admits that his argument is based on speculation; but speculation is not necessary, especially in light of the works of Schweinesbein and Immler. Admittedly, the Bavarians had discussed the possibility of using the talks to separate France from Sweden, but they meant this in a different sense: they hoped to lure France away from Sweden, not to reveal the talks in order to drive a wedge between the allies. See Immler, 66–67.

43. See Kraus, *supra*, footnote 45; Louis XIV to plenipotentiaries, 13 May 1645, *APW II B 2,* 100, pp. 321–23.

44. Kraus, "Kurfürst Maximilian," 28–30; Immler, *Kurfürst Maximilian I.,* 81–83.

45. Plenipotentiaries to Mazarin, 14 January 1645, *APW II B 2,* 13, pp. 49–50, and plenipotentiaries to Brienne, 1 April 1645, 68, pp. 217–18. See also the almost identical comment by Servien in an 22 April memorandum, *APW II B 2,* 90, pp. 300–301. In "Frankreich und die Pfalzfrage auf dem westfälischen Friedenskongreß," in *Études d'histoire européenne: Mélanges offerts à René et Suzanne Pillorget,* (Angers, 1990), 97–112, Andreas Kraus emphasizes the difference of opinion between Mazarin and Servien over the way to deal with Bavaria: Mazarin, claims Kraus, favored working with Bavaria on the basis of common interests, whereas Servien thought that Bavaria could not be brought to support French interests except through military pressure. It is true that Servien emphasized the differences in Bavarian and French interests, and above all the difficulties in getting Maximilian to separate from the emperor, more than Mazarin; this difference of opinion goes back at least to 1644 (see above, chapter 4, footnote 28). One might add that Servien's view of Bavaria was more realistic that Mazarin's in this respect. However, Kraus is incorrect to find in Servien's position a desire to separate Bavaria from the emperor that was fundamentally different from Mazarin's. Brienne had already spoken of separating Bavaria from the emperor in December, 1644; Mazarin was consistently interested in this goal, but did not pursue it with any particular single-mindedness after the Vervaux mission, only to drop it at the end of the year, as Kraus suggests.

46. Plenipotentiaries to Brienne, 25 March 1645, *APW II B 2,* 63, p. 204; Servien to Lionne, 26 March 1645, 64, p. 208; and Servien to Lionne, 22 April 1645, 89, pp. 296–97.

47. Mazarin to plenipotentiaries, 7 April 1645, *APW II B 2,* 75; 15 April 1645, 80; and Louis XIV to plenipotentiaries, 13 May 1645, 100; for Kraus, see "Kurfürst Maximilian I.," 30.

48. Mercy to Maximilian, 17 April 1645, KAA v. 2818, fols. 481r–82v.

49. Maximilian to Mercy, 17 April 1645, KAA v. 2818, fols. 473r–76v; 21 April, fols. 489r–489v; 23 April, fols. 510r–13v; 28 April, fols. 538r–41r; 30 April, fol. 543r; Immler, *Kurfürst Maximilian I.,* 107–10. Of Maximilian's restraint in fighting a battle, Immler writes that "in light of subsequent developments, it can not be ruled out that political motives secretly determined Maximilian to hold his generals to a stance of waiting." This assessment seems too cautious to me in light of the fact that Maximilian put the question of whether to attack to a vote of his privy council (see below); although Maximilian was virtually always cautious, it seems clear that he was concerned about the political repercussions of an attack, and deliberately avoided one until the results of Vervaux's mission became known.

50. Vote of the council of war, KAA v. 2818, fols. 561r–66r. See also Immler, *supra,* footnote 38. Tracy to Mazarin, 29 April 1645, CP All v. 46, fols. 378r–378v.

51. The best account from the French standpoint is in CP All v. 46, fol. 552r. See also Heilmann, *Feldzüge,* 197–218; Turenne, 39–50; Barthold, 508–11; Bérenger, *Turenne,* 212–14; Périni, 70–73; Jan Peters, ed., *Ein Söldnerleben im Dreißigjährigen Krieg: Eine Quelle zur Sozialgeschichte* (Berlin, 1993), 181. Sigfried Niklaus covers the campaign exhaustively from the German perspective in his "Der Frühjahrsfeldzug 1645 in Süddeutschland". However, he assumes too much in his reconstruction of the plans of Turenne and Mercy. On Turenne's side, this is understandable, since Niklaus uses no French sources. On the Bavarian side, however, it is less clear how Niklaus could believe that Mercy's campaign was a gradually unfolding plan designed to smash Turenne's army. He reads the eventually successful battle back into the beginning of to April explain Mercy's decision not to defend the Neckar (p. 139), and then explicitly states that by the end of April Mercy had achieved his goal of reuniting his troops and putting his army in a position from which to attack the enemy, who was in an apparently strong position. But to think that Mercy had been planning the attack for more than a week, let alone a whole month, is absurd in light of Mercy's desperate pleading to Maximilian on 17 April that he could not hold off Turenne and acutely needed remounts (see above, footnote 48). No doubt he was looking for an opportunity to attack, but it was a last-ditch measure designed to keep the Bavarians west of the Danube, and not a long-range plan that Mercy had held since the start of the campaign.

52. Servien to Lionne, 22 April 1645, *APW II B 2,* 89, pp. 296–97, and 20 May 1645, 106; Lionne to Servien, 6 May 1645, 98, and 3 June 1645, 120. Mazarin-d'Avaugour, 8 April 1645, CP Suède v. 7, fols. 269r–71v. Kraus ("Frankreich und die Pfalzfrage," 106) cites Lionne's letter in *APW II B 2,* 120 to show that Mazarin was personally hurt that Servien could say that he had let himself be misled by Maximilian. However, the letter clearly emphasizes Servien's personal criticism of Turenne for allowing the situation to degenerate; it is in this context that Lionne urged Servien to praise Mazarin's orders to repair the situation, and not, as Kraus makes it seem, in the context of Servien's statement that Bavaria had tricked France, which is tacked on almost as an afterthought in the next paragraph. Also note a letter from Mazarin to Stella de Morimont in Strasbourg from 24 May (CP All v. 46, fol. 518r)—and therefore before Lionne's letter to Servien cited above—that states, "the fault was not Turenne's for having advanced, but the German colonels'" for having been too spread out.

53. Plenipotentiaries to Brienne, 31 January 1645, *APW II B 2,* 28, p. 102. On the Dutch slowness at coming to Münster, see Israel, *Dutch Republic,* 353–60.

54. Servien to Lionne, 4 March 1645, *APW II B 2,* 53; Servien to Lionne, 11 March 1645, 57; and plenipotentiaries to Brienne, 18 March 1645, 59, pp. 192–93; Israel, *Dutch Republic,* 319–20; Wilhelm Tham, *Den Svenska Utrikespolitikens Historia,* vol.1, part 2, *1560–1648* (Stockholm, 1960), 333–39.

55. The numerous concerns over the East Frisian affair can be found in letters of (6 January Brienne to plenipotentiaries, *APW II B 2,* 6, pp. 23–24); (31 January plenipotentiaries to Brienne, *APW II B 2,* 28, p. 103); (18 February Brienne to plenipotentiaries, *APW II B 2,* 41); and (3 March plenipotentiaries to Brienne, *APW II B 2,* 49), among others. Amalie Elisabeth threatens to withdraw: Servien to Lionne, 4 March 1645, *APW II B 2,* 53, and plenipotentiaries to Brienne, 11 March 1645, 55, pp. 177–78; optimistic reports from Brienne: Brienne to plenipotentiaries, 4 March 1645, *APW II B 2,* 52, and 18 March 1645, 58; still

a problem on 22 July: plenipotentiaries to Brienne, 22 July 1645, *APW II B 2*, 172, p. 536; resolution of the problem: Brienne to plenipotentiaries, 26 August 1645, *APW II B 2*, 193, p. 611 (footnote).

56. Mazarin-plenipotentiaries, 21 January 1645, *APW II B 2*, 18, p. 77; Dutch still not in Münster: Longueville-Mazarin, 20 June 1645, *APW II B 2*, 144; Brienne-plenipotentiaries, 29 July 1645, *APW II B 2*, 174; Dutch want truce: plenipotentiaries-Mazarin, 3 March 1645, *APW II B 2*, 50. It had been Spanish policy at least since 1641 to try to make a separate agreement with the Dutch. For their part, the slowness of the Dutch in coming to the Congress was due mainly to the difficulty of getting all provinces and towns to agree on the instructions to be given to the plenipotentiaries; see Israel, *Dutch Republic*, 347–60.

57. Giving in to the Dutch on precedence: Louis XIV-plenipotentiaries, 21 Jan and 18 Feb, *APW II B 2*, 17, p. 73, and 42.

58. See August Heimer, *De Diplomatiska Förbindelserna mellan Sverige och England, 1633–1654* (Lund, 1893), 47–54. Sweden was in fact carrying on negotiations in the hope of gaining aid in their war against Denmark, but the war was over before Parliament was able to get involved. Because of this, and because of their concern of the French reaction, Sweden let the alliance idea drop.

59. Servien to Lionne, 15 January 1645, *APW II B 2*, 14; Lionne to Servien, 21 January 1645, 19; Mazarin to plenipotentiaries, 28 January 1645, 24; Lionne to Servien, 28 January 1645, 25; Brienne to plenipotentiaries, 21 January 1645, 16, and Louis XIV to plenipotentiaries, 21 January 1645, 17.

60. Oxenstierna and Salvius to Christina, 31 March 1645, *APW II C 1*, 311, p. 556 identifies the crucial change of opinion as occurring on 31 March. Their waxing impatience with the French, whose dilatoriness they attributed primarily to the conflict between Servien and d'Avaux, can be followed in the letters over the ensuing months, especially Salvius to Axel Oxenstierna, 3 April 1645, *APW II C 1*, 314; Rosenhane to Oxenstierna and Salvius, 14 April 1645, 316; and Oxenstierna and Salvius to Rosenhane, 17 April 1645, 318.

61. Plenipotentiaries to Brienne, 25 March 1645, *APW II B 2*, 63, and 1 April 1645, 68; Servien to Lionne, 25 March 1645, 64.

62. Plenipotentiaries to Mazarin, 14 January 1645, *APW II B 2*, 13; plenipotentiaries to Brienne, 11 March 1645, 56.

63. Unfortunately, the correspondence from the Swedish plenipotentiaries to their court breaks off abruptly on 31 March and is not recommenced until 12 May. The plenipotentiaries attribute the gap to a heavy workload of visits, but it is unfortunate at precisely the time when the second proposition was being negotiated with the French. The key disputes outlined below are mentioned in Oxenstierna and Salvius to Christina, 12 May 1645, *APW II C 1*, 326, and Oxenstierna and Salvius to Rosenhane, 15 May 1645, 328.

64. On the plenipotentiaries' desire to demand a return to the 1618 situation, see plenipotentiaries to Brienne, 7 January 1645, *APW II B 2*, 7, and plenipotentiaries to Mazarin, 14 January 1645, 13; on the court's reaction, Brienne to plenipotentiaries, 6 April 1645, *APW II B 2*, 71; Louis XIV to plenipotentiaries, 6 April 1645, 72; and memorandum from Servien, 15 April 1645, 84, p. 279. Kraus claims that Servien inserted the 1618 clause in the second proposition without permission from court, but this is contradicted not only by the court's 6 April memorandum, but also by Mazarin's later responses; if Servien had indeed gone against Mazarin's wishes on such a crucial issue, why did Mazarin never mention it? Kraus, "Frankreich und die Pfalzfrage," 105.

65. Plenipotentiaries to Brienne, 3 March 1645, *APW II B 2*, 49; Brienne to plenipotentiaries, 18 March 1645, 58; see also Dickmann, *Der Westfälische Frieden*, 332–34, and Goetze, 214–235, on Swedish idea of security.
66. Servien to Lionne, 15 April 1645, *APW II B 2*, 83. Dickmann's claim, *Der Westfälische Frieden*, 169–70, that France and Sweden avoided demanding satisfaction for fear of alienating the German estates is contradicted by this letter. Servien wrote a separate memo arguing in favor of the new method of negotiation; 15 April 1645, *APW II B 2*, 84.
67. Louis XIV to plenipotentiaries, 6 April 1645, *APW II B 2*, 72, pp. 230–31; court order forbidding mention of Protestant interests: Brienne to plenipotentiaries, 22 April 1645, *APW II B 2*, 86. See also plenipotentiaries to Brienne, 22 April 1645, 87; ibid., 13 May 1645, 101; Servien to Lionne, 13 May 1645, 102; Servien to Brienne, 20 May 1645, 105.
68. Swedish pressure: Servien to Brienne, 20 May 1645, *APW II B 2*, 105; ibid., 27 May 1645, 111; Servien to Rorté, 21 May 1645, 107. The Swedes actually referred to the favorable opportunity to deliver the proposition: plenipotentiaries to Brienne, 13 May 1645, Le Clerc, v. 2, 253. Mazarin's response: Brienne to plenipotentiaries, 27 May 1645, *APW II B 2*, 108; Lionne to Servien, 27 May 1645, 110; Louis XIV to plenipotentiaries, 30 May 1645, 114. Servien's apology: Servien to Lionne, 10 June 1645, *APW II B 2*, 127. Mazarin could be accused of inconsistency if one compares his handling of the first and second French propositions. However, essentially he seems to have held the consistent aim of wanting to see one version of each, whereas the plenipotentiaries sent him none of the first, and two of the second.
69. Plenipotentiaries to Mazarin, 3 June 1645, *APW II B 2*, 122; plenipotentiaries to Brienne, 10 June 1645, 126; Rorté to plenipotentiaries, 12 June 1645, 128; ibid., 14 June 1645, 131; plenipotentiaries to Rorté, 12 June 1645, 129; Servien to Lionne, 16 June 1645, 134. The Swedes also changed several words in their proposition, but soon forgot their differences with France as they became concerned that the emperor would advance negotiations with the French faster than with them: memorandum from St. Romain, 17 June 1645, *APW II B 2*, 139; Rorté to plenipotentiaries, 18 June 1645, 140; plenipotentiaries to Rorté, 18 June 1645, 141. For the French proposition, see Le Clerc, v. 1, 372–74. Note also from Goetze, 219, that the Swedes were not convinced of the need to reestablish Karl Ludwig in the Palatinate, which made agreement with France all the easier.
70. Cp. Heyner, 47.
71. Andreas Kraus, *Die Acta Pacis Westphalicae: Rang und geisteswissenschaftliche Bedeutung eines Editionsunternehmens unserer Zeit, untersucht an Hand der Elsaß-Frage (1640–1646)*, Rheinisch-Westfälische Akademie der Wissenschaften, Geisteswissenschaften, Vorträge, v. 269 (Düsseldorf, 1984), 19. His argument that the plenipotentiaries only wanted Breisach in April is invalid for three reasons. First, the plenipotentiaries were speaking in the context of relations with Bavaria; while they could argue that it was in Bavarian interests to leave France a passage into the Empire, it would have been difficult to make a case for the Bavarian interest in the French retention of Alsace. Second, the plenipotentiaries' letter of July 16 to the queen suggested strongly that they were already intending to retain all of Alsace; even if they were speaking in the context of what France held militarily and not of French demands, it is striking that the places they mentioned are almost all in their main instructions as French demands. Third, at best they can be expressing their own opinion; what the court thought was more important, and is completely unknown to us. Brienne to

plenipotentiaries, 1 April 1645, *APW II B 2*, 67; Longueville to Mazarin, 22 July 1645, 173; Servien to Lionne, 15 April 1645, 83, pp. 267–68.

72. D'Avaux to Anne, 9 December 1644, *APW II B 1*, 320; Servien to Brienne, 17 December 1644, 328, and 31 December 1644, 343.

73. Mazarin to plenipotentiaries, 7 April 1645, *APW II B 2*, 75; Servien to Lionne, 15 April 1645, 83; memorandum from Servien, 22 April 1645, 90; Lionne to Servien, 6 May 1645, 98. Kraus (*Die Acta Pacis Westphalicae*, 20–21) again uses his evidence very loosely and out of context here. First, he states that Servien, in a 31 December memorandum, was attempting to shift all of the blame for French annexation onto Bavaria. In fact, Servien not only does not mention such an idea, but also clearly states that Bavaria's intervention for French satisfaction was to be done in secret; thus, he could hardly have expected it to attract blame. Given Servien's usual completeness, if he did believe that his plan would work to French advantage in this way, it is hard to see why he would not have mentioned it. Second, Kraus claims that Servien pushed the annexation of Alsace on the court at precisely this time. To demonstrate this, Kraus cites Brienne's response to show that the court had taken up the annexation of Alsace as a demand; yet it is clear that Brienne speaks only of the annexation as a possibility, not a closed fact. Third, Kraus cites a royal memo from 6 April that empowered the plenipotentiaries to conclude a truce on *uti possidetis* conditions to show another step in the evolution of French demands. But the truce was solely a response to the Spanish negotiations and only incidentally affected the German situation; this is demonstrated by the fact that Mazarin wrote the very next day to ask the plenipotentiaries what conditions they could get regarding their German demands.

74. Plenipotentiaries to Mazarin, 17 June 1645, *APW II B 2*, 138; Louis XIV to plenipotentiaries, 1 July 1645, 155.

75. Immler, *Kurfürst Maximilian I.*, 105; Kraus, *Die Acta Pacis Westphalicae*, 20–23; Overmann, 437–38.

76. See also Wolfgang Hans Stein, "Das französische Elsaßbild im Dreißigjährigen Krieg," *Jahrbuch für westdeutsche Landeskunde* 5 (1979): 147.

77. Plenipotentiaries to Mazarin, 17 June 1645, *APW II B 2*, 138; plenipotentiaries to Brienne, 22 July 1645, 172; d'Avaux to Mazarin, 27 August 1645, 196 (in which d'Avaux speaks of the "Landgraviate of Alsace" a week after the French have detailed their demands to Bavaria in considerable precision). It might also be noted that the Bavarians used the term "Elsaß," even though they also clearly knew the complexities of the legal situation; KGR, v. 198, fasc.6, fols. 178r–79r, 5 August and Karl Jacob, *Die Erwerbung des Elsaß durch Frankreich im Westfälischen Frieden* (Strasbourg, 1897), 60–61. Kraus (*Die Acta Pacis Westphalicae*, 23) claims, in this context, that the 17 June letter of the plenipotentiaries to Mazarin was not known to Overmann. However, Overmann clearly deals with the letter in detail, including quoting from it at length; he merely uses a version misdated to 20 June (see *APW II B 2*, p. 433 for the dating problem). Where Overmann errs is in saying that the plenipotentiaries announced their demands to the mediators; in fact, they were merely asked by the mediators to elaborate their terms, and raise these as propositions for Mazarin to consider. Overmann, 436. See also plenipotentiaries to Brienne, 9 September 1645, *APW II B 2*, 210, p. 669, in which Contarini's ambiguous use of the expression "Flanders" caused the French some confusion.

78. Memorandum from Servien, 31 December 1644, *APW II B 1*, 345, pp. 832, 834; he did the same thing in a memorandum from 16 December 1644, *APW II B 1*, 329, p. 777.

79. Memorandum from Servien, 15 April 1645, *APW II B 2*, 84, pp. 275–76.
80. For a similar error on the part of the court, see Louis XIV to plenipotentiaries, 23 September 1645, *APW II B 2*, 219, pp. 701–2, where Philippsburg is mentioned, but not Breisach.
81. Plenipotentiaries to Mazarin, 17 June 1645, *APW II B 2*, 138; Louis XIV to plenipotentiaries, 1 July 1645, 155; plenipotentiaries to Brienne, 22 July 1645, 172. This demonstrates that, contrary to Dickmann's and Kraus's opinion, the policy of annexing Alsace was by no means a hard line taken by Servien while the court remained uncertain. Dickmann, *Der Westfälische Frieden*, 232–33; Kraus, "Die *Acta Pacis Westphalicae*," 20.
82. Louis XIV to plenipotentiaries, 4 January 1645, *APW II B 2*, 3; plenipotentiaries to Mazarin, 14 January 1645, 13. The plenipotentiaries' letter of 14 January (#13) actually crossed in the mail with the royal memo of 4 January(#3), which makes the plenipotentiaries' letter all the more striking, since it directly answered a point raised in the royal memo of which they could not have known.
83. Plenipotentiaries to Brienne, 15 July 1645, *APW II B 2*, 167; Longueville to Mazarin, 22 July 1645, 173; plenipotentiaries to Brienne, 12 August 1645, 185; and Longueville to Mazarin, 26 August 1645, 195; Dickmann, *Der Westfälische Frieden*, 233–35.
84. See, e.g., Brienne to Servien, 31 May 1645, *APW II B 2*, 116; Brienne to plenipotentiaries, 12 August 1645, 183. That the French viewed the battle as small, see plenipotentiaries to De La Haye, et al., 18 May, CP All v. 25, fols. 484r–85v.
85. Vervaux to Kurz, 15 April 1645, Kasten Schwarz (hereafter KS) 7981, n.p.
86. Memorandum from Servien, 15 April 1645, *APW II B 2*, 84, p. 284.
87. For a discussion of the Beratungsmodus debate, see Immler, Ruppert, and Dickmann, *Der Westfälische Frieden*, 186–89, as well as Le Clerc, v. 1, 380–89.
88. Mazarin to Turenne, 28 June 1645, *Lettres*, v. 2, 194 (cited in Heyner, 61).
89. On the orders to Enghien: Louis XIV to de Beauvais-Plesian, 15 May 1645, BN Mf v. 4171, fols. 278r–83v; Louis XIV to Enghien, 21 May 1645, BN Mf v. 4171, fols. 325r–36r; Mazarin to Enghien, 6 June, 7 June, and 11 July 1645, *Lettres*, v. 2, 73, 74, 79. Other defense measures: Louis XIV to Marsin, 14 May 1645, BN Mf v. 4171, fols. 283r–84v; Louis XIV to Turenne, 14 May 1645, 286r–286v; Louis XIV to Vautorte, 20 May 1645, 301v–7v; Louis XIV to Turenne, 21 May 1645, 307v; Louis XIV to d'Erlach, 25 May 1645, 336v–38. On the siege of La Mothe, see Braun, 141–42.
90. Beauregard-Mazarin, 5 June 1645, CP All v. 47, fols. 34r–34v, on the post-Herbsthausen situation and plans. On joining with Königsmarck: plenipotentiaries-Beauregard, 2 June 1645, CP All v. 47, fols. 6r–7r, stating that they want the Hessians and Königsmarck to go up to the Tauber with Turenne [rather more limited that their eventual demands]; plenipotentiaries-Beauregard, 18 May 1645, CP All v. 46, fols. 487r–487v, plenipotentiaries stating that Turenne needs the two Hessian brigades and will not do without them. Marsin-Mazarin, 11 June 1645, CP All v. 47, 76–76v, could not join with Turenne because Bellenave was not ready; he made a cavalcade into Germany, then returned to Speyer to await orders. News from (June 30 Speyer) in CP All v. 47, fols. 183r–84v, and July 2 (Frankfurt), 195r–195v.
91. Tracy-Mazarin, 4 July 1645, CP All v. 47, fols. 211r–12v: Geyso and Königsmarck agreed to stay with the whole force and march right at the enemy to force a battle. They all moved out on 6 July just before daylight. The best source for the allied plans is Enghien's undated memo in CP All v. 48, fols.

8r–20r. For the campaign up to Alerheim, see Heilmann, *Feldzüge*, 219–32; Aumale, 415–22; Barthold, 512–20; Turenne, *Mémoires*, 51–60.

92. Apparently Turenne had been upset with the town for attacking French stragglers after the battle of Herbsthausen; Barthold, 515; Heilmann, *Feldzüge*, 223.

93. Brienne noted that "we are so concerned lest the confederated armies separate, we want so much to prevent this, at least for a time, that we have given orders to Monsieur de Turenne to prevent it, forgetting nothing that he could do or offer that could deter Königsmarck." Brienne to plenipotentiaries, 8 July 1645, Le Clerc, v. 2, 88–89.

94. Mazarin to Enghien, 11 July 1645, *Lettres*, v. 2, 79.

95. For an excellent account of the battle, including a reprinting of most contemporary accounts, see Scheible, *op. cit.* Also Périni, 75–84.

96. Plenipotentiaries to Brienne, 29 July 1645, *APW II B 2*, 176; Jacob, 61–63; KGR, v. 198, fasc.6, fols. 176r–76v, 2 August, and 178–79, 5 August. It is not clear whether the Bavarian plenipotentiaries actually rejected d'Avaux's demands, or whether they were merely voicing their concerns to Maximilian. Maximilian himself could not tell, but made it clear in his letter that, if they had spoken to d'Avaux in the same terms that they wrote to him, they had gone too far. This is a point missed by Kraus ("Kurfürst Maximilian," 34–36), who, in his alacrity to show that Bavaria had not reached a secret reciprocal agreement with France, implies that the Bavarians did reject d'Avaux's demands. While there was certainly no fixed agreement, the general tenor of all the talks between the two sides was in this direction, as was consistently reinforced by Maximilian over the course of July and August.

97. Immler, *Kurfürst Maximilian I.*, 116, however, argues that the Alsace offer was not made because of the battle; see also Dickmann, *Der Westfälische Frieden*, 238.

98. Antoine III, comte de Gramont and Guiche, later duc de Gramont. Created marshal in 1641, he commanded French armies in Flanders, Champagne, Luxembourg, and Catalonia. His own extensive memoirs are an important source for the war. *Dictionnaire des maréchaux*, 204–5.

99. Anne to plenipotentiaries, 31 August 1645, *APW II B 2*, 200; Gramont to court, undated, *APW II B 2*, 200, pp. 643–44; Immler, *Kurfürst Maximilian I.*, 118–19.

100. Maximilian to plenipotentiaries, 9 August, KAA v. 3051, fols. 63r–68v (the full quotation runs, "so Ihr gleichfahls bey euch in geheimb zuhalten Unnd euch dessen allein selbsten vor euch pro re rata, wan andere Vermeinen, Unnd Vorgeben wolten, die sachen heroben in Reich stehen in Viel besseren terminis alß Sy de facto seindt zu bedrinen [?] wissent"); KGR, v. 198, fasc.6, fols. 178r–79r; Immler, *Kurfürst Maximilian I.*, 115–20. Interestingly, even the Bavarian *Landschaftsverordnung* (a representative institution) wrote to Maximilian after Alerheim urging him to conclude a separate truce with France. Though Maximilian rejected their interference in his policies, he could not but have been affected by their plea.

101. Jacob, 64; memorandum from the plenipotentiaries, 28 August 1645, *APW II B 2*, 198, pp. 630–33.

102. Ibid.

103. Possibly the French had phrased their demands ambiguously on purpose; see George H. Quester, "Wars Prolonged by Misunderstood Signals,"

Annals of the American Academy of Political and Social Science 392 (November 1970): 34–36, on the advantage of this.

104. Memorandum from the plenipotentiaries, 28 August 1645, *APW II B 2*, 198, p. 633. On the French understanding of Alsace, see Jacob, 64–68 and 170–71; Overmann, 439–42; Dickmann, *Der Westfälische Frieden*, 238–39 and 552 (where he discusses the important memo of Godefroy); Repgen, "Über den Zusammenhang," 70; Stein, "Das französische Elsaßbild," 131–56 (and especially 146–47 for the August, 1645 talks with Bavaria); and Rosenhane to Oxenstierna, 29 November 1644, *APW II C 1*, 251, *APW II B 2*, p. 397, footnote 1, and Brienne to Servien, 10 June 1645, *APW II B 2*, 124, p. 412 on Godefroy's presence. (Dickmann correctly notes this on p. 552, but then on p. 284 says that Godefroy had only been in Münster since the beginning of 1646. The date of Godefroy's arrival is given by Malettke, 206, as 24 November, 1644, and by Babel, 14, as September, 1644. Based on Rosenhan's letter of 29 November, above, the former date seems accurate.) See also d'Avaux to Mazarin, 6 April 1646, *APW II B 3*, 199, and 7 April 1646, 208; Longueville to Mazarin, 7 April 1646, 207; Mazarin to Longueville, 14 April 1646, 215, etc., for the later French understanding of the Breisgau and Sundgau. The French did get information from Paris before Vautorte's report arrived, but it was not sent until 19 August, and hence could not have arrived in time for the discussions of 20, 22, and 23 August with Bavaria; Mazarin to Longueville, 19 August 1645, *APW II B 2*, 191, p. 604. Though I am sympathetic to those who argue that the French did not have a very good understanding of Alsace at this time, I think Overmann errs when he says that, in his letter of 27 August, d'Avaux claimed that Upper and Lower Alsace was composed of four fiefs of the Empire, with as many seats in the Diet. It seems more likely, in the context of the entire letter, that d'Avaux was referring to East and West Pomerania along with Upper and Lower Alsace. Overmann, 439, footnote 1.

105. Kraus, *Die Acta Pacis Westphalicae*, 25 (I am reading "August" for "April," which is clearly a mistake), and *Kurfürst Maximilian I.*, 41.

106. Brienne to plenipotentiaries, 9 September 1645, *APW II B 2*, 206, p. 660.

107. Mazarin to Longueville, 19 August 1645, *APW II B 2*, 191; Longueville to Mazarin, 26 August 1645, 195; d'Avaux to Mazarin, 27 August 1645, 196; plenipotentiaries to Brienne, 28 August 1645, 197; Louis XIV to plenipotentiaries, 1 September 1645, 201.

108. Mazarin to Longueville, 12 August 1645, *APW II B 2*, 184. Mazarin probably got this idea from Vervaux; see Schweinesbein, 192–95.

109. Mazarin to Longueville, 9 September 1645, *APW II B 2*, 209, and 16 September 1645, 214; French irritation over Kötzschenbroda, Brienne to plenipotentiaries, 23 September 1645, *APW II B 2*, 218; royal memo stating that Maximilian must get over the "repugnance" he has for Swedish satisfaction, Louis XIV to plenipotentiaries, 23 September 1645, *APW II B 2*, 219.

110. Kraus's statement that "it was doubtless France who stalled the negotiations" is completely untenable. Kraus, *Die Acta Pacis Westphalicae*, 26. Immler, *Kurfürst Maximilian I.*, 83, 212, 488.

111. Plenipotentiaries to Mazarin, 29 August 1645, *APW II B 2*, 199; Louis XIV to plenipotentiaries, 23 September 1645, 219; plenipotentiaries to Brienne, 23 September 1645, 221; Steiner, 162, on the Swedish view of the Palatinate question in 1645.

112. Memorandum from the plenipotentiaries, 28 August 1645, *APW II B 2*, 198; Servien to Lionne, 2 September 1645, 205; Mazarin to Longueville, 9 September 1645, 209.

113. Mazarin to Longueville, 12 August 1645, *APW II B 2*, 184; ibid., 19 August 1645, 191; Longueville to Mazarin, 2 September 1645, 204; plenipotentiaries to Anne, 16 September 1645, 216; Louis XIV to plenipotentiaries, 23 September 1645, 219.

114. Louis XIV to plenipotentiaries, 23 September 1645, *APW II B 2*, 219, pp. 698–99.

115. Brienne to plenipotentiaries, 4 November 1645, *APW II B 2*, 249, p. 805; Longueville to Mazarin, 16 November 1645, 261, pp. 844–45.

116. Mazarin's initial terms, Louis XIV to plenipotentiaries, 1 September 1645, *APW II B 2*, 201; plenipotentiaries' memo to Mazarin, 29 August 1645, *APW II B 2*, 199; Bavarian rejections: memorandum of plenipotentiaries, 28 August 1645, *APW II B 2*, 198, and plenipotentiaries to Anne, 16 September 1645, 216; substitutions permitted: Louis XIV to plenipotentiaries, 23 September 1645, *APW II B 2*, 219, p. 702; two of three acceptable: *APW II B 2*, Louis XIV to plenipotentiaries, 14 October 1645, 237; plenipotentiaries insist on security, plenipotentiaries to Brienne, 18 November 1645, *APW II B 2*, 264, pp. 854–55.

117. Accepting divided quarters, plenipotentiaries to Mazarin, 29 August 1645, *APW II B 2*, 199; negotiations preferred to combat, Louis XIV to plenipotentiaries, 1 September 1645, *APW II B 2*, 201; changing attitude after Enghien's illness, Brienne to plenipotentiaries, Louis XIV to plenipotentiaries, and Mazarin to Longueville, 23 September 1645, *APW II B 2*, 218, 219, and 220.

118. Heilmann, *Kriegsgeschichte*, 695–96; *Feldzüge*, 290. The exact fate of the garrison is uncertain; Turenne wrote that it was sent to the Bavarian army, Enghien that it joined the French. Turenne, 69 and footnote 3.

119. Lahrkamp, *Jan von Werth*, 159–60; on Maximilian's questioning of von Werth's ability, Maier, 561 (footnote 160); Gramont, *Mémoires*, 263. For a negative assessment of von Werth's role at Alerheim, see Napoleon, 140–43. Lahrkamp points out that von Werth was "irreplaceable" as head of the cavalry; perhaps, but it seems clear that Maximilian's greater concern was over von Werth's abilities. In the immediate aftermath of the battle, one of his councillors proposed alternating von Werth and Ruischenberg; had von Werth truly been so important as head of the cavalry, it seems unlikely that this would have been suggested.

120. Immler, *Kurfürst Maximilian I.*, 116–17, 129.

121. Turenne, 69–70; Heilmann, *Feldzüge*, 290–305; Mazarin to Longueville, 23 September 1645, *APW II B 2*, 220; Champlastreux-Mazarin, 3 September [September falsely dated to August] 1645, CP All v. 48, fols. 29r–30v.

122. AG v. 94, fols. 103v–5v, 105v–10v; Turenne, 70.

123. Heilmann, *Feldzüge*, 692, footnote. His response to Turenne (Mazarin to Turenne, 18 August 1645, *Lettres*, v. 2, 86), while considerably more optimistic, is also laced with regret over the losses.

124. Le Tellier-Enghien, 19 August 1645, AG v. 94, fols. 105v–10v; Turenne-plenipotentiaries, 16 August 1645, CP All v. 48, fols. 87–r87v; Champlastreux-Mazarin, 3 September 1645, fols. 29r–30v; Millet-Mazarin, 9 September 1645, fols. 230r–31r; Millet-Mazarin, 19 September 1645, fols. 276r–77r.

125. Tracy to Mazarin, 14 September 1645, CP All v. 48, fols. 247r–247v; Turenne to Mazarin, 15 September 1645, fols. 249r–51r.

126. Ibid.; Heilmann, *Kriegsgeschichte*, 697. It is possible to read in many histories of the campaign that the French captured Heilbronn; thus Jules Roy, *Turenne* (Paris, 1896), 110, and even Bérenger's recent biography, *Turenne* (p. 221). The origin of this error seems to be the account of Roger de Rabutin (*Mémoires*

de Roger de Rabutin, Comte de Bussy, v. 1 (Paris, 1857), 109), in which he records that Heilbronn surrendered on 14 September. This source would probably have gone largely forgotten had not Paul Marichal made use of it, claiming, in a footnote to his popular edition of Turenne's memoirs, that Turenne had "forgotten" to mention the fall of Heilbronn (Turenne, *Mémoires*, 70). Bussy-Rabutin's memoirs, which give a day-by-day account, seem to have been based on a diary of some sort, and are otherwise accurate, so it is difficult to understand why he would have gotten it wrong; he even writes of celebrating in Heilbronn. Yet Turenne's memoirs, his letter of 15 September, and Mazarin's response (Mazarin to Turenne, 2 October 1645, *Lettres*, 95: "I am disappointed that the project of the siege of Heilbronn could not be executed as we desired . . . we would have bought the conquest of this fortress too dearly, because, after having conquered it, it would not have been possible for us to hold it"), not to mention Lotichium (693) and other pieces of evidence, leave little doubt that the town was not taken.

127. Turenne to Mazarin, 16 August 1645, CP All v. 48, fols. 87r–87v; Turenne to Mazarin, 15 September 1645, fols. 249r–51r; Peter Broucek, *Der Schwedenfeldzug nach Niederösterreich, 1645/46*, Militärhistorische Schriftenreihe v. 7 (Vienna, 1967), 19–22; Ruppert, 124–26.

128. Heilmann, *Feldzüge*, 308–9; Turenne, 72–76; Gramont-Mazarin, 16 October 1645, CP All v. 48, fol. 476r; Turenne-Mazarin, 23 October 1645, fols. 525r–525v; Bussy-Rabutin, 112–13; Aumale, 453; Napoleon, 140–43.

129. Bavarian resistance: plenipotentiaries to Brienne, 3 October 1645, *APW II B 2*, 229; French realization of Bavarian stalling: plenipotentiaries to Brienne, 8 October 1645, *APW II B 2*, 234; Maximilian's special envoy: Servien and d'Avaux to Longueville, 10 October 1645, *APW II B 2*, 235, plenipotentiaries to Brienne, 14 October 1645, 239, and plenipotentiaries to Brienne, 21 October 1645, 242; Servien criticizing Maximilian: Servien to Lionne, 21 October 1645, *APW II B 2*, 244, p. 778; Mazarin's excusing him: Mazarin to Longueville, 4 November 1645, *APW II B 2*, 250, pp. 807–9; plenipotentiaries' refusal to give in: 239 (as above).

130. For the Swedish reaction, see Oxenstierna and Salvius to Christina, 16 October 1645, *APW II C 1*, 405, pp. 786–88.

131. Complaint that Bavaria had lost interest: plenipotentiaries to Brienne, 21 October 1645, *APW II B 2*, 242; Bavaria demands guarantee of the Electorate: plenipotentiaries to Brienne, 4 November 1645, *APW II B 2*, 251; plenipotentiaries rebuked: Brienne to plenipotentiaries, 11 November 1645, *APW II B 2*, 256.

132. Mazarin to Longueville, 28 October 1645, *APW II B 2*, 246.

133. For Maximilian's side of the negotiations, see Immler, *Kurfürst Maximilian I.*, 126–36.

134. Louis XIV to plenipotentiaries, 1 September 1645, *APW II B 2*, 201, p. 645; Kraus, "Kurfürst Maximilian," 42–43, 49 ("das außerordentliche französische Werben um Bayern"); Immler, *Kurfürst Maximilian I.*, 121–22.

135. On France's frustration with Bavaria's changeability, Longueville to Mazarin, 2 September 1645, *APW II B 2*, 204, etc. (see above, footnote 113). For a further discussion of this issue, see chapter 9.

136. See Ruppert, 126–38, especially 126–31; Immler, *Kurfürst Maximilian I.*, 185–96. French attribute Trauttmansdorff's sending to Maximilian: Servien to Lionne, 21 October 1645, *APW II B 2*, 244, and Mazarin to Longueville, 28 October 1645, 246; view this as a positive effect in spite of the failed negotiations: plenipotentiaries to Brienne, 11 November 1645, *APW II B 2*, 258, and ibid., 18 November 1645, 264.

137. See Chéruel, *Histoire de France*, v. 2, 74–106; Hanley, 315–19. On the background of the financial situation, see Richard Bonney, *The King's Debts* (Oxford, 1981), 195–99.

138. The latter quotation is from Brienne to Longueville, 9 September 1645, *APW II B 2*, 207. Interestingly, however, Brienne concludes that the war will probably be ended by a truce rather than a peace; this contrasts with Mazarin's opinion, though Brienne, too, preferred a peace. Servien to Lionne, 5 August 1645, *APW II B 2*, 182; plenipotentiaries to Brienne, 12 August 1645, 185, pp. 588–89; Mazarin to Longueville, 19 August 1645, 191, p. 603.

139. Mazarin to Longueville, 9 September 1645, *APW II B 2*, 208.

140. Brienne to plenipotentiaries, 1 July 1645, *APW II B 2*, 154; Mazarin to Longueville, 22 July 1645, 170.

141. Plenipotentiaries to Brienne, 22 July 1645, *APW II B 2*, 172; Brienne to plenipotentiaries, 5 August 1645, 178.

142. Plenipotentiaries to Brienne, 12 August 1645, *APW II B 2*, 185, p. 589.

143. Servien to Lionne, 6 February 1645, *APW II B 2*, 36; Mazarin to Longueville, 26 August 1645, 194; Longueville to Mazarin, 9 September 1645, 211, and 7 October 1645, 233.

144. On Contarini, plenipotentiaries to Brienne, 21 October 1645, *APW II B 2*, 242; see also Mazarin to Longueville, 28 October 1645, 246, p. 788 on Venetian pressure; Mazarin on equilibrium: Mazarin to Longueville, 19 August 1645, *APW II B 2*, 191.

145. Servien, for example, wrote a letter on 11 November asking for a clarification on whether they could conclude with the emperor without Spain; similarly, Longueville noted that Contarini was pro-Spanish and hence opposed to any peace that would exclude Spain. Servien to Lionne, 11 November 1645, *APW II B 2*, 260, pp. 839–41; Longueville to Mazarin, 16 November 1645, 261, p. 847. Mazarin wrote on 22 July that Spain was ready to make peace at any price (Mazarin to Longueville, 22 July 1645, *APW II B 2*, 170); his latter comment is from a letter to the plenipotentiaries, 22 November 1645, *APW II B 2*, 266, pp. 866–67.

146. Mazarin to Longueville, 12 August 1645, *APW II B 2*, 184.

147. Immler, *Kurfürst Maximilian I.*, 133–34

148. Louis XIV to plenipotentiaries, 14 October 1645, *APW II B 2*, 237, p. 753; plenipotentiaries to Brienne, 28 October 1645, 247, pp. 979–78; ibid., 18 November 1645, 264, pp. 856–57; Mazarin to Longueville, 21 November 1645, 265, p. 860.

149. Plenipotentiaries to Brienne, 9 September 1645, *APW II B 2*, 210, pp. 670–71.

150. Brienne to plenipotentiaries, 23 September 1645, 218, pp. 695–96; ibid., 28 October 1645, 245, p. 783; 258, p. 834 and the footnote; Ruppert, 119–21. Le Clerc, v. 1, 276–77: This unattributed memorandum, dated to 1644, denies the possibility that Transylvania would make peace without Sweden. The Imperial treaties with Transylvania are recorded in Le Clerc, v. 1, 389–99.

151. Servien to Lionne, 5 August 1645, *APW II B 2*, 182, p. 572; Mazarin to Longueville, 26 August 1645, *APW II B 2*, 194.

152. On the Dutch arrival at the Congress, see Israel, *Dutch Republic*, 360. Rumors of Spanish-Dutch truce talks in Münster, plenipotentiaries to Brienne, 23 September 1645, *APW II B 2*, 221, and in Paris, Louis XIV to plenipotentiaries, 30 September 1645, 226, pp. 720–21. Rejection of Low Countries acquisition, Louis XIV to plenipotentiaries, 30 September 1645, *APW II B 2*, 227. Servien's

diatribe, Servien to Lionne, 21 October 1645, *APW II B 2*, 244, p. 779. Mazarin remains upbeat, Mazarin to Longueville, 20 October 1645, *APW II B 2*, 240.

153. Peak in relations with Sweden: Longueville to Mazarin, 12 August 1645, *APW II B 2*, 187. Concern over Kötzschenbroda: Longueville to Mazarin, 16 September 1645, *APW II B 2*, 217; Louis XIV to plenipotentiaries, 23 September 1645, 219, pp. 698–99; Servien to Lionne, 23 September 1645, 223, pp. 710–11.

154. Louis XIV to plenipotentiaries, 30 September 1645, *APW II B 2*, 226, p. 718; ibid., 7 October 1645, 231; plenipotentiaries to Brienne, 3 October 1645, 229. Another source of friction between France and Sweden at this time was the demand of de La Barde for the title of ambassador; Rosenhane to Oxenstierna and Salvius, 16 October 1645, *APW II C 1*, 406, and 24 October 1645, 417.

155. This was in addition to the regular French ambassador, Pierre Chanut, who had already been sent to Stockholm as the French ambassador on the week of 9 September; Brienne to plenipotentiaries, 9 September 1645, *APW II B 2*, 206. Complaints of Swedish inaction: Louis XIV to plenipotentiaries, 30 September 1645, *APW II B 2*, 226, and 21 October 1645, 241; rejected rumors: Louis XIV to plenipotentiaries, 21 October 1645, *APW II B 2*, 241, and plenipotentiaries to Brienne, 4 November 1645, 251; Rosenhan's talk: Mazarin to plenipotentiaries, 22 November 1645, *APW II B 2*, 266.

156. See Oxenstierna to Rosenhane, 21 September 1645, *APW II C 1*, 391; Rosenhane to Oxenstierna and Salvius, 17 October 1645, 406; and Rosenhane to Oxenstierna and Salvius, 10 November 1645, 430.

157. Mazarin to Longueville, 16 September 1645, *APW II B 2*, 214, pp. 687–88; Louis XIV to plenipotentiaries, 30 September 1645, 226, pp. 717–18.

158. That France wanted peace to turn against the Ottomans: Brienne to plenipotentiaries, 9 September 1645, *APW II B 2*, 206, and in the supplementary instructions of 23 November 1645 (267, pp. 887–88), it is listed as one of four reasons for France's desire for peace (see below). Servien's letters on the usefulness of the Turkish War (both against Spain, and to keep the Italian princes occupied): Servien to Lionne, 23 September 1645, *APW II B 2*, 223, and 11 November 1645, 260; the quotation is from Servien to Lionne, 8 November 1645, 255; Mazarin promises to be more accommodating: Louis XIV to plenipotentiaries, 30 September 1645, *APW II B 2*, 226; offering Spain the Turkish excuse: Mazarin to Longueville, 5 August 1645, *APW II B 2*, 179.

159. Brienne to plenipotentiaries, 13 May 1645, *APW II B 2*, 99, and Louis XIV to plenipotentiaries, 13 May 1645, 100, p. 324 argue that the emperor released Sötern because France was about to take the town; Brienne to Servien, 31 May 1645, 116, p. 398, notes that France might end the campaign by taking Trier, while Mazarin noted on 20 October (Mazarin to Longueville, *APW II B 2*, 240) that he had long been thinking of attacking the town that year. French suspicion of Sötern is evident throughout the year, notably in a memorandum from Servien, 27 May 1645, *APW II B 2*, 112, pp. 377–78; plenipotentiaries to Brienne, 8 July 1645, 160; plenipotentiaries to Mazarin, 8 July 1645, 161; Brienne to plenipotentiaries, 22 July 1645, 169; and plenipotentiaries to Brienne, 16 September 1645, 215. It seems to have been shared more or less equally between the plenipotentiaries and the court, though the plenipotentiaries were the ones to initiate the complaining. For a general discussion of the release of Sötern and the subsequent capture of Trier by the French, as well as the history of French relations with Sötern up to 1645, see Karlies Abmeier, *Der Trierer Kurfürst Philipp Christoph von Sötern und der Westfälische Friede*, Schriftenreihe der Vereinigung

zur Erforschung der Neueren Geschichte, v. 15 (Münster, 1986), 4–17 and 24–41. For a copy of the Imperial treaty with Sötern, see Le Clerc, v. 1, 343–44.

160. Longueville first pointed out the advantages of attacking Trier in the absence of quarters across the Rhine on 7 October (Longueville to Mazarin, 7 October 1645, *APW II B 2*, 233), and the plenipotentiaries' letter of the next day claimed that Sötern preferred a French garrison to the ravenous troops of Charles IV of Lorraine, who were considering quartering on the archbishopric again. Longueville reported the garrison to be only 400 on 4 November (Longueville to Mazarin, 4 November 1645, *APW II B 2*, 252; Abmeier, 30, reports its actual size as 250). Brienne noted on 11 November that the comments of the plenipotentiaries had helped the court decide to attack the town, though in that and his letter of 18 November, as well as Mazarin's letter of 20 October, it is clear that the court is most interested in gaining quarters—which they ultimately did not (Brienne to plenipotentiaries, 11 November 1645, *APW II B 2*, 256, p. 831; ibid., 18 November 1645, 263; and Mazarin to Longueville, 20 October 1645, 240). In his memoirs, Turenne says that the town surrendered on the second day the trenches were open; Abmeier, however, indicates that the garrison commander tried to hand over the keys as soon as Turenne approached. Turenne, 77. The question of French units quartering in Trier's territory is problematic. Though Abmeier (p. 34) implies that there was absolutely none of it, as regulated by the treaty of 29 November, Mazarin continued to suggest the lodging of two regiments along the Moselle, for which Sötern was to receive twenty thousand Reichstalers in compensation, as late as 8 and 9 December; Mazarin to Turenne, 5 December 1645, *Lettres*, 108, and Mazarin to Turenne, 9 December 1645, BM, v. 2215, fols. 210v–11r.

161. Servien to Lionne, 11 November 1645, *APW II B 2*, 260, pp. 839–41.

162. St. Romain to plenipotentiaries, 28 September 1645, *APW II B 2*, 224.

163. Dickmann, *Der Westfälische Frieden*, 241–43; Ruppert, 102–119.

164. Addition to main instructions, 23 November 1645, *APW II B 2*, 267.

165. See above on Bavarian influence on the emperor and the sending of Trauttmansdorff.

166. Mazarin to plenipotentiaries, 22 November 1645, *APW II B 2*, 266, pp. 866–67; Servien to Lionne, 16/21 December 1645, *APW II B 3*, 30, pp. 83–84.

167. Zeller, *De Christophe Colomb à Cromwell*, 259, speaks of "vertigo" in Mazarin's policies.

Chapter 8. 1646: Triumph and Continued War

1. CP All. 63, fols. 107r–11r. (I am using a transcript from the Vereinigung zur Erforschung der Neueren Geschichte in this case).

2. See, for example, the letter of the plenipotentiaries in plenipotentiaries to Louis XIV, 22 December 1645, *APW II B 3*, 31, p. 89; on the following discussion, cp. Dickmann, *Der Westfälische Frieden*, 265–66.

3. D'Avaux to Mazarin, 25 November 1645, *APW II B 3*, 5; Mazarin to plenipotentiaries, 16 December 1645, 25, p. 66; Mazarin to Longueville, 30 December 1645, 43, p. 131.

4. Servien to Lionne, 16/21 December 1645, *APW II B 3*, 30, p. 85.

5. A point that was, much later, approved by the plenipotentiaries: plenipotentiaries to Louis XIV, 7 May 1646, *APW II B 3*, 258.

6. Louis XIV to plenipotentiaries, 6 January 1646, *APW II B 3*, 50, p. 149; 52; Louis XIV to plenipotentiaries, 6 January 1646, Le Clerc, v. 3, and Mazarin to plenipotentiaries, 3 February 1646, 48. Actually, according to Lionne (Lionne to Servien, 6 January 1646, *APW II B 3*, 53), Mazarin had not yet read Servien's memo of 16–21 December. Possibly, then, he was anticipating that the Habsburgs would demand payment.

7. Plenipotentiaries to Brienne, 17 February 1646, Le Clerc, v. 3, 65–66.

8. Servien to Lionne, 14 April 1646, *APW II B 3*, 221; ibid., 14/19 April 1646, 228. These letters make all the more puzzling Immler's claim that Servien was opposed to paying the indemnity; Immler, *Kurfürst Maximilian I.*, 250.

9. Longueville to Mazarin, 18 April 1646, *APW II B 3*, 223; d'Avaux to Mazarin, 7 May 1646, 261. Longueville, like Servien, preferred an annual payment, since he believed that a lump sum would be too high; Longueville to Mazarin, 20 January 1646, *APW II B 3*, 79. Interestingly, Andreas Osiander, 68, has recently denigrated the French accomplishment in gaining Alsace by asserting firmly that they *bought* Alsace from the Imperials. Considered from one angle, this is an accurate assessment. However, approaching it from the point of view of the plenipotentiaries leads one to the conclusion that France conquered Alsace and voluntarily paid an indemnity in order to win greater legitimacy for it; after all, this was why they argued for the indemnity, and it seems very likely that they could have avoided paying it had they wished. This also undermines Osiander's claim that France was less concerned with consensus notions than other states (see conclusion, footnote 76); to the contrary, France was much more concerned with gaining legitimacy for Alsace than the Swedes were for Pomerania.

10. Mazarin to d'Avaux, 19 May 1646, *APW II B 3*, 274. The court, however, preferred to pay a lump sum, since France was not always able to pay its debts, and failure to make a payment would be an excuse for the Habsburgs to demand the return of Alsace. Lionne to Servien, 26 April 1646, *APW II B 3*, 246.

11. D'Avaux to Mazarin, 10 March 1646, *APW II B 3*, 165, p. 452.

12. The debate on the Ottoman threat was particularly sharp late in 1645; see also chapter 7. Mazarin repeatedly emphasized the value of sending soldiers instead of money, e.g., Louis XIV to plenipotentiaries, 9 December 1645, *APW II B 3*, 17, p. 46; Mazarin to plenipotentiaries, 3 March 1646, 139, p. 392; Mazarin to Longueville, 14 April 1646, 215. Servien also supported this policy (Servien to Lionne, 14/19 April 1646, *APW II B 3*, 228). The plenipotentiaries turned aside the mediators' 8 April request to provide money, saying they would have to write to court for permission; it was in this context that the court ordered them to remain firm on sending troops (plenipotentiaries to Brienne, 8 April 1646, *APW II B 3*, 210, and Louis XIV to plenipotentiaries, 21 April 1646, 232).

13. Longueville to Mazarin, 21 December 1645, *APW II B 3*, 28, p. 72; d'Avaux to Mazarin, 6 April 1646, 199; Brienne to plenipotentiaries, 3 February 1646, Le Clerc, v. 3, 48; plenipotentiaries to Brienne, 17 February 1646, Le Clerc, 65; plenipotentiaries to Mazarin, undated [a response to his letter of 3 February 1646], Le Clerc, 70–71; plenipotentiaries to Brienne, 10 March 1646, Le Clerc, 115–16; Dickmann, *Der Westfälische Frieden*, 265–66.

14. Servien to Lionne, 16/21 December 1645, *APW II B 3*, 30, pp. 83–84.

15. On the voting, see Dickmann, *Der Westfälische Frieden*, 257–59.

16. Plenipotentiaries to Brienne, 17 February 1646, Le Clerc, v. 3, 65, and plenipotentiaries to Mazarin, undated (see above, footnote 13), 70–71.

17. Brienne to plenipotentiaries, 17 March 1646, Le Clerc, v. 3, 126, and 7 April 1646, 144–46. For background on the French dispute with Strasbourg, see Stein, *Protection Royale*, 422–30 and 477–84.

18. Servien to Lionne, 11 November 1645, *APW II B 2*, 260, p. 840.
19. Livet, *L'intendance d'Alsace*, 109–10 and 120–22; Stein, *Protection Royale*, 518–19.
20. Reuss, *L'Alsace au Dix-Septième Siècle*, v. 1, 141–55 (quotation from p. 147).
21. Servien to Lionne, 31 January 1646, *APW II B 3*, 91, p. 234.
22. Brienne to plenipotentiaries, 3 February 1646, Le Clerc, v. 3, 48; Brienne to plenipotentiaries, 8 March 1646, *APW II B 3*, 152, p. 428 (quotation). Curiously, there was an intendant of Alsace, the Sieur de Baussan, but he was not asked; Livet, *L'intendance d'Alsace*, 96–99.
23. Plenipotentiaries to Brienne, 24 March 1646, *APW II B 3*, 186, p. 502; Servien to Lionne, 24 March 1646, 189; Brienne to plenipotentiaries, 14 April 1646, 213.
24. See Ruppert, 175–78; Louis XIV to plenipotentiaries, 21 April 1646, *APW II B 3*, 232. Stein, "Das französische Elsaßbild," 150–53, is no doubt correct when he states that the plenipotentiaries had a general idea of the legal situation in Alsace, but their repeated requests for information well into the heart of the negotiations indicate that they felt all too insecure on specifics and probably that they did not trust the information that they did have—which is very reasonable, considering Brienne's comment on the unreliability of the 8 March memo.
25. Mazarin to plenipotentiaries, 12 January 1646, Le Clerc, v. 3, 11; see below for examples of French awareness of Imperial orders, and for occasional misinformation on the orders. On Mazarin's spy, see chapter 2. On the Bavarians revealing Imperial orders to France, see Immler, *Kurfürst Maximilian I.*, 239, 241, and 247–48. Immler, an apologist for Maximilian, goes to great lengths to minimize the Bavarian role in passing along information to France; however, even he is forced to admit that, if one cannot answer that they did so with a clear "yes," "one shrinks from offering a simple 'no' in its place."
26. Louis XIV to plenipotentiaries, 6 January 1646, Le Clerc, v. 3, 7; Louis XIV to plenipotentiaries, 6 January 1646, *APW II B 3*, 50, p. 149; Le Clerc, v. 3, 10–11.
27. Mazarin to d'Avaux, 24 March 1646, *APW II B 3*, 184, p. 497, and 14 April 1646, 216.
28. Servien to Lionne, 5 December 1645, *APW II B 3*, 15; ibid., 16/21 December 1645, 30, p. 86; Longueville to Mazarin, 16 December 1646, 26, p. 69.
29. D'Avaux to Mazarin, 25 November 1645, *APW II B 3*, 5; ibid., 7 April 1646, 208; Servien to Lionne, 20 April 1646, 230. It is difficult to know whether the uncanny accuracy of Longueville's prediction was due to insight or luck, but it is striking.
30. Besides the evidence from footnote 27, see Servien to Lionne, 8 April 1646, *APW II B 3*, 211.
31. Mazarin to plenipotentiaries, 16 December 1645, *APW II B 3*, 25, p. 66.
32. Louis XIV to plenipotentiaries, 23 December 1645, *APW II B 3*, 34, p. 110.
33. Mazarin to Longueville, 14 April 1646, *APW II B 3*, 215; Mazarin to plenipotentiaries, 31 May 1646, 297. Both of these examples, however, come from later in the year, after Mazarin had been chastened by the Dutch question; it is possible that he was entirely sincere in wanting to downplay the French military situation.
34. Mazarin to plenipotentiaries, 3 March 1646, *APW II B 3*, 139, pp. 395, 397; Mazarin to Longueville, 5 May 1646, 255.
35. Mazarin to plenipotentiaries, 24 March 1646, *APW II B 3*, 182, p. 494; Mazarin to plenipotentiaries, 2 June 1646, 299.

36. Plenipotentiaries to Mazarin, 30 December 1645, *APW II B 3*, 46, p. 139; Servien to Lionne, 24 March 1646, 189, p. 517; plenipotentiaries to Mazarin, 14 April 1646, 220, and Louis XIV to plenipotentiaries, 21 April 1646, 232 on effectiveness of military pressure on Bavaria; Mazarin to plenipotentiaries, 16 December 1645, 25, p. 66.

37. Brienne to plenipotentiaries, 9 December 1645, *APW II B 3*, 16, and Mazarin to plenipotentiaries, 24 March 1646, 182; Bavarian resistance, plenipotentiaries to Brienne, 17 March 1646, Le Clerc, v. 3, 120. Though the Bavarians opposed the French acquisition of Alsace in principle, however, Maximilian realized that it was the fastest way to make peace.

38. Mazarin to Longueville, 14 April 1646, *APW II B 3*, 215; Louis XIV to plenipotentiaries, 21 April 1646, *APW II B 3*, 232; also, Longueville's negative assessment of the prospects: Longueville to Mazarin, 18 April 1646, *APW II B 3*, 223.

39. Longueville to Mazarin, 21 December 1645, *APW II B 3*, 28, p. 76; Louis XIV to plenipotentiaries, 23 December 1645, 34, p. 108; Mazarin to Longueville, 23 December 1645, 35, p. 114; plenipotentiaries to Mazarin, 27 January 1646, 86.

40. Servien to Lionne, 16/21 December 1645, *APW II B 3*, 30, p. 84.

41. Longueville to Mazarin, 30 December 1645, *APW II B 3*, 47, pp. 140–41.

42. Immler's rejection of the notion (which he attributes to Karl Jacob, although it was current even in the 1640s) that Maximilian sacrificed Alsace to gain the Upper Palatinate seems a matter of semantics. If Maximilian requested no more than "general support of his satisfaction" ("eine allgemeine Förderung seiner Satisfaktion"), it is quite clear what his "satisfaction" was to entail. The fact of Bavarian-French mutual support in matters pertaining to their satisfaction cannot be disputed, even if one can quibble about the details. Immler, *Kurfürst Maximilian I.*, 239–40.

43. Servien to Lionne, 1/2 December 1645, *APW II B 3*, 14; Mazarin to plenipotentiaries, 16 December 1645, 25, p. 66; Brienne to plenipotentiaries, 3 February 1646, Le Clerc, v. 3, 48–49.

44. Plenipotentiaries to Brienne, 17 February 1646, Le Clerc, v. 3, 66; d'Avaux to Mazarin, 24 February 1646, *APW II B 3*, 134, p. 368; ibid., 10 March 1646, 165, pp. 451–52; plenipotentiaries to Brienne, 10 March 1646, 163, p. 445. Longueville's complaint about the Bavarian plenipotentiaries on 27 January was directed not at their lack of good will, but at their ineffectiveness in carrying it out; in any case, this view was soon lost in the favorable reports that followed (Longueville to Mazarin, 27 January 1646, *APW II B 3*, 87, p. 226).

45. Immler, *Kurfürst Maximilian I.*, 219–22; Ruppert, 147–52.

46. Dickmann, *Der Westfälische Frieden*, 26, 51, 260, 271–72.

47. Dickmann, *Der Westfälische Frieden*, 268; Ruppert, 153–54; Mazarin's quotation is in Mazarin to plenipotentiaries, 16 December 1645, *APW II B 3*, 25, p. 64, and the sentiments are reiterated in Mazarin to Longueville, 3 February 1646, 99, p. 259 and Mazarin to d'Avaux, 3 February 1646, 100, p. 262.

48. Mazarin to Longueville, 23 December 1645, *APW II B 3*, 35, p. 113.

49. Mazarin to plenipotentiaries, 13 January 1646, Le Clerc, v. 3, 14; plenipotentiaries to Mazarin, 20 January 1646, 27–29; and Mazarin to plenipotentiaries, 10 February 1646, 62.

50. Plenipotentiaries to Brienne, 14 January 1646, Le Clerc, v. 3, 16, 18; Israel, *Dutch Republic*, 360–62.

51. Poelhekke, 244–60. Apparently there was a certain amount of conspiracy on the part of Pauw and Knuyt, perhaps under the influence of Spanish bribes,

to dramatize the offers by making them known at the same time. For the French perspective, see Mazarin to Brasset, 31 March 1646, Mazarin, *Lettres*, v. 3, 123, fols. 300r–301r, and the letters from d'Estrades's *Correspondance:* Mémoire for d'Estrades, February 1646, 138; d'Estrades to Mazarin, 26 February 1646, 139, and 27 February 1646, 140; and d'Estrades to plenipotentiaries, 2 March 1646, 141.

52. Plenipotentiaries to Anne, 24 February 1646, Le Clerc, v. 3, 82–84; Brienne to plenipotentiaries, 17 March 1646, 124.

53. Mazarin to plenipotentiaries, 17 March 1646, Le Clerc, v. 3, 129.

54. Plenipotentiaries to Mazarin, 30 March 1646, *APW II B 3*, 193, p. 520; Louis XIV to plenipotentiaries, 31 March 1646, 195, p. 525; Louis XIV to plenipotentiaries, 14 April 1646, Le Clerc, v. 3, 150–51, and plenipotentiaries to Louis XIV, undated [probably 14 April 1646], 153.

55. On the subsidy treaty: Brienne to plenipotentiaries, 7 April 1646, Le Clerc, v. 3, 144–46; concerns that the Dutch will not fight: Servien to Lionne, 24 March 1646, *APW II B 3*, 189, p. 508; Servien to Lionne, 3 May 1646, 253; plenipotentiaries to Louis XIV, 29 May 1646, 290.

56. Servien to Lionne, 3 February 1646, *APW II B 3*, 105, pp. 273–74.

57. A similar, but shortened, version is given in the plenipotentiaries' common dispatch from 10 February (plenipotentiaries to Brienne, 10 February 1646, Le Clerc, v. 3, 57–58), in which they summarize that "to whatever side victory goes, we could suffer prejudice" ("de quelque côté que la victoire tournât nous y pourrions souffrir du préjudice"). Mazarin's response in Mazarin to plenipotentiaries, 16 February 1646 [see chapter 2, footnote 22 above], *APW II B 3*, 115; Lionne specifically wrote to Servien that he would see some of his own ideas in Mazarin's letter (Lionne to Servien, 16 February 1646, *APW II B 3*, 119).

58. For example, see Mazarin to Longueville, 21 April 1646, *APW II B 3*, 233.

59. Servien to Lionne, 14/19 April, *APW II B 3*, 228.

60. Longueville to Mazarin, 6 April 1646, *APW II B 3*, 198; Mazarin to Longueville, 14 April 1646, 215. Similar sentiments may be found in Longueville to Mazarin, 7 May 1646, *APW II B 3*, 260, and Louis XIV to plenipotentiaries, 20 May 1646, 276; see also chapter 7.

61. Mazarin to Longueville, 8 March 1646, *APW II B 3*, 157, p. 436; ibid., 31 March 1646, 196, p. 526; ibid., 14 April 1646, 215; Mazarin to plenipotentiaries, 24 March 1646, 182, p. 495; Brienne to plenipotentiaries, 17 February 1646, Le Clerc, v. 3, 72–73.

62. Mazarin to plenipotentiaries, 16 February 1646 [see chapter 2, footnote 22 above], Le Clerc, v. 3, 52–53; Mazarin to plenipotentiaries, 3 March 1646, *APW II B 3*, 139, p. 391; ibid., 24 March 1646, 182, p. 494.

63. Wilhelm Kohl, ed., *Die Schwedischen Korrespondenzen: 1645–1646*, series II, section C, v. 2 of *Acta Pacis Westphalicae* (Münster, 1971), Christina to Oxenstierna and Salvius, 31 March 1646, 79, pp. 219–20. (Hereafter cited as *APW II C 2*.) De La Barde to plenipotentiaries, 21 January 1646, *APW II B 3*, 82, p. 216; ibid., 5 February 1646, 106.

64. Servien to Lionne, 16 January 1646, *APW II B 3*, 64, p. 180; Longueville to Mazarin, 17 February 1646, 124, p. 336.

65. Plenipotentiaries to Brienne, 14 January 1646, Le Clerc, v. 3, 16, 18.

66. Louis XIV to plenipotentiaries, 9 December 1645, *APW II B 3*, 17; Servien to Lionne, 23 December 1645, 40, pp. 124–25; ibid., 16 January 1646, 64, p. 175.

67. Longueville to Mazarin, 20 January 1646, *APW II B 3*, 79; Brienne to plenipotentiaries, 20 January 1646, Le Clerc, v. 3, 20; ibid., 27 January 1646, 29–30; and Mazarin to plenipotentiaries, 3 February 1646, Le Clerc, v. 3, 44.

68. Plenipotentiaries to Mazarin, 27 January 1646, Le Clerc, v. 3, 32–34; Dickmann, *Der Westfälische Frieden*, 253–54. In fact, the Swedes had reached no such agreement.

69. For Sweden's unhappiness with Turenne's military activity in 1646, see below; for Sweden's belief that France had secretly signed a truce with Bavaria, see Oxenstierna and Salvius to Christina, 4 June 1646, *APW II C 2*, 121, p. 300; for negotiations with the emperor, Rosenhane to Oxenstierna, 5 June 1646, *APW II C 2*, 122, pp. 301–2. What separates Sweden's paranoia from France's is the casualness with which Swedish ministers accepted what they imagined to be French disloyalty. Thus, in the aforementioned letter, *APW II C 2*, 121, the Swedish plenipotentiaries report that France is about to conclude a truce with Bavaria, which the Swedes oppose vehemently; nevertheless, it is the last item in the letter, and they add offhandedly that it is "all the more reason that we are thinking of travelling to Münster." This may be contrasted with French plans to carry on the war without Sweden if necessary; no similar plans seem to have been made by the Swedes.

70. For example, see Axel Oxenstierna to Johann Oxenstierna, 30 June 1646, *APW II C 2*, 136, and 9 July 1646, 144.

71. Yngve Lorents, *Efter Brömsebrofreden: Svenska och Danska Förbindelser med Frankrike och Holland, 1645–1649* (Uppsala, 1916), 38–52, especially 42–44.

72. Tham, 358.

73. Plenipotentiaries to Brienne, 3 February 1646, Le Clerc, v. 3, 39–40, and Brienne to plenipotentiaries, 17 February 1646, 74.

74. Official Swedish orders to this effect are included in Christina to Oxenstierna and Salvius, 20 February 1646, *APW II C 2*, 48, p. 153, and 14 April 1646, 87, pp. 237–38.

75. For Franco-Swedish relations in the first months of 1646, see P. Linage de Vauciennes, *Memoires de ce qui s'est passé en Suede, et aux provinces voisines, depuis l'année 1645 jusques en l'année 1655*, v. 1 (Cologne, 1677), 4–27.

76. D'Avaux to court, 24 February 1646, Le Clerc, v. 3, 84–91; Oxenstierna and Salvius to Christina, 12 February 1646, *APW II C 2*, 44, and 19 February 1646, 46; Dickmann, *Der Westfälische Frieden*, 253–54.

77. Mazarin to plenipotentiaries, 10 February 1646, Le Clerc, v. 3, 62, and plenipotentiaries to Brienne, 24 March 1646, 132; see also the Linage de Vauciennes reference above, footnote 75.

78. Mazarin to plenipotentiaries, 10 February 1646, Le Clerc, v. 3, 62; Louis XIV to plenipotentiaries, 7 April 1646, 146–47; Brienne to plenipotentiaries, 14 April 1646, 152.

79. Servien to Mazarin, 25 February 1646, *APW II B 3*, 135; Longueville to Mazarin, 6 April 1646, 198.

80. On Mazarin's concern over England, see Mazarin to plenipotentiaries, 24 March 1646, Le Clerc, v. 3, 137. Henrietta Maria arrived in Paris in November, 1644 (Roger B. Merriman, *Six Contemporaneous Revolutions* [Oxford, 1938], 173), and France signed a treaty with Charles I in the same year; it reaffirmed their support, but offered no assistance in his conflict with the Parliament. Dorothy A. Bigby, "An Unknown Treaty between England and France, 1644," *English Historical Review* 28 (1913), 337–41. Boris Porshnev has advanced the belief that Mazarin's concern over the fate of England's monarchy led him to conclude peace in 1648 against his will; see "Angliskaia respublika, frantsuskaia Fronda i Vestfalsky mir," *Sredniie veka* 3 (1951): 180–216. However, V.-L. Tapié correctly argues that such a conclusion is unwarranted; despite his support for the Stu-

arts, Mazarin was never so focused on England that he was willing to place it before France's Continental concerns. Tapié, *La Guerre de Trente Ans* (Paris, 1964–66), 405.

81. Immler, *Kurfürst Maximilian I.*, 227–33; plenipotentiaries to Brienne, 10 March 1646, APW II B 3, 163, p. 445.

82. Ruppert, 158–60.

83. Immler, *Kurfürst Maximilian I.*, 241–42; Ruppert, 161–64.

84. Longueville to Mazarin, 7 April 1646, APW II B 3, 207.

85. Mazarin to Longueville, 3 February 1646, APW II B 3, 99. Dickmann's comment that Servien "as ever advocated the most reckless policy of annexation" should be reconsidered in light of this letter; Dickmann, *Der Westfälische Frieden*, 269.

86. Longueville to Mazarin, 7 April 1646, APW II B 3, 207.

87. D'Avaux to Mazarin, 6 April 1646, APW II B 3, 199, and 7 April 1646, 208; Mazarin to Longueville, 14 April 1646, APW II B 3, 215; Servien to Lionne, 8 April 1646, APW II B 3, 211; Longueville to Mazarin, 7 April 1646, APW II B 3, 207. According to Overmann, 457, the Sundgau was in fact an inherent part of Upper Alsace.

88. Longueville to Mazarin, 6 April 1646, APW II B 3, 198; ibid., 7 April 1646, 207; Servien to Lionne, 8 April 1646, 211; cp. Dickmann, *Der Westfälische Frieden*, 270. In spite of Servien's comment, Longueville's general stance was in favor of giving up Philippsburg; see below. His demand for Strasbourg in the meeting with Trauttmansdorff is difficult to interpret, but it seems likely to be no more than an isolated attempt; his suggestion that it go to Mazarin—which was rejected by the cardinal on the grounds that it would look self-interested— is suggestive. In the same meeting, after all, Trauttmansdorff offered Longueville the Lower Palatinate as well as Alsace. Servien's fanciful plan to have Leopold Wilhelm, the emperor's brother and Bishop of Strasbourg, receive the Low Countries from Spain, and then hand over the bishopric as part of a marriage alliance, may have been a defensive manoeuvre to fit Longueville's generous offer to Mazarin into his own policy. Why else would he propose such a thing when he was opposed to the whole idea of getting the bishopric, which he argued could not be incorporated into the crown's domain because it belonged to the church, in the first place? Longueville also forced Trauttmansdorff to promise not to share his plan with anyone else, further indicating its exceptional nature.

89. Servien to Lionne, 8 April 1646, APW II B 3, 211. Dickmann (*Der Westfälische Frieden*, 269–70) errs in seeing in Servien's ideas a desire to occupy the east bank of the Rhine. For it is not the Forest Towns and the Breisgau that interest Servien, but the Forest Towns and the Sundgau—the latter of which is entirely west of the Rhine. The problem seems to be that Dickmann interprets Servien's statement of the necessity of assuring "toute la main droite" as meaning the right bank of the Rhine; but the rest of the quotation makes clear that he, in fact, meant the right flank of France's line of communication with Breisach. This accords with the demand for the Sundgau and the Forest Towns, which lie precisely in that direction.

90. D'Avaux to Mazarin, 7 April 1646, APW II B 3, 208.

91. For a discussion of these meetings, see Immler, *Kurfürst Maximilian I.*, 241–42; Jacob, 131–33; Joachim Foerster and Roswitha Philippe, eds., *Diarium Volmar*, part 1, *1643–1647*, ser. III, section C, v. 2 of *Acta Pacis Westphalicae* (Münster, 1984), 590–93; and Karsten Ruppert, ed., *Die Kaiserlichen Korrespondenzen*

1645-1647, ser. II, section A, v. 3 of *Acta Pacis Westphalicae* (Münster, 1985), 252, pp. 473-75. Dickmann (*Der Westfälische Frieden*, 269-70) strains a bit to see in the French demand of 8 April bits and pieces of the particular plans of Servien and Longueville, and in doing so gives more credit to the plenipotentiaries for the formulation of French demands than they perhaps deserve. The simpler explanation—that the demands were essentially those of the French instructions—seems more credible. (Cp. Ruppert, 161.) As has been shown above (footnote 89), Servien was not pushing annexation on the right bank of the Rhine, and therefore it does not make sense to see in the demand for Breisach a part of his plan; besides, Breisach had been the most important French demand at least since 1642. Moreover, we know that it was d'Avaux, and not Servien, who originated the demand for Neuenburg. Similarly, Benfeld, Saverne, and Philippsburg were not specific demands of Longueville. The only one that can even be traced to him is Philippsburg, and, as will be demonstrated below, he was perhaps less attached to it than any other plenipotentiary.

92. Joachim Foerster, ed., *Diarium Wartenberg*, part 1, *1644-1646*, ser. III, section C, v. 3 of *Acta Pacis Westphalicae* (Münster, 1987), 435-36; Immler, *Kurfürst Maximilian I.*, 242-43.

93. See APW III C 2.1, 591 and 593. The French were well aware of the importance of Turenne's approach to the Rhine: plenipotentiaries to Mazarin, 14 April 1646, *APW II B 3*, 220. Cp. Ruppert, 164-67.

94. Ruppert, 162-64; plenipotentiaries to Louis XIV, 14/19 April 1646, *APW II B 3*, 226.

95. This is no doubt one reason that there was a misunderstanding on its length. The French plenipotentiaries spoke of the truce as 3 weeks (plenipotentiaries to Louis XIV, 14/19 April 1646, *APW II B 3*, 226); Trauttmansdorff and Maximilian as four weeks (Ruppert, 163; Maximilian to Leopold Wilhelm, 18 May 1646, KAA v. 2846, fols. 443r-443v); and Mazarin even as six weeks (Mazarin to la Ferté-Senneterre, 24 May 1646, CP Suède 6, fols. 98v-100v, and Turenne, *Mémoires [pièces justificatives]*, 264-70). It is possible that the agreement was to last until the emperor's orders arrived, with no specific time limit set. In a talk with d'Avaux, Trauttmansdorff did say that it would take three weeks to get a response from the emperor; perhaps he was trying to gain an extra week somehow, though if he were, it seems that he would not have set the time limit at three weeks (d'Avaux to Mazarin, 18 April 1646, *APW II B 3*, 224). It is interesting that Le Tellier was not able to inform Turenne of the conclusion of the truce even in his letter of (27 April AG v. 99, fols. 197r-98v). See also Rousset, 49-50, for a misunderstanding that the truce caused with Sweden.

96. Mazarin to plenipotentiaries, 7 April 1645, *APW II B 2*, 175; see also the discussion surrounding the Vervaux mission and the 1645 campaign above, chapter 7.

97. Le Tellier to Tracy, 12 February 1646, BN Mf v. 4173, fols. 61r-70v; Le Tellier to Tracy, 13 February 1646 AG v. 99, fols. 55v-63v. The latter document is probably an inaccurate copy of the former, since it gives not only a different date, but also totals the troop count incorrectly.

98. Mazarin to Longueville, 8 March 1646, *APW II B 3*, 157, p. 436.

99. CP Suède, v. 7, fols. 276r-76v. See also Mazarin to Turenne, 14 April 1646, CP All v. 64, fols. 233r-34r, for a very positive view of the link-up.

100. Mazarin to plenipotentiaries, 24 March 1646, *APW II B 3*, 182, p. 495; Gaudin to Servien, 11 March 1646, MD v. 855, fols. 53r-54v.

101. Turenne to Mazarin, 27 April 1646, CP All v. 64, fols. 302r-3r.

102. Mazarin to Turenne, 30 April 1646, BN Mf v. 4173, fols. 226r–28r; Turenne, *Mémoires*, pp. 256–64.
103. Israel, *Dutch Republic*, 360–62.
104. However, it is doubtful that Turenne's army consisted of more than 8000 troops in total; see footnote 137.
105. The basic idea for going to Luxembourg had been present at least since 30 April (see above, BN Mf v. 4173, fols. 226r–28r); however, at that time it had been secondary, whereas by the orders of 27 May it took on far greater significance. (Turenne, *Mémoires*, pp. 264–70). See also the orders to La Ferté-Senneterre, 13 May 1646, AG v. 99, fol. 220v; 24 May 1646, CP Suède v. 6, fols. 98v–100v, and 26 May 1646, AG v. 99, fols. 260r–62v. It appears from these that Mazarin was uncertain what to do with La Ferté-Senneterre's forces (besides to protect Champagne) until late May, which again suggests that he really became interested in the Luxembourg plan at that time.
106. Plenipotentiaries to Louis XIV, 7 May 1646, *APW II B 3*, 258; ibid., 29 May 1646, 290; plenipotentiaries to Brienne, 14 May 1646, 266.
107. Turenne's supply problems: Brienne to plenipotentiaries, 26 May 1646, *APW II B 3*, 285; Mazarin's desire to conclude before a link-up is necessary: Mazarin to Longueville, 12 May 1646, 264; his enthusiasm for the Luxembourg venture: Mazarin to Longueville, 20 May 1646, 277, Louis XIV to plenipotentiaries, 31 May 1646, 296, Mazarin to plenipotentiaries, 31 May 1646, 297, and ibid., 2 June 1646, 299; evidence that the Dutch would fight: plenipotentiaries to Mazarin, 14 May 1646, *APW II B 3*, 267, and Longueville to Mazarin, 14 May 1646, 268.
108. Plenipotentiaries to Mazarin, 19 April 1646, *APW II B 3*, 227.
109. Plenipotentiaries to Louis XIV, 14/19 April 1646, *APW II B 3*, 226.
110. Servien to Lionne, 14/19 April 1646, *APW II B 3*, 228.
111. Louis XIV to plenipotentiaries, 26 April 1646, *APW II B 3*, 241.
112. Mazarin to Longueville, 21 April 1646, *APW II B 3*, 233; Mazarin to plenipotentiaries, 26 April 1646, 243; Louis XIV to plenipotentiaries, 26 April 1646, 241.
113. Travel time from Paris to Vienna took at least several weeks. The Imperial decision is noted in Ruppert, 171–72.
114. Mazarin to plenipotentiaries, 31 May 1646, *APW II B 3*, 297, and 2 June 1646, 299.
115. Orders permitting them to accept Philippsburg instead of Breisach: Brienne to plenipotentiaries, 26 May 1646, *APW II B 3*, 285, and Louis XIV to plenipotentiaries, 31 May 1646, 296. Mazarin's assessment of Philippsburg: Mazarin to Longueville, 29 May 1646, *APW II B 3*, 289, and 2 June 1646, 300.
116. Louis XIV to plenipotentiaries, 26 April 1646, *APW II B 3*, 241.
117. Immler, *Kurfürst Maximilian I.*, 268.
118. Plenipotentiaries to Brienne, 17 February 1646, Le Clerc, v. 3, 65, and plenipotentiaries to Mazarin, undated [see above, footnote 13], 70–71; Longueville to Mazarin, 17 February 1646, *APW II B 3*, 124, p. 336, and plenipotentiaries to Mazarin, 24 March 1646, 187.
119. Mazarin to plenipotentiaries, 16 February 1646 [see above, chapter 2, footnote 22], Le Clerc, v. 3, 56 (which was written before the plenipotentiaries' concerns of 17 February); Mazarin to plenipotentiaries, 3 March 1646, *APW II B 3*, 139, p. 390 (in response to the plenipotentiaries' concerns); Mazarin to Longueville, 3 March 1646, 140, p. 398.

120. Plenipotentiaries to Mazarin, 24 March 1646, *APW II B 3*, 187; Servien to Lionne, 8 April 1646, 211; Louis XIV to plenipotentiaries, 7 April 1646, Le Clerc, v. 3, 146–47.
121. Mazarin to Longueville, 14 April 1646, *APW II B 3*, 215, and Louis XIV to plenipotentiaries, 21 April 1646, 232.
122. Louis XIV to plenipotentiaries, 26 April 1646, *APW II B 3*, 241.
123. Mazarin to Longueville, 14 April 1646, *APW II B 3*, 215.
124. Louis XIV to plenipotentiaries, 26 April 1646, *APW II B 3*, 241.
125. Plenipotentiaries to Louis XIV, 4 June 1646, *APW II B 3*, 304; Servien to Lionne, 5 June 1646, 307; plenipotentiaries to Louis XIV, 14 June 1646, *APW II B 4*, 10; Immler, *Kurfürst Maximilian I.*, 260–61; Ruppert, 174–75; Jacob, 158; Brienne, *Mémoires*, 119.
126. Servien to Lionne, 5 June 1646, *APW II B 3*, 307; de La Barde to plenipotentiaries, 24 May 1646, *APW II B 3*, 284.
127. Johann Oxenstierna to Axel Oxenstierna, 19 March 1646, *APW II C 2*, 74; Oxenstierna and Salvius to Christina, 28 May 1646, 118.
128. Oxenstierna and Salvius to Christina, 14 May 1646, *APW II C 2*, 107. In fact, however, the Swedes were exactly wrong on this point: the emperor made no trouble about giving up all of Pomerania and very little about the bishoprics of Bremen and Verden, in contrast to his slow, piecemeal concessions in Alsace. What the Swedes do not seem to have appreciated is the significance of the fact that France was demanding territory directly from the emperor, whereas Sweden's demands, coming as they did from other German estates, hardly excited much concern in Vienna. Ruppert, 200–205.
129. Plenipotentiaries to Louis XIV, 4 June 1646, *APW II B 3*, 304; plenipotentiaries to Louis XIV, 14 June 1646, *APW II B 4*, 10; plenipotentiaries to Mazarin, 14 June 1646, *APW II B 4*, 11.
130. D'Avaux to Mazarin, 13 June 1646, *APW II B 4*, 8; ibid., 18 June 1646, 19; Longueville to Mazarin, 18 June 1646, 18; Servien to Lionne, 5 June 1646, *APW II B 3*, 307.
131. Plenipotentiaries to Brienne, 18 June 1646, *APW II B 4*, 17.
132. Servien to Lionne, 5 June 1646, *APW II B 3*, 307.
133. Brienne to plenipotentiaries, 15 June 1646, *APW II B 4*, 14; Mazarin to Longueville, 15 June 1646, 15; Louis XIV to plenipotentiaries, 22 June 1646, 23.
134. Louis XIV to plenipotentiaries, 26 April 1646, *APW II B 3*, 241, and 20 May 1646, 276.
135. Turenne's hawkishness manifested itself on other occasions as well: in 1647, when he favored attacking and crushing the Austrian Habsburgs rather than turning against Spain; in 1648, when he opposed the Peace of Westphalia, instead preferring to carry on the successful war against the Habsburgs; and, much later, in the Dutch War, which he helped bring about more than any other minister. On this last instance, see Paul Sonnino, "The Marshal de Turenne and the Origins of the Dutch War," in *Studies in History and Politics: Essays in European History in Honour of Ragnhild Hatton*, v. 4, ed. Karl Schweizer and Jeremy Black (London, 1985), 125–36.
136. Louis XIV to plenipotentiaries, 20 May 1646, *APW II B 3*, 276.
137. Reports from unknown sources put Turenne's strength at six thousand cavalry but little infantry (Gaudin to Servien, 12 May 1646, MD v. 855, fols. 119r–20v). Mazarin himself had given Turenne's strength as three thousand cavalry and four thousand infantry on 24 May (Mazarin to La Ferté-Senneterre, CP Suède v. 6, fols. 98v–100v).

138. Lahrkamp, "Bönninghausen," 336–47. Perhaps not unexpectedly, Lahrkamp accepts Bönninghausen's own figure of 3000 troops raised and calls the mission a success. Reports from the French, however, indicate that he raised only 540 infantry out of 2000 contracted; that he raised an extra company of cavalry (which was more remunerative); that the little infantry that he did raise ended up costing 64 Reichstalers per head instead of the 16 he promised; and that it took him almost a year longer than expected. Le Tellier to Tracy, 13 February 1646, AG v. 99, fols. 55v–63v and 9 April 1646, BN Mf v. 4201, fols. 142r–43r; Mazarin to Tracy, 28 April 1646, CP All v. 64, fol. 304r; Mazarin to plenipotentiaries, 23 May 1646, AG v. 99, fols. 256r–57v; Mazarin to Tracy, 26 May 1646, CP All v. 60, fol. 334r.

139. Mazarin to Meulles (13 January 1646, CP Suède v. 6, fol. 406r) indicates that Meulles had been left in charge of levying troops without realizing it, thus causing a delay; Mazarin to Tracy, 3 March 1646, CP All v. 64, fol. 29r; Mazarin to Meulles, 28 April 1646, CP Suède v. 6, fols. 408r–408v; Mazarin to Meulles, 1 May 1646, CP Suède v. 6, fols. 410r–410v. Mazarin's repeated pleas to Meulles continued up until the beginning of July (CP Suède v. 6, fols. 407v–13v). By 12 May, Mazarin was ordering that the troops had to be collected within 15 days, or Meulles would have to think of getting his money back, because there would be no use for them after then. Several contracts were, in fact, broken because the recruiters either failed to levy their troops on time, or else raised only cavalry. Plenipotentiaries to Louis XIV, 3 June 1646, KAA 2846, fol. 504r, puts the recruits from northern Germany at 4,000 infantry and 4,000 cavalry. These figures are interesting because they are surprisingly high given the complaints and broken contracts that accompanied them. Probably they are optimistic estimates; Tracy eventually brought fewer than 4,000 troops to join Wrangel, although he had lost at least 500 more along the way (19 July 1646, Tracy to Mazarin, in Turenne, *Mémoires [pièces justificatives]*, 283–84). But to the extent that they are true (and for this purpose the theoretical figures of the contracts matter more than the actual number brought into the campaign), they also demonstrate how far the actual composition of the recruits varied from the original plan of 6,700 infantry and 800 cavalry (see above, footnote 97); the attempt to limit the amount of cavalry they raised had, it appears, failed completely.

140. On Turenne's shortage of money, see Turenne to Mazarin, 27 April 1646, CP All v. 64, fols. 302r–3r; Turenne to Mazarin, 4 May 1646, Turenne, *Mémoires [pièces justificatives]*, 353–54; Turenne to Mazarin, 22 June 1646, CP All v. 66, fol. 82r. On the delayed preparations, Le Tellier to Turenne, 30 April 1646, AG v. 99, fols. 198v–201r.

141. Plenipotentiaries to Louis XIV, 7 May 1646, *APW II B 3*, 258; ibid., 29 May 1646, 290; ibid., 4 June 1646, 304; plenipotentiaries to Brienne, 14 May 1646, 266; Servien to Lionne, 29 May 1646, 292; Longueville to Mazarin, 4 June 1646, 305.

142. For background to the Hessian War, see Beck, 9–32. On the capture of Marburg, Hans H. Weber, 67–78.

143. Hans H. Weber, 97–99, admits that the strength of 3,216 cavalry and 7,918 infantry is overstated, but declines to offer a better estimate. He cites four cavalry and eight infantry regiments as being in Darmstadt service. Based on the total figures that he provides, average regimental size works out to approximately 1,000. But whereas that was the ideal, in fact regiments tended to have closer to 300 men. Using 300 as the average would produce total figures of about 1200 cavalry and 2,400 infantry, which correspond extremely closely to

the estimates made by the Imperial army (undated, KAA v. 2846, fol. 503r) of 1,000 cavalry and 2,000 infantry.

144. Oxenstierna to Christina, 23 April 1646, *APW II C 2*, 93, p. 253.

145. Heilmann, *Kriegsgeschichte*, 701–4; Barthold, 548–50; Turenne, 81; Immler, *Kurfürst Maximilian I.*, 311–12; 23 June 1646, Maximilian to Leopold Wilhelm, KAA v. 2846, fols. 510r–13r.

146. Immler, *Kurfürst Maximilian I.*, 309–10.

147. Maximilian to Georg, 26 May 1646, KAA v. 2846, fol. 485r; Leopold Wilhelm to Maximilian, 1 June 1646, KAA v. 2846, fols. 481r–481v and 11 June 1646, fols. 495r–96v.

148. Invasion of Westphalia: Leopold Wilhelm to Maximilian, 20 May 1646, KAA v. 2846, fols. 445r–48r, and Maximilian to Leopold Wilhelm, 22 May 1646, KAA v. 2846, fols. 456v–58r; attacking Marburg: Maximilian to Leopold Wilhelm, 6 June 1646, KAA v. 2846, fols. 469r–70v; and 11 June 1646, Leopold Wilhelm to Maximilian, fols. 495r–96v.

149. Maximilian to Leopold Wilhelm, 6 June 1646, KAA v. 2846, fol. 468v; Immler, *Kurfürst Maximilian I.*, 311–12.

150. Barthold, 551–52, on the missed opportunity. Leopold Wilhelm to Maximilian, 18 June 1646, KAA v. 2846, fols. 501r–2r; in this letter, Leopold Wilhelm indicates his desire to advance between the French and Swedish armies and, "with God's grace, to hope for a good strike [against them]." He also argued that, since the French and Swedes were carrying on their military preparations during the truce, it was essential for Bavaria to do so as well. While Maximilian approved Leopold Wilhelm's general advance against the Swedes, he noted that a lost battle would cause "unrecoverable damage" (Maximilian to Leopold Wilhelm, 30 June 1646, KAA v. 2846, fols. 516r–17r). Leopold Wilhelm was moved by such statements to be cautious himself. He indicated, for example, that he would not "let myself be engaged in any action unless I have a particular advantage" (Leopold Wilhelm to Maximilian, 26 June 1646, KAA v. 2846, fols. 514r–15r). For more on Leopold Wilhelm's caution and its effect on the campaign, see below. Swedish concerns at the large Imperial-Bavarian force are amply expressed by Salvius in his letter to Christina, 9 July 1646, *APW II C 2*, 143, p. 356.

151. The Swedes had already anticipated Turenne's inaction as early as the end of March: Salvius to Christina, 9 April 1646, *APW II C 2*, 84.

152. Longueville to Mazarin, 13 June 1646, *APW II B 4*, 7; plenipotentiaries to Mazarin, 14 June 1646, 11.

153. Louis XIV to plenipotentiaries, 22 June 1646, *APW II B 4*, 23; plenipotentiaries to Brienne, 25 June 1646, 28; Turenne, *Mémoires [pièces justificatives]*, 273. Mazarin's chiding of Turenne for misreading his orders and refusing to link up is ironic not only because Turenne in fact went through with the junction on receipt of the first instructions from Münster, but also because the orders were ambiguous in the first place. Perhaps that is why Mazarin felt it necessary to explain them again, and even admitted that they might not have been clear: "My intention," he wrote to Turenne, "if you read my letters well, and if I explained myself well, was nothing other than that you do everything possible to attack Luxembourg, without ruining anything with the Swedes, and that in making the junction you do not agree to anything wrong or unnecessary" (Turenne, *Mémoires [pièces justificatives]*, 274). Nor were the plenipotentiaries' orders, which left Turenne considerable leeway in the decision, especially clear and decisive. Nevertheless, the argument advanced by some (including Bérenger, *Turenne*, 232, and Chéruel, *Histoire de France*, v. 2, 316) that Turenne decided to

link up with Wrangel contrary to orders is even less tenable. The source of this error is apparently a passage from Turenne's memoirs; however, the passage is ambiguous, stating only that Turenne marched to join the Swedes once he learned that the Bavarian and Imperial armies had linked up, without stating explicitly that he was doing so contrary to orders. No doubt Turenne hoped to take advantage of the ambiguity to show his decisiveness—perhaps understandable in light of the fact that he was in favor of the link-up all along—but he stops short of outright lying. Chéruel, at least, notes contrary evidence by Nani, the Venetian ambassador, but he (wrongly) chooses to accept that Turenne advanced without orders. See also the letters from Mazarin in Turenne, *Mémoires [pièces justificatives]*, 288–90, and Le Tellier in BN Mf 4201, fols. 277r–77v, in which Turenne's delay in linking up is fully excused—but the fact that it needs excusing proves that he was rather too slow rather than too quick to advance toward the Swedes.

154. Turenne to Mazarin, 22 June 1646, CP All v. 66, fol. 82r.

155. Turenne to Mazarin, 17 June 1646, CP All v. 66, fols. 63r–64r; , Turenne to Mazarin, 22 June 1646, CP All v. 66, fol. 82r. The dates of arrival of letters are approximate in some cases. The plenipotentiaries' letter to Mazarin of 14 June was answered on 22 June; it therefore must have arrived in at most eight days, and more likely in seven, since it usually took a day to decode. Turenne sent his secretary to Paris on 17 June and he arrived on 22 June. Estimating the same five days for the return trip—he was almost certainly sent back on the same or the next day, along with Mazarin's letter dated 22 June—would put him back with Turenne on 27 June. Turenne states that he received the orders from the plenipotentiaries three days before his secretary returned, or, by this calculation, 24 June. That seems like a long time for a letter sent on 9 June, considering that the letter to Paris, a much longer distance, was sent four days later and arrived at least two days earlier. It is possible that Turenne could have been referring to the plenipotentiaries' second letter, which they report having sent in a letter to Brienne on 25 June. However, this seems unlikely, since Turenne's letter of 22 June to Mazarin makes no mention of any orders from the plenipotentiaries, and indeed urgently requests orders. Moreover, it must be borne in mind that military letters were insecure (see chapter 4), and since the most direct routes to Turenne from Münster would have passed through areas occupied either by the Imperial-Bavarian army in Hesse or the forces of the Archbishop of Cologne (which was safe for diplomatic correspondence), it seems unlikely that the second orders could have arrived so quickly, considering that they must have been sent after 18 June (when the plenipotentiaries wrote their last letters that did not mention them). Unfortunately, none of the correspondence between the plenipotentiaries and Turenne survives, so it is impossible even to calculate an average travel time for letters from Münster to Mainz or Oberwesel, where Turenne was stationed.

The explanation of Charvériat (*Histoire de la Guerre de Trente Ans, 1618–1648*, v. 2, Paris, 1878) that Turenne invaded Cologne in order to force the elector into neutrality has no foundation.

156. Turenne, *Mémoires [pièces justificatives]*, 277–79; CP All v. 66, fol. 82r, Turenne to Mazarin, 22 June 1646.

157. Turenne, *Mémoires [pièces justificatives]*, 278–79. Turenne left "about 1000" infantry, not counting a regiment of 300 stationed at Philippsburg (in addition to the garrison there), and two regiments of cavalry. Mazarin suggested leaving such a force in his letter of 29 June. Of course, it would have arrived too late

for Turenne, who probably left well before it was even sent. However, Mazarin may well have included similar, oral orders when he sent back Turenne's secretary (Turenne, *Mémoires [pièces justificatives]*, 274), if his passion for the Luxembourg venture alone had not been sufficient recommendation to Turenne.

158. For Swedish complaints, see, e.g., Rosenhane to Christina, 1 July 1646, *APW II C 2*, 137.

159. This was about the most the plenipotentiaries could have done, considering that they had received no letters from Turenne since 9 April, and consequently had no knowledge of the present state of his army. Tracy to Mazarin, 19 July 1646, Turenne, *Mémoires [pièces justificatives]*, pp. 283–84, and Wrangel to Turenne, 18 July 1646, 283; Longueville to Mazarin, 16 July 1646, *APW II B 4*, 73. Mazarin had had the same idea, but his orders, sent on 12 July, only arrived too late to have any effect; Mazarin to Tracy, 12 July 1646, Turenne, *Mémoires [pièces justificatives]*, pp. 281–82.

160. Plenipotentiaries to Brienne, 18 June 1646, *APW II B 4*, 17; Longueville to Mazarin, 18 June 1646, 18; ibid., 9 July 1646, 62; Ruppert, 184–85.

161. D'Avaux to Mazarin, 18 June 1646, *APW II B 4*, 19; see also ibid., 23 July 1646, *APW II B 4*, 83.

162. Mazarin to plenipotentiaries, 1 July 1646, *APW II B 4*, 45; Mazarin to Longueville, 20 July 1646, 79; see also d'Avaux to Mazarin, 23 July 1646, 83. The plenipotentiaries' statement is from plenipotentiaries to Mazarin, 16 July 1646, *APW II B 4*, 72.

163. Memorandum from St. Romain, 3 July 1646, *APW II B 4*, 52; Longueville to Mazarin, 16 July 1646, 73; Brienne to plenipotentiaries, 20 July 1646, 76; Linage de Vauciennes, 33.

164. Lionne to Servien, 6 July 1646, *APW II B 4*, 56; Linage de Vauciennes, 55–56, 60–61, 65–66. Oxenstierna did formally request leave, but Christina denied it on the grounds that it would take too much time to train a replacement.

165. Axel Oxenstierna to Johann Oxenstierna, 2 June 1646, *APW II C 2*, 120; 31 March 1646, 80; and 13 August 1646, 163.

166. Christina to Oxenstierna and Salvius, 31 March 1646, *APW II C 2*, 79.

167. Salvius to Gyldenklou, 7 May 1646, *APW II C 2*, 98; Christina to Oxenstierna and Salvius, 2 June 1646, 119.

168. Christina to Oxenstierna and Salvius, 18 July 1646, *APW II C 2*, 148, and 11 August 1646, 159.

169. Johann Oxenstierna to Axel Oxenstierna, 25 June 1646, *APW II C 2*, 133; 23 July 1646, 151; and 13 August 1646, 165. Axel Oxenstierna to Johann Oxenstierna, 11 August 1646, 160.

170. Plenipotentiaries to Louis XIV, 30 July 1646, *APW II B 4*, 91.

171. Mazarin to Longueville, 6 July 1646, *APW II B 4*, 54; d'Avaux to Mazarin, 16 July 1646, 74; Linage de Vauciennes, 39–40, 44. Interestingly, Mazarin later admitted to Magnus de La Gardie that France had kept Turenne from crossing the Rhine because of the slowness of the Dutch to enter the campaign; Magnus Gabriel de la Gardie to Oxenstierna and Salvius, 21 September 1646, *APW II C 2*, 187, p. 451.

172. For Johann Oxenstierna's view of the meeting, see Oxenstierna to Christina, 23 July 1646, *APW II C 2*, 150.

173. Plenipotentiaries to Brienne, 16 July 1646, *APW II B 4*, 70; plenipotentiaries to Louis XIV, 16 July 1646, 71; Longueville to Mazarin, 16 July 1646, 73; on de La Gardie, also memorandum from St. Romain, 3 July 1646, *APW II B 4*, 52; Göran Rystad, "Magnus Gabriel De La Gardie," in *Sweden's Age of Greatness,*

1632–1718, edited by Michael Roberts (London, 1973), 25; Tham, 359. De La Gardie's report of his meeting with Mazarin is found in Magnus Gabriel de la Gardie to Oxenstierna and Salvius, 21 September 1646, *APW II C 2*, 187. For the court's response, see Brienne to plenipotentiaries, 27 July 1646, *APW II B 4*, 86, and Louis XIV to plenipotentiaries, 27 July 1646, 87.

174. Longueville to Mazarin, 2 July 1646, *APW II B 4*, 49.
175. Mazarin to d'Avaux, 20 July 1646, *APW II B 4*, 80.
176. Lionne to Servien, 20 July 1646, *APW II B 4*, 81; Lionne to Servien, 27 July 1646, 89.
177. Plenipotentiaries to Louis XIV, 9 July 1646, *APW II B 4*, 60.
178. Plenipotentiaries to Louis XIV, 14 June 1646, *APW II B 4*, 10.
179. Servien to Lionne, 14 June 1646, *APW II B 4*, 12. Much of this went directly into the plenipotentiaries' common memoir to court on 9 July (Le Clerc, v. 3, 244–45).
180. At least, it outweighed the other factors in Servien's memo (above, footnote 179). Brienne's memoirs are, as usual, problematic on this question: he claims that Mazarin supported taking Alsace in sovereignty, but this is contradicted by Mazarin's letter of 7 September. Brienne, 119–21; plenipotentiaries to Louis XIV, 9 July 1646, *APW II B 4*, 60; Mazarin to d'Avaux, 7 September 1646, 146. It is also worth noting that in 1653–54, Vautorte was sent to the Imperial Diet in Regensburg with instructions to say that France was ready to hold Alsace as an Imperial fief in spite of the provisions in the Peace of Westphalia, which suggests that Mazarin indeed preferred to have it as a fief; Christian Pfister and M. Lavisse, "La Formation de l'Alsace-Lorraine," in *Pages Alsaciennes* (Paris, 1927), 20–21. Another issue, not raised by the plenipotentiaries until 1647 but about which they may have thought earlier, was that taking Alsace as a fief might cause the German estates to insist that France take the three bishoprics as a fief as well, the arguments being the same for both. Plenipotentiaries to court, 10 June 1647, BN Mf 15857, fols. 150r–62r.
181. Comte de Garden, *Histoire générale des traités de paix et autres transactions principales entre toutes les puissances de l'Europe depuis la Paix de Westphalie*, v. 1 (Paris, 1848), 212. A mere list of all works written on this subject would go on for pages; the most important treatments are those by Garden; Karl Jacob; Alfred Overmann; Fritz Dickmann; Konrad Repgen; and Andreas Kraus.
182. Ruppert, 171–79.
183. Meiern III, 36, p. 39.
184. Plenipotentiaries to Louis XIV, 14 June 1646, *APW II B 4*, 10.
185. Longueville to Mazarin, 13 June 1646, *APW II B 4*, 7. See also plenipotentiaries to Louis XIV, 9 July 1646, *APW II B 4*, 60, in which the plenipotentiaries note that their new demands "are reserved more for making the Imperials see reason than in the hope of actually obtaining them."
186. Stein, "Das französische Elsaßbild," and Malettke, "Diplomatie et Guerre: Les traités de Westphalie, Münster et Osnabrück 1643–1648," *XVIIe siècle*, no. 182 (1994): 169–70, argue that the French had a better understanding of Alsace than has been previously acknowledged. It seems clear that the French knew enough to realize that the final treaty was ambiguous, but a precise understanding cannot be attributed to them. See below on the preliminary treaty for further discussion of this matter.
187. D'Avaux to Mazarin, 18 June 1646, *APW II B 4*, 19.
188. For Mazarin's opinion, see Mazarin to d'Avaux, 29 June 1646, *APW II B 4*, 38; ibid., 20 July 1646; Mazarin to Longueville, 30 June 1646, 43; ibid., 6 July 1646, 54.

189. D'Avaux to Mazarin, 18 June 1646, *APW II B 4*, 19; Mazarin to d'Avaux, 29 June 1646, 38.
190. D'Avaux to Mazarin, 2 July 1646, *APW II B 4*, 50.
191. D'Avaux to Mazarin, 30 July 1646, *APW II B 4*, 92. See also ibid., 6 August 1646, *APW II B 4*, 102 for a further meeting between d'Avaux and Trauttmansdorff at the beginning of August.
192. Plenipotentiaries to Louis XIV, 9 July 1646, *APW II B 4*, 60; Rosenhane to Christina, 17 June 1646, *APW II C 2*, 129, p. 326. Rosenhane actually wrote that "emellan Franckrijke och churfursten af Trier hålles före vara allaredo een hemlig accord sluten öfver Philipsbourg i så motto, at churfursten det hafver cederat" ("between France and the Elector of Trier there is held to be already a secret accord concerning Philippsburg in such a fashion that the Elector has ceded it"). His use of the passive implies that it was the general opinion that France and Trier already had such an agreement.
193. Abmeier, 55–58.
194. Abmeier, 59–64.
195. Plenipotentiaries to Brienne, 2 July 1646, *APW II B 4*, 48.
196. Abmeier, 64–78.
197. Plenipotentiaries to Louis XIV, 30 July 1646, *APW II B 4*, 91.
198. Longueville to Mazarin, 16 July 1646, *APW II B 4*, 73; ibid., 24 July 1646, 84; ibid., 13 August 1646, 112; d'Avaux to Mazarin, 16 July 1646, 74; ibid., 23 July 1646, 83; ibid., 13 August 1646, 113; Servien to Lionne, 24 July 1646, 85; Mazarin to Longueville, 27 July 1646, 88; ibid., 10 August 1646, 107; plenipotentiaries to Louis XIV, 30 July 1646, 91; ibid., 13 August 1646, 111; Mazarin to d'Avaux, 3 August 1646, 96. It is interesting to contrast this attitude with that of Salvius, who wrote to Oxenstierna on 5 July that it was the best time to make peace because the armies were in a balance, and "both sides can conclude [peace] with reputation" (*APW II C 2*, 140).
199. Longueville to Mazarin, 13 August 1646, *APW II B 4*, 112; d'Avaux to Mazarin, 13 August 1646, 113.
200. D'Avaux to Mazarin, 23 July 1646, *APW II B 4*, 83; plenipotentiaries to Louis XIV, 30 July 1646, 91. Apparently there were some Dutch opposed to allowing Turenne to cross at Wesel (a town they controlled), so the court praised the plenipotentiaries' decision to go there to assure a rapid passage: Brienne to plenipotentiaries, 10 August 1646, *APW II B 4*, 105; Louis XIV to plenipotentiaries, 10 August 1646, 106; Mazarin to Longueville, 10 August 1646, 107.
201. Lahrkamp, *Jan von Werth*, 163. Peters, 183, notes the lack of food from the perspective of a common soldier.
202. Leopold Wilhelm to Maximilian, 18 July 1646, KAA v. 2902, fols. 22r–22v.
203. Maximilian to Leopold Wilhelm, 21 July 1646, KAA v. 2901, fols. 15r–11v. See also Maximilian to Leopold Wilhelm, 16 July 1646, KAA v. 2901, fols. 3r–4r; Leopold Wilhelm to Maximilian, 3 August 1646, KAA v. 2902, fols. 26r–26v.
204. Leopold Wilhelm to Maximilian, 3 August 1646, KAA v. 2902, fols. 26r–26v.
205. Leopold Wilhelm to Maximilian, 18 July 1646, KAA v. 2902, fols. 22r–22v; Leopold Wilhelm to Maximilian, 11 August 1646, KAA v. 2902, fol. 47r.
206. Maximilian to Leopold Wilhelm, 16 July 1646, KAA v. 2902, fols. 3r–4r; Maximilian to Leopold Wilhelm, 31 July 1646, KAA v. 2902, fols. 19r–21r.
207. Not only is his caution evident in this campaign, but ever since he took up command of the Imperial forces at the beginning of 1645, he had been

particularly concerned to conserve the army. Broucek, "Erzherzog Leopold-Wilhelm," 34.

208. Significantly, Leopold Wilhelm specifically noted that he decided not to attack the French at Bonamös in order to preserve the army. Accounts of the attack may be found in Turenne, *Mémoires [pièces justificatives]*, 296–301; ? to Mazarin, 18 August 1646, CP All v. all 66, fols. 257v–59r; Turenne, *Mémoires*, 85–88; and Leopold Wilhelm to Maximilian, 17 August 1646, KAA v. 2902, fols. 61r–62v. Lahrkamp, *Jan von Werth*, 165, footnote 14, rightly notes that the 1646 campaign is not as well understood as others in the war. The lack of a decisive battle has doubtless played a large role in its failure to interest modern historians; nevertheless, it was one of the most decisive campaigns of the century, and is badly in need of an in-depth study. Interestingly, Turenne specifically noted that their maneuver "should not bring less profit than victory in a great combat" (Turenne, *Mémoires [pièces justificatives]*, 301). The accounts of Barthold (552–53) and Heilmann (*Kriegsgeschichte*, 705) must be used with particular caution.

209. Leopold Wilhelm to Maximilian, 17 August 1646, KAA v. 2902, fols. 63r–63v.

210. ? to Mazarin, 18 August 1646, CP All v. all 66, fols. 257v–59r; Turenne, *Mémoires*, 89–90, and ibid., *pièces justificatives*, 302–4.

211. On Turenne's decision not to besiege Heilbronn, see CP All 66, Turenne to Mazarin, 4 September 1646, fols. 362r–63v; Turenne to Mazarin, 9 September 1646, fols. 378r–80r; and News from Frankfurt, 9 September 1646, fols. 374r–374v. On Turenne's request for reinforcements, see Turenne, *Mémoires [pièces justificatives]*, 299–301, 302–4, and the letters cited above in this footnote.

212. Ibid., and Turenne, *Mémoires*, 90–91.

213. Hans H. Weber, 107–17; News from Frankfurt, 9 September 1646, CP All 66, fols. 374r–374v, and News from Frankfurt, 23 September 1646, fols. 450r–450v.

214. Maximilian to Leopold Wilhelm, 19 August 1646, KAA v. 2902, fols. 51r–51v; Maximilian to Leopold Wilhelm, 27 August 1646, KAA v. 2902, fols. 69r–70v; Immler, *Kurfürst Maximilian I.*, 313–17; Heilmann, *Kriegsgeschichte*, 708–9.

215. D'Avaux to Mazarin, 20 August 1646, *APW II B 4*, 122.

216. Plenipotentiaries to Brienne, 20 August 1646, *APW II B 4*, 120; plenipotentiaries to Louis XIV, 27 August 1646, 130; Ruppert, 186–87; Dickmann, *Der Westfälische Frieden*, 292–93; Abmeier, 80–83. The French claimed to know the result of the Electors' decision before the vote; how this happened, if indeed it is true, is unknown. D'Avaux to Mazarin, 27 August 1646, *APW II B 4*, 132.

217. Servien to Lionne, 11 September 1646, *APW II B 4*, 152.

218. This is known as the "ita tamen" ("only to the extent, nevertheless, that") clause, from its first two words.

219. Philippe Dollinger, "Le Traité de Westphalie et l'Alsace," in *Deux siècles d'Alsace française* (Paris, 1948), 11; Reuss, *L'Alsace au Dix-Septième Siècle*, 167; Ruppert, 189–96. Most historians have attempted to resolve the contradiction in one way or another. Dickmann, *Der Westfälische Frieden*, 296–300, for example, argues that France obtained sovereignty over all Habsburg-controlled territory. But how could the Habsburgs surrender more control than they themselves possessed? Zeller's elegant solution (*Comment s'est faite la réunion de l'Alsace à la France*, 112–13) that the "ita tamen" clause was intended only to ensure that mediate estates did not escape French control founders, alas, on the actual French understanding of the treaty. Lavisse's attempt to explain away the contradiction (Ernest

Lavisse, *Louis XIV: Histoire d'un grand règne, 1643–1715* [1908; reprint, Paris, 1989], 20–22) is decidedly unconvincing, as is Malettke's argument ("Diplomatie et Guerre," 169–70) that the quality of Imperial rights changed when they transferred to France. Bardot, 62–72, is one of the few historians to tackle this issue directly and show that the French themselves considered it contradictory. See especially pp. 285–91 for a 1661 French memorandum that not only argues that the treaty was contradictory, but also says that Servien knew this.

220. Clive Parry, ed., *The Consolidated Treaty Series*, v. 1, *1648–1649* (Dobbs Ferry, New York, 1969), 299–300, 345 (in both Latin and English). I have modified the English translation slightly to make it clearer and more literal.

221. Bardot, 56.

222. Livet, *L'Intendance d'Alsace*, 122–23; Bardot, 73–74.

223. It is interesting to note that the plenipotentiaries felt that Spain was deliberately trying to get a vague peace treaty of which it could take advantage later: plenipotentiaries to court, 22 March 1647, BN 15863, 215–11v. See also Tapié, *Guerre de Trente Ans* (1989), 402.

224. Servien to Lionne, 11 September 1646, *APW II B 4*, 152; Ruppert, 193, 197–98; Konrad Repgen, "Aktuelle Friedensprobleme im Lichte der Geschichte des Westfälischen Friedens," in *Historische Klopfsignale für die Gegenwart* (Münster, 1974), 58–61; Dickmann, *Der Westfälische Frieden*, 295–96; Malettke, "Diplomatie et Guerre," 162–65 (basically following previous historians); plenipotentiaries to Anne, 17 September 1646, *APW II B 4*, 159 for the plenipotentiaries' high valuation of this accomplishment.

225. Plenipotentiaries to Mazarin, 6 August 1646, *APW II B 4*, 100; Brienne to plenipotentiaries, 10 August 1646, 105; Mazarin to Longueville, 17 August 1646, 117.

226. D'Avaux to Mazarin, 20 August 1646, *APW II B 4*, 122; plenipotentiaries to Louis XIV, 27 August 1646, 130; d'Avaux to Mazarin, 27 August 1646, 132; Mazarin to d'Avaux, 7 September 1646, 146.

227. Longueville to Mazarin, 3 September 1646, *APW II B 4*, 140; Brienne to plenipotentiaries, 14 September 1646, 153; Servien to Lionne, 17 September 1646, 161.

228. Plenipotentiaries to Brienne, 10 September 1646, *APW II B 4*, 148; Ruppert, 185–86.

229. Longueville to Mazarin, 16 September 1646, *APW II B 4*, 157; plenipotentiaries to Brienne, 17 September 1646, 158; plenipotentiaries to Anne, 17 September 1646, 159.

230. Oxenstierna and Salvius to Christina, 27 August 1646, *APW II C 2*, 172, and 3 September 1646, 176.

231. Salvius to Christina, 17 September 1646, *APW II C 2*, 186; Christina to Oxenstierna and Salvius, 22 September 1646, 188; Christina to Oxenstierna and Salvius, 29 September 1646, 192.

232. D'Avaux to Mazarin, 23 September 1646, *APW II B 4*, 168; Anne to plenipotentiaries, 29 September 1646, 178.

233. See Immler, *Kurfürst Maximilian I.*, 246–47, for a high valuation of Bavaria's role.

234. Plenipotentiaries to Brienne, 10 September 1646, *APW II B 4*, 148.

Chapter 9. Mazarin as Negotiator and Strategist

1. For the repeated concerns to prevent the Imperial negotiations from being concluded before the Spanish ones, see the plenipotentiaries' dispatches

in BN Mf 15857, 13 May 1647, fol. 117v; 10 June 1647, fol. 151v; 30 June, fols. 187v–89r.

2. See Riezler, *op. cit.*

3. Mazarin to Turenne, 27 October 1647, *Lettres*, v. 2, 220, and 14 December 1647, 232. See Rousset, 52, for Swedish criticism of Mazarin's dilatoriness.

4. Plenipotentiaries to court, 24 June 1647, Le Clerc, v. 4, 121; plenipotentiaries to Brienne, 5 August 1647, 141; Plenipotentiaries to court, 18 November 1647, BN Mf 15857, fols. 404r–6v; Dickmann, *Der Westfälische Frieden*, 447–48.

5. The plenipotentiaries sent letters of increasing urgency beginning in the middle of the year: BN Mf 15857, 31 June 1648, fols. 187v–89r; 19 July, fols. 217r–217v; 22 July, fols. 231v–36v; 5 August, 261v–66v; etc.

6. See plenipotentiaries' memo, February 1648, CP All. 107, fols. 263r–70v. Judging from the plenipotentiaries' letters, it appears that the decision to give up on trying to delay the peace until Spain was defeated was made in November, 1647, well before the monarchy's financial collapse and the beginnings of the Fronde; see especially their letter of 18 November 1647 (above, footnote 4).

7. Plenipotentiaries to Louis XIV, 6 March 1648, CP All. 107, fols. 301r–301v.

8. Mazarin to Servien, 23 October 1648, *Lettres*, v. 3, 104; Mazarin to Turenne, 6 November 1648, in *Collection des Lettres et Mémoires trouvés dans les portefeuilles du Maréchal de Turenne*, ed. Général Comte de Grimoard, v. 2 (N.p., 1782), 70–76. These letters show that Mazarin made peace because of his fear of Sweden defecting, not because of the Fronde, as well as that he would have preferred to continue the Imperial conflict until Spain made peace. It seems inherently unlikely that Mazarin could have been forced to make peace in the Empire because of the Fronde when he was willing to continue the conflict with Spain in spite of it.

9. Zeller, *Comment s'est faite l'Alsace*, 120–21, and *De Christophe Colomb à Cromwell*, 263.

10. For example, see Guth, 411, 413–15; Geoffrey Treasure, *Seventeenth Century France* (New York, 1966), 181; Livet, "Louis XIV and the Germanies," in *Louis XIV and Europe*, ed. Ragnhild Hatton (Columbus, Ohio, 1976), 62.

11. Henry Kamen, "The Statesman," in *Baroque Personae*, ed. Rosario Villari, trans. Lydia G. Cochrane (Chicago, 1995), 24.

12. Johannes Burkhardt, *Der Dreißigjährige Krieg* (Frankfurt, 1992), 42–50; Lee, 68, 70; see also Lossky, 50–51, and Bonney, *The King's Debts*, 195.

13. For example, see Lee, 66, and Peter Limm, *The Thirty Years War* (New York, 1984), 42, the latter of which does not mention any Alsatian territory besides the Sundgau.

14. Lee, 66.

15. Parry, 295, 341.

16. See Stein, *Protection Royale*, and *APW 1.1*. Diplomatic historians have generally agreed that Mazarin's gains outweighed at least Richelieu's intentions, e.g., Malettke, 383–84; Lavisse, 26–27; Dickmann, *Der Westfälische Frieden*, 232 (the rare exception is Lee, 19). This is to focus on France's material gains, but one could also add the substantial advantage of weakening the Empire (for which see Goetze, 258–59).

17. D'Avaux to Mazarin, 7 April 1646, *APW II B 3*, 208; Louis XIV to plenipotentiaries, 9 December 1645, 17, p. 44–45.

18. Servien to Lionne, 3 May 1646, *APW II B 3*, 253, and 14/19 April 1646, 228. On the eve of the conclusion of the treaty, de la Court exclaimed that

all the French ministers were ecstatic about having achieved things "judged impossible"; de la Court to Lionne, 13 October 1648, CP All. v. 110, fols. 69r–73r.

19. D'Avaux to Mazarin, 18 April 1646, *APW II B 3*, 224.

20. Plenipotentiaries to Anne, 17 September 1646, *APW II B 4*, 159; see also Brienne to plenipotentiaries, 14 September 1646, 153, and Mazarin to d'Avaux, 20 July 1646, 80.

21. Cf. Osiander, 66–72.

22. Cf. Textor, 27–28.

23. Perkins, 248; Treasure, *Seventeenth-Century France*, 178; and Saint-Aulaire, 309 are among those to note Mazarin's patience and stability.

24. Henri de Rohan, *De l'intérêt des princes et des états de la chrétienté*, ed. Christian Lazzeri (Paris, 1995), 172.

25. Mazarin to d'Avaux, 20 July 1646, *APW II B 4*, 80; also Mazarin to plenipotentiaries, 31 May 1646, *APW II B 3*, 297 on the need to be patient in the negotiations if nothing happens soon.

26. Heyner, 109.

27. Mazarin to Turenne, 17 April 1645, CP Suède 6, fols. 240r–42r.

28. Louis XIV to plenipotentiaries, 31 August 1646, *APW II B 4*, 135.

29. Mazarin to d'Avaux, 7 April 1646, *APW II B 3*, 203. See also Brienne to plenipotentiaries, 9 September 1645, *APW II B 2*, 206; plenipotentiaries to Louis XIV, 9 July 1646, *APW II B 4*, 60; Brienne to plenipotentiaries, 27 July 1646, 86; ibid., 28 September 1646, 175; plenipotentiaries to Brienne, 10 September 1646, 148; and Anne to plenipotentiaries, 29 September 1646, 178.

30. See above, ch.5; also plenipotentiaries to Mazarin, 30 December 1646, *APW II B 3*, 46, p. 139; Servien to Lionne, 24 March 1646, 189, p. 517.

31. Brienne to plenipotentiaries, 17 August 1646, *APW II B 4*, 115; plenipotentiaries to Brienne, 21 May 1646, *APW II B 3*, 279. See also Brienne's comment on George Rakóczy: "He takes up arms easily and lays them down with equal facility." Brienne to plenipotentiaries, 21 September 1646, *APW II B 4*, 162.

32. Mazarin to d'Avaux, 3 August 1646, *APW II B 4*, 96; see also Brienne to plenipotentiaries, 31 August 1646, *APW II B 4*, 134, and plenipotentiaries to Brienne, 10 September 1646, 148.

33. Longueville to Mazarin, 2 July 1646, *APW II B 4*, 49; Mazarin to d'Avaux, 20 July 1646, 80.

34. Louis XIV to plenipotentiaries, 17 August 1646, *APW II B 4*, 116.

35. See also Raumer, 607–8, on the dangers of putting too much emphasis onto a particular statement of goals in primary sources.

36. Longueville to Mazarin, 13 June 1646, *APW II B 4*, 7.

37. See, for example, their attempt to include Neuenburg as one of the Forest Towns (above, chapter 8).

38. Goetze, 203–4, came to a similar conclusion about Swedish demands.

39. There is some reason to believe that Sweden followed a very different pattern, the central government issuing orders that changed their territorial demands materially every few months; see Tham, 362–64. This is a matter that needs further verification and study.

40. Charlie Sheen, "A Survey of the Notion of Christendom, Principally in France, 1580–1690," Ph. D. Diss. (UCLA, 1970), 2, 43–45. It is worth noting, however, that his own research shows that, even in the theoretical literature, almost all authors were more interested in their own particular states than in Christendom (pp. 23–45, especially 29–30). See also the introduction for a discussion of other historians' appraisals of Mazarin as peacemaker. See also Pierre

Blet, "Die Idee der Christianitas im Frankreich des 17. Jahrhunderts: Vorstellungen und Wirklichkeit," *Gregorianum* 7 (1976): 285–305, for a similar assessment to Sheen's, although not touching much directly on Mazarin. Even those who do not defend Mazarin overtly as a pacifist, e.g., Tapié (*Guerre de Trente Ans* (1989), 392–93), consider him more "international" than Richelieu.

41. Dethan, "Wicquefort et Callières," 96; see also Heyner, 97.
42. Guth, 415; Laurain-Portemer, 48.
43. Lossky, 60–61; Zeller, *L'Organisation défensive des frontières*, 45 (however, see footnote 47); Kalevi Holsti, *Peace and War: Armed Conflicts and International Order, 1648–1989*, v. 41 of *Cambridge Studies in International Relations* (New York, 1991), 38: "essentially defensive and order-constructing: to provide themselves ... with defensible frontiers" (again, see footnote 51); Treasure, *Mazarin*, 242–43.
44. Mazarin to d'Avaux, 26 April 1646, *APW II B 3*, 245.
45. Brienne to plenipotentiaries, 12 May 1646, *APW II B 3*, 263; Servien to Lionne, 3 May 1646, 253.
46. Plenipotentiaries to Anne, 17 September 1646, *APW II B 4*, 159.
47. Among the few historians to view Mazarin as aggressive are Heyner, 109, and Grand-Mesnil, 8–9 (calling Mazarin's policy "constantly bellicose"). Zeller, *La Guerre de Trente Ans*, 157, states that the French were generally "annexionnistes" and Mazarin himself an "annexionniste convaincu" in spite of certain misgivings at the beginning of his ministry. This would seem to contradict, or perhaps to supersede, his earlier statements about Mazarin being primarily defensive; see above, footnote 43. The problem of French aggression is intimately related to the question of change or continuity between Richelieu and Mazarin. While few have made Richelieu out to be the pacifist that historians have claimed Mazarin was, there seems to be a general sense that he was less aggressive than Mazarin. Berger, for example, claims that "the French approach to the war had undergone a basic and fundamental change"; until the 1640s, the war "had been fundamentally defensive," but now became "an offensive war, with new goals" (9). Admittedly, he concentrates on the struggle with Spain from 1648, but the same is not true of Dickmann, *Der Westfälische Frieden*, 118–19. Kurt von Raumer, "Westfälischer Friede," *Historische Zeitschrift* 195 (1962): 610–11, and "Zur Problematik des werdenden Machtstaats," *Historische Zeitschrift* 174 (1952): 75–76, makes a fundamental advance in showing that Richelieu's policies are inseparable from the conditions of his time, and hence that one cannot necessarily claim that he was less aggressive than Mazarin simply because he proposed to annex less (since the military situation was also less advantageous; had Richelieu survived until 1648, he might well have advanced similar policies to those Mazarin did). Hermann Weber has advanced similar ideas in "Richelieu et le Rhin," and his student Wolfgang Stein has investigated the subtlety of the shift in French policy in his dissertation, published as *Protection Royale*.
48. Textor, 23 (citing Reuss, *L'Alsace au dix-septième siècle*, v. 1, 148).
49. Chapter 8, footnote 84. Stein, *Protection Royale*, 328.
50. See also Tapié, *Guerre de Trente Ans* (1989), 404.
51. One of the few historians to recognize this is Holsti, 32, who writes that "Mazarin was more interested in French aggrandizement and less concerned with constructing a general peace system for Europe" than Richelieu.
52. Fritz Textor, especially pp. 28–9 and 282–3, seems closer to the truth here than Zeller, *L'organisation défensive*, 46. Even without direct evidence of a policy

of conquest, it is clear that France was getting more than it needed for its own defense.

53. Lossky, 60–61; Schumann, 198. The following contrary analysis finds a rare ally in Treasure, *Mazarin*, 264–65.

54. Mazarin to Longueville, 28 October 1645, *APW II B 2*, 246, p. 789.

55. Mazarin to plenipotentiaries, 1 June 1645, *APW II B 2*, 118; Lionne to Servien, 1 July 1645, 156.

56. On Contarini, plenipotentiaries to Brienne, 21 October 1645, *APW II B 2*, 242; see also Mazarin to Longueville, 28 October 1645, 246, p. 788 on Venetian pressure.

57. Mazarin to Longueville, 12 August 1645, *APW II B 2*, 184; Louis XIV to plenipotentiaries, 9 December 1645, *APW II B 3*, 17.

58. See, e.g., Louis XIV to plenipotentiaries, 30 September 1645, *APW II B 2*, 226; addition to main instructions, 23 November 1645, 267, p. 887–88. For this section, see also chapter 7.

59. Servien to Lionne, 11 November 1645, *APW II B 2*, 260; ibid., 5 August 1645, 182. Also memorandum from Servien, 15 July 1645, 168.

60. Servien to Lionne, 23 September 1645, *APW II B 2*, 223.

61. Mazarin to Longueville, 5 August 1645, *APW II B 2*, 179. See also Osiander, 23–24.

62. Barozzi and Berchet, 267–70.

63. Mazarin to Longueville, 9 September 1645, *APW II B 2*, 208. Louis XIV also seems not to have taken the Turkish threat as his own responsibility; see V.-L. Tapié, "Louis XIV's Methods in Foreign Policy," in *Louis XIV and Europe*, ed. Ragnhild Hatton (Columbus, Ohio, 1976), 8–9.

64. Mazarin to Longueville, 20 January 1646, *Lettres*, v. 2, 114.

65. Osiander, 23. See also the comments by David English Carmack, "Law in French Diplomacy: From the Treaty of Westphalia to the French Revolution, 1648–1789," Ph. D. Diss. (University of Virginia, 1963): "The norms that France upheld were upheld only out of self-interest. Vital interests were never subordinated to community interests." I find Charlie Sheen's description of Louis XIV as a statesman for whom Christendom had "a distinctly French flavour" to fit Mazarin as well ("The Fate of the Concept of Christendom in the Policy of Louis XIV: an Example from the King's Negotiations with the Empire, 1680–4," *European Studies Review* 3 (1973): 283–9). (This article would appear to differ significantly with the conclusions of his dissertation; see above, footnote 40.)

Fritz Dickmann, "Rechtsgedanke und Machtpolitik bei Richelieu: Studien an neu entdeckten Quellen," in *Friedensrecht und Friedenssicherung: Studien zum Friedensproblem in der Geschichte*, (Göttingen, 1971), 73–74, rejects the idea of Richelieu as an unprincipled statesman, emphasizing instead his theological background and how seriously he took law and "the higher goals of the state." Dickmann may be right that Richelieu took religion and law seriously, but it is hard not to be struck by the fact that the law is a plastic concept in his hands and always works out to his advantage (and that of France); see Dickmann's own examination of Richelieu's thought on pp. 65–70 of the same article. Mazarin is not Richelieu, of course, but their line of thinking appears to have been quite similar.

This is not to sanction Steinberg's assertion of Thirty Years' War diplomacy that "all decisions of consequence were taken in the cold light of what at the time became known as *raison d'état*" (p. 2). Some ministers, including the Frenchman d'Avaux, clearly did let religion influence their politics; Mazarin, however, seems to have been among the more purely political actors. (This point is also made in Weber's "Friede und Gewissen," *op. cit.*) On the other hand, Steinberg is correct to note (p. 99) that there was a certain self-consciousness to the French emphasis on *raison d'état*, at least for Mazarin and Servien.

66. For a nuanced (perhaps excessively nuanced) view of the notion that Christianity was in sharp decline during the 1640s, see Dupront, especially 59–60.

67. Saint-Aulaire, 307–8.

68. Evan Luard, *The Balance of Power: The System of International Relations, 1648–1815* (London, 1992), 341. The Peace of Westphalia is often seen as a landmark on the road to secularization (e.g., Leo Gross, "The Peace of Westphalia, 1648–1948," *The American Journal of International Law* 42 [1948]: 39, on the "lip service" the treaty paid to the idea of a Christian commonwealth); one need not adopt this view, however, to believe that Mazarin was a very secular thinker. John O'Connor ("Politique et utopie au début du XVIIe siècle: le Grand Dessein de Henri IV et de Sully," *XVIIe siècle* no. 174 (1992): 33–42, especially 40) notes that even renowned pacifists such as Sully and Crucé were interested in French aggrandizement, and emphasizes that "The Age of Dissimulation" is an accurate title. Even such a devout person as Maximilian of Bavaria put his government over the interests of the church; Immler, "Kurfürst Maximilian I. und die Kirche: Aspekte seiner Finanzpolitik während des Dreißigjährigen Krieges," *Zeitschrift für Bayerische Landesgeschichte* 51 (1988): 387–409.

69. Corvisier, *La France de Louis XIV*, 30–33.

70. Perhaps unsurprisingly, Steinberg, 76, also differs with the idea of Mazarin as an internationalist: "Contrary to Richelieu's far-sighted concepts of the concert of Europe, the Italian-born Mazarin took a narrowly French view of European problems." What is especially interesting about this statement is that Steinberg cites Mazarin's Italian birth while arguing for his French outlook, another example of how Mazarin's foreignness is considered central to his policies, whatever one thinks of them.

71. Mazarin to d'Avaux, 12 May 1646, *APW II B 3*, 265.

72. Livet, *Guerre et Paix*, 80. Livet was referring to the negotiations at the Congress of Westphalia in general, but they seem particularly applicable to Mazarin.

73. Guth, 415; Saint-Aulaire, 239.

74. Chapter 4, footnote 5.

75. Brienne to plenipotentiaries, 12 August 1645, *APW II B 2*, 183, p. 578.

76. In making this argument, I differ sharply with Andreas Osiander, 67, where he writes that "France had a comparatively small stake in the creation and preservation of a stable international system." To the contrary, it was clearly in French interests to keep Europe at peace precisely because they needed to guard their gains: it was the Imperials who wished to reignite a war at the first opportunity to win back what they had lost. This is why Richelieu formulated his plan of collective security (Dickmann, *Der Westfälische Frieden*, 52–54), and why Mazarin was very sensitive to the opinions of allies and neutrals. See also Goetze, 252–57, on Sweden's almost identical problems.

77. Mazarin to d'Estrades, 3 March 1646, *Correspondance authentique*, 142, p. 303.

78. This is evident above all from the context of the war, but at least one letter shows that the French were aware of the lack of flexibility in their negotiating position: on 24 June 1647, the plenipotentiaries wrote to Brienne that "it

would doubtless be desirable if one could achieve even more, but it is not easy to change things once they have been concluded" (plenipotentiaries to Brienne, BN Mf 15857, fols. 172r–75r).
79. Mazarin to Servien, 23 October 1648, *Lettres*, v. 3, 104.
80. Mazarin to Longueville, 9 September 1645, *APW II B 2*, 209.
81. Dickmann, *Der Westfälische Frieden*, 272.
82. Servien to Lionne, 25 March 1645, *APW II B 2*, 64, p. 207.
83. Addition to main instructions, 23 November 1645, *APW II B 2*, 267, pp. 887–88; see also Longueville to Mazarin, 14 May 1646, *APW II B 3*, 268, where he notes that France's "friends are as jealous of her as her enemies."
84. On the French need for alliances, see also Hermann Weber, "Chrétienté et équilibre européen dans la politique du cardinal de Richelieu," *XVIIe siècle* 42 (1990): 7–16. Weber is one of the few remaining defenders of the idea that the Peace of Westphalia was based at least partly on a balance of power, along with Holsti, 26; see also Weber's "Une Bonne Paix," 48–49, and the older study of Gross ("The Peace of Westphalia," 27–28). While some, such as Osiander (42–43 and 80–82), have rejected the Peace of Westphalia as having any role in the balance of power, others see it as having helped *cause* balance of power ideas rather than *being caused by* them; see Luard, 2–5, and Konrad Repgen, "Der Westfälische Friede und die Ursprünge des europäischen Gleichgewichts," in *Von der Reformation zur Gegenwart: Beiträge zu Grundfragen der neuzeitlichen Geschichte*, ed. Klaus Gotto and Hans Günter Hockerts (Paderborn, 1988), 53–66, especially 55.
85. Laurain-Portemer, 21–22, 25.
86. Laurain-Portemer's main example is Mazarin's decision to return to war on Sweden's side in 1647 after Bavaria violated the truce. However, contrary to her assertion, Mazarin delayed the reunion for several months rather than linking up immediately (see Riezler, 531–32, and above, footnote 3); moreover, France still had an important outstanding demand (that the emperor be forbidden from aiding Spain after the peace), so it was in France's own interests to continue to war. Many historians have noted the importance of maintaining alliances for France's success in the war, e.g., Kerviler, 62.
87. O'Connor, "The Diplomatic History of the Reign," 151; also Livet, "Louis XIV and the Germanies," 66.
88. Zeller, *La Guerre de Trente Ans*, 210–11.
89. For example, see Holsti, *op. cit.;* see also the introduction to part I, footnote 26.
90. Pillar, 37; Michael Handel, *War Termination—A Critical Survey* (Jerusalem, 1978), 28–47, especially 35 and 37; Robert F. Randle, *The Origins of Peace: A Study of Peacemaking and the Structure of Peace Settlements* (New York, 1973), 116–57, 357.
91. Corvisier, "'Modernité' de la guerre de Trente Ans," 105–7, has noted the particularly flexible nature of Thirty Years' War alliances. This factor deserves further study as a stage in the development of modern coalition wars.
92. On the way Richelieu's alliance system delayed the negotiations, see Hermann Weber, "Une Bonne Paix," 61–69.
93. Pillar, 224–25.
94. Parker, *The Thirty Years' War*, 170–73.

Bibliography

Archival Sources

Bonn

Vereinigung zur Erforschung der Neueren Geschichte
Pre-publication editions of series 2, part B, volumes 3 and 4, and series 3, part B of the *Acta Pacis Westphalicae*.

Marburg

Hessisches Staatsarchiv, Marburg
Kriegssachen, 2218
Familienarchiv der Reichsfreiherren von Dörnberg, 4125

Munich

Bayerisches Hauptstaatsarchiv
Kurbayern Äußeres Archiv, 2788, 2795–96, 2818, 2846, 2849, 2890, 2902, 3051, 3054, 3056, 3058, 3065
Kasten Schwarz, 7679, 7981, 16402, 16406–7
Kurbayern Geheimer Rat, 197–9, 201

Paris

Archives du Ministère des Affaires Étrangères
Correspondance politique
Allemagne, vols. 23–28, 33–34, 45, 49, 53, 56, 60–68, 87, 98–103, 107–108, 110, 112–13, 118–23
Bavière, v. 2.
Suède, vols. 6–8, 12.
Mémoires et Documents
France, vols. 9, 23, 261, 406, 849, 852, 855–56, 1421, 1424, 1965
Bibliothèque Nationale, Manuscrits
Fonds français, 4169–71, 4173–74, 4176–77, 4198–203, 6180, 10640, 10647, 15857, 15863, 17948.
Nouvelles acquisitions françaises, 6210
Manuscrits italiens, 1827–29
Archives de Guerre
Correspondance, 89–90, 93–94, 97, 99–100, 107–8

Bibliothèque Mazarine
  Manuscrits, 2214–16, 1849
Wolfenbüttel
Herzog August Bibliothek
  Augustei, 11.8

Printed Primary Sources and Memoirs

Barozzi, Nicolò and Guglielmo Berchet, eds. *Relazioni degli stati europei lette al senato dagli ambasciatori veneti nel secolo decimosettimo.* Series 2, Francia. Volume 2. Venice, 1859.

Bérenger, Jean, Ph. Loupès, and J.-P. Kintz, eds. *Guerre et Paix dans l'Europe du XVIIe siècle: Textes et documents.* Paris, 1991.

Brienne, Henri de Loménie, comte de. *Mémoires du Comte de Brienne.* Collection des mémoires relatifs à l'histoire de France depuis l'avénement de Henri IV jusqu'à la Paix de Paris conclue en 1763. Edited by M. Petitot, vols. 35 and 36. Paris, 1824.

Brienne, Louis-Henri de Loménie, Comte de. *Mémoires de Louis-Henri de Loménie, comte de Brienne, dit le jeune Brienne,* edited by Paul Bonnefon. 2 volumes. Paris, 1916.

Dumont, Jean. *Corps Universel du Droit des Gens.* 8 volumes. Amsterdam, 1726–31.

Estrades, Comte d'. *Correspondance authentique de Godefroi comte d'Estrades,* edited by A. de Saint-Léger and L. Lemaire. Volume 1. Paris, 1924.

Gramont, Maréchal de. *Mémoires du Maréchal de Gramont, duc et pair de France.* Nouvelle collection des mémoires pour servir à l'histoire de France, depuis le XIIIe siècle jusqu'à la fin du XVIIIe. Edited by Michaud and Poujoulat, v. 7. Paris, 1839.

Le Clerc, Jean. *Négociations secrètes touchant la paix de Munster et d'Osnabrug.* 4 volumes. Amsterdam, 1726.

Mazarin, Cardinal. *Lettres du Cardinal Mazarin,* edited by Adolphe Chéruel. Vols.1–3. Paris, 1872.

Montpensier, Mademoiselle de. *Mémoires de Mademoiselle de Montpensier, Fille de Gaston d'Orléans, Frère de Louis XIII.* Collection des mémoires relatifs à l'histoire de France depuis l'avénement de Henri IV jusqu'à la Paix de Paris conclue en 1763. Edited by M. Petitot, v. 40. Paris, 1824.

Motteville, Madame de. *Mémoires de Madame de Motteville.* Collection des mémoires relatifs à l'histoire de France depuis l'avénement de Henri IV jusqu'à la Paix de Paris conclue en 1763. Edited by M. Petitot, vols. 36 and 37. Paris, 1819–1829.

Parry, Clive, ed. *The Consolidated Treaty Series.* Vol. 1, *1648–1649.* Dobbs Ferry, New York, 1969.

Pontis, Sieur de. *Mémoires du Sieur de Pontis.* Collection des mémoires relatifs à l'histoire de France depuis l'avénement de Henri IV jusqu'à la Paix de Paris conclue en 1763. Edited by M. Petitot, vols. 31 and 32. Paris, 1824.

Rabutin, Roger de. *Mémoires de Roger de Rabutin, comte de Bussy.* 2 volumes. Paris, 1857.

Repgen, Konrad, and Max Braubach (d.), eds. *Acta Pacis Westphalicae*. 3 series. Münster, 1962 ff.

Turenne, Viscount. *Collection des Lettres et Mémoires trouvés dans les portefeuilles du Maréchal de Turenne*, edited by Général Comte de Grimoard. 2 vols. N.p., 1782.

———. *Correspondance inédite de Turenne avec Michel le Tellier et avec Louvois*, edited by Édouard de Barthélemy. Paris, n.d.

———. *Lettres de Turenne extraites des archives Rohan-Bouillon*. Edited by Suzanne d'Huart. Paris, 1971.

———. *Mémoires du Maréchal de Turenne*, edited by Paul Marichal. Paris, 1909.

Vast, Henri, ed. *Les Grands Traités du Règne de Louis XIV*. Paris, 1893.

Secondary Sources

Abmeier, Karlies. *Der Trierer Kurfürst Philipp Christoph von Sötern und der Westfälische Friede*. Schriftenreihe der Vereinigung zur Erforschung der Neueren Geschichte, v. 15. Münster, 1986.

Allen, E. John B. *Post and Courier Service in the Diplomacy of Early Modern Europe*. The Hague, 1972.

Allen, Paul. "The Strategy of Peace: Spanish Foreign Policy and the *"Pax Hispanica,"* 1598–1609." Ph.D. diss. Yale, 1995.

Allmayer-Beck, Johann Christoph, and Erich Lessing. *Die Kaiserliche Kriegsvölker von Maximilian I bis Prinz Eugen 1479–1718*. Munich, 1978.

Anderson, M. S. *The Rise of Modern Diplomacy, 1450–1919*. New York, 1993.

———. *War and Society in Europe of the Old Regime, 1618–1789*. Leicester, 1988.

Anderson, Perry. *Lineages of the Absolutist State*. London, 1974.

André, Louis. *Michel Le Tellier et l'organisation de l'armée monarchique*. Paris, 1906.

Aumale, Duc d'. *Histoire des princes de Condé pendant les XVIe et XVIIe siècles*. Volume 4. Paris, 1886.

Babel, Rainer. "Der Westfälischer Friedenskongreß in französischer Sicht: Ein Tagebuchfragment Nicolas Doulceurs aus den Jahren 1647 und 1648." *Francia* 16 part 2 (1989): 13–27.

Bardot, Georges. *La question des dix villes impériales d'Alsace depuis la paix de Westphalie jusqu'aux arrêts de "réunion" du conseil souverain de Brisach, 1648–1680*. Paris, 1899.

Barker, Thomas M. *The Military Intellectual and Battle: Raimondo Montecuccoli and the Thirty Years War*. Albany, 1975.

———. "Ottavio Piccolomini (1599–1659): A Fair Historical Judgement?" In *Army, Aristocracy, Monarchy: Essays on War, Society, and Government in Austria, 1618–1780*, 61–111. War and Society in East Central Europe, v. 7. New York, 1979.

Barthold, F.W. *Geschichte des großen deutschen Krieges vom Tode Gustav Adolfs ab mit besonderer Rücksicht auf Frankreich*. 2 parts. Stuttgart, 1843.

Barua, Pradeep. "Military Developments in India, 1750–1850." *Journal of Military History* 58 (1994): 599–616.

Batiffol, Louis. "Richelieu et la Question de l'Alsace." *Revue historique* 138 (1921): 161–200.

Baxter, Douglas Clark. *Servants of the Sword: French Intendants of the Army, 1630–70.* Urbana, Illinois, 1976.

Beck, Kurt. *Der Hessische Bruderzwist zwischen Hessen-Kassel und Hessen-Darmstadt in den Verhandlungen zum Westfälischen Frieden von 1644 bis 1648.* Frankfurt, 1978.

Beik, William. *Absolutism and Society in Seventeenth-Century France: State Power and Provincial Aristocracy in Languedoc.* New York, 1985.

Beller, E. A. "The Thirty Years War." In *The Decline of Spain and the Thirty Years War 1609–48/59,* edited by J. P. Cooper, 306–358. Vol. 4 of *The New Cambridge Modern History.* Cambridge, 1970.

Bely, Lucien. *Espions et ambassadeurs au temps de Louis XIV.* Paris, 1990.

———. *Les relations internationales en Europe (XVIIe-XVIIIe siècles).* Paris, 1992.

Bély, Lucien, Jean Bérenger, and André Corvisier. *Guerre et paix dans l'Europe du XVIIe siècle.* 2d edition, 2 vols. Paris, 1991.

Bérenger, Jean. *Turenne.* Paris, 1987.

Berger, Peter Jonathan. "Military and Financial Government in France, 1648–1661." Ph.D. Diss. University of Chicago, 1979.

Bergin, Joseph. "Richelieu: A Prelate's Progress." *History Today* 41 (January 1991): 14–20.

Bernays, Isaak. "Die Diplomatie um 1500." *Historische Zeitschrift* 138 (1928): 1–23.

Bettenhäuser, Erwin. *Die Landgrafschaft Hessen-Kassel auf dem Westfälischen Friedenskongress 1644–1648.* Wiesbaden, 1983.

Bigby, Dorothy A. "An Unknown Treaty between England and France, 1644." *English Historical Review* 28 (1913): 337–41.

Biographie Générale, Nouvelle . . . , depuis les temps les plus reculés jusqu'à nos jours. 46 volumes. Paris, 1862–1866.

Birely, Robert. "Antimachiavellism, the Baroque and Maximilian of Bavaria." *Archivum Historicum Societatis Jesu* 53 (1984): 137–59.

Black, Jeremy. *A Military Revolution? Military Change and European Society, 1550–1800.* London, 1991.

Blet, Pierre. "Die Idee der Christianitas im Frankreich des 17. Jahrhunderts: Vorstellungen und Wirklichkeit." *Gregorianum* 7 (1976): 285–305.

Bonaparte, Napoleon. *Précis des guerres de Napoléon Ier.* Paris, 1965.

Bonney, Richard. *The King's Debts.* Oxford, 1981.

———. *Political Change in France Under Richelieu and Mazarin.* Oxford, 1978.

Bosbach, Franz. "Introduction." In *Die Französischen Korrespondenzen, 1645.* Edited by Franz Bosbach. Acta Pacis Westphalicae, series 2, section B, v. 2. Münster, 1986.

———. *Die Kosten des Westfälischen Friedenskongresses: Eine strukturgeschichtliche Untersuchung.* Schriftenreihe der Vereinigung zur Erforschung der Neueren Geschichte, v. 13. Münster, 1984.

Braun, Pierre. "La Lorraine pendant le gouvernement de La Ferté-Sénectère (1643–1661)." *Mémoires de la Société d'Archéologie lorraine et du Musée Historique lorrain* 56 (4th ser., v. 6) (1906): 109–266.

Broucek, Peter. *Die Eroberung von Bregenz am 4. Jänner 1647.* Militärhistorische Schriftenreihe, v. 18. Vienna, 1971.

———. "Erzherzog Leopold-Wilhelm und der Oberbefehl über das kaiserliche Heer im Jahre 1645." In *Aus drei Jahrhunderten: Beiträge zur osterreichischen Heeres-und Kriegsgeschichte,* 8–38. (Schriften des Heeresgeschichtlichen Museums Wien, v. 4). Vienna, 1969.

———. *Der Schwedenfeldzug nach Niederösterreich 1645/46.* Militärhistorische Schriftenreihe, v. 7. Vienna, 1967.

Burkhardt, Johannes. *Der Dreißigjährige Krieg.* Frankfurt, 1992.

Carmack, David English. "Law in French Diplomacy: From the Treaty of Westphalia to the French Revolution, 1648–1789." Ph.D. Diss. University of Virginia, 1963.

Carroll, Berenice A. "War Termination and Conflict Theory: Value Premises, Theories, and Policies." *Annals American Academy of Political and Social Science* 392 (November 1970): 14–29.

Carter, Charles H. "The Ambassadors of Early Modern Europe: Patterns of Diplomatic Representation in the Early Seventeenth Century." In *From the Renaissance to the Counter-Reformation: Essays in Honor of Garrett Mattingly.* Edited by Charles H. Carter, 269–95. New York, 1965.

Cate, Curtis. "The Making of a Marshal." *MHQ* v. 5 no.3 (Spring 1993): 26–35.

Chaboche, Robert. "Les soldats français de la guerre de Trente Ans, une tentative d'approche." *Revue d'histoire moderne et contemporaine* 20 (1973): 10–24.

Chagniot, Jean. "Ethique et pratique de la 'profession des armes' chez les officiers français au XVIIe siècle." In *Guerre et Pouvoir en Europe au XVIIe siècle.* Edited by Viviane Barrie-Curien, 79–93. Paris, 1991.

Charvériat, Émile. *Histoire de la Guerre de Trente Ans.* 2 vols. Paris, 1878.

Chéruel, Adolphe. "Le Baron Charles d'Avaugour, ambassadeur de France en Suède 1654–1657." *Revue d'histoire diplomatique* 3 (1889): 523–34.

———. "Henri Groulart, Seigneur de La Court: Sa correspondance relative aux négociations qui ont préparé la paix de Westphalie." *Revue des sociétés savantes,* 2d series (1860, pt. 2): 451–66 and 579–96.

———. *Histoire de France pendant la minorité de Louis XIV.* 4 vols. Paris, 1879.

Church, William F. *Richelieu and Reason of State.* Princeton, New Jersey, 1972.

Clausewitz, Carl von. *On War,* edited and translated by Michael Howard and Peter Peret. Princeton, New Jersey, 1976.

Colegrove, Kenneth. "Diplomatic Procedure Preliminary to the Congress of Westphalia." *American Journal of International Law* 13 (1919): 450–82.

Corvisier, André. *La France de Louis XIV: ordre intérieur et place en Europe.* 3d edition. Paris, 1979.

———. "'Modernité' de la guerre de Trente Ans." In *Destins et enjeux du XVIIe siècle.* Edited by Yves-Marie Bercé et al., 95–107. Paris, 1985.

Cousin, Victor. *La Jeunesse de Mazarin.* Paris, 1865.

Dedijer, Stevan. "The Rainbow Scheme: British Secret Service and Pax Britannica." In *Clio Goes Spying: Eight Essays on the History of Intelligence,* edited by Wilhelm Agrell and Bo Huldt, 10–63. Lund Studies in International History, v. 17. Malmö, 1983.

Des Robert, Ferdinand. *Charles IV et Mazarin (1643–1661).* Nancy, 1899.

Dethan, Georges. *La Vie de Gaston d'Orléans.* Paris, 1992.

———. *Mazarin: Un homme de paix à l'âge baroque, 1602–1661.* Paris, 1981.

———. "Wicquefort et Callières à l'ombre de Mazarin?" In *Guerre et Pouvoir en Europe au XVIIe siècle*, edited by Viviane Barrie-Curien, 95–103. Paris, 1991.

Dickmann, Fritz. "Rechtsgedanke und Machtpolitik bei Richelieu: Studien an neu entdeckten Quellen." In *Friedensrecht und Friedenssicherung: Studien zum Friedensproblem in der Geschichte*, 36–78. Göttingen, 1971.

———. *Der Westfälische Frieden*. 2d ed. Münster, 1965.

Dictionnaire des Maréchaux de France du Moyen Age à nos jours. N.p., 1988.

Dollinger, Philippe. "Le Traité de Westphalie et l'Alsace." In *Deux siècles d'Alsace française*. Paris, 1948.

Dulong, Claude. *La Fortune du Mazarin*. Paris, 1990.

Dupaquier, Jean. *Le Maréchal de Rantzau, 1609–1650: . . . son sang fut en cent lieux le prix de la victoire et Mars ne lui laissa rien d'entier que le coeur*. N.p., 1985.

Dupront, Alphonse. "De la Chrétienté à l'Europe: La passion westphalienne du Nonce Fabio Chigi." In *Forschungen und Studien zur Geschichte des Westfälischen Friedens: Vorträge bei dem Colloquium französischer und deutscher Historiker vom 28. April—30. April 1963 in Münster*, 49–84. Münster, 1965.

Du Toc, Fauvelet. *Histoire des secretaires d'estat, contenant l'origine, le progrés, et l'établissement de leurs charges, avec les éloges, les armes, blasons, et généalogies de tous ceux qui les ont possédées jusqu'à present*. Paris, 1668.

Ekberg, Carl. "Abel Servien, Cardinal Mazarin, and the Formulation of French Foreign Policy, 1653–1659." *International History Review* 3 (1981): 317–29.

Elliott, John H. "A Europe of Composite Monarchies." *Past and Present* 137 (1992): 48–71.

Enaux-Moret, Anne Marie. "Abel Servien, négociateur des traités de Westphalie: du parlement de Grenoble à la surintendance des finances, 1593–1659." Ph.D. Diss. Paris, 1968.

Engel, Josef. "Von der spätmittelalterlichen respublica christiana zum Mächte-Europa der Neuzeit." In *Die Entstehung des neuzeitlichen Europa*. Edited by Josef Engel. Handbuch der europäischen Geschichte, v. 3. Stuttgart, 1971.

Englund, Peter. *Ofredsår: Om den svenska stormaktstiden och en man i dess mitt*. Stockholm, 1993.

Evans, Peter, Dietrich Rueschemeyer, and Theda Skocpol, eds. *Bringing the State Back In*. New York, 1985.

Federn, Karl. *Mazarin*. Munich, 1922.

Fezer, Fritz, and Uwe Muuß. *Luftbildatlas Baden-Württemberg: Eine Landeskunde in 72 farbigen Luftaufnahmen*. Munich, 1971.

Fleitmann, Wilhelm. "Postverbindungen für den Westfälischen Friedenskongreß 1643 bis 1648." *Archiv für deutsche Postgeschichte* 1 (1972): 3–48.

Foerster, Joachim. *Kurfürst Ferdinand von Köln: Die Politik seiner Stifter in den Jahren 1634–1650*. Schriftenreihe der Vereinigung zur Erforschung der Neueren Geschichte, v. 6. Münster, 1976.

Foot, Rosemary. *A Substitute for Victory: The Politics of Peacemaking at the Korean Armistice Talks*. Ithaca, New York, 1990.

Frauenholz, Eugen von. *Entwicklungsgeschichte des deutschen Heerwesens*, edited by Eugen von Frauenholz. V.3, *Das Heerwesen in der Zeit des Dreissigjährigen Krieges*. Part 2, *Die Landesdefension*. Munich, 1939.

Gagliardo, John G. *Germany under the Old Regime, 1600–1790*. New York, 1991.

Gallati, Frieda. "Die Eidgenössische Politik zur Zeit des Dreißigjährigen Krieges." Part 2. *Jahrbuch fur Schweizer Geschichte* 41 (1919): 1–257.

Garden, Comte de. *Histoire générale des traités de paix et autres transactions principales entre toutes les puissances de l'Europe depuis la paix de Westphalie.* Volume 1. Paris, 1848.

Goetze, Sigmund. *Die Politik des schwedischen Reichskanzlers Axel Oxenstierna gegenüber Kaiser und Reich.* Volume 3 of Beiträge zur Sozial-und Wirtschaftsgeschichte. Edited by Wilhelm Koppe. Kiel, 1971.

Gonzenbach, August von. *Der General Hans Ludwig von Erlach von Castelen. Ein Lebens-und Charakterbild aus den Zeiten des dreißigjährigen Kriegs.* 3 vols. Bern, 1880.

Goodman, Allan E., ed. *Negotiating While Fighting: The Diary of Admiral C. Turner Joy at the Korean Armistice Conference.* Stanford, 1978.

Goubert, Pierre. *Mazarin.* Paris, 1990.

Grand-Mesnil, Marie-Noële. *Mazarin, la Fronde et la Presse.* Paris, 1967.

Greengrass, Mark, ed. *Conquest and Coalescence: The Shaping of the State in Early Modern Europe.* New York, 1991.

Grimmelshausen, Hans Jacob Christoph von. *Der aberteuerliche Simplicissimus Teutsch.* Stuttgart, 1985.

Gross, Leo. "The Peace of Westphalia, 1648–1948." *The American Journal of International Law* 42 (1948): 20–41.

Guth, Paul. *Mazarin.* Paris, 1972.

Gyllenstierna, Colonel E. "Henri de Turenne et Charles Gustave Wrangel." In *Turenne et l'Art Militaire.* Paris, 1975.

Hall, Geoffrey F., and Joan Sanders. *D'Artagnan: The Ultimate Musketeer.* Boston, 1964.

Handel, Michael. *War Termination—A Critical Survey.* Jerusalem, 1978.

Hanley, Sarah. *The Lit de Justice of the Kings of France: Constitutional Ideology in Legend, Ritual, and Discourse.* Studies Presented to the International Commission for the History of Representative and Parliamentary Institutions, v. 65. Princeton, New Jersey, 1983.

Harley, J. Eugene. "The Obligation to Ratify Treaties: Is Ratification Necessary for the Validity of a Treaty?" *American Journal of International Law* 13 (1919): 389–405.

Hart, B. H. Liddell. *Strategy.* 2d revised edition. New York, 1967.

Hartmann, Peter Claus. "Bayern als Faktor der französischen Politik während des Dreißigjährigen Krieges." *Um Glauben und Reich: Kurfürst Maximilian I. Beiträge zur Bayerischen Geschichte und Kunst, 1573–1657,* 448–455. V. 2, part 1 of *Wittelsbach und Bayern.* Munich, 1980.

Hatton, Ragnhild. "Louis XIV and His Fellow Monarchs." In *Louis XIV and Europe.* Edited by Ragnhild Hatton, 16–59. Columbus, Ohio, 1976.

Heilmann, Johann. *Die Feldzüge der Bayern in den Jahren 1643, 1644 und 1645.* Munich, 1851.

———. *Kriegsgeschichte von Bayern, Franken, Pfalz und Schwaben von 1506 bis 1651.* Munich, 1868.

Heimer, August. *De Diplomatiska Förbindelserna mellan Sverige och England, 1633–1654.* Lund, 1893.

Helly, M.A. *Deux Diplomates Dauphinois au XVIIème Siècle: Abel Servien—Hugues de Lionne.* Grenoble, 1924.

Heydendorff, Walther Ernst. "Vorderösterreich im Dreißigjährigen Kriege. Der Verlust der Vorlande am Rhein und die Versuche zu deren Rückgewinnung. Teil 2, 1639–1648." *Mitteilungen des Österreichischen Staatsarchivs* 13 (1960): 107–94.

Heyner, Georg. *Mazarins Bündnispolitik in Deutschland (1643–1648).* Marburg, 1946.

Holsti, Kalevi. *Peace and War: Armed Conflicts and International Order, 1648–1989.* Cambridge Studies in International Relations, v. 14. New York, 1991.

Howard, Michael. *War in European History.* New York, 1976.

Iklé, Fred Charles. *Every War Must End.* New York, 1971.

Immler, Gerhard. "Bayerisch-Spanische Beziehungen während des dreissigjährigen Krieges, insbesondere in den Jahren 1643–1645." In Johannes Greipl, Alois Schmid, and Walter Ziegler, eds., *Aus Bayerns Geschichte: Forschungen als Festgabe zum 70. Geburtstag von Andreas Kraus.* St. Ottilien, 1992.

———. "Kurfüst Maximilian I. und die Kirche: Aspekte seiner Finanzpolitik während des Dreißigjährigen Krieges." *Zeitschrift für Bayerische Landesgeschichte* 51 (1988): 387–409.

———. *Kurfürst Maximilian I. und der Westfälische Friedenskongreß.* Schriftenreihe der Vereinigung zur Erforschung der Neueren Geschichte, v. 20. Münster, 1992.

Irsigler, Ursula. "Einleitung." In *Die französischen Korrespondenzen, 1644,* edited by Ursula Irsigler and Kriemhild Gorozny. Series II, part B, v. 1 of *Acta Pacis Westphalicae.* Münster, 1986.

Israel, Jonathan I. *The Dutch Republic and the Hispanic World, 1606–1661.* New York, 1982.

———. "Olivares, the Cardinal-Infante and Spain's Strategy in the Low Countries (1635–1643): the Road to Rocroy." In *Spain, Europe and the Atlantic world: Essays in honour of John H. Elliott.* Edited by Richard Kagan and Geoffrey Parker, 267–95. Cambridge, 1995.

Jacob, Karl. *Die Erwerbung des Elsass durch Frankreich im westfälischen Frieden.* Strasbourg, 1897.

Jones, Colin. "The Welfare of the French Foot-Soldier." *History* 65 (1980): 193–213.

Kamen, Henry. "The Statesman." In *Baroque Personae,* edited by Rosario Villari, translated by Lydia G. Cochrane, 9–31. Chicago, 1995.

Kapser, Cordula. *Die bayerische Kriegsorganisation in der zweiten Hälfte des Dreißigjährigen Krieges, 1635–1648/49.* Schriftenreihe der Vereinigung zur Erforschung der Neueren Geschichte, vol. 25. Münster, 1997.

Kellenbrenz, Hermann. "Hamburg und die französisch-schwedische Zusammenarbeit im 30jährigen Krieg." In *Der Dreissigjährige Krieg: Perspektiven und Strukturen,* edited by Hans Ulrich Rudolf, 267–297. Wege der Forschung, v. 451. Darmstadt, 1977.

Kern, Fritz. *Die Anfänge der französischen Ausdehnungspolitik bis zum Jahr 1308.* Tübingen, 1910.

Kerviler, René. "Abel Servien." *Revue Historique et Archéologique du Maine* 2 (1877): 593–649; 3 (1878): 29–96, 167–245.

Kleinman, Ruth. *Anne of Austria, Queen of France.* Columbus, Ohio, 1985.

Kraus, Andreas. *Die Acta Pacis Westphalicae: Rang und geisteswissenschaftliche Bedeutung eines Editionsunternehmens unserer Zeit, untersucht an Hand der Elsaß-Frage (1640–1646).* Rheinisch-Westfälische Akademie der Wissenschaften, Geisteswissenschaften: Vorträge, v. 269. Düsseldorf, 1984.

―――. "Frankreich und die Pfalzfrage auf dem westfälischen Friedenskongreß." In *Études d'histoire européenne: Mélanges offerts à René et Suzanne Pillorget*, 97–112. Angers, 1990.

―――. "Kurfürst Maximilian I. von Bayern und die französische Satisfaction (1644–1646): Neue Quellen zu einem alten Problem." In *Land und Reich—Stamm und Nation: Probleme und Perspektiven bayerischer Geschichte. Festgabe für Max Spindler zum 90. Geburtstag*, edited by Andreas Kraus. Volume 2, *Frühe Neuzeit*. Munich, 1984.

―――. *Maximilian I.: Bayerns Großer Kurfürst.* Graz, 1990.

Krekeler, Heinz L. *Die Diplomatie.* Geschichte und Staat, v. 110–111. Munich, 1965.

Kroener, Bernhard. "Die Entwicklung der Truppenstärke in den französischen Armeen zwischen 1635 und 1661." In *Forschungen und Quellen zur Geschichte des Dreißigjährigen Krieges*, 163–220. Schriftenreihe der Vereinigung zur Erforschung der Neueren Geschichte, v. 12. Münster, 1981.

―――. *Les Routes et les Étapes: Die Versorgung der französischen Armeen in Nordostfrankreich (1635–1661). Ein Beitrag zur Verwaltungsgeschichte des Ancien Régime.* Schriftenreihe der Vereinigung zur Erforschung der Neueren Geschichte, v. 11. Münster, 1980.

―――. "Soldat oder Soldateska? Programmatischer Aufriß einer Sozialgeschichte militärischer unterschichten in der ersten Hälfte des 17. Jahrhunderts." In *Militärgeschichte: Probleme—Thesen—Wege*, edited by Manfred Messerschmidt et al., 100–123. Beiträge zur Militär-und Kriegsgeschichte, v. 25. Stuttgart, 1982.

Lahrkamp, Helmut. *Jan von Werth. Sein Leben nach archivalischen Quellenzeugnissen.* Veröffentlichungen des kölnischen Geschichtsvereins, v. 24. Cologne, 1962.

―――. "Lothar Dietrich Freiherr von Bönninghausen: Ein westfälischer Söldnerführer des Dreißigjährigen Krieges." *Westfälische Zeitschrift* 108 (1958): 239–365.

Langer, Herbert. *The Thirty Years' War.* Translated by C. S. V. Salt. Dorset, 1978.

Laurain-Portemer, Madeleine. "Questions Européennes et Diplomatie Mazarine." *XXVIIe siècle* 42 (1990): 17–56.

Lavisse, Ernest. *Louis XIV: Histoire d'un grand règne, 1643–1715.* 1908. Reprint. Paris, 1989.

Lee, Stephen J. *The Thirty Years War.* New York, 1991.

Limm, Peter. *The Thirty Years War.* New York, 1984.

Linage de Vauciennes, P. *Memoires de ce qui s'est passé en Suede, et aux provinces voisines, depuis l'année 1645 jusques en l'année 1655.* Volume 1. Cologne, 1677.

Livet, Georges. *La Guerre de Trente Ans.* Que Sais-Je, v. 1083. Paris, 1966.

―――. "Guerre et Paix (XVIIe siècle)." Ch. IX in *Documents de l'histoire de l'Alsace*, edited by P. Dollinger. Toulouse, 1972.

―――. *Guerre et Paix de Machiavel à Hobbes.* Paris, 1972.

———. *L'intendance d'Alsace sous Louis XIV, 1648–1715*. Strasbourg, 1956.

———. "International Relations and the Role of France 1648–1660." In *The New Cambridge Modern History*. V.4: *The Decline of Spain and the Thirty Years War 1609–48/59*, edited by J. P. Cooper, 411–34. Cambridge, 1970.

———. "Louis XIV and the Germanies." In *Louis XIV and Europe*, edited by Ragnhild Hatton, 60–81. Columbus, Ohio, 1976.

Lorents, Yngve. *Efter Brömsebrofreden: Svenska och Danska Förbindelser med Frankrike och Holland, 1645–1649*. Uppsala, 1916.

Losman, Arne. "The European Communications Network of Carl Gustaf Wrangel and Magnus Gabriel de la Gardie." In *Europe and Scandinavia: Aspects of the Process of Integration in the 17th Century*, edited by Göran Rystad, 195–200. Lund, 1983.

Lossky, Andrew. *Louis XIV and the French Monarchy*. New Brunswick, New Jersey, 1994.

Lotichium, J. P. *Theatri Europaei oder Historische Beschreibung aller Vornembsten und Denkwürdigsten Geschichten, so sich hin und wieder in Europa sonderlich im Reich Teütscher Nation von A. 1642 biß A. 1647 zugetragen*. Part 5. Frankfurt, 1647.

Luard, Evan. *The Balance of Power: The System of International Relations, 1648–1815*. London, 1992.

Lundgren, Sune. *Johan Adler Salvius: Problem Kring Freden, Krigsekonomien och Maktkampen*. Lund, 1945.

Lundkvist, Sven. "Die schwedischen Kriegs-und Friedensziele 1632–1648." In *Krieg und Politik 1618–1648: Europäische Probleme und Perspektiven*, edited by Konrad Repgen. Schriften des Historischen Kollegs, Kolloquien, v. 8. Munich, 1988.

Lutz, Luitpold. *Die Bayerische Artillerie von ihren ersten Anfängen bis zur Gegenwart*. Munich, 1894.

Lynn, John A. "Food, Funds, and Fortresses: Resource Mobilization and Positional Warfare in the Campaigns of Louis XIV." In *Feeding Mars: Logistics in Western Warfare from the Middle Ages to the Present*, edited by John A. Lynn, 137–59. Boulder, Colorado, 1993.

———. *Giant of the Grand Siècle: The French Army, 1610–1715*. Cambridge, 1997.

———. "The History of Logistics and *Supplying War*." In *Feeding Mars: Logistics in Western Warfare from the Middle Ages to the Present*, edited by John A. Lynn, 9–27. Boulder, Colorado, 1993.

———. "How War Fed War: The Tax of Violence and Contributions During the Grand Siècle." *The Journal of Modern History* 65 (1993): 286–310.

———. "A Quest for Glory: The Formation of Strategy under Louis XIV, 1661–1715." In *The Making of Strategy: Rulers, States, and War*, edited by Williamson Murray, MacGregor Knox, and Alvin Bernstein, 178–204. New York, 1994.

———. "Recalculating French Army Growth during the *Grand Siècle*, 1610–1715." *French Historical Studies* 18 (1994): 881–906.

———. "Tactical Evolution in the French Army, 1560–1660." *French Historical Studies* 14 (1985): 176–191.

Maier, Franz. *Die bayerische Unterpfalz im Dreißigjährigen Krieg: Besetzung, Verwaltung und Rekatholisierung der rechtsrheinischen Pfalz durch Bayern 1621 bis 1649*. New York, 1990. (In European University Studies, series 3, v. 428.)

Maland, David. *Europe at War, 1600–1650*. New York, 1980.

Malettke, Klaus. "Diplomatie et Guerre: Les traités de Westphalie, Münster et Osnabrück 1643–1648." *XVIIe siècle*, no.182 (1994): 153–70.

———. *Frankreich, Deutschland und Europa im 17. und 18. Jahrhundert. Beiträge zum Einfluß französischer politischer Theorie, Verfassung und Außenpolitik in der Frühen Neuzeit*. Marburger Studien zur Neueren Geschichte, v. 4. Marburg, 1994.

Masson, Bernard. "Un Aspect de la Discipline dans les Armées de Louis XIII: La lutte contre la désertion du soldat, 1635–1643." *Revue historique des armées* 162 (1986): 12–23.

Merriman, Roger B. *Six Contemporaneous Revolutions*. Oxford, 1938.

Mohr, Walter. *Geschichte des Herzogtums Lothringen*. Part 4, *Das Herzogtum Lothringen zwischen Frankreich und Deutschland (14.-17. Jahrhundert)*. Trier, 1986.

Montaigne, Michel de. *Essais*. Edited by Jean Plattard. Volume 1. Paris, 1959.

Mousnier, Roland. "Le Conseil du Roi de la mort de Henri IV au gouvernment personnel de Louis XIV." In *La Plume, la Faucille et le Marteau*, 141–73. Paris, 1970.

———. "Les crises intérieures françaises de 1610 à 1659 et leur influence sur la politique extérieure française, surtout de 1618 à 1648. In *Krieg und Politik 1618–1648: Europäische Probleme und Perspektiven*, edited by Konrad Repgen, 169–83. Schriften des Historischen Kollegs, Kolloquien, v. 8. Munich, 1988.

———. "Les mouvements populaires en France avant les traités de Westphalie et leur incidence sur ces traités." In *Forschungen und Studien zur Geschichte des Westfälischen Friedens. Vorträge bei dem Colloquium französischer und deutscher Historiker vom 28. April-30. April 1963 in Münster*, 33–48 Münster, 1965.

Müller, Hermann-Dieter. *Der schwedische Staat in Mainz, 1631–1636: Einnahme, Verwaltung, Absichten, Restitution*. V. 24 of *Beiträge zur Geschichte der Stadt Mainz*. Mainz, 1979.

Neveu, Bruno. "Correspondances diplomatiques et information." *XVIIe siècle*, no.178 (1993): 45–59.

Nicolson, Harold. *The Evolution of Diplomatic Method*. New York, 1954.

Niklaus, Siegfried. "Der Frühjahrsfeldzug 1645 in Süddeutschland (Schlacht bei Herbsthausen)." *Württembergisch Franken* 60 (1976): 121–80.

Noailles, Amblard Marie Raymond Amédée, vicomte de. *Le Maréchal de Guébriant (1602 à 1643)*. Paris, 1913.

Nova, Matías de. *Historia de Felipe IV, Rey de España*. Coleccion de Documentos Inéditos para la Historia de España, v. 86. Edited by José Sancho Rayon and Francisco de Zabalburu. Madrid, 1886.

O'Brien, Dennis H. "Mazarin's Diplomatic Corps, 1648–1661." *North Dakota Quarterly* 45 no.1 (Winter 1977): 31–42.

O'Connell, D. P. "A *cause célèbre* in the History of Treaty-Making: The Refusal to Ratify the Peace Treaty of Regensburg in 1630." *The British Yearbook of International Law* (1967): 71–90.

O'Connell, Robert L. *Of Arms and Men: A History of War, Weapons, and Aggression*. New York, 1989.

O'Connor, John T. "The Diplomatic History of the Reign." In *The Reign of Louis XIV: Essays in Celebration of Andrew Lossky*, edited by Paul Sonnino, 143–158. Atlantic Highlands, New Jersey, 1990.

———. "Politique et utopie au début du XVIIe siècle: le Grand Dessein de Henri IV et de Sully." *XVIIe siècle*, no. 174 (1992): 33–42.

Oman, Sir Charles. *A History of the Art of War in the Sixteenth Century.* New York, 1937.

Opitz, Eckhard. "Diplomacy and Secret Communication in the Seventeenth Century: Some Remarks on the Method of Gaining News in the Age of Absolutism." In *Clio Goes Spying: Eight Essays on the History of Intelligence,* edited by Wilhelm Agrell and Bo Huldt, 10–63. Lund Studies in International History, v. 17. Malmö, 1983.

Osiander, Andreas. *The States System of Europe, 1640–1990: Peacemaking and the Conditions of International Stability.* Oxford, 1994.

Osterbrauck, Willi. *Johann Reichsfreiherr von Werth, 1591–1652: Chronik eines umstrittenen Volkshelden.* Cologne, 1992.

Outrey, Amédée. "Histoire et Principes de l'Administration Française des Affaires Etrangères." *Revue Française de Science Politique* 3 (1953): 298–318.

Overmann, Alfred. "Die Abtretung des Elsass an Frankreich im Westfälischen Frieden." *Zeitschrift für die Geschichte des Oberrheins* bd. 58/9 (= N.F. Bd. 19/20) (1904–5), 79–111, 434–78; 103–45.

Pagès, Georges. *La Guerre de Trente Ans.* Paris, 1949.

Palmer, R. R. *A History of the Modern World.* 2d edition. New York, 1961.

Parker, Geoffrey. *The Army of Flanders and the Spanish Road, 1567–1659: The Logistics of Spanish Victory and Defeat in the Low Countries' Wars.* New York, 1972.

———. *Europe in Crisis, 1598–1648.* London, 1980.

———. "If the Armada Had Landed." In *Spain and the Netherlands, 1559–1659: Ten Studies.* Short Hills, New Jersey, 1979.

———. "In Defense of *The Military Revolution,*" in *The Military Revolution Debate: Readings on the Military Transformation of Early Modern Europe,* edited by Cliff Rogers, 337–65. Boulder, Colorado, 1995.

———. "The Making of Strategy in Habsburg Spain: Philip II's 'bid for mastery,' 1556–1598." In *The Making of Strategy: Rulers, States, and War,* edited by Williamson Murray, MacGregor Knox, and Alvin Bernstein, 115–50. New York, 1994.

———. *The Military Revolution: Military Innovation and the Rise of the West, 1500–1800.* New York, 1988.

———. "The Soldiers of the Thirty Years' War." In *Krieg und Politik 1618–1648: Europäische Probleme und Perspektiven,* edited by Konrad Repgen, 303–15. Schriften des Historischen Kollegs, Kolloquien, v. 8. Munich, 1988.

———. *The Thirty Years' War.* Boston, 1984.

———. "The Worst-Kept Secret in Europe? The European Intelligence Community and the Spanish Armada of 1588." In *Go Spy the Land: Military Intelligence in History,* edited by Keith Neilson and B. J. C. McKercher, 49–72. Westport, Connecticut, 1992.

—and Angela Parker. *European Soldiers 1550–1650.* New York, 1977.

Parrott, David. "The Administration of the French Army During the Ministry of Cardinal Richelieu." D. Phil diss. Oxford, 1985.

———. "The Military Revolution in Early Modern Europe." *History Today* 42 (December 1992): 21–27.

———. "Richelieu, the *Grands,* and the Army." In *Richelieu and His Age,* edited by Joseph Bergin and Laurence Brockliss. New York, 1992.

———. "Strategy and Tactics in the Thirty Years' War: The Military Revolution.'" *Militärgeschichtliches Mitteilungen* 38 (1985): 7–25.

Périni, Général Hardy de. *Batailles Françaises*. Volume 4, *Turenne et Condé, 1643–1671*. Paris, n.d.

Perjés, Geza. "Army Provisioning, Logistics and Strategy in the Second Half of the 17th Century." *Acta Historica Academiae Scientiarum Hungaricae* 16 (1970): 1–51.

Pepper, Simon, and Nicholas Adams. *Firearms and Fortifications: Military Architecture and Siege Warfare in Sixteenth-Century Siena*. Chicago, 1986.

Perkins, James Breck. *France Under Mazarin, with a Review of the Administration of Richelieu*. 2 vols. New York, 1902.

Pernot, Jean-François. "Guerre de sièges et places fortes." In *Guerre et Pouvoir en Europe au XVIIe siècle*, edited by Viviane Barrie-Curien, 129–50. Paris, 1991.

Peters, Jan, ed. *Ein Söldnerleben im Dreißigjährigen Krieg: Eine Quelle zur Sozialgeschichte*. Berlin, 1993.

Pfister, Christian and M. Lavisse. "La Formation de l'Alsace-Lorraine." In *Pages Alsaciennes*, 5–48. Paris, 1927.

Picavet, C.-G. *La diplomatie française au temps de Louis XIV (1661–1715): Institutions, moeurs, et coutumes*. Paris, 1930.

Piépape, Léonce de. *Histoire de la Réunion de la Franche-Comté à la France: Événements Diplomatiques et Militaires (1279 à 1678)*. Vol. 2. Paris, 1881.

Pillar, Paul. *Negotiating Peace*. Princeton, New Jersey, 1983.

Pillorget, René. "Die Bauernaufstände im Frankreich des 17. Jahrhunderts." In *Soziale und Politische Konflikte im Frankreich des Ancien Régime*, edited by Klaus Malettke. Einzelveröffentlichungen der Historischen Kommission zu Berlin, v. 32. (Studien aus dem forschungsprojektschwerpunkt »Soziale Mobilität im frühmodernen Staat: Bürgertum und Ämterwesen «am Fachbereich 13 (Geschichtswissenschaften) der Freien Universität Berlin, v. 2.) Berlin, 1982.

Poelhekke, Jan Joseph. *De Vrede van Munster*. The Hague, 1948.

Porshnev, Boris. "Angliskaia respublika, frantsuskaia Fronda i Vestfalsky mir." *Sredniie veka* 3 (1951): 180–216.

Porter, Bruce D. *War and the Rise of the State: The Military Foundations of Modern Politics*. New York, 1994.

Press, Volker. "Frankreich und Bayern von der Reformation bis zum Wiener Kongreß." In *Deutschland und Frankreich in der frühen Neuzeit*, edited by Heinz Duchhardt and Eberhard Schmitt, 21–70. Munich, 1987.

Quester, George H. "Wars Prolonged by Misunderstood Signals." *Annals of the American Academy of Political and Social Science* 392 (November 1970): 30–39.

Ramsay, Andrew. *Histoire du vicomte de Turenne*. 4 vols. The Hague, 1736.

Randle, Robert F. *The Origins of Peace: A Study of Peacemaking and the Structure of Peace Settlements*. New York, 1973.

Ranum, Orest. *The Fronde: A French Revolution 1648–1652*. New York, 1993.

———. *Richelieu and the Councillors of Louis XIII: A Study of the Secretaries of State and Superintendants of Finance in the Ministry of Richelieu, 1635–1642*. Oxford, 1963.

Raumer, Kurt von. "Westfälischer Friede." *Historische Zeitschrift* 195 (1962): 596–613.

———. "Zur Problematik des werdenden Machtstaats." *Historische Zeitschrift* 174 (1952): 71–79.

Redlich, Fritz. "Contributions in the Thirty Years' War." *Economic History Review* 12 (1959–60): 247–54.

Repgen, Konrad. "Aktuelle Friedensprobleme im Lichte der Geschichte des Westfälischen Fridens." In *Historische Klopfsignale für die Gegenwart*, 50–63. Münster, 1974.

———, ed. *Krieg und Politik 1618–1648: Europäische Probleme und Perspektiven.* Schriften des Historischen Kollegs, Kolloquien, v. 8. Munich, 1988.

———. "Über den Zusammenhang von Verhandlungstechnik und Vertragsbegriffen." In *Historische Klopfsignale für die Gegenwart*, 64–96. Münster, 1974.

———. "Der Westfälische Friede und die Ursprünge des europäischen Gleichgewichts." In *Von der Reformation zur Gegenwart: Beiträge zu Grundfragen der neuzeitlichen Geschichte*, edited by Klaus Gotto and Hans Günter Hockerts, 53–66. Paderborn, 1988.

Reuss, Rodolphe. *L'Alsace au Dix-Septième Siècle.* Bibliothèque de l'École des Hautes Études, fasc.116. Paris, 1897.

———. *Histoire d'Alsace.* 11th edition. Paris, 1916.

Riezler, Sigmund. "Bayern und Frankreich während des Waffenstillstands von 1647." *Sitzungsberichte der philosophisch-philologischen und der historischen Classe der k.b. Akademie der Wissenschaften zu München* 2 (1898): 493–541.

Roberts, Michael. "Gustav Adolf and the Art of War." In *Essays in Swedish History*, 56–81. London, 1967.

———. "The Military Revolution, 1560–1660." In *Essays in Swedish History*, 195–225. London, 1967.

Rohan, Henri de. *De l'intérêt des princes et des états de la chrétienté*, edited by Christian Lazzeri. Paris, 1995.

Roosen, William James. *The Age of Louis XIV: The Rise of Modern Diplomacy.* Cambridge, Massachusetts, 1976.

———. "Early Modern Diplomatic Ceremonial: A Systems Approach." *Journal of Modern History* 52 (1980): 452–76.

Rothenberg, Gunther E. "Maurice of Nassau, Gustavus Adolphus, Raimondo Montecuccoli, and the 'Military Revolution' of the Seventeenth Century." In *Makers of Modern Strategy from Machiavelli to the Nuclear Age*, edited by Peter Paret, 32–63. Princeton, New Jersey, 1986.

———. "Military Intelligence Gathering in the Second Half of the Eighteenth Century, 1740–1792." In *Go Spy the Land: Military Intelligence in History*, edited by Keith Neilson and B.J.C. McKercher, 99–111. Westport, Connecticut, 1992.

Rousset, M. *Recherches sur les Alliances et les intérêts entre la France et la Suède, rélativement aux circonstances présentes des affaires du nord et de l'Empire.* Amsterdam, 1745.

Rowan, Richard Wilmer. *The Story of Secret Service.* New York, 1939.

Rule, John C. "Review Article: Gathering Intelligence in the Age of Louis XIV." *The International History Review* 14 (1992), 732–52.

Ruppert, Karsten. *Die kaiserliche Politik auf dem Westfälischen Friedenskongreß (1643–1648).* Schriftenreihe der Vereinigung zur Erforschung der neueren Geschichte, v. 10. Münster, 1979.

Rystad, Göran. "Magnus Gabriel De La Gardie." In *Sweden's Age of Greatness, 1632–1718*, edited by Michael Roberts, 203–36. London, 1973.

———. "Die Schweden in Bayern während des Dreißigjährigen Krieges." In *Um Glauben und Reich: Kurfürst Maximilian I. Beiträge zur Bayerischen Geschichte und Kunst, 1573–1657*, 424–35. V. 2, part 1 of *Wittelsbach und Bayern*. Munich, 1980.

Sacchi, Henri. *La Guerre de Trente Ans*. Volume 3, *La guerre des Cardinaux*. Paris, 1991.

Sahlins, Peter. *Boundaries: The Making of France and Spain in the Pyrenees*. Berkeley, California, 1989.

———. "Natural Frontiers Revisited: France's Boundaries since the Seventeenth Century." *American Historical Review* 95 (1990): 1423–51.

Saint-Aulaire, Auguste, Comte de. *Mazarin*. Paris, 1946.

Salm, Hubert. *Armeefinanzierung im Dreißigjährigen Krieg: Der Niederrheinisch-Westfälische Reichskreis 1635–1650*. Schriftenreihe der Vereinigung zur Erforschung der Neueren Geschichte, v. 16. Münster, 1990.

Schaufler, Hans-Helmut. *Die Schlacht bei Freiburg im Breisgau, 1644*. Freiburg, 1979.

Scheible, Karlheinz. "Die Schlacht von Alerheim, 3 August 1645." *Rieser Kulturtage* 4, 1982 (1983): 229–72.

Schmidt, Hans. "Der Einfluss der Winterquartiere auf Strategie und Kriegführung des Ancien Régime." *Historisches Jahrbuch* 92 (1972): 77–91.

Schott, Rudolf. "Die Kämpfe vor Freiburg im Breisgau, die Eroberung von Philippsburg und die Belagerungen mehrerer Städte am Rhein im Jahre 1644. Zu einem Kupferstich von Cochin im Wehrgeschichtlichen Museum Rastatt." *Militärgeschichtliche Mitteilungen* 24 (Feb 1978): 9–22.

Schumann, Maurice. "Mazarin Européen." In *Mazarin*, edited by Georges Mongrédien, 153–68 and 179–99. N.p., 1959.

Schweinesbein, Karl. *Die Frankreich Politik Maximilian I. von Bayern, 1639–1645*. Munich, 1967.

Sheen, Charlie R. "The Fate of the Concept of Christendom in the Policy of Louis XIV: an Example from the King's Negotiations with the Empire, 1680–4." *European Studies Review* 3 (1973): 283–89.

———. "A Survey of the Notion of Christendom, Principally in France, 1580–1690." Ph.D. Diss. UCLA, 1970.

Solnon, Jean-François. *Quand la Franche-Comté était Espagnole*. N.p., 1983.

Sonnino, Paul. "The Marshal de Turenne and the Origins of the Dutch War." In *Studies in History and Politics: Essays in European History in Honour of Ragnhild Hatton*, v. 4. Edited by Karl Schweizer and Jeremy Black, 125–36. London, 1985.

Sörensson, Per. "Das Kriegswesen während der letzten Periode des Dreißigjährigen Krieges." In *Der Dreißigjährige Krieg: Perspektiven und Strukturen*, edited by Hans Ulrich Rudolf. Wege der Forschung, v. 451. Darmstadt, 1977. (Reprinted from *Historische Vierteljahrsschrift* 27 (1932): 575–600.)

Steckzén, Birger. *Karl Gustaf Wrangels Fälttåg 1646–1647 till och med fördraget i Ulm*. Uppsala, 1920.

Stein, Wolfgang Hans. "Das französische Elsaßbild im Dreißigjährigen Krieg." *Jahrbuch für westdeutsche Landeskunde* 5 (1979): 131–53.

―――. *Protection Royale: Eine Untersuchung zu den Protektionverhältnissen im Elsaß zur Zeit Richelieus, 1622–1643.* Schriftenreihe der Vereinigung zur Erforschung der Neueren Geschichte, v. 9. Münster, 1978.

Steinberg, S. H. *The "Thirty Years War" and the Conflict for European Hegemony, 1600–1660.* London, 1966.

Steiner, Jürgen. *Die pfälizische Kurwürde während des Dreißigjährigen Krieges (1618–1648).* Veröffentlichung der Pfälzischen Gesellschaft zur Förderung der Wissenschaften in Speyer, bd. 76. Speyer, 1985.

Stradling, Robert. "Conclusion: Second Thoughts." In *Spain's Struggle for Europe, 1598–1668,* 273–94. London, 1994.

―――. "Catastrophe and Recovery: The Defeat of Spain, 1639–43." In *Spain's Struggle for Europe, 1598–1668,* 197–212. London, 1994.

―――. "Seventeenth-Century Spain: Decline or Survival?" In *Spain's Struggle for Europe, 1598–1668,* 3–32. London, 1994.

―――. "Spain's Military Failure and the Supply of Horses, 1600–60." In *Spain's Struggle for Europe, 1598–1668,* 234–49. London, 1994.

Strasser, Gerhard F. "Diplomatic Cryptology and Universal Languages in the Sixteenth and Seventeenth Centuries." In *Go Spy the Land: Military Intelligence in History,* edited by Keith Neilson and B. J. C. McKercher, 73–98. Westport, Connecticut, 1992.

Tallemant des Réaux. *Historiettes,* edited by Antoine Adam. 2 vols. N.p., 1961.

Tapié, V.-L. "Louis XIV's Methods in Foreign Policy." In *Louis XIV and Europe,* edited by Ragnhild Hatton, 3–15. Columbus, Ohio, 1976.

―――. *La Guerre de Trente Ans.* Paris, 1964–66.

―――. *La Guerre de Trente Ans.* Paris, 1989.

Tessin, Georg. *Die Regimenter der europäischen Staaten im Ancien Régime des XVI. bis XVIII. Jahrhunderts.* Part 1, *Die Stammlisten.* Osnabrück, 1986.

Textor, Fritz. *Entfestigungen und Zerstörungen im Rheingebiet während des 17. Jahrhunderts als Mittel der französischen Rheinpolitik.* Volume 31 of Rheinisches Archiv. Edited by A. Bach and Fr. Steinbach. Bonn, 1937.

Tham, Wilhelm. *Den Svenska Utrikespolitikens Historia.* Vol. 1, part 2, *1560–1648.* Stockholm, 1960.

Thompson, James Westfall, and Saul K. Padover. *Secret Diplomacy: Espionage and Cryptography, 1500–1815.* Revised edition. New York, 1963.

Tingsten, Lars. *De Tre Sista Åren av det Trettioåriga Kriget jämte den Västfaliska Freden.* Militärlitteratur Föreningens Förlag, no.171. Stockholm, 1934.

Treasure, Geoffrey. *Mazarin: The Crisis of Absolutism in France.* New York, 1995.

―――. *Seventeenth Century France.* New York, 1966.

Van Creveld, Martin. *Command in War.* Cambridge, Massachusetts, 1985.

―――. *Supplying War: Logistics from Wallenstein to Patton.* New York, 1977.

Voltaire. *L'Ingénu et autres contes.* Paris, 1993.

Wagner, Eduard. *European Weapons and Warfare, 1618–1648.* Prague, 1979.

Weber, Franz. "Gliederung und Einsatz des bayerischen Heeres im Dreißigjährigen Krieg." In *Um Glauben und Reich: Kurfürst Maximilian I. Beiträge zur Bayerischen Geschichte und Kunst, 1573–1657,* 400–407. V. 2, part 1 of *Wittelsbach und Bayern.* Munich, 1980.

Weber, Hans H. *Der Hessenkrieg.* Gießen, 1935.

Weber, Hermann. "'Une Bonne Paix': Richelieu's Foreign Policy and the Peace of Christendom." In *Richelieu and his Age*, edited by Joseph Bergin and Laurence Brockliss, 45–69. Oxford, 1992.

———. "Chrétienté et équilibre européen dans la politique du Cardinal de Richelieu." *XVIIe siècle* 42 (1990): 7–16.

———. "Friede und Gewissen." In *Forschungen und Studien zur Geschichte des Westfälischen Friedens: Vorträge bei dem Colloquium französischer und deutscher Historiker vom 28. April—30. April 1963 in Münster*, 85–108. Münster, 1965.

———. "Richelieu et le Rhin." *Revue Historique* 239 (1968): 265–80.

Wedgwood, C. V. *The Thirty Years War*. London, 1938.

Weigley, Russell F. *The Age of Battles: The Quest for Decisive Warfare from Breitenfeld to Waterloo*. Indianapolis, 1991.

Wheeler, Everett L. "Methodological Limits and the Mirage of Roman Strategy." *Journal of Military History* 57 (1993): 7–41 and 215–40.

Wicquefort, Abraham de. *Memoires touchant les ambassadeurs et les ministres publics*. Cologne, 1676.

Wijn, J.W. "Military Forces and Warfare 1610–48." In *The Decline of Spain and the Thirty Years War 1609–48/59*, edited by J. P. Cooper, 202–25. V. 4 of *The New Cambridge Modern History*. Cambridge, 1970.

Zeller, Gaston. *De Christophe Colomb à Cromwell*. Part 1 of *Les temps modernes*. Volume 2 of *Histoire des relations internationales*, edited by Pierre Renouvin. Paris, 1953.

———. *Comment s'est faite la réunion de l'Alsace à la France*. Paris, 1948.

———. *La Guerre de Trente Ans et les relations internationales en Occident de 1610 à 1660*. Paris, 1947.

———. *L'Organisation défensive des Frontières du Nord et de l'Est au XVIIe siècle*. Paris, 1928.

———. "Le principe d'équilibre dans la politique internationale avant 1789." In *Aspects de la Politique française sous l'ancien régime*, 172–84. Paris, 1964.

———. "Saluces, Pignerol et Strasbourg: La politique des frontières au temps de la prépondérance espagnole." In *Aspects de la politique française sous l'ancien régime*, 114–27. Paris, 1964.

Index

Adami, Adam, prior of Murrhardt, 50
Alerheim, battle of, 44, 56, 62, 64, 69, 70, 74, 75, 81, 84, 86, 89, 90, 168–70, 173, 175, 177–78, 181, 185, 189, 194, 218, 230, 270
Alsace, 7, 261, 268, 271–72; administration of, 97–99, 104, 251–52; French acquisitions in, 185, 261–62, 271–72; French demand for, 34–35, 42, 105–6, 160–63, 171, 194, 196–201, 204–6, 213–17, 222–28, 236–40, 249–54, 269–70, 276, 278–79; garrisons, 89, 142, 165, 180; in military campaigns, 118–19, 124, 135, 160, 218; indemnity for, 47; landgraviate of, 104, 106, 172, 239, 250–51; ruining by war, 88, 92, 100
Amalie Elisabeth, Landgrave of Hesse-Cassel, 86–87, 123, 136, 155, 165, 167, 230–31. *See also* Hesse-Cassel
Amöneburg, 231
Anne of Austria, 113, 133, 207; power as regent, 28, 29, 30, 36, 37, 41, 108; relationship with Mazarin, 23, 29, 31, 40, 42
Armée d'Allemagne, 37, 48; in 1644 campaign, 128–29, 134–35, 137; in 1645 campaign, 142, 154, 178, 191; in 1646 campaign, 209, 217, 229; organization, 81–84, 100–102. *See also* Turenne
Aschaffenburg, 167, 247, 249
Augsburg, 69, 247

Baden-Baden, 53–54, 129
Baden-Durlach, 53–54
Bagno, Niccolò Guidi di, Papal nuncio in Paris, 45, 55, 145–46, 170, 216
Bailleul, Nicolas Léon de, surintendant des finances, 31
Bamberg, Imperial commander of Philippsburg, 130

Banér, Johan, Swedish general, 100
Bardot, Georges, 251
Baroque period, 23, 26
Basel, 105
Baussan, Philibert de, intendant in Alsace, 99, 252
Bavaria, 42; armed forces, 87; as part of Mazarin's strategy vs. Spain, 113; French propose territory on the Rhine, 105; French support for UP and electorate, 51, 183; French view of, 41; invaded by France, 92–93, 141, 247; military co-operation with emperor, 77, 88, 91, 135, 180–81, 218, 229–31; military forces, 87–91; plenipotentiaries, 37, 132–33, 169–72, 204–5, 216, 241; relations with France, 41, 54–55, 112–13, 132–33, 169–72, 204, 269, 280; secret council, 149, 169–70, 184; separate negotiations with France, 44, 181, 183–85, 188–89, 278; support for French territorial acquisition, 170–71, 194, 198, 201, 203–5, 208, 213–17, 249, 254; Truce of Ulm, 55, 254, 259; truce talks, 208–10, 227; war against France, 61–70, 78, 80, 84, 100, 116–19, 123–24, 126–32, 135–37, 148, 150–54, 165–68, 177–81, 203, 228, 231–33, 245–47, 264. *See also* Maximilian I
Beauregard, sieur de, French resident in Cassel, 53
Beck, Freiherr von, Spanish general, 123
Bélesbat, M. de, intendant in Alsace, 98
Belfort, 105
Benfeld, 98, 104–5, 161, 216, 222
Bergaine, Josèphe, Spanish diplomat, 155

Bergerac, Savinien Cyrano de, courier for Mazarin, 44
Bergin, Joseph, 23
Bergstraße, 167
Bernhard of Saxe-Weimar, general in French service (d.1639), 68, 81, 84, 99
Black Forest, 64, 119, 136
Black, Jeremy, 23–24, 56–57
Bohemia, 138, 180, 263–64
Bonamös, 245
Bonn, 233
Bönninghausen, Lothar von, mercenary hired by French, 229
Bouillon, duc de (Turenne's brother), 80
Bourbourg, 186
Brahe, Per, Swedish councillor, 52
Brandenburg, Elector of (Friedrich Wilhelm, The Great Elector), 51, 54, 142–43, 263
Breisach, 26, 63, 64, 65, 68, 73, 104, 119, 129, 136, 261, 263; French demand for, 41, 105–6, 161–63, 171, 194, 196, 205, 214–17, 221–24, 233, 249, 269–72, 279; French occupation and administration, 82, 89, 97–99; Habsburg decision to concede, 47, 224, 229, 262, 268; revolt in, 119–21
Breisgau, 104, 171–72, 196, 204, 214–17, 222
Bremen, 51, 236, 263
Brézé, duc de, *amiral de France*, 37
Brienne, Henri-Auguste de Loménie de, secretary of state for foreign affairs, 190; and secrecy, 46, 224; friendship with d'Avaux, 37; instructions to plenipotentiaries, 42, 108, 110–11, 122, 143, 156, 183, 187, 189, 204, 228; military views, 75, 173, 208–9, 275; role in government, 32, 265; territorial demands, 161, 163, 197, 200, 238, 242, 251, 271
Brünn, 65, 71, 191
Brunswick, House of, 53, 115
Burckhardt, Johannes, 260–61

Cabale des Importants, 30, 128
Callières, François de, 43
Cambrai, 271
Cambrésis, 271
Casale, 131

Catalonia, 76, 77, 194, 277; as French negotiating problem, 49–50; exchange project, 41, 49, 206, 220; orders to give in, 46, 49; war in, 118, 186, 264
Cérisantes, Marc Duncan, Swedish resident in Paris, 45, 52, 112, 149
Champagne, 134, 186, 262
Chanut, Pierre, French resident in Stockholm, 211, 235
Charles IV, Duke of Lorraine, 97, 136; at Tuttlingen, 101; in 1644 campaign, 119, 132; negotiations with Mazarin, 122–23, 137. *See also* Lorraine
Chavigny, Léon le Bouthillier, comte de, 33
Cherasco, Peace of, 28, 34
Chéruel, Adolphe, 23–24
Chigi, Fabio, papal nuncio and mediator, 145, 189, 206–7
Christian IV, King of Denmark, 109, 112, 211. *See also* Denmark
Christina, Queen of Sweden, 51–52, 209, 211–12, 235–36, 253–54
Church, William, 23
Clausewitz, Karl von, 26, 58
Colmar, 98, 105, 199
Cologne, city of, 233
Cologne, Elector of (Ferdinand of Wittelsbach), 87, 123, 169, 177
Condé, Henri II de Bourbon, prince de, 30, 31, 32, 46, 224
Constance, Lake, 119
Contarini, Alvise, Venetian mediator, 103, 214, 273; and Low Countries exchange, 206–7; French demand for Philippsburg, 249; proposes separate Imperial peace, 145, 187, 188, 253
Corvisier, André, 274
Courtrai, 48
Cousin, Victor, 25

D'Anctoville [sometimes spelled "d'Antouille"], sieur, 42, 49, 242
Danube River, 64, 67, 69, 79, 83, 90, 141, 148, 151–54, 167–69, 181, 209, 247, 249
Darmstadt, city, 167
D'Aumont, sieur, French military officer, 102, 127
D'Avaugour, Charles Dubois, baron,

French attaché with the Swedish army, 86, 152, 218, 232
D'Avaux, Claude de Mesmes, French plenipotentiary, 236, 265–67, 275; appointment as plenipotentiary, 33, 34; concern about intelligence leaks, 46; demand for Philippsburg, 161, 227, 241; difference of opinion with Mazarin, 39; discussions with Bavarian plenipotentiaries, 169–71; dismissal, 32; illness, 112; learns of Habsburg orders to concede Philippsburg, 47; Lorraine, 252–53; marriage alliance with emperor, 196; on military affairs, 73, 75, 76; praise of Mazarin, 262; predicts the Fronde, 201–2; progress of negotiations, 243, 249; quarrel with Servien, 35–38, 142–44; relations with Swedish plenipotentiaries, 52; religious views, 35; requests his recall, 143–44; role in council, 31; sovereignty in Alsace, 238, 251; Swedish demands, 234, 254; territorial demands, 214–16, 227; train, 38–39; trip to Münster, 103, 111; trip to Osnabrück, 142–43, 212, 259. *See also* French plenipotentiaries
Decapolis (ten towns in Alsace), 104, 171, 251
De La Gardie, Magnus Gabriel, Swedish envoy to France, 236
Denmark, 34; alliance with emperor, 109; invasion by Sweden, 108, 111–12, 116–17, 155; peace with Sweden, 135, 142; role as mediator, 103; treaty with France, 211. *See also* Christian IV
D'Erlach, Hans Ludwig, governor of Breisach, 72, 82, 99, 199; and Breisach revolt, 119–20; as governor of Breisach, 98; desire for command of the *Armée d'Allemagne*, 102; opinion on Neuenburg, 223
D'Estrades, Godefroi Louis, French attaché to Fredrik Hendrik, 207
Dethan, Georges, 24
D'Hémery, Michel Particelli, sieur, 31
Dickmann, Fritz, 22, 35, 54, 139
Dinkelsbühl, 69, 168, 178–79
Donaueschingen, 121

Donauwörth, 64, 126
D'Orléans, Jean-Baptiste Gaston de France, duc (Gaston d'Orléans); creation of Council of War, 72; knowledge of Philippsburg orders, 46, 224; relations with Charles IV, 97; role in government, 30, 31; role in army, 31, 118, 217
D'Oysonville, 72, 98–99, 119–20
Dunkirk, 77, 186

East Frisian affair, 53, 123, 155
Eberstein, Ernst Albrecht von, general for Hesse-Darmstadt, 247
Ehrenbreitstein, 176
Eilenburg, Peace of, 231
Einsiedeln, conference at, 54
Emden, Count of, 123
Enghien, Louis II de Bourbon, duc d', commander in Germany, 85, 264; correspondence with Mazarin, 79; in 1644 campaign, 118–19, 123–129, 131, 134, 136–37; in 1645 campaign, 142, 164–68, 177–79, 183, 265; in 1646 campaign, 217; military aggressiveness, 70; military campaigns of, 76, 80; Rocroi, 30, 100; role in government, 31
England, 277; and Low Countries exchange, 206; French favor Charles I, 213; possible alliance with Sweden, 50, 156
Englund, Peter, 25

Federn, Karl, 22
Ferdinand II, emperor, 87, 110, 114
Ferdinand III, emperor, 51, 53–54, 80, 99, 116, 156, 159, 162, 191–92, 194, 273, 276–77, 279; and Bavaria, 91, 113–14, 117, 127, 132–33, 146–47, 149–52, 171, 173–74, 176, 180–81, 183–86, 204; and plenipotentiaries' powers, 109, 133; and the negotiations, 47, 50, 105–6, 133, 138, 141, 144–45, 148, 157, 185–89, 193, 205, 237, 262; and Vervaux mission, 149–50; delays negotiations, 109–10; German estates, 53, 114–15, 139–40, 143, 164–65, 173, 198, 210, 249, 276, 281; Hesse-Darmstadt, 230; military control, 87–88, 90; military role, 78,

108, 117, 122, 127, 142, 169, 178, 180–81
Flanders, 29–30, 66, 76, 118, 129, 186, 194, 221, 271
Forest Towns (Waldshut, Rheinfelden, Säckingen, and Laufenburg), 105, 171–72, 196, 204, 214–17, 222
Franche-Comté, 104, 119, 142, 215
Franconian Alps, 64
Franconian Circle, occupied by Bavaria, 148; dominated by Maximilian, 88; representatives in Münster, 142
Frankenthal, 68, 81, 136, 141, 150, 232
Frankfurt, 115, 135, 148, 167
Frankfurt *Deputationstag*, 143
Frederik Hendrik, Dutch Stadholder, 53, 155, 207, 276
Freiburg, battle of, 62, 63, 66, 68, 69, 70, 74, 76, 78, 81, 90, 91, 124–26, 129, 132, 168, 270; public expectations after, 33
Freiburg, town of, 22; French plans to besiege, 79, 80, 127–28; in truce talks, 177; siege of, 76, 121–24, 137, 164
Friedberg, 245
Fronde (French rebellion), 22–23, 38, 260

Gagliardo, John, 56
Gallas, Matthias, Graf von, Imperial general, 63, 116, 135, 141
Garden, Comte de, 238
Gassion, maréchal, Jean, 118
Gazette de France, 45
Geleen, Gottfried Graf Huyn von, Bavarian general, 91, 170, 178, 231
Georg, Landgrave of Hesse-Darmstadt. *See* Hesse-Darmstadt
Gernsheim, 165
Geyso, Johann von, general for Hesse-Cassel, 86, 247
Giustiniani, Girolamo, Venetian ambassador in Paris, 117–18
Godefroy, Théodore de, French historiographer and adviser at the peace negotiations, 172
Gonzague-Nevers, Marie de, 191
Goslar, Peace of, 53
Goubert, Pierre, 22–23, 25–26
Graben, 181
Gramont, Antoine, duc de, 170, 178

Gravelingen, 118, 123, 137
Gronsfeld, Jost Maximilian Graf von, Bavarian general, 78
Grotius, Hugo, Swedish resident in Paris, 52, 112
Guébriant, maréchal, Jean-Baptiste Budes, duc de, 61–62, 64, 85, 100–101, 218, 220, 264
Gustavus Adolphus, Swedish king (d.1632), 22, 57, 73, 83, 90
Guth, Paul, 22, 24, 275

Habsburg archdukes, 105, 196–97, 214–15, 237
Habsburg, House of, 24, 31, 46–47, 109, 116, 122, 133, 160, 205–6, 281
Habsburgs, Austrian, 73, 80, 91, 104, 111, 114, 171–74, 185, 197–98, 200, 203, 208, 213, 230, 238–39, 250–51, 259–60, 262, 271, 277; attempt to divide France and Sweden, 51; discovery of French orders, 45–47; interception of French correspondence, 44; negotiating tactics, 49, 103; plenipotentiaries, 39, 109
Hague, The (also 's-Gravenhage, Den Haag), 103, 111, 233
Haguenau, prefectorate (or Landvogtei) of, 104, 171, 213–14, 239–40
Haguenau, town of, 105
Hall. *See* Schwäbisch Hall
Hamburg, city of, French recruits, 217, 229; French subsidy to Sweden, 116
Hamburg, preliminary treaty of (1641), 34, 103
Hamburg, Swedish-French treaty of (1641), 51
Handel, Michael, 278
Hanse (Hanseatic League), 115, 143
Harcourt, Henri de Lorraine, comte d', 186, 203, 209
Haslang, Georg Christoph, Freiherr von, Bavarian plenipotentiary, 54, 146, 170, 204–5. *See also* Bavaria
Hatzfeld, Melchior von, Imperial general, 117, 127, 130
Heidelberg, 69, 77, 93, 127, 167, 177, 220
Heilbronn, 62, 68, 70, 73, 77, 80, 84; in French-Bavarian truce talks, 177; in 1644 campaign, 127, 130–31; in 1645

campaign, 167, 178–81; in 1646 campaign, 220, 245, 247
Herbsthausen, battle of, 62, 69, 70, 75, 84, 93, 154, 159, 164–65, 169, 180, 265, 270, 275
Hesse-Cassel, alliance with France, 53, 276; armed forces of, 86–87; demands, 240, 280; in the peace negotiations, 115, 142; in 1644 campaign, 123, 134–36; in 1645 campaign, 155, 165–68; in 1646 campaign, 229–31, 243–45. *See also* East Frisian Affair; Amalie Elisabeth
Hesse-Darmstadt, 53, 229–30, 247
Heyner, Georg, 266
Hohentwiel, 68, 92, 121, 126
Holy Roman Empire (or Germany), 56, 66, 68, 73, 75–78, 81–82, 84–86, 92, 99–100, 102–3, 115, 133, 135, 155–56, 160, 163–64, 180, 190, 198–201, 204–5, 218, 221–23, 225, 227–29, 237, 242, 251, 259, 262–63, 267, 281; army, 61, 89, 218, 229–30; estates, 38, 47, 53–54, 103, 108–9, 114–15, 137–41, 144–45, 156–57, 160, 163–65, 173, 198–200, 210, 224, 237, 249–50, 276, 278, 280
Horn, Gustav, Swedish general, 90
Horst, Johann von der, Bavarian Statthalter in Lower Palatinate, 132
Höxter, 231
Huguenots, 193
Hungary, Ferdinand III as king of, 148

Immler, Gerhard, 149
Ingolstadt, 249
Isar River, 69
Italy, 56, 77, 84, 101, 103–4, 118, 163, 264

Jankov, battle of, 62, 89, 91, 142, 148–49, 151–52, 161, 165, 218, 270

Kamen, Henry, 260
Kempner Heide, battle of, 62, 100, 220
Kirchhain, 167
Kleinman, Ruth, 29
Kleve, 233
Knuyt, Johan de, representative for Zeeland and Frederik Hendrik, 53, 207

Koblenz, 176
Königsmarck, Hans Christoph Graf von, Swedish general, 167, 218, 231, 245
Korea, conflict in, 21
Kötzschenbroda, Truce of, 174, 190
Kraus, Andreas, 149, 173
Krebs, Dr. Johann Adolf, Bavarian plenipotentiary, 54, 146, 170, 175, 183, 204–5. *See also* Bavaria
Kreuznach, castle of, 62, 136
Kroener, Bernhard, 93
Krosigk, Adolf Wilhelm, Hessian plenipotentiary, 53

La Barde, Jean de, French resident in Osnabrück, 38; refused a seat in Swedish-Imperial talks, 210; report on Swedish negotiations, 226
La Court, Henri Groulart, sieur de, French resident in Osnabrück, 34, 38
La Ferté-Senneterre, Henri, duc de, governor of Lorraine, 92, 98, 220
La Force, Jacques Nompar, duc de, 97, 272
La Haye-Vantelet, Jean de, French resident in Constantinople, 189
Lamboy, Wilhelm Freiherr von, Imperial general, 245
La Meilleraye, maréchal, Charles de La Porte, marquis de, 31
La Mothe, 93, 165, 186
Landau, 137
Landsberg, 69
Languedoc, 251
La Thuillerie, Gaspard Coignet, sieur de, French resident in The Hague, 112, 211–12
Lauingen, 177, 247
Laurain-Portemer, Madeleine, 24, 271, 277
League, Catholic, 87
Lech River, 64, 69, 247
Lee, Stephen, 261
Lens, battle of, 70, 260
Leopold Wilhelm, Archduke of Austria, Imperial general, 63, 90, 91, 181, 230, 243–49
Lérida, siege of, 48, 65, 76, 77, 117
Le Tellier, Michel, French secretary of state for war, role in government,

32, 265; role in military administration, 83; role in military strategy, 72; 1644 campaign, 134; 1645 campaign, 180
Liège, bishopric of, 123
Linz, Peace of, 189
Linz, town of, 205
Lionne, Hugues de, Mazarin's secretary, 41, 122, 143, 146, 162, 208, 227; ally of Servien, 36, 37, 160; and French intelligence crisis, 46; on French military, 83, 154; withholds Servien's recall request, 144; urges immediate peace, 236
Lippe River, 233
Livet, Georges, 26, 275
Llorens, battle of, 186
Longueville, Anne Geneviève de Bourbon Condé, Madame de, 37, 266
Longueville, Henri II d'Orléans, duc de, 26, 35, 144, 173, 175–76, 203, 265–66; and French intelligence crisis, 47; and Lorraine, 253; and Sweden, 210, 212; difficulties in making peace, 236, 243; firmness in negotiating, 201–2, 214; military ideas, 48, 83, 100; opinion of Bavarian plenipotentiaries, 54–55; relationship with Mazarin, 28, 39; role in embassy, 34, 37–38, 144; role in government, 31–32; separate peace with Spain, 187; territorial demands, 41, 163–64, 197, 213–16, 224, 227, 238, 240, 269–70. *See also* French plenipotentiaries
Lorraine, duchy of, 9, 87, 105, 134, 172, 186, 218, 220, 238, 272; exclusion from peace conference, 225, 234, 252–53, 263, 277; French demands in, 38, 104, 161–62; occupation, 98; ruining by war, 88, 92; use for quarters, 135, 218. *See also* Charles IV, Duke of Lorraine
Lossky, Andrew, 24–25, 271–72
Louis XIII, king of France 1610–1643, 28, 30, 32, 34, 106, 108
Louis XIV, king of France 1643–1715, 22–23, 30, 90, 263, 277; accession, 28, 199; marriage alliance, 23, 196; minority of, 108; oath of loyalty to, 242; revolt during minority, 32, 118; royal orders in his name, 41

Low Countries. *See* Netherlands, Spanish
Ludwig, Landgrave of Hesse, 230
Luxembourg, 193, 220–21, 228, 233, 264
Lynn, John, 64
Lys River, 186

Magalotti, Pierre de, French general, 134
Main River, 68, 70, 86, 134, 136, 167, 231, 233, 243, 247
Mainz, city of, 67, 68, 73, 93, 131–32, 136–37, 142, 218, 221, 233, 276
Mannheim, 68, 93, 127, 135, 177
Mantuan War, 110
Marburg, 230–31
Marlborough, Duke of, 63
Marsal, town in Lorraine, 97
Marsin, Jean Gaspard Ferdinand, comte de, French officer, 165
Maximilian, Duke, late Elector, of Bavaria, 67, 157–58; abandonment of Munich, 69, 249; and 1645 campaign, 151–53, 169, 178; and 1646 campaign, 243–49; and 644 campaign, 126, 129–33, 137; and French satisfaction, 169–70, 203–5; and military intelligence, 77, 78, 79; and the battle of Freiburg, 126–27; and the Upper Palatinate, 138, 157; approaches to France, 113, 146–50, 169; as ruler of Bavaria, 54; as strategist, 59, 64, 70, 89–90; communication with Mazarin, 45; considered deceitful, 54, 75, 113–14, 175–76, 266–67; delay in sending representatives to conference, 114–15, 132–33; favors attacking France, 116–17; joins forces with emperor, 91, 230–31; military control, 87–91, 265–66; military goals, 88–89; pushes Ferdinand III to end the war, 185–86; stalls negotiations, 50; support for d'Avaux, 36; Truce of Ulm, 259; truce talks with France, 87, 169–70, 173–77, 181–85, 213, 227, 230–31. *See also* Bavaria
Mazarin, Jules, 21–22, 35, 170; 1646 truce, 209; and 1643 campaign, 100–102; and 1644 campaign, 118–19, 123–24, 127–29, 133–37; and 1645 campaign, 141–42, 152–54, 165–66,

177–83; and 1646 campaign, 217–22, 228–33; and Habsburg powers, 109, 133; and Hesse-Cassel, 86, 123, 136; and Low Countries exchange, 206–7; and Richelieu, 22–23, 28–30, 33, 106, 261–63, 274; and Sweden's Danish war, 112, 142; and Vervaux mission, 147–52; as negotiator, 10, 21, 259–64, 274–77, 279–81; as strategist, 59, 60–61, 66–68, 71–81, 117, 264–65, 275–76; Bavarian policy, 54–55, 92, 94, 113, 146, 173–77, 184–85, 203–5, 254; direction of government, 28–31, 32, 33, 34; Dutch policy, 110, 155–56, 189–90, 236; French territorial demands, 9, 99, 104–6, 161–62, 194, 214–17, 223–25, 238, 241, 251–52, 261–63, 268–70; German estates, 115; in the negotiations, 40, 49, 109–11, 138–41, 158, 160, 186–95, 201–3; intelligence and counterintelligence, 45–48, 78; Lorraine, 122–23, 137, 253; military management, 79–80, 265–66; ·.ew policy at the end of 1645, 18ᶠ -95; opinion of Maximilian, 113 175; relationship with Anne, 23, 29–32, 40, 42; relationship with Brienne, 42–43; relationship with different plenipotentiaries, 36, 39–41, 143; Spanish policy, 33, 113, 144–45, 186–89, 194–95, 221–22, 254, 259–60; Swedish policy, 109–11, 116, 136, 147, 150, 156–60, 174, 190–91, 209–13, 260, 276; willingness to compromise, 110–11, 133, 137, 140, 196–98, 270–74

Melander, Peter, Graf von Holzappel, Imperial general, 61, 91, 245

Melo, Don Francisco de, governor-general of the Spanish Netherlands, 117

Mercy, Franz von, Bavarian general, 63, 69, 178; and military intelligence, 78; complains that towns will not defend themselves, 67, 89; in 1644 campaign, 117–32, 135; in 1645 campaign, 148, 152–54, 165–68, 245; in Tuttlingen campaign, 101; on cavalry, 83; origin, 87; pitiless to French east of Rhine, 93; skill as commander, 90

Mergentheim, 67, 154

Mesmes, Henri de (brother of d'Avaux), 34

Metz, 129, 165

Meulles du Tartre, Claude, French resident in Hamburg, 217, 229

Milan, 194

"Military Revolution," 8, 10, 23, 56–57

Montmorency, revolt of, 97

Moravia, 263

Moselle River, 76, 119, 176, 193, 218

Munich, 69, 74, 169–70, 249

Nancy, 97

Nani, Giovanni, Venetian resident in Paris, 29, 32, 37, 273; role in French intelligence leaks, 45–46; view of Sweden, 50

Napoleon Bonaparte, 26, 72

Navarre, 33

Neckar River, 68–69, 134, 167, 181

Netherlands, Spanish, 22, 87, 99, 104, 205; exchange project for Catalonia, 41, 49, 190, 195; military campaigns in, 76–77, 82, 117, 137, 155, 189, 217, 221, 223, 259, 264

Neuenburg, 216, 222, 276

Nidda River, 245

Nördlingen, battle of, 64, 66, 98

Nördlingen, city of 69, 70, 168, 177

Nördlingen, second battle of. *See* Alerheim

Nuremberg, 78

O'Connor, John, 277

Oñate treaty, 205

Osiander, Andreas, 274

Ottoman Empire, 188–89, 191–93, 197–98, 272–73

Overmann, Alfred, 172

Oxenstierna, Axel, Swedish chancellor, 88, 191, 281; alliance with France, 51; low opinion of France, 211; Swedish satisfaction, 235–36, 279; withdraws from Rhine, 98

Oxenstierna, Johann, Swedish plenipotentiary, in the negotiations, 139, 174, 191; negotiations with French, 212, 226; relationship with Savlius, 52; relationship with Servien, 52; requests leave to return home, 235; trip to Münster, 112, 158, 236

Paderborn, 231
Palatinate, Electoral, as a negotiating point, 51, 160; Karl Ludwig, ruler of 51–52, 160, 175, 242; Lower, 52, 69, 99; Lower, French conquest of, 129–32, 136; Upper, 51, 138, 183, 204, 225
Palmer, R. R., 25–26
Paris, Treaty of (1641), 122
Parker, Geoffrey, 57, 280
Parlement of Paris, 29, 32, 34, 186
Parrott, David, 23–24, 56–58, 64
Passau, site of Imperial military conference, 116
Pauw, Adriaan, representative for Holland, 53, 207
Peñaranda, Gaspar de Bracamonte y Guzmán, conde de, Spanish plenipotentiary, 191; and Low Countries exchange, 206; sent to Congress, 146; urges Trauttmansdorff to stall, 206, 213, 221, 223
Pforzheim, 135
Philip IV, king of Spain, 28, 145, 206
Philippe Bourbon (brother of Louis XIV), 30
Philippsburg, 26, 63, 64, 68, 71, 73, 178–81, 261; French demand for, 40–41, 161–63, 171, 194, 196, 199, 205, 214–15, 223–24, 237, 240–43, 249, 254–55, 268–70, 276, 278; French occupation and loss, 98; French permission to concede, 45–46; French siege of, 128–32, 136–37; garrison of, 89, 134; Habsburg orders to concede, 47, 262; military role, 92
Picardy, 129, 271
Piccolomini, Ottavio, Spanish general, 126
Pillar, Paul, 277–78
Pinerolo, 205, 213
Plenipotentiaries, French, 26; and Bavaria, 171–72, 176–77, 181, 183–84, 200, 203–4; and Charles IV, 122; and Turenne, 79, 228–32; and Vervaux mission, 147, 150–51; concern about opposition to territorial demands, 198–99; convince Swedes not to withdraw from conference, 110; exclusion of Spain, 253; in the peace negotiations, 115, 140–41, 142, 157–60, 201–2; indemnity to archdukes, 196–97; on the battle of Freiburg, 123, 132–33; opinion of Chigi, 189; opinion of Maximilian, 113–14; oppose Mazarin's Spanish policy, 144–45; orders, 106, 108; praise of Mazarin, 263; territorial demands, 162–65, 222–23, 225–26, 255; trip to Osnabrück, 158–59. *See also* Servien; d'Avaux; Longueville
Poland, 236
Polhelm, Winand von, Hessian representative in Paris, 45, 53
Pomerania, 51, 158, 236, 254, 263, 279
Pont-à-Mousson, 180
Portugal, 194, 252, 277; and Low Countries exchange, 206; French orders to give in on, 46, 49
Postrema Declaratio, 242, 249, 254
Prague, Peace of, 87, 192–93
Pyrenees, Peace of (1659), 24

Rackóczy, George, Prince of Transylvania, 189. *See also* Transylvania
Rain, battle of, 74
Rain, town of, 69, 247, 249
Randle, Robert, 278
Rantzau, Josias, comte de, French general, 100–101
Ranum, Orest, 24
Regensburg, town of, 100, 249
Regensburg, Treaty of, 39, 110
Rheinfelden, battle of, 90, 99
Rhine River, 63, 64, 67, 69, 78, 80, 84, 89, 164, 200, 203, 263; French unwillingness to cross, 82; French pushed back west, 91, 93, 220; French intervention near, 97–98; in negotiations, 105, 161, 171–72, 176, 196, 214–15, 223, 241; 1643 campaign, 101; 1644 campaign, 118–22, 128–32, 134–36; 1645 campaign, 141–42, 149, 165, 180–83; 1646 campaign, 209, 220–21, 228–29, 232–33, 243
Richelieu, Armand-Jean Du Plessis, cardinal-duc de, French first minister 1624–1642, 22–24; and initial instructions to plenipotentiaries, 106; *assecuratio*, 140; compared to Mazarin, 262–63, 265, 274; death, 28; foreign policy, 33; goals in Thirty Years' War, 261–62; meets Mazarin, 28; military administration, 56; re-

fuses to ratify treaty of Regensburg, 39, 110; relations with Alsace and Lorraine, 97–98, 267; relations with Anne, 29; treaty with Weimarians, 82, 99, 220
Ries, 64
Rivière, Abbè de la, advisor to Gaston d'Orléans, 30
Roberts, Michael, 56–58
Rocroi, battle of, 70, 89, 100, 116
Roderich of Württemberg, 101
Rohan, Henri de, 266
Rorté, baron de, French resident in Osnabrück, 38
Rosas, 186
Rosen, Reinhold von, French general, 84, 101, 119, 124
Rosenhane, Schering, Swedish resident in Münster, 52, 112, 191, 211, 241
Rothenburg-ob-der-Tauber, 67, 69, 89, 93, 154, 167
Rottweil, 68, 70, 100
Ruischenberg, Johann, Freiherr von, Bavarian military officer, 178
Russia, 235
Russo-Japanese War, 278

Saavedra, Don Diego, Spanish plenipotentiary, 191
Saint Romain, Melchior Harod de Senevas, marquis de, French diplomat, role in embassy, 38; trip to Sweden, 211–12, 235
Saint-Aulaire, Auguste, comte de, 23–24, 274–75
Salvius, Johan Adler, Swedish plenipotentiary, 139, 191, 212, 226; and French subsidy, 116; complains of Vervaux mission, 147; friendship with d'Avaux, 52; relationship with Johann Oxenstierna, 52; Swedish satisfaction, 235; trip to Münster, 110, 112
Saverne, 105, 171, 216, 222
Saxony, Electorate of, 87, 263; and excellence title, 143; treaties with Sweden, 174, 190, 231
Schneider, Johann Balthasar, representative for Colmar, 199
Schorndorf, 69, 80, 247
Schumann, Maurice, 23–24, 272

Schwäbisch Hall, 67, 69, 180–81
Séguier, Pierre, French chancellor, 31
Sélestat, town in Alsace, 89, 105
Servien, Abel, marquis de Boisdauphin, comte de la Roche-, 265, 274; and Bavaria, 208, 213, 266; and Spain, 45, 145–46; and Sweden, 52, 112, 115–16, 210, 277; appointment as plenipotentiary, 34; in the negotiations, 111, 138–40, 157–58, 165, 201; Lorraine, 253; on Alsace, 196–97, 199, 200, 237–38, 250; on military affairs, 73, 75–76, 83, 119; opinion of Brienne, 42; opinion of Turenne, 84, 150–51, 154, 229; Ottomans, 192, 273; quarrel with d'Avaux, 35–38, 142–44; relationship with Mazarin, 39, 41, 143–44, 262; religious views, 35, 159; reports intelligence lead, 45; role in council, 31; territorial demands, 161–64, 198, 215–16, 222–23, 225, 227, 250, 271; train, 38–39; trip to Münster, 103, 111. *See also* French plenipotentiaries
Sheen, Charlie, 270
Silesia, 51, 263, 279
Soissons, Charles II de Bourbon, comte de, 80
Spain, 23, 28, 30, 89, 100, 243, 264, 272–73; and Catalonia, 50; and French satisfaction, 205–6, 213, 221; and mail system, 43–44; attacks on Mazarin, 33; exclusion from peace, 103, 109, 113, 144–45, 186–89, 223, 225, 234, 252–53, 259–60, 281; French spying on, 45, 47; French view of, 187–90, 194–95, 203, 254; in 1644 campaign, 117; in 1646 campaign, 220–22, 227; in 1647 campaign, 259; in the negotiations, 103, 109–11, 133, 137–38, 144–46; in Trier, 192–93; marriage alliance, 196, 206; negotiating tactics, 46, 201; relations with Bavaria, 113; separate peace with Dutch, 47, 53, 111, 155–56, 206, 213, 220, 279. *See also* Peñaranda; Saavedra; Philip IV
Spanish Netherlands. *See* Netherlands, Spanish
Speyer, bishopric of, 129, 242
Speyer, town of, 68, 131, 137, 181

Steinberg, S. H., 56
Steinheim, 247
Strasbourg, bishopric of, 104, 171, 215
Strasbourg, town of, 78, 98, 104, 199, 213, 251–52
Sundgau, region in Alsace, 104–5, 171–72, 196, 214–16, 222, 239, 261–62
Swabia, Imperial Circle, 61–62, 69, 88, 101, 127, 148, 180, 183, 190, 247, 263
Swabian Alps, 64
Sweden, 193, 259–60, 267, 276–77; and Hesse, 53, 86, 230; and mail system, 43, 281; and the Palatinate, 51–52; desire for Weimarian troops, 82, 220; in 1645 campaign, 142, 165, 167; in 1646 campaign, 208–9, 218–22, 228–33, 243–47; invasion of Bavaria, 54, 69, 74, 91; invasion of Denmark, 108–9, 111–12, 115–17, 123, 135; military co-operation with France, 80, 85–86, 91, 100, 152, 177, 183–84, 218–19, 227–30, 265; military forces of, 86, 88; military involvement, 97–98, 104, 190; opposition to a truce, 175, 183, 205, 209, 213; peace negotiations, 103, 109–10, 138–39, 142, 156–60, 164, 174, 198–99, 226–27, 234–36, 240, 253–54, 263; Protestant policies, 50–51, 157–60, 209–10, 225; relations with England, 156; relations with France, 35, 37, 50–52, 111–12, 115–16, 142, 156–60, 190–91, 195, 209–12, 225–27, 276; war against the emperor, 78, 86, 88, 100, 116, 148; war aims, 51, 114, 137. *See also* Salvius; Oxenstierna, Axel; Oxenstierna, Johann; Christina; Wrangel; Torstensson
Switzerland, 54, 64, 105, 171, 215

Thionville, 100
Thirty Years' War, 21, 24–25, 56–58, 63, 65, 71–72, 74, 218, 273
Three Bishoprics (Metz, Toul, and Verdun), 42, 104, 249–50, 252, 254
Torstensson, Lennart, Swedish general, 71, 86, 90, 108, 116, 135–36, 141, 148, 180, 218, 221
Tracy, Alexandre de Prouville, marquis de, *lieutenant-général* in the *Armée d'Allemagne*, 93; communication with plenipotentiaries, 48; in Tuttlingen campaign, 101; in 1644 campaign, 124, 134; in 1645 campaign, 154, 180; in 1646 campaign, 233; role in supplying AA, 85, 92
Transylvania, 142, 189
Trauttmansdorff, Maximilian Graf von, Imperial plenipotentiary, 259, 269, 280; arrival in Münster, 185, 193; concession of Breisach, 47, 272; French satisfaction, 185, 201, 205, 213–17, 221, 223, 228, 234, 241; on Mazarin, 263; spies in his household, 45; strategy in the negotiations, 198, 210, 276, 279
Treasure, Geoffrey, 22, 24, 26
Trier, city of, 192–94
Trier, Elector of (Philip Christoph von Sötern), 171, 267; French capture of Trier, 192–93; imprisonment in Vienna, 53, 139–40; negotiations over Philippsburg, 42, 49, 161, 192, 225, 241–43, 249; release, 192
Turenne, maréchal, Henri de la Tour d'Auvergne, vicomte de, 73, 189, 261, 267; after 1646, 259–60, 264–65; and military intelligence, 77–79; as commander of the *Armée d'Allemagne*, 61, 81, 84–85, 101–2; as tactician, 70; communication with plenipotentiaries, 48; co-operation with Enghien, 85; co-operation with Wrangel, 85–86; in 1644 campaign, 118–24, 126–29, 131, 133–36; in 1645 campaign, 141–42, 148–51, 164–68, 178–83, 192; in 1646 campaign, 203, 209–10, 213, 217–23, 228–33, 236, 243–49, 254; lack of discipline among troops, 80, 92; military campaigns of, 76, 80; military strategy of, 61–62, 73–74; relations with Mazarin, 80–81; suppresses Weimarian mutiny, 82
Tuttlingen, battle of, 68, 70, 73, 77, 81, 84, 89, 91, 101, 102, 108, 117–18, 121, 122, 193, 270

Überlingen, 92, 119–20, 164
Ulm, Truce of (1647), 55, 68–69, 80, 91, 177, 259
Ultima generalis declaratio, 249
United Provinces of the Netherlands,

role in passing on French information, 45; relations with Sweden, 50; relations with France, 52–53, 110–11, 189–90, 207, 276; do not want peace, 108; negotiations with Spain, 53, 111, 155, 189–90, 206, 213, 220, 280; in 1644 campaign, 118–19, 129; slowness in sending representatives to Münster, 155–56, 189–90, 193, 206–7, 279; in 1645 campaign, 155; in 1646 campaign, 207–8, 221, 223; after 1646, 259; peace with Spain, 47, 236, 264, 276–77, 279; relations with Denmark, 155; Catalonia/Low Countries exchange project, 190, 195. *See also* Pauw; Knuyt; Frederik Hendrik

Utrecht, Peace of (1713–1714), 21

Van Creveld, Martin, 57–58
Vautorte, François de, French intendant along the Rhine, 99, 200
Venice, 34, 188, 191, 272. *See also* Nani, Contarini
Verden, 51, 236, 263
Verdun, Treaty of (843), 22
Versailles, Peace of (1919), 21
Vervaux, Johannes, SJ, confessor to Maximilian of Bavaria, 44, 146–52, 161, 165, 169, 184, 217, 267
Vesoul, 119
Vic, Treaty of (1632), 97
Vienna, Congress of (1814–1815), 22
Volmar, Isaac, Imperial plenipotentiary, 201, 213, 250
Voltaire, 56

Von Werth, Johann, Freiherr, Bavarian general, 70, 87, 90, 100, 168, 178
Vosges mountains, 171, 222
Vulteius, Johann, Hessian plenipotentiary, 53

Wallenstein, Albrecht Wenzel Eusebius von, Imperial general (d.1634), 22, 60–61, 83, 87
Warburg, 167
Wartenberg, Franz Wilhelm Graf von, Bishop of Osnabrück, 216
Weimarian army, 74, 81, 82, 84, 85, 99, 101, 220; attempted reform of, 102; in 1644 campaign, 121; rebellion, 259
Wesel, 233
Westphalia (Imperial Circle), 61, 87, 119, 123, 167, 231, 245
Westphalia, Peace of, 7–10, 21–25, 51, 80, 91, 99, 103, 140, 238, 260, 270, 278, 280–81
Wicquefort, Abraham de, 271
Wildenstein, castle of, 99
Will, George, 21
Wimpfen, 167, 181
Wismar, 236
Wladislaw IV, King of Poland, 191
Wolfenbüttel, battle of, 100
Worms, 68, 122, 131–32, 137
Wörnitz River, 64
Wrangel, Karl Gustav, Swedish general, 86, 231–33, 236, 243–48, 254, 259–60, 265
Württemberg, Duchy of, 54, 68, 130–31, 134–36, 154, 177, 247

Zeller, Gaston, 26, 277
Ziegenhain, 247
Zusmarshausen, battle of, 50